The biography of Bishop Constantine Bohachevsky, told with great empathy, is skillfully woven into the larger history of the Ukrainian Catholic Church, across three political regimes and two continents, with the Vatican in between. The story is larger than life because it recounts the institutionalization of the Ukrainian Catholic Church in the United States as part of the process of formation of a global Ukrainian Catholic Church within global Catholicism.

—JOSÉ CASANOVA, GEORGETOWN UNIVERSITY

Constantine Bohachevsky was bishop, later metropolitan, of the Ukrainian Catholic Church in America from the mid-1920s until the early 1960s. He was an institution builder whose hard work produced admirable and enduring achievements. He was a modest, self-effacing man, yet he was assailed from many sides. He stood firm and true to his institutional vision thanks to a steadfast faith in the beneficence of God's will. His tale is told here by a professional historian at the height of her powers, who also just happens to be the niece of the great churchman. Martha Bohachevsky-Chomiak has written a model work of transnational, Ukrainian and American, history that illuminates issues too often neglected in both Ukrainian studies and the scholarship on American Catholicism. Extensive research, genuine readability, important messages—it's all in this book.

—JOHN-PAUL HIMKA, UNIVERSITY OF ALBERTA

Ukrainian Bishop, American Church is a successful example of a biography presented against the background of the history of the community that the subject represented and served. Dr. Bohachevsky-Chomiak masterfully demonstrates the goals and aspirations that animated the activity of the bishop and his community: they desired to preserve the Ukrainian national-cultural and especially religious-ecclesiastical heritage. The fruit of meticulous research and evaluation of a great amount of source material, including archives, results in a profound and comprehensive analysis of the life of Metropolitan Bohachevsky. The light, transparent style not only successfully veils many years of complex labor, but makes the book more attractive to a broad reading public.

—LILIANA HENTOSH, LVIV NATIONAL UNIVERSITY, UKRAINE

Like much of the history of the largest Eastern Catholic rite, this is an unknown and yet riveting chapter, in which both the Vatican and the Ukrainian Church discover how a national church becomes international. Bohachevsky-Chomiak has tamed her polyglot sources into a beautifully written narrative: clear prose graced with understatement and spiced with occasional irony.

—JEFFREY WILLS, UKRAINIAN CATHOLIC UNIVERSITY

Ukrainian Bishop,
American Church

MARTHA
BOHACHEVSKY-CHOMIAK

Ukrainian Bishop, American Church

CONSTANTINE BOHACHEVSKY AND THE UKRAINIAN CATHOLIC CHURCH

The Catholic University of America Press

WASHINGTON, D.C.

Cataloging-in-Publication Data available from the Library of Congress
ISBN 978-0-8132-3636-0

To the cohort of the dedicated clergy
raised by Metropolitan Bohachevsky, especially
Archbishop-Major Lubomyr Cardinal Husar,
Bishop Basil Losten, and
Bishop John Stock

CONTENTS

ILLUSTRATIONS

PREFACE

I am a niece of Archbishop/Metropolitan Constantine Bohachevsky. I met him when I was ten, and I was in my early twenties when he died in 1961. I remember him vividly, as children and adolescents do.

The family relationship places me as a historian at a disadvantage. My father thought otherwise, and encouraged me to work on Constantine's biography very early in my professional career. I demurred, pleading lack of sources. Hurt, my father wrote a short biography of his brother, apologizing profusely for its limitations. He felt his brother's story should be told for the good of the community, if not the world. He was concerned that the contemporary Catholic European clergy overlooked the American experience of the Ukrainian Catholic Church in the United States in their deliberations about the future of the Catholic Church. He worried that this oversight would cost the Ukrainian Catholic community dearly.

When the Ukrainian Catholic Church was legalized and Ukraine became independent in 1991, I presumed the story of the Ukrainian-American Catholic Church would be thoroughly studied by others. I worked on my own projects.

On a frigid February 27, 2002, at a reception following the consecration of yet another in the row of new Ukrainian Catholic bishops, Lubomyr Cardinal Husar, the archbishop-major of the resurrected Ukrainian Catholic Church, literally pushed me against an empty niche in the wall in the baroque St. George's archeparchial residence in Lviv. The Russian Orthodox clergy had just vacated the residence; the sauna had been removed, as well as most of the furniture. The great room was bare, but for Soviet-issue dining-room chairs that lined the main perimeter of the walls. It was cold. With few preliminaries His Eminence informed me that it was my duty, as a historian and as a member of the Church—not to mention of the Bohachevsky family—to prepare a scholarly biography of Constantine

Bohachevsky, who also happened to have been one of his teachers. Like my father, the cardinal-major argued that my familiarity with both America and Europe gave me added advantages that would ease the research. Cardinal Husar kindly promised to help with access to the archives. I did my best to protest, provided alternative scholars, argued objectivity, and procrastinated. But in the end I proved too weak to withstand the pressure from both then a living patriarch and a long-deceased father.

I turned my attention to this topic slowly, without ardent excitement. I had other time-consuming commitments that could not be dropped. That changed when I finally stepped into the Secret Vatican Archives. I was shocked by how little of the American story was known, even by the best-informed clergy. In trying to uncover my uncle's life, I also came across hidden alleys of the community, both in Ukraine and in America. Thus the project turned into a study of the relations of the church and the community, a story of a conflict of church and state in the absence of both an official state and a fully established church.

The Ukrainian Catholic Church is generally discussed in terms of its relevance to Ukrainian nationalism or its relationship to the Vatican. My modest goal is to contribute a closer look at a part of the church for what it was and what it strove to be. This is a book about how the Ukrainian Catholic Church fought for its autonomy during the lifetime of one bishop on two continents and under different political systems. As I reconstructed the bishop's life, I had to chart the contours of his world, which has not been much noticed. Bohachevsky lived his life through his work, where his imprint is evident. As a person, however, mountaineer that he was, he tread very lightly, leaving little evidence of himself beyond that work. I focus on an individual whose principled life resonates beyond Eastern Europe and its world-scattered immigrants to illustrate yet another aspect of Catholic Christianity. This is but one book on the lives of many people whose experiences deserve further study. I trust the life of this bishop in his changing church will help open doors for other subjects, and encourage more study of the varied world of Catholicism in its local practice. I drew on a variety of sources, most used here for the first time. Some of the archival collections are not yet fully catalogued. Many sources contradict each other. Predictably, the flowery published descriptions of festivities embroider the events they claim to document. In this field, the view back is often as murky as the road ahead.

Through the long years of research and writing, I experienced many kindnesses, both professional and personal. Let me acknowledge at least some of them. Fittingly, a book on a bishop owes primary expressions of gratitude to the late Metropolitan Major Lubomyr Cardinal Husar, for nudging me onto the subject, and to Bishop Basil Losten, for constant and substantive support. Bishop Paul Chomnycky made me feel at home in the hospitable complex of St. Basil Seminary in Stamford, Connecticut. I appreciated that the Ukrainian Catholic University in Lviv, Ukraine, invited me to test the topic in seminars and courses. My thanks to all, especially to Bishop Borys Gudziak and Oleh Turij.

I am indebted to Muriel Joffe for unfailing support and to Frank Sysyn for years of cooperation; to Liubov Abramuik Wolynets and Anna Krawchuk for unearthing sources; to Lilliana Hentosh for guiding me in the Vatican; to Myroslava Diadiuk and Lesia Stefanyk-Decyk for help in the Lviv archives; and to Olha Dudykevych for delving into the family genealogy. Special thanks to Very Rev. Robert Hitchens, rector of St. Josaphat Ukrainian Catholic Seminary; Rev. Ivan Kaszczak, a model priest who studied the Ukrainian Catholic clergy, and to Jeffrey Wills and Rev. Peter Galadza for reading early chapters; and to Andrew Sorokowsky and Borys Hlynsky for selfless translations from Latin and French. Several individuals shared their research, holdings, and reminiscences: Oleksandr Lushnytsky, Christine Kulchytsky, Yuri Danyliw, and Roman Ferencewych. I especially want to thank Ania B. Savage and Stephanie Chopek Sydoriak, friends and readers of unfinished chapters, my sister, Maria Odezynskyj, and my eldest niece, Rostia Stoecker, for their comments, and George Bohachevsky for holding on to the newspapers.

My heartfelt gratitude to Tamara Stadnychenko Cornelison and Mary Ann Szproluk for their editing and encouragement, and to Louise A. Mitchell for the final polish. Adrian M. Oryshkevych stepped in to help with the footnotes and to draw up a bibliography, and Paul Salvi did a good job with the photographs. This book intrigued my late husband, Rostyslav Chomiak. He riffled through my sources and was frustrated by my unwillingness to share the story publicly before the completion of the book. My daughters, Tania and Dora, their husbands, Lucantonio Salvi and Daren Chapin, and my grandchildren, Paul, Lianka, Katia, and Stephen, made certain that I knew I have a loving family.

NOTES ON TERMINOLOGY AND TRANSLITERATION

RUS', RUTHENIAN, RUSYN, UKRAINIAN

Political entities do not necessarily reflect nations, and ethnicities are not consistent in naming themselves. The tenth century name for Ukrainians was Rus' or Rusychi, which eventually became "Rusyn." The Latin variant is Rutheni or Ruteni; in English, Ruthenian. The name stuck in parts of the land, while in others the newer term "Ukrainian," coined in the twelfth century, came into use. Ukraine's neighbors sought to negate the existence of a separate Ukraine, as a construct and a state, and denied the congruence of Rusyn and Ukrainian. Ukrainians began immigrating to the United States where in most (but not all) areas where Ukrainians lived, the term "Ukrainian" supplanted "Rusyn." The dynamic immigrated with the new settlers and became a factor in the development of the Ukrainian Catholic Church in the United States.

"Rusyn," "Ruthenian," "Trans-Carpathian," "Carpathian" are used more or less interchangeably to refer to Ukrainians from the Carpathian and Trans-Carpathian areas. Some of them consider themselves Rusyns in addition to being Ukrainian.

The Ukrainian Catholic Church (historically known as the Ruthenian Catholic Church of the Byzantine Rite) dates itself from 988 when Prince Volodymyr made Christianity the law of the land. As part of the organized Catholic *ecclesia*, however, it was established in 1596, becoming an example of how ecclesiastical unity of the Orthodox Eastern Churches with the Western papacy could be restored without violating Eastern practice. The Ukrainian Church recognized papal primacy, but kept its Eastern ritual and its Church Slavonic language of worship. It entered into union with Rome, hence it is sometimes also called "uniate," but present-day Ukrainians resent this old term. By reestablishing the tie to the papacy, the Ukrainian Church strengthened its access to Western scholarship, art, and cultural values and modes of behavior. Thus, an Eastern Church became an identifiable Western cultural marker in Ukraine, without losing is Eastern visage.

The papacy and the Ukrainian Catholic Church, using Latin in correspondence until well into the twentieth century, also kept the terms "Ruteni" or "Rutheni" in documentation. The Ukrainian Church in the US was loath to initiate a formal change of the name from Ruthenian to Ukrainian independently of the home country. It was only after the metropolitan-major of Halych, during the Second Vatican Council, petitioned the pope that the term "Ukrainian Catholic Church" was formalized and the older term, Rutheni, dropped. The Byzantine Catholic Metropolitan Church in the United States, however, continues to use the terms Rusyn and Ruthenian.

In this book, I use Halychyna as a broad shorthand for Western Ukrainian lands, excluding Bukovyna and Zakarpattia, to avoid confusion with the clearly delineated Austrian Habsburg province of Galicia/Galitzia/Galizien, which included a Polish population. This Galicia has lately become a renewed subject of study. In contrast, the historic Halychyna had fluid boundaries, a Ukrainian majority, a large Jewish, and smaller Armenian and Karaim populations, and remains understudied. While I used "Galicia" in my previous publications, the term "Halychyna" better reflects my focus in this book—the specifically Ukrainian Catholic population in Europe and in the United States.

Because my topic and my sources deal with Ukraine, I use the currently incorrect place names for the cities of Pzemysl (which is in Poland) and Stanislaviv (which is now known as Ivano-Frankivsk and is in Ukraine).

ECCLESIASTICAL TERMS

"Diocese" (from the Latin) or "eparchy" (from the Greek) mean the same thing and tend to be used interchangeably. They refer to a recognized, clearly delineated ecclesiastical unit headed by a bishop or eparch. At present, when writing about Eastern Christianity, scholars favor the Greek usage, so I try to use it even though the term "diocese" was frequently used in the 1920s and 1930s in Ukraine.

An "exarchate" is a separate ecclesiastical unit directly under papal jurisdiction through a papal congregation. The exarchate, while functioning on territories of a Catholic ordinary, is not subject to the local Catholic Church authorities, but rather to its own bishop or a suitably empowered cleric. Long-term exarchates are sometimes referred to as dioceses. An exarchate, in contrast to a diocese—or, to use the Eastern variant of the term, eparchy—is a temporary church organization either located in a missionary territory or for a minority population.

Two or more eparchies in an ecclesiastically defined territory may be gathered into a "metropolitanate" headed by a "metropolitan," which in the West tends to be correlated with an archbishop. The metropolitan possesses certain specific ecclesiastical powers, but mostly functions as a *primus inter pares*. Officially, the Western Ukrainian metropolitan had the title of Halych and All Rus', but since the see was in Lviv, I simplify and use metropolitan of Lviv. Today, the head of the Ukrainian Catholic Church is a metropolitan-major of Kyiv, referred to as patriarch.

TRANSLITERATION

I use a modified Library of Congress transcription. Some of the players in this story, however, used other systems when they signed themselves in English. I have tried to honor their usage in writing their names as they wrote them, thus violating any attempt at consistency in the transcription. I trust the reader will understand. The Prockos, father and son, are a case in point. The Rev. Pavlo Protsko transliterated his name with a "ts," while the son simplified it to Procko. Thus both names are used. The following four letters cause the most problems, since both variant transliterations are used, even interchangeably, by individuals and authors alike. I have tried to use the "i" variant, but I cannot vouch for consistency.

Я ia, ya
Ю iu, yu
Ї ii, yi
Й y, j, i

ABBREVIATIONS

AES   Archivio degli Affari Ecclesiastici Straordinari, on
       Poland and America

ASV   Archivio Segreto Vaticano

CEC   Archive of the Congregation for the Eastern Church

LAL   L'vivs'ka Naukova Biblioteka im. V. Stefanyka
       Akademiii Nauk Ukraiiny, Viddil rukopysiv [Lviv
       Academic Library of the National Ukrainian Academy
       of Science, Manuscript Division]

PKEL   Protokoly Konferentsii Epyskopiv Lvivskoho
       Peremys'koho Stanislavivs'koho 1902–39 [Minutes
       of the conferences of the bishops of Lviv and
       Peremyshl]. Lviv Academic Library of the National
       Ukrainian Academy of Science, Manuscript Division,
       f. 9, Special Collections, spr. 106

TsDIA, Lviv Derzhavniy Istorychniy Archiv u Lvovi [The Central
       Ukrainian Historical Archive, Lviv]

UMAS   Ukrainian Museum and Archive, Stamford, Conn.

Ukrainian Bishop,
American Church

A Papal Choice and a Papal Charge

Today, the Ukrainian Catholic Church is the most numerous Eastern Catholic church in the world. In large measure that is due to the development of that church in the United States in the twentieth century. As it established itself in the United States, the Ukrainian-American Catholic Church provided visibility as well as support to the embattled Ukrainian mother church in Europe. Constantine Bohachevsky, the first archbishop/metropolitan of the Ukrainian Church in the United States, played a critical role in its consolidation and growth.

In 1924, Pope Pius XI sent a forty-year-old, freshly appointed bishop, Constantine Bohachevsky, to the United States with the task of transforming the contentious Ukrainian Catholic Church there into an orderly eparchy. Many of its congregants at the time were threatening to convert to Orthodoxy. The sudden request by none other than the pope to accept an appointment as a bishop to America astounded Bohachevsky, who had thought he was being tapped for missionary work in the East. Bohachevsky's acceptance changed the trajectory of his life and had a formative impact on the development of the Ukrainian Greek Catholic Church. Bohachevsky took the papal challenge a step further: he worked successfully to institutionalize his church within the United States. When the papacy recognized the existence of this church on par with that of the larger American Roman Catholic Church of the Latin rite, the United States officially became a country of many different Catholic rites.

The apogee of that recognition came on November 1, 1958, when Pope John XXIII recognized the Ukrainian Catholic Church in the United States as a developed archbishopric/metropolitanate, a fully embedded Catholic province in the United States. Although Bohachevsky's nomination in 1924 was divisive, the beginnings of his tenure contentious, and his legacy slow to gain recognition, upon his death in 1961 his contributions to the church and the Ukrainian community were indisputably recognized in the United States and abroad.

The Latin rite that passes for Roman Catholicism in the United States is only one rite of the Catholic Church. There are fourteen other rites that are mostly clustered in the Eastern or Byzantine segment of the Catholic Church. They adhere to Catholic doctrinal stipulations and accept the primacy of the Roman papacy, differing with Western Catholicism only in what are known as incidentals—liturgical practice, vestments, and most visibly the right of married men to enter the priesthood.

Fissures in the Christian faith developed as soon as the Christian community expanded and built its institutional frameworks. The split in 1054 between the pope and the patriarch of Constantinople proved to be the most pervasive of the early conflicts within Christianity, resulting in the division of Christians into "Orthodox" and "Catholic," Eastern and Western. The initial disagreement came to encompass the whole entity of the Christian church. It exists to this day, as do various attempts to overcome it, most of them unsuccessful. The Eastern Catholic Churches, while sharing Western theology, have retained more of the traditions of the original undifferentiated Christianity and thus may be better positioned to bridge the East-West divide.

When the split between Western and Eastern Christianity occurred, Kyiv, the heartland of Ukraine, was battling the Mongols, and Moscow had not yet been founded. For the next three centuries the whole Eastern European area, like the rest of Europe, was in turmoil. Dynastic, regional, and religious wars produced lively religious polemics and shifting political entities. Kyiv had accepted Christianity from Constantinople in 988, before the split with Rome. After the split, the Kyivan church remained under the patriarch of Constantinople. In 1596, part of that church withdrew its allegiance to the patriarch and joined the Catholic Church headed by the pope in Rome. This event marked the founding of what, for simplicity, I call in this book the Ukrainian Catholic Church.

Known historically as the Ruthenian Greek-Catholic Church of the Byzantine Rite or, somewhat dismissively, the uniate church, this church was established in Kyiv when Ruthenian Orthodox bishops aligned themselves with the Catholic Church. The Byzantine Eastern rite admitted the primacy of the Roman pope and the doctrine of the procession of the Holy Ghost, but the church kept its ritual, discipline, and language, and the right of married men to become priests. Now known mainly as the Ukrainian Catholic Church, this church continues to use different historical names—Greek Catholic of the Byzantine rite, Ruthenian Catholic, and Eastern Catholic. From its inception at the end of the sixteenth century to its emergence from the Soviet catacombs in the critical 1990s, the development of this specific Catholic Church was repeatedly undercut by political persecution and even Catholic clerical opposition to its existence. There have been occasions when members of the Catholic hierarchy questioned its legitimacy. The Ukrainian Church itself was subject to internal disagreements, some violent, as during the early decades of Bohachevsky's tenure and in the years after his death as well. Nevertheless, the church not only survived, but expanded far beyond its original borders.

The 1596 Union of Brest that formally established the Ruthenian Catholic Church of the Byzantine rite, in which Ruthenians and Belarusians participated, is still an object of heated debates. The Russian Orthodox Church never formally recognized its legitimacy, although at the historic meeting with Pope Francis in Cuba in February 2016, Kiril, the patriarch of Russia, mentioned in passing that the "uniate" church had the right to exist. In the West, countries in which the Latin rite was dominant often considered the Byzantine Catholic Churches as being somehow second-rate and of questionable loyalty to Roman Catholicism. (In official Catholic Church, pre-Vatican II parlance the Orthodox Church was considered "schismatic.") The papacy, on the other hand, valued the Byzantine Catholic Church as a potential instrument for Christian unity with the East and occasionally provided it with active support, especially in the development of its educational institutions.

The universal Catholic Church is not a national organization, and its churches are not organized in national units. The bishops of the church, the key administrative links in the vast organization that culminates in the papacy, are given geographical titles drawn from places in which the original, ancient Christian communities once flourished, some of which would be hard pressed to be considered Christian today. Thus, Catholic bishoprics do not necessarily reflect the existing political entity; instead a sense of Catholic unity despite shifting geographical borders is ideally perpetuated within the church administration by drawing upon ancient communality. At the same time, however, by supporting the rights of local Catholic churches vis-à-vis a civic authority, the Vatican inadvertently promotes nationalism. In Western Europe, civic and political consciousness developed in the shadow of Christian churches and challenged ecclesiastical authority. Our ideas of civil society as well as our definitions of tolerance emerged from the age-long struggle between the church and the state that in turn chiseled our understanding of both. This dynamic was largely absent in Eastern Europe, except that we find it in the part of Western Ukrainian territories from which most of the Ukrainian Americans came. Once the political entities from which they emigrated—the Habsburg Austrian Empire and the Russian Empire of the Romanovs—disintegrated, the immigrants were often as confused as American immigration officers about the ethnic make-up of Eastern European states, as well as their own identity.

Ukrainian immigration to the United States coincided with the rise of political and national awareness among Ukrainians in all parts of Eastern Europe, ruled until 1918 by multinational empires. National awareness manifested itself in the rise of civic movements and organizations which grew in importance with the decline of political stability in the area. The proliferation of civic organizations challenged the role of the Catholic Church in the Western Ukrainian territories, where that church had historically channeled Ukrainian public expectations. In Europe, Ukrainian Catholics traditionally had modest institutional aspirations, generally limited to the recognition and exercise of their rite and language. There was no independent Ukraine to speak in the name of its people until 1991, nor were ethnic Ukrainian territories united under one power. Regional difference, important in the Eastern European agricultural communities, emerged even more sharply among immigrants, most of whom had little schooling and limited opportunity to be well informed about the world and its politics.

During the aftermath of the First World War, Ukrainians fought for not only religious, but also cultural and especially political rights. Meanwhile, the Ukrainian Catholic Church in Europe became a more active player at the Vatican. Ukrainian interests conflicted with many aspirations of the Russians, Poles, Hungarians, Romanians, and eventually even the Czechoslovaks, each of whom claimed the same lands Ukrainians considered their own patrimony. Some of these countries were officially Catholic, and all recognized the papal power to name Catholic bishops. Ukrainians in all countries increasingly turned to the Vatican for help in upholding their national as well as religious rights.

For Ukrainians, Catholic and non-Catholic, the papacy acted as a lifeline to the outside world. During the revolutionary turmoil that intertwined with World War I the Ukrainian Catholic Church played a visible, albeit never a determinant, role in the fate of Ukraine. That the relatively small Ukrainian Greek Catholic Church could do so was largely due to the person of Archbishop/Metropolitan Count Andrey Sheptytsky. Sheptytsky took over the Lviv Metropolitanate in 1901 as a thirty-five-year-old and proved to be a dedicated, if not always successful, representative of Ukrainian aspirations until his death in 1944. Fully at home in Roman salons, Sheptytsky was equally sensitive to the needs of Ukrainian immigrants. It was largely thanks to his efforts that Soter Ortynsky was nominated as the first bishop of the Ruthenian/Ukrainian Greek Catholic Church in the USA. Ortynsky came from Halychyna, although at the time more Ruthenian Carpathians had immigrated to the United States than those from the Halychyna territories.[1] The Ruthenians resented the Halychanyn pressure to call themselves Ukrainians rather than the older term Rusyns. They complained to the Vatican, which objected to all outside pressure.

After the end of World War I, Halychyna became a bone of contention between the Poles and Ukrainians for the whole interwar period. Ukraine fared badly on all fronts. The Polish armies, with French help, proved victorious over the Ukrainians, as the rest of Ukraine folded into the Soviet

1. For an overview of the Ukrainian immigrant experience in the United States, see Myron B. Kuropas, *The Ukrainian Americans: Roots and Aspirations 1881–1954* (Toronto: University of Toronto Press, 1991).

Union. The new Polish government tried to move quickly to consolidate all the territories it considered Polish—which before the war had been administered by three different empires: Austrian, German, and Russian—into one centralized Polish state. Local administrators rode roughshod over the non-Polish parts of the state. Ukrainians in Halychyna, however, insisted on the legitimacy of the old Habsburg laws that provided some autonomy for Ukrainians. The Poles maintained that their de facto control of the territories voided previous legal systems, although the terms of the peace agreement assured the continued validity of the Austrian laws for a couple of decades. The Ukrainian Catholic Church, occasionally with the support of the papacy, adhered to the former interpretation of legality and disagreements ensued.

It was in this setting that Constantine Bohachevsky had lived and worked as a young priest. In February 1917, Metropolitan Sheptytsky named Bohachevsky vice-rector of the seminary in Lviv. The next year, on October 11, 1918, he was formally installed as the pastor and canon of the cathedral in Peremyshl, with official imperial Habsburg approval, just before the last Habsburg emperor abdicated.

The Vatican recognized that some governments had a legitimate interest in the appointment of bishops for their territories. The Habsburg Monarchy had been one such state. By recognizing the cultural concerns of their ethnic groups, the Habsburgs helped to politicize them not as Habsburg subjects, as the Habsburgs wished, but as members of distinct nationalities. When the monarchy disintegrated in 1918, the successor states—among them, Czechoslovakia, Yugoslavia, Hungary, Romania, and Poland—faced growing nationalist conflicts. The tension between wanting both multinational lands and a culturally unitary state was reflected in church policies and had an impact on the religious life of the immigrants in America.

The political remaking of Europe after the First World War profoundly affected the structure of the Catholic Church. In the immediate period following the end of the First World War and the collapse of the Habsburg, Romanov, and Ottoman empires, the political and religious scene in Eastern Europe and the Near East underwent major political changes and population shifts. Moreover, after the Russian Revolutions of 1917–18, apprehension about the spread of Soviet communism caused even greater consternation among churchmen and politicians in Europe and the United States. The Catholic Church saw the fall of tsarism, which had administered the Russian Orthodox Church as a government institution, as an opportunity to revitalize the search for Christian church unity.

Before the First World War, the papacy had become very interested in Eastern European and Balkan territories because a renewed movement for the reconciliation of the Catholic and Orthodox branches of Christianity arose there around the turn of the twentieth century. Ukrainian churchmen, most visibly Metropolitan Andrey Sheptytsky, the dominant presence in the Ukrainian Catholic Church, worked on restoring the unity of Christendom. Sheptytsky spent part of the First World War in Russian captivity, and then travelled through central Ukraine. He had to leave his see in Lviv when the new Polish Republic claimed sizeable Ukrainian territories. As an apostolic legate to the Americas, Sheptytsky gave the Vatican first-hand information about the fate of Ukrainian Catholics in the United States and their urgent need for a new bishop after the death of Bishop Soter Ortynsky in 1916. Sheptytsky feared that without a bishop the whole Ukrainian-American Catholic congregation might opt for a version of Ukrainian Orthodoxy, which offered a greater possibility for local governance. The emigration of Russian religious thinkers to the Balkans and to Paris following the Russian Revolution created additional interest in the Eastern traditions of Christianity and offered another glimmer of hope that Christian unity could be achieved.

At the same time, the Vatican feared that Eastern Catholics might be attracted to Orthodoxy, so the path to Christian unity (ecumenism had not yet become a household word) was narrow and fraught with potential danger. There was also a fear in the Vatican that Orthodoxy, or what was then referred to as "schismatic apostasy," would prove attractive to other disgruntled Catholics. The Ukrainian Catholic Church, with its ritual proximity to Orthodoxy, gave that church power beyond its numbers. Ukrainian Catholics, especially in America, could always threaten to turn to Orthodoxy if they felt slighted by the Vatican, as some Ukrainian Catholics in Canada had done in 1918 when they set up their own Orthodox church. The Orthodox, in turn, saw Rome's treatment of the Eastern Catholics as a litmus test on how the Vatican would treat the Orthodox, should the two branches of Christianity reunite. Both the Ukrainian Catholic Church and the Vatican officials realized the importance of filling the American bishopric for the Ukrainian Catholic Church, but the churchmen in Rome and Lviv could not find a suitable candidate for the post.

The consecration of a bishop is a religious rite but his appointment has secular dimensions. The reasons for the choice of a bishop interest even the irreligious. In the post-World War I world, the rise of new nation states increased the number of players and complicated the already complex issues within the countries and in their dealings with the papacy. The pope, who nominates all bishops, now had more factors to consider in making his choice. After the peace settlement, regional Catholic churches found themselves in two or three different countries, and the Vatican was drawn into the internal policies of the successor states of the Austro-Hungarian, Russian, and Ottoman empires. The three empires contained a patchwork of nationalities and religions. Ukrainians did not have an independent state, but the Ukrainian Greek-Catholic Church, still formally calling itself Ruthenian, had parishes in most countries in Eastern Europe and the Balkans. In serving these congregations the Ukrainian Church took on national characteristics.

Despite the failure of Ukrainians between 1917 and 1923 to fashion and preserve an independent state, the Ukrainian Catholic Church grew into greater visibility in the first half of the twentieth century, both in Europe and in America. Ukrainians had joined the great migration to America toward the end of the nineteenth century. By the 1880s, the laity had started organizing Catholic churches, and they asked the mother church for priests. The first officially authorized Ukrainian Catholic missionary priest celebrated his first liturgy in the United States in 1884 in the mining town of Shenandoah in Pennsylvania. The first bishop, Soter Ortynsky, consecrated in 1907, died in 1916. Although the Vatican addressed the need to appoint another bishop for Ukrainian Catholics in the United States as soon as it learned of Ortynsky's death, the parties could not agree on a satisfactory candidate. Rome ran into numerous difficulties before the final recommendation could be made. Meanwhile, Ukrainian Catholic Americans appealed to the Holy See with petitions and letters, arguing not only for a bishop, but for one who would establish a Ukrainian Catholic seminary to train American-educated priests in the traditional faith. The young priests, in turn, would preserve the church for the younger generation.

As the decision on the appointment dragged on, fear grew within the Vatican walls that if the Ukrainians in America continued without a bishop, the three hundred Ukrainian parishes and the 231 priests of the Ukrainian churches in the United States that served half a million Ukrainian Catholics might join *en masse* a newly founded Ukrainian Orthodox church. An exodus on such a scale would undermine the Vatican's quest for unity with the East and reflect badly on the whole Catholic Church.[2]

Pope Benedict XV died in 1922, having failed to stop the war or broker a just peace. The new pope, Pius XI, knew Eastern Europe first hand and understood the importance of the Ukrainian immigrant community in the United States, especially in its relation with the Eastern European Orthodox world. He sympathized with the spiritual needs of the immigrants, and charged the newly founded Congregation for the Eastern Church[3] to expedite its recommendation of episcopal candidates for the American-Ukrainian Church. Between 1922 and 1923 the congregation held four formal sessions to review all the documentation on the possible candidates for that appointment. Finally pressured to decide, the cardinals held their last very lengthy session on the appointment in the first days of February 1924. On February 14 they formally recommended the appointment of not one, but two bishops for the Ruthenian Greek-Catholic Church of the Byzantine rite in the United States, as the church was known officially. The cardinals knew full well that the American Catholic clergy were not very happy when the first Ukrainian bishop was sent to the United States in 1907. American Catholic clergy resented the Ukrainian Greek-Catholics of the Byzantine Rite, with their married priests and rowdy congregations. Why then did the pope send them two bishops some twenty years later? The answer to this question had as much to do with the situation in Europe as with the United States.

Ukrainian Catholic immigrants to the United States came from two

2. A petition asked specifically for a seminary "so that our children be taught by American trained priests," sent through Pietro Fumasoni-Biondi, the apostolic delegate to the United States; AES, America, pos. 181–91, fasc. 35, 8. For an introduction to the Ukrainian Catholic Church in the United States, see Bohdan P. Procko, *Ukrainian Catholics in America: A History* (Lanham, Md.: University Press of America, 1982). Ivan Kaszczak presented a new edition of this work (Poughkeepsie, N.Y.: Maar Printing Service, 2016).

3. Technically, the name was the Congregation for the Eastern Church, but the term was often used in the plural, and this form officially became its name in 1967.

different areas within the Habsburg Empire. Those from the Hungarian Trans-Carpathia referred to themselves as Ruthenians or Rusyns; those from Halychyna preferred using a newer term—Ukrainian. Bishop Ortynsky had sought to mitigate the differences between the two immigrant groups in America as they set up Catholic parishes. But even with full episcopal powers, which he only received in 1913, the bishop could not settle disagreements. When he died in 1916, it became more difficult to maintain an orderly exarchy. And at Rome, as soon as the news of Ortynsky's death reached Europe, Hungarian representatives began lobbying the Vatican to appoint a bishop amenable to Hungarian concerns.[4] The Vatican, although sensitive to local concerns, resented outright pressure and worried that the Hungarian candidate would alienate the Ukrainians from other areas.

In earlier meetings on the appointment, the cardinals of the Congregation for the Eastern Church supported the Lviv Metropolitan Andrey Sheptytsky's recommendation of Bishop Dionysius Njaradi, the bishop of Kryzhovychi, which was then in Yugoslavia but with responsibility over churches in Czechoslovakia and Hungary. Metropolitan Sheptytsky thought Njaradi was an ideal candidate—experienced, diplomatic, well connected, industrious, and honest. And he worked with both camps—Ukrainian and Ruthenian. Sheptytsky stated his view forcefully: "Njaradi is the best candidate, the only one who because of his virtues, energy, and gravitas would be gladly accepted by all priests, the only one who would be capable of resurrecting and rejuvenating the eparchy. His only flaw—lack of English language—could be readily mitigated by his having good advisors."[5] The Hungarian government did not object to Njaradi.[6]

4. For an overview of Hungarian policies toward Ukrainians in the United States, see Osyp Danko, "Natsional'na polityka Madiarshchyny sered Rusyniv Zakarpattia v Spoluchenykh Shtatakh Ameryky," *Ukraiins'ky Istoryk: Zhurnal Istorii Ukraiinoznavstva* (New York) nos. 1–4 (1999): 191–208.

5. The eight-page letter that Metropolitan Sheptytsky wrote to Cardinal Isaiah Papadopulos, at the time chair of the Congregation for the Eastern Church, on March 1, 1923, had high praise for Njaradi, but most of it dealt with the changes that would have to be made in five different jurisdictions once Njaradi left for America. CEC, vol. 117, Prot. 9863/9831 and 737/32 [Rigotti, 151–59].

6. But Hungarians in the United States, who learned of this possibility, mistrusted Njaradi "because it is rumored that he is a propagator of Galician Ukrainians." M. Juhasz, president of a Ruthenian fraternal society, to Bishop Antonii Papp of Mukachiv; AES, Poland, pos. 81–91, fasc. 355.

Njaradi, who was a frequent visitor to Rome, also had personal support in high Vatican circles. So, after the cardinals in the Congregation for the Eastern Church re-read Sheptytsky's letters and other pertinent material, they accepted the metropolitan's suggestion of Njaradi as the only viable candidate for bishop.

When offered the American post, Njaradi said he would go to America if ordered by the pope, but he would rather work with his own now scattered flock that needed additional attention because of the complexity of the border changes.[7] The Vatican officials felt that the experienced, independently wealthy, well-liked bishop could not be spared for what was generally still considered to be a missionary post in far-off immigrant America. The political rearrangement of Eastern Europe and the Balkans was of greater import than the internal tensions within the Ukrainian immigrant community. After his candidacy for the American post was withdrawn, however, Njaradi became a very active adviser during the final deliberations on the nomination of a bishop for America. He had first-hand experience of dealing with Ruthenian/Ukrainian churches in different areas. He suggested separating the Ruthenian and Ukrainian administrations for the time being. His suggestion of naming two bishops for Ukrainian Catholics in the United States carried the day. After another review of all the possible candidates, and a brief note of objections to each, two names were forwarded to the pope: Basil Takach, the rector of the seminary at Mukachiv, and Constantine Bohachevsky, the vicar-elect of the Peremyshl Diocese. (The city is now in Poland and is known as Przemysl.)

At an audience on February 14, 1924, Pope Pius XI accepted the recommendation for the two bishops, but asked that the decision not be made public immediately.[8] Polish Catholics in America had been clamoring for a Polish bishop, but the papacy on principle refrained from naming bishops for ethnic or national considerations. At this time, however, there happened to be a suitable candidate of Polish origin for a vacant bishopric in the United States, and the pope wanted to announce it before the

7. Njaradi to Cardinal Giovanni Tacci, chair of the Congregation for the Eastern Church, April 1, 1924; CEC, vol. 117, Prot. 12941/1291 [Rigotti, 261–64].

8. The pope, on May 3, 1924, asked Pietro Fumasoni-Biondi that the nomination of the Ruthenian bishops not be made public for a month or so, until a bishop of Polish nationality be named for the United States; AES, America (1921–25), pos. 181–91, fasc. 35, 36.

Ukrainian nominations became public. In the process, information on the appointment of the two Ukrainian bishops failed to reach the Ukrainian Catholic administrator in the United States.

Bohachevsky was immediately thrust into civic as well as religious leadership. He had headed the Peremyshl Civic Committee when none of the laity would risk taking the position, and firmly defended the eroding rights of Ukrainians, including the use of Ukrainian language in schools and local government, as well as the freedom to practice one's religion. Although the new Polish Republic was a Catholic state, it pressured Ukrainian Catholics to change their rite to Latin, especially if they wanted a government job. The Polish Republic sought to make Polish the exclusive state language—even in the records of the Ukrainian Church. Polish officials resented what they considered Bohachevsky's obstinacy and waited for a chance to catch the priest breaking a law. The excuse for Bohachevsky's arrest came on June 20, 1919. A Ukrainian clerk in Polish government service, bypassing the Ukrainian Catholic Church, petitioned the government to change his rite from Eastern Catholic to the Latin Catholic. Bohachevsky, as pastor of the cathedral, refused to honor the request on legal grounds. Bohachevsky was arrested, paraded on foot through the whole city to the police station across the river San, and incarcerated in the local military jail.[9] After a week of this treatment, he was transferred to the prison in Modlin, and a month later to Dobie, near Cracow, for another month. While in prison, he was punished for preaching in Ukrainian. In both prisons, physical violence was routinely used against the prisoners.

Between prison transfers Bohachevsky managed to see Achille Ratti, the papal nuncio (who in 1922 would become Pius XI) in Warsaw. The obviously beaten and starved Bohachevsky made a lasting impression on the future pope-he referred to him in a letter as "an apostolic man."[10] Through direct Vatican intervention, Bohachevsky was freed on September 1, 1919, after a two-month imprisonment. He was given three days to make it back

9. The family story of Bohachevsky's arrest, told in general terms along with descriptions of arrest and mistreatment of other family members, is confirmed, in detail in Kotsylovsky's formal letter to the papal auditor Carlo Chiarlo, September 10, 1923; ASV, Warsaw, vol. 224, 365r. I drew additional information from my meetings with Bishop (clandestine) Vasyl Hrynyk in Peremyshl in the winter of 1976.

10. Achille Ratti to Pietro Gaspari, quoting the letter he wrote to General Haller on July 20, 1919; ASV, Warsaw, vol. 194, 1003.

to Peremyshl. Incarceration strengthened Bohachevsky's pro-Vatican sentiments even as it made the Vatican more aware of his person and of Ukrainians. Poland's short-sighted anti-Ukrainian policies were especially evident in Bohachevsky's case because of his steady climb up the Catholic hierarchical ladder. The Polish authorities even froze Bohachevsky's income as they accelerated their policies of active discrimination of minorities. That made it difficult for the pope to normalize relations with the Polish Republic—how could the pope sign a treaty with a nominally Catholic government that persecuted other Catholics?

The appointment of Bohachevsky gave the pope a gracious way out of an awkward situation with the Polish government, while at the same time it expanded the structure of the Ukrainian Church. Bohachevsky possessed all the qualities that the papacy wanted in a Catholic bishop—he was practical, modest and pious, loyal to the Vatican but capable of independent action; and it seemed his proven Ukrainian patriotism would make him very acceptable to his people. His public behavior in the face of adversity, demonstrated by preventing public demonstrations, even on his behalf, that would have served as pretext for armed government intervention, especially impressed the Vatican officials. He was decorated by the Habsburgs, climbed the local Ukrainian church ladder, and at the same time was actively involved with the working-class population. No one questioned his piety, his loyalty to Rome, nor his scholarship. He knew classical Greek, Latin, some Hebrew and Italian and French, had excellent Ukrainian, Polish, Church Slavonic, and German; and he could read Russian. As Njaradi, he did not know English—but that could be remedied. The more the cardinals studied Bohachevsky, the more his candidacy appealed to them. Meanwhile, in Peremyshl, Bohachevsky was completely ignorant that he was an object of such high-level discussion.

Although the appointment of a Ukrainian bishop for the United States had been talked about for years, no one predicted the selection of two bishops. Once the news about Takach leaked out, there was no need for anyone to speculate about a second appointment. By mid-April, Reverend Xavier Bonne in New York already knew of Takach's appointment, as did the Prague press and the Czechoslovak government.[11] Only on May 26,

11. Rev. Xavier Bonne to Rev. Enrico Benedetti, the recording secretary of the Congregation for the Eastern Church, April 28, 1924; AES, America, pos. 181–91, fasc. 35, 37.

1924, did Pietro Fumasoni-Biondi—the apostolic delegate in Washington—inform Rev. Petro Poniatyshyn—the administrator of the Ukrainian Catholic Church in the United States—of the dual appointment. Bohachevsky was to become the bishop in Philadelphia, and Takach in a city to be determined; but since no specific dates of arrival were given, speculation about the appointments continued.[12]

Both nominees were consecrated as bishops at a joint ceremony on June 15, 1924, at the Greek church of St. Athanasius in Rome. The two agreed to travel together to be met jointly in New York by the Ukrainian/Rusyn Catholic congregation. The Vatican and Ukrainian Catholic authorities agreed that this would demonstrate the cooperation of the bishops and offset criticism that Rome was dividing the Ukrainian Catholic Church. Both bishops came to America specifically to minister to the Ukrainian Catholics living there. They came willingly to serve and carry out the important work of the church. They were optimistic and energetic, trusted in God, and hoped for the best.

Bohachevsky was told to expect major difficulties, but he thought the difficulties would be minor, since the major problem that plagued the church in the United States, the tension between the Ruthenians and the Ukrainians, was to be resolved. Not briefed on the specifics in the exarchy, he did not initiate contact with any of the priests, since he did not know where each stood. He waited to see how he would fit into the new setting and looked forward to consolidating the church and working with the community. Once in America, in the first few months, he even considered that the situation in the Ukrainian Catholic Church in the United States was not as dire as had been presented to him, but he was quickly proven wrong. It would take him a full decade to reach his goals of consolidating the church and working with the community. A conservative cleric, who placed his hopes on education as much as in Providence, Bohachevsky was thrown into the maelstrom of the American jazz age and the Great Depression. At one point he would lose a third of his congregations, and there was even an attempt on his life. After the end of World War II, he, a militant proponent of clerical celibacy, would welcome over one hundred married clergy and their families into his diocese.

12. Pietro Fumasoni-Biondi to Rev. Petro Poniatyshyn, May 26, 1924, copy, UMAS.

For all his modesty and the missionary simplicity of his life, Bohachevsky found himself thrust simultaneously into Vatican politics and the tumult of American immigrant life on his very first trip to both Rome and America. In the United States the odds were stacked against him—he did not know English and was totally ignorant of American law and customs; he lacked diplomatic skills and was averse to back-room deals; his oratory was down-to-earth; and his pedantic habits clashed with the culture of American industrial cities. His two attempts at public self-defense failed, and his reliance on prayer, reason, and good works showed little immediate success. His opponents, in contrast, were sophisticated in presenting their arguments, clothing them in patriotism and democracy, and reaping immediate results.

Bohachevsky cared little about the image he projected. He even considered the details of the construction of the metropolitanate (the bricks and mortar part, with its growth spurts and the inevitable fissures) as only the underpinnings of what was most important—the missionary service to his people. What mattered to him was the church as an instrument for the salvation of his people—their souls as well as their spirits, an incubator for eternity. Once the Roman Pontiff saw fit to call upon him, the Rev. Constantine Bohachevsky of Halychyna, to become the bishop for the Ukrainian Catholics in the United States, he became duty incarnate; and the life he led was one of service. He prodded his faithful and especially his priests, at times not very gently, to make certain that the growth of the church came from below, that the people were aware of what it was that they were building, and that they not limit the church to beautiful buildings.

Bohachevsky succeeded because, as far as he was concerned, he had been destined to prevail. God's Providence was on his side. His direct papal appointment to the missionary post of the Ukrainian Catholic exarchate in the United States validated Bohachevsky's calling to the priesthood. He saw himself and his work as an integral part of two forces that made up his world—the Catholic Church and the Ukrainian people. He focused his sight on making the people in his care aware that they too were active instruments of God's design, individually responsible for their fate. This goal required a Catholic education and the support of their own strong church. Since neither was available for Ukrainian Catholics in the United

States at the time of Bohachevsky's arrival, he had to create the church infrastructure and the schools. At the same time, he worked to make the United States and its Latin-rite Roman Catholic Church more aware and respectful of the Ukrainian presence.

When the Soviet Union, in 1946, had forcibly abolished the Ukrainian Catholic Church in Ukraine, arresting and executing its leadership and pushing the church underground, the role of the American church became even more important. In Western Europe, the Ukrainian churches functioned in small émigré communities, while the Ukrainian Church in America effectively emerged from its own catacombs of immigrant slums unto public recognition in the Vatican and in the United States.

Two years after Archbishop-Metropolitan Bohachevsky's death, on January 23, 1963, Cardinal (since 1949, in pectore) Joseph Slipyj was freed from Soviet incarceration and transported to Rome. Ten years later, when two of Bohachevsky's most dedicated clerics—John Stock, "the Pastor to the Displaced Persons," and Basil Losten, who would facilitate the training of Ukrainian priests from Ukraine in the Ukrainian institutions in the United States—were ordained bishops, some of the Philadelphia faithful protested violently, viewing these appointments as a slight to Cardinal Slipyj. A new period of unrest that engaged mostly the post-World War II émigrés began in the Ukrainian Catholic Church in the West. The issue was the establishment of a patriarchate and the recognition of Cardinal Slipyj in that seat. The church survived this painful interlude.

In Ukraine, when it was very much a part of the USSR, the laity identified religious rights with human rights, and fought for both in any way they could. By 1989, there were increasing signs of the church emerging from the catacombs. When the mother church legalized itself after four decades of Soviet repression, the Ukrainian Church in the United States provided a model for church structure, and the Ukrainian-American seminary welcomed students from the newly independent Ukraine. The proclamation of Ukraine's independence in 1991 changed the Ukrainian Catholic Church dramatically. As the Ukrainian Catholic Church in Ukraine became legal, it not only reclaimed Western Ukraine, but quickly moved back to its original territories in Kyiv and the East. Two priests from the Philadelphia Archdiocese, one following the other, became the archbishops-major in independent Ukraine. Myroslav Cardinal Lubachivsky (1914–

2000) and Lubomyr Cardinal Husar (1933–2017) retraced Bohachevsky's steps back to Ukraine and began working there to organize the emergent structure of a resuscitated Ukrainian Catholic Church.[13] Both had worked with Bohachevsky. Lubachivsky, of the last generation to be ordained by Sheptytsky, had worked long years in the Cleveland area developing Ukrainian Catholic schools and churches. Cardinal Archbishop-Major Lubomyr Husar had been a student at the seminaries that Bohachevsky had spent his lifetime building.

I doubt that Bohachevsky, known for his lengthy prayers and short sermons, ever allowed himself to hope for such a turn of events in Ukraine within the lifetime of his own clergy.

13. Husar had been a student at St. Basil's Seminary. Bohachevsky tested his knowledge of theology prior to ordination, but Bishop Ambrose Senyshyn ordained him because, as Bohachevsky pointed out, at the time the exarchy was already divided and the ordinary bishop had the right to consecrate the priests in his diocese.

CHAPTER 1

An Embedded Priesthood

Constantine's generation was among the last of the wide network of traditional clergy families in the Ukrainian Catholic Church, and his family history provides a typical example of this class. His father, Sylvester, was what was known as a "modern" priest—a scion of a priestly family, but one who had received a higher education, read secular books, liked mathematics, and developed an understanding of the economic needs and social aspirations of the farmers whom he served. The family seat was in Pluhiv, a village in the low Carpathians in which for about two hundred years a Bohachevsky, or a man married to a Bohachevsky, had been a pastor. Constantine's father Sylvester along with his brother Petro tried to make it on their own, without family help. They took adjoining parishes in the lowlands, closer to Lviv. Constantine, the second of Sylvester's seven sons, was born on June 17, 1884, at Manaiiv, the small village in the Zboriv area of Halychyna, the heartland of Western Ukraine in the Austro-Hungarian Empire. But as the family grew Sylvester could not make ends meet. He returned to the highland villages where he cared for two or three parishes at a time and where he was closer to his own family and the in-laws, the Zarytskys, who can be considered to personify the richer and more conservative wing of the class.

The villages in which Constantine grew up were small, all had less than one hundred households. They were picturesque, steeped in historical lore, knitted with each other by bonds of family and expanded hospitality. Constantine's childhood was a happy one, and he retained only fond memories of his large extended family and of the whole atmosphere of his youth. By the time he became an adult, however, the society in which he flourished was rent by wars, economic crises, and internal tensions. Yet the strength that the young boy drew from his seemingly inauspicious surroundings, buttressed by the religious practices of his church, sustained his very productive life until his death, on January 6, 1961, at Philadelphia, Pennsylvania. His core beliefs and identity were firm and unwavering, strong enough to survive war, prison, adjustment to America, and the open hostility of his flock.

HALYCHYNA, NOT GALICIA, AND ITS CHURCH

Constantine's childhood must be viewed in the larger setting of Ukrainian life in Halychyna, the Ukrainian Church there, and his extended family. A century before Constantine's birth, the Habsburg rulers who had acquired parts of the Polish Commonwealth, expanded the Ukrainian, medieval, political entity of Halych to include a part of ethnic Poland, and popularized the Latinized name of the new province as Galicia/Galitzia. At the time of his birth the area was still largely rural. Although there were Polish villages, Ukrainians constituted the majority of the population in the original Halychyna, the eastern part of expanded Galicia. In addition to Ukrainians and Poles, there were a very large established Jewish minority and smaller populations of Armenians, Karaims, Czechs, and Germans.

The Ukrainian population there was, with few exceptions, composed of Catholics of the Greek rite, or uniates.[1] The very name of the church is often the subject of debate. In Bohachevsky's time it was called the "Greek-Catholic Church of the Byzantine Rite," a name approved by the

1. For a historical overview of this part of the Catholic Church, see Bohdan Bociurkiw, *The Ukrainian Greek Catholic Church and the Soviet State (1939–1950)* (Edmonton: Canadian Institute of Ukrainian Studies, 1996), 1–21. For a fuller presentation from a traditional Western Ukrainian standpoint, see Gregory Luznytsky [Luzhnytsky], *Ukraiins'ka Tserkva mizh Skhodom i Zakhodom* (Philadelphia: Providence Association of Ukrainian Catholics, 1954). On the relationship of the Catholic Church and the broad Ukrainian national movement, see John-Paul Himka, *The Greek Catholic Church and the Ukrainian society in Austrian Galicia* (Cambridge, Mass.: Harvard Ukrainian Studies, 1986); and his *Religion and Nationality in Western Ukraine: The Greek Catholic Church and the Ruthenian National Movement in Galicia, 1867–1900* (Montreal: McGill University Press, 1999). For a broader look, see Serhii Plokhy and Frank Sysyn, *Religion and Nation in Modern Ukraine* (Edmonton: CIUS, 2003).

Habsburg monarchy when it annexed the territory at the end of the eighteenth century. At times the adjective "Ukrainian" or "Ruthenian," an older variant of the same name, was included for greater specificity. The term "uniate" was also used, but for some it seemed a term of opprobrium. The largest cities in eastern Halychyna were Lviv, Peremyshl (now Przemysl, Poland), and Stanyslaviv (now Ivano-Frankivsk, Ukraine). Other towns in Halychyna were remnants of medieval trading towns, with little new industry and a small middle class. The urban population was mixed, predominantly Poles and Jews, a growing Ukrainian minority, and a sprinkling of Czechs, Armenians, and Austrian officials. The Ukrainian Catholic clergy, which was largely salaried by the state, performed basic administrative functions, registering births, marriages, and deaths, and setting up schools. Since the salary was inadequate for the type of leadership roles the state and the society expected, the parish clergy supplemented their income by traditional means, running farms and expecting payment, which was set by the ecclesiastical authorities, for their individual priestly services. Historically, the Ukrainian Catholic priests in Halychyna were subject to church discipline, to the will of the local authority (which was in a state of flux as the Habsburg bureaucracy removed some feudal arrangements of the nobility over their holdings), and to a lesser extent, to the good will of their flock. In some villages, the landowner continued to exercise the right to approve pastors even after the First World War.

The clergy were the major contact of the village with the outside world. They provided spiritual guidance and encouraged the establishment of secular clubs, schools, and small economic cooperatives.[2] Ukrainian clergy considered it their duty to socialize their flock into the broader entity known as "the people" or "the nation." Their wives were their primary helpers, dispensing rudimentary hygiene knowledge, "fancy" cooking skills, and sometimes setting up cooperative daycare for children. The Catholic priests were the foremost part of the emerging Ukrainian intelligentsia. They were not aware that they were "creating" a nation; they

2. The modern Western Ukrainian cooperative movement should be dated from the successful attempt of the Peremyshl Ukrainian Catholic clergy to establish a widows' and orphans' benefit society for their members at the beginning of the nineteenth century. A brief discussion in Martha Bohachevsky-Chomiak, *Feminists Despite Themselves: Women in Ukrainian Community Life, 1884–1939* (Edmonton: Canadian Institute of Ukrainian Studies, 1988), 50–53.

were merely asserting their own identity along with the villagers.[3] The people—hence the nation—already existed, they just needed to know who they were. The village priests, from whom most of Western Ukrainian intelligentsia came, were at times even worse off financially than wealthy peasants. Yet money never determined clergy status—at least not openly. Religious, civic, family, and educational factors intertwined. The profession was almost but not quite hereditary, but the priests saw themselves as having a calling, not a profession. The calling was not limited to religion.

The Catholic Church played a dual role in Western Ukraine. On the one hand, it was one of the major agents of change in the country, especially in the villages. At the same time, by insisting that all development occur within the confines of church dogma, it perforce limited that development. The church, even more than the government, introduced official documentation into the personal lives of the villagers by recording and notarizing births, marriages, and deaths. The same church insisted upon formalities (such as marriage banns) that publicized personal decisions. Church rituals, especially public processions, served as models for organizing village life. As a public institution, the village church became the visible symbol of group identity. Hence, even before a fully secular society emerged, there existed a group identity that referred to itself by the historic term "Ruthenian." Slowly within Constantine's childhood, that term was first supplemented and eventually supplanted by the more modern term "Ukrainian."

Within its own sphere, the Ukrainian Catholic Church saw itself as a defender of the identity and welfare of its people. While the Catholic Church offered tools for modern life, whether literacy or rudimentary administration, it also warned of the perils of modernity. Since Ukrainians had not created a fully secular society before the emergence of modern democratic strivings, the Ukrainian Catholic Church was increasingly drawn into political and societal battles. The secular intelligentsia that emerged formulated its views within the context of that religious world. Overall, the church fought against liberalism. Its own view of democracy was one that was compatible with church teachings and vision.[4]

3. For a fuller discussion of the Ukrainian Catholic clergy, and its decline as a separate caste, see Andrew Sorokowsky, "The Greek-Catholic Parish Clergy in Galicia, 1900–1939" (Ph.D. diss.; University of London, School of Slavonic and East European Studies, 1990).

4. *Rerum novarum*, Pope Leo XIII's encyclical that focused on urban workers, was

All aspects of political, cultural, and religious life in Halychyna were dominated by rival Polish and Ukrainian nationalisms, land shortage, and economic want. Although Ukrainians in pre-World War I Halychyna were intellectually as enmeshed in the struggle between conservatism and modernity as any other group in Europe, they couched the rhetoric of that debate in terms of national rather than human rights. Modernity had a tinge of socialism and even slight ripples of atheism. These trends contributed to the formation of a secular intelligentsia that despite their criticism of the church was shaped by the specific climate of Ukrainian Catholicism in Halychyna. Social responsibility colored the work of anyone who claimed social standing, and an almost religious, optimistic certainty pervaded the group. For lack of a better term, these people came to call themselves intelligentsia. The Western Ukrainian intelligentsia put its efforts into various projects that could lead to immediate results, even if small. Unlike the neighboring Russian intelligentsia, the Ukrainian intelligentsia was not alienated from the people but rather evolved with them and their local organizations. Headed by either members of the Catholic clergy or the secular intelligentsia, cooperatives, workshops, acting groups, self-help circles, and choirs dotted the Ukrainian countryside. On the other hand, European fin-de-siècle decadence, Scandinavian existentialism, dramatic philosophical breakthroughs, and even local, Lviv, mathematical innovations had only a limited impact on what passed for the Ukrainian creative society in Halychyna.[5]

The Catholic Church structure was as hierarchical as the Austrian Empire when, at the end of the eighteenth century, it took over a land that included Poles, Ukrainians, and Jews. As in any large hierarchical structure the center did not always control all its disparate parts. The secular Habsburgs helped the church formalize education of priests, and thus made it easier for all qualified graduates of high schools, regardless of social status, to seek entrance to the seminaries. Clerical education of Ukrainian Catholic priests led the clergy to identify not only with the church but also with its people.

---

promulgated in May 1891. It coincided with the first politically motivated street demonstration of Ukrainians in Halychyna in Stryj, where Constantine and his older brother Volodymyr would attend the high school.

5. See Stanislaw Ulam, *Adventures of a Mathematician* (Los Angeles: University of California Press, 1975).

The last decade of the nineteenth century witnessed the penetration of socialist ideals in the area. Popular wisdom now argued that people were meant to create their own rule and to have a democratic national polity or even a sovereign state. A national ideal could thus be part of the new socialist striving. Contact with Ukrainian intelligentsia from tsarist Ukraine broadened the scope of cultural activity and moved the Western Ukrainian national discourse from its clerical Halychyna roots into a broader, secular context. This was aided by the romanticizing of the Zaporozhian Cossack lore. Children of the Catholic clergy began to enjoy greater mobility and more open career choices. Organized political parties, grounded in ideological principles, arose in Halychyna in the last decade of the nineteenth century and sought to replace the clergy as "the voice of the people." The clergy considered freethinkers to be the next wave of the corrupting influences with which God repeatedly tested the world. Yet many Catholic priests organized public actions, demonstrated for the universal right to vote, joined political parties, stood for office, and propagated programs of social welfare, without giving their actions an ideological tinge. The tensions between the upper- and lower-class clergy, while present in private and even in correspondence, did not emerge in the public sphere.[6]

Economic and social changes in Halychyna were gradual and comparatively nonviolent. Within Constantine's immediate environment the changes involved secularization of Ukrainian community life in the sense that the leadership in the village passed from the priest to the secular teacher. At the turn of the twentieth century the expansion of educational facilities and the professionalization of clergy education broke its relatively closed ranks. An influx of candidates for priesthood from outside

6. An unusually sharp example comes from a letter that Bishop Josaphat Kotsylovsky wrote to his vicar, Bishop Basil Lakota, on January 20, 1927, referring to an action that Metropolitan Sheptytsky took toward Bohachevsky: "[Giving Bohachevsky's letter to the person whose actions Bohachevsky questioned] was so obnoxious, so vile. He might as well, as in the pre-Zamosc times, told his servant to whip [Bohachevsky] as the gentry had done toward our fathers. Issues of lord and peasant exist among the church hierarchy, somewhat in the nature of the land question [use of forests and grazing fields by the peasant farmers]." Archiwum Panstwowe w Przemyslu (formerly Wojewodske Archiwum Panstwowe), Archiwum Grecko-Katolickiego Biskupstwa, Syg. 9484. The recently discovered, alleged memoirs of Bishop Khomyshyn—Hryhoriy Chomyshyn, *Dva Tsarstva*, ed. Wlodzimierz Osadczy and Rev. Ihor Pelehatyj (Lublin: Petit SK, 2016)—openly discuss class tensions within the Ukrainian Catholic Church, but the authenticity of the publication is hotly disputed.

the clergy families masked the exodus of the sons of the clergy into other professions, once they had the opportunity to do so. Individual priests scrambled for bigger and richer parishes to feed their growing families and to meet the changed aspirations of their sons to be educated in professions other than priesthood. The priests not only spread the word of God but also educated the people. By the end of the nineteenth century the clergy saw their personal aspirations as a natural and compatible part of the national aspirations.[7]

Despite the eventual cultural and political preeminence of Lviv, Halychyna's major Ukrainian city, at the end of the 1890s, the hub of Western Ukrainian political activity centered on the southwestern towns, especially Stryj and to a lesser extent the larger Stanislaviv, today's Ivano-Frankivsk. This was the area in which Constantine grew up and where he received his formative high-school education. We need not go into the minutiae of Austrian electoral processes; suffice it to say that while the central government in Vienna proclaimed the expansion of electoral rights and developed plans for a better publicly sponsored educational system, the local authorities attempted to hem in the implementation of those rights. Ukrainians took to the street to demand modest goals—universal electoral rights and education in their own language. When Constantine was still young, the first public political rally was held at Stryj in 1890. Soon, rallies, meetings, concerts, religious ceremonies, sports events, all began serving as expressions of Ukrainian solidarity. When the authorities tried to prevent public demonstrations, the priests held outdoor pro-

7. The Ukrainian language memoirs of Rev. Fylymon Tarnawsky (December 4, 1862–September 24, 1948) provide a frank presentation of the life of the Ukrainian Catholic clergy. My father, Danylo Bohachevsky, made a typed copy of one version of the manuscript; the following quotation is from the unpublished text: "In those days at St. George Cathedral, one's connections determined one's fate. That depressed and demoralized [us]." My translation from Tarnawsky, *Spomyny* [*Memoirs*] (1820s–1940s), 109, unpublished manuscript version in the possession of the author. Parts of Tarnawsky's memoirs were published as *Spohady: Rodynna Khronika Tarnavs'kykh*, ed. Anatol Bazylewycz and Roman Danylewycz (Toronto: Dobra knyzhka, 1981). Personal connections often determined appointments. Sylvester Bohachevsky in an undated letter turned to a layman, Oleksander Barvinsky, one of the leading democratic political activists, to ask for help in expediting his transfer to a promised larger parish. In another letter, dated July 9, 1892, Bohachevsky asked Oleksander Barvinsky to help Vasyl Sen'kiv, a poor Manaiiv boy, enter a high school. LAL, Barvinsky File, nos. 664–5 and 167/11.

cessions and open-air services. When locally hired thugs tried to stop the peasants from going to vote, the priests organized processions of electors who solemnly marched to the voting places, carrying a cross and religious banners. Austria was a Catholic country as well as a monarchy, and both *lèse majesté* and blasphemy were public crimes.

THE BOHACHEVSKY FAMILY

Ukrainian Catholic priests can be married men. The right to keep married clergy was one of the major conditions under which Ukrainians, then still known as Ruthenians, joined Rome's fold in the year 1596. Their sons traditionally studied for the priesthood and married within the clergy milieu, and their daughters generally married seminarians who after marriage received holy orders into priesthood. For almost ten generations the relatively closed group of married clerics and their families had preserved as best they could both the Eastern rite of the Catholic Church in Europe and a sense of a Ukrainian identity. The system worked in an agricultural society with limited educational and professional opportunities.

The Bohachevskys were a typical family within the declining tradition of Ukrainian Catholic hereditary rural clergy. The immediate surroundings of Bohachevsky's childhood and youth belied the standard picture of Halychyna as being economically backward and socially unstable. The generation of Constantine's parents combined organized religion, popular education, and social involvement in poor but refined surroundings. Their social circle was open, widespread and informal, weaving idealism and practicality with old-fashioned gentility. These were the unsung priests who mixed modern card games and politics in the evenings, and were equally at ease praying the Liturgy the next morning.

In contrast with Bohachevsky's adult life, his childhood was stable. Both his parents were active in local community life, easily adjusting to new parishes. His mother organized and led choirs, and his father, in addition to being the parish pastor, was active in politics and experimented with bee keeping. Sylvester Bohachevsky, Constantine's father, received a formal higher education that went beyond purely liturgical issues.[8] As

8. The Austrian monarchy financed seminaries for the Ukrainian Catholic Churches after the regime confiscated many church holdings. The use of Ukrainian language in

an activist priest, he used his church education for the physical and social welfare of his flock. Sylvester, in typical enlightened Habsburg fashion, saw no conflict between his civic and sacerdotal duties. He tried, within the confines of church regulations and Christian ethics, to carry through policies of social responsibility, working assiduously to reduce rampant alcoholism in his parishes. When he took over as parish priest in Manaiiv in 1887, the village, which consisted of eighty households, had eleven taverns. Five years later the bars had dwindled to three. Sylvester set up a village center, a lending library, and a school. He was active in organizing a democratic Ukrainian political party, canvassed the villagers on the importance of electoral rights, and set up a local cooperative for farm products. Additionally, he established a branch of the public education society, Prosvita. The community appreciated his work even two decades after he left the village.

Thanks to his fun-loving nature, Sylvester wooed a bride from a clerical family of better social and financial standing. Olena's father was Oleksiy Zarytsky, the pastor of Tura Velyka, in the hilly Boyko area of Halychyna. During Constantine's lifetime, Oleksiy remained the pastor; later the parish passed to a son-in-law, Rev. Kornylo Dudykevych. Although Sylvester Bohachevsky was not as well off as Olena's father, she never complained. Judging from family memoirs, the Zarytskys helped the Bohachevskys both financially and in kind, at one point giving them livestock.[9]

From family descriptions, Olena Bohachevsky emerges as a very strong woman. In the first decade of marriage, she organized and ran village

---

high schools and the university in Lviv were major goals of Ukrainians from 1772, when the Austrian monarchy took control over Halychyna, to the very collapse of the empire. Prior to the Austrian takeover, Ukrainian Catholic priests schooled outside the home were still somewhat of a novelty among the clergy. Most Ukrainian Catholic priests essentially had been apprenticed with their father or other clerical relatives. For a fuller discussion, see Ivan Kaszczak, The Education of Ukrainian Catholic Clergy (1882–1946) (Lviv: Svichado Press, 2007).

9. The Zarytskys hailed from Tura Velyka; the Bohachevsky family claimed its origin from near-by Pluhiv. The Zarytskys kept their gentry papers and maintained an upper-class household. One of their sons became an opera singer in Berlin, where he signed his name with a von. The extended family embraced a moderate democratic activism, supporting liberal political reforms, expansion of educational opportunities, and land reform, but rejected socialism. See, for instance, death notices of Rev. Omelian Bohachevsky (1833–July 2, 1893), Dilo, no. 137; and his wife, Anna (née Pisets'ka) Bohachevsky (1842–October 14, 1891), Bat'kivshchyna, 1891, no. 41, LAL, f. 167, op. 11, od. zb. 309, 15.

FIGURE 1. OLENA BOHACHEVSKY,
NÉE ZARYTSKA (1862–1944)

church choirs and put on theatre performances. She treated the children she bore matter-of-factly, keeping the infants at her feet on the bed so she would not have to leave the bed to nurse. But after bearing seven of them—it can be assumed that there were no more than seven because we have no information about miscarriages or infant deaths—Olena withdrew from community affairs. She smoked heavily; and in later years, she had her grandchildren help her roll her cigarettes. She and her husband took schooling seriously, scrimping to send the boys to the gymnasium in Stryj, and then to the first Ukrainian language gymnasium, in Lviv.

Large families were the norm for the times. The Bohachevsky's first three sons, all born in Manaiiv, carried names of historical significance: Volodymyr (1882–1952), Constantine (1884–1961), and Danylo (1890–1985). They were named, respectively, after the ancient Kyivan prince who made Christianity the state religion in 988, the Byzantine emperor who legalized Christianity in Constantinople some five hundred years earlier, and the Western Ukrainian king who received his crown from the papacy in 1253.

They were all born while their father was socially and politically most active. As the size of the family strained family resources, Sylvester had to ask his church superiors to assign him to multiple parishes, and the family had to move a number of times. The younger boys were born in the picturesque Carpathian low hills. Oleksa (1893–1920) was named in honor of the maternal grandfather, while Ivan (1896–1956), Omelian (1898–1985), and Petro (1900–1920) carried the names of their uncles. As was the tradition at that time of high infant mortality, Constantine was christened "by water" a few days after his birth. Petro Bohachevsky, Sylvester's brother, who at the time was the pastor of the neighboring Harbuziv, performed the short baptismal rite. Omelian Bohachevsky, the pastor of Pluhiv and a patriarch of the family, celebrated the subsequent rite which included confirmation of the infant. Constantine's godparents were Rev. Fabian Zhukovsky and Mrs. Olympia Holovkevych, the wife of the judge in Manaiiv.

During Constantine's childhood and youth, the Bohachevskys were continually strapped for money. Sylvester, who came from a poorer branch of the Bohachevskys, struggled for the first decade of his married life not to rely upon his wife's family. Nevertheless, in the search for larger parishes that could feed the growing family, the Bohachevskys moved closer to the family seat of their better off in-laws, the Zarytskys. Once the family moved closer to the in-laws, Sylvester accepted their financial help. In 1895 the family moved to Lyubyntsi,[10] near Stryj, and then to Krasne.[11] Five years later Sylvester asked to be transferred to Petranka.[12] Sylvester explained his predicament to Metropolitan Andrey Sheptytsky—"my family needs and duties have reached a breaking point; I can barely manage to make ends meet."[13] The financial advantage of these parishes was that the priest had the right to sell lumber from the adjoining state forest.[14] Sylves-

10. The village, in the mountain range between Stryj and Skole, had been founded near a third-century B.C. settlement.

11. Krasne, founded in 1556, draws its name from a local river.

12. Petranka expanded in the mid-eighteenth century, thanks to an increase in its salt and linen production.

13. Sylvester Bohachevsky to Metropolitan Andrey Sheptytsky, March 8, 1910, from Krasna (now Krasne). He adds "I ask your Excellency's grace, which I, as heretofore, will always return by working with all my power in the vineyard of Christ." TsDIA, Lviv, f. 358, 2, spr. 110.

14. Austrian laws allowed harvesting of timber for sale in a direct ratio to the number of new saplings. That eased the financial burden somewhat for the head of the large

ter continued his civic and economic activism in the mountain villages. He encouraged beekeeping as a small business venture. He took an active part in organizing electoral campaigns and sought Metropolitan Sheptytsky's help in dealing with government authorities. He was not loathe to intervene with Sheptytsky to ask for the appointment of a particular person as postmaster[15] or to plead for support for the daughter of a deceased priest.[16] In each of these cases one of the salient strengths for the supplicant was adherence to the Ukrainian nation. At the same time, Sylvester boasted to the metropolitan in Lviv that the influence of the Radical Party in his parish (at the time he was writing about Krasne) had declined. "In church," he wrote, "I was careful to influence my parishioners purely in a Christian spirit."[17] At one point, when the Polish ferry keeper refused to serve the Ukrainians, Sylvester dramatically forded a flooded river with a delegation of the electors, raising his cross and standing on the wagon.[18] He had to make certain that the electors cast their votes. Since political demonstrations were forbidden, the presence of a priest in a chasuble could transform a public gathering into a religious activity.

Sylvester was a firm believer in the benefits of physical activity. He en-

---

family. For the most part, the villagers survived on a natural economy, eking out adequate subsistence from the crops and animals that they raised. Serfdom had been technically abolished in the 1790s. It crept in again until it was finally abolished in 1848. Social and economic repercussions remained in the dues that had to be paid under the guise of rent and taxes to the manorial owners of the village land. The villagers owned the land, but the plots, inadequate to begin with, were subdivided among the sons who had little opportunity to leave the villages. The land could not sustain a growing population. Land hunger exacerbated poverty, highlighting illiteracy, infant mortality, and growing alcoholism among the peasants. The programs of land distribution, which subdivided the estates were slow and mired in politics.

15. Sylvester Bohachevsky to Metropolitan Andrey Sheptytsky, November 30, 1911, Sylvester argued that Onufrey Kinakh, a local Polish resident, was a solid army veteran who, unlike other Poles in the village, regularly frequented the Ukrainian Catholic Church. TsDIA, Lviv, f. 358, op. 2, spr. 110, pp. 36–38.

16. Sylvester Bohachevsky to Metropolitan Sheptytsky. The exact date of this letter is not clear in Sheptytsky's correspondence, TsDIA, Lviv, f. 358, op. 2, spr. 110.

17. Sylvester further boasted about his sons—one already a lawyer who regularly goes to church, as do all his children; moreover, his parish regularly buys Catholic journals. Sylvester Bohachevsky to Metropolitan Sheptytsky, June 6, 1910, TsDIA, Lviv, f. 358, op. 2, spr. 110.

18. Danylo Bohachevsky, *Na vozi i pid vozom: Spomymy halyts'koho advokata* (Toronto: Dobra Knyzhka, 1976), 23.

couraged his sons to help out on the farm and promoted hiking through the region's mountain ranges. It was a custom adopted by Constantine, who enjoyed long walks, which for some of his companions seemed like strenuous hikes, throughout his life, though he also feared heights and preferred to avoid narrow winding mountain paths.[19] Constantine would promote physical activity and sports in schools and seminaries.

Much information on Constantine's childhood comes from Danylo, his junior by six years, a sizeable difference by Danylo's own admission.[20] By the time Danylo became aware of his childhood, Constantine was off to the gymnasium. The boys had the run of the whole house; the parlor doubled as a classroom and a game room. The formal tone of the lessons was offset by mealtime conversations. Evenings were spent either debating some issue (such as the morality or immorality of hitching train rides without paying), doing mathematical puzzles, or playing parlor games, including card games, which some clergy excoriated. Unlike his brothers, Constantine did not pick up the card game habit. The household was noisy, especially during the summer when each of the brothers was likely to bring a friend or two to spend the summer in the mountains. Naturally, farm work had to be done first, with the boys priding themselves on their ability to wield a scythe. Horses were strictly for farm work, and if the boys wanted to go to a party or to visit friends, they went on foot. Constantine especially enjoyed gatherings of the extended family, while his brothers were willing to walk ten miles to go to a dance.

The picture of the young Constantine that emerges from his early years is that of a quiet boy. He had weak lungs, rich golden hair, and inquisitive dark eyes. He grew up to be of average height and weight. Although he did not share his father's propensity for mischievous pranks, he willingly put up with them. He was close to his mother, sharing some of her personality traits—both were serious, independent, and strict. Constantine was clos-

19. Osyp Nazaruk to Viacheslav Lypynsky, April 15, 1926, in *Viacheslav Lypynsky: Collected Works*, vol. 7, *The Letters of Osyp Nazaruk*, ed. Ivan L. Rudnytsky (Philadelphia: W.K. Lypynsky East European Research Institute, 1976), 382.

20. In addition to his memoirs, *Na vozi*, Danylo Bohachevsky wrote *Vladyka Konstantyn Bohachevsky: Pershy Mytropolyt Ukraiins'koii Katolyts'koii Tserkvy v ZSA* (Philadelphia: America, 1980). Danylo's memory was reinforced by Fylymon Tarnawsky, who, in his memoirs, described Sylvester Bohachevsky's hospitality, as well as his love of hunting. In his memoirs, Danylo focused on public events.

est in age, but not in personality, to Volodymyr, his senior by two years. The ebullient and handsome first-born Volodymyr would later become the family reprobate—dropping out of the university, amassing extensive debts that the father felt obliged to pay off, and emigrating to America in disgrace around 1905. Compared to the rest of the boisterous brood, Constantine was a bookish loner. Except for hiking, he was not readily drawn to the physical exertions on which the younger boys thrived. As a young boy, he initiated the tradition of the youngsters helping in the community reading room; and he enjoyed reading newspapers out loud or tidying up the place. Constantine loved the small hilly villages. They were home. He was especially drawn to the area near Stryj where he spent his youth.[21] Each village, regardless of its size or location, had its complex history, dating back to the fourteenth century. Each had stories of battles with the Mongols, a Cossack tale, and a version of a Robin Hood. Most had a Jewish quarter, and occasionally a Polish landlord and a small Polish population.

Halychyna, overwhelmingly rural, was overcrowded, and had poor land and an inequitable land-holding system. Both the Habsburgs and later the Polish Republic struggled with the division of the land holdings that dated to the early modern times when Western Europe needed grain. Land hunger propelled the emigration to America, and land poverty shadowed all aspects of life in Halychyna, from health to politics. Constantine grew up very aware of the plight of the villagers, as much as of the financial difficulties of his own father in raising his large family.

A PRODUCTIVE DICHOTOMY

Like many similar families the Bohachevskys prided themselves on two mutually exclusionary characteristics: gentry lineage and closeness to the village farmers. This somewhat anomalous pairing was possible because the old Polish-Lithuanian Commonwealth, which included the ter-

21. Constantine's uncle, another Omelian (1868–March 23, 1902), was mourned in Dilo, no. 60, 1902, for his selfless work as a teacher at Mariampol, near Halych. A follow-up note, in Dilo, no. 65, 1902, is signed by the immediate family of the deceased: wife Julia (Iryna); daughter Natalia (Lunia); brothers Sylvester and Theodore; sister Olha Bohachevsky; and cousin Olena Dudykevych; Ihnat Spyrydonovych, father-in-law; and Kornylo Dudykevych, brother-in-law.

ritory of Halychyna, once had a large gentry class. In later times people remained conscious of their once elevated social position despite their present impoverished state. Because status was not contingent on political power, this self-styled gentry was relatively fluid and varied socially and economically. This group was especially susceptible to the popular romanticism laced with mild nationalist tones that swept Europe in the mid-nineteenth century. Embracing the use of the vernacular, these men and women focused on educational and agricultural projects that would benefit the peasants. The myth of gentry status helped many Ukrainians avoid feeling inferior vis-à-vis the richer Poles they encountered. It helped foster the self-help projects that bonded peasants and priests and softened the social and political radicalism of the Ukrainian intelligentsia once it discovered socialism as an ideology. In a related manifestation of this sentiment of *noblesse oblige*, some of these "gentry" families chose to cement their solidarity with the "people" by destroying whatever documentation of gentry status they might have had, including deeds, proclamations, and heraldic symbols. It was a rather odd fashion that, among other things, permitted nongentry families to claim gentry status without much proof. The Bohachevskys were among those who legitimately claimed modest gentry status, but they were equally proud that one of their ancestors had destroyed proof that this claim was true.[22]

The clergy enjoyed a higher social status than the peasants, even when richer peasants were better off than the clerical families. The clergy had to live up to their social standing, dress and entertain appropriately, and send their children off to schools they could scarcely afford, without dipping into the pockets of the faithful. There is no dearth of descriptions of clergy overcharging peasants for their services in the name of the Deity and the church. Socially the clergy sought to emulate the upper classes. They held balls and receptions; embraced French cuisine and Western clothes, and enjoyed card games, dancing and parlor games. Those who could afford it traveled abroad. Families and friends visited often. Adults

22. Constantine's father, as well as two of his uncles, Theodor and Petro, all priests, carried on a lively correspondence on personal and political issues with Oleksander Barvinsky, a community activist. At one point, Petro asked Barvinsky to put in a good word about him to the metropolitan, who objected to Petro's political activism, LAL, Barvinsky File, nos. 664–65.

unobtrusively organized parties for the young people. A well-balanced life meant mastering good social graces, cultivating intelligent conversation, and exhibiting moderation in everything. Most considered open ambition crass, but that did not hinder one from seeking a better position. Scholarship might be praised, but was certainly not widely emulated. The secondary-school curriculum favored classical languages and the humanities and sought to instill lessons of nobility, patriotism, and individual responsibility.

Ukrainians never thought to doubt that they were a part of Europe: a nation composed of God-fearing people as any other European nation. The prevailing wisdom was that only accidents of geography, the predatory nature of imperialist neighbors, the laziness of the people exacerbated by drunkenness, and lack of education prevented the area from being a flourishing part of Europe. The Catholic Church, which Italians considered a bastion of conservatism and the prime enemy of nationalism, became the visible rallying force of national cohesion for Galician Ukrainians in the Habsburg Empire.

The Bohachevskys lived up to the claim of clergy activism. Reverend Teodor Bohachevsky, Constantine's uncle, was elected to the Halychyna parliament in 1902, where his passionate defense of Ukrainian political rights against the encroachments of the local Polish administrators gained him recognition beyond the confines of his district and stood in the way of his getting a more lucrative parish.[23] He accused the Polish administration of using the local political powers that they had gained from the Viennese government to oppress Ukrainians.[24] An aunt, Olha Bohachevsky, was among the first dozen women in Halychyna who went into teaching.[25] She worked under the double burden of being a Ukrainian woman in a profession overseen by Polish men.[26] Omelian, a younger

23. Theodore Bohachevsky and Sylvester Bohachevsky married two Zarytsky sisters. Theodore was a member of the Galician Regional Parliament and a leading activist organizer of public demonstrations for the introduction of universal suffrage. He was recognized for his political efforts; see newspaper mentions in LAL, f. 167, op. 11, and od. zb. 313, f. 15.

24. See Vasyl Lencyk, "Ukraiins'ke katolyts'ke dukhoventstvo—ostoia natsionalnoii substantsiii," in Beresteis'ka Uniia (1596–1996) (Lviv: Logos, 1996), 33.

25. Olha Bohachevsky was an indefatigable Ukrainian activist teacher. She also tried her hand at writing; see Zhinocha Dolia (Kolomyia), March 1, 1928, 3.

26. On May 12, 1905, Reverend Theodore Bohachevsky, then the pastor of Letsivka,

brother of Sylvester, was a folklorist who earned early membership in the Shevchenko Scientific Society.[27] Another uncle, Rev. Petro, was a frequent contributor to Ukrainian newspapers. In 1891, Petro and Sylvester used the region's major Ukrainian paper, Dilo, to solicit volunteers to prepare sermons focusing on the needs of the peasants.[28] Petro Bohachevsky died of a heart attack before the project was completed. Sylvester had little time for it, as his own family needs continued to grow.

The Bohachevsky clan took Ukrainian patriotism for granted; at home they spoke phonetic, vernacular Ukrainian, with a strong admixture of Church Slavonic.[29] Constantine's aunt, Olha Bohachevsky, exemplified the

requested a transfer to a town with a railroad, such as Skole, Styniava, or Holyn. He argued that he had served over twenty years in remote villages, had proven his dedication to the church and to the people, and needed to be closer to "communication." The letter alludes to earlier talks with the metropolitan, and although it does not refer directly to Theodore's political activity, the undercurrent is there. In a later letter, dated December 19, 1910, after the transfer was complete, Theodore warmly greeted Sheptytsky on the feast day of St. Andrew, his patron saint. LAL, Barvinsky File, no. 666; see also TsDIA, Lviv, f. 167, o. 11, od. 3b. 313, item 15. Today there are Bohachevsky Streets in Holyn and Skvyra, named in honor of Theodore Bohachevsky.

27. When he died, Dilo, (no. 60, 1902) praised him for "knowing how to combine his professional obligations with the sacred duty of each upstanding Rusyn who cares for the welfare of the people. He tackled community activities [narodne dilo] and courageously worked for the welfare of the poor. His outspokenness, determination, and energy warmed the indifferent and the depressed, encouraging them to struggle and work for Rus-Ukraine."

28. Petro Bohachevsky, pastor of Harbuziv, co-signed the call, Dilo, no. 291, 1891. The existing Ukrainian books of sermons were traditionally didactic, and the Polish and German ones were not much different. The Bohachevsky proposal reads like a community agenda. It is worth quoting in full since the choice of topics differs dramatically from those in conventional preacher handbooks at the time. "The aim of the proposed collection is to engender genuine piety. Along with that, the signatories want to awaken or rather to stimulate a sense of human dignity and national awareness. [We want to help] overcome the peasants' unwillingness to develop an orderly approach in their relationship to government institutions and to awaken a desire for self-help in economic poverty, by forming cooperatives to focus on the principles of better nutrition, [as well as] to teach them how to raise their children in a Christian patriotic spirit, especially to be able to eradicate in future generations all the prevalent drawbacks—corruption, egotism, and greed." Petro Bohachevsky died soon after posting the note. He had written articles on the condition of Ukrainian Catholic parishes in Dushpastyr (Lviv, 1895, issues 1, 2, 3, 5, 8, 9), published in Pravda (Lviv), and was active in local politics as a member of the Zolochiv District council.

29. This information is gleaned from my father's accounts of the times; see Danylo Bohachevsky, Na vozi. The Bohachevskys spoke Ukrainian at home, although the women did much reading of popular literature in Polish. The Zarytsky elders at the time spoke

family's "progressivism." She repeatedly lost her job as a teacher because of her ethnicity and gender, but continued to actively promote women's rights and women's access to higher education. Constantine would also become an active promoter of women's education.

The Austrian government mandated that each village have an obligatory three-year school for all boys and girls. Initially run by the priest or cantor, by the end of the 1890s professional lay teachers increasingly took over these functions. These schools did not offer sufficient preparation for entry into the gymnasium, the secondary school that was a prerequisite for entry into a university. Consequently, all seven Bohachevsky brothers, in addition to attending the village school, were also home taught.[30] Following the custom of progressive priests, Sylvester included one or two of his sons' village companions in these sessions to prepare willing village children for entry to the high school. The lessons included the Greek and Latin classics in translation that would prepare the boys for the study of the originals in the gymnasium.[31] The elder Bohachevsky stressed both humanities and mathematics and paid special attention to a structured approach to study. He eschewed corporal punishment; a suitably firm glance was sufficient to quell unacceptable behavior.

Because the gymnasia were located in towns, village children, whether from the clergy or the peasantry, had to board either at the school or more frequently with local families. The first Ukrainian language gymnasium, established in Lviv in 1863, had a limited enrollment and, by contemporary

---

Polish at home, while the Dudykevych family opted for an older Ukrainian with Church Slavonic admixtures. None of them were linguists so they ended up speaking a personalized regional dialect.

30. The elder Bohachevsky boys, Volodymyr and Constantine, were tutored by Illya Kokoruz (1857–1933) a foremost classical philologist who was one of the founders of the Alliance of Ukrainian Schools (Ridna Shkola) and later became the headmaster of the Lviv Gymnasium which the younger Bohachevsky boys later attended.

31. The support of the village youth was not only limited to tutoring. Thus Sylvester Bohachevsky, while himself strapped financially, wrote to Oleksander Barvinsky on September 7, 1892, requesting financial help for Vasyl Senkiv, a son of the local smith. LAL, Barvinsky file, item 665.

standards, was far from home. Constantine and his older brother Volody-myr were sent to a closer state gymnasium in Stryj where Polish was the language of instruction. They boarded at the home of a clergy widow who, in exchange for products raised at the Bohachevsky parsonage, housed and fed the boys. Such mutually beneficial arrangements were widely practiced in Halychyna.

The course of study in the gymnasium included eight years of Latin and six of Classical Greek, advanced courses in German grammar and literature, eight years of history, a solid grounding in geography, and eight years of mathematics. Polish history and literature were part of the official curriculum. Religion classes were held separately for Ukrainian and Polish children. It was presumed that the former would be Eastern rite, the latter Latin. Ukrainian history, culture, and literature were studied both formally and informally. Theatre productions and collecting folklore texts and artifacts supplemented these studies. As a gymnasium student, Constantine most enjoyed searching for old religious artifacts, manuscripts, and rare books in the churches that dotted the low hills where his father was stationed. Constantine was very active in the gymnasium. He joined a secret student organization and debated political issues.[32]

As Austria-Hungary modified its administration, Polish parties gained political dominance over the province of Halychyna/Galicia—a result of the juggling act that characterized the administration of the Austro-Hungarian Empire with its fifteen recognized languages. The local Polish administration sought to strengthen Polish presence by creating Polish-language schools in historically Ukrainian areas. To counteract what they considered Polish encroachments, Ukrainians became adept at using constitutional means to advocate and press for Ukrainian-language educational institutions. At the beginning of the twentieth century, the Ukrainian political community within the Habsburg Empire first and foremost demanded Ukrainian language schools. In a speech delivered on June 28, 1910, Metropolitan Andrey Sheptytsky, who as head of the Ukrainian Catholic Church in the Habsburg realm was an ex-officio member of the Austrian Upper House, formally called for the establishment of a Ukrainian university. The Poles viewed his speech as an irresponsible and incendiary

32. Fylymon Tarnawsky, "Potriyny Iuviley Preosv. Konstantyna Bohachevskoho," *Nova Zoria*, August 9, 1934, 3.

act. When peaceful moves proved inadequate, Ukrainians resorted to public demonstrations. Nevertheless, the political opposition of the Poles, lack of funding and economic backwardness made it very difficult to establish Ukrainian-language schools and dormitories.

For Western Ukrainians of Constantine Bohachevsky's generation, electoral and educational rights were inextricably intertwined. The promotion of education in the native language to eradicate illiteracy and to foster a national identity was a major political goal for them. The political activists realized that without an informed electorate, universal suffrage, their other major goal of the time, would to be meaningless. Equally intertwined were activities that Ukrainians characterized as social or communal. The Ukrainian word *hromada* (society) has the same broad spectrum of meaning as "society" and "social" do.

Constantine's immediate milieu took for granted that anyone with his advantages of birthright and education would aim to lead a life that was socially useful and personally satisfying. Constantine's father, uncles, and aunts promoted activities that expanded civic and educational rights for Ukrainians in the Austrian Empire, and Constantine naturally adopted many of their convictions. Throughout his life, he stressed the importance of education and worked to establish Ukrainian Catholic schools. For him, however, education went beyond pedagogy and the acquisition of knowledge. True wisdom balanced knowledge with Christian ethics. People with this wisdom would be capable of turning a tottering society into a just state.

BECOMING A PRIEST

Constantine was a diligent student. He passed the dreaded "matura" at first try on June 16, 1903. The nine-person committee gave him high grades—mostly fours on a scale of five—except in Polish and German languages, where he got a "gentlemanly C" in the words of his brother.[33] Constantine earned the highest grade—exceptional—in Ukrainian liter-

33. Danylo, who prided himself on his "gentlemanly Cs," gleefully mentioned that Sylvester praised Constantine's tenacity in study even as he did not gauge him to be exceptionally gifted. There seems to be little credence to this claim, which reflects more on my father than on Constantine.

ature and language and in philosophy. Such grades assured him entrance to the university, and everyone presumed that he would choose a scholarly career. But Constantine surprised them. Upon graduation in 1903, he chose to enter the seminary. His family and friends were baffled: he had not discussed priesthood as a profession. Moreover, he did not have a good singing voice nor was he a particularly effective public speaker. These two qualities, the elite jokingly opined, were the major qualifications for a good priest.

What made Constantine decide to become a priest? Sons of priests of Constantine's generation, unlike those of previous generations, had the option of entering secular professions. But it was an option constrained for most students by monetary considerations. According to his brother Danylo, their father did not pressure his sons, although he would have liked at least some of them to become priests. However, he did expect them to become well-educated, socially and politically active members of their Ukrainian community. Perhaps the increasingly erratic behavior of Constantine's older brother, Volodymyr, may have swayed his conscientious younger brother to continue the family tradition for males to enter the priesthood. On the other hand, it is more likely that Constantine had a genuine desire to become a priest. Certainly the course of his life would prove that supposition. What would be surprising was Constantine's decision to be ordained a celibate. Married clergy were the norm for Ukrainian Catholics, and young men who wanted to take orders as celibates were at times dissuaded by their elders from taking that step.[34]

The Ukrainian Catholic Church went through important changes before Constantine became a priest. A century before his birth, the reform of the monastic orders provided a more effective upper clergy. During his infancy the Ukrainian Church began modernizing the ecclesiastical administration. As he matured, the academic level of seminary instruction rose. By the time he began his clerical career, the old hereditary clerical parish system was breaking down. Finally, during his lifetime the role of the priest in the Ukrainian community in Halychyna changed.[35] As the

34. Rev. Fylymon Tarnawsky, later chancellor in the United States, was talked out of celibacy by an older priest. He notes that only his mother supported his initial desire to remain celibate. Tarnawsky, *Spomyny*, 84.

35. See Kaszczak, *The Education of Ukrainian Greek Catholic Clergy*.

population became diversified, the focus of the pastor's role expanded to include guidance for the more educated and less easily satisfied flock. Publications aimed at the clergy now focused on the importance of the priest in the development of society.[36] Constantine knew he would be a different priest than his ancestors to meet the challenges facing his church.

By the time Bohachevsky became a full-fledged seminarian, the atmosphere at the university became more politically charged. A year before he entered the university, about four hundred Ukrainian students, half of them theology majors, had withdrawn from the university, noisily protesting the mistreatment of Ukrainians by Polish authorities.[37] To prevent a repetition of the student strike, younger seminarians were barred from participating in extracurricular activities at the university.[38] Nevertheless, student protests continued on a smaller scale, and the seminarians, as well as the overall population, became more aware of public protest as a means to be used to attain political goals.

The seminary program, which Bohachevsky pursued from 1903 to 1905, reflected the standard European classical education of the time. As a particularly gifted seminarian, Constantine also attended the University of Lviv faculty of theology, and signed up for philosophy courses. There he studied courses on church history and dogmatics in greater depth than

36. This is amply evident from the discussions of the Halychyna bishops who met regularly in the inter-war period. The minutes of the meetings of the conference of the Lviv, Peremyshl, and Stanislaviv bishops, PKEL (Okremykh nadkhodzhen'), op. 1069. Also see the letters of Constantine Bohachevsky to Sheptytsky, TsDIA, Lviv, Sheptytsky correspondence, f. 358, op. 2, spr. 99.

37. Among those were Yosyf Botsian, who would later serve with Bohachevsky at the Church of the Transfiguration in Lviv and eventually become bishop of Lutsk; Tyt Halushchynsky, who would become a noted Basilian educator; and Ivan Liatyshevsky, who became assistant bishop of Stanislaviv. See Sorokowsky, *The Greek-Catholic Parish Clergy*, 85.

38. Sheptytsky was criticized by his own priests. The Ukrainian-Catholic upper clergy were predictably concerned about the young seminarians' direct exposure to the "secularization" that they would experience in the university. On Sheptytsky's help of the students, see Wolfdieter Bihl, "Sheptyts'kyi and the Austrian Government," in *Morality and Reality: The Life and Times of Andrei Sheptyts'kyi*, ed. Paul Robert Magocsi (Edmonton: Canadian Institute of Ukrainian Studies, 1989), 18. On Sheptytsky's theology, see Peter Galadza, *The Theology and Liturgical Work of Andrei Sheptytsky (1865–1944)* (Rome: Pontifico Instituto Orientale, 2004); and Andrii Kravchuk, *Christian Social Ethics in Ukraine: Legacy of Andrei Sheptytsky* (Edmonton: Canadian Institute of Ukrainian Studies Press, 1997); on his political views, see Liliana Hentosh, *Mytropolyt Sheptyts'ky, 1923–1939: Vyprobuvannia Idealiv* (Lviv: Klassyka, 2015).

was done at the seminary, and also took classical Hebrew and introductory Arabic, Syriac, and Chaldean, ancient Ukrainian literature, the Vulgate, and some social studies. Moral theology, homiletics, and canon law, as well as an introduction to Austro-Hungarian legal practice rounded out his formal studies.

A devotee of the extracurricular, Constantine helped run the seminary library and a more informal reading room, worked on editing parts of the religious journals the seminary published, and liked evening discussions on current political developments informally run by the Venerable Isidore Dolnytsky, an eminent religious scholar.[39] Bohachevsky read widely in the standard philosophical and historical classics, mainly German. He followed the current political issues—elections, parties, platforms, anticlericalism, liberalism; and he was particularly vocal in defending the rights of Ukrainians within the university. At one of his oral examinations, he insisted on using Church Slavonic quotations as a language of equal value to Latin for ecclesiastical purposes, despite the demand of one Polish examiner to use Latin exclusively. Constantine replied in perfect Latin that matters dealing with Ukrainian Church ritual need to be discussed in Church Slavonic, although the young seminarian said that he intended to communicate with his flock in Ukrainian.[40]

Bohachevsky fit well into communal dormitory life. He liked the Spartan atmosphere of the seminary, headed at the time by Rev. Hryhory Khomyshyn (who would soon become bishop at Stanislaviv). Lviv, the city of dreams for provincial society, held no particular attraction for the young Bohachevsky beyond his interest in searching for church antiques. He enjoyed active work and had a positive outlook. He honed his powers of concentration, which served him well later in life. He was thrifty, took care of his personal needs and clothes, and showed an ingenious practical bent. For example, he devised various ways of waking himself up silently at 4 A.M. so as not to wake up others. One method was to use an intricately constructed mechanical device connected to a large clock that jerked his covers at the pre-set time.

Bohachevsky's real passion, however, was looking for old church arti-

39. LAL, f. 451, op. 1, spr. 9, *Khronika seminarii za 1898–1913 rr.*, a handwritten list for 1903–4 catalogs the books borrowed.
40. Danylo Bohachevsky, *Vladyka Konstantyn Bohachevsky*, 17.

facts. He would share his findings with Metropolitan Andrey Sheptytsky and Ilarion Sventsitsky, the director of the museum Sheptytsky founded. With the permission of his father and the Krasne village church council, Bohachevsky sent the Lviv Museum a rare zinc and lead chalice and a collection of parish and school registers from the eighteenth century. In Holyn, the home village of his mother, and in nearby Kropyvnyk, he found antique textiles, including two complete sets of vestments. Later, his first posting in Semyhoniv yielded the antimisium of Bishop Joseph Shumliansky from 1747, as well as washed-over frescoes.[41]

While a seminarian, Constantine spent part of his summers with the family, in the hills of the lower Carpathians. In later years, he would look back on these summers with a nostalgic fondness, despite the fact that his studiousness was an object of family fun—his rambunctious younger brothers played practical jokes on him, pranks he good-naturedly tolerated. In conversations with his brothers in later years, he focused on holidays and events with the extended family and friends. He vividly remembered minor details and recalled names his brothers had forgotten.

INNSBRUCK

Upon completion of the seminary program, Metropolitan Sheptytsky offered Bohachevsky a fellowship for graduate work at the University of Innsbruck and at the Canisianum, a Jesuit university founded in 1858 at Innsbruck specifically for Eastern Catholic students. The three years Bohachevsky spent at Innsbruck between 1905 and 1908, and the extended trips he took there until 1910 in preparation for his doctorate marked the final formative period of Bohachevsky's education.

Sheptytsky's financial support came with the tacit understanding that the recipient personally inform the metropolitan of his progress. Bohachevsky regularly wrote to Sheptytsky through his postdoctoral research at Munich in 1913. From this correspondence, we get a glimpse of a young man who would one day become a metropolitan himself, a young man not yet fully prepared for the loneliness of his chosen profession.

Sheptytsky, nineteen years Bohachevsky's senior, assumed a father-

41. Letter of Bohachevsky to Sheptytsky, December 30, 1909, TsDIA, Lviv, Sheptytsky correspondence, f. 358, op. 2, spr. 99, Letters of Constantine Bohachevsky, 21–22v.

ly role in Constantine's life. Bohachevsky's letters reveal a vulnerable and touchingly frank young man. His neatly handwritten concise letters were reverential but not obsequious.[42] They were direct and to the point. He varied headings—sometimes Excellency, Bishop (*Archyierey*), Master (*Vladyko*)—but most frequently, the simple Your Excellency. At first, Bohachevsky signed himself "Kost." By the end of 1909, he transitioned to the more formal Konstantyn Bohachevsky. In his letters, the young Bohachevsky is open about his physical, emotional, and financial insecurities. He has trouble breathing, his stomach hurts so much that he suspects some abnormality, he tires easily. He notes periods of sadness. He complains of lassitude during meditations, of exhaustion and heat. The illnesses about which he complains (weakness, stomach pains, lassitude, lack of an appetite) are best cured, by his own admission, at home, where he heads whenever he can. The rare times of doubt about his vocation, which he admits, he diagnoses as the result of overwork and exhaustion. Each time, he snaps back to work within a week. In greeting Sheptytsky on the occasion of his patron saint Andrew's feast day (December 12, old-style calendar), young Constantine's visceral connection with his native land bursts forth in the romantic rhetoric of the time: "[I am now] far from Halychyna . . . only sweet memories linger of our Ruthenian holidays. Yet deep down in my soul I feel more clearly than ever the solemnity with which our clan marks the holydays."[43]

Constantine was very conscious of the gaps in his education and aware of the faith that his superiors put in him. He studied hard, noting that the academic demands at Innsbruck were more rigorous than those at Lviv. Even some of the religious practices were challenging. In one of his first letters he complains that it was difficult to maintain absolute silence for eight days, one of the requirements of a religious retreat. He proudly boasts of accomplishing this feat as a step toward his spiritual growth. "I left for Innsbruck anxious and insecure. How could it have been otherwise? [I] was young and already venturing for the first time into such distant lands, [alone] among foreigners and strangers [which] is not among

42. TsDIA, Lviv, Sheptytsky correspondence, f. 358, op. 2, spr. 99, Letters of Constantine Bohachevsky, 1–42.

43. Constantine to Sheptytsky, undated, but the signature and text suggest 1907, TsDIA, Lviv, f. 358; op. 2, spr. 99.

the most pleasant experiences. But, thank God, here I . . . found out that things are not as fearsome as they appear . . . [sic]"[44]

While Bohachevsky was at Innsbruck, Sheptytsky made a clandestine journey to the Russian Empire as part of his life-long ambition to heal the rift of 1054 between the Roman Catholic and Orthodox Churches. Bohachevsky's correspondence illustrates how anxious Sheptytsky was to learn how the Russians studying at Innsbruck fared and what the Jesuits were saying.[45] Bohachevsky's laconic replies show a remarkable lack of interest in behind-the-scenes activities. As to the politics of the institution, Bohachevsky's information is skimpy, noting this or that rumor but failing to go into details about its reliability or ramifications on specific people. He mentions student unrest at the university in 1908, but notes only that even the theology faculty had to be closed because of potential disturbances. He writes that the rector banned the subscription to Dilo, the major Ukrainian newspaper, but does not protest the decision. Instead, he suggests that another publication, such as the "Peoples' Word" (Narodne Slovo), could be a replacement.[46] Compared to the detailed missives that a Russian Catholic priest, Leonid Fedorov, sent Sheptytsky, or even to other clerical correspondence of the time, the young Bohachevsky's letters are more than laconic.[47] He refused to take up Metropolitan Sheptytsky's requests for fuller background material, reporting only what he knew, which was little.

Innsbruck made a strong impression on Bohachevsky. He liked everything about it—the order, the cleanliness, the river, the hills, the general structure of life. He does not mention the buildings, but relishes the collegiality of the Innsbruck academic community. Companionship, easy

44. Constantine to Sheptytsky, undated, TsDIA, Lviv, f. 358; op. 2, spr. 99, pp. 35–36, misfiled with an envelope from Munich. Handwriting and signature are from the Innsbruck period.

45. Sheptytsky was especially interested in Aleksandr Sypiagin, a Russian Catholic, a member of the first short-lived Russian Parliament in 1905, who changed his rite from Latin rite Catholic to that of the Eastern (uniate) rite. He spent a few months at Innsbruck. See Mytropolyt Andrey Sheptyts'ky i Hreko-Katolyky v Rosii, vol. 1, Dokumenty i materialy, 1899–1917, ed. Yuri Avvakumov and Oksana Hayova (Lviv: Ukrainian Catholic University Press, 2004), 117.

46. Constantine to Sheptytsky, May 6, 1908, TsDIA, Lviv, f. 358; op. 2, spr. 99, p. 10.

47. For Fedorov's correspondence, see Avvakumov and Hayova, Mytropolyt Andrey Sheptyts'ky.

access to publications, and accessibility of the faculty exceeded his expectations. The friendly atmosphere in the monastery dormitory impressed him most: "I can safely say that the monastery is built on the trust of prefects and students. I have never seen such cordial coexistence and mutual respect of each other."[48]

Unlike many other beneficiaries of Sheptytsky's largesse, Bohachevsky was painfully aware of the financial cost of his stay. He counted every penny. He communicated financial difficulties without embellishments, simply informing Sheptytsky of increases in tuition. He apologized for not qualifying for a "certificate of poverty" that would have reduced the cost of tuition covered by the metropolitan. Because Constantine felt that the expense was not academically justifiable, he even gave up a proposed trip to Rome.

At Innsbruck Constantine set a primary goal of acquiring as much knowledge as possible in the shortest time, so as not to squander money. He enrolled in courses taught by the most eminent professors, he focused on philosophy, where he knew he needed guidance. With the help of his Swiss fellow university students, he studied French and worked on his Italian as well. It did not occur to him to study English. He planned his courses carefully and rigorously studied for his examinations, refusing to break his concentration even to accommodate an audience with Sheptytsky.[49] He found dogmatics more trying than moral philosophy, but by the fall of 1908 he had passed all the necessary examinations. He began working on his dissertation.

For his doctoral thesis Bohachevsky chose to study the epiclesis—the invocation to the Holy Spirit in the Byzantine rite Eucharistic Canon, which follows the consecration of the host. This prayer, whose origin is a matter of debate, is a call for the Holy Spirit to reassert the initial Consecration. It is one of the areas of worship that is markedly different between

48. Constantine to Sheptytsky, undated, TsDIA, Lviv, f. 358; op. 2, spr. 99. This appears to be the first letter of Constantine to Sheptytsky, not dated and misfiled in f. 358, p. 2, spr. 99, as being on p. 35. Bohachevsky uses the term "konvikt" for monastery, as it was frequently used at the time.

49. Constantine to Sheptytsky, from Krasna, near Petranka, October 25, 1908, TsDIA, Lviv, f. 358; op. 2, spr. 99). He writes that he is studying moral philosophy six to eight hours a day, and if he breaks the rhythm, it would be difficult to take the "rigorozy"—the doctoral examinations.

the Eastern and Western practice. Bohachevsky hoped that by studying the sources of the period prior to the sixteenth century, he would be able to date the epiclesis. He also hoped to gain access to Russian synodic discussions on the epiclesis and study how the debate developed in Ukrainian and Russian Church literature.[50]

Meanwhile at Lviv his older brother Volodymyr, embarrassing the family and undermining their finances, emigrated to the United States where he publicly rejected Catholicism. This was apostasy, and Sylvester took the news very hard. Constantine suggested that his father should ask Sheptytsky to have someone in America talk to Volodymyr. The intervention worked.[51] The elder Bohachevsky then began writing more frequently to Sheptytsky. Having almost lost a son—spiritual loss being equal to physical death for him—Sylvester wanted Sheptytsky to see that the family was a close one despite the lapses of the oldest son.

ORDINATION TO PRIESTHOOD

Although Constantine had fulfilled all the requirements for ordination to priesthood, he did not want to rush the ordination. However, Metropolitan Sheptytsky was anxious to have the studious seminarian ordained as soon as possible. The young man pleaded with the metropolitan to postpone his ordination, protesting that he was recovering from a nasty cold.[52] The real reason for the delay was financial—with several siblings left to educate, the family simply could not afford the dowry that the families of unmarried clerics generally provided prior to ordination.

With or without the dowry, Sheptytsky insisted on as quick an ordination as possible. The ceremony was held on January 31, 1909, at St. George Cathedral. The ordination increased the family's financial difficulties. The

50. Constantine to Sheptytsky, from Munich, December 8, 1912, TsDIA, Lviv, f. 358; op. 2, spr. 99.

51. Relieved, Sylvester wrote an unusually emotional letter to Sheptytsky, dated May 11, 1907: "My son in America came to his senses and broke away from those independents. . . . The Almighty in His mercy removed this sorrow, which pressed my breast as a millstone. Now that I received this joyous news, I must thank your Excellency for honoring my request and sympathizing in my sorrow. I remain forever dedicated to my most worthy Arch-Pastor.—Sylvester Bohachevsky, Pastor." TsDIA, Lviv, f. 358, op. 2, spr. 110, pp. 26–27.

52. Bohachevsky noted that he did not have a fur coat to wear under the vestments during the ordination ceremonies, and "St. George's [Cathedral] in winter is very cold,"

debts incurred by Volodymyr had already depleted the household budget; Constantine's decision to remain celibate drained it even further because there would be no bride's dowry, which traditionally funded the household essentials. The younger brothers wanted to study at the university but knew that lack of funds would keep them in the village; they might, at best, travel to Lviv only to take exams. But Constantine would need at least a china service and after some discussion, the parents presented him with a silver-plated set, a decision most likely prompted by concerns that Constantine, a bachelor, would chip fine china. The idea of having to buy silverware and china for a brother who had already lived at Innsbruck and who had the personal support of the metropolitan upset Danylo, the next in line. He had just enrolled at Lviv University, had plunged full force into the student political movement, and now wanted his chance to attend the university at Lviv. Danylo's protest was so voluble that he had to be quieted by his parents.[53]

A NEOPRESBYTER

After the ordination Constantine Bohachevsky, officially titled "neopresbyter," was to shepherd seventeen seminarians who were preparing for ordination before embarking on a trip to work in the United States. On February 5, 1909, he was appointed assistant pastor of Semyhoniv, a tiny village in the vicinity of his father's parish. He was also working on his dissertation. While Bohachevsky served there, Sheptytsky stopped by briefly, as the metropolitan visited other surrounding village churches. Bohachevsky wrote movingly about the experience when he learned of Sheptytsky's death. Towards the end of his life, Bohachevsky recalled that during that first year of his priesthood he also witnessed the consecration of an older colleague from Innsbruck, Nykyta Budka, as the first Ukrainian bishop of Canada, never thinking that he would work in America, and that Bishop Budka would come to visit him in Philadelphia.[54]

Constantine to Sheptytsky, December 28, 1908, TsDIA, Lviv, Sheptytsky correspondence, f. 358, op. 2, spr. 99, pp. 19–20v.

53. Danylo Bohachevsky, *Na vozi*, 52.

54. From a speech Bohachevsky delivered on the fiftieth anniversary of Ukrainian settlement in Canada in *Propamiatna Knyha z nahody zolotoho iuvileiu poselennia Ukraiins'koho*

Bohachevsky plowed into pastoral duties with all his energy, hearing confessions, visiting parishioners, and hunting for archeological treasures. Nevertheless, he still had time to complete his dissertation, which he modified because there was no hope to get access to Russian synodal decisions on the epiclesis. Bohachevsky refocused his research on the Last Judgment as presented in the Greek patristic theology, beginning with Clement of Alexandria. Later he narrowed the topic to the "Logos apud Sanctum Ioannem in Prologo et Philonem Alexandrinum." He drew his information from a variety of sources, including the works of Russian scholars. His meticulous research earned him a doctorate in sacred theology with honors. He received his doctorate in divinity from Innsbruck University on November 19, 1910. Within two months, on January 12, 1911, Sheptytsky appointed him an official book censor at the Chancery. By fall, with the opening of the new academic year, Bohachevsky was an adjunct professor in the theological department at the University of Lviv. The appointment, in the accepted academic use of the intimate you, was written in Polish and signed by the head of the theology department, Dr. Kazimierz Wais.

Bohachevsky continued his post-doctoral work at the Ludwig Maximillian University in Munich in the academic year 1912–13 through a grant from the Austrian Ministry of Religion and Education. He researched the writings of Clement of Alexandria, as well as the then-popular literature on the Sophia as the Wisdom of God. By the beginning of 1913, he got bogged down among the redactions of Clement and spent his last months at Munich attempting to date all the extant texts. Bohachevsky enjoyed the life he carved out for himself at Munich. It centered on the monastery where he stayed and on the university where he did his research. He wrote that it was "difficult to imagine better working conditions" than those in the faculty reading room at the university library.[55]

While at Munich, Bohachevsky unwittingly took his first step toward

---

narodu v Kanadi (Yorkton, Saskatchewan: Redeemer's Voice, 1941), 3–4. On Budka, see Athanasius D. McVay's God's Martyr, History's Witness: Blessed Nykyta Budka, the First Ukrainian Catholic Bishop of Canada (Edmonton: Ukrainian Catholic Eparchy of Edmonton and Metropolitan Andrey Sheptytsky Institute of Eastern Christian Studies, 2014).

55. Constantine to Sheptytsky from Munich, March 8, 1913, TsDIA, Lviv, f. 358; op. 2, spr. 99. pp. 27–28).

becoming a missionary. He was shocked to discover that there were no Ukrainian rite services for the many migrant workers from Halychyna. The contrast of the comfort of his life and the hardships of the laborers in the same city made an indelible impression upon him. The local Latin Catholic clergy denied him permission to hold services and referred him to papal authorities. Bohachevsky immediately asked Metropolitan Sheptytsky for guidance.[56] Instead, Sheptytsky recalled Bohachevsky to Lviv to his duties as dean of studies at the seminary, in effect unwittingly ending one of his star pupils' research career.

A PRIEST FOREVER IN A CHANGING WORLD

Bohachevsky's career in the Ukrainian Catholic hierarchy started conventionally enough. As a celibate priest, with a doctorate from Innsbruck, he was on the road to what at the time was considered an excellent career. Metropolitan Sheptytsky continued to take an interest in him. Bohachevsky was thus able to pursue his scholarly studies. But Constantine did not seem to be driven by ambition. He did not position himself for better appointments, nor did he adjust his views to suit his superiors to curry favor and attract attention. His sense of duty overshadowed all other considerations.

Constantine came of age within a Catholic Church, which was expanding its role as a purely spiritual entity to one increasingly attentive to social concerns. Beginning with Pope Leo XIII, the universal Catholic Church sought to reestablish itself as a moral force in society. Within the Austrian Empire, which was officially a Catholic state, the Ukrainian Catholic Church used its position to lobby actively for equal rights for Ukrainians.[57]

56. Ibid., p. 28: "Not knowing the will of Your Excellency."

57. Thus, for instance, the bishops, at their conference meeting, decided to send an official delegation to the emperor to discuss measures that would assure that "the Halychany—, especially Rusyny, would be treated equally in the upcoming Parliamentary election." PKEL, minutes of January 12, 1906, p. 6. A few weeks later the bishops wanted assurance that recruits to the Army could celebrate their holy days according to the Julian calendar. PKEL, minutes of April 23, 1906, p. 7. In a later strongly worded comment, the bishops authorized the metropolitan to call the attention of the Habsburg governor in Galicia to Polish encroachments into Ukrainian electoral districts. PKEL, minutes of November 12, 1906, which was held at Peremyshl.

Bohachevsky, like his father before him, considered himself a "reformist" priest. Scholarship for him was an essential adjunct of the faith, and in good Thomistic fashion, he saw no conflict between the two. In the early years of his priesthood, his sermons were long and flowery, full of poetic imagery, scholarly references, and fiery exhortations.

Constantine's correspondence with the metropolitan displays characteristics that would become his hallmarks: directness, thoroughness, and brevity in communication. Ascetic, thrifty, and practical in his personal life, he did not consider these qualities extraordinary; he had begun to expect them of others as well. His faith by this time was direct and structured. Gone was the youthful listing of his ailments along with his plans. He had learned to keep his emotions well hidden from public view. The transformation steered the young Constantine to rely on God and to seek the Godhead in silence and in prayer.

CHAPTER 2

Priestly Service in
Times of War

On October 1, 1913, Bohachevsky returned from his research in Munich to continue as dean of academic programs at Lviv Seminary and adjunct professor of theology at Lviv University, where he taught courses in catechetics and methodology.[1] Concurrently he had administrative tasks at the chancery. At the very beginning of the year, January 22, 1914, Sheptytsky formally nominated Bohachevsky to the "Commission on ritual matters . . . which are to be the subject of the next archeparchial synod."[2]

1. I had four major sources on Bohachevsky's priestly career: First of all, a hand written *curriculum vitae* of Bohachevsky prepared for Kotsylovsky in 1924. Second, I had Bohachevsky's original personal documents or copies of such documents which had been given to Hryhor Luzhnytsky for his proposed biography on Bohachevsky. Oleksander Lushnytsky kindly passed them on to me. The quotation is from a typed letter marked as No. 886/Syn[od], addressed to Bohachevsky and signed by Metropolitan Sheptytsky, now in my possession. Third, I checked the information I had against parts of the Sheptytsky holdings at the TsDIA, Lviv, f. 451, op. 2, spr. 49: Correspondence of the Greek Catholic Metropolitanate. Finally, I had some notes and many memories of lengthy conversations I had with Bishop Vasyl Hrynyk (December 27, 1896–May 31, 1977) in Peremyshl in March and April, 1977. Hrynyk had worked closely with Bohachevsky in Peremyshl. He had spent decades in Polish and Soviet jails, but his memory was clear. He volunteered his reminiscences, correctly presuming that as Bohachevsky's niece, I would be interested in them. A biography by Igor Halagida, *"Szpieg Watykanu:" Kaplan greckokatolicki ks. Bazyli Hrynyk* (Warsaw: Instytut Pamieci Narodowej, 2008), focuses on Hrynyk's activities after 1939.

2. Typed letter marked as no. 886/Syn[od], signed by Metropolitan Sheptytsky. Copy in possession of the author.

This scholarly working group was determining primary texts and Eastern church rituals. Feeling secure in what appeared to be a predictable career in Lviv that merged pastoral concerns and scholarly pursuits, the young priest looked forward to another grant from the Ministry of Religion and Education through the Department of Theology of Lviv University to continue his research at Berlin University in the autumn of 1914. That was not to be.

For Constantine the first shock of 1914 was personal: the sudden death of his fifty-year-old father, Sylvester, on May 19, 1914, a few months before the outbreak of World War I. Constantine returned to Pobuk, Petranka, and Kamin, in the low Carpathians, to close up parish affairs and await the new pastor. He managed to fence in the large iron cross erected on his father's grave in Petranka before the outbreak of the First World War in August 1914.

In the first months of the war, the Russian Imperial Army, in a short-lived but long-remembered rapid advance, overran most of the area where Ukrainians lived. In the army's wake, the Russian imperial government deported the major Ukrainian political leaders, as well as thousands of peaceful residents. Metropolitan Andrey Sheptytsky was among the first to be deported to Russia, and the Ukrainian Catholic Church in Halychyna remained without a formal archbishop/metropolitan during the First World War.

Bohachevsky escaped that fate. Judging from my father's rather sketchy memoirs, the Russian units roaming the Carpathians around the villages where the elder Bohachevsky had been a pastor were for the most part good-natured conscripts who occasionally helped needy villagers. During the first days of the tsarist occupation of the villages that formed his parish, Bohachevsky locked the church in Pobuk, refusing to hand over the keys to a Russian Orthodox priest who had arrived with the tsarist army to spread Orthodoxy in the region. Danylo recounts Constantine announcing that the Orthodox priest would have to shoot him before he entered the church.[3] The commanding tsarist officer proved to be a moderate, opposed to the chauvinist policies espoused by the Orthodox clergy who accompanied the Russian army. The officer sent the priest away and requisitioned

3. Danylo Bohachevsky, *Na vozi i pid vozom*, 54.

rooms in the parsonage for himself. He became more of a guest than a part of an occupying army, spending hours with Constantine, his mother, and his younger brothers. The incident was an example of civilized behavior at a time when the two empires were about to disintegrate. The area remained under Russian occupation until December 15, 1915, when the Russians retreated. This lengthier stay in the area in which he grew up gave the adult Bohachevsky a painful opportunity to see at close range the hard life in the villages.

After his father's death Constantine became responsible for his mother and his five brothers. All but the youngest, Petro, were eventually drafted into the Austrian Habsburg army and all later served in Ukrainian military units. Oleksa died of typhoid on the battlefields of Southern Ukraine and Danylo was interned by the victorious Poles after almost making it to Kyiv via Odesa with the Ukrainian Halychyna Army. Omelian and Ivan eventually made it home from the Italian front.

In 1914, within half a year, Constantine had lost his two most important authority figures: his father and his metropolitan. He now saw his world without the filter of available parental support. Back in Lviv in December 1915, he found an apartment near Assumption Church, handy for his mother and Petro, who was finishing up high school and tutoring on the side to supplement the family income. Petro would die of influenza during the Polish-Ukrainian war in 1920.

Constantine was now pro-rector of the seminary, the director of the spiritual development of the seminarians, as well as the administrator of the Church of Transfiguration (Preobrazhennia). On May 5, 1916, he was named adviser to the episcopal see and took the required oath of service. In February 1917, he was named vice-rector of the seminary. Nomination to these positions required approval of the Austro-Hungarian emperor; those regarding Bohachevsky were among the last documents the young Karl Habsburg signed.

SHEPTYTSKY'S VISION OF CHURCH UNITY

Bohachevsky's work was influenced by Metropolitan Sheptytsky, who was the dominant personality in Western Ukraine. Before World War I Sheptytsky had been in the forefront in bringing the cause of Ukrainians to the

FIGURE 2. PEREMYSHL CLERGY

attention of the Habsburgs. After the war, under different governments, he continued to promote Ukrainian issues, perpetuating the preeminent public role of the Ukrainian Catholic Church in Western Ukraine. Clergy played a critical public role, particularly with the changing front lines of World War I and the wars that followed. The physical church remained in the public eye, as did the clergy's ability to organize religious activities with public overtones, reinforcing the historic role of the church in the preservation of Ukrainian culture. Most political regimes permitted religious, but not public, gatherings and processions. Hence, religious gatherings had national and political underpinnings.

The involvement of Sheptytsky in what would later be dubbed the ecumenical movement expanded the image of the Ukrainian Catholic Church. Sheptytsky's vision went beyond Ukrainian affairs. He was unquestionably the single most important Ukrainian cleric of modern times, but hardly typical of the church he led—an anomaly rather than an example of the Ukrainian Catholic priestly milieu. Indeed, much of Sheptytsky's achievement lies precisely in his ability to work within the secular Ukrainian community in implementing his grand religious vision. Working to actively build a union of all Christians, he was convinced that Christ's prayer "All shall be one" (Jn 17:20–21) was a realistic goal and not merely a prayerful exhortation. From this perspective, he promoted a dialogue between the Catholics and the Orthodox. As a preliminary to the hoped-for union of Christian churches, he stressed the need to educate Ukrainian Catholic priests in Eastern theology. Sheptytsky sought to understand the Orthodox legacy and to inculcate that understanding in his priests. It was through the prism of sympathetic understanding that he hoped to bring the vast lands of the Russian Empire into a union with Rome.[4]

4. Sheptytsky's role within the context of the ecumenical movement has not yet been adequately studied. An exceptional personality, he chose to identify with the Ukrainian Catholic Church and that is the aspect of his life that has received the most public scrutiny. Although his rich, aristocratic Ukrainian family had for a number of generations identified with Poland, Sheptytsky was charismatic enough to overcome the initial Ukrainian mistrust to his background. He spent his fortune on Ukrainian charities. His breeding and law education permitted him to establish an international presence for the Ukrainians if not in Europe, then at least in the Catholic Church. He was a spokesperson for the Ukrainian cause, as well as for the unity of churches. It is only now, with access to the archival holdings being opened, that the latter aspect of his activity can be studied. The publication of the first volume of materials dealing with his contacts with Russia is an early step in

Catholics in the Austrian Empire saw two ways of healing the ancient rift between Eastern and Western Christianity. One, promoted by most of the Polish clergy, envisaged the fusion of Eastern Orthodoxy into Latin Catholicism, with scant attention to ritual differences. A small group of Russian Catholics favored this approach. (We should remember that before the reforms of Vatican Council II there were few ritual and no linguistic differences in the Latin-rite Catholic Church throughout the world, because Latin was the language of worship and public prayers were centrally prescribed.) A more nuanced approach to the reestablishment of Christian unity supported the fostering of the Eastern brand of Christianity within the larger framework of the Catholic Church. The Ukrainian Catholic Church, with its adherence to Eastern ritual and its acceptance of papal primacy, could serve as a model.

The Ukrainian Catholic Church that shaped Constantine Bohachevsky saw itself as a link with an Orthodox East uncorrupted by autocracy and a means for Latin Catholicism's reconciliation with Eastern Orthodoxy. Rome viewed this potential as a major reason for supporting a separate Ukrainian Catholic Church rather than pursuing a policy of benign neglect that would have (or at least could have) resulted in the Polonization of the Ukrainian Catholic Church and its diffusion into Latin Catholicism. The Vatican had long paid lip service to the unifying role Ukrainian Catholics could play in the attempt to bring the errant Orthodox back into the Catholic fold. And in fact, the more the Ukrainian Catholic Church became the national church of Ukrainians, the more actively it moved toward cleansing itself of Western ritual influences. Hence, although communion with the East was the long-term goal of the elite Vatican clergy, the more immediate result was to strengthen the Ukrainian Church as a discrete unit within Catholicism. Simultaneously, the cleansing of the Ukrainian Catholic Church from the Latin overlays in its rituals contributed toward the strengthening of its public and political role. This ritualistic "orientalism" had little to do with forging ties with the Orthodox. On the

---

this study. See Avvakumov and Hayova, *Mytropolyt Andrey Sheptytsky i hreko-katolyky v Rosiyi*; and Andrii Kravchuk, *Christian Social Ethics in Ukraine*. Before World War I, Pope Pius X verbally gave Sheptytsky authority to act in the pope's name to promote Eastern Catholicism among the Russian Catholics and the Orthodox. Not everyone recognized the validity of that charge.

contrary, the divide between the two was seldom breeched, and only by the uppermost levels of the clergy on both sides.

It is not clear with whom Sheptytsky shared his grand vision; the most open accounts on the matter come from like-minded non-Ukrainian Catholics. Moreover, while the metropolitan participated in joint activities with the Orthodox on an international level. Sheptytsky's public pronouncements in Halychyna mentioned unity of the two churches in general terms, even as he busied himself with unity endeavors. The metropolitan was faced with the very practical needs of training the clergy to carry out the grand aims of Christian unity that he and his confreres envisaged. In May 1911, Metropolitan Sheptytsky informed the Ukrainian bishops about the "recently established missionary school at the Seminary of the Holy Ghost in Lviv for the training of missionaries to the United States and Canada. Currently it holds eight candidates."[5] The bishops periodically raised the need for missionary schools, some indeed were established, although little information about them exists.

At home in Halychyna, Sheptytsky's sermons focused mostly on the dangers of secularization and on the need for vigilant public expression of one's faith. Based on his public statements, one could conclude that Sheptytsky was fully on the side of the traditionalists who rejected modern science and against the so-called modernists, who sought to reconcile science and religion. At the same time, however, one must remember that Sheptytsky had been born into a well-connected aristocratic family with diverse ties; he had an excellent education, and had traveled extensively. Coming from such a background, it is unrealistic to expect that he would simply write off the cultural forays of the so-called modernists. Indeed, it was this broad worldview and experience that prompted Sheptytsky to invite Prince Maximillian of Saxony from Switzerland to lecture in Lviv— the same Maximillian who had run afoul the papacy for his very liberal views and for his criticism of the pope who had postponed full episcopal rights to the first Ukrainian bishop in the United States.[6] This side of

5. PKEL, spr. 106, p. 16. That same meeting also charged Hegumen Platonid Filas to expand the network of missionary schools for priests, and to establish a missionary society. See also TsDIA, Lviv, f. 359, op. 1, spr. 267, and pp. 3–4.

6. Liliana Hentosh, *Vatykan i vyklyky modernosti: skhidnoievropeis'ka polityka Papy Benedykta XV ta ukraiins'ko-pol'sky konflikt u Halychyni (1914–1923)* (Lviv: Klassyka, 2006), 184–85.

Sheptytsky was not commonly known, however, even among the higher Ukrainian clergy.

It is almost ironic, then, that the strengthening of the Ukrainian Catholic Church—which for Sheptytsky was to have been a path toward the spiritual unity of all Christians—became for secular and nationalist Ukrainians a sign of patriotism and loyalty in itself, a visible embodiment of their national existence. The movement to cleanse the Byzantine rite of its Latin accretions was particularly lively in the Ukrainian Church in the decades bracketing the World Wars.

INSIDE THE LVIV METROPOLITANATE

During Constantine Bohachevsky's tenure at Lviv, the Ukrainian Catholic Church faced two major internal problems. One was the need to streamline its administrative system and root out petty corruption. The other was to update and codify liturgical texts and church regulations, which had been altered through various redactions. Sheptytsky commissioned scholars to study and establish authoritative liturgical texts for the church rites. Bohachevsky was co-opted to work on a project that began with an early six-person textual study group. In 1914, a formal textual editing commission was created, and Sheptytsky appointed Bohachevsky as one of its members. The work was renewed after the First World War, and continues to this day.[7]

The context of the major discussion within the Ukrainian Catholic lay congregations was the rejuvenation of Eastern rite ritual practices within the Catholic Church. The idealized Eastern-church culture had no template and could be subject to personal interpretation. The agenda focused on removing signs of Latin practices that had either crept in or were in-

7. Galadza, The Theology and Liturgical Work of Andrei Sheptytsky, 270. The commission, announced on January 22, 1914, and headed by Isidore Dolnytsky, was charged to prepare for the archeparchial synod. World War I cut short the work of this committee. The aged Dolnytsky was arrested at the beginning of World War I for alleged pro-Russian views. See a collection of letters, documents, and memoirs published as Litopys rodu Dolnyts'kykh: Dokumenty, Materialy, Spohady: Henealohichne doslidzhennia, ed. Oleh Dolnyts'ky (Lviv: Ukrainian Catholic University, 2004), 476–77. The commission was transferred to Rome in 1938 and headed by Eugène Cardinal Tisserant. The documents were not published until the 1950s.

troduced earlier, at times forcefully. In addition to textual and liturgical matters, practices that might be viewed as secondary took on major importance before and after the First World War—the use of statues, placement of flowers on the altar, the correct placing of icons on the sacred screen that divides the altar from the nave (the iconostasis), the length and fullness of the vestments, the type of head covering the priests wore and whether they should grow beards. Some of the practices borrowed from the Latin rite, such as the Corpus Christi processions, services to the Sacred Heart, May services to the Virgin, or Stations of the Cross, became popular within Ukrainian congregations, especially among women. Even purists could not decide where the cultural boundaries lay.

By the beginning of the twentieth century, the traditional Russophiles, with their glorification of an idealized Eastern church culture strong enough to stem Polonization, were no longer popular in Halychyna. Local government administrators, however, used vigilance about Russian agents as an excuse to arrest Ukrainians. The arrest of the Russophile priests during the First World War briefly revived this dying trend, although its influence became limited to the Transcarpathian region where conservative White-Russian émigrés established a foothold.

The first decade of Bohachevsky's priesthood coincided with a dramatic expansion of cultural life among the Ukrainians in Halychyna. The great war of ideas between the modern secularists and the traditionalists who defended the public role of the church had some resonance in Halychyna. Public discourse came to include topics other than those set by the Church and local convention. Eastern Ukrainian literary works, which were published in Halychyna owing to the ban on Ukrainian-language works in Russia, popularized a world without Catholicism and created a challenge for the clerical leadership in the public sphere. Gradually, sons of priests who themselves did not become priests felt entitled to speak out on issues relating to Church practice. By the late 1920s, the laity in Halychyna actively discussed Church policy on social and political issues, and within the next decade an active Catholic Action organization was established.

The two church-related issues that stimulated the most ardent debates within the Ukrainian community were clerical celibacy and the use of the vernacular. In the early twentieth century, the laity began to press for the use of vernacular Ukrainian rather than the traditional Church Slavonic in all facets of worship, not only in sermons and hymns. This issue is still debated.

The debate on celibate clergy also crested and waned throughout the century.[8] The official position on married clergy—that is, that married men could receive Holy Orders—was a key provision of the Union of Brest (1596). Over time Latin Catholics used this provision to impute a second-rate status to the Ukrainian Church. In 1891, there was an attempt to get the Ukrainian clergy to accept a resolution supporting the moral superiority of celibate clergy over married clergy. That move failed. Nevertheless, the argument for preferring celibate clergy gained support in the twentieth century. Bishop Khomyshyn of Stanislaviv was the most outspoken proponent of making celibacy mandatory for Ukrainian clergy. Bishop Josaphat Kotsylovsky (sporting a magnificent beard that manifested his dedication to the Eastern rite) also saw the advantages of a clergy unencumbered by family constraints but did not make celibacy mandatory for priesthood. Both of these bishops saw celibacy as a means of creating more effective and better educated clerics. Sheptytsky formally agreed to promote celibacy for the Greek Catholic Church at a meeting of bishops in 1919 but refrained from making any public pronouncements on the matter and, unlike his own bishops, readily continued to ordain married men into the priesthood.[9] The financial difficulties of the married Ukrainian

8. All Ukrainian bishops expressed support for clerical celibacy in their meetings, but it was not until 1922, when information on the proceedings of the conference was leaked to the press, that a public outcry among the laity and clergy broke out. See Andrew Sorokowsky, *The Greek-Catholic Parish Clergy*, 92–96; John-Paul Himka, *Religion and Nationality in Western Ukraine* (Montreal: McGill-Queens Press, 1999), as well as his presentation of the pertinent documentation in "The Issue of Celibacy at the Lviv Provincial Synod of 1891: Unpublished Documents from Lviv and Przemysl (Peremyshl) Archives," in *Mappa Mundi: Zbirnyk naukovykh prats' na poshanu Yaroslava Dashkevycha z nahody yoho 70-richchia*, ed. Ihor Hyrych et al. (Lviv: Kots Publishing, 1996), 648–70.

9. At what is numbered the twenty-eighth conference of bishops, the metropolitan put his signature under the first point which read: "We recognize the general need for celibacy of the clergy in our Halychyna Province, and . . . we have decided to introduce it. The Conference . . . will study the time and means it could be realized." PKEL, minutes of August 24, 1919. At the next meeting, held on September 24, 1919, at Lviv the bishops did agree that all seminarians accepted that year would be ordained celibates. PKEL, minutes of September 24, 1919.

clergy, the conflicts arising from the choice of positions, as well as individual and official attempts to be more in tune with the rest of the Catholic Church, made the clergy raise the issue again. The higher Ukrainian clergy, for their part, feared that celibacy would promote an influx of peasant and workers' sons to the clergy, lower the standards, and diminish the quality of Ukrainian cultural life. These sentiments were rarely as clearly expressed as by Rev. Oleksandr Zubrytsky, a canon of the Peremyshl cathedral, in a confidential memorandum to Sheptytsky.[10]

For most Western Ukrainians, however, any attempt to introduce priestly celibacy was seen as a means to limit the Ukrainian educated class. Some even pointed out the work of the wives of priests as an argument to preserve the married clergy. Sons of priests who did not enter priesthood were the prime candidates for secular professions; an unmarried clergy would considerably reduce the size of this class.

Bohachevsky was an outspoken proponent of celibacy. In a memorandum he wrote in June 1918, he praised virginity and argued that this level of total selfless dedication was essential for priests to commit themselves fully to their calling.[11] He was convinced that only clergy who were thoroughly and exclusively dedicated to their work would save the nation and its church.

Bohachevsky was an ascetic man, modest in his needs and not given to expressions of personal sentimentality. His thrift, which stemmed from conviction as much as from need, became legendary. Working in the chancery of the metropolitan, he was the consummate model of the efficient cleric, showing little inclination for chitchat. In the seminary, he was a conventionally strict disciplinarian. He insisted on promptness, hoping in this manner to root out lassitude, which he considered the major draw-

10. Aleksandr Zubryts'ky, a priest in the Peremyshl diocese, wrote between the summer of 1929 and July 15, 1930, a number of confidential memoranda to Metropolitan Sheptytsky mostly to criticize Bishop Kotsylovsky. See "Statti i zamitky sviashchennyka Zubrytskoho z Peremyshlia," in TsDIA, Lviv, f. 201, op. 4b, spr. 2915; see esp. "Zapyska shchodo prymusovoho vvdenia tselibatu hr.kt.klyru v dvokh eparkhiakh Halytskoyi provitsiyi," ibid., pp. 27–29, quotation from p. 6 verte.

11. Bohachevsky outlined his views on clerical celibacy in a handwritten reply to a query on the issue titled "My view," filed under "Statutes, Lists, Correspondence and Other Matters relating to the Activities of the Spiritual Seminary at Lviv, 1924–1934." TsDIA, Lviv, f. 201, op. 48, spr. 2164, pp. 104 and verte.

back of Ukrainian men. He also insisted on a program of physical activity, which was unusual at the time. He dragged his often unwilling charges on long hikes. He attended Lviv cultural events and corresponded with Oleksander Barvinsky, the artistic metre of Lviv's conservative cultural community. As a result of all this activity, his research into the patristic origin of the epiclesis suffered.

At the same time, Constantine collected old church artifacts, working diligently on the museum that the metropolitan was organizing. He developed extracurricular cultural programs on ethnography and church architecture for the seminarians. Bohachevsky's model for Eastern-rite churches was epitomized in the wooden ones of the Carpathians, which he scoured for historical artifacts and old church documents. Based on this model, his ideal church would have old icons, censers with bells, and massive hand-dipped beeswax candles. Into this idealized picture he also admitted embroidered coverlets, banners, and flags, but rejected statues and other material modes of public religious sentiment that he felt detracted from the austere beauty of the rite.

As pastor of Transfiguration Church, Bohachevsky was assisted by Rev. Havryil Kostelnyk, a confidante of Sheptytsky, who most vocally supported a pro-Eastern cultural approach in ritual matters,[12] and by Reverend Yeremak, who hailed from Volyn, an ethnically Ukrainian area that had been within the Tsarist empire (it also had a Polish minority). Bohachevsky remained the pastor of Transfiguration until June 1916. This church, built in the 1890s exclusively with donations from all Ukrainian political and social groups, became a symbol of Ukrainian patriotism. Located two blocks from Lviv's magnificent opera house, the imposing stone

12. Havryil Kostelnyk was the most active proponent of Eastern traditions in the Ukrainian Catholic Church. He argued to preserve and if necessary reintroduce Eastern Christian rituals, linguistic forms, and even parts of dogma by pointing out that in his native Balkans the older Ukrainian settlers who still preserved nineteenth-century versions of Byzantine worship remained steadfast in their Catholicism, while the recent Halychyna Ukrainians who settled in Yugoslavia were more likely to become Orthodox. See Sorokowsky, The Greek-Catholic Parish Clergy in Galicia, 216 ff. Kostelnyk in 1946 spearhead the signing of the forced renunciation of Catholicism in favor of the Orthodox Church and soon afterwards was killed. See recent articles on Kostelnyk by Maria Kashuba and Iryna Mirchuk, "Havryil Kostelnyk," in Beresteys'ka Uniia: statti i materialy, ed. Maria Kashuba and Iryna Mirchuk (Lviv: Logos, 1996), 210–13; and Iryna Mirchuk, "H. Kostelnyk i Ukrayinska natsionalna ideia," in Rizdvo Khrystove 2000 (Lviv: Logos, 2001), 201–4.

structure in the Byzantine style drew its parishioners from the Ukrainian bourgeoisie, the growing working class and the secular intelligentsia, thus visibly demonstrating the changes within the Ukrainian polity.

IVAN FRANKO'S DEATH

It was during this time that the poet Ivan Franko died, on May 28, 1916, just as the military front—the Germanic empires battling the Russian one—was passing through Lviv. On his deathbed the ailing writer refused the repeated ministrations of three priests who tried to get him into a Catholic heaven; Franko declined in the knowledge that his place in the national pantheon was secure. The Ukrainian youth in Halychyna idolized him to such an extent that a "cult of Franko" arose. Ukrainian high school youths, too young to be drafted, announced they would march in Franko's funeral procession, even if no priest participated. Under Austrian wartime regulations processions were permitted only for religious burials. If there would be no priest—and Franko had stipulated that he did not want one—the local Polish authorities were authorized to imprison Ukrainians participating in the funeral procession. After painful deliberations, with canon fire increasingly audible, the priests decided that Franko had to have been emotionally unstable at the time of his death and delegated one elderly priest to bury the poet in accordance with the ritual of the church, skirting church regulations of the time that a Christian who denied his Christianity openly could not receive a Christian burial.[13]

13. The chancery priests decided that Franko was no longer clear-headed, and Franko's body was laid to rest with the ministrations of one priest and a cortege of the poet's mourners. The clergy kept no notes and later rumors developed about the burial. Franko was a complex personality, and not well read by the priests. He was, however, a hero for the young. To use the title of a recent study on the poet, Franko consciously sought to mold himself as the *Prophet in His Country*; Yaroslav Hrytsak, *Prorok u svoiïy zemli* (Kyiv: Krytyka, 2006). His prolific poetry and readable short stories, novels, and newspaper articles, as well as his extremely popular children's tales made him a household name. The clergy, however, knew only his fashionable anticlerical ditties. Franko's daughter would later recount that Metropolitan Sheptytsky had visited Franko, and after his death held a church prayer for him. The metropolitan had power to do that as a high church official. His priests did not think they had that authority.

Meanwhile, the Austrian Army was short of German- and Ukrainian-speaking chaplains. Bohachevsky's service in the army had been deferred a number of times. On June 23, 1916, three weeks after Franko's death, the extension on Bohachevsky's deferment was lifted. He was called up to serve as a chaplain in the 30th Infantry Regiment stationed on the Italian front. That appointment had no relation to Franko's death, although years later an unfounded rumor emerged that Bohachevsky had been sent to the front because he would not bury Franko.

Through the summer and winter, until February 22, 1917, Bohachevsky trudged with the army through the Armentera Mountain Range and into the Sugan Valley, scenes of some of the bloodiest battles of the Great War. According to Reverend Ivan Lebedovych, and as reflected in other accounts, Bohachevsky threw himself into the fray very courageously, determined, as he was, to be with the front-line recruits.[14] He repeatedly risked his life to comfort wounded soldiers and minister to the dying. Such observations were confirmed when, on March 12, 1917, Bohachevsky was awarded one of the last crosses for bravery, second class with sword and ribbon, that the new Habsburg Emperor Karl gave out.[15]

Bohachevsky experienced firsthand the wretched conditions of the Austrian Army. He also knew of the terrible internment camps in which the Austrian government, fearing a resurgence of pro-Moscow sentiment, detained alleged Russophiles, including elderly priests, as soon as the hostilities began in 1914. (This policy angered Ukrainians and ensured the continued existence of that diminishing faction.) Brutality mixed with squalor, inefficiency, and illness contributed to high death rates at these camps. When Bohachevsky returned from the front, he was still one of the

14. Rev. Ivan Lebedovych, *Polevi dukhovnyky Ukraiins'koii halyts'koii armii* (Winnipeg, self-published, 1963). The bishops' conference on April 23, 1906, sought to ensure that the Ukrainian soldiers in the Austrian Army would be able to adhere to the Julian calendar during the holydays.

15. The award was a special "Geistliche Verdienstkreuz II Klasse am weissroten Bande mit Schwerten" issued by the emperor. The distinction was duly noted in the Lviv *Archeparchial Bulletin*, July 25, 1917, no. 9, 101. When Danylo was transported as a Polish prisoner of war, Constantine offered to change places with him, suggesting Danylo put on his cassock and escape.

youngest highly placed priests in the Lviv chancery. Now an experienced military man, he was sent to inspect the areas of the camps in September and October of 1917. Bohachevsky did not discuss this period of his life, though he kept, as a painful memento of the trip, the sewn cluster of stamped pages that the German military authority issued him at every inspection point as a permit to travel.

The nine-month period spent in the trenches and trudging through the western Carpathian foothills followed by the firsthand experience of the camps had a profound impact on the relatively sheltered Bohachevsky. His upbringing in a supportive and loving family had isolated him from the ugliness of life, and he was squeamish about life's uncomfortable physicality. The gore and dirt of trench life must have been wrenching, as were the violent deaths he repeatedly witnessed. Bohachevsky emerged from the ordeal even more disciplined, steeled, and demanding of himself. He had become a hardened veteran in an unstable world. To the end of his days, he remained proud of his straight spine and light tread.

Upon demobilization on February 23, 1917, Bohachevsky resumed his duties at the seminary, the university and the chancery. He immediately organized supplementary lectures on Ukrainian studies, including a segment on the importance of archeological findings in churches and the surrounding cemeteries. With the rector, Rev. Joseph Botsian, he sought to create an island of peace, at least in the seminary.[16] He returned to working in Sheptytsky's museum. His work there merited him an honorable mention from the museum's director, Dr. Ilarion Sventsitsky.[17] Meanwhile, Sheptytsky returned from Russian captivity and a triumphant trip through Ukrainian territories in 1917. One of Metropolitan Sheptytsky's

16. Rev. Botsian accompanied Sheptytsky during his exile to the Russian Empire, at the end of which Sheptytsky consecrated him as bishop of Lutsk, on the basis of the powers verbally granted him by the pontiff. This appointment was not recognized by the Polish government, which claimed the right to block ecclesiastical appointments. Sheptytsky was trying to reassert Ukrainian Catholicism in the Volyn area, in which the tsarist regime in the 1830s forcefully implemented Orthodoxy. The Poles tried to limit the influence of the Ukrainian Catholic Church while promoting Latin rite Catholicism. Botsian died in 1926 at Lviv.

17. At one point Bohachevsky physically threw out a Polish official who taunted Ukrainians in the Lviv Ethnographic Museum funded by Sheptytsky. Danylo Bohachevsky, *Vladyka Konstantyn*, 20, quoting Vasyl Lencyk, "Ukrayinsky Muzey v Stemfordi," *America*, January 30, 1973.

first acts at home was to consecrate a fellow Basilian, Josaphat Kotsy-lovsky, as bishop of Peremyshl on September 23, 1917.[18]

Bishop Kotsylovsky needed young priests in Peremyshl to develop the diocese there according to the same organizational plan that the diocese of Lviv pursued. He persuaded Bohachevsky to move to Peremyshl, appealing to his sense of duty and also offering him an immediate promotion that would increase his salary. Sheptytsky countered by offering Bohachevsky the rectorship of Lviv Seminary. As tempting as this offer was, Bohachevsky felt that he could be of more use in Peremyshl.[19] Sheptytsky was surprised by Bohachevsky's choice. No one declined the Lviv metropolitan.

In terms of career advancement, Bohachevsky was well along the way within Sheptytsky's entourage. However, he never showed any partic-ular interest in the clerical camps that formed within the inner circle at St. George Cathedral. Nor was he ever enamored with the city of Lviv. There were also other considerations. Bohachevsky had to support his young-er brothers and his mother, and Peremyshl offered immediate advance-ment. Most important, Bohachevsky shared many of Kotsylovsky's views on key issues. On June 29, 1918, Bohachevsky moved himself, his mother, and the youngest brother to Peremyshl.[20] After the war, it was to this new

18. Bishop Josaphat Kotsylovsky (1876–1947) was an outsider among the Ukrainian clergy. Unlike most Ukrainian priests who chose their profession early in life, the young Kotsylovsky had served as an Austrian army officer, had a reputation for rowdiness, and had fathered an illegitimate child whom he supported financially. He was thirty-one when he became a priest in 1907. In a further unusual move Kotsylovsky entered the Basilian order five years into his priesthood. Thin, tall, with a long gray beard, he looked as severe as his reputation. He zealously defended the independence of the church as well as all church rules, promoted de-Latinization of the Ukrainian Catholic rite (a popular move among the intelligentsia) but also insisted on a return to a stricter Eastern prayer discipline (a decision that did not garner even much lip service, let alone support) and argued for celibate clergy. He promoted a Western style of education for priests. The most open attack on Kotsylovsky came in an eighty-page brochure published in Lviv in 1927 and reprinted in 1929 under the auspices of Ivan Gotia. Kotsylovsky was executed in a Soviet prison, refusing to join the Orthodox Church. There is a reliquary of him in the Church of St. Basil in Kyiv, a mile or so from the prison in which he had been kept. Kotsylovsky was declared blessed, an inter-mediary step to sainthood, by St. John Paul II in June 2001, during the pope's visit to Kyiv.

19. Kotsylovsky boasted in letter to the papal auditor, Monsg. Carlo Chiarlo, dated Sep-tember 10, 1923, that Bohachevsky chose Peremyshl over rectorship in Lviv. ASV, Poland, no. 224, p. 329.

20. I wonder if Kotsylovsky was aware of the number of brothers that the new assistant

Bohachevsky household in Peremyshl that his three remaining brothers, veterans of Ukrainian armies, returned from Polish internment camps.

The official release of Bohachevsky from his duties as vice-rector of the seminary at Lviv, which Sheptytsky issued only on October 24, 1918, included praise for his "zealous, dedicated, and selfless execution of the functions of vice-rector of the seminary during extremely difficult war times."[21] Even greater difficulties were to come for all concerned. Although Bohachevsky did not have the requisite age and time in service, he was nominated by his superiors—a nomination that had to be approved by the pope—to become an eparchial canon. He formally advanced to that position in Peremyshl.

THE WAR AFTER WORLD WAR I

Bohachevsky's six-year tenure in Peremyshl (1918–24) roughly coincided with repeated Ukrainian attempts, some military, to gain independence and political recognition both as a sovereign state in the East, as a newly independent Ukraine that emerged from the ruins of the Romanov Empire, and in the West as a successor state of the dissolved Habsburg Empire.

November 11, 1918, the date that marked the end of the Great War, meant little for Ukrainians. Ten days earlier, Lviv Ukrainians proclaimed national independence, and war with the Polish factions erupted. In both the Russian and Austrian empires Ukrainians were caught in the middle of a series of civil wars and total social disarray. Their lands were still being fought over by outside parties. There was fighting in all parts of Ukrainian lands, and many Ukrainians fought in formal armies, militias,

---

would host in the lean post–World War I years. Constantine's younger brothers, who joined him as they were either demobilized or freed from Polish prisons, caused further tension with the families of the canons who lived on episcopal property. Family lore has it that as the various Bohachevsky brothers, in differing stages of de-mobilization or job search, came to stay with Constantine in Peremyshl, they ran afoul not only of the canons, but also their pets. Omelian hoped to study engineering, John searched for a job as an accountant, Danylo, although he never said so openly, felt the pressure that Constantine was under and left Peremyshl soon after he was freed. He made ends meet by clerking, opened a legal practice, and did get a doctorate in law from Lviv University.

21. Among the documents I received from Oleksander Lushnytsky.

or anarchic groups, or just to stop marauders, or formed brigand bands of their own. The post–World War I hostilities involved civilians in greater numbers than even during the world war. The breakdown of civil order put the weak and especially minorities at risk. And when a semblance of peace came in 1923, it was not on the terms most Ukrainians had envisaged.

In the period between the disintegration of the Romanov Empire in 1917 and the consolidation of the Communist Party of Russia's power over the territories of the newly established Union of the Socialist Soviet Republics in 1922, Ukrainians established a number of independent governments, but were unable to maintain any of them when faced with the onslaught of better equipped hostile armies. The Russians fought their civil war while mounting campaigns to reconquer Ukrainian territories. Ukrainians in Eastern Ukraine could not rally around one government to defend their sovereignty. The Ukrainian National Republic, too weak to roll back a Russian-financed Ukrainian communist regime, sought an understanding with the new Republic of Poland at the cost of Western Ukrainian lands after the Western Ukrainians lost their military bid of independence to Poland. Yet, even though the Bolsheviks emerged victorious from the chaotic ruins of the Russian Empire, they had to agree to the establishment of a Soviet Ukrainian Republic. This Ukrainian communist state, built on the assumption of parity with the alleged state of Russian workers, also fell victim to a renewed centralized regime in Moscow.

Back in October 1918 even the most skeptical expected the dissolution of the Austro-Hungarian Empire. The only issue was whether the dissolution would be peaceful or violent. The three Ukrainian Catholic bishops of Halychyna—Metropolitan Sheptytsky and Bishops Khomyshyn and Kotsylovsky—were among the founders of the Ukrainian National Committee that worked for an orderly transfer of Austrian power to the local units, including Halychyna proper and Volyn. The National Committee planned to make a claim to be one of the Habsburg Empire's legal successors in Western Ukrainian lands. But on November 1, 1918, a younger group of Ukrainians in Lviv proclaimed the creation of an independent Ukrainian republic (which was eventually consolidated with the Ukrainian People's Republic, whose capital was Kyiv). A war between the Ukrainians and the Poles erupted in Halychyna, which remained a bone of contention between the Poles and Ukrainians throughout the whole interwar period. Ukrainians claimed the right to be Ukrainian in lands the Poles claimed to be their own, Unlike the Poles, who mustered armed support from France, Ukrainians lacked all outside support. The Polish armies, with French help, proved victorious.

The new Polish Republic government tried to move quickly to consolidate the territories it considered Polish, which had been administered by three different empires, into one centralized Polish state. Local administrations rode roughshod over the non-Polish parts of the new state. Nevertheless, Ukrainians hoped that the Wilsonian principle of self-determination of nations would influence the peace arrangements for Western Ukrainian territories. The Allied decision in March 1923 to cede the Western Ukrainian areas of Halychyna and Volyn to Poland directly, not even as a mandate, came as a shock to the Ukrainians.

It was a period of undeclared but bloody confrontations and skirmishes during which heroic deeds were quickly celebrated in popular music and art, and heinous crimes went unpunished. Daily existence was extremely difficult—hunger, disease, poverty, and physical dangers undermined the already strained resources of the people. In a desperate measure, a faction of Ukrainians allied to the Polish Republic fought the Soviets, but were forced to abandon Ukrainian territories. As various attempts to establish a Ukrainian state failed, the population came under foreign control.

Ukraine fared badly on all fronts, and Bohachevsky, as other young men, felt the failure personally. They had fought and lost. Even Sheptytsky failed in 1918 to convince the Polish bishop of Lviv for both clerics to proclaim a ceasefire. In November 1918, a year after Sheptytsky's triumphant return to Halychyna from Russian internment, the Catholic Polish Republic arrested him on charges of sedition. To extricate the pope from an embarrassing situation, early in 1920 Sheptytsky went to Rome for the standard five-year *ad limina* visit of each bishop to the pontiff. Once Sheptytsky was in Rome, the pope asked him to serve as the apostolic emissary to Ukrainian Catholics in Brazil and Argentina. Sheptytsky used the opportunity to travel also to the United States and Canada, where the Vatican empowered him to collect funds on behalf of the war orphans in Ukraine. The metropolitan tried to lobby in America and in Europe for the Ukrainian cause, while Western Ukrainians refused to admit the legitimacy of Polish rule.

Despite numerous failed endeavors, for a large segment of Ukrainians in this period the hope of imminent independence flickered and occasionally burned. The Ukrainian intelligentsia never abandoned their belief in some sort of independence for at least a part of Ukraine. In Peremyshl, which both the Poles and Ukrainians claimed to be theirs, the standoff was particularly sharp. After they lost the war with Poland, Ukrainians insisted on the legitimacy of the old Habsburg laws that provided a degree of rights for Ukrainians. The Poles maintained that their de facto control of the territories voided the previous legal systems, regardless of whether the new borders were recognized internationally. The Ukrainian Catholic Church, on occasion supported by the papacy, adhered to the former interpretation of legality. This legal limbo would be further complicated by the death of Pope Benedict XV in 1922; by the attempts of Metropolitan Sheptytsky, in 1923, to return to his see in what was now to be Poland; and by delays in crafting a concordat between the new Republic of Poland and the Papal See. Unbeknownst to him, all three of these events had a direct bearing on the future career of Most Reverend Dr. Constantine Bohachevsky, canon and pastor of the Peremyshl cathedral, president of the seminary, apostolic protonotary, and appointee vicar of the Peremyshl Eparchy.

PEREMYSHL

Dating from 1087, present-day Polish Przemysl (Peremyshl) was the seat of the oldest Ukrainian Catholic bishopric.[22] The Ukrainian cathedral in Peremyshl was well cared for, and the eparchy was run by staid, conservative clergy families. Peremyshl's strategic geographic position made it a major Austrian military garrison, which contributed to a building boom prior to World War I that the local Ukrainian Church used to its advantage. During World War I Peremyshl became, after Verdun and Antwerp, the third most heavily fortified city in Europe, the site of major battles. The city had a higher per capita proportion of Ukrainian residents than did Lviv. Its sizeable Ukrainian middle class succeeded in building schools

22. The cathedral was claimed by both Poles and Ukrainians, and in late 1996 the Polish Latin Catholic clergy had a Byzantine cupola of the cathedral destroyed. It is now a Latin-rite church. Subsequently, the Polish government transferred another Peremyshl church to the Ukrainian Catholic rite. There is a Ukrainian bishop in Peremyshl now, although not at the original cathedral.

and economic cooperatives for the city's Ukrainian population, as well as the first Ukrainian insurance program for the families of the Catholic clergy. It also had a strongly entrenched Ukrainian Catholic upper clergy. Peremyshl had a tradition of effective bishops, especially Julian Pelesh, who had close personal relations with the Habsburg court.

A building boom in the 1890s changed Peremyshl into an industrializing city through the influx of a labor force from the villages. After the Bolsheviks came to power in Ukraine, many émigrés from central and eastern Ukraine settled here. The clergy feared the spread of socialist ideas among the working population as well as Ukrainian Orthodoxy among the elites and communism among the workers. The strategic location of Peremyshl made both the Habsburg and the subsequent Polish governments, as well as the local population, very conscious of security. The Habsburg concentration camps for alleged Russophiles, formed in the first days of World War I, were located in the territories of the Peremyshl bishopric. The arrest of the Ukrainian conservative clergy and other major figures of the area deepened the rift between Poles and Ukrainians.

Josaphat Kotsylovsky's appointment, on October 23, 1917, as bishop of Peremyshl, ruffled the Ukrainian clerical elite. Although Kotsylovsky's father had been a member of the Galician Sejm, as a farmer he was considered an upstart. The married, clerical elite of Peremyshl did not take kindly to such a man becoming their bishop. With his military background and a neophyte's desire for quick results, Kotsylovsky wanted to modernize the church. He immediately took a very active role in the bishops' meetings, although he was, after all, the junior bishop of the three.[23] He became frustrated by the leisurely pace of his fellow bishops and stymied by growing opposition of the Peremyshl prelates to his plans of expanding the seminary. Moreover, upon his arrival as the new Peremyshl bishop, Kotsylovsky had run afoul of the established, local clerical families who resided in the buildings connected to the cathedral. The canons with their families traditionally occupied comfortable apartments on cathedral property while the diocesan seminary had no room to grow. Kotsylovsky proposed that the elder canons relinquish their cathedral apartments in order to

23. At their February 20 and 21, 1918, meetings the bishops made decisions on clerical education, religious practices, the Catholic press, and relations with monastic orders, PKEL, February 1918, 24–26.

house the expanded seminary.[24] Kotsylovsky was also shocked to discover that the cathedral church did not have a separate treasury but relied on the support of the Society of St. Joseph, which had clerical and lay members. He insisted that the cathedral and all things related to it should be fully subject to the bishop's authority.

Kotsylovsky wanted to address the needs of the church and those of the new city residents at once. Immediately upon his accession he started to rationalize the church administration, control its finances, institute a merit system within the clerical hierarchy, and establish a full-scale local seminary on the grounds of the chapter housing. He addressed lax practices in the administration of the cathedral parish as well as of the whole diocese. As a Ukrainian patriot, in light of the defeat of Ukrainian armies, the failure of Ukrainian diplomatic initiatives, the disintegration of community structures, and the collapse of the economy, Kotsylovsky decided that the only thing he could do was strengthen the church by creating an educated and dedicated clergy that would once and for all firmly establish this church in Peremyshl and within universal Catholicism.[25]

Bishop Kotsylovsky also started on the wrong foot with the broad lay congregation. Not aware that new patriotic songs were sung in the churches, he attempted to leave the cathedral during the singing. An irate crowd barricaded and heckled him by singing more patriotic songs until he was rescued by the police. The bishop's frequent curative trips to Switzerland did not help his public image either. Knowing this, Kotsylovsky looked for support outside his diocese. He brought in a young priest from Stanislaviv, Hryhory Lakota, as a professor at the Peremyshl seminary.[26] His eye also fell on Constantine Bohachevsky whom he had seen at various meetings. Kotsylovsky offered the young priest a promotion as well as a free hand in expanding the preparatory Peremyshl seminary into a full one.

24. The canons suggested alternate buildings for the seminary, but Kotsylovsky insisted on buildings abutting the cathedral. The canons eventually lodged a formal complaint which dragged on through church channels, documentation in Archiwum Panstwowe w Przemyslu, Kapitula Greckokatoticka w Przemyslu, 1772–1946, z. 143, jed. 512.

25. For an introduction to Ukrainian Peremyshl, see *Peremyshl': Zakhidny bastion Ukraiiny*, ed. Bohdan Zahaykevych (New York: America, 1961).

26. Hryhory Lakota (1883–1950) became Kotsylovsky's vicar, was arrested by the Soviets in 1947, died at the Vorkuta labor camp on December 11, 1950, and was proclaimed blessed by Pope John Paul II in 2001.

Bohachevsky agreed with Kotsylovsky that Ukrainians needed effective institutions more than dramatic actions. He had proven his courage under fire, but was not converted to the idea that individual heroism in the field was the most effective road to national liberation. The war experience reinforced Bohachevsky's conviction that only an educated, properly motivated, and hard-working population could succeed in creating a viable Ukraine. Ukrainians had a limited arsenal of state-building institutions; in Western Ukraine, one of the most important was the church. The trauma of the First World War, the economic collapse of an already impoverished region, and the roller coaster of changing governments challenged the church to be an agent of stability. As an insider, Bohachevsky saw the weaknesses in the Ukrainian Catholic Church. The intelligentsia, on the other hand, saw the church as a rich and stable organization that could be used as a public platform to express social and political goals. This disparate interpretation would fuel conflicts between the church and the public in Peremyshl. And in contrast to Sheptytsky, who always stretched out his arms to everybody, Kotsylovsky seemed aloof and severe.

Aware that a move from Lviv might be considered a setback in Bohachevsky's career path, Kotsylovsky held an elaborate welcoming ceremony for Bohachevsky and Lakota to the diocese on June 29, 1918, at which Bohachevsky was invested as a canon. Three months later, on October 11, 1918, Bohachevsky was also formally invested as the pastor of the cathedral in another pompous ceremony. Bohachevsky was two years shy of the minimum age for promotion to canon, so a papal dispensation had to be requested for the appointment, which gave an additional sheen to the title. The formal investiture of Bohachevsky as canon of the Peremyshl cathedral was one of the last events that took place while Peremyshl was still part of the Habsburg Empire and could draw on government funds. Bohachevsky, in addition to overseeing the administration of the Peremyshl cathedral, worked to expand the seminary curriculum from a two-year to a four-year program and increase the library holdings. He ran everything from the curriculum to milk delivery, encouraging the seminarians to develop their own extracurricular activities.[27]

27. As an example, the supplier of milk to the seminary argued to Bohachevsky in

In Peremyshl the Ukrainian community, both church and secular, welcomed Bohachevsky warmly as a dedicated Ukrainian patriot. The upper ecclesiastical hierarchy saw the young prelate as a welcome counterpoint to Kotsylovsky. Soon after his arrival, the elite and the upper hierarchy presented him with an exquisitely crafted gold chalice. They knew of his interest in art and national politics, and they welcomed the young man's involvement in public affairs.[28] Like many Ukrainian clergy, Bohachevsky now lived with his mother, an arrangement the established Peremyshl clergy strongly approved. The fact that the new prelate came from an old clerical family, and was not, like an increasing number of Ukrainian Catholic clergy, a first generation priest, was also a positive factor for the Peremyshl elite. The fact that the young prelate took care of his younger siblings, three of whom returned from Polish prisoner-of-war camps, was another favorable consideration. The older priests, counting on Bohachevsky's clergy lineage and family connections, hoped the young priest would temper the bishop's zeal for reform.

TO CARE FOR THE NEEDY

At Peremyshl, Bohachevsky was immediately thrust into civic as well as religious leadership. During the Polish takeover, he chaired the Ukrainian Civic Committee, since none of the secular intelligentsia would risk such high-profile work while the Polish–Ukrainian war was raging. He and his committee sought to aid the Ukrainian civil servants who had been fired by the new Polish government by actively lobbying to get Ukrainians reinstated to their positions. As head of the relief committee, Bohachevsky coordinated reconstruction projects and oversaw the relief effort. In addition to his clerical functions, Bohachevsky focused on the narrower needs of the war-ravaged Peremyshl and its growing poor. He worked hard to ease economic and social conditions in the area. He also immediately established a grammar school on cathedral grounds and worked

---

April 1919, that he ought to continue because his family had done the job before the war, Archiwum Panstwowe w Przemyslu, AGKB, 9305, z. 142, pp. 327–29.

28. Bohachevsky kept up his contacts, especially with Oleksander Barvinsky, and even a month before his appointment as bishop recommended a Rev. Theofil Kalynych as an organizer for the Christian-Social Party which Barvinsky sought to revive. Bohachevsky to Barvinsky, March 1, 1923, and April 14, 1924, LAL, Lysty do Oleksandra Barvinskoho.

closely with the Basilian nuns to establish day care facilities, orphanages, and schools elsewhere in the city.[29] The river San cut the city in half, and worker families clustered on the bank opposite the city center, where rents were cheaper. Bohachevsky focused on that area. He actively channeled funds for orphans and began planning for day care and schools there. He encouraged the organization of domestic workers and opened a dormitory for the young peasant women who flocked to the city in search of employment. Bohachevsky even promoted the founding of a lay auxiliary of the Basilian monastic order, which was administered by Rev. Vasyl Hrynyk, to help the poorest Peremyshl suburbs—Vovche and Perekopane—organize community projects.[30] To a greater extent than at Lviv, Bohachevsky directly addressed the economic and social needs of the Ukrainian urban population. The new surroundings set off its poverty making it difficult for Bohachevsky to enjoy the leisurely drawing-room life of the higher clergy or to pursue his museum interests. His time was so stretched that he declined requests to lead public prayers at political demonstrations he considered counterproductive. That behavior led to sharp criticism in the Ukrainian press. Like Kotsylovsky, Bohachevsky had his own vision of what was good for Ukraine and what was good for the church, and he would not do other people's bidding. More than ever he realized that the church needed to practice the faith through social and educational programs.

Kotsylovsky appointed Bohachevsky to audit the cathedral finances. The audit lasted over a year and resulted in the separation of the cathedral treasury from that of the lay and clerical Society of Sts. Joseph and Nychodem. Bohachevsky opened the society's membership to the nuns of the Order of St. Basil the Great, a ploy to get the majority necessary to change the by-laws so that the pastor of the cathedral would be *ex officio* president of the society. The intelligentsia resented the inclusion of nuns

29. TsDIA, Lviv, f. 376, op. 1, spr. 36.

30. Rev. Vasyl Hrynyk (1896–1977) remained in Peremyshl, and after the forced relocation of the western Ukrainians in Poland further west into formerly German territories, ministered half clandestinely to the Ukrainian Catholics in Poland. He was arrested by the Polish communist government after he had written to Bishop Ivan Buchko on the situation of the Ukrainian Church in Poland. By the 1970s he was able to return to Peremyshl where he ministered as an *in pectore* bishop to a greatly diminished and terrorized Ukrainian population. Personal conversations with the author, 1976.

on the board of directors and objected to the restructuring.[31] To demonstrate their opposition, they sabotaged one of the public committees that Bohachevsky was putting together to build a Ukrainian Catholic church in the newer, poorer part of Peremyshl.

Other conflicts arose between church leaders and their secular flock. As the Eastern Ukrainian Orthodox émigrés settled in Peremyshl, the local intelligentsia openly admired the Ukrainian patriotism of the emergent Ukrainian Autocephalous Orthodox Church because of its use of the vernacular. The Peremyshl diocese, in contrast, promoted the veneration of St. Josaphat Kuntsevych, who had been killed by hostile Orthodox crowds in the seventeenth century.[32] The secular community in Peremyshl considered this veneration offensive to Eastern Ukrainians and hence unpatriotic.

LIMITS OF CATHOLIC UNITY

The Polish Republic strove to consolidate its diverse lands by making Polish the exclusive state language—even in the records of the Ukrainian Church. Within the old Austrian Habsburg administrative system, which was legally still in force, the parish priest performed some of the state administrative functions, such as keeping registers of births, marriages, and deaths. The government sought to reinforce its military victory over Halychyna and parts of Volyn with a corresponding cultural victory, through the policy of Polonization. The new government demanded that records of birth, marriage, and death be kept in the Latin alphabet in Polish, or at a minimum, in Latin. Kotsylovsky argued that the old legal system was still in place and mandated that the priests in his diocese continue using Ukrainian for such records. Bohachevsky concurred. He was resolute in his use of the Ukrainian language and continued to function—as was his

31. The Society of Sts. Joseph and Nychodem engaged in fund-raising and charity work, supported publications, and provided a forum for public life. It had a sizeable account at its disposal and Kotsylovsky wanted closer oversight of the funds. "Statti i zamitky sviashchennyka Zubrytskoho z Peremyshlia" in TsDIA, Lviv, f. 201, op. 4b, spr. 2915, pp. 27–29.

32. St. Josaphat Kuntsevych was popular among the Halychyna Ukrainian Catholics. See for instance PKEL, minutes of October 16, 1923, p. 34, where Bishop Botsian of Lutsk is singled out for promoting this veneration.

legal right—within the old Habsburg legal codex. He refused to honor any requests for change of rite without due cause.[33] In the meantime, he continued his relief work, setting up community structures and schools, and providing economic support to the needy. A priest in a cassock and Roman collar still commanded respect, even from the new Polish policemen. Nevertheless, because the Ukrainian priests were so visible in public life, local officials, determined to assert their power, harassed and arrested Ukrainian clergy at the slightest provocation. In Peremyshl, they focused on Bohachevsky and waited for a chance to catch him breaking a law.

The excuse for Bohachevsky's arrest came on June 20, 1919. A Ukrainian clerk in Polish government service, bypassing the Ukrainian Catholic Church, petitioned the government to change his rite from Greek Catholic to Latin. Bohachevsky, as pastor of the cathedral, refused to honor such requests, although the number of requests increased as it became obvious that jobs went more readily to those who were of the Latin rite. Bohachevsky was summoned to the local administrative office the following day. Upon arriving, Bohachevsky insisted that he be addressed in Ukrainian, as was his right under the law. An enraged city official yelled, "I will not speak in this swinish language. You murdered our nuns." Bohachevsky protested the treatment and insisted that a report be drafted, but it was drafted in Polish, so Bohachevsky refused to sign it and left. That afternoon Bohachevsky was arrested, paraded on foot through the town to the police station across the river San, and incarcerated in the local military jail, reputedly in the company of prostitutes.[34]

The police resorted to the extreme measures they would use more broadly in the 1930s. Bohachevsky was charged with violating the law by using Ukrainian in church documents. He was kept incommunicado, severely beaten, and publicly mocked. After a week of this treatment, he was transferred to the prison in Modlin, and a month later to Dobie, near

33. ASV, Warsaw, vol. 224, fol. 323–30. Although both the Polish and the Ukrainian creeds are Catholic, the change of rite from one to the other had to be approved by church authorities. The tendency was for Ukrainians to change rites to avoid persecution or get better treatment. The Vatican opposed this practice, and instituted regulations that made it difficult to change rites.

34. Kotsylovsky to the papal auditor Carlo Chiarlo, September 10, 1923, ASV, Warsaw, 224:365r. The local governor, Stanislaw Zimny, used Bohachevsky's case as a stepping stone to replace Kazimierz Hrabowski as governor of Lviv.

Cracow, for another month. He was also punished for preaching sermons in Ukrainian in the jails. In both prisons, physical violence was routinely used against the prisoners. Bishop Kotsylovsky detailed the treatment Bohachevsky endured in a letter to the papal nuncio:

They [the guards] treated him badly. In the first [few] days they would not permit anyone to visit him, nor to receive anything from the nuns; he did not have a bed or bedding. In the presence of other prisoners, Sergeant Lukasiewicz mocked him verbally, using language that ought not to be repeated here. During the mandatory walks in the prison courtyard, the guard ordered Bohachevsky to repeatedly fall to the ground and get up, just for his amusement. [Other guards] spat in his face.[35]

Between prison transfers Bohachevsky managed to see Achille Ratti, the papal nuncio (who in 1922 would become Pius XI) in Warsaw. The obviously beaten Bohachevsky made a strong impression on the future pope. In a personal letter Ratti berated General Josef Haller, the hero of the Polish victory, for his army's mistreatment of Ukrainians and for establishing a system that abused such men as Bohachevsky. Ratti characterized Bohachevsky as "an apostolic man."[36] Bohachevsky's rank made his case more visible than those of other arrested Ukrainian activists and priests. Sheptytsky and Kotsylovsky forcefully protested the arrest. Monsignor Giovanni Genocchi, the erstwhile papal envoy, corroborated reports on the public and police violence against Ukrainian priests in the new Polish Republic.[37] Through direct Vatican intervention, Bohachevsky was freed on September 1, 1919. He was given three days to return to Peremyshl. While he was incarcerated his residence was robbed.

Prison weakened him physically, but Bohachevsky remained immovable on the position of rite and language. He found legal loopholes that allowed him to establish a day care and a school for the growing Ukrainian working-class population of Zasiannia, the western part of the town. The

35. Kotsylovsky to Warsaw papal nuncio, Lorenzo Lauri, April 4, 1924, in reply to a Vatican inquiry about anti-Polish sentiment among Ukrainian clergy, specifically relating to Bohachevsky. ASV, Warsaw, 224:365–66.

36. ASV, Warsaw, vol. 194, fol. 104:1003. In a quick reply to Ratti, General Haller dismissed the charges, saying that soldiers will be soldiers and Ukrainians are known for their unnecessary complaints.

37. ASV, Warsaw, vol. 224, fol. 323r, 324rv, 329r, 330rv. I am also drawing on my conversations with Bishop Vasyl Hrynyk of Peremyshl in winter 1976 and spring 1977.

local government, in response, kept fining him and sentencing him to renewed prison terms (which were suspended), and eventually withholding his salary altogether.

In contrast to many states, the Vatican knew of the existence of Ukrainians, and at the end of World War I even emerged as a defender of Ukraine.[38] Incarceration of Ukrainian clergy made the Holy See more aware of the plight of Ukrainians in the Polish Republic. Metropolitan Sheptytsky and Bishops Khomyshyn and Kotsylovsky lodged formal protests with the Vatican about Polish discriminatory policies and arrests of Ukrainian priests. Once the Vatican had learned more about Ukraine through the firsthand experience of its envoys, Vatican representatives organized a relief effort for Ukrainians, which was seen as more proof that the Vatican now cared for Ukrainians who were being unjustly treated by their Polish Catholic brethren. For its part, the Ukrainian Catholic Church, and especially Sheptytsky, more actively demonstrated interest now in its Orthodox brethren. As late as March 1923, the bishops' conference in Lviv offered to ask the pope's permission to send Catholic priests to Soviet Ukraine to offset the influence of the Orthodox Autocephalous Church on the Catholics there.[39]

The death of Pope Benedict XV in January 1922 and the fact that the new pope, Pius XI, had firsthand knowledge of Ukraine kindled Ukrainian hopes amid an otherwise bleak situation. Bohachevsky, in attending to his duties as pastor of the cathedral, continued running into problems with the local police, often under fatuous pretexts. One example of this involved his stance on children of mixed Ukrainian-Polish marriages, often in conjunction with his unyielding stance on language. According to church law, girls born of a mixed marriage followed the rite of the mother whereas boys followed that of the father. Change of rite was permitted only in exceptional cases. Bohachevsky insisted on following the letter of

38. Pope Benedict XV had actively opposed World War I, to the extent of even inviting representatives of the feminist Women's League for Peace and Freedom to visit Rome. The league's representative, Mary Sheepshanks, later visited Halychyna to study the situation there first hand. Benedict's successor, the former nuncio in Poland, Cardinal Achille Ratti, who became Pope Pius XI in 1922, had been very favorably inclined toward the creation of the Polish state. His closer acquaintance with the region led him to see the extent of Polish government abuses of the minorities. For a fuller discussion see Hentosh, *Vatykan ta vyklyky modernosti*, esp. 255–58.

39. PKEL, minutes of the bishops' meeting in Lviv, March 16, 1923.

the law and would not grant a simplified change of rite even when Ukrainians requested it. Moreover, within the terms of the law, Bohachevsky was still within his rights in issuing baptismal documents in Ukrainian, although the local government insisted on Polish. Bohachevsky would not budge even if the parents asked for a Polish-language baptismal certificate from the Ukrainian Church. In December 1922, Bohachevsky was again sentenced to jail, but the sentence was commuted to a fine.

As reforms in the Peremyshl diocese were carried out, Bohachevsky's public role became even more complex—in addition to his difficulties with the Polish administration, he was increasingly criticized by the elder canons and the lay intelligentsia. As pastor of the cathedral he led a procession in 1921 to the nearby hamlet of Pykulychi to pray at the graves of Ukrainians who had died in the internment camp, as well as the soldiers buried there. The Polish administration could not stop a religious procession. The following year, however, some leaders of the Ukrainian intelligentsia announced a march with clergy participation without conferring beforehand with the clergy. Kotsylovsky was out of the country at the time, and Bohachevsky, fearing a provocation, forbade the priests and seminarians to take part in what appeared to be an inadequately planned undertaking of which church representatives had not been informed, let alone invited. Nevertheless, the two elderly cathedral canons (Oleksander Zubrytsky and Omelian Mryts) saw an opportunity to win support from Ukrainian society and announced that, despite their age and infirmity, they would lead the march.[40] The press used this event to criticize the bishop, the vicar, and the church for a good year.[41] Kotsylovsky, on the other hand, cited the criticism of his protégé as proof of how insubstantial were Polish accusations that Bohachevsky was inciting "Ruthene terrorism":

The older canons [who most actively opposed Bohachevsky's nomination as vicar] are widowers who cannot, as per the wish of the Holy See, administer the seminary and the monasteries. For this reason it is not surprising that along with the recognition and honors for his work, Rev. Bohachevsky at the same time has

40. Danylo Bohachevsky, Na vozi i Na vozi i pid vozom, 75–77.

41. The march was held in 1922, but articles about it continued to be published throughout the following summer, 1923, in Ukraïnsky Holos, a Peremyshl weekly. Kotsylovsky sent the following issues to the nuncio: May 28, 1922, no. 22; June 18, 1922, no. 25; and June 10, 1923, no. 23, V. ASV, Warsaw, 224:356.

become an object of attack and hatred. The views of our newspapers, especially those who try to influence the way in which community activist intelligentsia think the Ukrainian national church [should be] structured, and [the views] of the Polish government converge in their assessment of Dr. Bohachevsky.[42]

Meanwhile, the elder priests increasingly resented Kotsylovsky's plans for the expansion of the seminary. They lodged a formal complaint that Bishop Kotsylovsky had overstepped his powers, first to the metropolitan, then to the Vatican. The matter dragged on for several years, but in the end, the Vatican found no evidence that the bishop's activities were objectionable. Following this decision, the papal nuncio personally traveled from Warsaw to Peremyshl at the end of December 1923 to persuade the canons to work with Bishop Kotsylovsky.[43] Kotsylovsky addressed all further issues in the ongoing disputes with the cathedral canons through official church channels, which involved both written and oral communication. As a result, Peremyshl became well known in Rome.

THE CONCORDAT AND SHEPTYTSKY'S RETURN

The Polish Republic had pledged to adhere to the legal conventions of the Austrian Empire, honor the linguistic and cultural rights of its ethnic minorities, and ensure freedom of worship. But the new republic repeatedly violated its pledge. As Polish oppression grew, so did Ukrainian, lay pressure on the church to be more proactive in the national movement. Bohachevsky's drawn-out case dramatically and openly illustrated the violations of the local Polish officials toward the population. He became a *cause célèbre* as the highest-ranking cleric to be openly maltreated by the regime. Rallies required prior police permission, which was generally denied. Ukrainian society, which considered the Polish administration an occupation force, thought of new ways to demonstrate its opposition. Marching to the cemeteries, they would carry wreaths of thorns; when the government outlawed this practice, the wreaths were covered with flowers. Along the same lines, not so subtle changes with an opposition subtext were introduced into gymnastic exercises, scouting, and sports.

42. Kotsylovsky to Lauri, September 10, 1923, ASV, Warsaw, 224:340.
43. The nuncio, Lauri, to Kotsylovsky, undated note, ASV, Warsaw, vol. 224, unpaginated note.

Although Halychyna's political fate was for all purposes sealed by 1921 owing to the superiority of the Polish Haller Army, Ukrainians continued to count on some degree of autonomy within the post-Habsburg space. Halychyna's status as a Polish territory was not formally legalized until March 15, 1923, the day that the Allied Council of Ambassadors announced that all of Halychyna would go to Poland. That decision to put Poland in charge of Halychyna further radicalized Ukrainians. It strained the relations between the Ukrainian laity and its clergy because many Ukrainians looked to the church for resolute statements, if not actions, in defense of Ukraine and its people. Kotsylovsky feared the worst—the establishment of a nondenominational Ukrainian national church, Orthodox infiltration, and the spread of atheism: "The postponement of the return of the metropolitan [to Halychyna] exacerbates the destructive rumors that bode no good for our church. Our church is facing a time of great challenges. The schismatics profit from their policies. Nor is there a lack of proselytizers for a national church."[44]

Ukrainians held protest meetings in all cities in Western Ukraine against the decision to cede the Western Ukrainian territories to the reestablished Polish Republic, as soon as the information reached the cities and villages of Halychyna. The apostolic visitator Giovanni Gennochi was in Lviv at the time, with the assignment of studying conditions firsthand. The expected Ukrainian protests were peaceful, but the response of the police was violent, giving Genocchi ample evidence and enabling him to inform the Vatican of the brutal tactics that the Polish regime used against the Ukrainian population.[45]

The Allied decision on the fate of Halychyna, as unpalatable as it was for the Ukrainians, opened the way for Metropolitan Sheptytsky to return to Lviv toward the end of the summer of 1923. His journey was far from simple. As Sheptytsky negotiated to reenter his Lviv See with the help of Vatican diplomacy, Kotsylovsky, under the guise of needing health care, served as a courier between Lviv and the Vatican. During his absences from Peremyshl, Kotsylovsky relied on Bohachevsky in such delicate matters as Sheptytsky's plan to slip into Halychyna unobtrusively. Bohachevsky revealed parts

44. Postscript to a letter to Carlo Chiarlo, the papal auditor, August 31, 1923, ASV, Warsaw, 224:342 v.

45. Memorandum of Genocchi, August 31, 1925, AES, Poland, pos. 40, fasc. 49.

of that original plan only in 1945, after Metropolitan Sheptytsky's death was confirmed. The story appears in a brief note in the Philadelphia Eparchial News.[46] After Sheptytsky managed by skillful diplomacy and some arm-twisting to get a Polish visa, he was to travel incognito in his rail car attached to a regular train and thus slip into Lviv without being called to the attention of the local government officials. Both Sheptytsky and Kotsylovsky feared that any information about Sheptytsky's return would on the one hand enable the Polish regime to block the travel, and on the other provoke Ukrainians into anti-Polish demonstrations that would lead to more bloodshed. Kotsylovsky drew Bohachevsky into the conspiracy, and the two in the middle of the night walked down the steep hill to meet Sheptytsky's train from Vienna when it made a refueling stop in Peremyshl. However one of the railway workers, who knew Bohachevsky from his work in Zasiannia, whispered that the conspiracy had failed. Information of Sheptytsky's travel had slipped out, and his car had been unlinked at the Polish border. The two would-be conspirators, Kotsylovsky and Bohachevsky, surreptitiously returned to their homes. Complex negotiations were needed before the increasingly ill Sheptytsky finally made it home to his see in Lviv.

Eventually, the now ill Metropolitan Sheptytsky was able to return to Lviv, with many detours and amid great difficulties. As demanded by the new Polish law, Sheptytsky pledged his loyalty to the Polish Republic, but managed to do so without fanfare and thus avoid the additional declarations that his bishops had been forced to make.[47] The government in turn promised to adhere to the principles of Christian justice. Nevertheless, Polish repression against Ukrainians became even more violent as the interwar years progressed. The Polish authorities justified this trend as a valid response to growing Ukrainian opposition.[48]

46. Constantine Bohachevsky, "Pomynalne slovo," Eparkhiial'ni Visti, August 1945, 25.

47. The bishops' conference of October 16, 1923, formally welcomed Sheptytsky back to his see, PKEL, 34. It seems only one conference (the 31st, February 16–17, 1922) was held without Sheptytsky, PKEL, 34.

48. AES, Poland, vol. 634, files 19 and 20, also AES, vol. 634, file 30. Ivan Buchko, at the time Sheptytsky's helper, wrote numerous reports to the Vatican documenting government abuse of Ukrainians.

During this difficult time Bohachevsky climbed steadily up the clerical ladder, reaching levels that merited papal approval. On March 23, 1923, the same date that Polish rule in Halychyna was formalized, Bohachevsky received an official document of his appointment as apostolic protonotary, a high-ranking position in the ecclesiastical court system. Kotsylovsky wrote to Bohachevsky formally: "I have the honor to inform your Excellency about this highest recognition by the Sacred Congregation for the Eastern Church."[49]

The papacy had become even more entangled in the Polish-Ukrainian standoff a few months earlier, when on January 15, 1923, Kotsylovsky appointed Bohachevsky his vicar-general. By tradition and law that appointment, to the second highest position in the eparchy, had to be approved by the government, but the approval was generally taken for granted. Ukrainian Catholic bishops simply informed the state authorities of their choice, tacitly expecting government approval. There was no immediate government opposition to the nomination of Bohachevsky as Kotsylovsky's vicar.

However, the elder canons, who had long resented being passed over in favor of the young upstart, complained to the metropolitan's office, to the nuncio, to the Congregation for the Eastern Church, and even to the pope. All four parties disregarded the dissatisfaction of the aged Peremyshl clergy, but the representative of the Lviv governor, the Peremyshl *voevoda*, Stanislaw Zimny, became interested in their complaints. In July 1923, six months after Bohachevsky's nomination as vicar, the Lviv governor, Kazimierz Hrabowski, challenged Bohachevsky's nomination. Through his representative in Peremyshl, the Lviv governor informed Kotsylovsky that Bohachevsky's appointment was illegal and therefore void and ordered Bohachevsky to be immediately removed from all his posts. Hrabowski had several objections to the technicalities of the appointment and shared them directly with the Vatican nuncio. The primary charge was that Bohachevsky threatened the national security of Poland:

49. Kotsylovsky to Bohachevsky, letter (in the author's possession) among Bohachevsky's personal papers naming him protonotary *ad instar Participantium*. The papal letter reached Peremyshl on May 14, 1923; and Kotsylovsky immediately had the nomination delivered to Bohachevsky.

We have official proof that Bohachevsky, as a canon and pastor of the Greek Catholic chancery in Peremyshl always exhibited and continues to show enmity to the Polish state and to the Polish government, which proves, beyond doubt, that he does not want to recognize, despite the decision of the Council of Ambassadors in March 1923, that Little Poland [Malopolska] is part of the Polish Republic. The above person carries on agitation to fan national hatred among the residents of Eastern Galicia, which is unseemly for a cleric. At each step he makes the work of the Polish administration difficult despite our directives and regulations. Instead, he treats the administration in a provocative and frivolous manner, by which behavior he wants to demonstrate that he does not recognize neither the Polish state nor the Polish language. That was why he was arrested, as a person dangerous to public and civic order, and later he was fined administratively a number of times. Hence this is scandalous behavior, and his actions, were he to remain a canon and pastor of the cathedral chapter, would endanger public order.[50]

This letter came when Kotsylovsky was out of the country. The new nuncio to Poland, Lorenzo Cardinal Lauri, summoned Bohachevsky to Warsaw in early August. Monsignor Carlo Chiarlo, the apostolic auditor, was also present at the meeting to review the charges. Both Vatican officials were satisfied that Canon Bohachevsky had not violated the law in any manner. To the contrary, Bohachevsky had provided persuasive firsthand information on the abusive treatment and harassment of Ukrainians by Polish authorities. The Vatican representative suggested that Bohachevsky raise this matter directly with Czeslaw Andrycz, the head of the department of religion in the Polish Ministry of Foreign Affairs, while Chiarlo contacted the Polish minister of Foreign Affairs directly. Both Vatican officials promised to look into the matter, and the nuncio's notes ended with a twice-underlined phrase "what to do in the matter of Bohachevsky."

And indeed, the Polish Ministry of Internal Affairs, in a communiqué to the nuncio, supported Zimny in his charge that Bohachevsky continuously refused to accept the decision of the Council of Ambassadors affirming Polish rule in Halychyna. They accused the priest of actively fomenting opposition to the regime and demanded his removal from all posts within

50. Voevoda Zimny, on behalf of the presidium of the Lviv governor, July 20, 1923, ASV, Warsaw, no. 13962/923, p. 320. Polish officials maintained that the appointment violated the statutes of 1874, since the government had not been duly informed of the appointment. The governor maintained that he had learned about the appointment incidentally, only through a letter from a staffer at the chancery.

fourteen days and the confiscation of his salary. The confiscation demand was redundant; Bohachevsky had not been paid the state salary due him for more than two years. The Republican government made the case to the papal nuncio in Warsaw that Bohachevsky was a threat to the security of the state.[51] The case dragged on, sharply dividing the Peremyshl clergy.

Despite the problems with the Ukrainians, the Vatican wanted to formalize its relations with Poland by signing an official concordat. The Polish lobby at the Vatican was strong, certainly in comparison with that of Ukraine, which did not speak in a single voice. The complaints of the dissatisfied Peremyshl canons, moreover, provided additional justification for the Polish government to insist that the Vatican dismiss Bohachevsky. Canon Levytsky wrote a formal protest to the Congregation for the Eastern Church that was apparently so vicious that the congregation would not send Kotsylovsky the copy he requested. The other canons opposed the nomination because Bohachevsky was too young.[52] This combined opposition from the Ukrainian clerics and the Polish government was enough to persuade the Holy See to delegate a formal inspector to look into the matter. In anticipation of this, the nuncio advised Kotsylovsky to arm himself "with fortitude and toleration . . . because we all know that canons can cause serious problems for their bishop, and even make the bishop's life quite bitter."[53]

VATICAN SCRUTINY

The Vatican began a formal inquiry into the propriety of Bohachevsky's nomination as the Peremyshl vicar-general. When Kotsylovsky returned to Halychyna from his recuperation in Davos, Nuncio Lauri sent him a copy of the note from the Vatican requesting the bishop to reply in detail to the charges levied against Bohachevsky. These included "fanning hatred among the population which speaks [many] different languages" and "impeding in a particularly insolent fashion the work of the local administration."[54]

51. AES, Poland, vol. 634/22, 50–52.
52. February 14, 1924, ASV, Warsaw, 224:353.
53. Note unnumbered, ASV, Warsaw, vol. 224, after p. 323.
54. Ministry of Internal Affairs of Poland, no 1/2494, dated Warsaw, August 22, 1923, ASV, Warsaw, 224:340.

Lauri formally charged the special investigator, Carlo Chiarlo to make certain that Kotsylovsky answer all of the questions Rome posed about Bohachevsky.

Kotsylovsky's fiery temperament was well known, and the auditor, Carlo Chiarlo went out of his way to impress upon him the need to reply to the Vatican's note temperately. The auditor feared that what was an embarrassing situation could soon escalate into something far worse. Chiarlo's overriding concern was that Bishop Kotsylovsky, thinking that the papacy distrusted the Ukrainians, would publicize the charges. That would provoke the Ukrainian side to engage in demonstrations that the Polish government would suppress. That would make the Vatican's position even more awkward. Chiarlo assured Kotsylovsky that the inquest was more routine than hostile.

Kotsylovsky held his temper. In his reply to the auditor, dated September 10, 1923, the bishop defended the legality as well as the worthiness of his choice of vicar. His arguments were equally directed toward the objections raised by the Polish regime and those raised by the Ukrainian opposition, as well as to the Holy See. The bishop of Peremyshl argued that in appointing his vicar he had followed exactly the same procedures as those used by Sheptytsky, which the Lviv governor had not questioned. Nor had the authorities challenged Kotsylovsky's appointments of the Reverends Pynylo, Voytovych, Zubrytsky, and Levytsky as canons in a procedure that paralleled that used in Bohachevsky's appointment. "But even if one were to apply the regulation of May 7, 1874," Kotsylovsky continued, playing the legal scholar:

I can't even consider the possibility of a government veto to Bohachevsky's appointment. By no means can Bohachevsky be suspected in any of the possible actions that would justify his removal. His conduct, previously as now, is characterized by equanimity and proper respect to all without exception. The sole count on which Bohachevsky could be considered guilty—and that was pointed out to him during a meeting of the [Ukrainian] bishops, is that he used and continues to use the Ukrainian language in registering births and in all official correspondence. That was the reason he was arrested in Modlin, and also he was fined for this a number of times (the last occasion was the previous July when he was already the pastor of the cathedral).

As if he were not forceful enough in denying the charges against Bohachevsky, Kotsylovsky then added: "I officially declare that all the charges against Bohachevsky are false." Kotsylovsky appreciated Lauri's intervention on behalf of the Ukrainians, but he could not overlook the major issue: "as of today not a single step was taken to implement the promises given by the Minister of Religion to Your Excellency; nevertheless I hope that it will be done soon, given the dismissal of the governor of Lviv, and other [personnel] changes in the Ministry of Religion."[55]

Meanwhile, Bohachevsky suggested that the governor simply drop the charges against him. That could end the whole case. But the Lviv governor lamented that the matter was out of his hands; indeed, he seemed visibly unhappy that Warsaw had become involved in his local affairs. "Bohachevsky had a very bad feeling from the meeting," Kotsylovsky relayed to the nuncio.[56]

During this time Bohachevsky was not only not paid, but was repeatedly fined for using Ukrainian in church records. Despite this severe financial hardship he continued in his duties. The regime refused to budge, but there was no discreet way in which Kotsylovsky could be asked to withdraw Bohachevsky's appointment without provoking a Ukrainian reaction that would without doubt lead to renewed bloodshed. The stalemate dragged on.

A POPE'S PROBLEM

The confrontations between a Ukrainian Catholic bishop and the Polish Catholic governor in a Catholic country whose establishment the new Pope Pius XI had openly supported reflected badly on the pontiff. At the same time, there was also increasing pressure on the Vatican to appoint a bishop for Ukrainian Catholics in the United States. The Ukrainian-American Catholics, eight years without a bishop, feared that their believers would flock to the newly established Ukrainian Orthodox Church in America. As things turned out, the unrest in the Peremyshl eparchy would have unin-

---

55. Kotsylovsky to Lauri, October 10, 1923, ASV, Warsaw, 224:343–44. For good measure Kotsylovsky also included the May 5, June 10, and June 18, 1922, issues of *Ukrayinsky Holos* (Peremyshl) directed against him, Bohachevsky, and Bishop Khomyshyn of Stanyslaviv.

56. Kotsylovsky to Chiarlo, ASV, Warsaw, 224:342.

tended international implications and lead to dramatic consequences for the Ukrainian immigrants in the United States.

The Holy See was faced with a complex set of issues: the appointment of a Ukrainian vicar in Poland whom the Polish government refused to recognize prevented the Vatican from signing a simple concordat with the new Catholic state. The new pope, Pius XI, who had once championed the freedom-loving Poles, now found himself in an embarrassing situation—Catholic Poland was oppressing Ukrainian Catholics. Meanwhile, on distant shores, a Ukrainian-American Catholic Church had been without a bishop for over eight years. The Ruthenian faction, buttressed by the new Hungarian state, and the Halychanyn faction demanded a bishop for America, presumably one for all, since none of the groups were recognized formally to merit a separate bishop. To make matters worse, the imminent establishment of a new Ukrainian Autocephalous Orthodox bishopric in the United States threatened the very existence of the fragile and unstable Ukrainian-American Catholic Church of the Byzantine Rite. Afraid that Ukrainian Catholics could turn to Orthodoxy at any minute, Catholic Church officials at the highest level realized that a Ukrainian Catholic bishop had to be appointed to the United States immediately.

Toward the end of March 1924, Bohachevsky was summoned again by the papal nuncio to Warsaw for what he presumed would be another by now routine discussion of his behavior vis-à-vis the Polish regime. He packed lightly for an overnight trip, but included all the documentation about his arrests and fines that he had insisted the officials copy for him. In Warsaw, Bohachevsky was met not only by the nuncio, but also by Kotsylovsky, who had just come back from Switzerland via the Vatican. Both excellencies confronted Bohachevsky with a question: Would he be willing to take on the difficult task of working as a missionary bishop?

At the time, there had been much talk about the expansion of the Ukrainian Catholic Church in the East—first into the Volyn territories, which had been Catholic until the 1830s, and then into the fabled Ukrainian steppes. Bishop Khomyshyn even discussed plans to appoint a Catholic bishop to one of the Soviet Ukrainian cities.[57] The realities of that expansion, the work of Sheptytsky as well as that of others, the establishment of small missionary training centers for priests, were not

57. PKEL, meeting of December 1923.

publicly discussed outside a small circle of those actually involved. So although Bohachevsky never spoke of what went on in his mind at the time that the question of missionary work was posed to him, he probably thought of work in the East. He replied in the clear-cut manner for which he was known, "Yes, of course I will."[58] He was then told he would be appointed bishop of the Ukrainian Catholic Church in the United States, an appointment that came as a total surprise.[59]

Bohachevsky was also told he could not return to Peremyshl because he would be arrested, and that would place the pope in an even more awkward position. Moreover, his arrest would provoke Ukrainian demonstrations and subsequent government repressions. In consideration of these arguments, Bohachevsky accepted a temporary clandestine appointment as a papal emissary to the Vatican. With no official government documents—the Habsburg Empire was no more and the Polish Republic had not yet issued passports—on March 30, 1924, Bohachevsky was secretly whisked out of Poland to the Vatican. From a routine trip to the Warsaw nuncio, without even having a chance to pack or to say goodbye to his mother, Bohachevsky headed for Rome via Prague. Kotsylovsky kept the papal nuncio in Warsaw abreast of each step of Bohachevsky's undercover journey to Rome.[60] The border crossings were new, each posing the danger that an eager, local official might expose a precarious diplomatic balancing act. Having arrived safely at Rome, Bohachevsky immediately set out to learn English. His official appointment as bishop of Amiso was dated May 8, 1924.

58. Danylo Bohachevsky, in his *Vladyka Konstantyn Bohachevsky*, 24, wrote that Constantine did not ask for an elaboration of the appointment as missionary bishop but just immediately agreed. The Ukrainian Catholic bishops, at their meetings, did talk of petitioning Rome for missionary bishops for Ukraine. See PKEL, minutes of December 10, 1923.

59. Danylo Bohachevsky, *Vladyka Konstantyn Bohachevsky*, 24, referring to "Otets Konstantyn Bohachevsky," *America* (the Philadelphia Ukrainian Catholic daily), December 20, 1964.

60. Kotsylovsky to Lauri, March 25, April 1, April 9, 1924, ASV, Warsaw, 244:368, 443, and 448.

CHAPTER 3

An Unexpected Nomination

Constantine Bohachevsky arrived at the Vatican on March 30, 1924. It was his first trip to Rome. He would spend four months here before leaving for America. He was asked not to disclose the reason for his arrival, which was very easy for him to do. The Vatican denizens had no reason to pay attention to his stay: a relatively young cleric from the periphery of Europe where, as was often the case, the canons disagreed with their bishop. One would think that a cleric who had worked with the new pope, Pius XI, before he had become pope, would use the time at the Vatican to explore the inner workings of the bureaucracy with which he would henceforth be in direct contact. Bohachevsky's value system, however, was different. He was appointed to minister to his people in the United States, and he would use the time to prepare himself for that job by learning some English. His facility in English would benefit his congregation more than having contacts in Rome. He never doubted that the pope would do whatever was needed for Ukrainians, without prompting.

That is not to say that Bohachevsky disregarded the levers of power. He merely trusted the Vatican and felt no need to explicate the obvious. Bohachevsky considered the most crucial part of his appointment the charge to establish a seminary for the training of Eastern-rite priests in America as quickly as possible. Implicit in this charge was the decision about whether that exarchate should set roots in the United States or should it rather minister to a temporary immigrant population. As long as there were no specific institutions for the training of Ukrainian Catholic priests, the Ukrainian Catholic Church in America could be viewed as simply ministering to a migrant population, in much the same fashion as other Eastern Catholic churches in the United States. The establishment of a seminary would institutionalize a Catholic Church that was different from the Latin rite in the United States. That was Bohachevsky's charge, and that would determine his actions for the rest of his life.

To take a very long view of the issue, the erection of the Ukrainian Catholic archbishopric in the United States in 1958 broke the tradition set in the Lateran Councils of the twelfth century. The councils had stipulated that in the European areas in which Latin-rite Catholicism predominated, there should only be one archbishop per area; all other Catholic bishops, regardless of their rank would automatically be the leading bishop's vicars or suffragans. Whether the Lateran decisions had any bearing on America was unclear, but the scrappy Ukrainian immigrant churches in Pennsylvania's black-coal belt moved the United States into the Eastern tradition as far as the Catholic Church structure was concerned. The United States, disregarding geography, kept the Eastern Christian practice, where it was normal to have multiple bishops of different rites or churches in the same city.

The American Latin-rite Catholic Church was less wary of alternate rites in 1924 than it had been in 1907, when the first Ukrainian Catholic bishop had been appointed. At the time, the papacy had still been running the American Catholic Church as a missionary territory. It was only on June 29, 1908, that Pope Pius X asserted the Catholic Church of the Latin rite, that is, the American Roman Catholic Church, to be a full-fledged member of the Catholic *Ecclesia*. The decision was not widely popularized, since American bishops had managed their churches by themselves quite effectively for almost three hundred years. The papal act was seen as mere formality. By 1924, the year that the two Eastern-rite bishops for the Byzantine churches were appointed, the American Latin Catholic Church was secure in its inner structure in the United States and in the manner of its recognition by the Vatican. So in contrast with 1907, in 1924 many of the Latin-rite American bishops were relieved that the Ukrainian churches would have bishops to keep order within their congregations.

Within the Ukrainian communities, the appointment the bishop in 1924 was one of the most discussed clerical appointments in the Ukrainian

Catholic Church. It was not Bohachevsky but the appointment itself, which was the object of public speculation. Although there was no direct information on which candidates for the post had been considered, nor even how any Catholic bishop was chosen, many people on both sides of the ocean claimed to have bits of reputedly relevant information that made the rounds through the rumor mill.

In contrast with the nomination of the first Ukrainian bishop to the United States in 1907, which had been largely Sheptytsky's choice, in 1924 there were more priests in the United States who could have considered themselves quite ready for the episcopal staff. Joseph Zhuk, former rector of the Lviv seminary, former vicar-general in Bosnia, and claiming to be an intimate of Metropolitan Sheptytsky, arrived in the United States via Canada in 1922 amid speculation of an imminent appointment. Other priests, either celibate or widowers, had toiled in America long enough to claim due recognition. Many priests in America shed old-world formalities on such appointments, while their congregations went even further in trying to integrate American democracy into the administration of the Ukrainian Catholic Church. The priest in America did not enjoy the status he did in Europe, nor did priests necessarily hold ecclesiastical authority and those who wielded it always in high regard. In America, both the pastor and his congregation developed a broader variety of acceptable interactions between the two than had been practiced in Europe. Certainly, the seven-year episcopal interregnum in Ukrainian Catholic America was an important factor in undermining all centralization of the exarchy and increasing the informality in the parishes. The periodic meetings, the correspondence, the sheer number of candidates that were considered and rejected also contributed to the popularization of the process, and interest in the man who won out in the end. I have no way of telling how much of this history and pre-history Bohachevsky knew. Ostensibly it made no difference to him, but all the talk influenced the society in which he was to function.

A NEW POPE AND OLD ISSUES

World War I jolted the Vatican bureaucracy into formalizing its relations with the Eastern churches. Faced with growing complications with its many Eastern churches as well as an influx of those who claimed to be monks from the Near East, in 1917 the Vatican replaced the Committee for the Eastern Church in the Congregation for the Propagation of the Faith with a new, separate, and stronger entity, the Congregation for the Eastern Church. While the pre–World War I deliberations of the Committee on the Eastern Church were often carried out by correspondence, the Congregation for the Eastern Church relied more on formal meetings. The Ukrainian Greek Catholic Church came under its purview. One of the first tasks of the new congregation was to prepare the information that the Holy Father would need to nominate a suitable bishop for the American Ukrainian Church. The cardinals reviewed the existing materials—prepared reports, minutes, notes, memoranda, specific pleas, and counterarguments. They formulated three questions that had remained topmost in the earlier deliberations:

1. Whether, and which, of the candidates presented should be proposed to the Holy Father for the succession to Msgr. Ortynsky, as ordinary for the faithful of the Ruthenian rite living in the United States.

2. Whether the chosen bishop should be explicitly enjoined to conform to what has been decided by the Sacred Congregation for Propagation of the Faith regarding the seminary for the formation of Ruthenian priests in the United States.

3. Whether, and how, to ensure the goods and properties belonging to the Ruthenian community to prevent the dispersal of the same upon the death of the bishop.[1]

This was the agenda that Achilles Cardinal Ratti, as Pope Pius XI, in 1922, inherited after the death in January of Benedict XV, who had shepherded the Vatican during the immediate post–World War I disarray. Pius XI had been, among his many positions, a papal representative to the newly independent Poland and had become personally familiar with the ethnic makeup of the area. Upon his accession, he directed the Congregation for the Eastern Church to speed up the nomination of the Ukrainian/Ruthenian bishop to the United States and at the same time to study how a seminary for that church could be established. We need to keep in mind that at the time Ukrainians and Poles were in various stages of the armed confrontation that began in 1918.

1. AES, America (1916–17), pos. 205, fasc. 11, p. 523.

Meanwhile, within the Ukrainian immigrant community in the United States, rumors about the candidates for the bishopric surfaced, causing further tensions among the Ukrainian priests and increasing fears of mass apostasy. The imminent erection of a Ukrainian Autocephalous Orthodox diocese in the United States suddenly made Orthodoxy very palatable to patriotic Ukrainian Catholics. The attractiveness of Orthodoxy grew as the newly established Ukrainian Orthodox Church took steps to bring its bishop to the United States. Giovanni Bonzano, the papal representative to the United States, on leaving the country in 1917, predicted a "complete ruin" of the Ukrainian-American Catholic Church and a mass defection to Orthodoxy unless a Catholic bishop were immediately dispatched.[2] In a panic, the Ukrainian Catholic priests drafted petitions warning Rome of a mass exodus of Ukrainians in the United States to Orthodoxy unless a bishop were appointed.[3] In a similar panic, the Ukrainian Catholic priests in America drafted similar petitions.

Metropolitan Sheptytsky, who had left his see in 1918 to avoid open confrontations with the new Polish Republic, returned from his visitations in America at the end of 1922. Ill but nevertheless deeply involved in political attempts to get better terms for Western Ukrainians, he spent the first half of 1923 in Rome. These attempts cost him the cardinal's hat, and undermined his influence in the inner sanctum of the Vatican.[4]

Many American Catholic bishops had opposed the initial appointment in 1907 of Soter Ortynsky as the Ukrainian Catholic bishop to the United States. A decade later, some American Roman Catholic bishops, and even some Ukrainian priests, felt that the best way to help the Ukrainian Catholic Church in the United States would be to place it under the jurisdiction of the Roman Catholic bishops. Rome worried as much about the rise of popular nationalisms as it feared all government influence upon the church. The cardinals were concerned about Ukrainians, especially the

2. Bonzano to the Congregation for the Propagation of the Faith, September 23, 1917, AES, America (1916–17), pos. 205, fasc. 11.

3. Petitions from the Ukrainian immigrants from Halychyna and from the Carpathian areas requesting the nomination of a bishop, CEC, Protocolli 12119/ 12025, f. 117; also AES, America (1923–25), pos. 188–91, fasc. 35, pp. 15–20.

4. Avhustyn Babiak, *Podvyh Mytropolyta Andreia Sheptyts'koho iak Apostol'skoho vizytatora dlia Ukraiintsiv (1920–1923) i ioho Vzaiemyny z uriadom Pol'shchi* (Trenton: Socita Scientifica Sevcenko-Ucraina, 2013), 128–40.

Halychanyns who were not known for their attachment to the Holy See. Giovanni Genocchi served as the "apostolic visitor" to the Ukrainian National Republic in 1920 and in 1923 was appointed "the apostolic visitator for the Ruthenians in Halychyna." Genocchi was favorably disposed to the Ukrainians. Nevertheless, even he expressed concern in a private letter: "It seems that the Ruthenians have the same endemic illness as other Eastern-rite Catholics: they confuse rite and religion, and many of them think that by changing the rite they change religion, sacrificing one for the other. Even worse, the Ruthenians in Halychyna, as the majority of Orthodox Russians, [think that] to change to the Latin rite means to become Polish."[5]

The members of Congregation for the Eastern Church tried hard to reconcile the often-conflicting information stemming from Warsaw, Lviv, Peremyshl, Vienna, and the American cities. Since no one had an exceptionally strong candidate whom others would support, the congregation honestly pleaded a lack of suitable candidates as the major reason for the long delay in the appointment to replace Bishop Ortynsky.

Metropolitan Sheptytsky had stimulated attempts to unite the Eastern and Western churches through the agency of the Ukrainian Catholic Church. The Vatican understood the attraction of Catholicism in its Ukrainian variant to potential Orthodox converts, yet it did not support Sheptytsky's work unconditionally. Few in the close papal circle shared Sheptytsky's interpretation of the mandate which he received from Pope Pius X to establish Catholic churches in Orthodox territories.[6] Bonzano was even asked if Sheptytsky's visit to America had occasioned political protests among the faithful.[7] While on the one hand Rome welcomed

5. Apostolic visitator in Poland Giovanni Genocchi to Pietro Cardinal Gasparri, April 16, 1923, AES, Poland, pos. 27–29, fasc. 36.

6. CEC, Prot. 8950/22 [Rigotti, 165]. Bonzano to the pope, November 20, 1922; the Scapinelli Ponente of 1923. AES, America (1916–17), pos. 205, fasc. 11; and also AES, Poland (1922–28), pos. 18–21, fasc. 32; and AES, Poland (1922–25), pos. 25–27, fasc. 35.

7. Polish authorities presumed that Sheptytsky would work against them even in the United States. Answering a query to that effect, Bonzano assured Pope Pius XI that "in the United States Sheptytsky worked exclusively as a spiritual guide and did not engage in political agitation." Bonzano addressed his letter to the pope, it went through the usual channels. Memorandum in preparation for a papal audience, November 9, 1922, CEC [Rigotti, 168–69]. (There is no specific protocol number on this document but previous note CEC, Prot. 9086/9058, is related to the topic.)

the possibility of a union with the world's vast Russian Orthodox community—which to some seemed almost palpable during the first disorganized years after the breakup of the Romanov Empire—church union through the Byzantine rite as practiced by the Ukrainian Church was not a popular idea. Although this matter did not directly relate to the situation in the United States, it further complicated the appointment of a Ukrainian Catholic bishop there. Ironically, Sheptytsky's attempts to promote the Western Ukrainian Republic in its desperate efforts at independence diminished his influence within inner Vatican circles. The diplomatic and military successes of Poland immediately after the war further undermined the potential significance of the Ukrainian Catholic Church in the quest for Christian unity. Regardless of what the Polish government policies toward Ukrainians were, the Polish Roman Catholic Church was considered to be pro-Vatican. Metropolitan Sheptytsky, on the other hand, was perceived in Rome as more of a visionary for unity with the East than a pragmatic diplomatic player, and thus treated accordingly.[8]

After the Polish-Ukrainian War began the metropolitan could not return to his own see. To avoid further tension, the pope appointed Sheptytsky as apostolic visitor to Ukrainians in Argentina and Brazil, and permitted him to collect donations in North America for the war victims in Europe. Many Western Ukrainians falsely presumed that the metropolitan had been named vicar to Ukrainians in both Americas. In any case, the American appointment, from 1921 through 1922, gave Sheptytsky a chance to work for both the Ukrainian Church and its war-weary home country from abroad. The funds he raised in his extended travels alleviated the plight of some orphans in war-torn Ukraine. At the same time, the first-hand information about the Ukrainian Church and its priests in the Americas strengthened Sheptytsky's argument about the need for a bishop for the Ukrainian Church in the United States. During his stay in the United States, Metropolitan Sheptytsky became acquainted with many Ukrainian priests, but he could not recommend any of them wholeheartedly for the

8. The information that the Vatican received in the unsettled post–World War I years was understandably not always reliable. For instance, the Polish Commonwealth informed the Vatican that Bohachevsky had been incarcerated from 1918 to 1922. This may be an oversight, but more likely it was done to undermine Bohachevsky's nominations as vicar and then as bishop. AES, Warsaw, 228, vol. 1, 448; and AES, Russia, 634, fasc. 20 and 22.

position of bishop. It brought home the painful realization that none of the mission priests Sheptytsky had sent to the United States had developed leadership qualities. The metropolitan spent a grueling summer in Brazil and Argentina, and when he returned to the United States in July 1922 he found the Ukrainian political situation unchanged and the bishopric still vacant. Giovanni Bonzano, the apostolic delegate in Washington, even suggested that Sheptytsky should stay on as bishop in the United States since the Lviv Metropolitanate could be run by his vicar.[9] The administrator of the Ukrainian Church in America, Rev. Petro Poniatyshyn, and Rev. Havryil Martiak, his vicar who dealt with the Rusyns, reported great difficulties even with their closest priests. They feared immediate mass apostasy.

Even Sheptytsky became disheartened with the Ukrainian community in the United States. Moreover, the metropolitan had fallen ill in Chicago, and had a difficult time recovering as he kept up with his travels. In the face of these circumstances, a weary Sheptytsky drafted his own preliminary analysis of the situation in a frank letter to Isaiah Papadopulos, the assessor of the Congregation for the Eastern Church, dated October 24, 1922.

The fact that the faithful have been without a bishop for almost seven years in itself is leading the eparchy to ruin. The half measures of the administrators may likely lead to more scandals. The administrators are incapable of maintaining discipline, which is visibly deteriorating. Bad priests who now enjoy complete freedom do not want a bishop for fear of losing that independence. Episcopal properties are under lock and key, and church properties in some of the major centers of immigrant life are endangered. The people feel abandoned, comparing themselves to abandoned sheep. [Although] Roman Catholic bishops are appointed within three months, . . . with the Eastern rite it is not clear if a bishop will or will not be appointed. . . . The faithful think that the Roman Curia does not care at all about them. . . . They see that the administrators tolerate abuses, think Rome tolerates them also, they are disillusioned, brought to the brink. Many people have abandoned the church. Schismatic and Protestant propaganda does its terrible disservice. . . . I have assured the Ukrainian-American clergy that there are no grounds to the rumors of the abolition of the [Ukrainian Cath-

9. Memorandum in preparation for papal audience, November 9, 1922, CEC, vol. 117, Prot. 8950/8924 [Rigotti, 166–69].

olic] dioceses. Their concern is all the greater because they know that a [Latin] Catholic bishop in Canada expressed the wish that Bishop N[ikola] Budka (who is coming with me to Rome) be recalled and the Ruthenian colonies be subordinated to the Latin bishops. The Canadian bishops discussed this matter at their conference. Here [in the United States] as in Canada it is necessary to explain over and over again that—which the Roman Congregation [for the Eastern Church] knows well—the abolition of the Ruthenian diocese in Northern America would mark a great triumph of the Ukrainian nationalist schism, which has a strong tendency to organize itself in Canada, in the United States, as well as in Ukraine, where they call it Ukrainian Autocephalous Church.[10]

In contrast to the American situation, Sheptytsky felt he could influence the political fate of Halychyna. He returned to Europe in December 1922. Before he reported to the Vatican, he went to Paris to try to argue the Ukrainian cause before the diplomats who were deciding on the status of Halychyna as part of the postwar settlement. In Rome, after this unsuccessful diplomatic foray, Sheptytsky was confronted by the March 1923 announcement that Halychyna had been declared part of the Polish Republic. Within two weeks, the Metropolitan nevertheless made another effort at Paris for the Western Ukrainian Republic. Rightly fearing unrest in Lviv, the metropolitan was eager to return to his see but had to wait for clearance from Polish authorities.[11]

During this critical time in another letter to Papadopulos, Sheptytsky expounded his detailed plan for personnel appointments in Europe and the United States.[12] He recognized the importance of the American see and argued that only an experienced elder bishop could deal with the difficult Ukrainian exarchy in the United States. Sheptytsky was convinced that only the fifty-year-old Bishop Dionysius Njaradi of Kryzevich had the experience to exercise the necessary authority effectively.

Njaradi hailed from the Vojvodina, which the Habsburg Empire

10. The letter was not circulated or known, hence the long citation. Sheptytsky to Papadopulos, October 24, 1922, CEC, vol. 117, Prot. 9863/9831; an earlier draft of the letter, with handwritten corrections, in CEC, vol. 117, Prot. 8950/8824 [Rigotti, 147–53].

11. A workable compromise was brokered at the Vatican that permitted Sheptytsky to return to Lviv. AES, Poland (1923–33), pos. 40, fasc. 49. Fullest discussion to date in Hentosh, *Mytropolyt Sheptyts'ky, 1923–1939*, 35–50.

12. Sheptytsky to Papadopulos, October 24, 1922, a typed, edited, eight-page draft of the letter, signed by Sheptytsky, CEC, vol. 117, Prot. 9863/9831 and 727/32 [Rigotti, 152–59].

had acquired in one of the wars with the Ottomans in the second half of the eighteenth century. This heterogeneous area was a theater for Catholic and Orthodox enmity. (The Muslim issue is extraneous to our story.) The Habsburgs had encouraged Ukrainians to emigrate from the Transcarpathian region to Vojvodina, hoping in this way to weaken the independence-minded Catholic Croats. A movement for union of the Orthodox with the Catholic Church was most active here. Njaradi, a professor at the Zagreb Greek-Catholic seminary, became bishop for Eastern-rite Catholics in the Vojvodian area in 1915. He was consecrated in Rome by Chaldean, Bulgarian, and Syrian bishops, which underscored the ecumenism of the Ukrainian/Ruthenian prelate. Njaradi had been very been helpful to Vatican officials during the confusing postwar period when the multi-national states of Yugoslavia, Czechoslovakia, and the diminished Hungary were created.

By his own admission, Njaradi was favorably received in Rome and had a reputation for being a well-versed pro-Vatican moderate.[13] The Vatican valued his ability to function within the changing political framework. For Sheptytsky, however, Njaradi was an ideal candidate for America—experienced, diplomatic, well connected, industrious, and honest. He could work with both camps—Ukrainian and Ruthenian. Forcefully, the metropolitan restated his view that "Njaradi is the best candidate, the only one who because of his virtues, energy, and gravitas would be gladly accepted by all priests, the only one who would be capable of resurrecting and rejuvenating the eparchy. His only flaw—lack of English language—could

13. Dionysius Njaradi was born on October 10, 1874, in the town of which he was appointed bishop—Rusky Kerestur, Baczka, then under Austro-Hungarian rule. It became Yugoslavia, and now is in Serbia. The town still has the Ruthenian cathedral, but is now the village Ruski Krstur. Ukrainians refer to it as Kryzhovic, Ruthenians as Ruski Krstur. Its Latin variant is Crisiensis. As was mentioned above, Njaradi was consecrated bishop in 1915 in Rome by Syrian, Bulgarian, and Chaldean bishops. There was no Ukrainian Catholic bishop available in Rome at the time. During the disintegration of the Austro-Hungarian Empire, he served as the apostolic delegate to Priashiv, Czechoslovakia, and also continued in his home diocese. *Entsyklopediia Podkarpatskoj Rusy*, ed. Ivan Pop (Uzhorod: Izdadelstvo V. Padiaka, 2001); and the English edition *Encyclopedia of Ruthenian History and Culture*, ed. Paul Robert Magocsi and Ivan Pop (Toronto: University of Toronto Press, 2005); also Petro Stercho, *Karpato-Ukraiins'ka Derzhava* (Toronto: Shevchenko Scientific Society, 1965), 85; and Augustin Stefan, *For Justice and Freedom*, book one (Toronto: Toronto Free Press, 1973), 286–88. Njaradi died on April 14, 1940; some maintain he may have been poisoned.

be readily mitigated by his having good advisors."[14] Sheptytsky was so certain that Njaradi would be appointed to the United States that he spent a large part of his letter addressing the concerns of the Ukrainian Catholic Church in Eastern Europe, which now had to adjust to changing political configurations. He thought ahead: "[Njaradi's] nomination could become effective only at the moment that a replacement for the position in Kryzevich is finalized, in case the Serbian government not approve the choice. The same can be said about the Priashiv eparchy in which Njaradi is the apostolic administrator. The bishops for both areas should be announced the very same day that Mons. Njaradi's appointment to the United States is made public."[15]

Unlike most Ukrainians who looked to the immigrants to America mainly for financial support, Sheptytsky recognized the importance of the United States for Ukrainians.

I well realize that Rev. Njaradi is needed both in Kryzevich and in Mukachiv, but even if he were able to continue his previous administration of both sees—which he himself considers impossible—I think his work in these eparchies will be of lesser import than the work in the Ruthenian Eparchy in the United States because there are more Ukrainians in the United States [than in Kryzhovic and Mukachiv]—500,000 souls in one, as compared to the 150,000 and 40,000 in the other two. [Also] the Ruthenian émigrés exercise a great negative influence on all Ukrainian eparchies in Europe.[16]

With these suggestions Sheptytsky considered the matter of a bishop in the United States to be settled. It never occurred to him that Njaradi might not accept the American post.

Sheptytsky realized how difficult it would be to be a Ukrainian Catholic bishop in America.[17] But he also judged the church in America to be of

14. Metropolitan Sheptytsky to Isaiah Papadopulos, Rome, March 1, 1923, CEC, vol. 117, Prot. 9863/9831 and 727/32) [Rigotti, 152–59].

15. Ibid.

16. Ibid.

17. Earlier, Sheptytsky had offered almost *pro forma* possible suggestions for the position of the Ukrainian-American bishop noting the problems with each: Rev. Joseph Chaplynsky had reconsidered becoming a monk and instead became a secular priest, which was considered to be a mark of immature judgment. Joseph Zhuk, with an impressive career that included service in Lviv and Vienna, had even moved in May 1922 to the United States. But Zhuk's open ambition and nonpriestly behavior alienated his supporters, and made

greater potential significance than the restructuring of the southwestern parts of the Ukrainian Catholic Church. Sheptytsky knew that although Njaradi would not leave his eparchy gladly, "he would be ready to accept the cross of the American bishopric if directed by the Holy Father—and it certainly would be a cross for him." To sweeten the bitter pill, Sheptytsky argued that Njaradi should immediately be made a titular archbishop to bolster his authority in the United States. He then examined the changes that would have to be made in Europe if Njaradi left for America. The metropolitan ended his lengthy missive by repeating that Njaradi was "the only candidate who could be capable of administering this eparchy and dragging [the Ukrainian Catholic Church in the USA] out of its moral misery."[18] Sheptytsky then highly recommended that Basil Takach replace Njaradi in Europe. Sheptytsky specifically warned that under no circumstances should Poniatyshyn, the administrator of the exarchy, be appointed bishop, although Njaradi, as archbishop, should make certain that both administrators, Poniatyshyn and Martiak, received some formal titles to offset their disappointment that neither had been appointed bishop.[19]

Sheptytsky found himself in an unenviable position. He had pushed hard for a Ukrainian bishop for the United States, and now could not recommend any of the priests he had sent there. Unlike many in his entourage, the aging metropolitan sensed the growing importance of the United States, although he never really liked the brash, young country. If the fabled metropolitan ever lost heart, now was that time. He placed his hopes on Njaradi and turned his own attention back to European affairs.

---

him unsuitable for the bishop's crozier. Almost in desperation, Sheptytsky also suggested that any one of the prominent Basilians could fill the American vacancy. Among the possible successors to the Pioneer Bishop were Bishop Hryhory Khomyshyn, the Basilian Abbot Platonid Filas, as well as another Basilian, Josaphat Kotsylovsky, not yet bishop of Peremyshl when first suggested. The Ruthenians protested against a number of specific names, imputing simony and nepotism to none other than the two administrators, Martiak and Poniatyshyn. None of these suggestions remained in the hopper when the final decision was made. CEC, vol. 117, Prot. 9863/9831 [Rigotti, 160–64].

18. Ibid.

19. Poniatyshyn's request for permission to attend the Paris Peace Conference to represent "the political interests of Ukrainian-Halychanyns" perturbed the apostolic legate in Washington and therefore was rejected by the Vatican. Giovanni Bonzano to Cardinal Nicolò Marini, secretary of the Congregation for the Eastern Church, December 5, 1918, AES, America, pos. 40, fasc. 50.

The final decision on the American nominations coincided chronologically with the difficulties Sheptytsky faced in trying to return to his see in Lviv.[20]

The Allied decision on March 15, 1923, acknowledged Polish control of Halychyna. That decision sealed the final failure of Ukrainian diplomacy to gain independence. Pius XI upheld the decision with the stipulation that the Polish Commonwealth honor the rights of its minorities, including those of the Ukrainian Catholic Church.

Poland was pressured to permit Sheptytsky to return to Lviv. After many complications, he arrived at Lviv at the beginning of October 1923. The critical political, social, and humanitarian crisis in Halychyna immediately required his whole attention.[21] The Vatican, faced with multiple problems connected with post-World War I diplomatic shifts, including the replacement in January 1923 of the apostolic legate to Washington, Giovanni Bonzano, by Cardinal Pietro Fumasoni-Biondi, was ready once again to postpone the decision on the appointment of a Ukrainian bishop for the United States.

The Ukrainian-American clergy could not let the matter slide. The popularity of the new Ukrainian Orthodox bishop among Ukrainian Catholics increased the likelihood that they would turn to Orthodoxy. Fumasoni-Biondi sent the Vatican a lengthy letter in Latin drafted by the administrator Poniatyshyn, all six of his consulter priests, and the chancellor (a Ruthenian, Valentyn Balog). They spelled out the danger to Rome: the failure to nominate a Catholic Ukrainian bishop when the Autocephalous Orthodox Ukrainian Church has its own bishop in the United States would lead to mass defections of Catholics into Orthodoxy.[22] By the end of 1923, an

20. As seen in the previous chapter, Polish authorities used their interpretation of Bohachevsky's activities in Peremyshl as proof that the Ukrainian Catholic Church headed by Sheptytsky actively undermined the Polish government. AES, Poland (1923–33), pos. 40, fasc. 49. See also CEC, Prot. 5015/5008 and 12559/12427 on the diplomatic preparations for Sheptytsky's trip to the US [Rigotti, 305–8].

21. Sheptytsky to Papadopulos, January 22, 1924, CEC, vol. 117, Prot. 12559/12427 [Rigotti, 308].

22. AES, America (1923–25), pos. 188–91, fasc. 35, pp. 23–29.

additional series of printed petitions initiated by the Providence Fraternal Association of Ukrainian Catholics in America arrived at the Washington office of the Vatican legation. The Minneapolis branch of the association hit the papacy's most vulnerable spot: "With their intensive propaganda of nationalistic ideals they [the Orthodox Russians and Ukrainians] announce the appointment of a Ukrainian Orthodox bishop; they assail the Holy See for apparently not paying adequate attention to the affairs of the Ukrainian Catholic Church of America. They exploit the absence of a Ukrainian bishop appointed by Rome for their own purposes."[23]

Fumasoni-Biondi made the case for the appointment of a naturalized American citizen. He argued that the new bishop should know English, be well versed in American property law so as not to be dependent upon the local priests, and above all, be able to withstand growing American nationalism, distrust of immigrants from Latin and Eastern European countries, and the escalating popularity of the Ku Klux Klan. He pointed out that the "Catholic Church [in the United States] is accused of encouraging foreign immigration to America and passivity [regarding] Americanization."[24] Hence, he feared that a non-American Ukrainian Catholic bishop would be at a double disadvantage. Fumasoni-Biondi downplayed the severity of disagreements between the Ruthenians and the Halychanyns, most likely reflecting the views of the leaders among the Ukrainian clergy. Unaware of earlier discussions, Fumasoni-Biondi proposed the candidacies of Stefan Vashchyshyn, Joseph Chaplynsky, or Poniatyshyn. None of them met the standards of the congregation.[25]

The first year of Pope Pius XI's tenure was interspersed with Ukrainian issues. The Vatican offered assistance, both material and political, to Ukrainians. With the defeat of all Ukrainian armies in 1921, Ukrainians had no international presence. Moreover, Sheptytsky could not get a visa to go back to Lviv. It took over six months of intricate negotiations and a number of failed attempts, for the by now very ill Sheptytsky to reach Lviv. This time he stopped at Peremyshl.

23. CEC, vol. 117, Prot. 12119/12025, [Rigotti, 229–38].

24. AES, America (1923–25), pos. 188–91, fasc. 35, p. 21.

25. Ibid., p. 21 verte; see also CEC, vol. 117, Prot. 12119/12331, January 18, 1924 [Rigotti, 239–42].

The Congregation for the Eastern Church discussed the appointment of a bishop for Ukrainian Catholics in the United States at three of its plenary meetings between 1922 and 1923. They held their last meetings on this appointment in early February 1924. The cardinals and other members of the Congregation for the Eastern Church studied the older reports made to the Congregation for the Propagation of the Faith prepared by Cardinal Diomede Falconio and Giovanni Bonzano, apostolic delegates in America in 1911 and 1912, respectively, and all the subsequent material. They weighed the interests of Hungary and rejected the criticisms of the late Ukrainian Bishop Ortynsky. All agreed on the need for a bishop for the Byzantine Church in the United States, and continued to discuss specific names. Among the top contenders now were Canon Mykola Rusnak, the vicar in Priashiv; and two Mukachiv canons, Yuri Szabo and Petro Hebey. Sheptytsky's earlier suggestions were again considered, but since they had not been strong ones, they were not followed through. Sheptytsky had once suggested that it would be wise to choose a priest who already knew the American scene and recommended Volodymyr Petrivsky, who had served as Ortynsky's secretary, or Joseph Chaplynsky. Again the recommendations were not strong enough to offset the objections.[26]

Other possible solutions were considered, none too persuasively. A few American Roman Catholic bishops were willing to serve as bishops for the Eastern-rite clerics. Other Roman Catholic bishops offered to finance the Ukrainian Church in the United States should the Ukrainian clergy be brought under their jurisdiction because "in their essence the [Ukrainian] faithful are deeply Catholic."[27] But the vast majority of Ukrainian Catholics not only opposed any Roman Catholic jurisdiction over the Ukrainian Church but also saw any such attempt as a direct attack on its integrity.

Cardinal Pietro Fumasoni-Biondi, the apostolic delegate in Washington at the time of the most heated discussions of the Ukrainian-Catholic issue, argued forcefully against any administrative fusion of the Latin and

26. AES, America, pos. 188–91, fasc. 35, pp. 1–22. My thanks to Dr. Andrew Sorokowski for preparing the translations.

27. Fumasoni-Biondi to Pope Pius XI, March 3, 1924, AES, Austria, vol. 224, pos. 188–91, fasc. 35, pp. 20–21.

Byzantine rites. American Roman Catholic bishops already complained that the Vatican had not issued specific directives on how to deal with the Ukrainian priests working in the bishops' dioceses. American bishops knew little about the specifics of the Eastern rite, and their own faithful were simply scandalized by the Ukrainians with their married clergy and their faithful, ending parish disagreements in street fights.

The cardinals in the Congregation for the Eastern Church reread Sheptytsky's letters, but only his suggestion of Njaradi was sufficiently persuasive. The cardinals returned to the earlier deliberations. The late Pope Benedict XV had thought of nominating Josaphat Kotsylovsky, but Kotsylovsky had been chosen as bishop of Peremyshl. Pope Pius XI felt it would be unwise to move the bishop now. The cardinals considered one of the Belgian Redemptorists who had worked in North America, but the Ukrainian Americans regarded these priests as foreigners despite their having become Eastern-rite Catholics. Rev. Schryivers was suggested as a temporary papal visitator.[28] However, in the end Njaradi once more emerged as the only viable candidate.

Njaradi clearly did not want the post. When offered the American nomination, he said he would of course go if the pope ordered him, but he would rather work with his own scattered flock.[29] The Vatican decided that the political rearrangement of Eastern Europe and the Balkans was of greater import than the internal tensions within the Ukrainian immigrant community in America. The pope and the cardinals agreed that Njaradi was indispensable at his present post formally in Kryzevich, which also included territories in Hungary and Czechoslovakia. During the final deliberations on the nomination of a bishop for America, Njaradi went from candidate to a very active adviser.

Pope Pius XI was known to have lobbied for an independent Poland. Now, by persecuting Catholic Ukrainians, this Catholic state made it im-

28. AES, America, pos. 188–94, fasc. 35, pp. 4–19.

29. Njaradi to Cardinal Giovanni Tacci, chair of the Congregation for the Eastern Church, April 1, 1924, CEC, vol. 117, Prot. 12941/1291 [Rigotti, 262–64]. An additional factor in the Vatican decision was that the Hungarian government, as well as the Union of Ruthenian Greek Catholic Fraternal Societies, mistrusted Njaradi "because it is rumored that he is a propagator of Galician Ukrainianism." M. Juhasz, president of the Ruthenian fraternal society to Antonii Papp, the bishop of Mukachiv, AES, Poland, pos. 88–91, fasc. 355.

possible for the Holy See to sign a concordat normalizing relations with Poland. The pope was also faced with the intransigence of the Polish administration, which had refused to confirm the appointment in May 1923 of Constantine Bohachevsky as vicar of Peremyshl.[30] A special papal emissary to the area had documented Polish mistreatment of national minorities, including the arrests of Ukrainian Catholic priests. This was an embarrassment for the pope. As deliberations were held on the appointment of the American bishop, the tension between the Poles and Ukrainians in Halychyna, especially in Peremyshl, percolated beyond the Congregation for the Eastern Church. It looked as if Pius XI would be a weak pope who could not even sign a concordat with the new state he promoted, Poland.

In one fell swoop, Bishop Njaradi solved both problems for the pope—the fate of the Ukrainian cleric whom the Poles refused to accept and the nomination of a bishop for Ukrainians in the United States. Picking up on the difficulties raised by Poniatyshyn and Martiak, Njaradi suggested that the pope appoint not one, but two Ukrainian bishops for the United States.[31] One would minister to the people who came from the Carpathian regions and called themselves Ruthenians, the other would serve the Ruthenian Ukrainians from Halychyna. Njaradi recommended both Basil Takach, the rector of the seminary in Mukachiv, now in Czechoslovakia, and Constantine Bohachevsky, the nominee for vicar in Peremyshl, Poland, to fill these posts.[32]

Takach had already been studied as a possible candidate for the American-Ukrainian bishop, but Bohachevsky was an unknown in the Vatican. Bohachevsky's arrest by the Polish authorities in 1919 had caused concern in Rome but that was assuaged by assurances from the legate in Warsaw that Bohachevsky was neither a political radical nor pro-Orthodox. Njaradi pointed out that that Polish administrative opposition to Bohachevsky's appointment as vicar of Peremyshl was also partly

---

30. Carlo Chiarlo met with Bohachevsky personally in July 1923 to assess the nature of Bohachevsky's difficulties with Polish law enforcement and found nothing objectionable in Bohachevsky's activities. AES, Poland, vol. 224, p. 320; also AES, America, pos. 188–191, fasc. 35, p. 1.

31. AES, America, pos. 188–91, fasc. 35, point 5, p. 3.

32. Ibid., also point 14, p. 19.

fanned by the Ukrainian Peremyshl canons who opposed whatever Bishop Kotsylovsky did. The high Vatican clerics at these meetings sympathized with the bishop, not with the canons.[33] Kotsylovsky was contacted again, this time to provide basic information on Bohachevsky—proof of baptism, vitals on education and ordination, and the like. Bishop Kotsylovsky even handwrote a *curriculum vitae* for the priest whom he had lured away from Metropolitan Sheptytsky's Lviv and who was to be his vicar.

The Roman cardinals wrestled with the possibility of alienating American Roman Catholic clergy by catering to the needs of the Ukrainian Catholic immigrants. Cardinal Raffaele Scapinelli who was in contact with the Latin Catholic Americans opposed the appointment of two bishops on practical grounds:

An argument against the appointment of two bishops lies in the fact that American [Latin] Catholic bishops have a very hard time accepting one Ruthenian bishop, and most likely will not accept the appointment of two well. We should listen to their [American bishops'] views, before making this decision. There is a further impediment—Ruthenian churches . . . are often mixed, so the delineation of the territories of the two bishops will be most difficult.[34]

The cardinals weighed the options: continued scandals in the Ukrainian Church due to the in-fighting between the Halychanyns and the Ruthenians, going against the wishes of the American Roman Catholic bishops, and letting the pope fend for himself in the tricky Ukrainian-Polish confrontation. After more discussion of the negative repercussions that the tensions between Ukrainian and Ruthenian Catholics had upon the Latin-rite Catholics in the United States, the cardinals reluctantly agreed to recommend the appointment of two Byzantine rite bishops in the United States. They expected the Roman Catholic bishops to comply with the decision.

The pope demanded a recommendation; the cardinals' tempers were frayed, they needed to explain the failure to provide a recommendation. In the last background note to the pope, the cardinals laid the long delay in the appointment of the bishop for Ukrainian Catholics in the United States squarely on the shoulders of the Ukrainian priests and the Hungarian government: "The true reason for the eight-year delay in providing a successor

33. Ibid., p. 35.
34. Ibid., pp. 8 and 14.

to Msgr. Ortynsky has been the difficulty in finding an ideal person: the Ruthenians from Hungary absolutely desire one of their nationality. The Hungarian government exerted pressure, but the congregation did not accept their candidate."[35] Cardinal Raffaele Scapinelli tried to put a more positive slant and reported: "This appears an especially propitious time to appoint a bishop because none of the governments are lobbying their own candidate. The question remains: should we appoint one or two bishops for America. But there is a new factor now: the arrival of the Orthodox Ukrainian bishop has fanned national-patriotic sentiments."[36]

After Njaradi's candidacy for the American post was withdrawn, his suggestion of naming two bishops for Ukrainian Catholics in the United States carried the day.[37] The final meeting of the Congregation for the Eastern Church on the appointment of the Ukrainian bishops to the United States, held on February 14, 1924, was long, but the Congregation for the Eastern Church at its plenary reached a decision.[38] Two names were forwarded to the pope: Basil Takach, the rector of the seminary at Mukachiv, and Constantine Bohachevsky, the vicar-elect of the Peremyshl diocese.

The decision on the two nominations was presented to Pope Pius XI that very day in a formal audience. The follow-up audience was somewhat confusing. The elderly assessor of the Congregation for the Eastern Church, Isaiah Papadopulos, had the mistaken impression that the decision was for one bishop to be the primary and wanted to know which of the two had been chosen.[39]

The solution was understood to be a temporary one, but given the Catholic regulations on the episcopate it could not be so documented. Later correspondence of individual Vatican officials clearly suggests that

35. Ibid., p. 1.
36. Ibid., p. 13.
37. CEC, vol. 117, Prot. 10323 [Rigotti, 834–37].
38. The following are mentioned as having participated in the decision: secretary of the Congregation at the time Cardinal Tacci; Cardinals Scapinelli, Willem Van Rossum, Franz Fruhwirth, Bonzano, Francis Aidan Gasquet, Camillo Laurenti, and Franz Ehrle were the other participants. Papadopulos for some reason is not listed in the copy of the documents in CEC, but is included in the documentation in AES, America (1923–25), pos. 188–91, fasc. 35, pp. 1–29.
39. AES, America (1923–25), pos. 188–91, fasc. 35, p. 19.

the cardinals expected the Ukrainians to patch up their differences and eventually fuse the two dioceses. Njaradi's solution had the added incentive of helping the pope out of a tight situation. Njaradi suggested two bishops, both of them in exarchates, which were not as permanent as dioceses, thus leaving open the possibility of reuniting the Ukrainian Catholic branches at some later date.[40]

BOHACHEVSKY IN ROME

The decision of February 14, 1924, to appoint two bishops was not made public immediately.[41] In the case of Bohachevsky, it remained a closely guarded secret largely to spirit the cleric secretly out of Poland before the Polish nationalists could sabotage the appointment. Bohachevsky travelled incognito with different Vatican colleagues and ended his clandestine journey to Rome around April 2 or 3, 1924, with no major incidents. The arrival of yet another priest in Rome was too minor a matter to merit any interest. The ostensible reason for Bohachevsky's sudden trip to Rome was for him to iron out the difficulties that Kotsylovsky, his bishop, had with his canons. Few in Rome considered tension between the bishop of Peremyshl and his advisers in any way exceptional enough to merit any interest.

Bohachevsky easily escaped public notice in Rome. He spent much of his time closeted at the Basilian monastery at the Piazza Maria dei Monti studying English. "He is in Rome, in the Ruthenian College—and no one knows why he came here, and he can mask his presence by pretending to have come to inform about the problems between the Peremyshl bishop and the cathedral chapter," wrote one surprised record keeper of the Congregation for the Eastern Church.[42] True to his later behavior, Bo-

40. Njaradi's proposal was discussed both in private and at a plenary session of the Congregation for the Eastern Church in December 1923, and January 1924, AES, America (1923–25), pos. 188–91, fasc. 35, pp. 18–19.

41. The pope, on May 3, 1924, asked Fumasoni-Biondi that the nomination of the Ruthenian bishops not be made public for a month or so, until a bishop of Polish nationality be named for the United States, AES, America (1923–25), pos. 188–91, fasc. 35, p. 36.

42. Enrico Benedetti, the recording secretary of the Eastern Congregation, to Rev. Bonne in New York, June 30, 1924, AES, America, pos. 188–91, fasc. 35, p. 33. Bohachevsky's presence at the Basilian residence is attested by his laconic signature in the guest book of the Basilian Order in Rome.

hachevsky did not use the time at the Vatican to build alliances, or to at least study firsthand the workings of the Holy See. Instead, ensconced within walking distance of the Coliseum, he diligently drilled English vocabulary. In a few years, the new bishop would have reason enough to remember the martyrs who had made the Coliseum holy.

The appointment of a Ukrainian bishop had been talked about for years, yet no one predicted the appointment of two bishops. By mid-April Reverend Xavier Bonne in New York already knew of Takach's appointment, as did both the Prague press and the Czechoslovak government.[43] Once the news about Takach leaked out, there was no need for anyone to speculate about a second appointment.

Only on May 26, 1924, did Pietro Fumasoni-Biondi, the apostolic delegate in Washington, inform Rev. Petro Poniatyshyn, the administrator of the Ukrainian Church in the United States, of the dual appointments. Bohachevsky was to be the bishop in Philadelphia, and Takach in a city to be determined. No specific dates of arrival were available for either bishop.[44]

Both nominees were consecrated as bishop at a joint ceremony on June 15, 1924, at the church of St. Athanasius in Rome. Bishops Kotsylovsky of Peremyshl, Njaradi of Kryzevich, and Ivan Melle, the archbishop of the Greek Catholic Church in Rome, officiated. It is a measure of the new bishop that there is no list of attendees, or a written report on the ceremony. For that matter, Bohachevsky did not seem to have brought up the event in later conversations.[45] I suspect that in the Holy City with its high concentration of churchmen this ceremony, so regal in other places, seemed routine. Cardinal Giovanni Tacci, the secretary of the Congregation for the Eastern Church, informed Cardinals O'Donnell of Boston and Hayes of New York of the appointments.[46] Bohachevsky, we recall, sent his metropolitan a clipping of the publication of his nomination in *L'Osservatore Romano*. Sheptytsky, in his personal letter of congratulations, predicted that the new bishop would have great difficulties, and then asked him matter-of-factly to deliver some documents to his archivist in Rome.[47]

43. Letter to Benedetti, April 28, 1924, AES, America, pos. 188–91, fasc. 35, p. 37.
44. Fumasoni-Biondi to Poniatyshyn, May 26, 1924, copy, UMAS.
45. Danylo Bohachevsky, *Vladyka Konstantyn Bohachevsky*, 24.
46. CEC, vol. 117, Prot. 13769/13755 [Rigotti, 257–60].
47. Sheptytsky to Bohachevsky, May 28, 1924, UMAS.

There is a moving, albeit laconic postscript on Bohachevsky's appointment. The note taker in the Eastern Congregation commented, most likely to Father Xavier Bonne, that:

During the last papal audience of the assessor for the Eastern Congregation [Isaiah Papadopulos], the Holy Father let it be known that he wanted certain sums of money to be given to the two Ruthenian bishops to America. Now, after careful research it came to light that Takach has ample family funds. The situation of the other one is totally different. Not only does he not have any family resources, he does not have any savings, no resources from his diocese, since for a year and half he has not been receiving the salary from the government that as the vicar general and canon of the cathedral chapter should be his. He did not have the funds necessary to order a ring and a cross, so the Holy Father gave him those. For more than three months he has been living in Rome, in the Ruthenian College—and all he spent was barely $200. I think it is necessary to give him 10,000 lira to buy the necessities that are suitable for a bishop before his journey.[48]

Bohachevsky received the money in time to make the purchases needed to arrive in New York suitably dressed. He would encounter ample crosses during his life in America, in addition to the one he received from the pope.

Bishop Kotsylovsky struggled mightily with his conscience before he let "his best priest" be considered for bishop for the United States.[49] Kotsylovsky, for all his saintly qualities, was a severe taskmaster with a difficult personality. His colorful past and a seemingly terminal illness made him difficult to work with. Kotsylovsky appreciated that Bohachevsky found ways to minimize the tension.

On the other hand, by freeing the pontiff's hand in the awkward Polish situation, Kotsylovsky now had a rare chance to be of direct service to the pope. Contact between the bishop of Peremyshl and Metropolitan Sheptytsky was very spotty in the immediate post–World War I period, and their relationship eventually became quite strained. I found no communication between Sheptytsky and Kotsylovsky about Bohachevsky's appointment. Kotsylovsky, after only brief reflection, recommended Bohachevsky to the Holy See in the strongest possible terms. He went so far

48. Enrico Benedetti (mostly likely to Father Xavier Bonne), April 1, 1924, AES, America, pos. 188–91, fasc. 35, p. 37.
49. Kotsylovsky to Lauri, September 10, 1923, ASV, Warsaw, 224:332 verte.

as to handwrite Bohachevsky's curriculum vitae for his vicar in Italian the sooner to introduce him to the Vatican clerics. When the die was cast and Bohachevsky crossed the Polish border into Czechoslovakia, Kotsylovsky wrote to the papal nuncio in Warsaw: "May God be with him and with me, and may God repay me for the loss of such a priest."[50]

Bohachevsky possessed all the qualities that the papacy wanted in a Catholic bishop: he was practical and pious, loyal to the Vatican but capable of independent action, and it seemed his proven Ukrainian patriotism would make him very acceptable to his people. His public career, chaplaincy on the front lines, and the persecution he suffered at the hands of the Polish regime left no doubt about his Ukrainian patriotism. It was his behavior in the face of adversity, the quiet fortitude with which he met arrest and discrimination, the responsible common sense he demonstrated by preventing public demonstrations on his behalf that would have served as a pretext for armed government intervention—these qualities tipped the scales in Bohachevsky's favor. Bohachevsky was praised for his piety, his administrative skill in implementing practical projects for his parishioners, and his loyalty to Rome. He had worked with the parish and the bishop to establish a daycare facility and school in the working-class district of Peremyshl. At the same time, he stood up effectively to radical factions on the right and the left.

Perhaps an important, immediate reason for his appointment was that Pius XI remembered the gaunt, erect, brown-eyed transfer prisoner in Warsaw whom he had characterized as "an apostolic man."[51] The appointment of Bohachevsky gave the pope a gracious way out of an awkward situation with the Polish government, while at the same time it expanded the structure of the Ukrainian Church.

Sheptytsky wrote a quick note to Bohachevsky on May 28, 1924, when L'Osservatore Romano ran the notice of the episcopal appointment. The metropolitan asked Bishop Kotsylovsky to deliver this letter personally, so Bo-

---

50. Kotsylovsky to Lauri, April 1, 1924, ASV, Warsaw, 244:448. There was no mention of any discussion about the Bohachevsky appointment, although in an earlier letter Kotsylovsky specifically pointed out that Sheptytsky also considered Bohachevsky the best priest of his diocese, Kotsylovsky to Lauri, September 10, 1923, ibid., p. 334.

51. Ratti to General Haller protesting arrests of Ukrainian civilians and clergy, July 20, 1919, ASV, Poland, 194:1004.

hachevsky could have his blessing before the actual ordination. "God will allow Your Excellency to suffer greatly for God's cause [spravy], but Your Excellency will have the satisfaction that your work and sacrifice will save this whole poor people."[52] Then Sheptytsky requested that Bohachevsky pass on some papers to be filed in the Sheptytsky archive in Rome, without bothering the Holy See about the information in it, although Bohachevsky should familiarize himself with it. The letter ends "with expressions of the highest regard and fraternal love in Jesus Christ, Andrey, M[etropolitan]."

The formalities of the appointment were minutely carried out. In Warsaw, Kotsylovsky was duly sworn by the legate, Archbishop Lorenzo Lauri in the presence of the auditor Carlo Chiarlo. Bishop Kotsylovsky submitted written answers to the twenty-six standard questions in the *Processus Inquisitionis super qualitatibus promovendi ad episcopalem dignitatem*. Rev. Basil Lakota, who would later, as Kotsylovsky, die a bishop-martyr, served as the second recommender. His answers, also in Latin, were handwritten.[53]

Kotsylovsky noted that Bohachevsky's name was misspelled in an earlier document, neither the first nor the last of such occurrences until Bohachevsky, upon arrival to the United States, decided upon a transcription of his family name. Kotsylovsky singled out Bohachevsky's mother for special praise for "heroically submitting to Divine Providence in all calamities that befell her."[54] Two of Bohachevsky's brothers had died in the war, and Bohachevsky supported education of the youngest two. The family was well-known in the community, produced Catholic priests, including the candidate's father as well several uncles, one of whom had also served as a deputy to the Habsburg Provincial Diet. Kotsylovsky noted Bohachevsky's scholarship, but also stressed how productive his social and educational work was despite the political and financial difficulties under which he labored."[55] Lakota, the second formal witness, had known Bohachevsky since 1903 when they both roomed in the seminary dormitory in Lviv. Since 1918, the two men worked hand in hand in Peremyshl. Lakota knew more intimate details of Bohachevsky's life than Kotsylovsky. Where the

52. Sheptytsky to Bohachevsky, May 28, 1924, unpublished, UMAS.

53. Both documents in AES, Poland, vol. 108, pp. 370–446.

54. Answer to point 4. *Processus inquisitionis super qualitatibus Rev.-mi D.D. Constantini Bohacevskyj*, AVS, Nuntiatura Apostolica Poloniae, vol. 108.

55. Ibid., answer to point 14.

bishop noted two brothers living with the candidate, Lakota more correctly referred to three. Lakota also praised Bohachevsky's active social life.

The testimony was duly compiled, stamped in red wax, sealed, and filed away. There was no opposition to Bohachevsky's appointment. The young man had all reason to think that his education, experience, and especially his selfless dedication and zest for work would enable him to live up to the high expectations of his recommenders. He accepted the appointment humbly, but with the full realization that he had been made bishop by none other than the successor of Peter. He always wore the cross and ring the pope had given him, although he never disclosed the donor publicly.[56]

The formal act of appointment of Bohachevsky and Takach, dated May 8, 1924, maintained parity between them. The dual appointment was justified purely by the disagreements between the Ukrainians and the Ruthenians. Once the cardinals made their decision, they wanted the two men to leave for America as quickly as possible. The cardinals specifically told the nominees that rules could be bent to expedite their departure:

Taking into consideration everything that pertains to your convenience, we permit you to select a consecrating bishop of your rite, one who is in communion with the Holy Apostolic See. . . . In case two other invited Catholic bishops, united with Rome, cannot be had, you should be assisted by two priests, likewise of your rite who are constituted in some high office or ecclesiastical dignity, we grant a full and absolute faculty to the consecrating bishop selected by you to give you the afore mentioned consecration.[57]

Nevertheless, towards its end, the document again made certain that the whole procedure be a Catholic one. The official nominating text repeated the injunction "unless you first make the profession of the faith and depose the oath according to the exemplars given by the Apostolic See you cannot receive the said consecration."[58]

The cardinals also established that the bishop for the Halychanyns

---

56. Family information supported by a personal conversation with Bishop Basil Losten held at his office at St. Basil Seminary, Stamford, Conn., October 30, 2012.

57. I quote from the English translation of the official document found in UMAS, Chancery Archive. The document, dated "May 8, in the third year of our Pontificate," is signed by Cardinal Octavius Cagiano, the chancellor; Francis Bersani, administrator of the apostolic chancery; Julius Campori, the protonotarius; Raphael Visiti, protonotarius; P. Mansia, scriptor apostolicus; and Alfredus Liberati, promotor.

58. Ibid.

FIGURE 3. CONSECRATION OF BISHOPS BOHACHEVSKY AND TAKACH

reside in Philadelphia, while the other bishop make his residence else-where. The diocese was to be divided by parishes—a simple majority vote of the parishioners ought to decide the choice of exarchy. Obviously, none of these decisions could be made preemptively from Rome. The division of the diocese would be done only after the two bishops arrived on American soil.[59] In a separate letter to Bohachevsky, the assessor of the Congrega-tion for the Eastern Church reinforced that as bishop Bohachevsky was invested with full powers. For good measure, Msgr. Papadopulos enjoined the new bishop to confide in the pope on all important matters.

To avoid potential unrest by misunderstanding the status of each of the two new bishops, both bishops agreed to travel to America together to be met jointly in New York by the whole as yet undivided Ukrainian/Rusyn Catholic congregation. The pertinent Vatican and Ukrainian Catholic au-thorities agreed that this would best demonstrate the cooperation of the

59. Ibid.

bishops and offset the criticism that Rome divided the Ukrainian Catholic Church. The Vatican cardinals also maintained that Takach should first ease his successor in Mukachiv into his position and address the ecclesiastical shifts necessitated by the political changes in Eastern Europe before he left for America. After the episcopal consecration, Bishop Takach returned home to Priashiv to prepare for the long journey to America. Thus, despite the provisions for haste and the fears of the rapidly growing crisis in the American church, the departure of the two bishops to the United States was postponed by almost two months.

Bohachevsky, too, would have liked to go back to Peremyshl and maybe pack. In addition to professional issues, Bohachevsky had been caring for his mother and supporting the education of his two younger brothers. With his move to the United States, his mother would not be able to keep the clerical apartment in which she lived. Bohachevsky relied on Bishop Kotsylovsky to bring his mother the news and on a brother who was just beginning a law practice to care for their mother. Constantine did not seem to have contacted his older brother Volodymyr, who had escaped to America from his creditors, leaving his father and Constantine to clear the family name.

Despite the secrecy of his appointment, Bohachevsky did receive some congratulatory letters through the diplomatic post, a mere glimmer from the life that the new bishop had constructed for himself, his mother, and his younger brothers in Peremyshl. The high clerics from Lviv sent their regards, as did the children from the daycare in Peremyshl. The Catholic youth group from Peremyshl sent thanks for his work and prayers for the success of the service that awaited him in America. There were cards from the priests with whom he had studied and served early in his career, and a few letters from his current fellows. One colleague reported on measures to cheer up Bohachevsky's mother, who took the departure of her second son to America quite badly. There seems to have been some talk of her possibly coming to America, but nothing could be considered before Bohachevsky's arrival in the United States.

Bohachevsky stayed on in sweltering Rome, waiting and learning English, worrying that his new diocese was rapidly disintegrating as he struggled with elementary English in the heart of Italy.[60] He did not feel

60. Sergei Dabych to Bohachevsky, August 1, 1924. This letter, as the subsequent ones, were found unfiled in UMAS.

comfortable in Rome where he was utterly dependent on others. He did not consider it seemly to follow up on his acquaintance with the pope. For political reasons he could not communicate with the church back home, or with his family. And he did not want to establish contact with the church in the United States before Takach had done the same.

Each day, Bohachevsky expected to hear from Takach, who was handling all the travel arrangements for both because Bohachevsky had neither the documentation nor the money. But more than a month passed before Bohachevsky received a handwritten letter from Mukachiv, dated July 15, 1924, apologizing for the delay. Takach could not speed up all the visits he had to make in order to arrange for the administrative flow of the Catholic Church in Yugoslavia, Hungary, and Czechoslovakia. Meanwhile, he asked Bohachevsky to get him the necessary papal documents, as well as an antimension with the holy relics of a saint and a painting or a photograph of the pope to take to America.

Takach assured "his Dear Brother," as he addressed Bohachevsky, that the proposed new bishop for Mukachiv, Petro Hebey "is a man of our orientation."[61] To underscore the connection of the new Mukachiv bishop with the rest of the Ukrainian Catholic Church, Takach accompanied his successor on a formal trip to Lviv, Stanyslaviv, and Peremyshl to meet with the three Ukrainian Catholic bishops. That—and the need to assure Ukrainian Catholic representation at a Christian Unity meeting in Velehrad—justified the postponement of the departure for New York. Takach apologized for not writing "and for postponing our departure, I can only say that I had to make that long journey [because of] very important religio-political reasons." He assured Bohachevsky that passage from Cherbourg, on August 2, was reserved, and that "I will give you all the other necessary information, and if I can, even send you the ticket, [when I will be] in Prague on the twenty-first." Takach promised that Njaradi would also get in touch with Bohachevsky and asked for confirmation of the receipt of his letter, so he would not worry needlessly.[62]

Two other intriguing letters date from this period—one on June 19, the other August 1, 1924—from Archimandrite Sergei Dabych, a Poltava native

61. Takach to Bohachevsky, July 15, 1924, UMAS. Petro Hebey [Gebe, Gebey] (1864–1931) was consecrated bishop of Mukachiv on July 16, 1924.
62. Ibid.

with two Moscow University doctor of philosophy degrees in law and in theology, who as an Orthodox monk converted to Catholicism in 1923. These letters offer proof of Bohachevsky's continued interest in Metropolitan Sheptytsky's big project of re-establishing Christian unity in Russia, Belarus, and Ukraine. Later, in the United States, Bohachevsky would try to integrate other such priests into the Ukrainian Catholic Church.

Dabych lived in Paris but had to leave France because of visa irregularities. He offered Bohachevsky his apartment. From Bruges, Dabych worried why Bohachevsky had not gotten in touch with him and apologized profusely if for any reason he had offended him. It is not clear if Dabych wanted to go to the United States or if he just presumed Bohachevsky would go to Paris to seek other prospective converts to Catholicism.[63]

The only American who contacted Bohachevsky seems to have been a slightly older, fellow high school student from Stryj, Rev. Mykhaylo Kindiy. Kindiy was an assistant pastor in Newark, the New Jersey parish run by Rev. Poniatyshyn, the administrator of the exarchy. The letter, addressed to the "Reverend Mitered priest Bohachevsky," points out that while the "American press" wrote about Bohachevsky's nomination, "to this day there is no official affirmation—the apostolic delegate in Washington knows nothing nor do the newly appointed American cardinals [Patrick J. Hayes and George W. Mundelein]—I am very much interested if this is indeed the case."[64] Kindiy tried to jog Bohachevsky's memory about the golden times they had shared in the high school in Stryj.

More importantly, Kindiy asked for information because "rumors here are rife. Some even maintain that you were already consecrated the week after Easter, and that both of you will be in the US before the end of May." The priest ended with a breezy "sincere brotherly greeting." In the post-scriptum he noted that the administrator was also in the dark "not knowing if you should be congratulated and when to prepare for your arrival. . . . This makes all [of us] uneasy, [you should] write or telephone [us]."[65] Bohachevsky apparently did not answer this letter, careful, as he

63. Dabych died three years later. I have not found any more of his correspondence with Bohachevsky.

64. Rev. Mykhaylo Kindiy to Bohachevsky, UMAS.

65. Kindiy to Bohachevsky, May 2, 1924, UMAS. There are no notations, nor an envelope.

was, not to break ranks with Takach. Thus the Ukrainian-American community had most of the summer to speculate about who was made bishop and why.

On the eve of Bohachevsky's consecration, Bishop Khomyshyn, his former seminary prefect and now bishop of Stanyslaviv, offered him the most specific advice the younger man ever received. Khomyshyn had not been to America, but the incidence of emigration from his see was proportionally higher than from the Lviv metropolitanate, which made Bishop Khomyshyn feel knowledgeable about the United States.

Khomyshyn's letter was dated June 3, the feast of St. Constantine, which was the only personal holiday Bohachevsky acknowledged. Khomyshyn, shocked by stories about the moral decline of the priesthood in America—cohabitation, simony, and intrigues between the Carpathians and the Halychanyns—cheered his new clerical colleague: "But that should not trouble you—where the need is great, so is God's aid."[66] Then Khomyshyn offered Bohachevsky seven pointers:

1. Work closely with Takach, disregarding any rumors manufactured to prevent cooperation.

2. Be very circumspect. Avoid joining any faction for at least three years regardless of how attractive the faction appears—many will try to compromise you as they did Bishop Ortynsky.

3. Attend to the spiritual needs of the priests first, raise their moral level, only then turn to the laity.

4. Try at all costs to reduce the tension between the Halychanyns and the Ruthenians.

5. Organize your own seminary as quickly as you can.

6. Wear Ortynsky's liturgical robes.

7. Keep up contact with the old country.

Khomyshyn ended by asking Bohachevsky to "consider these few thoughts. God give you courage to endure till the end and thus save your soul."[67] Khomyshyn's letter expanded on Metropolitan Sheptytsky's terse warning of the difficulties that the new bishop would face in America.

66. Khomyshyn to Bohachevsky, June 3, 1924, UMAS.
67. Ibid.

Bohachevsky finally left Rome in August for Cherbourg, there to board the ship bound for Amsterdam to take part in the twenty-seventh International Eucharistic Congress. He felt a sense of relief that the wait was at last over; he was on the road to the place that the Roman pontiff had sent him.

CHAPTER 4

Church and Society in
a New Land

Bohachevsky came to the new world of the United States willingly to minister specifically to the Ukrainian Catholics living there. He looked forward to consolidating the church and working with the community. Although the picture of the Ukrainian Catholic Church in the United States that had been presented to him was not a pretty one, the new bishop was optimistic and energetic. He trusted God and loved his neighbor and hoped for the best. He thought the difficulties would be minor, since the major problem that plagued the church, the tension between the Ruthenians and the Ukrainians, had been resolved for the time being. Within the first few months, he even considered that the situation in the church was not as dire as people had warned. He was to be proven very wrong.

To understand why it took Bohachevsky a decade to reach his two immediate goals—to consolidate the church and to work with the community—we need to take a closer look at the formative period of the Ukrainian Catholic Church in the United States: from 1884, when the first Ukrainian Catholic parish was established (and coincidentally the year of Bohachevsky's birth) to 1924, when the Ruthenian Catholic Exarchate was divided into two exarchates and Bohachevsky was appointed as exarch to Ukrainian Catholics from Halychyna in the United States.

Bohachevsky and Takach were told that there were about three hundred Catholic churches of the Byzantine rite in the United States. The number was somewhat inflated, since not all churches were parishes, nor were the congregations stable. The laity had set up many of the parishes, at times not paying much attention to legal or canonical regulations. As soon as a group of Western Ukrainian Catholic immigrants found fairly stable work, they turned their attention to getting a priest for the church they wanted to build. Although the immigrants came from various parts of Ukraine, they all came from a nonindustrialized, agriculturally patriarchal society that had not yet become a fully moneyed economy. With no knowledge of city life, the immigrants were immediately dropped into a dynamic urban environment.

Unlike the slightly earlier Jewish emigration from the same areas, few Ukrainians understood the opportunities a money-based economy offered. What they knew and what justified their hard physical labor was the church. They did not think much about it; they just knew the church was there. Every village had a church, and the church had to have a priest. America was no different. The immigrants would have their churches. This personal attachment to the church was both the strength and the weakness of the Ukrainian Catholic Church as an organization. The personal involvement that built parishes also contributed to their disintegration in times of internal tensions or external demands, such as money needed for the upkeep of the local priest and the faraway chancery.

The immigrants knew little about the structure of the Catholic Church. Few realized that in Europe the state partially supported the Catholic Church financially. While some learned about the legalities of establishing a corporation in the United States, none were aware of church regulations. An individual, or more frequently a group of faithful, would chip in to buy or build a church or a church hall and then would encourage a priest to come. In America the community shouldered the livelihood of the priest and his family. In the absence of a bishop, who had the power of the burse and hopefully some funding and who could therefore establish an equitable remuneration schedule, the priests had to fend for themselves. Ukrainian priests coming to America had to have formal permission from their bishop, but they did not receive any funding. Once in the United States, they were to present themselves to the Roman Catholic bishop of the area in which they ministered.[1] These procedures, set to assure cleri-

1. In the last decades of the nineteenth century, when Ukrainian immigration to the United States began and before the establishment of the Congregation for the Eastern

cal discipline, were often broken for practical, rather than ideological reasons. America was just too big, and Latin Catholic bishops were not always forthcoming toward what seemed to them itinerant clergy. There were a few high-profile cases in which the lack of understanding by the Latin-rite Catholic clergy led Ukrainian Catholics to join the Orthodox Church.[2] Discipline was hard to enforce, and the life of the priest was usually hard. On occasion the Latin clergy helped their fellow priests, but these were few and hardly documented.

Church congregations in the United States were more mobile than in the home country, and parishes were mostly urban, thus lacking the moderating social power of the settled, agricultural community of Eastern Europe. Parishes arose haphazardly as availability of work drew larger congregations. The creation of splinter parishes by dissatisfied factions

---

Church, the Sacred Congregation for the Propagation of the Faith approved each Ukrainian Catholic priest serving in the United States, and notified the respective Latin Catholic bishop. The size of the United States and the mobility of its population undermined the premise of the regulation even if it were universally followed. Despite repetitions of the regulation, some Ukrainian Catholic priests came to America without authorization, and in America most Ukrainian priests had difficulties presenting themselves to Latin bishops. In 1890 the Propagation of the Faith mandated that each Ukrainian Catholic priest going to America have written permission of their local bishop before leaving their home diocese and upon arrival present himself to the Roman Catholic bishop in the United States in the area in which he would work. The provision was reiterated by Pope Leo XIII a number of times, thus proving its ineffectiveness. One reason priests were disinclined to follow the letter of the law was purely logistical. Ukrainian priests serviced different congregations in different states, and the need to go to each ranking area bishop was not only tedious but often impossible. Nor were the busy Roman Catholic bishops overjoyed at the prospect of meeting with Eastern-rite priests. Most of the American clergy had little knowledge of Eastern Catholicism; almost all found the idea of married clergy shocking, and the mandatory meetings of Roman Catholic bishops and Ukrainian Catholic priests at times led to verbal clashes.

2. Gerald P. Fogarty, SJ, *The Vatican and the American Hierarchy from 1870 to 1965* (Collegeville, Minn.: The Liturgical Press, 1982), 64, the numbers vary from 10,000 to as high as 90,000. In a less dramatic case, Bishop Michael J. Hoban of Scranton, Pennsylvania, for instance, excommunicated the Ukrainian Catholic priest, John Ardan of Olyphant, Pa., in 1902, instituting a nasty court case over church property. Ignorance of the Eastern rite led to a personal confrontation between two strong-minded clerics, Bishop John Ireland and the Ruthenian priest, later bishop, Alexis Toth. The former failed to recognize the canonicity of the latter, and the irate Toth led an exodus of about a quarter million Ukrainian Catholic immigrants to the Russian Orthodox Church in the 1890s alone. See also Fogarty's "The American Hierarchy and Oriental Rite Catholics, 1890–1907," *Records of the American Catholic Historical Society* 85, nos. 1–2 (March–June 1974): 17–28.

contributed to the administrative difficulties of the Ukrainian Catholic Church for decades. Indeed, the initiative to create a parish often came from a secular congregation that might be transient. Conversely, when employment in an area waned, so did the parish and the pastor's livelihood. In either case, ownership of church property was not clear, and churches and halls were often heavily mortgaged. Although immigrants asked the upper clergy in Halychyna for priests, they did not ensure the priest's livelihood.

Most Ukrainian Catholic priests came to the United States at the request of their bishop to perform missionary service for their kinspeople in America. But there were priests who came because there was no available parish at home or for other personal reasons. Oleksa Prystay, a forty-five-year-old, married priest decided to go to the United States in 1907 when he read that a boyhood friend of his, (Stefan) Soter Ortynsky, was made bishop for Ukrainian Catholics in the United States. Prystay was having severe political and financial problems in Halychyna, and after consultation with his wife, left her with the children and became a missionary in the United States. Later in retirement Prystay, who was distantly related to Bishop Bohachevsky and very critical of him, wrote a four-volume memoir, after the Great Depression deprived him of his once considerable savings.[3] His highly subjective, firsthand account describes how Ukrainian Catholic priests fared in the United States before 1930. The book was well received in Europe. Another, much shorter account by Rev. Konstantyn Andrukhovych was less widely read. Andrukhovych, whose tenure preceded Bohachevsky's arrival in America, wavered in his loyalty to the Catholic Church. He turned to Orthodoxy in America, but then returned to the Catholic Church when he went back to his native Carpathian Mountains.[4] Both priests gave heart-wrenching accounts of how badly the parishioners

3. Oleksa Prystay, Z Truskavtsia u svit khmaroderiv, was published in four volumes, the first three by Dilo, a daily newspaper in Lviv, in the years 1933–36, and the fourth by the Naukove Tovarystvo im. T. Shevchenka [Shevchenko Scientific Society] in Lviv in 1937. Both publishers represented important Ukrainian institutions—Dilo was the premier Halychyna Ukrainian newspaper and the Shevchenko Scientific Society was the premier, public, academic Ukrainian organization. Prystay dedicated the second volume to Metropolitan Sheptytsky, the other volumes carry no dedication. The volumes were later reprinted by other publishers. I used the original version.

4. Konstantyn Andrukhovych, Z zhytia Rusyniv v Amerytsi. Spomyn z rokiv 1889–1892 (Kolomyia: n.p., 1904). His records are at TsDIA, Lviv, f. 489.

FIGURE 4. PROCESSION

treated the clergy. Among other things, they described secular parish committees that locked priests out, cheated them of money and property, and ridiculed them. Swindlers, under the guise of democratic rule, also manipulated the unsuspecting priests as well as the faithful. Disorganization in the church facilitated the growth of Orthodox parishes. Unrest jumped like wildfire from parish to parish until the beginning of the 1930s. Both chroniclers placed a great deal of blame for these conditions on the church hierarchy, especially on the bishops.[5] And, of course, both stressed

5. Andrukhovych complained that neither Cardinal Sylvester Sembratovych nor Rev. Ivan Voliansky helped him, although toward the end of his life he did concede that

their own dedication to their church, and emphasized the deep attachment Ukrainian immigrants had toward their ancestral worship.

Andrukhovych compressed his memories of America into one small volume. Published in Kolomyia, Halychyna, it did not sell well—first because Andrukhovych had dallied with Orthodoxy, but more importantly, because the priest was very critical of the Ukrainian intelligentsia in the United States. He complained:

[In the last decade of the nineteenth century] there developed the so-called secular intelligentsia. Oh God! These people in free America really flipped. They defined freedom by not recognizing anybody's honor, and did not really show any intelligence at all, only lack of manners and pushiness. They interfered in church matters and made such scenes that I read about these devilish activities with terror and surprise. They had nothing to lose, and convinced of their intellectual superiority over the simple folk [prostoliudynom] they demoralized simple minds, awakened passions that led to disorder only to fish out some dollars for themselves from these muddy waters. . . . These people called meetings, bought whisky; and everyone talked but no one listened.[6]

The four-volume memoir of Rev. Prystay, which appeared in two editions and was widely read, provided more detail on the situation in the Ukrainian Catholic churches. Prystay began his memoirs after he lost his life savings in the stock market crash, circumstances that heightened his criticism of the society to which he had dedicated his life. The examples he provided—of charlatans becoming priests, of priests resorting to duplicity, of illicit economic and sexual affairs, of switches from Catholicism to Orthodoxy and back again, of autonomy run amok, and of good deeds going punished—might have come from any American frontier tale. But they were shocking to staid Eastern European ears. The behavior of congregations toward the clergy changed under the impact of American mores, as did that of priests toward the parishioners. Individual priests and laity were more likely to lobby for causes involving their own smaller ethnic enclaves and to contact higher authorities with their complaints.

---

he misjudged Sembratovych. Prystay charged Bohachevsky with lack of social grace and failure to provide clerical hospitality and also complained that Andrey Sheptytsky did not offer him the help he needed. Prystay, Z Truskavtsia u svit khmaroderiv, vol. 4 (Lviv: Naukove Tovarystvo im. T. Shevchenka, 1937), 207.

6. Andrukhovych, Z zhytia Rusyniv v Amerytsi, 86.

At the beginning of the nineteenth century, the Ukrainian Catholic clergy in Western Ukraine had created a fund for the economic support of widows and orphans of priests. In the United States the clergy made a few attempts to organize themselves for other purposes as well. On occasion, the Ukrainian-American clergy demanded self-government and a say in the appointment of a bishop. In the absence of a bishop for their own rite, in July 1899 the clergy and lay activists even tried to create a functional self-government for the Ukrainian Catholic Church in the United States. Ten priests and fifteen parish representatives (out of a total of sixty churches and forty-four priests) established, with lay participation, the society of Sts. Cyril and Methodius, which was intended to oversee and coordinate the activities of the Ukrainian Church in America. Bohdan Procko, the pioneer historian of the Ukrainian Catholic Church in the United States, considered this meeting "the first serious attempt to introduce lay control over the church, a principle which troubled the Ruthenian Church in the United States for many years to come."[7] The Cyril and Methodius Society included both Ukrainian and Ruthenian priests. The former, like their flock, were in the minority, but the priests from Halychyna had drive and a goal—they wanted to make the Ruthenians aware of their Ukrainian identity. Their insistence on the use of the term "Ukrainian Church" rather than the traditional "Ruthenian" undermined the organization but that did not hamper the activist priests. Some published their demands and established an autonomous Ruthenian Church, arguing for an elected bishop in America, or better yet, a patriarch.[8]

That move, together with the continued real danger that dissatisfied Catholic clergy and faithful might turn to other faiths, especially Orthodoxy, troubled the Vatican and persuaded it to go against the wishes of the American Latin-rite Catholics. Although the American Roman Catholic clergy demanded that local and minority churches be integrated into a single hierarchic structure in the United States, the Vatican, after a decade of deliberation, appointed a bishop for Ukrainian Catholics. In June

7. Procko, *Ukrainian Catholics in America*, 14.

8. Association of the Ruthenian Church in America, *Unia v Amerytsi* (New York: Association of the Ruthenian Church in America, 1902). Ivan Ardan (1871–1940), Ivan Konstankevych (1859–1918), and Anton Bonchevsky (1871–1903) emerge as the leaders in this phase of the movement.

1907, Pope Pius X, through the Congregation for the Propagation of the Faith, appointed Metropolitan Sheptytsky's candidate, Soter Ortynsky, to be bishop for all Ukrainian Catholic immigrants in the United States. Formally, however, Ortynsky was considered an auxiliary of the Latin-rite Catholic prelate in whose diocese Ukrainian parishes were located, which was seen as a limitation of his power.[9]

The apostolic letter *Ea semper* from Pius X also included a clause expressly forbidding the ordination of married men in America.[10] This document immediately became a foil for accusing the papacy of violating Eastern-rite privileges. It was sometimes referred to a "bulla," since it was meant to serve as a foundational document of the Ukrainian exarchy. Metropolitan Sheptytsky was unhappy about both limitations and tried to limit their impact. At Ortynsky's consecration as bishop on May 12, 1907, all Ukrainian Catholic bishops—Sheptytsky, Konstantyn Chekhovych, Hryhory Khomyshyn, and Ortynsky—jointly protested the limiting terms of the appointment. As the Conference of Ukrainian Bishops, they formally warned the papacy that subordinating the Eastern church in the

9. See Rev. Lev I. Sembratovych, "Yak pryshlo do imenuvannia nashoho pershoho epyskopa v Amerytsi," in *Iuvyleyny Al'manakh Ukraiins'koii Hreko-Katolyts'koii Tserkvy u Zluchenykh Derzhavakh z nahody 50-littia yiyi istnuvannia* (Philadelphia: America, 1934), 103–7. Sembratovych stressed the important role that Sheptytsky's personal contacts in Rome and availability of funds necessary for travel had in the approval for the Ukrainian bishopric. Sembratovych, Sheptytsky's secretary at the time, was privy to all the formal and informal moves in which Sheptytsky engaged to overcome the opposition of the Hungarian administration, American clergy, and individual Catholic Poles at the Vatican to establish a separate Ukrainian Catholic diocese in the United States. According to the *Ea semper* of 1907, which established the Ukrainian-American exarchate, the Ukrainian bishop was to be formally the vicar of each bishopric in which Ukrainian Catholic churches were located. No married priests were to serve in the United States. Ortynsky, nevertheless, consecrated some married men as priests, as did Sheptytsky on his second visit to America in 1921. Ortynsky did receive full episcopal powers in 1913.

10. In a pastoral letter (actually a speech) in 1908, Ortynsky complained that his position vis-à-vis the Roman Catholic bishops was also weakened by the refusal of some parishes to turn over deeds of their churches to him. See a précis of Ortynsky's letter in *America* (Ukrainian Catholic newspaper, Philadelphia), July 14, 2007, 6 and 23. See also *Temporary Diocesan Statutes of the Byzantine Rite Apostolic Exarchate of Philadelphia, PA, USA*, vol. 1 (Philadelphia: Bishop's Chancery Office, 1953), 11. In an attempt to bolster Ortynsky's position, the Ukrainian Bishops' Conference, on April 19, 1909, sent a letter to Ortynsky asking him if the metropolitan should intervene to the Vatican on his behalf. PKEL, minutes of the April 19, 1909, 11.

United States to local Roman Catholic ecclesiastical authority could push its faithful into Orthodoxy.[11]

Bishop Ortynsky tried to play the traditional role of the ideal Ukrainian Catholic clergyman—to use the Gospel as a means of finding a balance between a meaningful life and a just society. That goal became increasingly difficult in a society whose core values were changing. Financing the activities of the church was a major problem, made all the more difficult since neither Lviv nor the Vatican were open about money matters and Ortynsky had little practical experience managing money or establishing a stable institution in a volatile society.

Together with the parishes, the immigrant society, often under the tutelage of Catholic priests, developed an alternate community structure—the community cooperative insurance societies that came to be known as fraternal organizations. The fraternal insurance cooperatives stored funds, lent money on a short-term basis, provided burial funds, and used some of the proceeds for community needs. Community needs had to be defined—a hall, an evening school, and more nebulous work for the common good, which often meant for some benefit to the mother country. Ukraine, it must be remembered, did not exist as a separate entity. The fraternal organizations were established before Ortynsky's appointment, which gave those organizations a sense of historic primacy in the articulation of the common cause. The relationship between the two organizations—the Catholic Church and the fraternal organizations—would color the next half-century of Ukrainian life in the United States.

In the early twentieth century a tension between the immigrants from Halychyna and those from Ruthenia developed when the two groups were thrown together as one community for the first time. The Ruthenians themselves came from two different parts of the Austrian Monarchy—

11. PKEL, December 2, 1907, 10. At this meeting Sheptytsky also raised the need for more missionaries for future work in the East and elsewhere. The threat of mass conversion to Orthodoxy was an effective means that the Ukrainian Catholics had to pressure the Vatican for expanding that church's rights.

one controlled by Hungary, the other, such as Halychyna, under Habsburg rule, consequently they had to make adjustments to each other, not only to the Ukrainians. The Ruthenians—using the old term for Ukrainians—came to America before the Halychanyns, and often before the popularity of the modern Ukrainian movement reached their ancestral villages. The immigrants from Halychyna came later, some touting their modern Ukrainian identity. Often Catholic priests from Halychyna felt that it was their civic duty to point out to the Carpathian Ruthenians that they and the Halychanyns were members of the same Ukrainian nationality. The growing tension between the Ukrainians and the Ruthenians was not a matter of language—at the time the difference was regional rather than linguistic, given the Ukrainian language spoken in Halychyna. Rather, the Ukrainian activists wanted the Ruthenians to be equally active in their social and political concerns. This desire is best illustrated by the five priests from Halychyna, the so-called American circle, who in the early twentieth century chose priestly celibacy for national, rather than religious reasons—it was a decision that better positioned them to raise the national consciousness of the Ukrainian flock in America without irritating American Catholic sensibilities.[12] Another priest, Hryhoriy Hrushka, frustrated by Ruthenian unwillingness to identify clearly with any Ukrainian cause, established the Rus'ky narodny soyuz in 1894 as a secular organization that soon was transformed into the Ukrainian National Association (UNA). It cut off all relations with the Carpatho-Ruthenians who adamantly refused to call themselves Ukrainians. Nominally an insurance credit union, the UNA grew to be a major social institution with substantial financial resources. Earlier Hrushka founded the newspaper *Svoboda*, which became the major Ukrainian voice in the United States. Although the clergy played an important role in the development of the UNA before 1907, and between 1916 and 1924 when, following Ortynsky's

12. One of these priests, Konstantyn Andrukhovych (*Z zhytia Rusyniv v Amerytsi*) recounts how after voting in the Austrian parliamentary elections for Franko in 1897, he, Ivan Ardan, and Anton Bonchevsky resolved at all costs to go to America to work for the national enlightenment of the Ukrainian immigrants in America. See Bohdan P. Procko, "Role of the Catholic Church in the Adjustment of Ukrainian Immigrants in America, 1884–1914," in *The Ukrainian Heritage in America*, ed. Walter Dushnyck and Nicholas I. Fr.-Chirovsky (New York: Ukrainian Congress Committee of America, 1991), 97–102; and Myron B. Kuropas, *The Ukrainian Americans*, 87–88. See also Oleksa Prystay, *Z Truskavtsia*, 3:93–98.

death, there was no bishop in the United States, the UNA tacitly opposed the growth of a strong rival autonomous Catholic Church structure, both under Bishop Ortynsky and later under his successor.[13] In spite of the dramatic differences between the old country and the new, the laity and the clergy each sought to replicate the mother church according to their own vision of it. The scene was set for a tug of power between the priest and the parish, as well as among the parishioners.[14]

In the United States, Bishop Ortynsky preserved the vision of the priest as the leader of the community. Reinforced by the example of Metropolitan Sheptytsky's growing authority within Ukrainian society in Halychyna, Ortynsky plunged into community life as energetically as he had into the task of building a solid church infrastructure. He tried to unite the Carpathian Ruthenians and the Halychany Ukrainians through ecclesiastical, social, and financial organizations. But he could not control the fraternal organizations, which functioned as cooperative insurance and credit unions. Although the Ukrainian National Association made Ortynsky its honorary chairman as a sign of cooperation, the bishop found some statements made by the board members objectionable, and he resigned his membership in the UNA. Instead, in 1912 Ortynsky established the Ukrainian Catholic Association, Providence (commonly known as the Providence Association), a separate Catholic fraternal and insurance company.[15] He also set up an informal credit union, but unfortunately overlooked the legal strictures on banking in the United States. Despite many difficulties, he established an orphanage and struggled to create a

13. For a brief introduction, see Rev. Walter Paska, "The Ukrainian Catholic Church in the USA," in Dushnyck and Chirovsky, *The Ukrainian Heritage in America*, 75–83; and Procko, "Role of the Catholic Church in the Adjustment of Ukrainian Immigrants," Dushnyck and Chirovsky, *The Ukrainian Heritage in America*, 95–102. On Bishop Ortynsky, see Ivan Kaszczak, *Bishop Soter Stephen Ortynsky and the Genesis of the Eastern Catholic Churches in America* (Philadelphia: CreateSpace Independent Publishing Platform, 2016).

14. There were other views. Rev. Fylymon Tarnawsky was one of the few clerics who voiced the need to adjust the administration of the Ukrainian Church to the new American surroundings. He noted that the young, Ukrainian, immigrant priests in America did not understand how the church was run, nor did they realize that the church needed to be independent of all outside control. Tarnawsky, *Spomyny*, 159.

15. The bishop's insistence that all members of the association profess the Catholic faith led to the establishment of the separate Ukrainian Workingmen Fraternal Union that attracted socialists and progressives. Communists kept to their own organizations.

seminary for the training of Ukrainian priests in America. In an attempt to have a neutral meeting ground to bring the Halychany and the Carpathians together, he created a civic organization called the Ruska Rada. Community consensus broke down over the name.

Priests, meanwhile, had to maneuver in an American society that had not adjusted to the concept of multiple identities. Ortynsky found it hard to administer the far-flung parishes, and complaints from some priests about Ortynsky reached Metropolitan Sheptytsky. The metropolitan planned to attend the Eucharistic congress in Montreal in 1910 and combined that with a visit to the Philadelphia exarchate. As was his custom, Sheptytsky asked Reverend Vasyl Merenkiv to provide him with a preliminary confidential report on the Ukrainian Catholic Church in the United States and Canada. The lengthy and critical report could have easily described the situation that Bohachevsky would encounter fifteen years later: "The situation of our church, bishop, and priests is hopeless. Everyone realizes it—priests and bishop. There really was never such hell as here and such headaches. The crisis is hopeless and all encompassing. The chaos begins in the bishop's chancery and ends in the most remote parish. Everyone blames this desperate condition on obstacles they cannot change. Hence they cannot find a way out."[16]

Merenkiv blamed American materialism, the clergy's highhanded treatment of parishioners, as well as the primitive attacks on Protestantism that alienated Americans from Ukrainian immigrants. He accused the Ukrainian clergy in the United States of "toadyism, servility, lack of trust, undue suspicion, bribery, and corruption." All this, he continued, is "a sign that moral foundations were washed out, replaced by gain as the goal of the day." But mainly he accused Bishop Ortynsky of bad management practices. Conceding that Bishop Ortynsky was "energetic, religious, and an effective missionary," the priest nevertheless noted that he would have liked to see in the bishop "more caution, careful thought, selfless dedication, and love." That, he continued, would enable Ortynsky to construct a lasting foundation for a "building which, while not finished, would be

16. Rev. Vasyl Merenkiv to Sheptytsky, with note from Sheptytsky "answered," TsDIA, Lviv, f. 358, op. 2, spr. 210, pp. 20–34. The segment on the Ukrainian Church in the United States runs from p. 20 to half of p. 28. The letter itself is not dated, but Sheptytsky's signature and note "replied" is dated October 1911.

well founded and strong."[17] Merenkiv conceded that that the bishop tried hard to become a leader of his people but could not establish authority over the community. In a passage underlined, presumably by Sheptytsky, Merenkiv recommended "choosing *appropriately qualified persons to help* [Ortynsky], *and paying them accordingly.*" Surprisingly, Merenkiv argued that the Ukrainian clergy should be subject, at least for the time being, to the local Roman Catholic bishops. "It is easier to deal with ten English bishops than with fifty Ruthenian parishes, committees, meetings." In his view, the chronically litigious relations between bishop, priests, and communities made civic or ecclesiastical organization impossible: "Only when the local parishes see that behind their leader, be he called vicar-general, stands the justice of the state, and that the bishop, the lawyer, and the priest say one and the same thing, then independence [from the Roman Catholic hierarchy] *de facto* would be at least a small step toward independence *de jure.*"[18]

17. Ibid., 23.

18. Ibid., 26. The brutal criticism continued: "It seems that the situation is so critical that a sudden, determined, radical step could change the course for the better. I will be frank: Either change the person or change the tactics" (ibid., 27). Merenkiv did not hide his criticism of Ortynsky, noting that "it was a pity Dr. Josef Zhuk had been too young when the nomination had been made." Both of Vasyl Merenkiv's subsequent suggestions could have served as a lesson for Constantine Bohachevsky fifteen years later, had he been aware of them. "As to tactics, they flow from the events. One needs to be subtle. At this time one needs first and foremost to abjure all kinds of newspaper polemics and instead present real acts and serious food (for the soul), and the truth will win out by itself. Then we should choose qualified persons to assist us and *reimburse them suitably* [this was underlined, presumably by Sheptytsky]. Finally, we should sacrifice ourselves and not touch money issues, take what they give us . . . and document in our own paper how much and for what purposes the donations were made." (ibid., 28). He went on to note that new priests should be specially trained for work in the United States, taking into consideration principles according to which local priests were trained. Only then would the Ukrainian Catholic clergy get a chance to win back the good will of their flock. As if to underscore an already-made point, Merenkiv noted that the hatred of the clergy by their parishioners is not social or socialist, it is "simply elemental" (ibid., 28). With that scathing comment, he turned his report to Canada, where he gauged the situation to be much better.

Sheptytsky used his visit in the summer of 1910 to bolster Ortynsky's position. The metropolitan blessed the Cathedral of the Immaculate Conception of the Virgin Mary in Philadelphia and a site for a seminary in southern Virginia, near Yorktown. The choice of the name for the cathedral reflected a desire to stress the Catholicism of the Greek Catholic rite, since the Orthodox resented the fact that the papacy independently had made Mary's immaculate birth a dogma, thus violating the principle of Christian unity.[19]

While friendly crowds met Sheptytsky, the civic leadership of the community openly rebuffed the metropolitan in order to prove its non-denominational status. Nonetheless, the trip to the United States armed Sheptytsky with strong arguments for his case that the Ukrainian bishop needed to exercise full ecclesiastical authority on his own. As a result, on August 17, 1914, by the decree *Cum episcopo*, the Congregation for the Propagation of the Faith confirmed Bishop Ortynsky's full ecclesiastical jurisdiction over all Ukrainian-American Catholics.

With the knowledge that he would have full episcopal authority Ortynsky crossed the Atlantic and travelled to the Hungarian part of the Habsburg Empire to negotiate funding for a Ukrainian Catholic seminary in the United States. The outbreak of World War I almost stranded him. He was barely able to return to America with empty hands. This undermined his credibility as a community leader.

World War I speeded up the secularization of the Ukrainian-American community. A group of Ukrainian-American immigrants convened a "Ukrainian parliament" that not only drew up a fully secular program but also pointedly dispensed with both the bishop and public prayer as part of its proceedings. Cut off from communications with his home country and drawn into complications regarding property and personalities, Ortynsky lost control over individual parishes in which the parishioners could not find a common voice. He proved unable to spark community cohesion

19. The belief that the Virgin Mary, the only mortal so blessed, was born without original sin was officially proclaimed by Pope Pius IX in 1854 as a dogma. The provincial synod at Lviv celebrated the proclamation in 1891 to manifest adherence of the Ukrainian Church to the doctrine.

around the church. He could not do the impossible—use the traditional Halychyna definition of Ukrainian to mean also Catholic. After his return to the United States, Ortynsky suffered repeated bouts of pneumonia. He died on March 24, 1916. His premature death cut short the simmering clergy rebellions against him, all opposition to him was conveniently forgotten; instead there were rumors that the bishop had been murdered. Speculation about the bishop's replacement surfaced immediately, as did a run on the credit union Ortynsky had established.

The clergy, aware of the administrative crisis in the church, again tried to create a clergy organization that would set the tone for community action. In October 1916, the priests from Halychyna held a congress at which they established the Society of St. Paul, whose main goal was to promote the inner growth of the clergy.[20] They proposed to hold retreats, popularize religious publications, foster religious vocations, and, most importantly, "to make the laity aware of the financial needs of the church."[21] When the priests passed on to community affairs, however, the Halychanyns protested the use of the term "Rusyn" by the Ruthenian parishes. For good measure, they also alerted the apostolic delegate to financial abuses in the Ruthenian Church.

20. The initiative for the new clergy organization—or to activate Bishop Ortynsky's old Rada—came from Revs. Zakhariy Orun and Volodymyr Chaplinsky, with the close collaboration of Maksym Kinash, Oleksander Ulytsky, Volodymyr Dovhovych, Mykola Pidhoretsky, and Vasyl Hryvniak. Procko, *Ukrainian Catholics in America*, 43; I supplemented the account with information from a handwritten draft "of the minutes of the First Organizational Meeting of the St. Paul Society held in New York, October 10, 1916," in the papers of Volodymyr Dovhovych. The notes, taken by a different hand in the same file, are marked on the "Consultations of delegates of the Central Organizations in the matter of [establishing] a 'Ukrainian Council,' held in New York City, November 1, 1916." The minutes are not signed and this version has corrections in pencil. The priests gave presentations on the turn to Orthodoxy, on the orphanage, and on part-time primary schools. They agreed that the faithful opposed funding a seminary, but felt that eventually they would realize the importance of having a diocesan seminary. At the same time, the priests from Halychyna charged that the Carpathian Rusyns were lax in adhering to church regulations. The Halychanyns considered asking the apostolic delegate to urge the Ruthenian administrator to follow canonical regulations more closely. In this notetaking, the Rus'ka Rada was rendered as Ukraiinska, and on one occasion with the addition "national" or "people's" (*narodna*).

21. UMAS, in a sheaf of handwritten notes that the librarian at UMAS thought would be of interest. "To foster in the people support towards a seminary and make the broad masses aware of the problem, so that they would support the chancery financially."

At the same time, with the help of the civic organizations, the clergy leadership resuscitated Bishop Ortynsky's old Rada as an "all-Ukrainian committee" of all émigré organizations with no regard to religious affiliation. It was to be thoroughly American in the sense that "American politics [polityka] [aim] to organize citizens [sytyzeniv]."[22] Nominally, the Carpathian Rusyns and the Halychanyn Ukrainians were cooperating, the former bereft of the clandestine financial support that the Hungarians had been channeling and the latter cut off from direct political news from home.

PONIATYSHYN AND THE PUBLIC
ROLE OF THE CHURCH

The death of Ortynsky rekindled the fear that the Ukrainian Catholics without their own upper clergy would turn *en masse* to Orthodoxy. The Congregation for the Propagation of the Faith moved swiftly. In secret from the Hungarian and Polish clerical "lobbyists" in the Vatican, the pope acceded to the request that the Ukrainian-American clergy elect its own clergy administrator until a bishop was named. The clergy elected Reverend Petro Poniatyshyn, a Halychanyn, as administrator, and Reverend Havryil Martiak, from the Carpathian branch of the church, to be his vicar.[23] At a meeting with the apostolic delegate, Giovanni Bonzano, the two administrators decided that it would be wiser to work as co-administrators—each responsible for the faithful who came from their respective areas of origin. This very complex approach, based on the place of birth of each congregant, could not work smoothly in a society that

22. The founding congress (z'iizd) was chaired by Rev. Ivan Konstankevych, Rev. Lev Levytsky was the vice-chairman, and Revs. Ivan Velyhorsky and Volodymyr Derzhyruka served as secretaries. The priests were concerned that the community was channeling its resources into the Ukrainian language evening schools, while the spiritual needs of the people were not being adequately addressed. The society proposed to handle social, educational, and immigration matters. The founders specified sixteen points of activity including the establishment of a Ukrainian theatre and museum in the United States, as well as a correspondence bureau. The Rada would speak for the Ukrainians in America, focusing on social, educational, and immigration matters.

23. Brief discussion in Rev. Walter Paska, "The Ukrainian Catholic Church in the USA," 75–83.

was based on availability of work, even though the two administrators cooperated with each other. Not all the clergy practiced the same degree of cooperation.

The outcome of the election angered Rev. Stefan Dziubay and other Ruthenian clerics, who had presumed that the top position in the Ukrainian Catholic Church in the United States would alternate between the two branches. The anger spread to the informal church cooperative created by the late bishop Ortynsky where the faithful deposited their monies.[24] There was a run on the shares of what had essentially been a private banking venture. Poniatyshyn managed to control the potential scandal, largely through the advice of a Roman Catholic lawyer and with the help of insurance monies that Ortynsky's brother donated to the church.

Dziubay, hurt by being passed over, became an Orthodox bishop and proceeded to ordain "numerous priests with doubtful qualifications" who further managed to muddy church waters.[25] The loyal Rusyn Catholic clergy, however, proceeded to elect Rev. Havryil Martiak as the new vicar. In practice, Martiak dealt with the Ruthenian clerics, while Poniatyshyn handled the pastors from Halychyna. Officially, both priests, Poniatyshyn and Martiak, were considered to have been nominated by the pontiff through the Congregation for the Propagation of the Faith. Making the

24. The bishop had used the funds to buy the cathedral, the cemetery, eight houses, and some Austrian stock bonds. Then the bishop wanted to buy yet another house for his residence, but decided to do that through an intermediary, Mr. Julian Chupka, Esq., so that the price would not go up. By the time the house was bought, Bishop Ortynsky had died. Rev. Vasyl Stetsiuk, the cathedral pastor and Ortynsky's secretary, did not inform his successor, Rev. Maksym Kinash, of the details of the house ownership. When Mr. Chupka died there was a danger that his widow would not honor the arrangement and would legally claim ownership of the property. Kinash persuaded her to cede the deed of the house to him. Thus Kinash became the owner of a house that had been purchased with borrowed church money for a proxy buyer. Kinash, as pastor of the Ukrainian Catholic Cathedral in Philadelphia wrote to Bohachevsky on October 12, 1924, that Ortynsky had planned to establish a Ukrainian bank, but never went through the state legalities. When he died there was a run on the investments and Ortynsky's brother, the beneficiary of the bishop's life insurance of $50,000, used the money to cover the costs of the credit union. UMAS, Chancery Archive.

25. The quotation is from Procko, *Ukrainian Catholics in America*, 41. In the last years of the Austro-Hungarian Habsburg Empire, Hungarian laymen actively tried to influence the Vatican's choice of appointment of a Ukrainian bishop. Dziubay's career in the Catholic Church may have fallen victim to the Vatican's resentment over the Hungarian lobby, as much as to his unpopularity among the Halychyna clergy.

clergy complicit in how the Vatican could reconcile expediency and adherence to a strict hierarchic principle may have empowered the clergy to justify their cutting administrative corners.

Poniatyshyn inherited a fiscally complex exarchy over which he had very limited powers: he could not sell property or dispose of large sums of money, nor establish the seminary or discipline the clergy.[26] Because of legal complications with Ortynsky's will, he did not have access to needed funds. The resurrected Rada, Ortynsky's civic organization, which the clergy had hoped to shepherd, had no independent financial backing and became dormant. Poniatyshyn tried to maintain contact with his priests through the publication of *Eparchial News*,[27] but quickly ran into difficulties with the local church committees that, in his words "did not want to understand that the church is governed by law, and not by the wishes of sundry individuals."[28]

Petro Poniatyshyn had spent his whole priestly career in the United States. He had been ordained by Sheptytsky in 1902, and by the following

26. In writing about his tenure, Poniatyshyn stressed that his major difficulties were establishing discipline among the priests and preventing church property from falling into private hands. He pointed out how helpful Latin Catholic bishops were in sorting out property issues. Poniatyshyn had severe difficulties in countering first the well-funded Tsarist Orthodox activities and then the newly founded Ukrainian Autocephalous Orthodox Church among Ukrainian Catholic parishes. Lack of ecclesiastic discipline and America's vast territories, as well as the impact of the American revivalist movement, made it easy for charlatans to act as priests. See Petro Poniatyshyn, "The Ukrainian Church and the U.N. Association," in *Propamiatna Knyha: Vydana z nahody soroklitnioho Iuvyleiu Ukraiins'koho Narodnoho Soiuzu (Jubilee Book of the Ukrainian National Association in Commemoration of the Fortieth Anniversary of Its Existence)*, ed. Luka Myshuha (Jersey City, N.J.: Svoboda Press, 1936), 287–99. See also Poniatyshyn, "Iz chasiv administratsiii eparkhiii," in *Iuvileyny Al'manakh Ukrayins'koii Hreko-Katolyts'koii tserkvy*, 110–14.

27. The September 15, 1920, issue of *Eparchial News* marked the first of the issues published under Poniatyshyn's editorship. To stress continuity with Ortynsky, Bohachevsky numbered the publication as the fourth issue.

28. See Poniatyshyn, "Iz chasiv administratsiii eparkhiii," 110–14. The longer Poniatyshyn's tenure as head of the church grew, the weaker his power became. His regulation that church funds should be kept separate from publicly collected donations was not followed, and parish finances were difficult to disentangle. In April 1917, on the eve of All-American Ukrainian Day (April 21) when Ukrainians had the permit to collect funds nationwide, Poniatyshyn published, as regulation no. 423, a special leaflet for the clergy, explaining that a special committee should be created in each church for the purpose of collecting the monies. All collected funds were to be sent to the Ukrainian Alliance in Yonkers, NY, which was empowered to deal with the details. Copy of the leaflet in UMAS.

year was in Ramey, Pennsylvania. He felt at home in the United States and was one of the few Ukrainian Catholic clerics who personally befriended American politicians. He liked New York and New Jersey, and avoided Philadelphia, although it was the seat of his administration. He delegated Rev. Maksym Kinash to take over as pastor of the Philadelphia cathedral to free him from administrative duties. He was able to work closely with the community organizations and especially with *Svoboda*, the mouthpiece of the increasingly important Ukrainian National Association, the new name adopted by the all-Ukrainian fraternal organization, the Ruthenian Council.[29] In 1918, Poniatyshyn headed a new civic organization—the Ukrainian National Committee (Komitet) in the United States. The committee, supported by the UNA, was to serve as the united voice of the Ukrainian community. Poniatyshyn took pride in his ability to muster united political activity from Ukrainian immigrants, especially in the immediate post–World War I years, and to keep the Catholic Church and the community on an even keel during the period of the failed liberation wars in Ukraine from 1917 to 1923. Poniatyshyn worked with the Ukrainian-American intelligentsia to promote the Ukrainian cause. His community successes—the establishment of an office for the Ukrainian National Committee, the participation of some of its members in informal peace deliberations in Versailles, and especially the support that Poniatyshyn garnered for Ukrainians in Washington through the help of the Jersey City congressman James A. Hamill—were impressive.

Meanwhile, Metropolitan Sheptytsky's life and activities continued to give greater prominence to the public role of the Ukrainian Catholic Church—first, his ordeal as a political prisoner of tsarist Russia, then as an exile displaced from his land by a hostile Polish government, next as a pilgrim-petitioner before the world on behalf of his people, and, finally, as a formal envoy of the pope to Ukrainians in Brazil, with visits to North America in 1921–22.

In the years following the armistice of November 11, 1918, Ukrainian-American activity centered on bringing the Ukrainian cause before the

29. There were thus three major Ukrainian fraternal insurance organizations in the United States—in the order of size of membership, they were the Ukrainian National Association; the Ukrainian Catholic Association, Providence; and the Ukrainian Workingmen's Association.

victorious Allies. It was a continual uphill struggle of a large part of the Ukrainian immigrants. Poniatyshyn understood that he was in a position to magnify his voice. He had become friendly with Congressman James A. Hamill, and through Hamill he managed to arrange a meeting with President Warren G. Harding's incoming secretary of state, Charles Hughes. Owing to Poniatyshyn's efforts the State Department at least acknowledged the receipt of numerous communications from various Ukrainian groups.[30] When Poniatyshyn did not receive Vatican permission to travel officially to the Versailles Peace Conference negotiations, Congressman Hamill sought to represent Ukrainians in Paris. Most important, Poniatyshyn was instrumental in getting President Woodrow Wilson to officially designate April 21, 1917, as Ukrainian Day, with the right to solicit street donations for that cause. Within the context of the time, Poniatyshyn had reason to consider himself a successful Ukrainian leader, as well as an effective churchman.

The prospect of the establishment of an independent Ukrainian state following the 1917 Russian Revolution and the fall of the Habsburg Empire in 1918 made Ukrainian-American community organizations more active politically. Through monetary contributions, street demonstrations, and other types of public pressure the immigrant community convinced itself that it was making a tangible contribution to the cause of Ukraine. The very limited resources of the immigrant community were increasingly channeled into the public sector, while the needs of the church, the clergy, and even families were judged to be secondary.

The First World War ended in the rapid disintegration of empires— Hohenzollern Germany, Habsburg Austria-Hungary, Ottoman Turkey, and Romanov Russia—that made it possible for many people from those areas to make their way West. The peace that followed was much more difficult than previous diplomatic settlements because the victors tried to establish peace on new principles of the self-determination of nations

---

30. There were many petitions from the Western Ukrainian Republic headed by Evhen Petrushevych. The fullest available discussion is in Oleksander Pavliuk, *Borot'ba Ukraïiny za nezalezhnist' i polityka SShA* (Kyiv: Akademia Press, 1996), see esp. 113–15. Myron Kuropas commented: "Father Poniatyshyn compromised his moral authority within the clerical community precisely because he was perceived more of a political rather than a spiritual leader: [Poniatyshyn was] dynamic and productive . . . in the political arena. . . . [Priests] came to perceive Father Poniatyshyn more as a politician than as their spiritual director." Kuropas, *The Ukrainian Americans*, 306.

and the democratic equality of states. While the Peace Treaty of Versailles was being hammered out, a different series of wars broke out in Eastern Europe. Paramount in Western eyes was the fear that the new communist regime in Russia threatened to spread the revolution of the working classes worldwide, even, if necessary, by military action. Although communist revolutions in Germany and elsewhere failed, the Ukrainian National Republic became the first victim of the Russian communist campaign to spread the revolution by force.

Political instability offered chances for migration, including renewed opportunities to come to the United States. The first Ukrainian immigrants had come to the United States for clearly economic reasons; those who followed added social and political agendas. Both groups included a few individuals and subgroups that sought to undermine the Ukrainian Catholic Church. More, however, inadvertently increased the administrative and financial disorder in the Ukrainian Catholic parishes by their well-meaning attempts to help. Factions proliferated. Sometimes there were problems with the cantors, who also ran the informal Ukrainian language schools for children and whose salaries were often higher than those of priests. And while most of the priests sent to the immigrant communities worked selflessly, there were not a few cases of priests unworthy of the name and priests who turned to Orthodoxy either for money or out of pique against the Ukrainian Catholic hierarchy. American society, with its vast array of churches and denominations, fostered both lay and clerical independence. It nurtured mobility and an interest in practical economics, both of which could breed mismanagement as much as efficiency in church administration. Parishes changed hands, priests strapped for funds created consumer cooperatives or even banks that they could not control. The chaos, of course, did not go unnoticed, and the priests involved, as well as the church itself, were frequently criticized. Parish fights migrated to the streets, and at times police intervention was necessary. The Latin Catholic clergy protested to the papal delegate about the bad name that rowdy Ukrainians gave to all Catholics.

The clergy worked through informal networks and tried to meet periodically, but lack of coordinated planning and the distances between parishes stymied these efforts. Nevertheless, some of the priests were uncomfortable that little time and energy were left for traditional religious practices. The parish church continued to be a forum for community groups and political parties, while the church administrative structure, without a bishop and clear organizational guidelines, remained nebulous. The growing tensions within the American Catholic Churches expanded the role of the apostolic delegate to the United States, as he was increasingly called upon to conciliate between the Catholic rites.

By trying to replicate the role of the priest as both a community and a church leader, the Ukrainian-American clergy missed their opportunity to establish their own strong clergy association. Lacking a financial base and dependent upon the good will of the parish, the clergy also failed to develop a sense of their own clerical community. The priest stood alone, geographically separated from friends and dependent upon communities that increasingly questioned his right to authority and knowledge. The younger priests were celibate in a society that did not have a social network of extended family or a closely knit community. Aging priests had not planned for old age. There were the usual suspected concubines, a field day for the rapidly developing Ukrainian-language yellow press. The unstated role of the church as the purveyor of tradition and identity was increasingly taken over by the "nation." And those who spoke in the name of the nation did not necessarily need the blessing of higher authorities.

NEW HOPES

The Great War and the failed hopes it engendered for an independent Ukraine politicized the Ukrainian community both at home and abroad. The Ukrainian Catholic Church in the United States, as the most visible Ukrainian-American organization, was pressured into public activity. The victory of the Poles over the western Ukrainians compromised Catholicism for some Ukrainians owing to Poland's anti-Ukrainian policies. By the end of the war, Ukrainian political activists, many of whom were recent arrivals from Eastern Europe, veterans or victims of the wars, speeded up the formation of secular organizations. The revolutions in Europe polarized émigré politics, which became ideological and contentious because of lack of opportunities for concrete action. Democratic nationalism was the most popular tendency, and its leaders were more dynamic than the conservative churchmen preferred. The Ukrainian-American community pushed hard to

bring the aspirations of their countrymen to the attention of the world powers through lobbying, petitions, demonstrations, and mass meetings. They
expected all Ukrainians abroad—in Europe and in America—to be active in
publicizing the cause of Ukraine in political terms. The continued crises in
the home country made this kind of activity all the more important.

The Ukrainian Catholic Church—whether housed in its own building
or in rented space—remained the locus of social life for the Ukrainian
immigrant community. For some, the priest remained the father figure;
as for some priests the bishop was a father figure. Metropolitan Sheptytsky intuited that relationship and moved slowly to introduce changes
that would restructure the church as a formally administered corporation
rather than a benefice or a family. His successors—on both sides of the
Atlantic—faced a modern world that necessitated an immediate change
of approach. Modernity meant hierarchic administration and a monetary
economy, a disintegration of the old paternal system, and a clear delegation of authority as well as separation of tasks. The variety of churches that
American separation of church and state made possible gave the dissatisfied faithful less drastic options than total rejection of the faith.

Most importantly, since the congregation built the church and supported the priest, for Ukrainians in the United States the church became
the first school of political and social action. Thus, ironically, the separation of secular from ecclesiastical authority also made it easier for the
church to become politicized. As it was, the Ukrainian Catholic Church
in the United States was torn by regional and ideological predilections
during its long formative period.

Two additional factors—neither of them necessarily recognized or articulated by the parties involved—should be mentioned when discussing
the first fifty years of the Ukrainian Catholic Church in America. The early
priests who came to work as missionaries were often young men with little
experience in hierarchic structures. The church they knew predated the
administrative centralizing procedures that Metropolitan Sheptytsky established. These priests embellished their memories of the motherland,
viewing it as a relaxed peaceful Arcadia where villages supported their
priests. Second, the priests tended to see the bishop in this idyllic scenario
as a supportive presence who would succor them in need, provide spiritual
and material comfort, and heed their advice.

The hopes for an imminent independent Ukraine and the belief that Ukrainian-American public opinion might affect the course of events brought the church even closer to the struggle for Ukrainian liberation. The weaker the prospects for an independent Ukraine, the stronger became the pressure on the church to engage in the struggle. The more settled the Ukrainian immigrants became in the United States, the more they became conscious of the political impact they might have on Ukraine's political fate. This conviction was bolstered by the arrival of emissaries of various Ukrainian governments-in-exile and institutions. Those who could, turned their energies and their money toward helping war-torn Western Ukraine rebuild, and even those who could do little engaged in public discussion on ways to help the motherland. Regardless of their own political proclivities, the Ukrainian public expected religious figures to be publicly and politically active. After the victory of the communists in Russia and the establishment of the Union of Socialist Soviet Republics (USSR), the situation was further complicated by the arrival of pro-Soviet activists in the Ukrainian émigré community. For example, the future Soviet dissident Nadia Surovtseva was sent to the United States in the early 1920s to sway Ukrainian-American public opinion toward the new Soviet regime.

At the same time that it was dealing with the broad issues of Ukrainian nationalism, the Ukrainian Catholic Church faced the lure of a renewed Orthodoxy, one part of which, no longer supported financially by a tsarist government, now was more attractive to Western Ukrainians. The founding of the Ukrainian Autocephalous Church in 1921, and especially the establishment of an Orthodox Ukrainian eparchy in the United States, headed by Bishop John Teodorovych in 1924, significantly increased the attraction of Orthodoxy to Ukrainian immigrants.

The unsuccessful struggle for an independent Ukraine contributed to a mood of malaise and unrest in the Ukrainian-American community. As we have seen, Sheptytsky was disheartened during his final visit to the United States in 1922.[31] Nevertheless, Western Ukrainians did not give

31. The July 14, 1922, report of the Lviv director of the police to the Warsaw Ministry of Internal Affairs, relayed information from Ukrainian-American sources that Sheptytsky along with the Ukrainian Catholic priests and the Vatican were very critical of Polish policies. Archiwum Akt Nowych, Warsaw, Syg. 879, p. 147.

up hope for the independence of at least Western Ukraine. The Western Ukrainian People's Republic (known as ZUNR), while nominally united with the Ukrainian Peoples' Republic, created and maintained a separate diplomatic corps in exile in the hope of being treated by the Allies as a successor state and therefore eligible for self-government in the territory that Ukrainians occupied. ZUNR dispatched a representative, Lonhyn Tsehelsky, to the United States, to lobby the American government.[32] He opened a diplomatic mission in Washington in 1921, which Luka Myshuha then ran until 1923.

ZUNR had no money, and Tsehelsky addressed a regular gathering of priests on July 16, 1923, trying to get them to create a support group for ZUNR. Since there were socialists in the government, after some discussion, Poniatyshyn pointed out that it would be better not to mix politics with the church. It is illustrative that Tsehelsky viewed his presentation to the clergy as the first meeting of "intelligent individuals [*inteligentnykh odynyts'*], the likes of which had not been held before in America."[33]

POLITICAL DEVELOPMENTS IN THE
UKRAINIAN IMMIGRANT COMMUNITY

Poniatyshyn's political leadership of the community ended in the early 1920s with the arrival of two more representatives of ZUNR. The president in exile, or as he was known by his formal title "Dictator," Evhen Petrushevych, working from Vienna, sent Osyp Nazaruk and Luka Myshuha to America to fundraise for his strapped government. Both men would later play a critical role in the early years of Bohachevsky's tenure as bishop in the United States. After seeing the disintegration of ZUNR, they both re-

32. Lonhyn Tsehelsky (1875–1950), a lawyer popularly elected to the last Austrian Parliament, played a major role in Ukraine's attempt to gain a voice at the Versailles Peace Conference. He was appointed to represent the Western Ukrainian National Republic in Washington, D.C. Tsehelsky complained repeatedly that he had neither money nor directives from the ZUNR, and was even reduced to handing out Presbyterian leaflets to earn money to pay the secretary. Nazaruk to Lypynsky, November 1, 1925, in Lypynsky, *Collected Works*, 335.

33. Rev. Volodymyr Dovhovych, notes from the meeting, July 16, 1923, UMAS. Dovhovych has four pages of notes on the Tsehelsky presentation and the discussion that followed. Tsehelsky did not consider it proper as a representative of the ZUNR to fundraise in the United States. He also disagreed with the friendly policies ZUNR had begun to take toward Soviet Ukraine, and he severed his connection with ZUNR.

alized that the only way for them to survive would be through journalism or politics. Nazaruk, who was originally sent to Canada but quickly made his way to Chicago, was a journalist; Myshuha became one as a way to continue his public career.

Osyp Nazaruk, Bohachevsky's senior by one year, had been a participant in the Ukrainian Liberation struggle and the author of a first-hand report titled *A Year in Greater Ukraine*.[34] A stormy socialist in his youth, Nazaruk later played a key role in the Ukrainian Radical Socialist Party. As such, he took part in organizing the revolt against Hetman Pavlo Skoropadsky in Kyiv in 1919. While on his fundraising mission for ZUNR through Ukrainian settlements in Western Canada, Nazaruk underwent a major spiritual crisis, and this radically changed his worldview. In line with his changed beliefs Nazaruk—never one to do anything halfway—gravitated toward the conservative Hetman movement and the organized Catholic Church.[35] He renounced socialism as a false and underdevel-

---

34. *Rik na Velyki Ukraiini* (Vienna: Ukraiinsky Prapor, 1920).

35. Osyp Nazaruk (1883–1940), a tanner's son who graduated with a law degree from the University of Vienna, began his public career as a radical socialist. He fought with the Ukrainian volunteer army in the aftermath of the First World War, participated in the overthrow of the conservative Hetman regime, and served in the diplomatic service of the Western Ukrainian National Republic. Disillusioned at the defeat of the Ukrainian Republic, he experienced a dramatic intellectual crisis while fundraising in Western Canada, and became a practicing Catholic, a monarchist, and a close collaborator of Viacheslav Lypynsky, the foremost spokesman of Ukrainian conservatism. He discussed his return to the Catholic faith and his new conservative politics in a series of newspaper articles in Chicago. Nazaruk's change of views reflected the earlier path of one of the major radical activists in Halychyna, Dr. Vasyl Okhrymovych, whose book *Choho ia navernuvsia* (Lviv, 1920) became a bestseller and was republished in 1926. Nazaruk was known for his bluntness, for publicly expounding his views in periodic press as well as in popular brochures and patriotic fiction, some of which is popular in contemporary Ukraine. The most important sources on the man and his period: Nazaruk, *Rik na Velyki Ukraiini* [*A Year in Greater Ukraine*]; and Nazaruk, *Hreko-Katolytska Tserkva I Ukraiins'ka Liberal'na Intelligentsia* [*The Greek-Catholic Church and the Ukrainian Liberal Intelligentsia*] (Lviv: Pravda, 1929). His letters to Lypynsky from the United States provide an invaluable source of information on the events and the flavor of the era. Nazaruk prided himself on being a man of the people who understood the views of the common farmer from Halychyna. He reinforced Lypynsky's analysis of the basic conservatism of Ukrainian peasants, and defended the Catholic Church and the Hetman. As a disillusioned socialist, he spent a number of years trying to build up a structured and disciplined monarchist movement in the United States. In 1927 he returned to Ukraine and edited one of the major Catholic newspapers. He broke with Lypynsky on personal issues, but not with the conservative cause. He died in 1940. An avid note taker and letter writer,

oped ideology, and became an openly practicing Catholic and a supporter of a parliamentary monarchism best personified by the conservative
philosopher Viacheslav Lypynsky. Nazaruk wrote a series of brochures
explaining his change of heart. Toward the end of 1922, he moved to Chicago where he edited the mouthpiece of the growing monarchist Hetman
movement in the United States.

Nazaruk was a self-made man, uncharacteristically forthright and energetic in a society whose upper crust practiced a studied air of ennui. He
was a passionate man who lived his convictions and decided that only the
Catholic Church could withstand the communist onslaught on humanity
and culture. Nazaruk's high regard for the Catholic Church did not blind
him to the weaknesses of its clergy. He was particularly brutal in his assessment of the Ukrainian Catholic clergy in the United States:

Most of our clergy not only are not clerics in the full meaning of the term, but
[they] are not even Christians! They are pagans—vindictive, envious, quarrel-
some, demagogic, with no inner discipline, materialists—that's how they were
raised. Even in seminaries, instead of thinking and talking about their high
calling, they talked and thought about rich girls and lolled about. Then they got
married and saw their parishes as sources of money. These are the words of Rev.
Tarnawsky who knows them [such clerics] well and shares my views.[36]

Luka Myshuha (often referred to in contemporary sources as Myshuga)
was a worldly man, a dandy given to handmade suits and restaurant
meals, even while his personal circumstances forced him to live hand-to-
mouth in a boarding house. He enjoyed being taken for Baron Rockefel-
ler when he strolled down the then-still fashionable Fourteenth Street to
Lüchow's, his favorite New York restaurant.[37] Three years younger than
Bohachevsky, he preceded the bishop by three years in his arrival in the
United States. Myshuha cultivated the image of a national statesman, never compromising his public *persona*—self-confident, lordly in demeanor;
he maintained an aura of the committed public servant, the upscale face
of a downtrodden nation. Consciously or unconsciously, he appeared to

Nazaruk's unpublished daily notes in separate notebooks survived the Soviet period by having been shelved into other books and manuscripts. They are only now being discovered,
and have only partially been studied.

36. Nazaruk to Lypynsky, January 14, 1925, in Lypynsky, *Collected Works*, 266.

37. Antin Dragan, *Luka Myshuha: Korotka biohrafia* (Jersey City, N.J.: Svoboda, 1973), 87.

remain above the fray that he controlled through the only available means he had—the press and public opinion.

Myshuha had many reasons to consider himself superior to the average cleric. He owed his privileged youth to the financial help of his famous opera-singer uncle, who, through his Western European employment, financed the youth's upbringing and travels, and a first-rate education that culminated in a doctorate in law from Vienna University. In the company of his uncle, Myshuha had taken part in a pilgrimage to the Holy Land organized by Sheptytsky. During the journey, despite his youth, he sat in close proximity to the high-ranking prelate at a number of meals. Although he was saved from the Austrian draft, he served in the Sichovi Striltsi (Sich Riflemen) toward the end of the Great War and then emigrated with the defeated Ukrainian National Republic. Myshuha drafted the memoranda that Sheptytsky used in his meetings with U.S. officials and was present at the White House during the *pro forma* encounter between President Warren Harding and the metropolitan. Regardless of his official position, Myshuha considered himself a representative of one of the erstwhile Ukrainian governments and had close contacts with the emerging Ukrainian underground in Poland. He and his confreres felt that the church—as the best-organized Ukrainians abroad— should work in close cooperation, if not under the direction of, the state representative. Although a Catholic, he did not join any parish. Like other representatives of the Ukrainian organizations, he viewed churches as a conduit to collect needed funds from the public. It was at this critical stage, in 1922, that Luka's uncle, the tenor Oleksander Myshuha, died. His largesse had financed his nephew's career. Suddenly Luka was left with no financial backing.

Nazaruk and Myshuha, both law graduates of the University of Vienna and political colleagues, kept in touch as they both sought to solve the major problem facing both: lack of funds for themselves as well as for the Ukrainian cause, as each of them interpreted it.[38] The last-ditch attempt of the Eastern Ukrainians to draw on Polish help to defeat the

38. Luka Myshuha (1887–1955), a lawyer by training, spent his whole life in Ukrainian community work. He served briefly in the diplomatic service of the Western Ukrainian People's Republic, and from 1926 was on the editorial board and editor of the Ukrainian National Association's daily, *Svoboda*. He came to be highly regarded for his work and commentary. Nazaruk's initial assessment of Myshuha, written privately to Lypynsky, described Myshuha

Soviets failed. The Western Ukrainian government in exile headed by Petrushevych, hoping for recognition well into 1925, even toyed with the Ukrainian Socialist Soviet Republic, which made Lonhyn Tsehelsky, the official representative in United States, resign in protest around the end of 1921. Myshuha became Petrushevych's man in the US.[39]

In 1922 Myshuha had been instrumental in reorganizing the Ukrainian Committee, the outgrowth of Bishop Ortynsky's Rada, into an entity known as the United Ukrainian Organizations of the United States (Alliance). It was nominally headed by Rev. Volodymyr Spolitakevych and had a twelve-member board of directors, but Myshuha was its prime mover. The organization's headquarters were in the Ukrainian Community Hall in Philadelphia, a block away from the cathedral. The Alliance never achieved the status that the fraternal organizations had. Providence and UNA, both on a firm financial basis, were the real powers in the community affairs of American Ukrainians. Providence reflected the Catholic Church; UNA claimed to speak for all Ukrainians. The UNA establishment credited its organization with initiating the modern era in Ukrainian life in the United States.[40]

---

as basically honest but small minded, wary of upsetting the support of the "half-intelligenty" on whom he relied (Nazaruk to Lypynsky, December 22, 1924, in Lypynsky, *Collected Works*, 232). According to Nazaruk's October 15, 1924, letter to Lypynsky, Myshuha at the time was showing signs of possible cooperation with the Hetman movement. Writes Nazaruk: "I am intently carrying on a correspondence with him [Myshuha] for he would be a valuable asset [*zdobutok*]—loyal [*virny*], determined [*kharakterny*], and energetic [*rukhlyvy*] and quick-witted [*sprytny*], although he lacks a political education. Intelligent by nature. Solid and honest. We've been in correspondence for a while now" (ibid., 228). Nothing came out of Nazaruk's attempts to draw Myshuha to the conservatives, and the two became arch-polemicists. As their viewpoints diverged Nazaruk considered Myshuha's political views primitive and accused him of an inability to think in long-term goals, which ability he, Nazaruk, and the whole Hetman movement had. Once it was clear that Myshuha gravitated toward the nationalist wing of the Ukrainian political spectrum, Nazaruk's view changed drastically, as seen in a letter to Lypynsky, written in January 1926, "Myshuha is a total zero in political knowledge and thinking; he simply functions under the pressure of former President Petrushevych. Functions badly. I have a sense that Petrushevych dirtied himself [*opohanyvsia*], and Myshuha is his mirror image. Now Myshuha and his fellow villager Rev. Spolitakevych wrote a statement against Bolshevism. I doubt it was genuine," (ibid., 353).

39. Nazaruk to Lypynsky, March 26, 1925, wrote full of irony: "Petrushevych must have made Myshuha new promises, in the sense of 'Japan recognizes us' or something else of that ilk." Ibid., 311.

40. See Poniatyshyn, "Iz chasiv administratsiii eparkhiii," 110–14, 159.

As the community developed a central organization, the local Catholic parishes became even more politicized. There was much talk about who might be the new bishop. Rev. Joseph Zhuk, who had enjoyed high clerical positions in Europe and had emigrated to Canada in 1920, moved to Philadelphia in 1923. Those allegedly in the know about the Vatican marked him as the next bishop. Rumors proliferated.

By the time Bohachevsky arrived, a clerical culture, formed on Ukrainian civic traditions and American mores, had developed in the United States. The America Bohachevsky came to in 1924 was very different from the America Bishop Ortynsky met when he arrived in 1907. Still, Bohachevsky inherited all the problems that Ortynsky had encountered. The clergy faced particular difficulties: the congregations were not stable, since workers followed jobs; parishes in the United States were not homogenous; churches were more likely to experiment with the administrative structure and challenge the authority of the priest; non-Catholic Ukrainian churches were growing faster in the United States than in Europe, undermining some parishes; Latin-rite Catholic priests resented the strange Ukrainian Catholicism as the presence of Catholic priests of different rites who were not under episcopal discipline could undermine the consolidation of the Latin Catholic Church; and Orthodoxy remained a viable option for the dissatisfied. Some Ukrainian Catholic priests, moreover, viewed American Catholicism through European eyes, as a church lacking a scholastic tradition and cultural seasoning.

Contemporaries likened the situation in the Ukrainian Catholic Church in America to a wild jungle that needed clearing. The nuncio, Pietro Fumasoni-Biondi, was especially disturbed by the disorder in the Ukrainian Church in the United States. On January 16, 1924, he wrote that Poniatyshyn and Martiak lacked all authority, "and even people who are generally favorably well-disposed [to the church] are losing heart and are ready to go to another church."[41]

The buoyant and optimistic, forty-year-old Bishop Bohachevsky knew little of this story when he stepped firmly onto a New York pier on August 15, 1924. He would learn it soon enough.

41. AES, America, pos. 188–91, fasc. 35, p. 7. From a preparatory memorandum for Pope Pius XI.

CHAPTER 5

The First Steps of a
New Bishop

After attending the twenty-seventh International Eucharistic Congress in Amsterdam in 1924, in a show of concord the two new Ukrainian bishops sailed together on the *Mauritania*—Constantine Bohachevsky from Halychyna (Galicia) to the Ukrainian parishes and Vasyl Takach from the Carpathian lands to the Ruthenian parishes. During their talks on the Atlantic crossing, they worried that neither knew the United States or their eparchies. Takach was aware that he had supportive clergy waiting for him; Bohachevsky had little information on how he would be met. Both bishops presumed that all the necessary notifications of their arrival had been sent.

That was not the case for Bohachevsky. His nomination was still not widely known, since no one had expected the nomination of two Ukrainian bishops to the United States. The authoritative Catholic journal *Nyva* in Lviv announced the appointment of Takach as the bishop for the American church. There was either a lack of communication or an attempt to keep the arrival of Bohachevsky in as low a key as possible not only in the Vatican, but also within the Ukrainian Catholic community.

Poniatyshyn, the administrator of the Ukrainian Catholic Exarchy, surprisingly embarked on an extended visitation of the eparchy at the time of the expected arrival of the bishops. He did not leave an itinerary. When the apostolic delegate, Pietro Fumasoni-Biondi, informed the Ukrainian Catholics of the United States of the appointments of their new bishops by a letter dated May 26, 1924, Poniatyshyn could not be reached. Instead, Rev. Mykhaylo Kindiy on behalf of the chancery in Philadelphia, sent Bohachevsky an informal congratulatory letter with a reminder of their shared, fun-filled school days and a promise of special concern: "We would be greatly obliged if you send us precise information about the date of your arrival and the name of the vessel. . . . News about your appointment has been bandied around for a long time throughout America, [but] we got the official affirmation only today—I, as a Stryj native, am particularly overjoyed, because I know you from our Stryj school days."[1] The letter must have surprised Bohachevsky. It is reasonable to presume that he would have interpreted such a letter, written on behalf of the chancery as either a slight or a reflection of the informality of American mores. The courtesies of the time as well as church protocol demanded a more formal acknowledgement of his nomination from his new exarchy.

Because of Bohachevsky's unusual legal status, Takach handled the specifics of their travel. The Congregation for the Eastern Church informed the Roman Catholic bishops in the United States of the appointments, but not of the dates of arrival. Bohachevsky, meanwhile, presumed suitable arrangements were being made. Unintentionally, Takach's desire to do the right thing by formally visiting the bishops in Halychyna, postponed the bishops' travel to the United States. While the Ruthenians had already collected money for their new pastor's arrival, Poniatyshyn sent a circular to the Halychyna clergy informing them of the imminent arrival of the bishops only on June 23, 1924. He suggested that the Ukrainian priests donate at least $10 each as a welcoming gift for their new bishop, and send the funds to his office in Newark.[2] He then took another visitation trip.

1. Congratulatory letters to Bohachevsky from Ukraine were found in an unmarked file at UMAS in 2010. Cardinal Tacci, the secretary of the Congregation for the Eastern Church, informed Cardinal O'Connell of Boston of the appointment of the two Ruthenian bishops. O'Connell replied on June 31, 1924, that the two bishops would be warmly welcomed. Poniatyshyn wrote to the New York Roman Catholic Chancery on July 29, 1924, asking for more information on the arrival of the Ukrainian bishops. The Chancellor, Thomas G. Carroll, of the New York diocese replied that they "should like to have timely warning." CEC, Rutheni, f. 12658, p. 117 [Rigotti, 257]. Ten years earlier, in 1912, there had been a similar mix-up in the announcement of Nykyta Budka's nomination as bishop of Ukrainian Canada. See McVay, God's Martyr, 68–79.

2. The "Gift of Love" donations, published in the Eparkhiial'ni Visti, October 1924, listed the clergy donations averaging $10 each (Antin Lotovych gave $50 and Mykhaylo Pazdriy

The *Mauritania* reached New York Harbor on August 14, 1924. Since the Ruthenians knew the arrival date of their bishop, a welcoming delegation chartered a small vessel that kept the *Mauritania* company through its last afternoon at sea. A small Ukrainian representation joined in at the last minute, but their names have not been preserved. Appropriate speeches and prayers were shouted from the boat, and all present sang both the informal Ruthenian anthem "I Am a Ruthenian" and the Ukrainian "Ukraine Has Not Perished." After immigration and disembarkation, the formal welcoming ceremonies were held on the 14th Street pier of Manhattan at nine o'clock in the evening. Bishop Nykyta Budka from Canada; Monsignor Carroll, representing the vacationing Patrick J. Cardinal Hayes; Rev. Poniatyshyn, the episcopal administrator; and his vicar, Rev. Havryil Martiak greeted the two bishops and escorted them to a dinner at the Pennsylvania Hotel, some twenty blocks away.

Neither of the new bishops was in much of a festive mood. No one knew how the parishioners would take to the division of the parishes. For all their prayers of brotherhood, both bishops were concerned about potential flare-ups among their undivided faithful. Nor did the fact that the Ukrainians were in the dark about the welcoming ceremonies help create a closer bond. Nothing in Bohachevsky's behavior suggests that he accused Takach or his staff of ill will in their failure to inform the Ukrainians in a timely fashion of the bishops' arrival, or if indeed the fault lay with them.

Attuned to awaiting concerns, both bishops departed the very next day for their new sees. Bohachevsky made his way to Philadelphia on a train he would soon get to know intimately. He was accompanied by Bishop Budka. Bishop Takach was taken by his advisers to look at possible sites on which to build his diocese in northwestern Pennsylvania. Both Ukrainian bishoprics would be in Pennsylvania, where many Ukrainian Catholics settled. A Vatican plan for the Ruthenian diocese to locate in New York City could not be implemented.

Bohachevsky insisted that his formal installation be held on his first Sunday in Philadelphia, August 17, 1924, in the Cathedral of the Immaculate Conception of the Blessed Virgin Mary, which remained his see until his death. The church had been acquired by Ortynsky and blessed by Shep-

---

$25), and the special collection in churches averaged about $20. Poniatyshyn, Zhuk, and Kinash are not listed.

tytsky, and Bohachevsky drew comfort from that continuity. Its home-liness and absence of Eastern architecture did not trouble Bohachevsky even in his later years. Since there was no time for preparations for the festivities, no invitations were sent out. The chancery placed an announce-ment in the *Philadelphia Record* for the August 17 edition. There is no men-tion of Bishop Budka at the ceremonies, although there is a photograph of him and Bohachevsky dated August 1924 sitting in the garden of the Orphanage of St. Basil in Philadelphia.[3] Budka, a close associate of Met-ropolitan Sheptytsky, must have been a source of comfort for Bohachevsky during the first few days in America. It was his consecration as bishop that Bohachevsky witnessed in his first year of priesthood.

The cathedral, while a mere two miles from the heart of Philadelphia, hugged the sidewalk. The surrounding solid redbrick row houses were modest, a far cry from Lviv and dramatic Peremyshl. The houses were not set back. Even the bishop's residence had the requisite three marble steps straight from the sidewalk to the front door. The office windows were eye level with the passing crowds. The only patch of greenery was a little gar-den up the block that the Basilian nuns kept at the orphanage. The area was flat, the blocks evenly rectangular, and the din and dust constant. Bo-hachevsky accepted the site as it was and quickly adjusted to the surround-ings. He did not complain, and soon even gave up the bishop's residence to be used for a badly needed dormitory. But when later he looked for sites for schools, he searched for greenery and fresh air.

Bohachevsky's self-deprecating behavior on arrival did, in fact con-fuse the clergy, in much the same fashion that a century later Pope Fran-cis's housing choice shocked the Roman Curia. A certain degree of pomp around the person of the bishop is generally expected. The Ukrainian priests also looked for signs of personal sympathy, largesse, and hos-pitality from the new bishop. Sheptytsky and Ortynsky, after all (as the American press picked up at the time), had sported titles of nobility; Bo-hachevsky had the mere middle class "Dr." before his name. He had no private funds, and he presumed, quite correctly, that his new diocese was equally short. In contrast, the public (and this included the clergy) as-sumed that the bishop had money. They could not fully understand why

---

3. McVay, *God's Martyr*, 380.

he had chosen not to arrange a proper welcoming ceremony or at least wait to prepare a suitably festive installation.

Despite the lack of preparations, the bishop's installation was well attended, and even included an organized group of Lithuanians, who shared the Ukrainians' resentment of the Poles.[4] We know little about the ceremony, but we know that the new bishop wore his predecessor's exquisite silk and brocade vestments, which he continued to wear through the mid-1930s. The vestments were too long for him, so he folded them over his waist. Not exactly comfortable, but serviceable; and the new bishop was not going to waste money needlessly. Two photographs from the occasion—both taken by an amateur—were published in the 1934 Ukrainian Church almanac. In both, the too-tall staff covers Bohachevsky's face. Two altar boys hold up the bishop's mantle, which is also too long. The other photograph shows that, despite the haste, the cathedral was decorated and the crowd ample. At the entry doors, Bohachevsky is accompanied by one priest. In his sermon, the new bishop promised to continue the work of Bishop Ortynsky and professed his service to God, people, and the papacy. He established his scholarly credentials by a judicious use of quotations from the Scriptures. He stressed that he came to America through the agency of none other than the pope to "fulfill the will of the Successor of Christ, the Holy Father Pius XI."[5]

Unlike most Ukrainian immigrants to America, who thought their stay would be temporary, Bohachevsky arrived in the United States with a firm intention of staying in the country. He spoke not of coming to the United States, but rather "of settling with you, my dear and esteemed priests and faithful in this New World." In ascending Ortynsky's orphaned post, Bohachevsky asked for prayers to continue the pioneer bishop's work jointly

4. See Kasys Vidikavskas's note, "Lytovs'ka delegatsiia na pryvitanni Epyskopa Kyr Konstantyna," on the Lithuanian delegation at the greeting of Bishop Kyr Constantine, in *The Jubilee Almanac of the Ukrainian Greek-Catholic Church 1934* (Philadelphia: America, 1934), 114–15. While no editor of the almanac is mentioned, the title page reads, "Vydannia Yuvileynoho Komitetu Ukraiins'koii Hreko-Katolyts'koii Tserkvy u Zluchenykh Derzhavakh. Zakhodom o Volodymyra Lotovycha, sekretariia Komiteti [Publication of the Jubilee Committee of the Ukrainian Greek-Catholic Church in the United States. Through the efforts of Rev. Volodymyr Lotovych, secretary of the Committee].

5. *Eparkhiial'ni Visti*, October 1924, 1–2. Bohachevsky's pastoral letters had no title, but always had the full address to "The Reverend Clergy and the Faithful."

with the faithful. He left no doubt that his first duty was the salvation of souls of the faithful, which required a strong and effective church. In closing his remarks, he stated that he was looking forward to working with a free community that was, unlike its counterpart in Ukraine, unencumbered by outside pressure:

My duty is to serve the Lord God, foster His renown, [strive for] the welfare of our Holy Catholic Church, and to care for the salvation of the flock entrusted to me. I want to be a Good Pastor, and the good pastor always considers the good of his people who moved to a new homeland where, as in the old country, they love the Lord God and serve Him, because only then will [the people] be a great and renowned nation.[6]

The bishop's goals were clear-cut, and he thought that he stated them clearly. He wanted the community to know that his interest was the church and that this church was his link to Ukraine. He did not consider it necessary to stress his patriotism given all that he had gone through. The new bishop was young, energetic, and eager to learn, and ready to travel to meet his far-flung flock in person.

EPISCOPAL CONCORD

Bohachevsky and Takach saw the church as an autonomous corporation with specific goals. Above all, the Catholic Church was for them a communion of faithful practitioners, not merely a vehicle of tradition. They both considered the reinstatement of order in the parishes and discipline among the priests as their primary immediate goal. The new European bishops did not waste any time on preliminary niceties. Within ten days of their arrival in the United States, they took care of all the necessary ecclesiastical formalities. Bohachevsky and Takach held a formal meeting with Poniatyshyn, the episcopal administrator, and his vicar, Havryil Martiak, in the diocesan office at 818 North Franklin Street. The Ukrainian Catholic newspaper *America* reported that the bishops were joined by Valentyn Balog, the chancellor, and by several diocesan consulters: the Reverends Valentyn Gorzo, Myko-

6. Text in *Eparkhiial'ni Visti*, October 1934; and in Isidore Sochotsky, "The Ukrainian Catholic Church of the Byzantine-Slavonic Rite in the USA," in *Ukrayins'ka Katolyts'ka Mytropolia v Zluchenykh Derzhavakh Ameryky, 1 Lystopada, 1958*, ed. Miroslav Kharyna (Philadelphia: Archbishop's Chancery, 1959), 232–33.

FIGURE 5. FRANKLIN STREET BACKYARD, 1924

la Pidhoretsky, Lev Levytsky, and Maksym Kinash. Bishop Takach asked that both papal nomination *bullae* be read in the original Latin and in the Ukrainian translation.[7] The reading of the papal *bulla* formally established the two Ukrainian Catholic exarchates in the United States. *America* reported: "As of August 26 both bishops took over the administration of the heretofore single eparchy of the Ruthenian rite [*rus'koho obriadu*]."[8]

7. *America*, September 28, 1924.

8. Isidore Sokhotsky, "Ukraiinska Katolytska Tserkva vizantiys'ko slovians'koho obriadu v ZDA," in Kharyna, *Ukraiins'ka Katolyts'ka Mytropolia*, 229. Sokhotsky has the Philadelphia exarchate receiving 144 churches and 102 priests, while the Carpathians end up with 155 churches and 129 priests. In describing these events, I specifically use the terms "consultors" and "Ruthenian" as they are used in the *America* article written before the direct intervention of Bishop Bohachevsky in church and community matters; within a year, the

The appointment of two rather than one bishop for the Ukrainians in the United States should have troubled the Ukrainian secular community from the start. This was, after all, a community that preached a single united Ukraine, from the Carpathian Mountains to the Don River. Instead, the Halychyna intelligentsia tacitly accepted the establishment of a separate Ruthenian diocese. Overall, the secular community took on a waiting strategy toward both bishops.

The two bishops traveled jointly to some parishes in which parishioners voted on their choice of exarchy. Other parishes made the decision without the bishops' presence. Discussions took place in each parish and did not lead to any organized altercations between the factions. The process proceeded peacefully, although often with rancor. In view of later developments, this relatively peaceful process was surprising. The division was not easy. It entailed people and property in each parish, since parishes included both Ruthenians and Ukrainians. The Ruthenians did not lay claim to the cathedral and nearby buildings, a noble gesture that left Bohachevsky with a financial situation he did not at first understand. According to church practice, an eparchy is established in perpetuity, but an exarchate could be viewed as an administrative stop-gap measure. As minority churches, however, exarchates can have a lengthy life. The bishops decided that the best way to delineate the two exarchies would be for the individual parishes to vote by a simple majority of the parishioners on the choice. It was a matter of self-identification—that is, whether a parishioner considered himself Ruthenian or Ukrainian—which for both bishops meant the same nationality but different administrative units. For many of the faithful, unfortunately, the matter was not so simple. Most likely, both bishops saw the division as a temporary measure that would eventually be adjusted. They both were aware of the attendant complexities and both tried to minimize disruptions.[9]

Both bishops needed peace to develop and grow into the unity that all desired. Relations between the two bishops remained friendly, but never close. They realized that they faced the same difficulties and that little

---

use of these terms would be considered "Polonizing tactics" of the bishop. The two administrators were relieved of their posts on September 1.

9. I have not been able to find much specific information on the actual division of the parishes, except for a few lists of the 140 parishes that Bohachevsky compiled in 1931.

would be gained from rivalry between them or from pressuring communities to join this or that eparchy. The dual appointment was a seemingly workable arrangement—by separating the Ruthenians from the Ukrainians, it had removed one of the internal tensions in the Ukrainian Catholic Church. It took more than a decade for both exarchies in the United States to develop into well-structured administrative organizations.

Bohachevsky had been warned that the exarchy was in complete disarray. He was told to salvage as much as possible of the holdings of the church as quickly as he could. Given Sheptytsky's criticism of the Ukrainian-American clergy, Dionysius Njaradi's unwillingness to take the appointment, and the negative assessments of the Congregation for the Eastern Church, Bohachevsky expected immediate problems. He may or may not have been familiar with criticisms of Ortynsky's tenure, specifically Ortynsky's difficulty in maintaining discipline among his priests. He thought he would face some opposition from the more radical Ukrainian Americans. Instead, the crowds that came out to see him during the first months of his tenure pleasantly surprised him. The new diocese, even halved by the agreement with the Ruthenians, did not seem as bad as it had been suggested. The novelty of the experience buoyed up his innate optimism, which would be quickly tested.

The Ruthenians in the United States turned their attention to local affairs. The clergy briefed Bishop Takach and began building his residence and cathedral. In contrast, many of the Halychyna clergy in the United States, including Rev. Poniatyshyn, were deeply involved in raising awareness for the Ukrainian cause in addition to raising funds for the homeland. They had demanded a bishop to replace Ortynsky but did little to prepare for the new bishop's coming. Presumably, they felt that since the residence and the cathedral already existed, there was little for them to do before the new bishop arrived. There was a general presumption, quite false, that the bishop would have funds to care for the entire flock.

Upon arriving, Bohachevsky began travelling through the country to get a sense of America. He found out quickly that that ownership issues had to be handled locally, parish by parish. Once the parishes determined which exarchy to join, the bishop's office had to make certain that they were duly incorporated. Legally the bishop was to be sole owner of all real estate, including the churches the individual communities established.

This caused major difficulties. Titles and responsibilities were sometimes ambiguous, communities tried to control their priests, and the exarchy did not have funds to regulate salaries. Some communities locked out priests they disliked. There were times when trustees turned off light in the buildings, especially for married clergy with children, as a cost-saving measure. There were cases of parishioners refusing to accept a priest with a family. The correspondence of the priests among themselves presents a tale of woe concerning their treatment by the trustees.

Bohachevsky understood that without a stable and predictable central administration the parish clergy would be vulnerable to outside pressures. Without the moral and financial support of such an administration, parish priests were dependent upon the good will of congregations whose lay leaders might want to control church finances. The bishop hoped to overcome the pattern of outside control, fully understanding that this challenge meant self-reliance. Lacking funds, Bohachevsky would have to rely on the church itself. Thus, the very institution he was to create, strengthen, and lead was to be his major source of revenue as well as support. To that end, he needed to have full control over the finances and properties of the church. As it was, he could not even get reliable information on the church's financial state.

Very quickly, Bohachevsky realized that things were not how he saw them at his first visit. The Ukrainian Catholic Church in the United States was on the verge of bankruptcy and faced the loss of cathedral property. Many parishes were badly mismanaged. The bishop struggled to understand the system of ownership of the churches from the various examples that were presented him as well as from his travels. He learned that living conditions varied from parish to parish. Some priests subsisted on boiled potatoes; others bemoaned the absence of decent restaurants. All needed money, and all worried about their future. Many complained about the location of their parishes and the nastiness of their parishioners. Some priests wanted to be transferred; others preferred remaining where they were. Most priests were good men, but the training they received at Lviv in missionary work for America was woefully inadequate.

Knowing that the clergy in the United States did not receive any monies from the state (as was the case in Europe), Bohachevsky wanted to make certain that each priest had information on insurance policies available to the clergy in the United States. Earlier attempts of the clergy to create self-help cooperatives had failed, so the bishop recommended that the clergy buy into an insurance cooperative plan developed by Rev. Lev Chapelsky through the Omaha Nebraska Clergy Casualty Company. A 75 percent participation would ensure retirement benefits for all priests in the diocese.[10] For all their complaints, however, few priests availed themselves of this insurance since many preferred private arrangements for their old age. This proposal did not garner even the minimum necessary support, and the fate of aged clergy remained on the agenda of the diocese long after the proposal was forgotten.

As the bishop traveled through his parishes, he was impressed not by America's promise, as he had expected, but by the poverty and lack of education of his own congregation. Optimistically, Bohachevsky at first followed up each visitation with personal letters separately to the pastor and to the congregation. The faithful were generous, often at the cost of their families, but the lives they led had little prospect for advancement. The Ukrainian-American community, long accustomed to supporting the old country, was now faced with representatives of various, and for the most part conflicting, Ukrainian national, religious, and political goals. Requests for money grew, even as the financial situation in the United States worsened. Bohachevsky had not been fully briefed on the financial situation of the diocese, and his first attempts to understand this situation were slow and halting. From the available evidence, it is hard to ascertain why this task was so difficult—part of the problem likely stemmed from the fact that there was no single person fully responsible for or even fully knowledgeable about the diocesan finances. Neither Ortynsky nor Poniatyshyn had the knowledgeable personnel and the necessary funds to run an effective financial policy. On the other hand, it is also possible that there were concerted or random attempts to subvert Bohachevsky by not providing him with the information he needed. In any case, it became obvious that Bohachevsky had inherited a financial mess.

The muddle included Bishop Ortynsky's will and his credit union. It was difficult to grasp the complications with Bishop Ortynsky's will and the claims of Ortynsky's brother and executor, Joseph. To make matters

10. Circular dated November 10, 1926, UMAS.

worse, the second executor of Ortynsky's will, Rev. Mykhailo Guriansky, the aged pastor at Olyphant, Pennsylvania, was too feeble to come to Philadelphia to explain the intricacies of the financial arrangements or to have the bishop visit him. As mentioned earlier, Ortynsky had set up a credit union without paying attention to legal considerations. He had invested the parishioners' money in what he thought would be solid Austrian bonds, but these could not be cashed in once Austria became an enemy of the United States. The money vanished when the Austro-Hungarian Empire disintegrated. When creditors began asking for their money, Poniatyshyn used the argument that nothing could be done until a new bishop was appointed. Bohachevsky's arrival removed this pretext and precipitated the threat of public disclosure of the illegality of Ortynsky's "bank." Were this to come to light, the scandal in the Ukrainian Catholic Church would drag in the entire Catholic Church. Understandably, the chancery did not want to advertise the details of the transactions. The Ukrainian cathedral was in debt by the then-astronomical sum of $120,000 for the buildings it occupied. Bishop Ortynsky had bought, by proxy through Rev. Maksym Kinash to forestall a price increase, a building for $12,000 in which the cathedral pastor and his daughter resided.[11] It was now in arrears and subject to foreclosure. The proxy's widow now threatened to take over the title, which was in her husband's name, and expose the ploy. The dead bishop's make-do approaches with limited resources violated both state and canon law. The potential scandal in the Ukrainian Church would reverberate in the whole Catholic Church in America.

Bohachevsky asked Kinash to provide a written report on the cathedral finances, which he received on October 13, 1924, five months into his tenure. In a two-page, single-spaced "Explanation of the matter of the sale of the house and the drawing of the debt," Kinash wrote: "After Ortynsky's . . . death there remained a debt to the people in the sum of $176,000, in addition to the bank debt of $12,000. The late bishop used the people's

11. Rev. Maksym Kinash, fourteen years Bohachevsky's senior, came to the United States in 1914 after spending two years in Canada. Kinash had been ordained in 1895 by Sheptytsky's predecessor, Sylvester Cardinal Sembratovych. Kinash contributed to Ukrainian newspapers and was extremely helpful during the episcopal interregnum. Nazaruk, however, in a letter dated April 1, 1926, accused Kinash of withholding useful information from Bohachevsky, Lypynsky, Collected Works, 387.

and [other parish] churches' 'deposits' to buy the church [cathedral], the cemetery, and eight houses. The ninth house was bought after the bishop's death and registered in the name of the administrator."[12] The memorandum revealed that the Ukrainian Catholic Church was the owner of almost half a block of real estate within a two-mile radius of the city hall but could not meet its payments on that mortgaged property. We do not know Bohachevsky's reaction to the memorandum, but Kinash initially fared badly with the bishop for claiming a church building as personal property. Rumors flew around the community about a secret letter written by Ortynsky, which may or may not have been another will, or perhaps some clandestine correspondence from Rome to Ukrainian priests in America. Bombarded with bits and pieces of background information he could not decipher, Bohachevsky was thrown into a financial vortex. His English was as rudimentary as his understanding of the American financial and legal structure, but he was astute enough to realize that he had not been given the full story from any one source or at one sitting—he had to piece it together himself. What he gradually discovered was that the Ukrainian Catholic Church in America had committed two violations of American law: engaging in illegal banking and real estate ownership under false pretenses. The situation was unpleasant, and for a legalist such as Bohachevsky it was intolerable. Fresh on American soil, he must have had nightmares that the entire Ukrainian Catholic population would be expelled. In desperation, he considered declaring bankruptcy and starting anew. The erstwhile diocesan legal counsel, William J. Kearns, steered the new bishop from this path. Why Kearns had not been contacted earlier remains a mystery.

It was Kearns, who had developed a personal friendship with Ortynsky and served as counsel for Poniatyshyn, who cut the Gordian knot of Ortynsky's financial legacy. He did so in a two-page letter dated September 25, 1925—that is, more than a year after Bohachevsky's arrival in the United States. In this letter, Kearns clearly spelled out the financial intricacies after Ortynsky's untimely death. The delay in providing this information to the bishop is difficult to understand, but the letter was prompted by

12. Victor J. Pospishil, *Final Tally: A Report on the Unremarkable Life of a Catholic Priest in the Twentieth Century* (Matawan, N.J.: self-published, 2001).

Bohachevsky's attempt to hold one of Ortynsky's executors responsible for a debt of $25,968.50 and to probate the will.

Kearns explained to Bohachevsky that a review of Ortynsky's will would result in a scandal of major proportions for the whole American Catholic Church, and not only its Ukrainian part. The lawyer impressed upon Bohachevsky the legal responsibility of the individual bishop for the diocesan finances and all other affairs.[13] The lesson was so persuasive that as late as the 1950s, Bohachevsky personally added up all the contributions that came to the chancery, regardless of their size. After Kearns's explanations the bishop had a better footing on the shaky ground that was his new diocese. Rev. Merenkiv, in a personal letter to Bohachevsky written sometime later, reaffirmed the bishop's financial rights.[14] The bishop's immediate financial task was to make certain that all church property was legally owned by the diocese, that is, his own hands. He was, after all, responsible before God and the law.

Bohachevsky dealt with the finances, although he was not used to such sums. He learned the economic needs of his eparchy quickly, but at the same time he could not forget the situation at home. As 1924 drew to a close, he managed to send Metropolitan Sheptytsky $478.89 from what should have been his salary. He added a request that the Lviv chancery acknowledge the received sum. In addition, he sent his mother her monthly $5.[15]

As Bohachevsky delved into the legal and financial status of the eparchial properties, he uncovered other irregularities that threatened the existence of the church. This forced the bishop to take executive actions

13. Kearns to Bohachevsky, September 25, 1925, UMAS. Thanks to Rev. Ivan Kaszcak for finding it. Kinash had expected that by the time of Bishop Ortynsky's death all the eight houses should have been paid off, the debt to the congregation to have been reduced to $21,000, and the debt to the bank to $13,000. On closer study, however, Kinash found that only $70,000 remained of the original $176,000 worth of deposits. The remainder Bishop Ortynsky had invested in Austrian stock, apparently unbeknownst to his advisers. There was a danger of a run on the deposits made to the Ukrainian Catholic Church, as indeed the public began to demand the money they had deposited. Fortunately, Joseph Ortynsky, the late bishop's brother, used the insurance money that should have been his to bail out the church and a scandal was averted. I have not had access the financial records of the church and base the above on Kinash's letter.

14. Merenkiv to Bohachevsky, December 1, 1926, UMAS.

15. The money was divided into $262 for orphans and Catholic schools, $132.51 for invalids, and $84.38 for Ukrainian grammar schools. UMAS.

to prove his adherence to U.S. law in running the church: he suspended a number of priests and fired Dmytro Shtohryn, a trustee of the Providence Association. In response to these actions, *America* published several articles that, in vague terms, questioned the new bishop's actions. The popular voice of the Ukrainian Orthodox Church in the United States, *Dnipro,* was more direct, writing about: "The vassals of Rome—the Pole Sheptytsky and the uneducated clowns in *America* who can't write proper Ukrainian, or any other language for that matter . . . and now the new bird, Bohachevsky—they are resorting to U.S. law, to bailiffs and sheriffs, to get their churches back."[16]

The lesson Bohachevsky learned from this predicament was to make certain, as quickly as possible, that church holdings be legally entrusted to the church. Thus, during his visitations and even without them, Bohachevsky collected all liens on each of the churches in his diocese and tried to have the churches registered in his name, a move that would legalize church holdings. He began checking that churches and church organizations alike adhere to existing legal practices.

The chancery office, as we have seen, was run from both Newark and Philadelphia. It was understaffed. Its doors were open to all without any appointments, making it noisy and very informal. Routine matters were often disregarded because of emergencies that proved false or of little consequence. Taking the hierarchic administrative structure of the church for granted as a precondition for order, Bohachevsky began to work on creating a stable, predictable administration. Later celebratory literature would present the picture of a determined forty-year-old cleric marching head on towards his next assignment.

Bohachevsky considered his priests to be his independent co-workers in a joint enterprise, and eventually they all were. He changed the administrative structure of the Philadelphia exarchate. He managed the central office—the chancery and its staff. The effectiveness of the whole enterprise—the church, in common parlance—was dependent upon local activities and the leadership of the clergy. It took the bishop and his helpers a little under a decade to establish the necessary conditions and links in and among the parishes to get the exarchate to function well.

16. "Nechesni pakholky Rymu" [Wily serfs of Rome], *Dnipro,* February 13, 1926.

Bohachevsky's major problem proved to be internal opposition to his appointment, which he at first refused to recognize. He refused to admit publicly that there were priests in the exarchy who would not reconcile themselves to his appointment. The bishop's approach and personality made the road to his ultimate success difficult and slow. He considered his administrative approach self-explanatory, rational, and obvious. He was not adept at explaining his actions and felt that he did not have the luxury of time to argue his case at length. He simply saw the threat to the existence of the Ukrainian Catholic Church in the United States and tried to eradicate it.

The bishop realized that his quick actions to institute a highly structured administrative order, even though effective, were not welcomed. But he firmly believed that quick action in the first months of his tenure would be more likely to assure compliance than Ortynsky's gradualism. He surrounded himself with priests who shared his opinions on structural reform: Within a few months he appointed the Reverend Stefan Vashchyshyn as chancellor, and put reverends John Kutsky, Anton Lotovych, Ivan Ortynsky, Pavlo Protsko, Oleksander Pyk, and Lev Chapelsky on his advisory board. Except for Vashchyshyn, these were all relatively young priests. The elder priests resented the appointments.[17]

THE MISSIONARY BISHOP

The bishop made two dramatic decisions within three months of arrival. The first was financial: the bishop would be fully responsible for all church finances, church property would be held legally by the exarchy, not by the various committees. Collections made on church grounds had to be approved by the bishop, and monies collected for Ukrainian causes had to go through his hands. The second concerned spiritual matters. Bohachevsky reinstituted the Lviv archdiocesan regulations requiring the

17. Vashchyshyn (1876–1928) came to the United States in 1909 from the area around Sokal, which at the time was part of the Peremyshl diocese. Ivan Kutsky (1885–1944) came from the Lviv diocese to the United States in 1913; Antin Lotovych (1882–1949) came from the Lviv diocese in 1912; Pavlo Protsko (1889–1949) came from Peremyshl to the United States in 1922, Oleksander Pyk (1884–1938) came from Lviv in 1914 (chancellor, 1927–37]; Ivan Ortynsky (1883–1946) came from the Peremyshl diocese to the United States in 1913.

periodic testing of the clergy on their knowledge of the dogma and regulations of the church, a practice that had lapsed in the United States.[18] The first decision alienated the various groups that collected donations for their causes in the churches; the second threatened the complacency of the priests. It would have been awkward to protest Bohachevsky's compliance of a Sheptytsky regulation. But the community could openly protest the celibacy requirement for posting in the United States, and the calendar issue (Julian versus Gregorian) always sparked a meeting.

Celibacy was a nonissue for Bohachevsky. The papacy had already spoken on this matter, and in Bohachevsky's view, *Roma locuta, causa finita.* That he personally felt celibates were better priests made it easier for him to live with the regulation. But he had no trouble working closely with married priests. The calendar was another matter altogether. The decision on which calendar to use—the old calendar introduced by Julius Caesar in 46 B.C. or the new one approved by Pope Gregory XII in 1582—remained one of the most contentious issues for Ukrainian Catholics. This was and still is a topic on which the whole community, Catholic or not, feels competent to comment.

Bohachevsky personally preferred the old Julian calendar. For him the calendar was a tool, similar to a wheel or a ruler. He quickly realized that its continued use within the American economic and educational system created a major hardship for practicing Ukrainian Catholics. Even Sheptytsky and the clergy in Halychyna had been considering the need to bring the Ukrainian Catholic Church in line with the calendar that was in use worldwide, but they could not because the Ukrainian public tended to identify the use of the Gregorian calendar with attempts to Polonize the population.[19] There was no such impediment in the United States; on the contrary, there was mounting pressure among Ukrainian Catholic parishioners to change the calendar to conform to life in America. Bohachevsky, although a traditionalist by inclination and conviction, could defer to the people's choice. He agreed that each parish, by majority vote,

18. On November 1, 1924, Bohachevsky in an eight-line statement marked "No 469. Ispyt konkursovy dotychno nauky [Periodic examination on scholarship]" merely reaffirmed the validity in the United States of the Lviv regulations of 1891 concerning the periodic assessment of clergy qualifications. *Eparkhiial'ni Visti*, November 1924, 5.

19. PKEL, minutes of May 8, 1925.

could determine whether to continue using the current calendar or change to the new calendar. He promised, however, that the cathedral would honor the Julian calendar if there were even a single traditional parish left in the diocese.[20]

From his very first days in Philadelphia, Bohachevsky insisted on adherence to regulations, routine, and order that most found too rigid. He personally maintained all documentation related to bringing priests from Europe to the United States. He did not want his diocese to become a haven for illicit clerics or charlatans who were flocking to America from crumbling empires in the Near East and Eastern Europe. Lacking a secretary, he carefully wrote his first official letters by hand, agreeing that this or that priest should come to the United States. He insisted on proof that the immigrant priest had his home bishop's permission for the move.[21] In his early optimistic first months, Bohachevsky announced that each Thursday would be an "open-door time" for anyone who had church business with the bishop. He had to modify this practice because of abuses.

Throughout his inaugural year, the bishop dealt with legal and personnel issues involving the clergy and faithful. He was always careful to stress that he would build on Ortynsky's legacy and that he was of one mind with the church in Halychyna. Recognizing the vastness of the United States and how scattered the Ukrainian Catholic faithful were, he hoped the clergy would keep him informed and the congregations engaged. Bohachevsky commended Poniatyshyn's resumption of the publication of *Eparchial News*. This publication was to link all priests and provide them with useful and necessary information. It also charted the development of the diocese and served as a major venue for the bishop's pastoral letters. Bohachevsky presumed the good will of the priests and their understanding of his vision. He misread many of the priests, however, especially in how they perceived his initiatives. For instance, when presented with a suggestion, the bishop invariably countered that the speaker should follow up on his idea to see if it worked. He came to use this phrase often, not realizing

20. This decision served as a basis for accusing Bohachevsky of Latinizing the rite as late as the mid-1960s. See the Volodymyr Kubijowych-Danylo Bohachevsky polemics, Danylo Bohachevsky, *V im'ia pravdy: Peredruk stattey z Shliakhu* (Philadelphia: Apostleship, 1965).

21. See Archiwum Panstwowe w Przemyslu, Archiwum Biskupstwa Grezko-katolickiego w Przemyslu, 1921–46, f. 142 (5339).

that some took it as a rejection of the idea rather than its encouragement. They wanted the bishop to develop a plan of action for the proposed idea, to take it over and implement it. The bishop, however, expected the priests to take chances with their own projects. He did not communicate this sentiment clearly, and some priests tended to await instructions from above.

The pope had specifically charged Bohachevsky with establishing a seminary for his exarchy as quickly as he could. The bishop shared that view because he saw that America needed local priests. The realization that the Ukrainian Catholic Church had no funds with which to build the schools it needed transformed Bohachevsky into a missionary priest and changed the way he lived.

While still in Rome, Bohachevsky had corresponded with an Austrian colleague about the possibility of cooperative projects on clergy education. Once in Philadelphia, all Bohachevsky found of the seminary were some young boys, badly housed in the overcrowded orphanage (run by the Basilian nuns), who attended high-school classes in Roman Catholic or public schools. He wrote to his older Innsbruck colleague, who had requested a photograph of the Philadelphia seminary, that much still had to be done and he would have to wait before any joint projects could begin. He did not mention the photograph—what was there to photograph? Bishop Bohachevsky could do little. And he did what little he could, which had dramatic consequences for the way the bishopric was run. Bohachevsky changed the image of the bishop from lord bishop to missionary bishop. He realized that his exarchy was, after all, still not organized. It was still a mission territory, hence he decided to live as a missionary.

Bohachevsky concluded that since the Ukrainian Catholic Church in America would survive primarily on the largesse of a poor, working-class congregation, he as the bishop, would do away with the expected trappings of episcopal life. He had no need for the nonessentials which he did not have—the silver coffee service, the twelve-piece dinner setting—he had no reason to entertain, he did not need a living room, a salon, a dining room. He had the office, and all his dealings would be in the office and in the churches. Until there was a congregation that could support the training of its priests in its own institution, Bohachevsky would live on the third floor of the chancery and rely on the nuns to feed him. If he were thinking of a public image, then most likely he saw one in the positive light of a selfless worker in Christ's new fields. And that is how the silent majority of churchgoers saw him. The Ukrainian elite, however, saw him as an uncivilized eccentric.

Soon after settling affairs with Bishop Takach, Bohachevsky had the bishop's residence refashioned into a boys' dormitory as a pro-seminary for the high-school boys. He moved his quarters into the rooms above the chancery, which he occupied until the mid-1940s. He used the chancery office as an audience room and the formal salon. The bishop's two spartan rooms did not even have a couch, and he slept on an iron bed. Neither the roof nor the windows were insulated, but he would not bother with renovations. He did not need the extra comforts. He would live a simple life until his people built the schools that would give them a foothold toward a better life.

Bohachevsky worked consistently, with determination, discipline, and careful attention to detail. He made certain that he himself lived up to the highest standards in all respects. There was no salon in which to chat with visitors over a cup of tea. His own needs were minimal, and he did not appreciate others spending money on his behalf. The desolation of his war-torn country and the poverty of his immigrant flock—the two critical issues always on his mind—justified asceticism as a way of life for him.

Bohachevsky's approach may be reconstructed from the pastoral letters in the monthly *Eparchial News*, published during the first turbulent years of his episcopate. One of his longest and most telling pastoral letters was written in his first November in the United States. Full of Church Slavonic quotations (immediately followed by the Ukrainian translations), the letter reflected the emotional oratory on which Bohachevsky was raised, a melding of religion and patriotism. The bishop acknowledged that there was much work to be done, expressing his belief that this would be accomplished with the help of God and with the support of the faithful. He stressed the importance of hard work and ennoblement through suffering. While praising the immigrants, the letter exhorted them to "value scholarship and wisdom" and to seek God and His truth: "Follow Christ, my nation . . . preach the word of God to places where neither our voices nor church bells can reach. [Preach] above all by your holy, exemplary life." The service ideal that guided Bohachevsky made him conscious of his duty to lead his people onto the path of moral betterment. He felt he could perform that duty with the help of God, who in the words of Paul to the Philippians (Phil 4:13) "makes it possible for me to achieve everything through Jesus Christ who strengthens me."[22] A statement such as this could easily be considered boastful.

The bishop's matter-of-fact oratory was easily misunderstood. His love of "my dear Ukrainian land, my beloved—even if poor and enslaved—Ukrainian nation [and] my family,"[23] is a strong undercurrent in all his pastoral letters, not its focal point. Having grown up in a multinational country, Bohachevsky saw no tension between being a Ukrainian and living an American life. He did not think it necessary to discuss the obvious. His many critics would use this lack of emotion as proof of lack of patriotism. Bohachevsky's patriotic rhetoric focused not as much on the love of the motherland, as on the need for hard work and sacrifice to help Ukraine achieve her full potential among nations. Ukraine was constantly on his mind, and he sent what he could to Ukrainian causes—wounded veterans and orphans highest on his list and the unadvertised recipients of Bohachevsky's welcome funds. In connection with this, he issued a directive to hold a collection for the needy in the home country—"The anniversary of the November 1 proclamation of an independent Ukraine in Lviv" provided a suitable occasion to raise funds for the needy in Halychyna—"to fulfill your Christian and national duty . . . the old country is asking us for help, which we as good Christians and sincere Ukrainians cannot refuse."[24] Marking an anniversary of the proclamation of the Western Ukrainian Republic in 1927, Bohachevsky called on young men and women to dedicate themselves to their nation by joining the religious.[25] At the same time, however, he realized early on (and to a greater extent than did his fellow Ukrainian Americans) that unless the Ukrainian

22. Eparkhiial'ni Visti, November 1924, 4 and 5.

23. First pastoral letter, Eparkhiial'ni Visti, October 1924, 1–4. Bohachevsky's pastorals did not have titles, at best there was a reference to the holy day or other occasion for it. The first one began with the listing of his formal title, "Constantine Bohachevsky, Dr. Sacred Theology. By the grace of God and the blessing of the Apostolic See Bishop for the Greek-Catholic Ukrainians from Halychyna in the United States." He continued with the traditional in Halychyna greeting, "To Reverend Clergy and Faithful: Peace and Apostolic Blessing."

24. Ibid., 11.

25. Katolytsky Provid, October 1927.

immigrants in the United States became educated and thus able to reach a better standard of living, help from them would be only a pittance of what was needed. His greatest task was to balance the two demands: tending to the needs of his flock in the United States and mustering support for a beleaguered and desperate Ukraine. His iron will kept romantic sentimentality at bay, though no doubt contributing in the long run to keeping even potential supporters at arm's length.[26]

COMMUNITY PRESSURES AND
GROWING DISCONTENT

In the fall of 1924, not long after Bohachevsky arrived in America, protests of Polish misrule in Halychyna escalated into terrorist acts. One faction of the emerging Ukrainian nationalist movement gravitated from political protest into assassinations. Initially, there were no leaders, but within a few years, the movement transformed itself into a centralized Organization of Ukrainian Nationalists, which in turn splintered within a few years. Although ostensibly unrelated to our biography of the new bishop, the first years of his tenure were fashioned by the glow of the distant burning fields, the image of the suffering Motherland, and the pull of popular sociopolitical currents on the faithful. Frustrated by the failures of diplomacy, Ukrainian youth in Halychyna applauded individual terrorist actions that the church condemned. Bohachevsky's clerical colleagues in Halychyna shared their concern about the radicalization of Ukrainian political life. In the United States, conservatives such as Osyp Nazaruk saw the dangers of a leaderless movement spiraling either into anarchy or authoritarianism. Others, among them Luka Myshuha, supported such activities as a legitimate response to illegitimate actions and a way of mobilizing the youth. All Ukrainian political factions expected that it was the duty of the American Ukrainian community to support their move-

26. Even as late as 1948 he permitted himself only a fifteen-minute first meeting with each surviving brother and his family when they came to the United States. He could not trust his self-control, and he did not want to break down, even before family members. Only a handful of priests saw his tears. Rev. Hrynyck recalled the bishop crying for lack of better conditions for his seminarians, and Rev. Tarnawsky apparently shared some of his intimate moments with the bishop with my father, Danylo.

ments.[27] Other tensions followed, sparked again by the émigré community's view of the church as a public, quasi-political entity and its bishop as a potential instrument for strengthening one political view over another. Most of these leaders consistently considered their own political goals of the moment far more pressing than the growth of the church. They resented the bishop's control of church finances, and his failure to adjust his schedule to suit the needs or wishes of the community leadership. The emerging Ukrainian-American civic organization, the Rada that had been founded by the clergy, had become a gathering place for the leadership of the fraternal societies and the political groups. It called itself the Alliance (Obyednannia). Some of its leaders tended to view it as the arbiter of Ukrainian-American causes, and therefore all organizations, including the Catholic Church, should defer to its schedule and its assessment of immediate activities.

The bishop, from his first step on American land, considered the church independent of civic control. That did not mean abandonment of the "Ukrainian cause"—only its pursuit on the terms of the church. On this point, the tone was set when Bohachevsky would not cancel a scheduled dedication of a new Ukrainian Catholic Church in Stamford, Connecticut, on October 28, 1924, to attend an Alliance congress in Philadelphia. The bishop sent his greetings and statements of support, but his absence was viewed as a snub to the organization and even to the community.

The bishop made a schedule and adhered to it. Some activists in the community resented his absence from rapidly arranged community gatherings. Bohachevsky felt that there were few public functions at which his presence was imperative. Moreover, he did not want to place himself in the awkward position of being at the beck and call of community leaders, something his predecessor Soter Ortynsky had done almost routinely.

27. In a letter to Viacheslav Lypynsky, dated October 5, 1924, Nazaruk linked Myshuha and Evhen Reviuk, the editor of *Svoboda* in New Jersey, to the Ukrainian right-wing radicals: "The point is that these youths in the home country who believe that they will save the Ukrainian 'state' with this sort of 'struggle' want money from here [the United States]. The psychosis is so strong that even very serious persons (obviously I cannot entrust their names to the mails) have been swept by it." Nazaruk to Lypynsky, October 5, 1924, in Lypynsky, *Collected Works*, 221.

Bohachevsky wanted to be informed of the agenda of all meetings that he was expected to attend. Because community meetings were often called at the spur of the moment, the standing request for a preliminary agenda was enough to cause some meeting organizers to question the bishop's love of Ukraine.

In the 1920s, Ukrainian nationalism was closely linked to the then-popular school of democratic socialism and bore no stigma of social extremism. In Eastern Ukraine, Ukrainian nationalism had been strong enough to force the Bolsheviks to create an ostensible Union of Soviet Republics rather than one unified Russian state. Thus, the Soviet Socialist Republic of Ukraine was formed. Ukrainian political parties differed in their assessment of how to deal with that state. Ukrainian immigrants in America—undereducated and underpaid—were prime targets for communist propaganda. Communist public relations on behalf of the new regime in Ukraine were carried out by such effective activists as Myroslav Sichynsky, who had escaped to the United States after assassinating Governor Andrzei Potocki, and Nadia Surovtseva, who made a special trip to the United States to agitate among the Americans for support of the Soviet State. For a time, even the Western Ukrainian Peoples' Republic, which Myshuha came to represent, was flirting with the Ukrainian Soviet state. In contrast, Bohachevsky, like his brother-bishops in Halychyna, was very concerned about the spread of leftist, materialist ideologies among the Ukrainians. Bohachevsky's political predilections were conservative, and his preferred *modus operandi* was the use of legal channels.

Bohachevsky quickly became aware that the Latin-rite church in America was losing its half-hearted battle to preserve the ethnic characteristics of individual churches. In November 1920, the American archbishops jointly sent a strong letter to Rome noting their objections to ethnic considerations in episcopal choices: "It is of the utmost importance to our American nation that the nationalities gathered in the United States should gradually amalgamate and fuse into one homogeneous people and, without losing the best traits of their race, become imbued with one harmonious national thought, sentiment, and spirit, which is to be the very soul of the nation."[28] In the United States, Poles were not a threat

28. Fogarty, *The Vatican and the American Hierarchy*, 213.

to Ukrainians. The Eastern rite, with its independence from the jurisdiction of American, Latin-rite clergy gave the Ukrainian Catholic Church an advantage toward preserving their singularity. In Bohachevsky's eyes, the true enemies of Ukrainians in the United States were godlessness and materialism as well as the godless regime in Ukraine. It was these that he would battle in his pastoral work in the New World.

It is not clear how much Bohachevsky knew about the specific competing claimants to the position of Ukrainian Catholic bishop in the United States. He did not feel threatened by other claimants to the position and acted with certainty in the exercise of his episcopal power. Nor do we know if and how he worked to smooth the disappointments of such claimants as Joseph Zhuk, Petro Poniatyshyn, or Ortynsky's secretary, Volodymyr Petrivsky. He may not even have been aware of their expectations.

From the start, Bohachevsky's open frankness and his strict adherence to a timetable, not to mention his quick athletic gait, appeared strange, especially to the older clergy whose manners still reflected the cultivated taste of the prewar period. Some immediately decided that the bishop was aloof, and resented his goal-oriented efficiency. Most Ukrainian clergy in the United States nostalgically remembered the days before Sheptytsky's administrative modernization. Many expected an old-fashioned, benevolent, and kindly bishop who would commiserate with their difficulties over a pleasant meal and a glass of good wine. Instead, they got one who demanded more sacrifices and less small talk.

The small but hard-core intelligentsia was equally disappointed. They thought the bishop understood the primacy of political considerations over the church's needs. Instead, the bishop focused on the needs of the Ukrainian-American Church and helped only causes in the old country that he considered essential, the veterans and the orphans. The community, in turn, failed to be interested in Bohachevsky's scholarly exegesis of the faith. Nor would it respond to his attempt to move the poet-priest Markian Shashkevych to more prominent place in the national, secular iconostasis. In the early nineteenth century, this priest had preached and published in the vernacular rather than the customary Church Slavonic, bringing down ire from the conservative upper clergy at the Lviv Cathedral. In America, the lay organizations did not even show much interest in marking Ortynsky's memory, not to mention the mild-mannered Shashkevych, who died soon after his major publication appeared.[29] Many immigrants from Halychyna continued to be involved in the internal affairs of the home territories, supporting this or that cause or faction. Because the Ukrainian Catholic Church was the largest organization in the Ukrainian immigrant community, activist and civic organizations used church facilities for fundraising and even meetings. Few within the Ukrainian community realized the bishop's lack of personal resources, nor were they aware that the church and its parishes were in serious financial difficulties.

One reason the clergy knew little about Bohachevsky was that the information that the Ukrainian community in the United States received about events in Ukraine came from personal letters and from newspapers with spotty coverage. The papers focused mostly on Lviv. Events in Peremyshl (where Bohachevsky was posted before coming to the United States) were rarely covered. Nor was the church at the center of public attention; while the political fate of Halychyna was still debated, all else (including the church) was to some extent peripheral. Thus any information about him would most likely have come from the Lviv clergy, who would find no compelling reason to stress Bohachevsky's public activity. Moreover, the Ukrainian community was unaware of the degree of personal hostility that Peremyshl's Polish administration had directed at Bohachevsky and Kotsylovsky. The withholding of Bohachevsky's salary for almost two years by the Polish regime was certainly not common knowledge in the United States.[30] The American-Ukrainian clergy were, on the other hand, privy to rumors of disagreements on ecclesiastical matters, which were circulated in both lay and clerical circles, and were also influenced, to some degree, by the run-of-the-mill anticlericalism, which was still in fashion among the Ukrainian elite including, as unlikely as it seems, the clerical families. Relations between Bishop Kotsylovsky and

29. In February 1925, Bohachevsky lauded Ortynsky's achievements. He directed his priests to prepare sermons on Ortynsky and to carry out a special collection for the orphanage in the late bishop's memory. The secular organizations did not follow suit, although later various individuals would stress Ortynsky's public role.

30. See the July 2, 1924, report of the Wojewodstwo lwowskie—wydzial prezydialny to the Ministry of Religion and Public Enlightenment [Ministerstwo Wyznan religijnych i oswiecenia publicznego], Archiwum Akt Nowych, Warsaw, MSZ Syg. 5335 A, pp. 73–104.

Metropolitan Sheptytsky became increasingly strained, and Bohachevsky was linked to Kotsylovsky. The intelligentsia in Ukraine sided with Sheptytsky, and some of the animus against Kotsylovsky rubbed off on his former vicar. Since Kotsylovsky was criticized at home, Bohachevsky was fair game in America.

Other obvious problems compounded Bohachevsky's early tenure. Immigration officials noted that Bohachevsky spoke English. But his English was the result of a crash course in Rome and must have been rudimentary at best. His understanding of the American legal system was equally sketchy. He knew little about America, not even having read the popular German novels about American Indians. He never enjoyed clerical politics, and he continued to disregard popular politics. He feared that the church would be used by outsiders, and that made him very wary of offers of help. In all, he was ill-equipped for the complex situations that would soon demand his attention.

Bohachevsky had few reliable sources about the state of his exarchy or about the power configurations within the Ukrainian community. He presumed the exarchy would be able to function on its own, with the support of the faithful and the distant good will of Metropolitan Sheptytsky. When he arrived at Philadelphia, he was immediately faced with conflicting assessments about the Ukrainian community in the United States from individuals with vested business and political interests. He was continually told different versions of the same situation. He could not determine what was happening in his exarchy. Even his own brother Volodymyr came with Luka Myshuha, the leader of the moderate nationalists, not to offer their support to the bishop but to get paid jobs. Neither had the necessary qualifications, and both were rebuffed. Both took the rejection badly and made it appear as a rejection of cooperation with the Ukrainian community.[31]

The monarchist-conservative wing in the United States bid for cooperation was more refined. On the pretext that Stephen Hrynevetsky, M.D., a leading member of this wing, had a car, he and Nazaruk met Bohachevsky at the train station when the bishop first visited Chicago in October 1924. After a day of joyful community ceremonies—a huge throng at the church

---

31. The black sheep of the family, Volodymyr had been living in the United States for about a decade and a half. At the time, he ran a real estate business in Philadelphia.

that included two hundred white-clad, little girls and an organized para-military—the bishop met the monarchist delegation again at 11 P.M. It was, in some respects, an odd meeting, which began with Nazaruk chiding the bishop for delivering "not a sermon, but a nationalist rally speech" during the liturgy. Nazaruk spelled out the political situation to the bishop in two points—the first being that the conservatives wanted to cooperate with the church and the second being that the Hetman monarchist-conservative movement encompassed a broad Ukrainian community. The context of the conversation was Ukrainian rights in Europe, not the Catholic Church in America. The bishop's response was measured. He was a man of the church, and political activity was not his primary task. But the bishop could assure them that the Vatican had no objection to Ukraine's independence: "There is no opposition to a Ukrainian State. Now as far as the specific form of government [to support] we must see which way the people will go. The church will adapt itself either to a monarchy or a republic."[32] In writing to the chief ideologist of the monarchist movement, Nazaruk concluded that the bishop should be left in peace to build the church rather than be courted to become involved in political matters.[33]

Not all community activists were inclined to let the church develop at its own pace, however. The possibility of a Ukrainian state, or at least of autonomy for Ukrainians in Poland, was still real enough for the émigré Ukrainians to justify public action in America on that behalf. Many activists sought to draw the bishop and the hierarchy into their causes, which always gave primacy to current worldly needs rather than to religious growth or the needs of the church. All wanted the bishop to be involved in community af-

32. Nazaruk related the conversation to Lypynsky as if Bohachevsky were speaking. The Hetman faction did not want to participate in the formal greeting of the bishop so as to be able to maintain religious neutrality, especially since their leaders were Orthodox. But exigency prevailed: there were more Catholics than Orthodox even in the Ukrainian, monarchist stronghold in Chicago. Most likely, however, the major consideration in the decision on who was to meet the bishop was a very practical one—Hrynevetsky had a car, the pastor did not. Nazaruk to Lypynsky, October 15, 1923, Lypynsky, *Collected Works*. Nazaruk credited himself with convincing the bishop not to deliver rally speeches but to focus on religious matters in his sermons.

33. Nazaruk raised other issues—the need for schools, for a seminary, the level of the Catholic clergy. The bishop asked for a written set of recommendations and ended the meeting at 1 A.M. to meet with his clergy. That meeting ended at sunrise. Nazaruk was impressed with the bishop's energy, the priests, I suppose, less so.

fairs and the community to take part in discussing the affairs of the church.

The bishop set his mind to creating and maintaining a modern, streamlined office and efficient administration. He set up a rigid appointment schedule, and adhered to it, turning away both clergy and laity who had no appointments. He expected promptness and insisted on neatness in documents submitted to him. These policies seemed rigid and downright unfriendly to many of the immigrants, especially the priests, who were unaccustomed to such a structured way of doing things. To some priests, his matter-of-fact approach seemed curt, his energy aggressive, and the simplicity of his living arrangements miserly. At formal dinners in his honor, the bishop asked for modest meals, taking into consideration the needs of the mother country. The older clergy, remembering (albeit heavily sentimentalized) meetings with Sheptytsky, viewed Bohachevsky's formal approach to dealing with priests as inhumane.[34] But Bohachevsky was convinced that only adherence to procedure would protect his diocese from the chaos that engulfed it and from the petty immigrant squabbles.

Bohachevsky defined his role as a Ukrainian within the Catholic context. He never wavered in his endeavors toward the creation of a fully functioning Ukrainian Catholic Church in the United States, "which its parish churches, schools, seminaries, and libraries will defend."[35] Despite some of the clergy's passive resistance and generally covert questioning of his policies, Bohachevsky placed his hopes on the priests. He wanted them to be as excited as he was about his new diocese. He thought more of them would show initiative, embrace and expand the plans of reform, and be the fiery leaders of their uprooted faithful that they had promised to be. But many priests were exhausted, underpaid, and drawn in different directions. Some did not share their bishop's clarity of purpose. Instead, they came to him with complaints and expected his sympathy. Some of the older priests did not understand Bohachevsky's plans; others clearly resented his appointment in the first place. Bohachevsky began to rely on younger

34. The pace in America may have been faster, but then the disorder in the new land was also greater. Rev. Poniatyshyn, whose public role in establishing friendly contacts with American politicians was exceptional, had had severe difficulties in managing his clergy and finances. Thus in a letter to Bohachevsky, dated September 3, 1926, Poniatyshyn explained that he did not mail the Peter Pence because the donations were too paltry, UMAS.

35. Protsko to Nazaruk, April 14, 1937, UMAS.

priests, and brought in colleagues from Peremyshl. Bohachevsky quickly realized that not only the faithful, but even some clergy were ignorant of the tenets of the Catholic Church. He sought to remedy the situation by his own personal visitations to all his parishes and by retreats. He also made certain each issue of the monthly *Eparchial News* was published on time and provided informative literature on elements of the faith as well as current regulations. Under Bohachevsky's early tenure, the articles in the *Eparchial News* reminded the priests of the intimate relationship of religion to culture and of the duty of the clergy to ensure that their faithful understand how Christianity had historically been—and by implication continued to be—the defender of true learning as well as of social progress.[36]

Bohachevsky also tried to raise the self-confidence and prestige of the priests, to rekindle belief in the higher nature of their calling. In the November 1924 issue of *Eparchial News*, he presented his vision of the good priest, one who is constantly striving to better himself, who is diligent in the preparation of his sermons, who adheres to the customs of the Eastern rite, who is prompt and thorough. The bishop stressed that he was one with the clergy as he coaxed them into ambitions of self-growth. The title of the first direct article that Bohachevsky wrote to the clergy was "What Would the Diocesan Chancery Like to See in Each Priest," and the context focused on the importance of continued spiritual education and the fact that the bishop himself was a priest:

We priests graduated from theological studies, passed our examinations, but is this enough? Man must study until death, and priests must do so even to a greater degree, since a priest must teach others, provide a good example, and draw mankind to heaven. And how can he do that if he does not continue the study pertinent to his calling, does not take in the spirit of God, virtues and asceticism? We priests need to educate ourselves constantly; we must be spiritual lights, because God Himself demands that as well as does our nation for whom we work.[37]

In addition to the obligatory daily prayers, Bohachevsky recommended at least fifteen minutes daily of readings from spiritual literature. He suggested that the clergy not only order Ukrainian books and periodicals for

36. Such articles included a defense of religion as an essential human need, the cultural role of Rome, how Christianity could preserve humanity from cultural crisis, etc.

37. Bohachevsky, "Shcho Ep. Ordynariiat radby bachyty u kozhdoho sviashchennyka," *Eparkhiial'ni Visti*, November 1924, 7–8.

themselves, but also arrange for their sale in parishes. The bishop singled out *Bohoslovia* and *Dushpastyr*; the American *Missionary*, a Basilian monthly; and the Canadian *Redeemer's Voice*, published by the Redemptorists.[38]

Bohachevsky personally knew the tension inherent in the priestly profession—finding the balance between meeting the spiritual and civic needs of the congregation and finding time for one's own spiritual growth. While the role of the Ukrainian priest as the spokesman of the community was increasingly challenged, the community and political organizations nevertheless expected the Ukrainian Catholic Church in the United States to participate in public activities that others had defined on the presumption of shared common goals. Although repeatedly undermined, this presumption was rarely questioned. The clergy was often drawn into disagreements within the community that could develop into a disagreement between the pastor and the congregation.

To strengthen the connection between the bishop and the clergy, *Eparchial News* published articles on the relationship of the clergy to the bishop. One such article was penned by Rev. Myron Zalitach, a respected "old-timer" in the United States, and provided a historical background on the development of the position of the bishop. Stressing the close relationship between the bishop and the priest, Zalitach underscored that the bishop was simply a priest and that it was only with the growth of the church that the bishops had been forced to take on more administrative functions. Bohachevsky viewed this and similar articles as a means to create a camaraderie, to bridge administration and the spiritual development of the diocese as a unit.[39]

Also, in his first months Bishop Bohachevsky began to institute clerical discipline, rigorously and consistently. Even under Ortynsky, but especially during the administration of Poniatyshyn (who had to establish mission churches to prevent the takeover of communities by the autocephalous Orthodox), some Ukrainian priests behaved improperly. Bohachevsky's introduction of more rigid rules of clerical propriety, including the testing of the clergy, was seen as an encroachment by the

38. Ibid. *Bohoslovia* was published in Lviv by the seminary and by *Dushpastyr* in Uzhhorod.

39. Myron Zalitach (1876–1946) emigrated to Canada in 1916 and came to the United States in 1920; "Ditochi bratsva," *Eparkhiial'ni Visti*, October 1925, 10–12.

bishop's office. Nevertheless, Bohachevsky followed the practice of the home-country bishops and personally checked for cleanliness in the churches, being firm about what he perceived as an especially shameful practice—using the altar as a storage cabinet. Bohachevsky was a strict disciplinarian and expected his priests to live up to high standards, an expectation that many viewed as harsh and blind to local demands. On the other hand, there were those critical of Bohachevsky for readily accepting prodigals to the fold and for not disclosing reasons for the suspension of priests or the termination of other personnel.

Even as Bohachevsky sought to get his bearings in the new territory, the Ukrainian Catholic hierarchy in the home country continued to clarify some specifics of liturgical and sacramental practice and texts. During this time, the Ukrainian Catholic Church still focused on the nature of its own church vis-à-vis the Byzantine East and the Latin West. Although Metropolitan Sheptytsky kept a fatherly distance from the growing public discussion on vestments, rituals, and canonical texts, emerging periodically with a wise and moderating position, the bishops and canons engaged in increasingly public debate on celibacy, public devotions, the Sacred Heart, statues, and flowers in the churches. Such practices as devotions to Mary in May and the Sacred Heart of Jesus in June, as well as the installation of confessionals, which in the 1960s came to be derided as Western imports, were practiced in Western Ukraine and even personally promoted by Sheptytsky. Communion for children without the preliminary confession (an Orthodox practice) was rare in Catholic Ukraine (although at times practiced by Sheptytsky among intimates) and almost unheard of in the United States. All these issues—which can be viewed as complex or trivial, depending on one's sentiments—became objects of lively discussion on both sides of the ocean. In America, these discussions lacked the scholarly finesse of theological debates, but nevertheless dominated the Ukrainian-American public discourse. Bohachevsky, as one of the members of Sheptytsky's commission on the editing of the liturgical texts, was keen to rid the Ukrainian Church of Latin accretions. In this respect, however, he exhibited the same concern for people's sensibilities as he had in his decisions on the calendar. He was slow to remove statues, flowers, and even the Infant of Prague. He encouraged enclosed confessionals, explained elaborate First Communion ceremonies to honor the wishes of the congregation, and engaged in other such "Western" practices.

The relationship of the Eastern tradition with Western Catholicism was complicated by a lack of specificity in terminology: "Eastern" and "Catholicism" were still almost universally confusing, and there had been no useful results in efforts to define or redefine either. Both of Bohachevsky's mentors, Sheptytsky and Kotsylovsky, engaged in lengthy three-cornered polemics among themselves and with Rome, debating their respective interpretations of these terms and the greater matters they represented. Back in prewar Lviv, Bohachevsky had sided more with what came to be known as Westernizing tradition in the structuring of the church. A neat, hierarchic structure appealed to him.

The other side of the coin came to be known as the "Byzantinists," they chose to favor an idealized version of Orthodox tradition manifested more readily in liturgical worship than in public practice. Digging for the lost tradition stimulated both experimentation and different interpretations of textual variants. Still, both sides were within the confines of Catholic theology and both equally supported the uniate church. Eventually however, within the simplified American-Ukrainian context of the time, Bohachevsky could easily be portrayed as an avid "Latinizer," although he and Kotsylovsky pushed through significant "Eastern practices." For the sake of unity with the East, Sheptytsky was willing to adjust aspects of Catholic practice that earned him criticism for too sharp a turn toward Orthodoxy.

Public opinion was very much involved in what seems to us today arcane discussions on the versions of liturgical and other ritual texts to be used and the specifics of liturgical worship. The ingrained tradition of worship, yet equally ingrained varieties in its performance, contributed to the popularity of heated discussions on the specifics of worship. The topics seem obscure to the general reader, but the fact that there was dissention within the Ukrainian Catholic Church interested the Ukrainian intelligentsia. The interest had its echo in the United States where Roman Catholic ignorance of other rites within the Catholic Church manifested itself often as open hostility to Eastern-rite Catholics. The Ukrainian public often reduced the clergy to "Latinizers," who could be anyone whom one opposed, and others, who generally were simply viewed as "ours." This already simplified discussion among the Ukrainian laity in Europe, when transferred to the United States immigrant community—which was largely uneducated and not privy to the niceties of textual analysis of seventeenth-century manuscripts—led to simplification of the issues. Such philosophical discussions, once a matter of great interest to Bohachevsky, were now remote from the day-to-day operations of his American diocese and his current responsibilities.

Early in his tenure, Bohachevsky began almost weekly visitations to parishes, often related to pressing issues of property. But once these issues were addressed, he turned his attention to other aspects of parish workings. Chicago was one of the first Ukrainian communities that the bishop visited, twice in 1924, first in September and again in October. The city boasted one of the largest centers of Ukrainian diaspora and the largest Ukrainian church to date that was built in a traditional Ukrainian style. It was in Chicago that Bohachevsky became acquainted with the American Ukrainian conservative movement, as vibrant a force in émigré political life as the democratic movement. It was also in Chicago that Bohachevsky first met Nazaruk, who was at the time editor of a conservative Ukrainian newspaper and who apprised the bishop of the work of Lypynsky, the chief ideologue of the conservative Hetman movement.[40] Nazaruk hoped Lypynsky's scholarly works would persuade the bishop, as the representative of the church abroad, to support the conservative movement. Bohachevsky demurred, citing official church policy. Nevertheless Nazaruk was impressed by the young Bohachevsky, whom he considered bright, lively, energetic, and hard working. This perception was reinforced by the bishop's formidable schedule while in Chicago—from confessions and services beginning at six in the morning to meetings with the public and clergy until well past midnight. Nazaruk's only reservation about the bishop was that he seemed too complacent about the public life of the Ukrainian immigrants and that his sermons had too much patriotic rhetoric. Nazaruk equally impressed Bohachevsky. He did not mind the journalist's rough edges, rather enjoying his frankness; and he relished Nazaruk's open enthusiasms and admired his prodigious output. This

40. Hetman Pavlo Skoropadsky was more of a figurehead, but the movement had its followers among Catholics, even though Skoropadsky was Orthodox. Later Bohachevsky would be impressed by the young Danylo Skoropadsky, the hetman's son.

mutual admiration was grounded in compatible interests and personalities: Both liked "straight talk," and both loved being active outdoors. They were workaholics, both masked their personal emotional vulnerability under the steely stoicism of the time, both knew dire poverty first-hand, and both were genuinely dedicated to God and their country.

Visits to other cities followed, but for all his travels, Bohachevsky's home was Philadelphia, the city most closely associated with Sheptytsky and Ortynsky and a major center of Ukrainian Catholic community life in the United States. The hub of Ukrainian political and religious life in Philadelphia was the section of North Franklin Street lying between Girard Avenue and Spring Garden Street. A mere block away from a largely Jewish shopping area, it was the magnet that drew all fragments of Ukrainian society into a proverbial town square—the cathedral and the bishop's residence on one end and the Ukrainian Citizens' Club on the other, closer to busy Girard Avenue, which was one of the city's most traveled arteries. Everybody knew everybody and everybody's business, and émigré politics on the local (and even would-be national) level were formulated here. The presence of a new bishop rejuvenated interest in church affairs, and the collapse of all political attempts at Ukrainian self-determination fed that interest. The consensus in the émigré community was that the Ukrainian Catholic Church was a political force as well as a religious entity. This view was one of several factors that would make Bohachevsky's work difficult.

As the bishop worked on strengthening the diocese, which he considered to be his primary duty, the secular intelligentsia scrambled for money for what they considered to be projects of primary national importance. The bishop did not consider the two to be at odds but made no special moves to curry favor beyond the Catholic community. Bohachevsky understood that at least for the immediate future, hopes for any Ukrainian political power would have to be deferred. Once the Vatican signed a concordat with the new Polish Republic in February 1925, the Ukrainian bishops in Halychyna, headed by Metropolitan Sheptytsky, would have to reconcile themselves to Polish rule. The Ukrainian bishops in Halychyna did pledge loyalty to the Polish Republic, but at the same dropped any discussion of updating the calendar. They also speeded up work on trying to establish a Catholic university in Lviv to offset growing cultural secularism and political radicalism.

Bohachevsky kept in contact with Ukrainian Catholic dignitaries in Halychyna and followed the political situation there closely. Rev. Theodosius Halushchynsky, the Basilian abbot, personally informed him of plans to educate the Ukrainian population to promote an understanding of Polish-Ukrainian relations and related social issues, as well as about the dangers of ideological thinking. Halushchynsky hinted at attempts to create a moderate political party in Halychyna.[41] The church did not openly support any of the Ukrainian parties and maintained the position that it should be able to work with whatever form of government the people in Ukraine would ultimately choose. Under Bohachevsky's tenure as bishop, the delicate balance between church and state was very shaky, and the experiment to create a Ukrainian Christian political organization was not tried in the United States.

It is safe to assume that given Bohachevsky's principled (and quite visibly hostile) relationship with the new Polish regime, he did not expect to have his patriotism toward Ukraine questioned in the United States. He felt no need to advertise his incarceration (which he could have easily presented as martyrdom for Ukraine), nor his bravery in the war. Proper behavior at the time frowned on any self-aggrandizement, but equally scorned lack of due civility. Bohachevsky was convinced that the life he lived made his decency and patriotism self-evident. Bohachevsky was, by nature, a humble and modest man. But he came from a conservative part of the world where society was deferential to authority, taking secular and religious titles seriously. Within this conservative framework, the highest clerics used their full titles and were accorded public deference, and Bohachevsky soon discovered that this conservative tradition had its uses. As the highest representative of his church in the United States, the new bishop, despite his personal modesty, used his full title in public, a custom that emphasized that his position (as contrasted with his person) was an important one, recognized internationally, and certainly valid within the national community. Following the accepted custom in Europe, Bo-

---

41. Halushchynsky wrote to Bohachevsky on August 25, 1925, detailing how the proposed organization would function. Presumably Bohachevsky had been involved in the early plans for this undertaking. UMAS. Halushchynsky's report on the committee to establish a Ukrainian Christian organization is dated October 6, 1925; TsDIA, Lviv, f. 358, op. I, spr. 42.

hachevsky prefaced his first public statements with his full title and the source of his authority: "By the will of God and the grace of the Holy Father." He also used all his formal titles in the first documents and leaflets he promulgated. The radical opposition, which was particularly active in the 1920s, viewed this behavior as upper-class pomposity, inappropriate in democratic America, and adequate proof of the bishop's aloofness. The young men, who felt themselves to be representatives of the whole Ukrainian society and its governments-in-exile, buoyed up by the freshness of American democracy, resented Bohachevsky's public manifestation of authority. For them, the papacy carried little diplomatic weight. There was, moreover, a vocal segment of Ukrainian-American society that resented Catholicism and saw even the venerable Metropolitan Sheptytsky in Halychyna as nothing but a Polish count whose brother was a Polish general.

The atmosphere in the six-block area of Philadelphia that constituted Ukrainian downtown during Bohachevsky's first winter in the United States was one of tense but undifferentiated expectation, and the backlash to Bohachevsky's tone, position, and antecedents was evident from the start. The Ukrainian-American newspapers covered few of the bishop's activities—visitations, sermons, and the consolidation of the diocese. It was as if a shroud of silence enveloped the bishop. Even *America*, the mouthpiece of the Providence Association, of which the bishop was the titular head, buried the few news items about him deep in gray-tone text on middle or back pages. Ukrainians in America, it seems, were more focused on the situation in Halychyna and on the mistreatment of Ukrainians. The newspaper published some world news but little information on local events, with the exception of concerts and amusing tidbits. Priests placed paid announcements to call attention to the visitations of the bishop.

As early as February 1925, barely six months after Bohachevsky's arrival in the United States, the radical *Ukrayinsky Holos* charged that the bishop was a Polish agent. A poem in a local Polish American newspaper, the *Gwiazda Polarna*, that welcomed Bohachevsky was enough proof. Others considered Bohachevsky's participation in joint services with the Latin-rite Catholics, some of whom were Polish-Americans, as treason.[42]

42. Ivan Hundiak, editor of *Dnipro* (Chicago), to an unknown recipient at *Ukrayinsky Holos*, Peremyshl, February 2, 1925, TsDIA, Lviv, f. 309, op. 2, spr. 113. Hundiak was a Catholic

Bohachevsky was accused of not reacting forcefully when he was referred to as Ruthenian rather than Ukrainian, although often that was done in local American newspapers that appeared after the bishop's parish visitations. Some in the community felt that the bishop should be more proactive in correcting the American press in this matter.

Public criticism of Bohachevsky continued along other paths. The bishop's emphasis on the special role of the clergy, specifically those who were celibate—which ensured that their dedication was not be diluted by domestic considerations—was taken to be Polish-inspired. *America*, the Providence Association's tri-weekly, published articles attacking clerical celibacy, pointing out that Bishop Takach consecrated married men and that Sheptytsky was doing nothing to stop the practice. Most Ukrainian Catholics, including the clergy, viewed married priests as the backbone of Ukrainian society, the incubator of its elite, the guardian of its moral fiber. However, priests in the United States were more aware of the financial difficulties of raising a family on a limited income and were less inclined to engage in the relative merits of married and unmarried clergy. But an article by the Belgian Redemptorist Rev. Leo Van arguing the advantages of the unmarried clergy elicited criticism to the effect that this priest, as a foreigner, could not grasp the importance of married men entering priesthood.

Concurrently, there were those who advocated the introduction of the vernacular into church services, something the Ukrainian Autocephalous Church had already done. The Catholic Church at the time did not use, and for the most part did not even discuss, the use of the vernacular. Bohachevsky opposed the move, knowing that a good half of the faithful considered English and not Ukrainian to be their native tongue. The new bishop's concession to modernity to permit the use of the Gregorian calendar fed the argument that Bohachevsky wanted to Polonize the Ukrainian Church. Bohachevsky was also accused of selling the Ukrainian

---

priest who became Orthodox and worked closely with the Orthodox Ukrainian bishop in the United States, Teodorovych. According to Nazaruk's diary, Poniatyshyn's contacts in Rome promised him that Rome would get Bohachevsky to "change his tune" (*perekrutiat*). Nazaruk was convinced that Poniatyshyn had a back channel to the Vatican. This part of Nazaruk's handwritten diary for December 1926 has been recently discovered under a wall insulation at the Ukrainian National Historical Archive in Lviv, where it survived undetected during the Soviet period. It has not yet been fully processed, as attempts are being made to collect as many of the diary's fragments as possible.

Catholic Church to the Vatican by Latinizing the Eastern rite and of taking money for his own purposes.

Considering the brutal treatment he had suffered in Poland and his own strained finances, all of these charges were so ludicrous that Bohachevsky refused to take them seriously. He pressed on with his extensive agenda, insistently focusing on the need to build, maintain, support, or enhance Ukrainian Catholic schools in the United States, from grammar schools to a seminary. He encountered resistance and fragmentation in the community. The debate on education pitted the proponents of after-school courses for children run by cantors against those who wanted full-time parish schools run by nuns. The community part-time schools were considered democratic and patriotic; the nuns were viewed as not educated enough to run effective schools. The bishop countered by bringing more capable and better-educated nuns to the diocese and by successfully promoting parish schools. And whereas the vocal public kept stressing the need for primers and basic education, Bohachevsky insisted on promoting higher education, including high schools, colleges, and especially a seminary.

Many in the Ukrainian-American intelligentsia wanted the Ukrainian Catholic priests to educate the children in Ukrainian and publish primers to be available to all. Religious education was secondary. In 1925, Prystay (who would later be quite critical of Bohachevsky) offered a rebuttal to this intelligentsia viewpoint by writing a series of articles criticizing community-run schools in the United States "because they are run mostly by committees of illiterates."[43] The nationalist wing in Halychyna raised the same criticism of the Catholic Church for not being patriotic. In Europe, however, the Ukrainian Catholic Church was merely one among many players; in the United States, quite the opposite, it was a major player in the Ukrainian community (and perhaps even the sole organized player) that alternately played with or against the intelligentsia.

Overall, Bohachevsky's early educational decisions were sharply criticized from their inception for being elitist and unpatriotic. The bishop ignored his critics and moved full speed with as many resources as were available into the construction of a whole system of Catholic education. The work of the Basilian nuns had impressed him from his very first days

43. *America*, January 29, 1925.

in Philadelphia. One of them had even written to him about how helpful Americans are, "indeed, they are a holy people [who] value and help the religious."[44] Within this context, Bohachevsky soon realized that the eparchy needed nuns who would run the Catholic schools that would ensure the continuation of the Ukrainian Church in the United States. He expanded on Ortynsky's initiative by increasing the number of Ukrainian religious, inviting the Basilians to take over some of the larger urban parishes. He worked closely with the Basilian nuns, serving as the spiritual guide for the American-born novices. He persuaded the apostolic delegate to permit the nuns to conduct fundraising in the Roman Catholic dioceses to help them maintain the orphanage. In this and other ways, the Basilian nuns became the bishop's major helpers in implementing his vision of the church in America.[45]

Another event in Europe in the spring of 1925 directly influenced the relations between the Ukrainian Catholic Church and the Ukrainian community in the United States. Under the terms of the concordat that the Vatican had signed with Poland, the Ukrainian bishops in Halychyna had to take an oath of loyalty to the Polish Republic. Obviously, Ukrainian Americans found the loyalty provision offensive. By what we can only call a vast stretch of imagination, the Ukrainian intelligentsia in the United States made Bohachevsky responsible for the Vatican's recognition of Polish authority in Halychyna and Volyn. The signing of the Polish-Vatican Concordat became further proof of the American-Ukrainian bishop's pro-Polish sentiments. American newspapers, including the major daily *Svoboda*, accused Bohachevsky of undermining Ukrainian organizations by not routing church-collected contributions through the Alliance and for Polonizing the Ukrainian Church by permitting Gregorian calendar celebrations. The bishop was loathe to defend himself from such ludicrous charges, but a defense was necessary. Somewhat unexpectedly, he found an aggressive defender in Nazaruk. This support was propelled by a curious series of events and nonevents.

In April 1925, Bohachevsky's first Easter in the United States, *America*

44. Sister Mytrodora, OSBM, of St. Basil's Orphanage, to Bohachevsky, July 7, 1924, UMAS.

45. Rev. Paul Protsko to Osyp Nazaruk, April 14, 1937, Lysty sviashchennykiv, TsDIA, f. 406, op. 1, spr. 25.

did not run the bishop's traditional pastoral letter. Instead, it published a patriotic editorial that linked the Ukrainian national revival to the resurrection of Christ.[46] The criticism of the bishop escalated when it became clear that he would consistently implement his decision to handle church finances, including the relief funds collected in the churches, thereby excluding the Alliance, the nominal central Ukrainian-American organization at the time. *America* structured its reporting from abroad to reflect critically on the thrust of the bishop's actions, alleging that he did not want to help the suffering home country. The leftist, as well as the vocal Ukrainian Orthodox press picked up on the criticism and directed it at the whole church structure. Local church committees and communities became involved in the polemics. The struggle often devolved upon the ownership of church property, with personal attacks against the bishop.

Bohachevsky sought to rally his priests by holding a retreat at South Orange, New Jersey, where Sheptytsky had held one during his first trip to the United States. He felt that the criticisms leveled against his policies were to be expected and would eventually diminish, as the church grew stronger. The retreat drew fifty-two clerics, but only Prystay, ten years later in a personal letter, remembered that his was the only voice pleading with the bishop to have more public discussion of his plans. Prystay also claimed that his pleas served only to alienate the bishop and got no support from the clergy.[47] This claim is somewhat suspect, as it seems unlikely that Bohachevsky could intimidate the clergy this early in his tenure. By the end of Bohachevsky's first year, Prystay, his later critic, pointed out that Bohachevsky was being hounded in the same manner that had brought Ortynsky to an early grave:

That's how it was during the lifetime of the deceased Bishop Ortynsky, so it is after his death, [a death]—no offense to the present editors—which *Svoboda*, with

---

46. *America*, April 18, 1925. In later issues, to stress their adherence to Catholicism, the editors reminded the regional officers of the Providence Fraternal Insurance Association that all members were in duty bound to make their annual confession, and that the secretaries should ensure that the duty be fulfilled.

47. Prystay to Rev. M. Kovalsky, November 17, 1934, TsDIA, Lviv, f. 789, op. 1, spr. 66. Prystay accused Bohachevsky of refusing to participate in a planning strategy with a select group of priests. Bohachevsky refrained from meeting with groups, especially when the group was only part of a larger gathering.

its venerable editors at that time also hastened. The same situation is beginning now, the full circle all over again. . . . Gentlemen editors! Whether you attack the bishop, or your own clergy, whether Catholic or Orthodox, or if you attack another Ukrainian organization, only to cater to your own personal interests and likings, . . . know that you are attacking the Ukrainian nation. . . . Without much thought you are hitting the most important part of the national organism, its head; and you are using a primitive weapon, the newspaper that is already compromised by the assassination of Bishop Ortynsky. That is a sin (in the eyes of God) and a farce (in the eyes of cultured nations).[48]

Although the Alliance lacked a financial base, its dynamic leader My-shuha, by adroit tactics and skillful use of *Svoboda*, created a public forum that eventually structured itself as the authoritative voice of the community. It was initially built on the idea that the Ukrainian Catholic Church, both historically and at the time in question, was an integral part of the Ukrainian public community. As such, the church hierarchy and parishes were expected to adhere to the will of the people. The argument that the will of the people could be gauged through local self-proclaimed representative meetings was buttressed by the public understanding of American democracy, democratic socialism, and sentiment to the homeland that so urgently needed monetary help. At the same time the community leaders feared street power. Myshuha complained to Nazaruk about problems running an organization with "six priestlings [*popyky*]" and his fear that the "people would rise, and no one would be able to hold them back."[49] But his main complaint was that Bohachevsky undermined the Alliance financially by sending church funds directly to Sheptytsky's offices.

Events came to a head on the anniversary of Ortynsky's death, when Bohachevsky again tried to hold a public event to honor his predecessor. The response was tepid at best. The bishop realized that his Catholic missionary work should begin with the Ukrainian Catholic Church itself. He used the date—March 13, 1926—to cross the Rubicon and hire Nazaruk as editor of *America*. This move would dramatically change the situation.

48. An open letter of Rev. Prystay, as quoted in *Svitohliad Ivana Franka: Chy mozhe khrys-tians'kiy narid priyniaty i shyryty kul't ioho?* [Ivan Franko's Worldview] (Philadelphia: n.p., 1926), 31–32; see also TsDIA, Lviv, f. 789, op. 1, spr. 66, Sprava Onufria Kovalskoho.

49. Myshuha to Nazaruk, December 14, 1925, TsDIA, Lviv, f. 359, spr. 291, ark. 12.

CHAPTER 6

An Iconoclastic Bishop

Through the first two years of his tenure, Bishop Bohachevsky could not make his voice heard above his opponents, nor was he strong enough to rally a mass movement in support of the church. Increasingly frustrated, he watched as his eparchy was torn apart by squabbles over control of the local churches. He felt he had to act before the ramshackle structure that he inherited disintegrated completely. But how could he act, if he did not know who was behind the rumors and who organized demonstrations? The bishop thrust and parried ineffectually, not knowing which way to turn, which crisis to address first. The opposition hid behind the double screen of anonymity and patriotism, and had to be drawn out. For Bohachevsky, the opposition was merely an unfortunate but inevitable difficulty that the Ukrainian Catholic Church in the United States encountered as it established itself in the New World. The bishop's opponents, however, used the disarray in the first years of Bohachevsky's tenure as the definition of the man.

The core of the disagreement between Bohachevsky and those who claimed to speak in the name of the people centered on the autonomy of the Ukrainian Catholic Church within the context of the Ukrainian community. In the absence of a Ukrainian state, Ukrainians living in America created their own virtual statehood, endowing it with communal powers. They expected the local church to reflect their views and their priorities. Needs of Ukraine and of organizations deemed patriotic took priority over local needs. Within the Ukrainian-American milieu during this time, the concept of separation of church and state was considered to be part of a liberal worldview, hence anathema to most Ukrainians. Rhetorical usage within this social context identified liberalism with libertarianism and sexual profligacy.

Bohachevsky believed that by strengthening the church he was also promoting the solid core of the nation, caring for its moral well-being, and providing it with a sense of a larger home. In most of his pastoral letters, he argued that the people, as an ethno-national unit, needed continuous moral growth to remain a strong nation. To be fully productive the people needed education, which, as its by-product, would contribute to a better standard of living. The intelligentsia leadership, on the other hand, posited that the voice of the people (as they heard it at the moment) was indeed the will of the community. Hence, some community leaders viewed the bishop's attempts to consolidate the church as a lack of interest in what they considered to be the most important function of the immigrants: to help the cause of Ukraine now by supporting their political group, their vision, and often, themselves.

The concept of authority and what it entailed was somewhat amorphous within Ukrainian society. Leaders in the community allegedly accepted public functions only from a sense of duty and at the insistence of their supporters, while the bishop openly took responsibility as leader of the church. His voluble espousal of authority appeared authoritarian, and he was perceived to be power hungry. The bishop envisaged a traditional, hierarchic Catholic Church, free from outside interference and emotionally buttressed by the metropolitan and the pope. The pope and his legates, after all, had spoken up for the Ukrainian Catholic Church and its clergy during the post-World War I period—the only recognized political power to do so. He saw the church in America as a missionary church that had to advance the spiritual growth of the congregation while building the structure of the church. As all other bishops at the time, Bohachevsky viewed his authority over the exarchy as his prime responsibility. He was to maintain order in the church, and through the church in society. At the same time, Bohachevsky saw himself very much a member of Ukrainian society.

His opponents—they were numerous and included his older brother, the intelligentsia, and many members of the clergy and faithful alike—

FIGURE 6. CONSTANTINE BOHACHEVSKY, 1924

did not have as clear a goal. Political and personal ambitions within the Ukrainian-American community at the time were played out through struggles to gain influence in the fraternal insurance societies, the community centers, and the churches. Except for the bishop's attempts to assure that church properties be incorporated in his name, the community culture was amorphous—no one admitted a desire to lead, much less to control, this or that entity. The only socially recognized power was the equally amorphous "people," the *narod*. The term in Ukrainian can embrace nation, crowd, or ethnicity. Few public orators felt a need to be specific in the use of this term, but everyone, including Bohachevsky, used it in a positive sense.[1]

Bohachevsky and the leaders of the Ukrainian-American intelligentsia lived within different time frames. The bishop continually saw eternity, and within its scope he was secure in God's Providence, who cared for him, for the church, and for Ukraine. Of this he was genuinely convinced. He was equally certain that for the time being little could be done politically to alter the fate of Ukraine. The country was depleted, the people, exhausted. Things would change when God's will dictated they should change. Then good people would put their well-honed skills to good use, and those in America send Ukraine real support. Meanwhile, Ukrainian-Americans should make use of all opportunities in America to develop themselves, their church and society, and help Ukraine as much as they can (which given their poverty, was little). Time for the bishop was a gift to be used for growth, and the United States an area in which the Ukrainian Catholic Church could flourish unimpeded by hostile powers.

The leaders of the secular Ukrainian community, proudly seeing themselves as the "intelligentsia," had their own developmental blueprints for an independent Ukraine. There were many plans, often at cross-purposes, but there was a somewhat generic frame of reference that enabled the temporary cooperation of their various proponents. For one thing, community leaders all worked under time pressure, always seeing the nation on the

1. The term for "state" as a sovereign political entity in Ukrainian is *derzhava*, which was used to translate both the country the United States of America (*Zyednani Derzhavy Ameryky*) and the individual American states. In common parlance, Ukrainians in America resorted to referring to the forty-eight states by the sloppy but useful *steyt*. But it is the Germanic *Shtaat* that became the accepted literary norm in Ukrainian.

verge of destruction, always hurrying to adapt to changing circumstances. Both cataclysmic and minor events necessitated immediate action. And a large part of this adjustment was that the self-proclaimed democratic segments of the Ukrainian intelligentsia in the United States saw themselves as the legitimate representatives of Ukraine. And although they often disagreed with each other (sometimes violently), they would all feel comfortable signing their names to a commentary penned by Emilian Reviuk: "We [Ukrainians] began our historical journey on a lowly level, but reached high stakes . . . and considerable achievements."[2]

For the Ukrainian intelligentsia the times were always liminal and critical. Both Ukraine and its Ukrainian-American community were in danger of losing their identity at that critical moment—the former to its myriad enemies, the latter to inevitable assimilation. The self-proclaimed voices of the community were convinced that something had to be done immediately to mitigate, if not avert, the tragedy of the day. And each group or individual claimed to have the necessary solution to the problem, if only the community would listen. In each case, the support of the organized church, at least as far as fund raising went, was essential to success. Invariably, the bishop stood in the way.

Despite his nominal authority as leader of the Ukrainian Catholic Church in America, Bohachevsky was impeded by glaring disadvantages. The priests who had expected the nomination for themselves were interested in having the bishop fail. Critical information was withheld from him, either consciously or through oversight. Bohachevsky had no friends in America. He did not know English. He was unfamiliar with American law and free-market finances, he had little experience with crowd politics, and he knew nothing about American libel law. He was immediately identified with the Vatican, and at times, the Vatican made decisions that were not conducive to building support for the bishop, either in the lay community or among his own priests. One example of this was Rome's position on the sticky matter of married priests. Whereas the Congregation for the Eastern Church, on June 21, 1926, reaffirmed the independence of the Eastern church from local Roman Catholic control, it also reinstated

2. Emil Revyuk, "Development of Ukrainian-American Political Outlook," in Myshuha, *Jubilee Book of the Ukrainian National Association*, 323.

the requirement that Eastern Catholic priests in the United State be celibate. The latter requirement was also incorporated into the *Ea Semper*, the 1929 papal edict that again reaffirmed the equality of Eastern and Western Catholicism.

Bohachevsky was also hemmed in by his own personality. He was not outgoing in a profession open to public expression of emotion. He was a private person who unrealistically expected gentlemanly behavior from his peers and professionalism from his priests. The bishop was a hard worker, but incapable of sophisticated maneuvering. He got by on little and expected others to have the fortitude to do the same. None of these characteristics won him supporters. They alienated many who could derail his work. Four major groups actively opposed the bishop: his own clergy (especially those passed over for promotion); the secular intelligentsia that needed funds for its respective causes; the Orthodox Ukrainians in the community; and finally, the atheists, including the communists.

When Bohachevsky arrived in Philadelphia, the clergy, not knowing what to expect, were more neutral. Most soon learned not to cross him, which cut the bishop off from important sources of information. Bohachevsky established his authority so effectively that close friendship with him was difficult, even had he sought it. Very few priests volunteered specific advice, although in administrative matters, he followed the advice of the priests he worked with most closely, even in the rare instances when he disagreed with it.

Clerical opposition was aimed at the person of Bohachevsky, not at the episcopate. The leaders of the clerical opposition were under the impression that they would have the support of the Vatican or at least of the Lviv hierarchy in removing him. They adopted the position of preserving their loyalty to the Catholic Church and to Rome while focusing on the bishop's alleged inability to handle his eparchy. The probable leader of this group, Rev. Joseph Zhuk, recognized he could not act openly without violating clerical discipline and thus putting himself out of the running for the episcopal nomination once Bohachevsky was gone. He had to exercise his influence behind the scenes, through priests who lacked Zhuk's sophistication. The initial goal of the opposition was to demonstrate Bohachevsky's incompetence. This could be accomplished by proving that parishes demanded Bohachevsky's recall or—the ultimate threat—that the parishioners were converting to Orthodoxy. The strategy was to undermine the bishop until he resigned of his own volition or until a wrathful congregation ejected him, the more violently, the better.

The Ukrainian Catholic clergy's motivation was complex. They were subject to canonical discipline, but they also did not want to alienate their parishioners. Many of them, without subjecting their views to rigid intellectual analysis, were comfortable with placing the church within the cultural framework of the state, or lacking a state, a secular nation. Thus, there was a tacit agreement that the Ukrainian Catholic Church was an integral part of the Ukrainian nation, subservient to that nation's needs.

The motivation of the political leadership was straightforward: Lay Catholics did not want to diminish the church; they wanted it to serve the people, as they saw fit. The secular intelligentsia saw the church as a financial and organizational base. Its leaders considered themselves the primary interpreters of Ukrainian patriotism, and as such, deserving of compensation for their labors for the common cause. The church would deal with the spirit, but they had knowledge about everything else.

Unrest in the parishes among rank-and-file Ukrainian Catholics provided opportunities for those who sought to undermine Ukrainian Catholicism. Ukrainians (including Catholics) who wanted to strengthen and expand the Ukrainian Orthodox Church opposed Bohachevsky for patriotic reasons—their hope was that the Orthodox Church could unify all of Ukraine, as well as its immigrants, better than could the Catholic Church, which was regional. This hope emerged against the broader backdrop of Eastern and Western church politics, specifically with the establishment of the Ukrainian Autocephalous Orthodox Church. For the first time in modern times, Ukrainian Catholics—faced with a potentially attractive and patriotic Ukrainian Orthodox Church—were losing their purported monopoly on religious patriotism. Eastern Orthodoxy, which always had adherents within the Western Ukrainian cultural setting, became a more palatable choice for some than the tsarist-controlled Orthodoxy had ever been. The two branches of the Orthodox Church—Ukrainian Autocephalous and the Moscow Patriarchate—monitored the Catholic process with great interest, hoping that the tension between the bishop and his flock would again weaken the Ukrainian Catholic Church in America, in much the same way as it had been weakened by the turmoil surrounding the appointment of the first Ukrainian-American Catholic bishop in 1907. There was also a threat from Protestant churches in America, which were more successful in recruiting converts among Ukrainian Catholics than they were in Europe.

Finally, there were the atheist opponents, those who opposed religion in general and especially the Ukrainian Catholic Church and would continue to use any means to undermine this church. Atheism was more popular in the United States than in the home country, and its adherents often had financial backing from outside sources. Even so, full-scale atheism did not attract many Ukrainian immigrants, and atheists therefore limited themselves to ridicule of religion. Nor was the Western Ukrainian society in the United States secularized enough to openly disregard the Ukrainian Catholic Church. Few were willing to work for a national church administered through some version of community control, in other words, either Protestantism or Autocephaly.

The conscious or unconscious cooperation of all strands of opposition almost destroyed the weak fabric of the church Bohachevsky inherited even before he had a chance to formulate, let alone implement, the basic tenets of his own vision. Although the opposition failed to block the bishop's policies, it succeeded in coloring the public perception of Bohachevsky and thus undermined the recognition, especially in Halychyna, of the success of his projects. The public nature of this fight also made cooperation of the two Ukrainian-American Catholic eparchies—Ruthenian and Ukrainian—difficult. At the same time, the abject nature of this fight served to justify merely *pro forma* public participation in religious practices and prevented the church from fully developing its mission to serve as the spiritual fount for its members. The nature of the struggle can best be characterized by the fact that it is referred to in Ukrainian-language sources of the time by the word "*fayt*," the Ukrainian transliteration of the English word "fight."

Both the personalities and the policies of the protagonists contributed to the extreme nature of the hostilities. The bishop was convinced that only a firm church structure could save the Ukrainian Church. The intelligentsia, and especially Luka Myshuha, was equally adamant that without funding from the American immigrants, the Ukrainian cause would fail. Myshuha had lost his considerable financial backing upon the death of his uncle, but this did not modify the manner of his work. The only significant difference was that his funds now had to be locally drawn. For that he needed amenable parishes.

Only Bohachevsky, however, was charged with intolerance and fanaticism. His personality, understated as his rhetoric, especially on the point of Ukrainian patriotic sentiments, did not endear him to the generally gregarious intelligentsia. Indeed, his direct conversational style made many wary of him. Moreover, Bohachevsky had learned from Ortynsky that conciliatory moves toward the community led to an escalation of public demands on the church, and this (among other things) dictated his decision to choose the lonely life of a righteous leader, keeping his vulnerabilities hidden under what Poniatyshyn characterized as "his steadfast will and the iron consistency."[3]

Initially, Bohachevsky faced the problems that all Ukrainian bishops before and since have encountered: the extent of ecclesiastical power of the Ukrainian Catholic Church within the structure of the universal Catholic *Ecclesia*, and the role of the Ukrainian Catholic hierarchy as keepers of the national cause. Few bishops, however, faced such bitter, prolonged, and personalized opposition as Bohachevsky did. The attacks on him, even within the context of émigré politics, were unprecedented, both in the number of unsubstantiated charges and in scale and virulence. Bohachevsky was acutely aware of his personal responsibility—as bishop— for his eparchy. For the first time in his life, he had no immediate superior (other than his God and the pope) to guide his actions. He may have hoped for open support from Sheptytsky, but the metropolitan, involved with other weighty issues, did not pay much attention to the United States, now that it had a bishop. Bohachevsky did have the express support of Rev. Vasyl Merenkiv, the experienced priest whom Sheptytsky trusted enough to ask for confidential information on Ortynsky during that bishop's lifetime.[4] Another small source of comfort was the fact that the disgruntled

3. Poniatyshyn, "Z chasiv administratsiii eparkhiii," in *Iuvileyny Al'manakh Ukraiins'koii Hreko-Katolyts'koii Tserkvy u Zluchenykh Derzhavakh z nahody 50-littiia iiii istnuvannia, 1884–1934,* ed. Volodymyr Lotots'ky (Philadelphia: America, 1934), 114.

4. Vasyl Merenkiv had been consecrated by Sheptytsky in 1904 and came to the United States in 1910. He reinforced Bohachevsky's understanding of his legal rights by a letter he wrote to him October 1, 1926: "Not only does the chancery have full legal edict [*ydykt;* sic] to the church properties [*propertiv*] by right of inheritance according to the will of the last

clergy were not openly leading the protests. Also, enough financial support was coming in to the exarchate to allow it to function. Bohachevsky could even send money for orphans and veterans to the home country. He was firmly convinced that his policies would strengthen the Ukrainian Catholic Church in the United States, that the majority of the laity, although passive would support the church, as would most of the clergy. He felt that once the clergy and laity understood what he was trying to accomplish, they would share his views when he had the opportunity to present them.

The public digs against the bishop that began with his arrival in America at first did not seem important enough to warrant denial. One of the first assaults was published in *Dnipro*, a leftist publication of Ukrainian émigrés from the territories of the former Russian Empire. It called attention to a poem in a Polish-American newspaper (*Gwiazda poliarna*) that welcomed the bishop to America. In some quarters, that was proof that Bohachevsky was pro-Polish if not a covert Pole himself. Even Bohachevsky's support of the orphanage set up by Ortynsky was used against him: the orphans in Ukraine, after all, were more needy than those in the United States. In the ensuing squabbles over the issue of orphans, rather primitive attempts to subvert the bishop or simply to collect money emerged: individuals masquerading as agents of the bishop's orphanage campaign demanded money in his name. As early as April 1925, Bohachevsky felt compelled to issue a statement that the eparchy had not authorized people to collect money for the American orphanage. The official statement further explained that were the eparchy to introduce this practice, the collectors would have proper documentation and the support of local priests.[5]

Another public outcry arose over the fact that the Basilian nuns now adhered to the updated Gregorian calendar, whereas the cathedral still followed the Julian one. This distinction, and the fact that the orphanage run by the Basilian nuns, located a few houses down the block from the cathedral and the residency, had indeed become a second home for Bohachevsky served as the pretext for scurrilous verses (later reprinted in the

---

bishop, but even without such ... the Philadelphia properties were acquired by donations from the whole society, even the Magyar parishes." Merenkiv to Bohachevsky, October 1, 1926, UMAS.

5. *Eparkhiial'ni Visti*, February 11, 1925, 3.

Soviet press) about the bishop and the nuns. *Svoboda* also had a field day describing how the bishop celebrated Easter with the nuns, only to walk down the block to don black vestments for the Lenten services. The communist paper went further and gleefully described how the bishop was "hopping around with the nuns in the morning celebrating Easter, while in the evening across the street in his cathedral he mourns the death of Christ."[6] Bohachevsky nevertheless remained true to his promise not to change the calendar in the cathedral parish if even one parish continued to opt for the old style.

The nuns also became the object of ridicule, and one striking example should suffice. On June 3, the feast day of St. Constantine the Emperor and his mother, Empress Helena, the Ukrainian Philadelphia orphans collected the magnificent sum of $5 to donate to the Chinese Catholic Charities so that a little Chinese boy could be christened Constantine. That was the practice of most Catholic missions at the time, but *Svoboda* took the bishop to task for agreeing to such a waste of money, which of course could be better spent in Ukraine. Defending the donation to the Chinese charity, Nazaruk explained at length that the orphanage had to work hand in hand with Catholic Charities, without whose assistance the orphanage would be unable to care for the children. As to *Svoboda*'s complaints about the bishop spending time with the children, he argued, what could be better? He further observed that Myshuha had never contributed a penny toward the upkeep of the orphanage. Nor had he, for that matter, joined any Catholic parish. Such stories made good copy.

The fact that Bohachevsky on occasion appeared in public with Latin-rite prelates, some of Polish origin, was seen as proof that the bishop was colluding with the enemy. Bohachevsky was charged with selling the Ukrainian Catholic Church to the Vatican by Romanizing the Eastern rite and was further accused of using this money for his own purposes. Considering the brutal treatment that Bohachevsky had endured in Poland, the charges were too ludicrous to take seriously. Nevertheless, they hurt. The accusations multiplied, mainly focused on events that seem exceedingly minor by today's standards.

6. The examples are drawn from a convenient brochure prepared by Osyp Nazaruk and published in Philadelphia, *Nash Epyskopat v Amerytsi i Borot'ba Proty Neho* [Our Bishopric in America and the Attacks Against It], in 1926.

The barbed comments soon escalated into open attacks. Bohachevsky was accused of a variety of crimes and shortcomings—he was pro-Polish, he was taking over church property for himself, his goal was to destroy the Ukrainian Catholic Church, he was tampering with tradition by permitting parishes to change calendars, by supporting the Basilian nuns he was weakening the church, and he was not as good a pastor as his predecessor. Bohachevsky, moreover, was accused of failing to live up to Ortynsky's legacy, and of not standing up for the rights of Ukrainians before the Polish government and the papacy.

Bohachevsky's centralization of church holdings was perceived as an aspect of his grasping nature; his office practices were a sign of his inhumanity; his insistence on schedules and promptness, a sign of rigid inflexibility. "As early as 1925 articles began to appear urging Bohachevsky 'to remain close' to his people."[7] Such calls were often anonymous.

Bohachevsky viewed many of the attacks directed at him during the first years of his tenure as part of a "culture war" in which science and modernity were challenging traditional faith. His frame of reference was historical. In the 1880s, the newly expanded Hohenzollern Germany had sought to control the Catholic Church. In addition to its political component—church/state conflict—the attempt reflected the clash between a modern secularized worldview and a more traditional religious one. Although deeply hurt by the personal nature of the attacks against him, Bohachevsky saw the broader picture: the efforts of a secular community to dictate to the church. His erstwhile mentors, Bishop Josaphat Kotsylovsky of Peremyshl, as well as Bishop Hryhory Khomyshyn of Stanislaviv, were being subjected to similar attacks. Basil Takach, his fellow Ruthenian-American bishop, would suffer similar indignities five years later from his congregations. As the more extreme form of nationalism grew in Halychyna, even Metropolitan Sheptytsky was not exempt from accusations of lack of patriotism, just as had been the case in the early years of his episcopal tenure.

The two major Ukrainian-American newspapers, *America* and *Svoboda*, fed the drama by commentary more than reporting. Yet the unrest in the parishes stemmed not as much from disagreement about church issues as

7. Kuropas, *The Ukrainian Americans*, 306.

about the control of church finances. The written documentation, however, consists mainly of printed public statements that repeat the general accusations against Bohachevsky. Some of the handwritten petitions or the few letters to the bishop in untutored hands reveal the confusion of the time and the desire of the laity to avoid physical confrontations: some ask the bishop not to visit their parish; others complain of the bishop's failure to visit this or that parish during particularly contentious fights.

In later historical analyses, this stormy period was either briefly mentioned or glossed over. The treatment of individual priests by hostile communities was overlooked, and the attacks on the female monastic orders totally disregarded. At the time, however, the Basilian nuns in Philadelphia, and especially their titanic work with the orphanage and in schools, were singled out for vicious attacks. Still, the entire struggle was personified in Bishop Bohachevsky, as if he alone had been responsible for all the discontent and resulting turbulence. By personalizing the struggle, the community absolved itself of historical memory, simultaneously refusing to analyze its sources and ramifications. The rationale was simple: if one person could be blamed for everything that caused discontent, the removal of that person would solve all problems.

DRAWING OUT THE OPPOSITION

By acting decisively, Bohachevsky opened himself up to attack. The decisions he made and the resulting actions were calculated—he wanted to demonstrate his ability to govern the eparchy and to draw out the people who were leading the opposition. The genuine fear of a possible mass conversion of Ukrainian Catholics to Orthodoxy that troubled Rome (and which indeed had prompted the Vatican to agree to appoint two Ukrainian bishops for the United States) pushed Bohachevsky to accelerate his centralization policies. By the beginning of 1926, viscerally unable to stand idle and watch the steady attrition of the Ukrainian Catholic Church structure, Bohachevsky began to assert his power, dramatically and emphatically.

The initial drama was prompted by the threat of investigation by the State of Pennsylvania of the Providence fraternal insurance association that Bishop Ortynsky had founded. By 1925, it numbered over ten thousand members and served as the financial backbone of the Ukrainian-American Church.[8] It was also the publisher of *America*, which appeared three to four times weekly, and ran articles on all topics except those that positioned the bishop in a favorable light. Providence was in danger of being shut down by the U.S. government for dubious banking activities, which purportedly included subsidizing the newspaper with monies collected for insurance purposes. Bohachevsky at first toyed with the idea of declaring bankruptcy for Providence; he even feared that the eparchy would have to declare bankruptcy. His relations with the Providence Association had never been smooth, and the threat of investigation by the state exacerbated the tension.

The Providence Association had a complex governing board composed of elected laity and clergy, and the bishop had an *ex officio* vote that could be easily overridden. By January 1926, Bohachevsky had gained greater control of Providence and engineered (by vote) the dismissal of the two members held responsible for the mismanagement. By proving his ability to discipline the administration, the bishop avoided a legal suit. At the same time, he disciplined Reverends Kinash and Pidhoretsky for financial mismanagement of cathedral funds.[9] He reinstated Rev. Maksym Kinash a few weeks later, but Pidhoretsky by this time had joined the Orthodox priests.

Bohachevsky had scored a financial and moral victory. The disciplinary action and the reinstatement were meant as a clear signal to the clergy that the bishop in America would function the way bishops in the home country did. He would expect the same type of support from his priests. Now firmly in control of Providence and *America*, Bohachevsky gained the forum he needed. The bishop had emerged as an active player in the struggle for control of the church's material wealth. Now he had to move beyond his comfort zone of church and culture into émigré politics. He had proved he was not afraid to take on the leaders of the community. But the community was unstructured, and there were no clear battle lines. These were, after all, Ukrainians' first hands-on experiences with direct democracy.

8. Lypynsky to Nazaruk, April 3, 1926, Lypynsky, *Collected Works*, 382.
9. This was more in the nature of pro-forma disciplinary action. Because of the complex mortgaging schemes of the buildings that Ortynsky had used as security for his credit operations, the two priests had to pretend to buy and sell the houses, formally illegal acts.

Luka Myshuha and Osyp Nazaruk personified the two major political currents in the immigrant community. Bohachevsky represented the church, which he maintained was not a player in community politics. All three—Bohachevsky, Myshuha, and Nazaruk—were Ukrainian patriots, recent newcomers to America, none of them had emigrated to America for the sake of emigrating, but to perform specific tasks.

Luka Myshuha emerged by design or by happenstance as the leader of the secular organizations of immigrants from Halychyna. As such, his cooperation with Bohachevsky, the head of the Catholic Church in the United States, would have been natural. At the time, Myshuha lived in Philadelphia and was apparently engaged to marry the daughter of the cathedral pastor. Myshuha's offer to edit *America*, as well as his intervention on behalf of Reverend Kinash, the pastor of the cathedral, to secure real estate, reflected traditional public behavior in Halychyna. Within this framework, social relations and a certain degree of informality (reinforced by the fact that the political regimes and the laws under which Ukrainians lived had not been favorable toward them) had characterized both community and church activities, and Myshuha presumed Bohachevsky would follow that script. But Bohachevsky was a modern priest who saw the church as an autonomous corporation with specific goals. Above all, the Catholic Church was a communion of the faithful practitioners, not merely a vehicle of tradition. He could not hire Myshuha because Myshuha was not a member of any parish. Myshuha's argument that he would alienate Orthodox Ukrainians if he practiced Catholicism openly did not sway the bishop. Just as he would not hire his own brother, who had a decade earlier toyed with Orthodoxy, he would not cut corners to accommodate what some viewed as patriotism. Snubbed by the bishop, Myshuha turned his attention to trying to save the current civic association, the Alliance; when that failed, he used the Ukrainian National Association and *Svoboda* as his platform as well as his livelihood.

Myshuha felt he represented the people, although he feared populism (*narodovlastia*). He found the clergy too timid and complained to Nazaruk that it was impossible to run an organization with "six priestlings [popyky]." Nazaruk at one point thought Myshuha was trying to establish a national church, but that was not the case. Myshuha only wanted a church malleable to community pressure. From that perspective, the bishop's plan to strengthen the church without regard to how the community and political organizations were faring was treacherous.

The Ukrainian democrats agreed only on one principle: power to the people as we represent them. The people, however, spoke in many voices. Myshuha eventually emerged as a consensual community leader, pushing the clergy who supported him into an open confrontation with the bishop, which few priests wanted. Myshuha identified with the patriotic democratic nationalists, many of whom were also socialists, and he was not shy in pushing out older Ukrainian politicians, such as Lonhyn Tsehelsky, the erstwhile representative of the Western Ukrainian Republic. Myshuha was not interested in the church as a religious institution nor in the specifics of spirituality as practiced in the Eastern or Latin traditions. He viewed the church as an integral attribute of Ukrainian identity and felt himself personally empowered to implement how that identity should function in the United States. His thinking was "Eastern" in the sense that church, state, and society created a symphonic whole. In his view, that constituted the only genuine patriotic activity. He was confident that the bishop would actively support his work; when this did not materialize to the extent he expected, he accused Bohachevsky of not sending monies to Halychyna through the Alliance, the community organization Myshuha ran which came to depend wholly on local fundraising, a large part of which took place on church properties.

Myshuha preferred to work behind the scenes for the grand goal of Ukraine and the welfare of its community. He preferred the image he cultivated—the pensive grandee—rather than the real life he lived after the death of his wealthy uncle left him scampering for funds. Initially, Myshuha was not openly involved in the strife against Bohachevsky, although it was common knowledge that he was the force behind the movement to remove Bohachevsky from office. Nazaruk even arranged for a clandestine meeting with his erstwhile colleague to try to come to some agreement on the anti-Bohachevsky stance of Alliance, which at the time was Myshuha's sole means of support. Nazaruk failed to convince Myshuha to tamp down the attacks against the bishop and to try to stem the disorder in the parishes; the feisty journalist clearly realized that a full-scale battle between church and state was inevitable. Myshuha may have preferred to stand above the fray, but "myshuhizm," whether he liked it or not, was in open opposition to all the bishop stood for. Myshuha openly warned Nazaruk that "the force of the people will turn against you."[10]

Nazaruk, on the other hand, as a neophyte Catholic, had become very aware of the need of a strong church to be able to withstand the pressure of radical society. His experience in Eastern Ukraine during the revolutionary years 1918 and 1919 had led him to see the fragility of democracy before the power of the crowd, especially a skillfully manipulated mob. He saw the church as a spiritual institution and a stabilizing force. He was one of the few Ukrainian political activists to espouse openly the idea of the separation of church and state. Hence, the bishop would find him a congenial collaborator. Both Bohachevsky and Nazaruk liked clarity and direct action. The bishop had a clear goal for the church, but the Ukrainian-American community was not yet certain of the differing priority of its interests and interpreted the bishop's goal as being selfish and unpatriotic.

Bohachevsky's decisive handling of the Providence and cathedral financial crises excited the community. Although it was obvious that the road would be rocky, it was not clear which way the community would go. Community leaders bereft of resources, tried to gauge the direction the people would choose, which was a difficult task, as the people shifted directions. Nazaruk, a recent radical socialist, was primed to see communist operatives behind each public demonstration, and he may not have been far off the mark. In his detailed letters to Lypynsky, Nazaruk painted a picture of utter chaos in Philadelphia:

[There is a] revolution . . . everything is possible here: [after all, this is] emigration! Despite the fifty-story skyscrapers here this is the prairie, Wild Fields [a reference to the part of Ukraine the Cossacks conquered after the devastation of the Mongols and the inroads of the Tatars]. I am not surprised at the actions of the bishop: after all, these gentlemen are refashioning a Catholic newspaper into a Bolshevik cell![11]

10. Nazaruk to Lypynsky, April 3, 1926, in Lypynsky, *Collected Works*, 380–81. Myshuha used the word *narodovlastia* in the quoted phrase. It can be translated as "populism" with a radical tinge.

11. Nazaruk to Lypynsky, January 21, 1926, in Lypynsky, *Collected Works*, 367.

The bishop had the support of his closest collaborators and hoped for broader support, but his position was precarious. Nazaruk noted that his prospects of being hired to edit *America* appeared bleak:

It's still questionable if the bishop will win, because from what I hear the whole community in Philadelphia is roiling. Chaos cannot stand this bishop, who is educated in the Roman manner. Obviously! From the plebs to the canons—"revolution" is coming. I hear the cathedral is already empty; the nation is revolting by not coming [to church]! However, the bishop is very firm. But the cathedral is still in debt, and that can eat him up. He lives very frugally and packs his money into the orphanage and the seminary. Nice! But will he endure? Were he to fall the whole "black sea" of chaos would dance over him for a long time![12]

Nazaruk even resorted to Shevchenko's description of the chaos that the Cossacks could unleash to reflect the situation in Philadelphia:

What a beautiful "Cossack" people! It seems the people organically cannot stand order and authority. [The people] loves demagoguery from the time of Methuselah. It is so difficult to combat this. . . . Now Dr. Myshuga [sic] writes that the leaders should follow the people and that the bishop brings him, Dr. Luka Myshuga, shame, etc., etc. And the Catholic—"spiritual"—Ukrainians follow him against the bishop! Beautiful and unique.[13]

Bohachevsky continued his efforts to build an independent church, risking an open confrontation within the Catholic community. He insisted that *America* publish his Christmas pastoral letter on January 5, 1926. The bishop cleaned up the financial mess and brought order to the Providence Association finances. He held on to the cathedral, which had historic significance because it had been blessed by Metropolitan Sheptytsky himself. The bishop tried once more to rally the community by directing public memorial services on March 13, 1926, to mark the anniversary of Bishop Ortynsky's death on March 24, 1916. The services were held, but there was no outpouring of support for either of the bishops—Ortynsky or his successor.

Nazaruk, for his part, sought to popularize the conservative thinker, Viacheslav Lypynsky in America, arguing that his views would bolster the church. To make this Ukrainian, but Latin Catholic thinker amenable to

12. Nazaruk to Lypynsky, January 22, 1926, in Lypynsky, *Collected Works*, 367.
13. Nazaruk to Lypynsky, January 21, 1926, in Lypynsky, *Collected Works*, 368.

the Ukrainian Catholic clergy, Nazaruk published an interview with him in *America*. He hoped the political philosopher would boost Bohachevsky's panache with the intelligentsia.[14] But Lypynsky was never popular among Ukrainian intellectuals, and the American immigrants were no different.

On March 18, 1926, with great difficulty, Bohachevsky persuaded the board of Providence to hire Nazaruk as editor of *America*. It was a brilliant strategy, since Nazaruk was able to undermine the tactics of the opposition. He drew the leaders out into the open, including Luka Myshuha. With Nazaruk's appointment, Bohachevsky finally had the public voice that he needed to promote his program.

Nazaruk got to work immediately with all guns blazing. He drew out the disunited opposition and forced Myshuha to emerge from the sidelines. Nazaruk wanted Myshuha to admit that under the guise of patriotic activity he was using part of the money both to support a specific party as well as himself. Myshuha, on the other hand, felt that he, as any other rational person in his position, was working the best that he could in difficult circumstances. Any attempt to advertise this sad, existential condition he considered either heinous or stupid. He expected as a matter of course that the church would support him. Most likely, he had already discussed the matter with the person or persons who expected to be either bishop or close to the bishop's entourage. Nazaruk wanted this backroom politicking out in the open.

Fully aware that many on the staff of both Providence and the chancery would try to undermine his work, Nazaruk announced a strict editorial policy: He, the editor, would be responsible for all but the religious content of the publication. "As a lay person, I am not responsible for the religious content, which is in the purview of the church authorities." Nazaruk began reporting more directly on the efforts to discredit the bishop.[15] Nazaruk continued to describe how "populism wages a war against me . . . using extremely interesting means."[16] The picture that emerges is one of a society that is still in formation, many of its leaders untutored in the

14. Viacheslav Lypynsky, *Religiia i tserkva v istoriï Ukraïny* (Philadelphia: Narodna biblioteka Ameryky No. 17, 1925).

15. Nazaruk to Lypynsky, April 3, 1926, in Lypynsky, *Collected Works*, 382.

16. Nazaruk to Lypynsky, April 3, 1926, in *Lypynsky, Collected Works*, 380; See also Nazaruk writing to Lypynsky from Lviv, February 13, 1928, in Lypynsky, *Collected Works*, 454.

functioning of civic structures, quick to see slights, and keen to make certain that American freedoms not be violated. "They play nasty tricks on each other, like stealing notes for later use in petty blackmail."[17]

Within a week of assuming his role as editor of *America*, on March 30, Nazaruk published Bohachevsky's dramatic argument on why American Ukrainians need a seminary for the training of local priests. Instead of the standard connected paragraphs of sermons and pastoral letters, the new editor presented Bohachevsky's reasoning on "Why We Need a Seminary" in twelve well-defined points. The bishop made it clear that he was not dictating a policy but hoping for a discussion: "I submit this [plan] for our common good for consideration to all reverend clergy and to members of parishes to [expand] our organizations [and] to strengthen and enlighten our Ukrainian people."[18]

The arguments were simple, aimed at an unsophisticated reader. The text reflected how the bishop—very much in the tradition of Sheptytsky—wanted to integrate the needs of the Ukrainian Catholic Church in the United States with the traditional vision of Christianity as the vehicle of culture and progress. Bohachevsky began with the argument that cultured nations develop with the help of their churches, and unless there is a seminary to train the priests there can be no church. These cultured nations rely on well-educated clergy to promote a positive image of the country and its people. Ukrainians in America need American-born Ukrainian priests because, the bishop explained: "Priests from the old country find it hard to adapt to new conditions, . . . and they find it especially difficult to understand the psychological makeup of the young generation." He moved to what continued to be a major problem—the severe shortage of priests in the vast United States: "Whole American states, each the size of the entire Austria-Hungary, remain without [Ukrainian] priests . . . Alaska, Alabama, Oklahoma, Montana, and others."[19]

Then came the main point: Latin-rite schools will not accustom Ukrainian children to love their heritage; instead, they will encourage them to blend into the larger American Catholic society. Bohachevsky sought to

17. Nazaruk to Lypynsky, May 1, 1926, in Lypynsky, *Collected Works*, 387.
18. Bohachevsky, "Choho nam potriben Semynar" [Why We Need a Seminary], *America*, March 30, 1926.
19. Ibid.

rally the Ukrainian Catholic community to action by reminding it that the eparchy owned real estate in Philadelphia, real estate that could easily serve as a primary school. Other schools, including high schools, could be established with relative ease. What was needed was for each parish to support a candidate for the seminary or convent, thus assuring that there would be local American Ukrainian youths to serve the needs of their own society.

The bishop pointed out that despite all the difficulties four new monasteries had already been established during his tenure—in St. Louis, Chicago, Passaic (N.J.), and Philadelphia. He also reminded his readers that the Ukrainian population in Halychyna, even as it was brutally oppressed, supported its schools. Why then could not Ukrainian-American communities support at least one potential priest or nun from each parish? Why shouldn't the richer parishioners help the poorer ones who are ready for service? "Other societies have such noble people, surely we can also find them?"

Bohachevsky ended with assurances that supporting the needs of the local Ukrainian-American Church did not automatically mean abandoning support for the needs of the home country:

Finally, . . . there is no reason to think that collecting funds for the seminary will weaken our lay organizations. The opposite is the case! Generosity when unleashed will encourage others to similar noble actions. [Nor] . . . does it make sense to say that the nation needs only schools and not seminaries, or only lay organizations [and not religious ones]. The nation needs everything! And only when it has a well-funded church and lay organizations—seminaries, schools, sport clubs, economic, financial, and all others, will the nation be truly developed.[20]

The bishop expected a discussion that would popularize his plan of making Ukrainian immigrants more competitive by building schools in which they could reconcile their American and Ukrainian identities. Instead, the argument was waylaid by a charge that the bishop was not interested in Ukraine at all. Bohachevsky's call for a discussion was interpreted as an edict and instead of leading to a discussion, it heated up the polemics, provided more grist for discord in individual parishes, and did little to galvanize the clergy to support the bishop actively.

20. Ibid.

Nazaruk followed up Bohachevsky's call to education with a series of informative opinion pieces on politics and news items in which the bishop's position was favorably presented. The bishop's other helpers, including Revs. Konstantyn Kurylo and Kinash, buttressed his arguments. *America* began to highlight more frequently information on the work of the Basilian nuns, including news items about young women joining the order. Nazaruk reported clearly and simply, published unedited letters of semi-literate workers, and openly criticized the Ukrainian-language literary works which he did not consider good enough. The new editor saw a raw community of people striving toward a cultured life and presented their struggle. Realizing the impermanence of newspapers, Nazaruk collected both articles and testimonials about the disarray in the communities and the perfidious attempts to take over churches and published them in booklets that enjoyed mass circulation.[21] Because the polemics often included accusations that the church and the bishop were not patriotic Ukrainians because they used the term "Rutheni" in Latin, *America* launched into a series of informative articles on the history of the use of terms such as "Rus'," "Ukraine," "Russia," and the like. It was not only Americans who were confused by Ukrainians. Ukrainians themselves had problems with what name to use for themselves and their churches.

Some parishes and clergy continued to oppose Bohachevsky's fiscal policies. The older priests accused the bishop of favoring his own age group and predicted the near end of the Ukrainian Catholic Church in America. They chided the bishop for being too brash, too bold, too driven by the need for immediate results. At the same time he was scolded for being passive, for failing to react quickly, for not initiating enough out-reach programs. He was accused of being selfish and materialistic, even as his

---

21. Nazaruk published three brochures in defense of the bishop: *Nash Epyskopat v Amerytsi i Borot'ba Proty Neho; Svitohliad Ivana Franka;* and a small collection of an interview with Bishop Dionysius Njaradi and samples of *verbatim* letters of support for Bohachevsky, *Holos Ievropeis'koho Vladyky Preosviashchenoho Dioniziia: i inshi holosy pro nashi tserkovni spravy v Amerytsi* (Philadelphia: n.p., 1926), published in two thousand copies as a self-contained thirty-page brochure that served as continuation of *Nash Epyskopat.* The series ended in 1927 with the publication of a scathing criticism of the poet Ivan Franko: *A Few Reminiscences about Franko,* written pseudonymously by Volodymyr Levytsky, V. Lukych [pseud.], *Ivan Franko: Kil'ka spohadiv i kil'ka zdohadiv ioho suchasnyka i spivrobitnyka* (Philadelphia: Orphanage Publishing, 1927).

ascetic life in a small room above the chancery was derided for projecting a negative image of Ukraine and Ukrainians.

The situation at Woonsocket, Rhode Island, as it developed in the spring and summer of 1926, can serve as an example of the problems Bohachevsky faced. This textile town had attracted many immigrants and was home to a Ukrainian workers' community in its heyday, right before the 1929 stock market crash. There was always a shortage of Ukrainian Catholic priests in the United States, and the eparchy gratefully accepted all Halychyna could spare. Among these were men who did not fit the usual profile of a Halychyna priest. The parish priest sent to Woonsocket was Rev. Hlib Verkhovsky, an Eastern Ukrainian whom Sheptytsky himself had cultivated. The parishioners protested the "Mosco-Uniate Polish priest [batiushka]" who, as far as they were concerned, could not speak Ukrainian. They refused to attend his Easter services and tearfully sang "Christ Is Risen" outside the church, which they had nailed shut so that the priest would not defile it by his presence. Rev. Vashchyshyn, Bohachevsky's chancellor, personally explained that the Catholic Church, like Ukraine itself, was home to many nationalities, and that moreover Rev. Hlib was not Russian but a Ukrainian from a northeastern province that had been under tsarist domination. The committee hired a lawyer to gain control of the property. Bohachevsky preempted the move by personally collecting all the outstanding mortgages that the parish had against the church property.[22] For his opponents, this maneuver only served as proof that the bishop was a grasping miser who favored anti-Ukrainian priests.[23]

22. *Dnipro*, May 29, June 8, and 12, 1926, had a field day making fun of the Russian-speaking priest and encouraging the parishioners to boycott his services.

23. *Dnipro*, May 29, 1926, quoting *Woonsocket Call*, May 8, 1926, reported that the Ruthenian bishop would visit to try to calm the parish, and stop the strike against the priest, which had left barely twelve persons attending the Liturgy. *Dnipro* reported that the parish rejected Rev. Hleb Verkhovsky because he was not Ukrainian and could not speak the language. And if the bishop came to his support in person, the church community would strike. In its next two issues, June 5 and June 26, 1926, *Dnipro* reported that the bishop came to Woonsocket, scoured all the banks by car, paid the $20,000 outstanding mortgage and $2,000 for community loans, but did not stay for a meeting, proving that "The Union [Brest, 1596], invented by the Liachs [derogatory for Poles], now is showing its Polish horns." The meeting in Woonsocket of four hundred parishioners unanimously decided to run the priest out of town.

Discontent spread from parish to parish, the example of one successful withdrawal encouraging other parishes to announce their independence from the bishop. The individual demands and causes for the discontent varied. Generally, a community either liked or disliked the priest assigned to it and wanted the bishop to hear them out. Or they wanted to hold the title to the church. Or the property was so deeply mortgaged that it was not clear who owned it. Or there were multiple mortgages that were suddenly called in by the lenders that held them. In some localities, like Perth Amboy, New Jersey, it was the presence of activists from other communities who fomented discontent.

The memoirist Rev. Oleksa Prystay complained that none of the higher clergy were willing to tell the bishop what they thought he ought to do. Having worked with Bohachevsky when the bishop first arrived in America, Prystay felt he knew him well enough to accuse him of being "a stubborn, fanatic coward. He is afraid to show himself in places where there is some discontent, where his person could have saved the parish if only the bishop had come at the request of the pastor. . . . He does not want to meet with any delegations."[24]

Yet other priests advised the bishop to stay the course and not meet with self-appointed delegations, not to draw himself into the name-calling. Whatever the charge, Bohachevsky's response was always the same: prayer. He asked those few he trusted as well as those who were his fiercest opponents to pray hard so that the predictions of the decline of the Ukrainian Catholic Church in the United States did not materialize. The consensus among many priests and some faithful was that Myshuha was trying to make the bishop follow the directives of the Alliance. Nazaruk eventually began thinking that Myshuha was working to shift the Catholic Church into the Orthodox Autocephaly or even form an independent Ukrainian Church. Nazaruk fought Myshuha every step of the way. Reverend Konstantyn Kuryllo had a simpler suggestion: offer Myshuha a job at America or the Providence Association.[25]

24. Prystay to Nazaruk, June 15, 1929, Letters to Nazaruk, TsDIA, Lviv, f. 359, op. 1, spr. 303, p. 13. This was a five-page, single-spaced, typed letter.
25. Konstantyn Kuryllo, "A Priest Answers an Attack," Svoboda, July 16, 1926; see also Nazaruk to Lypynsky, September 17, 1926, Lypynsky, Collected Works, 398; and Nazaruk to Lypynsky, January 31, 1927, Lypynsky, Collected Works, 404.

As Myshuha and Nazaruk slugged it out to the delight of the reading public, the bishop attended to his daily duties. On his schedule were the twenty-eighth International Eucharistic Congress and the concomitant visit of Bishop Dionysius Njaradi to the United States, the dedication of Bishop Takach's new residence and church, and a retreat for all the priests of the eparchy. The congress was the first International Eucharistic Congress hosted by the American Roman Catholic Church. Few in the Ukrainian community realized its importance for the American Catholic Church, because smaller Eucharistic congresses had been held in the United States earlier that dimmed its international importance.

Latin-rite Catholic bishops, particularly those in the American Midwest who had Central and Eastern European roots, encouraged Eastern-rite Catholics to join forces with them to strengthen the wing of Latin Catholicism that wanted to keep local traditions and languages alive, in opposition to the Irish and Italians who favored homogenized English-language Americanization of the Catholic Church. His Latin-rite Catholic bishop-colleagues took Bohachevsky to see churches built in an "Eastern" style. Bohachevsky considered them courtesy calls.

Catholics in the United States were not formally discriminated against, but they, like Ukrainian Catholics, labored under adverse social pressure. This was particularly true of the East Coast Catholics, and it was the Irish Catholics and their Catholic brethren from southern and eastern Europe who felt the opprobrium of the upper-class urbanites the most. One antidote to this was that Catholic schools in the urban, immigrant ghettoes socialized children as much as they educated them. Slowly, Latin-rite Catholicism made inroads into upper American society. At the time, it was customary to hold special days of prayer that brought together clergy and laity from several parishes for public celebrations, and Roman Catholic celebrations began to be held in public areas rather than just in churches. Congresses affirming the reality of the Eucharist were particularly popular. Such congresses, on a regional scale, had been held in the United States prior to 1926. But the Eucharistic congress planned for June 1926 was to be different. It would be universal, with international representation, proving that Catholicism was not just an immigrant faith.

The twenty-eighth International Eucharistic Congress in Chicago was the first world congress to be held on American soil—a coming-out fete for American Catholicism.

Bohachevsky, as the exarch of the Ukrainian Catholics, received a formal invitation to participate in the Chicago Eucharistic congress. A newcomer to America, he presumed the pastor of St. Nicholas parish in Chicago, Rev. Fylymon Tarnawsky, should have a free hand in arranging the Ukrainian presence at the festivities.[26] Bohachevsky also encouraged clergy participation and hoped some Ukrainian priests would present papers at the event. The bishop presumed—wrongly, it turned out—that the priests would volunteer to take an active part in the preparations for the congress. After charging Tarnawsky with the task, Bohachevsky turned his attention to all the other issues facing him.

Tarnawsky had come to the United States in 1911 after the death of his wife, had served in Auburn and Cleveland, but was new to Chicago. The city had become a vibrant center of Ukrainian political activity and was still reeling from the fatal shooting on October 7, 1923, of its new pastor by the wife of the outgoing one.[27] A split in the parish led to the defection of a third of its members just as the building of the most grandiose Ukrainian church in America was being completed. Tarnawsky did all he could to assure that the Ukrainian Church was duly represented at the congress, but was barely able to get the support of the local priests, let alone get other clergy to spend their own funds to attend the congress. The Ukrainian clergy—underpaid, overworked, and pummeled by a community that could not find its center—showed little preliminary interest

26. Bohachevsky to Tarnawsky, October 22, 1925, UMAS Chancery Archive. Tarnawsky was twenty-two years older than Bohachevsky and was related to him. The older man, moreover, had wanted to remain celibate but was talked into marriage by his parents. He knew first-hand the adversity and the denigration married clergy experienced at the hands of some of the church committees. Through the years, Tarnawsky was like a father to the bishop, a source of both comfort and reinforcement of the correctness of his views and approaches.

27. The administrator, Petro Poniatyshyn, had transferred Rev. Mykola Strutynsky to Youngstown, Ohio. Strutynsky's wife, angered by the transfer, shot the incoming priest, Vasyl Steciuk, to death. Mrs. Strutynsky's brother, Myroslav Sichynsky, earlier had become a Ukrainian hero for assassinating, in 1908, a Polish official of the Habsburg government in Halychyna. Sichynsky escaped and settled in the United States where he became a member of the Communist Party.

in the congress. Only one Ukrainian Catholic priest prepared a paper, and he submitted it in Russian since he did not know English.[28] At the last minute, some Ukrainian priests did attend the congress, but did not bother to inform Tarnawsky of their plans before the event. The highest-ranking Ukrainian bishop at the congress was Dionysius Njaradi of Yugoslavia, who had come to America with a dual purpose: to bless Bishop Takach's new residence and attend the congress. Bishop Budka of Canada also attended, making his last extended trip to the United States before returning to Lviv in 1928.

Chicago's grand Ukrainian church had not yet been fully completed. Moreover, it was too small to hold the expected crowds during the planned solemn Eastern-rite episcopal liturgy. So Tarnawsky arranged that the Eastern-rite liturgy be held in the Roman Catholic cathedral, and Bohachevsky arranged for the presence of the papal nuncio. Neither of the arranged events took place. Permission to use the Roman Catholic cathedral was withdrawn days before the scheduled liturgy, and at the last-minute Luigi Bonzano, the nuncio, cancelled his plans to attend the Ukrainian liturgy. The Ukrainian intelligentsia, as well as the clergy, saw a Polish hand in the withdrawals.

The Byzantine liturgy took place at the yet unfinished St. Nicholas Church after all. It was solemn, moving, and well attended both by participating Eastern- and Latin-rite Catholic clergy as well as American Catholic laity. George Cardinal Mundelein donated the decorative bunting in the papal white and gold and the Ukrainian blue and yellow colors that adorned the church, and Bishop John F. Noll of Fort Wayne delivered the sermon.[29] There were four Ukrainian bishops, lay Ukrainians turned out *en masse*, and the choir was magnificent. In addition to the lengthy but well-executed services in the Ukrainian church, Bohachevsky participated, at the invitation of the cardinal, in the consecration of a new Roman Catholic church in Chicago built "in the Eastern style."[30]

28. The Ukrainian priest who prepared the paper was Rev. Hlib Verkhovsky. It could not be accepted because Russian was not a language used at the conference. Both *Svoboda* and *Dnipro* in their July 17, 1926, issues had a field day with this story.

29. Tarnawsky, *Memoirs*, 161.

30. This report is largely based on Nazaruk's letter to Lypynsky, October 15, 1924, in Lypynsky, *Collected Works*, 222–29.

Prystay, writing about these events later, complained about how paltry the Ukrainian celebrations looked in comparison to the novenas, processions, and picnics of the Latin-rite Catholics. He blamed the discrepancy on Bohachevsky's failure to do a better job of ensuring the proper level of Ukrainian participation. His observations are somewhat dubious as he and Rev. Ivan Kutsky were busy attending so many of the Latin-rite Catholic events that they barely managed to participate in the Eastern-rite liturgy.[31] Nor did Prystay mention that none of the Ukrainian priests, except Verkhovsky, volunteered a paper. Nonetheless, other evidence confirms that the Ukrainian part of the congress was not very well organized, especially when compared to the no-holds-barred magnificence that the Latin-rite Catholic Church in the United States showcased. Bohachevsky, rather than the local clergy charged with preparations for the event, took the heat, especially when it was discovered that the local clergy had not been given any funds to support their role in preparing for the congress.

The overall opening formalities, handled by the American Latin-rite Catholic Church, went well. The presence of the four Ukrainian bishops—Njaradi, Bohachevsky, Takach, and Budka—in their distinctive golden, dome-shaped miters, was dramatic enough to attract the attention of the American press during the opening ceremonies. But the American press, faced with an unusual multiplicity of rites, lumping them together, referred to Eastern Catholics as "Greek," thereby sprinkling salt on Ukrainian wounds. Later accounts also reveal another irritant: during the opening ceremonies one Latin-rite Catholic bishop was allegedly overheard to have said privately that Catholic unity demanded the immediate abolition of other rites in favor of the Latin variant. It is not clear who overheard the remark, but it later caused great consternation among Ukrainian clerics. They felt that Bohachevsky failed to challenge the offending remark on the spot, thus proving his indifference to the Ukrainian Church.

However, the most glaring scandal at the American Eucharistic congress—at least according to the Ukrainian Orthodox press—occurred at the special banquet for the clergy, which was hosted by the Latin Catholic archbishop. The precise wording of the invitation to the event is not

31. Prystay to Petrivsky, April 13, 1927, in Prystay, Z Truskavtsia u svit khmaroderiv, vol. 3 (Lviv: Dilo, 1936), 163–84.

known, but one can speculate that those who created it did not consider it necessary to specify that priests should come without female companions. When some of the Ukrainian clergy showed up for the evening banquet with their formally clad wives, the wives were denied access to the banquet. One can argue that the Ukrainian clergy who had lived in the United States for at least a decade should have realized that wives would not be appropriate in an all-male clerical gathering, but they apparently chose to ignore the problems the presence of wives might create. The Ukrainians felt that Bohachevsky was weak. The bishop should have insisted that the wives of the clergy join the formal dinner, or at least the bishop should have led the Ukrainian unmarried clergy out of the premises. I have not been able to ascertain if the other Ukrainian Catholic bishops had been invited to the event. They are not mentioned in the later polemics.

The incidents described above angered Ukrainians. They resented the fact that the American clergy did not give Ukrainians the use of the Latin-rite Catholic cathedral, as had been originally planned. The ungenerous treatment of married Ukrainian Catholic clergy and their wives provided Ukrainian journalists with juicy anti-Catholic material. The Ukrainian leftist press had a field day with the way things turned out—the snub to the wives reinforced their contention that the Ukrainian Catholic Church was not only unpatriotic, but also insignificant and weak. *Svoboda* and the other Ukrainian-American press organs touted the incident as proof of Vatican perfidy.

A few days after the Chicago congress, on July 5, 1926, the Ukrainian-American bishops, along with Bishop Njaradi, headed for the blessing of Takach's residence and consistory. The joyous solemnity of the occasion, and particularly the visible support of the Ruthenian congregation for their pastor, stood in sharp contrast to the tense atmosphere that pervaded Philadelphia's treeless, scorching Franklin Street that summer.

THE IVAN FRANKO ANNIVERSARY

The conflict between the intelligentsia and the church in the United States came to a head when Bohachevsky refused to mandate, and then forbade, formal church services to mark the tenth anniversary of Ivan Franko's death. Bohachevsky had not been able to mobilize the community to mark the tenth anniversary of Ortynsky's death, nor even to memorialize the "Awakener" of Western Ukraine, Rev. Markian Shashkevych; and he found the glorification of the atheist Franko misdirected. He questioned the propriety of holding up the popular poet as a model for the young. By speaking out against a "cult of Franko" in the community, Bohachevsky gave his opponents their most potent weapon. The opposition used the tenth anniversary of Franko's death to question Constantine Bohachevsky's Ukrainian patriotism.

Franko had become a national icon, idolized by Halychyna youth and fully aware of a "cult of Franko" that began during his lifetime. It blossomed full force in the 1920s. For Western Ukrainians Franko was a bard of Ukraine equal to Taras Shevchenko. His prodigious literary and scholarly output, as well as his political activism and peasant origin had made him a household name. In his youth, Franko, a brilliant and versatile writer, was a socialist; he made fun of organized religion and wrote popular anti-clerical poetry. By the time of Franko's death on May 28, 1916, there was little mention of the poet's very public rejection of organized religion. Slowly but inexorably, Franko's sharp edges of Marxism and atheism were quietly robed in nationalism's silvery patina. By the 1920s, a picture of Franko hung incongruously side by side with icons in Ukrainian-American households.

When Bohachevsky came to the United States, he was not aware that Franko had been elevated to a national icon. He took the poet and writer seriously, respecting his views even as he opposed them. Among other things, Bohachevsky knew first-hand that Franko had had ample opportunity, even on his deathbed, to return to God, and chose not to. Prior to World War I, as Franko's reputation grew, the leadership of the Ukrainian Catholic Church in Halychyna had already become very concerned about the spread of atheism and materialism in the land. At their meeting on July 11, 1904, the bishops of Halychyna, at Sheptytsky's initiative, created a commission that was to monitor all publications and counteract the spread of materialism.[32] They repeated the warning against the "bad Ruthenian press" in 1911, but could not decide on a scale of dangerous publications.[33] Bohachevsky, who had among his early positions been named

32. PKEL, July 11, 1904, 4.
33. PKEL, January 24, 1911, 15; they created the commission only to table the project at

an ecclesiastical censor, was very much aware of the concerns of the bishops. Kotsylovsky and Khomyshyn shared Bohachevsky's view of Franko; Sheptytsky did not. Shaped by these events and by his own role in them, Bohachevsky found the popularity of socialist ideas in the United States shocking, especially among the Ukrainian immigrants. During the war and postwar period, Bohachevsky had neither the time nor the inclination to pay attention to Franko's posthumous reputation. The home country was being torn apart by issues far weightier than Franko, and he had no reason to think that Franko would become a hero for the immigrants in the United States. He easily wrote Franko off as one of the cohorts of modern foes of the church, never imagining that in the immigrant community in the United States, Franko loomed larger than life. Now, suddenly confronted by the "cult of Franko," Bohachevsky became genuinely concerned by the threat to his flock's spiritual welfare. Celebration of Franko would deny the authenticity of all that the church stood for. Bohachevsky was most worried by the impact Franko's socialist writings might have on the youth he dreamt of grooming for religious service. He did not think it right to "sanitize" the poet, to close one's eyes to his atheism and unconventional life, and elevate him by holding memorial services in all Ukrainian churches.

Few others, however, were consistent enough to subject Franko to such scrutiny. Most wrote off Franko's atheism and used the poet as a patriotic symbol against Polish occupation. Nazaruk was an exception. The journalist saw that by condoning even a partial acceptance of Franko, the church would violate its own integrity. From this position, Nazaruk, who was himself a former socialist atheist who took part in the armed Ukrainian liberation struggle in Kyiv, presented the weaknesses in Franko's reasoning and character. He demonstrated that while some parts of Franko's output were very valuable, his other works prevented this excellent writer from being elevated to the role of Moral Hero. But this observation was tantamount to criticizing motherhood. Most Western Ukrainian immigrants chose to focus on Franko the writer, not Franko the social critic and forerunner of modernist decadent literature. Faced with these

---

the next meeting, May 9–10, 1911. The bishops worked on the text for over two years, see minutes of October 10, 1911, and April 29, 1912. In 1913, Budka from Canada also suggested that sins against the sixth commandment include the reading of "bad books."

attitudes, Nazaruk swept into an open attack on Franko, launching an assault even on the intelligentsia's holy of holies—the tenth anniversary of the poet's death. He also began to wage war openly against Myshuha who, Nazaruk was convinced, wanted to destroy him and the bishop as well.[34]

In the end, the failure to permit religious services for Franko to mark the tenth anniversary of his death made the bishop a traitor to Ukraine in the eyes of many. The Catholic practice of the time was that only Catholics in good standing with the church merited formal memorial religious services, but no one wanted to bother knowing what Franko thought of the church. Some kept their thoughts to themselves. The leadership of the Alliance, however, chose to interpret the bishop's failure to mandate prayers for Franko as opposition to the whole Ukrainian cause. They also chose to make their opinions on this matter public.

Under the signature of the board of the Alliance, the community coordinating council which Myshuha sought to lead, he announced a formal program marking the anniversary of Franko's death that included religious services. Rev. Vashchyshyn, who at the time was serving as Bohachevsky's chancellor while being on the board of the Alliance, publicly protested both the proposed celebration and the use of his name without prior approval in announcing the Franko memorial program. Myshuha put Vashchyshyn on the spot by sending him the following letter on Alliance letterhead. I quote it in its entirety because it reflects the tone Myshuha, ten years the priest's junior, used in his dealings with the clergy and the public:

I read in the newspaper, America, dated June 3, a statement in which you claim not to have signed the Alliance communiqué about the jubilee of Franko.

Herewith I have the honor to state that it is true that you have not signed this proclamation, as you have not signed other such proclamations, nor [have] you protested [against such procedure] earlier.

Ever since its establishment, the Alliance leadership had not sought the specific approbation of each member of the executive board, and this is the first questioning of this procedure during the four-year existence of the Alliance.

In view of your statement I must now ask you officially if you agree with the statement of the Alliance in the matter of the celebration of the tenth anniversary of the death of the great national teacher Ivan Franko, or not. Because when

34. Nazaruk to Lypynsky, July 1, 1926, in Lypynsky, *Collected Works*, 302.

your signature was included there was no doubt for a moment that you would agree with our resolution. Your recent statement makes me doubt my [earlier] presumption [about your view of Franko].

At the same time let me add that you were present to the very end of this meeting of the Alliance and did not express any protest about your signature.

Let me also add that at that meeting my proclamation about the Franko festivities was unanimously approved by acclamation.

Please send your answer to my question by return post, if possible.[35]

Myshuha's letter left no doubt that he sought to present the bishop as a small-town hick, incapable of understanding broad national needs. Vashchyshyn, who since his arrival in the United States in 1909, had served both in the mining areas of Pennsylvania and in the textile mills of Connecticut, was a well-known public figure. Having him on record to prove the bishop wrong in assessing Franko's public role would strengthen the Alliance's position. Vashchyshyn let Myshuha's letter slide. He still hoped that somehow the outbreak could be hemmed in.

The summer heated up when two typesetters of *America* resigned in protest of Nazaruk's proposed article on Franko's work, which they refused to set into type. (Nazaruk, among other things, had characterized some poems as decadent and morbid.) The typesetters, Teodor Sarakhman and Florian Shnurer, sent the text of their protest to *Svoboda*, which immediately published their statements in a brochure. Thus the bishop's call for a conversation on education was transformed into a discussion of the bishop's failures and limitations, especially when compared to the achievements of the poet who had died a decade earlier but who still lived in the hearts of Ukrainians.[36]

Recognizing that this was only an introductory salvo to a longer battle, Bohachevsky wanted Sheptytsky to go on record about the negative impact Franko had on Ukrainian society. But the metropolitan had met the poet and had dismissed his political views as shallow and irrelevant. In 1918, Sheptytsky, en route to Lviv from his exile in Russia, had even held a memorial service for Franko in Kyiv at the request of the poet's daughter.

35. Myshuha to Vashchyshyn, n.d. (most likely June) UMAS, correspondence of priests.
36. This brochure, titled *Svitohliad Ivana Franka* [*Worldview of Ivan Franko: Can a Christian People Accept and Propagate His Cult?*], published in the usual *America* brochure run of two thousand, has not made it into the vast literature on Franko.

Having done so, the metropolitan tacitly approved the actions of priests who held similar services for the atheist poet.

Bohachevsky did not have that option. Not only did he take Franko's atheism seriously, he also had to contend with lay activists in his American churches who shared his views and were scandalized that a socialist atheist who scoffed at the church would be publicly memorialized by that church. Another danger was that the worker population, which made up the majority of Ukrainian parishes, was particularly vulnerable to leftist propaganda.

Bohachevsky sought to explain all this to Sheptytsky while attempting to convince the metropolitan to tone down the Franko celebrations. Some time earlier he had written to Sheptytsky about the direction that one of the Ukrainian religious journals was taking. In this letter he apologized "for turning a second time to Your Excellency on a public matter, and perhaps I will need to do so again in the future." In what for him was an unusually lengthy three-page letter, which he addressed to Sheptytsky directly on November 16, 1926, Bohachevsky argued the necessity to extirpate the "cult of Franko."

Following the example of Lviv lay societies our local "Alliance," which for a number of years has been trying to break up the Catholic Church under the guise of church welfare, likewise proclaimed the "cult." As Your Excellency no doubt knows, all Catholic churches [in the United States] are supported exclusively by voluntary donations, I have risked in the name of the principles of our church to oppose this "cult" of an atheist within our nation. I was motivated in this decision not by any desire for struggle with the segment of atheistic intelligentsia, which consciously is splitting the Catholic Church—but rather by concern about the future. Because if we let these celebrations take root, we will not be able to stem the popularization and free distribution of his atheistic works and satires against our holy church and even against faith in God. Granted that passivity would give us temporary "peace," but in the future [this peace] would reflect brutally on the fate of the church and on the morals of the people.

Without mincing words, Bohachevsky continued:

Sadly, but very frankly, I am informing Your Excellency that the main argument of the atheists in their destructive agitation runs somewhat along these lines: "Why does Metropolitan Sheptytsky, in whose eparchy Franko died and was buried, not speak up against the "cult" of this "genius"? It is obvious [so the argument runs] that the metropolitan agrees with those who support, and not with those who oppose the dissemination of this "cult."

It is difficult, to be sure, to reply to this argument when, moreover, priests in the eparchy of Your Excellency take an active part in the celebrations of Franko and his "cult," while the press provides reports of their participation, with names of priests, that the local emigrants often know personally. And all of this without any news on what, if anything, the Lviv chancery [ordynariat] is planning to do to halt the participation of the clergy in this "cult."[37]

Not only was Bohachevsky's move unpopular, it also cost him dearly: "We are suffering major financial losses. *Svoboda* openly calls on people not to donate a penny to the church. . . . Even donations for the orphans fell." But he remained firm:

In addition to the principle in this matter, I am motivated also by fear about the future of that people whose morals and salvation have been entrusted to me, for it is clear, that if the above mentioned agitators weaken the prestige of the church, then many faithful will be demoralized and will succumb to all sorts of vices, that will shame the Ukrainian name in this our second fatherland that has accepted us so hospitably in its own land.

Finally, he pleaded:

To strengthen this request let me add, that there is no reason to fear public opinion in the matter [banning Franko celebrations in churches] because even the most leftist publications admit the justice of the principled stand of the eparchy in the struggle against the cult of Franko.

Bohachevsky signed the letter almost coldly: "With deep regard, Servant in Christ, Constantine, Bishop."[38]

Sheptytsky replied carefully and with much thought, but well after the worst of the confrontations. The draft of the letter to Bohachevsky is handwritten by a secretary, with many editorial changes, presumably in Sheptytsky's hand. The metropolitan began with the argument that the situation was not simple and could not be resolved simply, and that

37. Bohachevsky to Sheptytsky, November 16, 1926, TsDIA, Lviv, f. 408, op. 1, spr. 1249. Parts of the letters were first published in *Pravda pro Uniiu: Dokumenty I Materialy*, 2nd ed. (Lviv: Kameniar, 1968), 172–78. The selection was a useful document in the Soviet antireligious and antinationalist campaign.

38. Bohachevsky to Sheptytsky, November 16, 1926, TsDIA, Lviv, f. 408, op. 1, spr. 1249.

there were major differences between Halychyna and the United States. Bohachevsky, not Sheptytsky, bears primary responsibility for the salvation of Catholics in America. He, Bohachevsky, must make the decision he thinks best: "Life in your [part of the world] is somewhat different from ours, so you will have other considerations when considering 'the cult of Franko.' Therefore, I have no intention of judging your regulations about this matter. Locally, you can gauge the situation better and how to deal with it. I only want to explain [the original word 'justify' was crossed out] my own tactics toward the 'cult of Franko.'" Sheptytsky then argued that Franko's atheism was only a small part of his output and did not reflect the true nature of Franko, whom he characterizes as a thinker ("philosopher" is crossed out) of encyclopedic scope.

The places in which he [Franko] develops his materialism and atheism are weak, he was able to present patriotic and national themes better and more effectively, so much so that solid criticism has already rolled the dice that Ivan Franko will be remembered in the future only as a poet, nationalist, patriot. I had the occasion to persuade myself that ["my" crossed out] believers, subject to my jurisdiction, value Franko exclusively for his greatness as a national patriotic writer and not because of his atheism and materialism, which they [the faithful] reject.

The metropolitan further explained that forbidding the clergy to honor Franko would just backfire. Franko's poetry was already so popular that it was included in school curricula and was read widely by the public. Banning Franko would only make it easier for "the rabid" supporters of Franko to stress his atheism. "So if there is no hope to extirpate Franko's popularity in our nation, then I think it would be wiser to adhere to the proverb *quieta non movere*. Franko's atheism and materialism no longer have the power they had previously, neither among the old or the young."

Sheptytsky further pointed out that communism was not spread through Franko, but directly from Russian and Ukrainian sources. Because Ukrainians had fewer recognized great talents than the Poles, Sheptytsky considered that it was difficult to challenge Franko's position. In other words, because Ukrainians had so few recognizable writers and thinkers, it was better to overlook Franko's drawbacks and not take seriously those parts of his legacy that were not to the church's liking. After enumerating the reasons that he could not support Bohachevsky's position, Sheptytsky also hinted that had the bishops in Halychyna followed his suggestions, the fracas at home and abroad could have been averted:

Please believe me that I am very sorry I cannot help you in your difficult situation. But I cannot practice what I consider dangerous and senseless to be able to help you. If you had only turned to me before promulgating the ban [on the Franko celebrations], then it would have been easier to accommodate you. Specifically, I would have been willing for all our bishops in light of the popularization [of the] "cult of Franko," to have jointly, or separately, published a directive to the clergy and the faithful that Franko's worldview is hostile toward faith and church, and then the clergy could have suitably enlightened the faithful during the Franko celebrations.

Before ending with a suggestion that Bohachevsky disseminate publications that present Franko in the proper light, among them an article by Reverend Havryil Kostelnyk, Sheptytsky noted in the margin: "During the long years of my episcopate I learned through experience that one cannot achieve much by interdict. Better and more secure successes can be reached by teaching, which helps in the upbringing of the faithful."[39]

Sheptytsky's letter was not so much a slap on the wrist for Bohachevsky as proof that, as the local bishop, he had to be personally responsible for the salvation of the Ukrainian Catholic immigrants in the United States. Sheptytsky, after all, was not the pastor of the flock on this side of the ocean. He, Constantine, bishop, was personally responsible before God if his faithful strayed and he failed to bring them back to the straight and narrow. For the young bishop the seminal point of Sheptytsky's letter was the reassertion of Bohachevsky's responsibility.

Bohachevsky took Sheptytsky's advice, read more Franko, and on occasion even quoted a few phrases from the poet's patriotic quatrains. Eventually the bishop would outgrow his righteous adherence to regulations, but first he had to prove—to himself and his faithful, and to his superiors in the church—that his policies could prevail in the exarchate entrusted to him.

Nazaruk prepared another brochure on Franko, which was published late in 1927. In it Vasyl Lukych (a pseudonym of Vasyl Levytsky), who as a young man worked with Franko, also shared his views on what makes a

39. Ibid.

national hero.[40] He concluded that Franko was a superb editor and an effective teacher, but lacked the qualities essential for a Great Man. Lukych argued that Franko's poetry was uneven, and the poet often published his works raw, while holding high demands for others. Nor was Franko's scholarly and publicist output of world-class level. Where Franko excelled was in launching a senseless, destructive campaign against the church, which caused great harm to a generation of young people in Halychyna. What is more, argued Lukych, the spiritual crisis that Franko abetted had ultimately destroyed the poet.

"The cult of Franko" was more useful to Bohachevsky's opposition than any of the polemics against the bishop. In the heat of battle, few made distinctions between the analysis of Franko's writings and the veneration of the poet as a hero. The Alliance made the celebration of the Franko anniversary, which was to include services in the churches, a major goal of its agenda. That forced Chancellor Vashchyshyn's resignation from its board. The Providence Association withdrew from the Franko commemoration. The bishop was strong enough to persuade the Providence Association to demand an apology from the Alliance for defamation of his character, but too weak to make this happen effectively. On July 29, 1926, the leadership of the Providence Fraternal Association passed the following resolution:

Considering that his Excellency the bishop is the chief trustee of the Providence Organization and taking into account the fact that the Association Alliance came out against the Ukrainian Catholic bishop in its communiqué no. 18, titled "The new Greek Catholic bishop Dr. Constantine Bohachevsky has rejected all national work," that Dr. Myshuha frequently speaks out publicly against the person of our trustee, which shocks us and causes vociferous recriminations, the Providence Organization at its semi-annual meeting July 29, 1926, calls upon the Association Alliance: 1. To provide satisfaction and apologize to the Honorary President. 2. To charge Dr. L. Myshuha to apologize to [Bohachevsky] and withdraw his slanderous attacks.[41]

A note to the resolution explained that the Providence Association did not withdraw from membership in the Alliance, it merely asked for an

40. Lukych, *Ivan Franko*.
41. Resolution unanimously accepted. Text of the resolution in Nazaruk, *Holos Evropeiskoho Vladyky Preosviashchenoho Dioniziia*, 31, 32.

apology for falsely accusing the bishop of not supporting this organization or the whole Ukrainian movement. An apology for misrepresenting
the position of the church would have made it possible for the Providence
Association to continue working with the Alliance, thus providing a way
out of the impasse. But Myshuha was unwilling to admit that the Alliance
misinterpreted the bishop. Instead he now accused the Providence Association of arbitrarily withdrawing from the Alliance. But even that move
did not strengthen the Alliance enough for the organization to continue,
as more organizations withdrew from it.

In the end, no apology was made. Myshuha and his confreres felt certain that they were in the right in accusing the bishop of unpatriotic behavior, presumably hoping it would speed the bishop's resignation. They
were convinced that it was merely a matter of weeks before the bishop
would be removed. *Svoboda* also sought to undermine Nazaruk by playing up his socialist past.[42] But the major barbs were directed against
Bohachevsky and his anti-national activity: "the bishop is trying to control all the parish funds... which leads to court proceedings."[43] This
accusation, which formed the basis of the charge that the bishop was not
a Ukrainian patriot, was repeated in numerous publications and equally rebutted by Nazaruk. The basis for the accusation was Bohachevsky's
self-proclaimed focus on building up the Ukrainian Catholic eparchy and
establishing a seminary to encourage American-born youths to become
priests. Nevertheless, Nazaruk maintained that the real motive was the
bishop's success in establishing fiscal and ecclesiastical discipline in the
eparchy. As for Bohachevsky's being pro-Polish, Nazaruk's rebuttal was
that Bohachevsky was in a Polish prison when Myshuha was meeting with
representatives of the Polish government. And as for the claim that the
Vatican wanted to destroy the Ukrainian Catholic Church, Nazaruk argued, why had the pope appointed two Ukrainian Catholic bishops to the
United States, whereas the Poles had no specifically Polish bishop in the
country?

The opposition continued its attacks against Bohachevsky's patriotism, accusing him of not reacting forcefully when he was referred to as

42. Defense Committee of the Ukrainian Catholic Church, New York City, *Stan'mo pry
svoyim Archypastyri* [Let Us Stand by Our Archpastor], 3.

43. Anonymous article in *Svoboda*, December 3, 1926.

Ruthenian rather than Ukrainian. Usually, such stories in local newspapers appeared after the bishop left the area. The opposition also pointed to official Vatican correspondence, which used the historical "*Rutheni*," a term the intelligentsia considered an insult. There were also some voices calling for the introduction of the vernacular into the church service. Bohachevsky opposed the move knowing that a good half of the faithful would consider English, and not Ukrainian, to be their native tongue.

Open disregard of Bohachevsky's regulations spread. Some large parishes refused to make any church donations until the bishop changed his policies. Other priests paid chancery dues from their own pay, rather than risk the ire of the parishioners by collecting for the chancery. Nazaruk, afraid the bishop was too gentle and too soft to withstand the whirlwind raging against him, sought to strengthen the bishop's will in the face of the mounting opposition. The editor's articles were quickly made into pamphlets for easier distribution, as the attacks on the bishop spread through the larger parishes. Nazaruk suspected, in a letter to Lypynsky, that Myshuha most likely was working to establish a national Catholic autocephaly or even a nondenominational national church.[44]

None of Bohachevsky's conciliatory tactics worked. The fall was shaping up to be a stormy one. Early in August Bohachevsky held a retreat for more than fifty priests, and apparently only Prystay warned the bishop that opposition to him was more widespread than it appeared. Bohachevsky misread the ensuing silence as support of his policies. Nothing could have been further from the truth.

Disorder in the parishes spread full force like tumbleweed from town to town. Priests were placed in the most awkward positions, trying to meet the bishop's demands and at the same time reconcile their contentious parishioners. The bishop's apologists reacted to the charges made against him; they did not make the case for him. They, like Bohachevsky,

44. Nazaruk to Lypynsky, September 17, 1926, in Lypynsky, *Collected Works*, 398: "'Myshugizm' is triumphant because the society is ripe for it. Obviously, a fair number of the old priests support and wage war against the bishop. That is a fact. I am almost certain that Myshuga [sic] wants to establish conditions that would lead to autocephaly—in much the same fashion as the intelligentsia in Canada or [Petro] Karmansky in Brazil. . . . Extreme nationalism is responsible for this dissolution [*rozklad na tli natsionalistychnim*]." Karmansky was a poet and political activist.

used a traditional rhetoric that had already acquired a new meaning for their listeners. The bishop spoke of character, sacrifice, eternity; their audience heard nation, party, and country. State-building had recently failed for Ukraine; the church was the one building bloc that still endured in its pre-World War I form. Bohachevsky thought that deeds spoke louder than patriotic assurances. He expected to run on his record, but no one presented that record strongly enough to make an impact, and the bishop's personality as well as his cultural views prevented him from touting his case.

Bohachevsky defended himself publicly only once: at a sermon preached on the Sunday after Epiphany, January 23, 1927, at the cathedral in Philadelphia. Soon afterwards he left for Europe (on February 12, 1927) to perform a scheduled episcopal consecration in Rome and to take part in the bishops' conference in Lviv. Meanwhile, he prayed. His reaction can be understood only within the context of his worldview and the society he had left behind. He was not alone in his conviction that salvation can be achieved solely within the strict Magisterium of the church, but he was certainly one of the most consistent and literal interpreters of this doctrine. He relied only on God and his path to God was only through prayer. He prayed at monastic lengths, far longer than expected of uncloistered clergy. His fervor underscored his belief in a fiercely righteous God, awesome in the original meaning of the word. Awed by this God, Bohachevsky did not focus on his surroundings or those who tried to help him. His God may be testing him as far as public opinion was concerned, but the bishop kept his steadfast faith and never wavered in his belief that God stood with him. One can envision a hard-working, determined lonely figure in a black suit with a Roman collar trudging every week with his little black suitcase to a different church in a working-class neighborhood, knowing that he might be jeered, shoved, spat upon, have doors slammed in his face, rocks hurled with crude epithets and yet convinced that despite all appearances to the contrary he was doing God's work. As it turned out, he was right after all. His church eventually prospered, but not before he completed his own Gethsemane.

In the Gordian entanglements of this struggle, we can discern strands reflecting historical peculiarities of the Ukrainian experience, and others evolving from local American considerations. Many Ukrainians raised in the Ukrainian Catholic Church never considered the idea of the separation of church and state pertinent for their situation. Lacking a state, the church served as the only visible locus of public activity. The bishop defended traditional Catholicism in which the clergy played a leading, although not an exclusive role. He feared the disorder that had come from secular control of the individual churches, and worried that the authority of the church (as well as its resources) would be subverted for other causes. His opponents sought some if not total control over the laity and considered themselves the true representatives of the people, thus qualified to determine the boundaries of church activity and influence.

The polemics about the bishop became so heated that they trumped interest in communism, local politics, and even politics in the home country. The bishop's iron will and steely nerves were beginning to crack. He considered meeting with his opponents face to face after all. His advisers demurred, recalling the tragic results of Ortynsky's tactics. They feared for the church as much as for themselves, were the bishop to recognize the legitimacy of negotiations with his foes, as Ortynsky had tried to do. Their insistence on this position kept Bohachevsky on his narrow lonely path. He would not negotiate with an amorphous crowd, and the crowd could not structure itself into a stable functioning organization with a responsible elected leadership.

CHAPTER 7

The *Fayt*

Bishop Bohachevsky had planned to go to Rome and Lviv in the summer of 1926, his second in the United States. He looked forward to seeing his family and friends, and especially his fellow-bishops for the first time since his consecration. But his closest advisers insisted it was imperative for him to stay in Philadelphia. In their view, the opposition was waiting for a suitable moment to control the church. The bishop's absence from Philadelphia would provide an ideal chance to bring forth the claimant to the episcopate. Furthermore, in Europe Bohachevsky would be more likely to overestimate the opposition's willingness for a compromise, even as it continued its clandestine tactics. The advisers feared that mingling with the broader Ukrainian-European community might cloud the bishop's judgment and make him forget murky American conditions. That could lead to a repetition of Ortynsky's experience, only postpone the crisis, narrow the church's freedom of action, and further weaken the church in America and lead to its demise.

That spring, the assassination in Paris of Symon Petliura, the head of the Ukrainian National Republic in exile, had heightened the national fervor of the immigrants, awakened discussions on political systems for Ukraine, and increased pressure on the churches to support a political agenda. Bohachevsky at first dismissed the primitive leaflets against him as rantings of the extreme left, but as the summer progressed he realized the growing strength of the movement against the church. He spent the

235

summer in his stiflingly hot rooms on the third-floor walkup above the chancery. The tension dragged through the fall. The entry stoop to the chancery teemed with kibitzers who expostulated on the workings of the eparchy, the Vatican, and the world. Bohachevsky slipped out through the back alley to spend downtime with the orphans. The bishop held steady and did not permit himself to be provoked. Neither did the opposition. The uneasy stalemate held. People continued to mill in front of the chancery, sit on the stoop, and enumerate the bishop's shortcomings. By mid- September Bohachevsky even suggested that one of the lawyers ask the Philadelphia Office of Public Safety if there was any way to stop at least the distribution of hostile literature in front of the chancery office. There was not.

Through the summer, the Ukrainian Orthodox Autocephalous Church grew in popularity. It increased its use of vernacular Ukrainian to prove its Ukrainian patriotism and make itself more attractive to unhappy Catholics. There were rumors that prominent members of the Ukrainian intelligentsia had already created a National Ukrainian Church that included Catholics and Orthodox. How would the Catholic Church in America respond to these challenges?

At the same time the news from the home country was bleak: a rise of extremist sentiments among the youth, including a couple of assassinations; leftist trends among the intelligentsia, highlighted by increased emigration to Soviet Ukraine; Polish repression; disagreements between members of the clergy and among laity on clerical celibacy and the role of the church. Bohachevsky's erstwhile colleague Havryil Kostelnyk moved the discussion from liturgical matters to lay participation in church reforms, which foreshadowed the Vatican II *aggiornamento* still almost a century away. Bohachevsky, challenged by effective Orthodox and anticlerical moves, wrote to Metropolitan Sheptytsky, concerned that the articles in Kostelnyk's journal *Nyva* (The Field) contributed to the unrest in America and might even spread unrest to the Ukrainian Catholic Church elsewhere.

Bohachevsky received a lengthy reply, not from the metropolitan, but from Kostelnyk, who chided Bohachevsky for writing to Sheptytsky rather than to him. Kostelnyk commiserated with Bohachevsky's "difficult situation," but told him that the difficulties were of his own making. A different bishop, in his view, could have controlled the movement: "Do not worry," he opined, "about our archdiocese. There is no likelihood that the dangerous tendencies with which you threaten His Excellency [Sheptytsky] would develop here. At least [the Lviv church] is safe as long as the metropolitan is alive. He does not push people away, thus making them succumb to hostile agitation."[1] A very influential circle that advised Metropolitan Sheptytsky shared Kostelnyk's views.[2] Bohachevsky kept the letter but did not respond to Kostelnyk. Instead, he once again wrote to Sheptytsky, this time focusing on the Franko celebrations discussed in the chapter six. Meanwhile, Nazaruk kept up his barrage of polemical articles in *America*.

The crisis seemed to ripen by September 15, 1926, when the Alliance held a meeting in Philadelphia to plan the community's actions for the rest of the year. The Alliance claimed to represent the entire Ukrainian-American society, including the churches. Its leaders expected that all churches would become members of the Alliance and act in accordance with the policies determined by the meetings and the leadership. There was no agenda, short of a skeletal one of lofty goals. Bohachevsky was willing to cooperate with this organization on specific, clearly defined issues, but he did not consider it proper for the church to be directly affiliated with any organization that could by its vote compromise the church's position. Some of the activists chose to interpret the bishop's stand as opposition to the community.

A group of twenty-three community activists decided to bring the bishop, if necessary by force, to take part in the Alliance meeting. They marched directly to the office and when told that the bishop would not see them without prior arrangement, the twenty-three men, now reinforced

1. Rev. Kostelnyk to Rev. Kinash, June 6, 1929, UMAS. Oleksandr Lushnytsky has kindly offered to me Kostelnyk's letter to Bohachevsky from the Hryhor Luzhnytsky personal archive. In contrast to Kostelnyk's rosy view, Hegumen Theodosius Tyt Halushchynsky wrote to Bohachevsky about his difficulties in organizing a nonpolitical Catholic action group; Halushchynsky to Bohachevsky, December 12, 1926, UMAS.

2. Kostelnyk to Bohachevsky, November 17, 1926, a five-page, handwritten letter critical of Bohachevsky's policies. Kostelnyk edited the journal *Nyva*, which carried on a lively debate on church reform, clerical celibacy, and lay participation in the administration of the church. See especially *Nyva* (September 1925): 291–93. In a later issue, Kostelnyk summarized the discussion "Chy spravdi nova doba nashoii tserkvy?" *Nyva* (May 1926): 113–117. For good measure he included the beginning of another article, "Psykholohia viry" [Psychology of faith], in the same issue, pp. 175–181.

by others armed with picks and shovels, prepared to storm the chancery. The scene turned ugly. The priests directed Bohachevsky to the chapel, where he knelt at the altar to pray, while the crowd broke into the building. Earlier attempts at harassing the bishop had involved smashed windows, stone throwing, and ostentatious parading of opponents in front of his office. This time, however, organized violence threatened the person of the bishop. Eventually Vashchyshyn calmed the crowd.

Bishop Bohachevsky did not face the crowd personally. For this, he was accused of cowardice, and he later mulled over the arguments he might have used had he confronted his opponents. Each would-be confrontation, the priests knew, undermined the bishop's resolve not to negotiate with the crowd; and each negotiation, the priests also knew, would undermine the autonomy of the church. They feared that the bishop would change his tactics and go public, to repeat what they considered Ortynsky's failed policies that could later be characterized as appeasement. The church needed to be strong, even if in the process the bishop appeared weak.

The bishop's refusal to meet with the self-styled representatives in September spawned a "bishop is a coward, as well as a traitor" campaign. Unsanctioned meetings of parish communities became more frequent. The pressure on Bohachevsky was relentless. As soon as he took care of one issue, another difficulty arose. Toward the end of September, Fumasoni-Biondi, the apostolic delegate, questioned Bohachevsky by letter as to whether Nazaruk was the right person to edit *America*, a query that sent Bohachevsky to Washington within the week. By mid-November it was clear that a major public meeting of Catholic parishes would be held—with or without the bishop's blessing. To prevent this, Chancellor Vashchyshyn sent a memorandum to all the priests on November 19, 1926, forbidding their participation in nonsanctioned meetings.[3]

The priests closest to Bohachevsky feared a repetition of the drawn-out negotiations between the community leaders and the bishop that had contributed to the disorganization in the church and affected Bishop Ortynsky's health. They were still convinced that the opposition was only waiting for a suitable occasion to undermine the church to gain control

---

3. The document was dated November 10, 1926, but Bohachevsky held off with its proclamation. UMAS.

of its finances. A few priests sent strong letters of support to keep up the bishop's courage and steadfastness.[4] Vashchyshyn, the most conciliatory of Bohachevsky's close collaborators and at the time his chancellor, finally decided to expose the opposition by sharing with the bishop the gist of a conversation he had had with Luka Myshuha more than a year earlier. Had the speaker been any one but Vashchyshyn, Bohachevsky would have immediately dismissed the story. Vashchyshyn's tale at first left Bohachevsky speechless. Recovering his equilibrium, the bishop insisted on writing down the important points of the conversation. Vashchyshyn's account was summarized by hand on a sheet of lined paper. The resulting note provides one possible reason why Bohachevsky stood fast in the face of all the criticisms hurled at him.

From the note we learn that on September 22, 1926, as the mutiny of his parishes was brewing, Bohachevsky's chancellor, Rev. Vashchyshyn, in the presence of the Rev. Oleksandr Pyk and later joined by Rev. Pavlo Protsko, related the following:

Back in 1925 [24 crossed out] Dr. Luka Myshuga [sic] stated before the witness [Rev. Vashchyshyn] that he most likely would begin a war against the bishop mainly because the bishop did not transfer money [to Ukraine] through Dr. Myshuha, who is the secretary of the Alliance and thus takes part of the money for his salary. The witness, Rev. Vashchyshyn, had a feeling that the issue was mainly financial. Dr. Myshuha, furthermore, noted that he is not beginning the struggle that moment because of consideration for Rev. Vashchyshyn with whom he was friendly and whom he visited along with Rev. Kinash [the pastor of the cathedral]. Also [other] members of the Alliance stated before this witness that they would start a war, once they collect more facts.[5]

It is easy to understand why a principled priest like Vashchyshyn would not want to publicize such conversations. The bishop's chancellor was determined to prevent conflicts within the community. It is also likely that he had written off Myshuha's comment to the heat of the moment and to his financial difficulties. By the end of 1926, however, the situation between the church and its opponents was critical, and Vashchyshyn could

---

4. Rev. Vasyl Merenkiv to Bohachevsky, December 1, 1926; Rev. Mykola Simenovych to Bohachevsky, December, 1926; Rev. Mykhailo Lukasky to Bohachevsky, January 3, 1927, UMAS.

5. UMAS.

no longer remain silent: "Rev. Vashchyshyn further stated that Mr. Hryt-sai [spelled Hrytsei, Hrytsay, or Hrycey elsewhere] had told him, Vash-chyshyn, that it is a pity that the bishop hired M. Pashchuk [also at times spelled Pashuk] to administer the church properties. He recommended other candidates, including himself." The final paragraph of the document, written by the same hand but with a different pen presumably a day later, stated:

Rev. Paul Protsko said on September 23 [that is, the day after the events documented above] in the presence of Rev. A. Pyk that after the resignation of Rev. Kinash and after the hiring of M. Pashuk as accountant Mr. V[olodymyr] Bohachevsky appeared at his [Pyk's] office, along with Mr. Hrytsei to say that the bishop should have hired such an upstanding citizen as Hrytsei instead of Pashuk. Then Mr. Hrytsay suggested that Rev. Protsko remit money to the homeland through him, including all [other] funds that the bishop sent home.

These financial considerations, especially the machinations of his brother, whom Bohachevsky would not hire, were enough to convince the bishop that he had to stand his ground. He had no choice. There was adequate evidence that the movement against him was not just one of spontaneous local unrest, but rather a centralized one. Yet actual proof of clerical malfeasance was lacking. The bishop's hands were tied, and he was loath to accept unsubstantiated charges that highly placed clerics were scheming against their bishop.

The bishop neither notarized the document nor filed it in the chancery. Instead, Bohachevsky put the sheet among his private papers where it was mixed in with other miscellany. An archivist from Ukraine, for whom the entire story was totally foreign, came across it in the uncatalogued papers at the Ukrainian Museum and Archives in Stamford in the fall of 2004. The document (if it can be called one) raises serious questions. A handwritten sheet of lined paper, it has no title and no letterhead; the few slight corrections are scratched out or inked in. The signatures of Reverend Volodymyr Pyk, Reverend Protsko, and Bishop Bohachevsky ("Constantine, Bishop") are genuine. The text is at the same time strange and obvious in its simplicity. It tersely recounts a conversation about the origin of the movement against the bishop, and it helps explain the bishop's course of action. Armed with this information, Bohachevsky could have dragged his main opponent through the American courts. Instead, he let the text and the matter that inspired it languish. Why? Perhaps because he could not fully believe the allegations or (more likely) because he saw all the legal loopholes in a testimony that could be written off as hearsay, or possibly because his church and his people had behaved in a manner that would seem foolish to the vast American public and the whole Catholic Church. Bohachevsky did not have the heart to drag the Ukrainian Catholic Church in America even further into what others could belittle as a sandbox fight.

The conversation about Myshuha described above was meant to convince the bishop that there was indeed a concerted effort to dislodge him. The priests wanted him to see that he was correct in not meeting with the representatives of the twenty-three civic organizations who came to his door demanding an audience on September 15, 1926.[6] Another question that arises here is why would Vashchyshyn, a mature, experienced priest, bring up this dated piece of information at a critical time when new self-proclaimed parish representatives were accosting the chancery. Each delegation claimed the bishop's attention, but the bishop, uncertain of the delegates' legitimacy, saw no one. Bohachevsky was roundly and openly criticized for such tactics, so much so that he considered changing his policy and meeting with the delegates. But his advisers, again remembering Ortynsky's unhappy experience, remained determined to keep Bohachevsky from direct debates with an unruly mob.

The Myshuha incident imputes if not spurious then at least underhanded activities to persons who remained at the head of the Ukrainian-American community. Myshuha claimed to be an official representative of Ukraine, as the new representative of the Western Ukrainian People's Republic after the resignation of Lonhyn Tsehelsky. Theodore Hrytsei (also Hrycey), a notary public, had an insurance business that facilitated money transfers to Ukraine.[7] Rev. Joseph Zhuk was one of the most accomplished Ukrainian Catholic priests of the period. Bohachevsky must have found the information that Vashchyshyn brought to his attention embarrassing

---

6. Bishop Ambrose Senyshyn published a series of obituary articles in *Kovcheh*, February 1961, immediately after Bohachevsky's death, which presented a dramatic secondhand telling of Bohachevsky praying at the altar while the roaring armed crowd charged at the door. See also the *Newsletter of the Stamford Eparchy*, January 1961.

7. Hrytsei advertised his services: "a well-known pre-War truly Ukrainian notarial office," *Svoboda*, December 3, 1926.

and troubling. For one thing, it provided a clear-cut financial reason for the opposition of the intelligentsia leadership to his policies. It offered proof of the degree of opposition, something he could no longer ignore. But to admit how he had acquired such information would make the bishop party to backroom-style rumors that would undermine not only his position but also his sense of self. Bohachevsky might understand why Myshuha needed money, but to say so publicly would undermine the cause of the Ukrainian Republic as well as his own standing in a community that already doubted his commitment to the Ukrainian cause. The rumors of a plot against him that the bishop had cavalierly disregarded were proving to be true. Clearly, in September 1926 the bishop still relied on a gentlemanly code of conduct, on his part but also from Myshuha and the dissident clergy.[8]

Bohachevsky's adherence to this gentlemanly code contributed to the difficulty of fully understanding him, especially because he left no other written records about these episodes. We can only conjecture why he diverged from his earlier devotion to record keeping. Perhaps he felt that his life beyond church functions was not worthy of documentation; perhaps he was ambitious or vain enough to think that someone else, a mythical historian of the future, would do this for him. On the other hand, he may have been too embarrassed for himself and for his people to keep written records of contentious events. Or perhaps he was simply too tired to do so, or loathe to waste good paper and ink, since he came from an area where each good piece of paper that had a blank reverse side, was valued for the simple reason that there was a shortage of paper.

Svoboda kept up its line of argument, supporting the primacy of public service on behalf of current Ukrainian causes in the home country over local church policies in the United States. In its December 8, 1926, issue, *Svoboda* reprinted an article excoriating Bishop Kotsylovsky for his criticism of Franko and chiding the cleric for not being a genuine "citizen-bishop" like Metropolitan Sheptytsky.[9] This was a thinly veiled warning to Bo-

8. Nazaruk wanted the bishop to press charges, and there are a few other letters hinting that the bishop should have fought harder and openly criticized the opposition for using the church for collection of funds. Even ten years later, in a letter dated March 13, 1937, from Lviv, Nazaruk, writing to Rev. Adam Polishchak, bemoaned the bishop's unwillingness to fight. Nazaruk correspondence file, TsDIA, Lviv, f. 359, op. 204, pp. 33 and *verte*.

9. It was published as "Holosy presy" [Newspaper Voices], a popular eclectic column. Under the heading "Povorot do chornoii starosvichyny" [Return to Black Antiquity], the

hachevsky to become a citizen-bishop or face the consequences: backlash from the community and criticism from the church hierarchy. The movement to convene an all-American assembly of representatives of the Catholic parishes from the entire United States of America was gaining traction. Even the bishop's older brother, Volodymyr, wrote a one paragraph letter to *Svoboda* stressing that the bishop would not even help his brother, why would he support the people? Would the priests follow the chancery's instructions and refuse to participate or would they be swept up by the strong popular wave and succumb to the community's demands?

The movement against the bishop appeared to be local, but events in individual towns followed the same pattern. The local branch of the Ukrainian National Association generally worked through an *ad hoc* community committee to organize parish activists or town meetings and follow-up demonstrations. Information about meetings spread by word of mouth, leaflets, and notices in *Svoboda* and other publications. They were most popular in the eastern industrial belt and in the industrial towns of the American heartland linked by railroads. In Detroit, an *ad hoc* Committee of United Associations urged all Ukrainians to attend a meeting on October 10, 1926, "to ask Bishop Bohachevsky who he is—a Ukrainian, a Ruthenian, or a Byzantine? And who sent him to us—the Ukrainian People, or Rome, or Byzantium, or perhaps it was Warsaw?"[10] Leaflets proliferated, some urging meetings or other actions, others elaborating on the views of the writer. In response, *Svoboda* had devised a shorthand approach to covering even the very critical ones, for instance, the meeting held in Newark, New Jersey, on November 21, 1926. The article covering this meeting was succinct—by this time, the agenda at these meetings had become repetitively standard. The newspaper did not bother to elaborate on what caused the immigrants in Newark to meet. The article merely noted that among the issues considered to be of "national and church" importance were "clericalism, Ruthenianism, celibacy, concordat, Franko." The most

---

article criticized Bishop Kotsylovsky's policies, especially the prohibition of holding religious memorials for the poet, Ivan Franko, a militant atheist. This article was based on a December 2, 1926, article on Bishop Kotsylovsky in evening edition of Dilo, the Lviv Ukrainian daily. The term used was *hromadiane vladyky* [citizen bishops]. The term would again surface in the 1940s.

10. Leaflet at UMAS.

telling paragraph, however, went beyond these details. It was a call to action:

> But beyond all these matters the struggle continues about the one great, basic, major question, namely, should the politics of the [Catholic] Church be guided by the will of the nation, the faithful of this church, or according to the will of the hierarchy? ... The Ukrainian nation should stand shoulder to shoulder to support those priests who in this battle choose to go with the nation. And even if there are no such priests, the battle should continue [without the priests] because—when the shepherds turn into wolves, the lambs must graze themselves.[11]

The final phrase was part of a popular quatrain by the poet Ivan Franko.

The overarching questions remained unanswered. Would the bishop, who was still perceived by the settled immigrants as a lordly European outsider, and of questionable Ukrainian patriotism despite his prison sentences, now think about joining the crowds? Or would he simply drop everything and leave for Rome? As the large peoples' meetings grew ever louder, the priests who stood with Bohachevsky worried that the bishop was considering a meeting with the crowd.

FRANKLIN STREET BACK CHANNELS

A few weeks before the planned meeting, on November 23, 1926, Rev. Ivan Ostap, at the time pastor of New Kensington, Pennsylvania, warned Bohachevsky of a plot against him in his closest entourage. Addressed to "Your Excellency—Your Grace and Dearest Lord-Bishop!" the lengthy letter was self-serving and indicative of the pervasive rumormongering among the clergy and the faithful. Ostap warned the bishop that the radical "popyky-priestlings," as well as the priests in the chancery, meant to destroy him. He advised the bishop not to trust anyone. Ostap criticized the bishop for not permitting a meeting of priests and laity and for hiring Nazaruk, but offered his services to remedy these mistakes. He thought that the bishop should immediately establish a financial association exclusively for priests so that the priests would have job security and support in their old age. Meanwhile, Ostap knew that the priests had organized

11. *Svoboda*, February 24, 1927, 1.

their own secret association, and Ostap would try to "to sneak into it and 'quietly' vote in a better direction—but that has to be done very carefully and quietly! I'm trying to creep [wheedle] in, but I don't know if they will have me!" Ostap's letter ended with a warning that the bishop should burn the letter lest even his closest advisers see it.[12]

Ostap may have clinched the contention that there was an organized plot against the bishop, but like everyone else, he did not know who was behind it. His letter buttressed Bohachevsky's growing realization that he was dealing not with internal opposition but with a destructive movement aimed at the eradication of the Catholic Church. But Ostap's offer was too cryptic and underhanded for Bohachevsky to follow his advice. As far as the bishop and his advisers were concerned, the most likely suspects would be Myshuha and Rev. Joseph Zhuk; their interests coalesced—both would gain from the removal of Bohachevsky—but neither showed his hand. Rev. Petro Poniatyshyn was another likely contender for a promotion should Bohachevsky resign. Ostap, isolated between the two fronts, returned to Europe and led a quiet village life. The bishop kept the letter in the same way he had kept the note about Myshuha and Hrytsei: not numbered nor filed nor destroyed.

Rev. Fylymon Tarnawsky held on to Chicago, a major achievement for the bishop's camp while the large New York community battled it out on multiple fronts. Elsewhere, at the slightest provocation, planned or spontaneous gatherings were held in various towns, mainly on the east coast, but also in Cleveland, where the local priest saw Bohachevsky as Kotsylovsky's man, whose influence therefore had to be undercut. The disruptions that ensued spun out of control; at one point almost half of the faithful had broken with the bishop. Parishioners fought each other for control of church property, for defense of the church and for Ukraine, for this or that political grouping, but mainly for control of funds. Priests wavered, and families split on their assessment of the bishop or the pastor, or of the calendar. The Ukrainian community in the United States—and

12. Ostap to Bohachevsky, November 23, 1926, UMAS. The tone of the letter reflects the patriarchal relationship that characterized the church in Halychyna—the use of familial diminutives for ecclesiastical personages, the informality in the establishment of facts as well as tactics. The priest wanted a one-on-one relationship with the bishop, not an interview brokered through a church bureaucracy.

not only its Catholic component—became one roiling mass of discontent. Police intervention became more frequent, even when it was not requested. By February 1927 Bohachevsky even considered court action against *Svoboda*.[13]

The crisis reached its apogee as 1926 turned into 1927. On December 3, 1926, *Svoboda* confirmed rumors of the convocation of a congress to deal with matters of the Ukrainian Catholic Church, none of them doctrinal. The paper published a call for the congress without any clergy signatures or any sign of clergy participation. The announcement was practically a detailed indictment of Bohachevsky. To portray the tenor and substance, I am including my translation of the full version as published by *Svoboda*:

A CALL TO ALL UKRAINIAN-CATHOLIC PARISHES IN THE UNITED STATES

Horror and sadness grip each Ukrainian-Catholic when he sees the incredibly rapid disintegration within the Halychyna émigré Ukrainian Catholic Church. Within the year, eighteen churches either broke away entirely from the Catholic Church or split up.

More than 20,000 souls changed their religion, and tens of thousands more stopped going to our churches. No true Ukrainian can rejoice from this confusion that is tearing our emigration apart. None of us want disunity. Only Poland for its own purposes wants us disunited. It [Poland] wants to splinter our émigré unity in America. Poles [pejorative *Liach* is used] know well that disunity will sap our strength and religious discord will tear us asunder and that will result in the diminution and eventual cessation of our aid to our native land.

Taking all this into consideration, it is no wonder that Poland, which had a determining voice in the appointment of Bishop Bohachevsky, found him a useful tool for this goal.

People think so because:

1. Bishop Bohachevsky spoke out against the Alliance, which is an organization to help our country, especially in its struggle with Poland. It is obvious to all

---

13. In a February 4, 1927, letter to Bohachevsky, Rev. Ivan Kuts'ky reported on his discussions with a Mr. Smith, a lawyer who, according to Kuts'ky, argued cases before the Supreme Court. The lawyer maintained that Bohachevsky had a strong case. UMAS, Chancery Archive.

that these steps of the bishop are beneficial to the *Liachs*[14] who want above all to destroy the [Ukrainian] Alliance in America. Let's not forget that the Alliance met the bishop with friendship and respect and that, recognizing its noble goals, he promised to work with the Alliance. That he did not do. Does not this bishop, who was chosen and sent by Poland, realize that in this manner he is performing the work that the *Liachs* want?

2. Bishop Bohachevsky opposed the celebrations of Ivan Franko. The ban against [religious] services for this major dead national genius and the lies published by Nazaruk in *America* have only further splintered society. Who gains? Only our enemies, only Poland.

3. Bishop Bohachevsky presents himself before Americans as "Greek Catholic" or "Ruthenian bishop," and his trusted adviser Nazaruk is defending the use of such terms as Rus' and Rusyn in America. Who is afraid of the term "Ukrainian" if not the Poles, who call us "Rusiny," primarily to sever our ties with Greater Ukraine? There are other issues that trouble Ukrainian Catholics in America:

A. The bishop wants to introduce mandatory clerical celibacy, although Bishop Vasyl Takach [of the Carpatho-Ruthenians] is openly and bravely consecrating married men as priests.

B. In making parish appointments the bishop is not guided by the wishes of the congregation but by his own wishes, thus causing further havoc and discontent.

C. At a time when the whole nation, like Lazarus, extends its hand in supplication, the bishop orders a collection for a seminary knowing full well that if such a collection were successful it would be at the cost of aid to the native land, or even its complete cessation. Moreover, we think that the seminary planned by the bishop is totally unnecessary, and may even be harmful. One, it will be extremely costly, two, we are convinced that none of the students of Bohachevsky would be of any use to the national needs of Ukrainians in America.

We must express this same skepticism about the plan to bring in nuns to our parish schools because we know very well that only a few nuns have the qualifications necessary for teaching.

A few of the parishes [which need priests] can be staffed each year by two or three priests from the home country who could replace the dead clergy, we could get those who are persecuted in the old country because of their patriotism. But the people understand the goals of Bishop Bohachevsky, that he wants to get

14. A mildly derogatory word denoting Poles.

rid of all patriotic priests and man the parishes with priests who undermine all patriotic activity, and therefore we must oppose this [seminary] initiative.

A. We see that Dr. Osyp Nazaruk is the destructive and debilitating power behind the throne, who helps foment the ruin and annihilation in our émigré community. Only recently he was a fervent enemy of faith and church, who for long years through his speeches and publications ridiculed and blackened the church and now he is the major voice in our Catholic diocese in America. This is mockery over common sense, such ridicule of the faithful—that very fact alone should be enough to scandalize all who care for the faith and the church. Had the bishop even searched [wider] he could not have found a better person to destroy the Ukrainian Catholic Church. Even Poland could not find better means for its destructive work. But we won't repeat all that; everyone [already] knows from reading the lies published in *America*, *Sich*, and various brochures.

B. Bishop Bohachevsky is trying to seize all the diocesan properties for his personal control. He considers the best priest one who goes against his community, who initiates court proceedings, and who forces the parishioners to transfer all church property to the bishop. He ignores representatives of parishes, even if they are the most eminent men; he ignored the meetings of priests who gathered for retreats, he does not want to convene meetings of priests to have their counsel during this terrible "time of troubles"[15] because he [the bishop] says: I don't care, let there be only three churches left, but such as I want. Christ said that a good pastor will leave the 99 healthy ones to seek the lost 100th, but Bishop Bohachevsky would rather lose all 99 if only one were to his liking. What does this mean? Who profits from the disorder and discord in our society? Who wants us to splinter into opposing groups?

This is just a general sketch of the situation of the Ukrainian Catholic Church under the jurisdiction of Bishop Bohachevsky. The real situation can be gauged from what is happening in the cathedral—one part [of the faithful] organized an autocephalous parish, and the rest are just waiting around.

Noting all this and watching as everything is being quickly ruined in our church in emigration, we have decided to convene a congress of representatives of all Ukrainian Catholic Churches in the United States.

The congress will take place in the Citizens' Hall in Philadelphia on Wednesday, December 29, 1926. It will begin at 9 A.M. sharp. Each parish may send be-

15. The Russian term *smootnoe vremia*—"disorderly epoch or time of troubles"—refers to the period of dynastic crisis and foreign intervention in the sixteenth and seventeenth centuries.

tween one to three delegates. Let there be no unrepresented parish. The welfare of the church and of the emigration rests on this meeting. We must consult and find ways of saving the Ukrainian Catholic Church from disintegration, and the whole Ukrainian emigration from chaos and a religious war.

Each parish should immediately convene a public meeting and choose its delegates.

If a priest doesn't want, or rather, cannot announce this meeting, it should be convened by some other church organization or brotherhood. We do not want a revolt, no split, no changing of religions. We only want to heal relationships in our church; we want a bishop who will not be dependent upon Poland, which opposes us.

This moment will be carved in gold letters in the annals not only of the emigrant community but of Ukrainian history as a whole. We, on free soil, will serve as an example to our enslaved brethren on how to defend [our] faith and nation. We, the laity, will show the Apostolic See that although we are Catholics we will not permit our ancient rights and privileges to be curtailed.

Neither Rome itself, nor anyone else, has respect for fallen women and those who bow their spines before untruth and violence. We are fighting for truth and for human and national honor. Let Rome hear our manly protest against episcopal autocracy, let it hear the legitimate demands of our whole Catholic emigration and of our people in the old country.

Therefore let each honest parish that values the faith, in which the embers of love for the people have not died, hurry to this Congress.

Down with slavery.

Let us scatter darkness and prove that Catholicism does not kill off conscience and human dignity.

Love of our people and love of your church call upon you [to attend] the Congress. Do not let our faith be destroyed; nor our rite; nor our love for Ukraine.

As Ukrainians and as Catholics we are not breaking with Rome. By no means! We are only going to fight for our rights and privileges because we joined with Rome as equal with equals.

Philadelphia Pa., November 29, 1926

FOR THE ORGANIZING COMMITTEE OF THE UKRAINO-CATHOLIC CHURCH CONGRESS IN AMERICA

Teodor Hrytsey, Chrmn.; Ivan Vaverchak, vice-chrm. ; Mykhailo Darmohray, secrt.; Mykhailo Kotsiuk, Stefan Kutsyy, Dmytro Sedliar, Mykola Bishko

Attention! Please Note: To obtain credentials for the Congress and about all other matters contact the secretary at the following address:

M. Darmohray, 809 North Franklin St. Philadelphia, Pa.

An anonymous letter to the editor published in *Svoboda* on December 8, 1926, summed up the reasons for the protests against Bohachevsky. Under the banner headline "Let's save our church for our nation [*naroda*, sic]" is the following text:

We, Ukrainians in America, are living at a time of the rebirth of our national life. The planned Congress . . . will be one of the most important means of this renewal to strengthen the national spirit. The success of this Congress will determine not only the welfare of the Ukrainian Catholic Church, but in great measure the welfare of our whole emigration. Because most of our emigrants cluster around the churches it is important to know whether the religious circles support or destroy or stand apart from the national concerns. Our aid to the native land depends in large measure on how the clergy and their superiors view that aid. They are responsible in large measure for raising the national consciousness of the whole community.

Bohachevsky was the obvious impediment to the national cause of the church:

The bishop is convinced that the vast power of the Roman church will save him . . . so much so that he lovingly uses the Latin terms "diocese" and "consultors" rather than "eparchy" and *sovitnyky* [advisers]. He takes the lead in changing the calendar . . . and various other plans . . . that merely underscore . . . his vast ambition . . . and his servile attitude toward Rome. We cannot abandon the church. We need to figure out what to do. . . Every single parish must send its representatives to the Congress . . . [nationally] conscious believers have to choose delegates to prevent religious strife and moral degradation of our emigration. The people through its representatives will valiantly demand their rights from Rome and thus initiate the appointment of men who demonstrate love of their nation and who are capable of defending the rights and privileges of their church before the Apostolic See. The fate of our church is in our hands! Only those in whom the love of their land has died completely will not attend this congress.[16]

Nazaruk presumed that the anonymous voice was Myshuha's. The same issue of *Svoboda* published a shorter note, signed by Volodymyr Bohachevsky, the bishop's older brother, who sounded as categorical as his sibling. Volodymyr advised disregarding the bishop completely: "he is not

16. *Svoboda*, December 8, 1926, 2.

interested even in the fate of his own brother and his family. . . . Just get to work yourselves. You have to address the welfare of your own people and church yourselves. That is the only hope for a better future in America."[17]

It was by now obvious that the congress of the laity and any clergy that chose to participate had the replacement of Bohachevsky by a more amenable bishop as its immediate goal. But it also became clear that some of the organizers hoped the gathering would also result in a dramatic creation of a national church, free of the papacy and of high clerical interference. Along with the stated goals, clandestine directions to potential participants were circulated. None of these proponents, however, chose to use their names openly.

One document regarding the congress differed substantially from other complaints about the bishop. Its goal was the creation of a national Ukrainian church. Although not signed, the four-page, printed leaflet claimed to be written by Catholic priests who provided specific instructions to the delegates on how to behave at the meeting. The Catholic faithful were openly encouraged to break with a Latin Rome that had never been favorably disposed toward Ukrainians. The Ukrainian Catholic Church would be better off joining the Orthodox. The priests—or at least the writers of the "instructions"—exhorted the delegates to speak up to provide the popular pressure that the priests needed to break with Catholicism. That pressure did not materialize. Nor did the assurances that the priests would follow the flock if only the parishioners would choose Orthodoxy. No priest risked putting his name on the document. The leaflet was widely distributed.[18] However, because none of the priests signed the announcement, none could be held responsible for its publication.

This document reinforced Bohachevsky's uncompromising decision to forbid the proposed congress. Yet he still wanted to give the organizers a chance to modify their stand. He waited almost two weeks before promulgating the official decree (no. 778), dated the feast day of St. Nicholas, December 19, 1926, which banned the clergy, under the pain of sin, from participating in such meetings. He buttressed his interdict with scripture,

17. "Chy mozhe buty vyhliad na zminu?" [Can There Be Any Possibility for a Change?], *Svoboda*, December 8, 1926.

18. Copy with the author. My thanks to Yuri Danyliw for providing the leaflet to me.

Mathew 29: 18–19: "All power is given me, on earth and in the heavens."[19] The bishop reminded the priests that the tenets of the church state that lawful power resides in the Holy See, and the bishop is the papal executive. To underscore the importance of the decree, Bohachevsky formally promulgated it as a separate leaflet: "We, by God's grace and the blessing of the Apostolic Roman See, bishop for all the Greek Catholic Halychanyn Ukrainians in the United States of Northern America address all Honorable and Highly esteemed Spiritual Fathers, all praiseworthy church committees and all the faithful subjects of our episcopal jurisdiction with the following warning."[20]

The use of the royal "We" was too good an opportunity for the bishop's opponents to miss, and prompted parallels between the bishop and the Polish gentry who had lorded it over Ukrainian peasants and whom Franko had so passionately decried. Once again, Bohachevsky's reliance on convention backfired. More colorful criticism of the bishop appeared, with critics invariably making fun of all his titles. An additional flurry of handouts accused the papacy of suppressing Ukraine and made fun of religion in general.

Watching the mounting disorder, Bohachevsky once more questioned his own judgment. He simply could not comprehend that so many people could take the abject lies about his person seriously. He decided to break his silence, attend the meeting, and explain his position. He even thought of resigning publicly to put an end to the seemingly pointless polemics.[21] When Bohachevsky summoned his advisers—"Perhaps I could explain [the issues] as they really are," he reasoned—the closest ones, Pyk, Protsko, and Nazaruk, vehemently opposed him. Reverend Oleksander Pyk, "pale as death," flatly disagreed with his bishop: "[Our opponents] used up all the [available] arguments against the bishop. Now they are simply treading water. We should not give them more fuel for their arguments."[22] Nazaruk, the bishop's main apologist, reminded the bishop

19. Nazaruk, diary, TsDIA, Lviv, not yet filed.
20. Ibid.
21. Nazaruk to Lypynsky, January 31, 1927, Lypynsky, *Collected Works*, 404.
22. This account is drawn from one of the few contemporary sources of the time—Osyp Nazaruk's handwritten calendar-diary, discovered in TsDIA, Lviv, not yet filed. Two weeks before the congress, beginning on December 10, Bohachevsky held meetings with his close advisers, Rev. Oleksandr Pyk, Rev. Paul Protsko, and Osyp Nazaruk. Nazaruk advised

that it was not the priests or the faithful, but Myshuha and the intelligentsia who spearheaded the movement against the bishop for purely monetary reasons. They wanted to handle the collection of funds to be able to use the monies for the causes they considered important. The bishop should remember that the people were behind him, the bishop, although their voices had been drowned out momentarily.

Other advisers also argued that the congress would not go against Rome despite its criticism of Rome's policies and the concordat with Poland. The bishop's steadfastness and endurance had been tested to the breaking point, but the recollection of Ortynsky's unhappy experiences led him to keep his course. Bohachevsky was placated with the promise that Reverend Pyk would attend the congress. But when the time came Pyk decided not to attend the meeting, whose only goal was to remove the bishop.

The congress was held on December 29, 1926, in the Ukrainian Citizen's Club, two blocks up Franklin Street from the cathedral. *Svoboda* is the major source of information about its preparations and activities, as well as the post-congress assessment of what happened. The gathering was scripted but could not be controlled. The representatives were unruly. The agenda seems to have been prepared more by the Alliance leadership than by the clergy or lay activists. According to Myron Kuropas's reading of the sources, the congress included delegates from eighty-one Ukrainian Catholic parishes, each claiming to represent his entire respective parish, although by this time most parishes were divided. Kuropas also noted that there were two or three priests in attendance. I have only noticed Rev. Ulytsky mentioned in the *Svoboda* reports, which function as minutes. Kuropas summed up the resolutions of the congress in this manner:

After hearing a series of impassioned speeches about the celibacy issue, the church calendar, the Rome-Warsaw concordat, and the general decline of the

---

Bohachevsky not to participate in public meetings. In his notes, Nazaruk pointed out that Ortynsky too readily believed that his clergy went with the more radical demands of the society, when in fact most of the clergy supported a moderate stand. Nazaruk writes: "The limitless naiveté of Bishop Ortynsky. The [so called] article that seventeen priests signed. Calls all.—All answer— no! [The document submitted to Ortynsky had not been signed by the priests whose signatures appeared on the published version.] Now the situation is similar, instead of Dem[ydchuk] there is Myshuga." Quotation from the notes marked December 10, 1926, TsDIA, Lviv, unfiled.

Ukrainian Catholic Church in America under Bohachevsky's leadership, the congress passed resolutions, which called for

1. The recall of Bishop Bohachevsky by the apostolic delegate

2. The appointment of future Ukrainian bishops from among candidates recommended by the clergy and laity

3. The right of local parishes to hire and terminate priests and to maintain control over all church finances

4. The refusal to pay eparchial dues until Bohachevsky is removed [from office] and all due monies are placed in escrow by a newly formed church committee

5. The official change of the name of the church by Rome from "Ruthenian" to "Ukrainian" with the retention of the appellation "Greek Catholic" to distinguish it from the Latin-rite Catholic Church.[23]

The congress created a Committee for the Defense of the Greek Catholic Church in America. *Svoboda* triumphantly boasted: "[this] demonstrates that no longer can an autocratic church, which recognizes only blind obedience, rely on the Ukrainian 'serf.'"[24] Nazaruk, who mournfully predicted the eventual demise of the Ukrainian diaspora and its Catholic Church in the United States, noted that Tarnawsky was the only person who still steadfastly believed in Bohachevsky's ability to turn the tide.

In a repetition of the September march on the bishop, a group of the delegates, allegedly headed by Rev. Oleksa Prystay, headed down the block toward the bishop's residence, hoping to force Bohachevsky to face "the people's court." Bohachevsky's successor, Ambrose Senyshyn, described the most dramatic ending to the congress in an article published in the Stamford eparchial newsletter immediately after Bohachevsky's death in 1961. Senyshyn, of course, could not be a primary source (he arrived in the United States only in the 1930s), nor does he name his source. The dramatic description may be somewhat embellished, and it echoes the march of the Alliance delegates back in September.

According to Senyshyn, after voting by acclamation to accept the de-

23. Myron Kuropas, *The Ukrainian Americans*, 307–8; see also Procko, *Ukrainian Catholics in America*, 58–59; reports of the meeting in *Svoboda*, December 31, January 11, and January 12, 1927, on pages 1 and 4 in the three issues. The first lead headline summarized the presentation: "Kongress Ukraiintsiv Katolykiv – Velyky Suktses" [The Congress of Ukrainian Catholics – A Huge Success].

24. Report of the meeting in *Svoboda*, January 11, 1927.

mands of the congress, the participants (characterized by Senyshyn as a mob) went down Franklin Street to the bishop's office. The bishop, not recognizing the validity of the congress, refused to meet the delegates and retreated to his small chapel and prayed, ignoring the crowd in front of the building:

There was a time when these scandal-mongers created havoc in Philadelphia, attracting and instigating a mob on Franklin Street to drag the bishop to a civil court... I recall this bitter and shameful incident only to show the Ukrainian people how our metropolitan conducted himself during this period of horrendous insults from his own kind. He did not seek revenge, he did not call upon the police to apprehend the leaders, he did not prosecute them, but when the seething crowd sought to break into his residence—in that hour of his Gethsemane—he went into his private chapel and fervently prayed for many hours to the Eucharistic Christ, seeking comfort in his grave suffering. A great pain welled in his heart—not because of the injury done to his person, but at the thought of the awful tragedy of some of our leaders who stooped so low and who used such perfidious devises. It was prayer that gave the late metropolitan [Bohachevsky] strength to bear all this.[25]

The convocation of the Philadelphia congress on December 29, 1926, and the publication of the delegates' demands forced the leadership of the dissident clergy into the open. It also forced Bishop Bohachevsky to respond quickly and decisively. He played it strictly by the rules. The bishop excommunicated the major organizers of the gathering.[26] Since there was no direct proof that any priest took part in the public meeting, none was disciplined. Only after a lay committee to defend the church was formed, were the priests forced to take a stand.

Bohachevsky used the Christmas season to deliver his only public refutation—in the guise of a sermon—to the charges that the congress

25. Senyshyn, "On the Death of the Archbishop," *Stamford Eparchial Newsletter*, January 1961. The popularity of ecumenism was still a decade away. There is a background story. In the seventeenth century, at the height of the Catholic-Orthodox polemics in Ukraine, an enraged Orthodox mob hacked to death the Catholic archbishop of Polotsk, Josaphat Kuntsevich, while he was at the altar. Kuntsevich was sanctified, and despite his Belorussian ties, became especially venerated in Halychyna.

26. Philadelphia Chancery, excommunication, January 6, 1927, UMAS. It named Theodore Hrytsey, Mykhaylo Darmohray, and Mykhaylo Kotsiur from Philadelphia; Ivan Vaverchak from Perth Amboy; as well Dr. Luka Myshuha, Ivan Ivanyshyn, Hryhory Pyniuk, Mykhaylo Biyan, and Semen Yadlowsky.

had levied against him. He focused on the specifics of the charges against him. He argued against public control of the churches, defended the need for full-time Ukrainian Catholic schools, and addressed some of the complaints about abuses within the church. He tried to explain that the Vatican concordat with Poland was a diplomatic necessity that had nothing to do with the Ukrainian Catholic Church in the United States.[27]

Bohachevsky still hoped to sway the clergy to his side. He observed the festive Christmas and Epiphany celebrations with a smaller congregation than in the previous two years, but the violent demonstrations seemed to have subsided. Small contributions for the seminary were coming in, a sign that not all the immigrants opposed the bishop or his work. And to shore up the bishop's will, on New Year's Day in 1927, Dr. Stepan Hrynevetsky, himself an Orthodox, donated $1,000 (a substantial sum at the time) for the building of the seminary, proof that the bishop still had major supporters. Bohachevsky sent his usual St. Andrew's and Christmas greetings to Sheptytsky, perhaps hoping for a sign of support. None came, although Bishop Njaradi was back in Europe after his trip to America. While in America, Njaradi came to Bohachevsky's defense and agreed with him on what issues to raise at the bishops' conference. Back in Europe, Njaradi's praise of the work of the Ruthenian Church in the United States merely called more attention to the difficulties in the Ukrainian Church.[28] Nevertheless, Njaradi ultimately convinced Sheptytsky to agree to expand the format of the Ukrainian bishops' meeting to include the participation of Ukrainian bishops from all parts of the world. This was the issue Bohachevsky had wanted to raise at the planned March meeting of the bishops.[29]

Bohachevsky hoped, against all evidence, that he would still be able to sway the leadership of the Providence Association to his side at the organization's annual meeting on January 26 and 27, 1927. As Providence's titular head, he had the right to address it, and he prepared a well-crafted speech,

27. Eparkhiial'ni Visti, January 1927, 6–7.
28. Nyva, the journal Kostelnyk edited, printed a comment in its November–December 1927 issue (431–34) that leading Ukrainian priests in the United States rightfully protested the plans for a useless American seminary.
29. Minutes of the twenty-seventh meeting of Halychyna bishops, held April 30, 1927, PKEL. The bishops also reaffirmed the oversight of the clergy of lay organizations, especially the welfare ones.

drawing on reasoned argument and the gravitas of his episcopal position. He walked into the meeting room, began with a prayer, and delivered his speech, stressing the universality and importance of the church structure and its enduring sustainability. He mused that on the eve of Christ's crucifixion none of the apostles, the direct predecessors of all validly consecrated bishops, had come to Jesus' defense. Only Pilate defended Jesus, and yet Jesus and his Church had endured. Bohachevsky compared the Church to a mighty oak that loses leaves and fruit only to grow stronger. He mentioned Ortynsky's difficulties, emphasizing that the establishment of the Providence Association had been that bishop's final achievement. Graciously, the bishop thanked those who supported him, and left the meeting after delivering his speech.

Neither Bohachevsky's reliance on noble Roman stoicism nor Nazaruk's aggressive energy had much effect on the board of the Providence Association, which sided with the bishop's opponents. Nazaruk was dismissed as editor of *America* on February 1, and (perhaps with intentional irony) *America* published Bohachevsky's speech along with Nazaruk's farewell article. As the bishop, Nazaruk aimed for a dignified note: he worked "not in his name" but for God and for understanding His Supreme Will. He felt fully justified in defending the bishop, whose probity was recognized by the Ukrainian-American as well as the Canadian press. His own immediate goal, Nazaruk confessed, had been to shake Ukrainians' reliance on patriotic slogans, as if rhetoric were an adequate tool for gaining independence. He asked readers not to believe rumors that he, Nazaruk, would embark on a political career, emphasizing that he was turning his attention to scholarship instead. But Nazaruk kept a door open: he announced he would discuss his reasons for leaving the United States only when he wrote his American memoirs, something that never came to pass.

Angered by the dismissal of his defender, the bishop fired off a public letter accusing the trustees of improper behavior as well as of un-Christian sentiments toward Nazaruk. But he could not reverse the decision. On February 3, Rev. Antin Lototsky, a moderate, took over the position which he would keep for many decades as editor of *America*. The paper was again peppered with stories from Halychyna and with appeals to donate money for the Ukrainian primary schools there.

By this time, everyone knew Bohachevsky was leaving for Rome on the visit he had planned earlier. *Svoboda* falsely presented the trip as a recall, to keep the antiepiscopal fires burning.[30] Because Bohachevsky did not yet have American citizenship, he had to get a Polish visa to travel to Lviv. He was received warmly by Poland's envoy Jan Ciechanowski. The bishop predictably used the occasion to voice his objections to the Polish government's policy of nationalizing church property. The envoy, in an equally predictable move, diplomatically assured the bishop that that law would not be implemented. Of course, for the opposition this routine trip served as further proof of Bohachevsky's pro-Polish sympathies, although Myshuha's visit to the Polish envoy to get his visa the following year elicited no public comments.

AN ALTERNATIVE LEADER

Bohachevsky was careful not to be absent from the United States for long periods of time. He therefore postponed his departure for Rome until February 12, 1927, to take part in the next conference of Ukrainian Catholic bishops, which was to take place at Lviv, and to officiate at the consecration of the new Mukachiv bishop, Pavlo Hoydych. The Christmas holidays passed quietly in the various churches. Bohachevsky drafted all the necessary documents to empower his chancellor to function in his place during the bishop's absence.

The bishop's departure was seen by some clergy as justification for holding a clergy gathering, despite the fact that statutory provisions empowered the chancellor to exercise eparchial authority in Bohachevsky's absence. The priests waited until Bohachevsky sailed for Rome to hold their meeting without the participation of the laity. On February 23, 1927 (two weeks after Bohachevsky left for Rome), thirty priests gathered in New York in the Pennsylvania Hotel. Despite advance preparations, the meeting had an aura of urgency. Some priests could not make adequate last-minute plans to attend, so they telegraphed "their statements of solidarity."[31]

---

30. *Svoboda*, February 14, 1927, falsely reported that Bohachevsky had been summoned to Rome and left precipitously; see Nazaruk to Lypynsky, April 22, 1927, in Lypynsky, *Collected Works*, 410.

31. *Katolyts'ky Provid*, October 30, 1927, even Kostelnyk made fun of the gathering: "Bohato halasu znehevia," *Nyva* (July–August 1930): 318–20.

FIGURE 7. CONSECRATION OF BISHOP HOYDYCH, 1927

Svoboda, in its report on the event, pointed out that the decision to hold the meeting had been very sudden, perhaps to justify the low attendance. The *ad hoc* body of clerics referred to itself, in a nod to a wished-for Eastern practice, as "synodal priests." Of course, the Ukrainian-American exarchate, not yet fashioned a fully empowered eparchy, was in no position to convene a canonical synod. The Ukrainian Catholic Church in Europe had held a synod in 1907, in line with Sheptytsky's effective, yet understated reforms. There had been a particularly contentious meeting with large clergy participation in Lviv in 1890 that devolved onto the celibacy issue. Partial reports of this meeting leaked out in the early 1920s and were making their rounds among the intelligentsia. These discussions contributed to the American Ukrainian Catholic clergy's readiness to call their gathering synodal rather than just clerical. With the bishop gone—in infamy, as far as the dissident priests were concerned—their mood was one of exaltation. The dissidents seized upon Bohachevsky's absence to fashion a church that reflected the popular mood and planned to send their emissaries personally to the apostolic delegate in Washington, D.C.

At the very beginning of the gathering, the pastor of Brooklyn, Antin Lotovych, still hoped to derail a hostile meeting. He read the chancellor's letter forbidding the gathering and threatening serious consequences. Two priests, Andriy Strotsky and Roman Volynets, who had been under the impression that the chancery had sanctioned the meeting, walked out of the so-called synod. The solid core of twenty-six priests remained, and after their deliberations solemnly decided:

1. To address the Apostolic See through the delegate in Washington, that he [the delegate] inform Rome that the person of Bishop Constantine Bohachevsky is so unpopular among our emigrant community that his continued episcopate may cause a major exodus from the Ukrainian Greek-Catholic Church.

2. To affirm that as Ukrainians and as American citizens [we] protest strongly against all Polish interference in our church affairs, and especially when it comes to the appointment of bishops to our dioceses.

3. To proclaim our deep sympathy with the struggle of our nation for its state and for democratic institutions. To fulfill at least a crumb of our duties as patriot-priests, we solemnly affirm our duty to support as best we can all actions that strive toward the achievement of the above national goals.[32]

As a postscript, the organizers called for calm. They assured the Ukrainian Catholic faithful that the pope would agree to their demands since the movement was not directed against the church but only to remove one bishop.[33] The signatories further "urged Ukrainian Catholics to remain loyal to the church because the matter [of the bishop] will be settled soon."[34] In the interim—that is, until a new bishop could be ap-

32. *Svoboda*, February 24, 1927, 1.
33. *Svoboda*, February 24, 1927. The signatories were priests: J. Zhuk, M. Strutynsky, J. Sklepkovych, P. Haniak, L. Levytsky, A. Ulytsky, I. Zakharko, Y. Zatserkovny, P. Sereda, J. Boiarchuk, M. Kinash, Rev. Dr. Guliay, V. Spolitakevych, V. Petrivsky, O. Pavliak, M. Prodan, I. Teodorovych, M. Lysiak, D. Dobrotvir, V. Korytovsky, V. Dovhovych, Y. Dzendzera, Y. Pelekhovych, I. Shukhovsky, E. Bartysh, and V. Zholdak.
34. Two priests personally delivered the petition to the apostolic representative,

pointed by Rome with Ukrainian community participation and approval—the synodal priests proposed to direct the affairs of the church in the United States. They did not include the nominal head of the Ukrainian Catholic Church, Metropolitan Sheptytsky, in their deliberations. They turned directly to the papal delegate, ignoring Sheptytsky's pro forma authority. Fumasoni-Biondi, the delegate, lost no time informing Luigi Cardinal Sincero, the secretary of the Congregation for the Eastern Church, of the developments in Philadelphia. His report is dated February 26, 1927.

Joseph A. Zhuk, followed by Volodymyr Petrivsky, the late Bishop Ortynsky's secretary, were the first to sign the petition addressed to the apostolic delegate. According to the delegate's notes, Revs. Joseph Boiarczuk and John Shukhovsky delivered the petition quoted below:

The Ukrainian Greek Catholic Church in the United States is in a critical condition. The vast majority of the Ukrainian Catholics have turned against the bishop, C. Bohachevsky, who aroused their ire because of his high-handed methods in national and ecclesiastical affairs. He has made himself an impossibility as the head of our diocese as the *"persona odiomissima"* among our emigration [sic].

The Ukrainian Catholics in America feel an immense relief on account of the journey of Bishop Bohachevsky to Rome, because they expect that he will be revoked from his bishopric in Philadelphia.

The undersigned Ukrainian Catholic priests believe firmly, that only the revocation of Bishop Bohachevsky would prevent the entire series of scandals, which would certainly happen, if Bishop Bohachevsky would ever return to America.

We feel also, that to appease the aroused anger of our emigration no palliative means would be sufficient. As pastors, who are responsible for the salvation of souls, as catholic [sic] priests, we wish to get back to our faith and church, we felt it as our sworn duty to hold a general meeting of our clergymen to find a solution for those who are now in temporary apostasy.[35]

Fumasoni-Biondi. Text of the petition in *Svoboda*, February 25, 1927, a hand-copied version in the Warsaw Nunciature (Pos. 605r–6r). The Congregation for the Eastern Church filed its copy of the petition on March 15, 1927, Bohachevsky's hand written elaboration March 19, 1927. Both documents at CEC [Rigotti, 771–75, penciled numeration 718/466/28, overridden by No. 4345-g].

35. Quoted from the text filed at the Congregation for the Eastern Church. Joseph Zhuk (1872–1934) was prefect of Lviv seminary in 1902–7, its rector in 1907; vicar general to Bosnia 1908–14; pastor in Vienna 1914–20; in Toronto 1921–22, in Montreal 1923; in Philadelphia 1923. It is not clear when he moved to Carnegie, with frequent visits to New York.

The two "synodal" emissaries expected immediate approbation of the apostolic delegate to their demands. Instead, Fumasoni-Biondi spoke very firmly about the harm that the New York clergy gathering had caused—the priests had scandalized the faithful and undermined the Ukrainian Church's authority. "I told them one could not be in union with the papacy, and at the same time reject one's bishop." Fumasoni-Biondi was most shocked by the way Rev. Zhuk behaved—seizing churches to consolidate his power. That a faculty member of the Lviv seminary would engage in such activities was incomprehensible to the staid Vatican functionary. He decided that the Ukrainian clergy should be taught a lesson to wean the priests from their tendency to follow such "wolves."[36] Fumasoni-Biondi was convinced that Vashchyshyn and Bohachevsky's principled stand saved the diocese from the disarray that plagued it. Bohachevsky was in Rome when Fumasoni-Biondi's letter arrived at the Congregation for the Eastern Church. He immediately handwrote an elaboration of the situation. At the same time, other priests, headed by Vashchyshyn, circulated their hand-signed petition among the clergy in support of Bishop Bohachevsky, which was also duly studied.[37] A few months later Fumasoni-Biondi, at the insistence of the Congregation for the Eastern Church demanded that the returning priests publicly acknowledge the error of their ways to ensure that such behavior would not be repeated in "this unhappy diocese."[38]

The most likely challenger to Bohachevsky for the bishopric in the United States was Rev. Joseph Zhuk (1872–1934). The rumor that Sheptytsky supported Zhuk's candidacy, although baseless, was one of the longest lasting, believable rumors of the 1920s. Zhuk was a highly educated,

36. The Congregation for the Eastern Church filed its copy of the petition on March 15, 1927, with accompanying elaboration "On the difficult situation in the Ruthenian diocese of Msgr. Bohachevsky" in Italian. Bohachevsky's handwritten elaboration from Rome dated March 19, 1927, in Latin. Both documents at CEC [Rigotti, 771–5, penciled numeration 718/466/28, overridden by No. 4345-g]. Fumasoni-Biondi was particularly concerned because Rev. Volodymyr Petrivsky was secretary to Bishop Ortynsky. Petrivsky was firmly convinced that Rev. Vasyl Stetsiuk had poisoned Ortynsky. Mrs. Strutynsky, angry at her husband's transfer from Chicago, shot Rev. Stetsiuk point blank in the confessional. (She was the sister of Myroslav Sichynsky, the assassin of the ethnic Polish governor of Habsburg Galicia.) Bohachevsky treated the assassinated Father Stetsiuk as a martyr.

37. ASV, Warsaw, f. 194.

38. CEC [Rigotti, 685, marked by hand 576/28 .1927], Ruthenians, Prot. no. 3316.

socially adept, and well-positioned Ukrainian cleric whose family came from Austrian lands that eventually became part of Yugoslavia. He had been the prefect at the Lviv seminary when Bohachevsky was there. At the same time, Zhuk continued as vicar-general in Bosnia. During the First World War, Zhuk was pastor of St. Barbara Ukrainian Catholic Church in Vienna. From Vienna he moved in 1920 to Canada, one would suppose with Sheptytsky's permission. The following year he came to Philadelphia and then moved to Syracuse. To some observers, Zhuk's travels point to Sheptytsky's support of his candidacy for bishop in the United States, although Sheptytsky's letters from Rome show that this was by far not the case. Nevertheless, the rumors circulated, and Zhuk most likely believed them himself. For these and other reasons, Zhuk was forced to emerge as an open opponent of Bishop Bohachevsky at the clergy meeting in New York's Pennsylvania Hotel. Whether he wanted to do so or whether his hand was forced is immaterial. What does matter is that Zhuk became the *primus inter pares* of the clergy that claimed to speak for the church. Ortynsky's erstwhile secretary Volodymyr Petrivsky, then turning sixty-eight, became his right-hand man. Their high positions within the Ukrainian Catholic hierarchy played into the hands of those officials at the Vatican who doubted the Ukrainian Catholic Church's loyalty to Rome. Moreover, their actions undermined Sheptytsky's standing in Rome at a time the metropolitan most needed Vatican support.

There is ample evidence that Sheptytsky did not support Zhuk, but that was not known at the time. Zhuk, after all, had all the qualifications to consider himself an excellent candidate for bishop. If he felt that he had high backing for his nomination, Zhuk did not think it necessary to deal with Bohachevsky, whom he considered far from his equal. It is likely that he was waiting for a sign (from Lviv or from the Vatican) before openly challenging Bishop Bohachevsky. Circumstances—in particular, the struggle between Bohachevsky and the secular leaders in the United States—forced him to take sides earlier. There is no evidence that Zhuk and Bohachevsky met in the United States, although both had worked in Lviv.[39]

Repercussions and an escalation of hostility followed in short order. Vashchyshyn excommunicated Rev. Zhuk. After the Pennsylvania Hotel

39. I did not have access to documentation on Bohachevsky's early visitations.

meeting, Zhuk tried to rally the dissident priests and his own parishioners in Carnegie, Pennsylvania. He tried to establish a self-help fraternal
society for the priests and even published a newsletter of his presumed
eparchy, profusely apologizing for its modest scope. Neither venture succeeded. Nonetheless, Zhuk's considerable reputation in the community
and within the church continued to bolster the hope that he was the ideal
counter to Bohachevsky. Individual Ukrainian-American priests sought
to influence Zhuk not to break with Catholicism but to keep waiting for
Bohachevsky to be removed. But once *Svoboda* published the decisions of
the meeting with Zhuk's signature, Chancellor Vashchyshyn felt he had no
choice but to see Zhuk as a usurper to the bishop's staff.

THE BISHOP STRIKES BACK

Still in Rome, but by now fully apprised of what was happening in America, Bohachevsky at his audience with Pope Pius XI offered to resign his
episcopal power into the papal hands.[40] Whether or not the resignation
was formally tendered, it was not accepted. The bishop would return to
his rebellious see, despite the threat to his life that came in a letter apparently sent from Philadelphia to Rome. In Rome, Bohachevsky found
a sympathetic and understanding audience. Indeed, the Vatican clergy
understood his troubles, being fully aware of the difficulties that bishops
in the global ministry of the church often faced not only from enemies, but
from their own priests. Moreover, Ukrainians already had a reputation at
the Vatican for complaining about almost all of their bishops. The current
Ukrainian-American problem was turned over to the Congregation for the
Eastern Church for review.

40. I rely on the general account of the Ukrainian Catholic Church included in the celebratory publication in honor of the establishment of the archbishopric-metropolitanate:
Rev. Isidore Sochotsky, "The Ukrainian Catholic Church of the Byzantine-Slavonic Rite in
the USA," 199–286. The author was a close collaborator of Bohachevsky, and the publication
appeared during Bohachevsky's lifetime, so presumably with his approval. There are minor
editorial differences between the Ukrainian and English presentations. The English version
of the article reads: "Bishop Bohachevsky placed himself and his episcopal jurisdiction in
the hands of the Holy See." At the same time a threat that his life would be in danger if he
returned to the U.S. was received (281). In the Ukrainian version "His Reverence Constantine laid his powers [*povnovlasti*] in the hands of the Apostolic See" (240).

Bohachevsky's first full report to the congregation, although hand-written in Latin, was very professional. It reminded the readers of the difficult position of the whole Ukrainian Catholic Church; namely, that Ukrainians lacked a state in which the church could develop normally. The immigrant population reflected some of these difficulties, Bohachevsky commented, but as in the home church most of the Ukrainian Catholic clergy and faithful in the United States were good Catholics who worked hard to develop their church. Although some clergy vacillated, the bishop assured the Roman prelates that "many are returning to the fold. Once schools and especially a seminary will be established, the society, and the church should develop well."[41]

The congregation was impressed that "three years into his tenure [Bohachevsky] personally delivered his first diocesan report in which he concisely presented the condition of the clergy and the faithful."[42] What mattered greatly to the congregation was the quality of the clergy. The summary presented for the audience with Pope Pius XI on this issue reported that "Among the ninety-five [Ukrainian Catholic priests in the United States] only thirty-seven are celibate or widowers, of which twenty-nine are lay priests and eight are former monks. The rest are those who most likely left their [home] dioceses without the proper papal authorization."[43] The congregation studied the pertinent documents and concluded that under the circumstances Bohachevsky had acted as well as could be expected. The cardinals admired his courage and fortitude. They charged Fumasoni-Biondi to deal individually and directly with each dissident Ukrainian-Catholic priest to make certain that he understood church discipline.[44]

When it became obvious that the Vatican would support Bohachevsky and not the dissidents, most of the clergy returned to the fold. Zhuk, however, as the premier cleric in the dissent movement, was faced with a dilemma: either to accept Bohachevsky's nomination and carry on as if nothing had happened, or prove that he had acted not from personal am-

41. CEC, Prot. 576/28 [Rigotti, 672–77; 688–92].
42. CEC, Prot. 576 /27 [Rigotti, 688–92].
43. CEC, Prot. 576/28 [Rigotti, 672–77; 688–92].
44. AES, Poland, Prot. 792, specifically discussing "The very unruly Ruthenian priests in Mons. Bohachevsky's diocese."

bition but from religious conviction and become a convert to Orthodoxy. It was not an easy decision, and neither Zhuk nor the Vatican took it lightly. Zhuk did convert to Orthodoxy, and a few years later, in 1932, he was elevated to bishop. Bohachevsky asked the congregation and Sheptytsky to institute official clerical procedures against him, as detailed by *Cum data fuerit*. On his deathbed in 1934, Zhuk apparently confessed to a Catholic priest and died a Catholic, although there is some doubt if the Catholic priest did reach him in time.

Meanwhile, Bohachevsky had planned to go to Lviv directly from Rome, once Hoydych was consecrated bishop. The ceremony was delayed because of Hoydych's visa problems, while the bishops' conference was also postponed for other considerations. Very reluctantly, Bohachevsky had to cancel his trip to Lviv because he could not afford to be absent from Philadelphia at Easter. There is a rare note of open resentment in his later correspondence about the delay in the bishops' conference meeting.[45]

Whatever the scheduling problems, Bohachevsky's nonparticipation in the bishops' conference at Lviv was seen within the Ukrainian-American community as a sign of Sheptytsky's displeasure with the bishop. The conference was held at a time when Kotsylovsky and Sheptytsky disagreed on the publication of certain texts, and the disagreements were very much in public view. Eventually, even Cardinal Sincero had to intervene.[46] Although Bohachevsky felt the worst was over in his exarchy, he nevertheless girded himself for a protracted confrontation in the United States with the holdover dissident clergy. In a letter to Kotsylovsky, dated May 3, 1927, he wrote:

We have some breathing space in the United States from the dissident priests and their supporters. Father Zhuk was suspended before my arrival here [from Rome to the United States] and left to join Father [Lev] Levytsky in Cleveland. A part of the dissident priests returned to the fold. Some of the laity are trying to find out in a round-about way if I am ready to forgive them. They want to negotiate.... The opposition is running into difficulties from their own people, and their clergy are now squabbling about better parishes and positions.[47]

45. The meeting of the Ukrainian bishops elicited interest at the Vatican and bared the continued disagreements within the Ukrainian clergy. Meanwhile, Fumasoni-Bondi sent Bohachevsky an extremely gracious letter, dated August 3, 1927, encouraging him not to lose heart. The letter is filed at CEC with materials from the Papal Nunciature, [Rigotti 792–4].

46. Galadza, *The Theology and Liturgical Work of Andrei Sheptyts'kyi*, 312.

47. Bohachevsky to Kotsylovsky, May 3, 1927, UMAS. Kotsylovsky assured the Basilian

Kotsylovsky, who had felt the ire of the mob on his own person, was sympathetic to the plight of his erstwhile helper.

Nonetheless, the community's criticism of Bohachevsky was somewhat justified. The bishop's actions that had impressed the Vatican were precisely those that the Ukrainian immigrant communities found jarring. Parish priests were shocked by the drastic changes that transformed the chancery from a haven reminiscent of an idealized old-fashioned manor where priests could feel at home into an impersonal modern administrative office. After all, the Ukrainian priests came to America either out of duty or economic necessity; they had little time or inclination to analyze how the church was adjusting to changing politics, technology, and economy. Clearly the bishop, alone and under pressure, failed to consider the human repercussions of his radical reforms. On the contrary—he saw himself as very much a traditionalist. Moreover, Bohachevsky lacked diplomatic communication skills and had no staff that could effectively remedy that lack. Had the bishop been wiser and worldlier, he might have handled the opposition more adroitly. He might have been more flexible or might also have fixed the problem by hiring his potential critics. Moreover, he could have shown more empathy toward individual priests. Every priest thrown out of his church and home by irate mobs, every parish split by contentious court cases, every lonely priest who looked in vain for solace from his tight-lipped bishop was justified in accusing Bohachevsky of a lack of empathetic support and of failure to heed the specific advice each of them was ready to offer had he only been willing to listen. Yet hardly anyone did what each thought could have been done. Bohachevsky acted and took direct responsibility for his actions.

Rev. Prystay became the most outspoken of Bohachevsky's critics, but there was little substance to his criticism. He devoted no more than ten

Abbot Theodosius Halushchynsky that the information the abbot had from the United States alleging that Bohachevsky is behaving inappropriately, was definitely false. Kotsylovsky to Halushchynsky, May 24, 1927, TsDIA, Lviv, Lysty do Halushchynskoho, f. 684, op .2, spr. 217, vol. 1, 89–92. Kotsylovsky was also under fire for allegedly destroying the church and colluding with the Polish regime. Ivan Gotia published a Ukrainian copy of a forty-page memorandum to the pope from Peremyshl laity protesting Kotsylovsky's policies, supplementing it with a lengthy discussion of the situation in Peremyshl, all under the title In the Defense of the Rights of Our Greek-Cath. Church (V Oboroni prav nashoyi Hreko-katol. tserkvy [sic]). The eighty-page booklet, published in Lviv in 1929, touched on conditions in America.

paragraphs to Bohachevsky in his bestselling four-volume memoir. Revisiting one painful episode after another in his poverty-stricken, lonely old age, this chronicler-priest only ruminated on how the bishop could have averted tragedy, mainly by not focusing on Catholic education. Almost as an afterthought, at the end of his third volume, Prystay did mention that the bishop offered him a position at the chancery, which the priest declined immediately, convinced that he would have to compromise "his life-long principles."[48] The bishop's grandiose educational plans did not fit into the pioneer priest's worldview. Prystay admired the self-made Americans—the immigrants who succeeded without the benefit of higher schooling. Priests in Halychyna, faced with easily radicalized, undereducated, and unemployed youth, were themselves not inclined to tedious studies. They found solace in reading about the missteps of the Ukrainian-American higher clergy, and especially about the missteps of bishops opposed to married clergy.[49]

Strangely, however, one finds little Monday-morning quarterbacking about the leadership of the Ukrainian-American community, both at the time and subsequently. Bohachevsky remained the dogmatic and authoritarian prelate, perceived as a man who distanced himself from the people, despite the fact that the bishop's main support, both moral and financial, came from the parishioners. The attempts that the bishop had made to present his side of the story—the Christmas sermon on the eve of his first departure for Rome and the step-by-step apologia delivered to his priests at a closed retreat during Easter 1933—were not made public and had little impact. The bishop withdrew into prayer and self-imposed loneliness to such an extent that as late as 1952 he was overjoyed by the fact that a newly arrived priest pointed out an error in his arithmetic. Apparently no one in the bishop's immediate surroundings had ever dared to do anything like that before.[50]

48. Prystay, Z Truskavtsia u svit khmaroderiv, 3:234; and 4:200. See also Prystay to Nazaruk, June 15, 1929, TsDIA, Lviv, f. 359, spr. 1.303, p. 12.

49. The negative image of Bohachevsky in the Lviv Consistory administration would have momentous implications after his death. Cardinal-Patriarch Joseph Slipyj, freed from Soviet incarceration, was firmly convinced that the Ukrainian Catholic Church in the United States was still in its infancy and needed to be built by him ab ovo. This part of the story awaits its historian.

50. Pospishil, Final Tally, 219.

There is certainly more critical information about the bishop than there are sources on the way public opinion turned in his favor. In contrast to the movement against him, which spread because of organized community action, the reverse process was largely the result of individual decisions by families, rather than decisions made by the parish priests. We have little documentation on this reversal, short of anecdotal evidence and the public announcements about priests returning to the fold.[51] Ivan Kravs, an activist in the conservative movement, wrote to Osyp Nazaruk that "the bishop is on top. The other side is just a bunch of crazies [*variativ*]."[52]

The last attempt of some Ukrainian-American Catholic clergy to undercut Bohachevsky's authority was centered in Allentown, Pennsylvania. It failed to gather support and withered on its own.[53] The Congregation for the Eastern Church received only two more formal complaints about Bohachevsky—one on February 29, 1932, and the other, undated and handwritten in Ukrainian, in May of 1934. In the first, Petro Orshan, a parishioner who had led the split from the cathedral, provided lists of parishes that left because of the bishop, reinforcing these lists with the signatures of eighty persons. Orshan mainly complained about the bishop's high-handedness and concluded: "The bishop has become the most hated person among our people. This fact alone constitutes a serious setback for the Catholic faith."[54]

51. Stephanie Chopyk Sydoriak, whose childhood was spent in Boston, interviews by the author, August 2008. Her father was active in the Boston community and withdrew in solidarity with the movement against the local priest to an Orthodox church. A few years later, Mr. Chopyk announced that the whole family would return to the Catholic Church.

52. Ivan Kravs to Osyp Nazaruk, September 3, 1928, TsDIA, Lviv, f. 359, op. 1, spr. 267, p. 4, giving a sense of the polemics. Kravs goes on to commend Dr. Tsehelsky on his work in *Ukraiiinsky visnyk* in "cleaning out the Augean stables. He sure fashioned an effective whip against Myshuga, which made it necessary for him to leave the U.S.A." Kravs also wrote about an alleged "seventy-page manuscript of the late Ortynsky that recently surfaced in which Bishop [Ortynsky] denies that he is Polish and on paid service to the Italian pope, the charges levied against him by the 'progressivists.' This means that these chaotics have not managed to advance even an iota. It seems that this sort of lunacy [*liunatyzm*] returns every ten years or so."

53. This group—led by the priests Joseph Pelekhovych, Petro Sereda, Oleksandr Ulytsky, and Oleksandr Lysiak; and two civilians: Ivan Vaverchak and Hryhor Pypiuk—tried to reinstate Zhuk but failed for lack of public support. *Svoboda*, April 9, 1929; CEC, Prot. 526/527.

54. CEC, Prot. 576/28 [Rigotti, 721–29].

The second complaint to the congregation was written by Adam Zhurybida and transmitted by the newly appointed papal delegate to the United States, Amleto Cicognani. In his ten-page letter, Zhurybida wrote that he wished "to do his duty and provide some facts that illustrate the work of Bishop Bohachevsky." His main argument was very direct: "Bohachevsky opposed the Ukrainian people and tried from his very arrival to destroy all associations and all 'cultural' life."[55] The *New York Times*, on January 14, 1935, with a dateline of Carteret, New Jersey, carried a brief note that Oleksa Prystay was elected bishop to replace Zhuk, but that was not quite the case.

Myshuha, considered the bishop's major critic, did not document his role in church affairs. Instead, he always wrote in the name of the people. This is seen most clearly in the *Jubilee Book of the Ukrainian National Association*. Three years after Bohachevsky purchased property for a seminar and college, Myshuha and his associates gave their account of the Catholic Ukrainian-American religious world. This volume served as a counterpoint to the success of the bishop's activities by stressing the work of the organization known for opposing him in the previous decade. Myshuha's major article in the volume provided an overview of Ukrainian immigrants; he chose to title it "The Formation of the Worldview of the Ukrainian Immigrant in the United States," which he translated into English more fortuitously as "Development of Ukrainian-American Outlook." Myshuha often adopted a moral high ground and wrote in the name of the newspaper *Svoboda*. His view was nonetheless quite clear: "The only enlightened Ukrainians in the United States are the Ukrainian priests. They are primarily responsible for the future of our nation. And therefore all means have to be used to make certain that they understand their position and fulfill their duty . . . in church and outside of it."[56] At times reverting to the condescending (in Western Ukraine) terminology of "pip" for priest, Myshuha repeatedly cautioned his audience about venal clergy. While bemoaning lack of tolerance in the Ukrainian community, in the same breath he urged his readers to have nothing in common with the

55. CEC, Prot. 576/28; separate file for Zhurybida [Rigotti, 365–79, 720–39]. Zhurybida wrote in Ukrainian, and Vatican officials had to translate the text.
56. Luka Myshuha, "Development of Ukrainian American Outlook," in Myshuha, *Jubilee Book of the Ukrainian National Association*, 148–49.

pro-Russian and pro-Hungarian factions of the Ukrainian/Rusyn clergy.[57] He exonerated the Ukrainian émigré population from its opposition to Ortynsky, disregarded the major difficulties Ortynsky had had with the public, and presented a whitewashed picture of his tenure. The ideal period of *Svoboda*'s relations with the Catholic Church, as far as Myshuha was concerned, was under Poniatyshyn's administration, because Poniatyshyn "understood *Svoboda*'s spirit." That these relations later soured "was not *Svoboda*'s fault."[58]

Myshuha continued to hold Bishop Bohachevsky personally responsible for the unrest in the Catholic Church and hence in society at large. The bishop, as far as he was concerned, was not flexible enough to cooperate with the broad community, a view popularized by *Svoboda*. Myshuha felt justified in his didactic tone toward the clergy (and toward Bohachevsky) because he was convinced that he understood the critical role of the Ukrainians in the United States much better than did Bohachevsky. Moreover, he, Myshuha, represented the official government of Ukraine, the Western Ukrainian National Republic, and therefore the whole nation. In sympathy with Myshuha's perspective, the intelligentsia attributed exceptional importance to the newspaper *Svoboda*: "Tilling this soil [that is, the religiously minded Ukrainian immigrants], *Svoboda* needed in the first place to enlighten the immigration about its very name. . . . *Svoboda* . . . conscious of its historic mission for the Ukrainian immigration not only enlightens

57. Ibid., 154, 150.

58. The quotation is from Myshuha in ibid., 154. As proof of good will of the UNA, Myshuha noted that there was no conflict with Bishop Teodorovych, of the Autocephalous Orthodox nor with Bishop Joseph Zhuk, once he became an Orthodox bishop after he left the Catholic Church. According to Nazaruk, Myshuha at the time was showing signs of possible cooperation with the Hetman movement. Writes Nazaruk: "I am intently carrying on a correspondence with him [Myshuha] for he would be a valuable asset—loyal, energetic, and quick-witted, although he lacks a [a background] in political science. Intelligent by nature. Solid and honest. We've been corresponding for a while now," Nazaruk to Lypynsky, October 15, 1924, Lypynsky, *Collected Works*, 228. Nazaruk's attempts to draw Myshuha to the conservatives failed. A year and a half later, in January 1926, Nazaruk wrote: "Myshuha is a total zero in political knowledge and thinking; he simply functions under the pressure of former President Petrushevych. Functions badly. I have a sense that Petrushevych dirtied himself and Myshuha is [his] mirror image. Now Myshuha and his fellow villager Rev. Spolitakevych wrote a statement against Bolshevism. I doubt it was genuine. Now he [Myshuha] is writing private letters against me," Nazaruk to Lypynsky, one letter dated January 1 and 11, 1926, Lypynsky, *Collected Works*, 353.

[the immigrants] about their national origin, but also is instrumental in getting the clergy to organize."[59]

Dmytro Halychyn, who had immigrated before Myshuha, also stressed in the same publication that the UNA pioneers, "those *popyky radykaly*" who established the Ukrainian National Association, were guided by the interests of the Ukrainian immigrant workers. He went on to credit the UNA with "initiating a new era in the history of the development of the Ukrainian immigration, an era of struggle with darkness, ignorance, apathy, an era whose motto was to restructure the Ukrainian peasant mass into a labor class conscious of its rights and tasks."[60]

Given this reading of the early immigration period, it is no wonder that Myshuha expected the bishop to be deferential to his views and to what he saw as his expertise in issues related to Ukrainian-American society. Moreover, Myshuha was pressured to raise funds for the cause, as well as to provide for his own livelihood. The supporters of the Western Ukrainian government of Petrushevych, now in exile, continued well into 1925 to hope for recognition, and even toyed with contacts with the Soviet Ukrainian government.[61] Whatever the reality, they were firmly convinced that the struggle must continue full force under their leadership for the Ukrainian people to survive.

The closest Myshuha came to apologizing to Bohachevsky took place in August 1934. His letter to the bishop, now filed in the Chancery Archives at Stamford, is worth quoting in full:

Your Excellency!

My friends from our clerical circles ask me why I am not pursuing attempts to get the barricade that had been placed against my person by church authorities lifted. They say that even the good of the national cause necessitates that the matter be settled.

Obviously this matter is of some interest to me, as a believer and a member of our church. I think that the course of time has best proven that all my actions were guided by the welfare of our church, whose history is so closely tied

59. Myshuha, "Development of Ukrainian American Outlook," 43, 49, 146.
60. Dmytro Halychyn, "Fraternal Organizations in the Past and Present," in *Jubilee Book of the Ukrainian National Association*, 159.
61. Nazaruk to Lypynsky, March 26, 1925, Lypynsky, *Collected Works*, 311, "Petrushevych must have made Myshuha new promises, of the kind that 'Japan recognizes us' or something else of that ilk."

with our national life. Precisely this can provide Your Excellency the possibility to reconsider the decision that was to have placed me outside the Ukrainian Greek-Catholic Church.

Sincerely yours, Dr. Luka Myshuha[62]

This was hardly an apology. But in the spirit of Catholic theology, Myshuha did show signs of—if not contrition—at least willingness toward a resolution. Myshuha played this mini-Canossa card well. If the bishop refused to meet his outstretched hand, he, Myshuha, would get the community sympathy vote.

As usual, the bishop resorted to the law. He chose to interpret the letter as a petition of a penitent rather than a public statement and filed a memo into the Dr. L. Myshuha file no. 1057, dated August 28, 1934, at the chancery. Then the bishop held a meeting with the venerable Rev. Tarnawsky and filed a memorandum: "Rev. F. Tarnawsky [and] +K, Ep. [present at meeting to discuss the petition] Rev. Tarnawsky undertook to tell the penitent that before the ban can be lifted he has to express either in writing or orally his contrition before the bishop for all the evil he has committed and in this manner rescind and do restitution for all the harm toward my person. +K." Part 2 of the document is in Bohachevsky's neat hand: "Dr. Luka Myshuha in New York on September 2, 1934, offered his excuse to the bishop; on September 3, 1934, Rev. F. Tarnawsky received the power to absolve Dr. Luka Myshuha from the excommunication. Dated September 4, 1934." Bohachevsky accepted Myshuha's apology. The Myshuha file no. 1057 was closed.

A couple of alternate versions of Myshuha's apology to Bohachevsky nevertheless slipped from the rumor mill. In one, Myshuha joined a receiving line, and upon reaching the bishop, mumbled his apology. The guests streamed on, and the bishop kept the line moving. In another version, the bishop and Myshuha met on a pre-arranged train ride, where Myshuha apologized to the bishop. Obviously Bohachevsky did not get the public satisfaction he would have liked, but he did not insist on it. The bishop kept his silence, even after Myshuha died in 1955. Myshuha left no memoirs. Bohachevsky would not actively endorse *Svoboda*, nor would give the paper interviews.

62. Myshuha to Bohachevsky, August 1934, UMAS.

For the bishop this period had been difficult, though not difficult enough to define his tenure. He accepted the difficulties in whatever form they came—public ridicule or interminable court proceedings. The last major property court case in the exarchate was settled in 1938, while smaller settlements lingered into as late as 1952. Most of the priests and a fair part of the dissidents returned to the Catholic Church. Bohachevsky did not publicly dwell on this violent time. He seemed satisfied with public admission of wrong decisions made and a promise of clerical obedience. Nor did Bohachevsky try harder to explain himself or defend his behavior. He continued working, living his ascetic personal life and reaching out personally to the congregations during his almost weekly visitations as he built a renewed community. The east-coast Ukrainian intelligentsia never fully understood that the bishop was fashioning a God-fearing, and self-sufficient and responsible Ukrainian immigrant in America. Nevertheless, despite the firm grip Bohachevsky had on his emotions, it is more than likely that the whole "Fayt" experience, along with the disappointment of the aborted trip to Lviv in 1927, had a deep psychological impact. Signs of this exist. When Bohachevsky returned from Rome in April 1927, he realized that with Nazaruk's departure he would have no close lay associates in America. Nazaruk, who like Bohachevsky, readily dismissed psychological niceties, found the bishop lacking his earlier spunk: "he's not used to the chaos that reigns here. I think he'll resign soon."[63]

Bohachevsky did not resign. His character proved to be as strong as his spine remained straight.

63. Nazaruk to Lypynsky, May 20, 1927, Lypynsky, *Collected Works*, 411.

CHAPTER 8

The Critical Years

The two trips that Bishop Bohachevsky made to Rome in 1927 and in 1929 bracketed the most critical period of his tenure and determined the fate of the Ukrainian Catholic Church in the United States. Both trips reinforced Bohachevsky's view that the mother church was in no position to either help or guide its churches abroad. He continued to see the papacy as the powerful supporter of the Ukrainian Catholic Church in the United States. It helped that Bohachevsky understood that as a world institution the Catholic Church needed to balance the conflicting interests of its many members. His expectations were realistic.

Both Takach and Bohachevsky saw that at least for the time being the sensibilities of their congregations prevented joint actions of the dioceses, but that did not stand in the way of coordinating some of their activities. They agreed it would not be prudent for them to leave the country without a Ukrainian Catholic bishop. Takach had visited the Halychyna bishops immediately after his ordination in 1924, hence it made sense for Bohachevsky to make the trip in 1927. He timed his trip to Rome to participate in the consecration of Paul Hoydych as bishop of Mukachiv and then to attend the bishop's conference at Lviv. The first would demonstrate the unity of the Ruthenians and the Halychanyns, without aggravating the American Ruthenians. The second, the bishops' conference at Lviv, would underscore the link of the American exarchates with the mother church. Bohachevsky and Njaradi were to present their plan for expanding these meetings to include Ukrainian bishops worldwide at the Lviv meetings. But, as we saw in the last chapter, Bishop Hoydych's consecration was postponed until March 25, 1927, and then the bishops' conference was postponed until April 30, 1927. Bohachevsky could not stay for the conference because he needed to be in Philadelphia for the Easter celebrations. His absence at Easter would be perceived as indifference to his own diocese. His vicar, Rev. Vashchyshyn, bombarded him with letters from Philadelphia, urging his immediate return for fear of a renewed eruption.[1] The bishop's critics viewed his absence at the conference as a sign of official displeasure from Lviv. Nothing was further from the truth.

The bishops' conference in 1927 supported Njaradi when he presented his and Bohachevsky's suggestion of broadening this conference to include all Ukrainian bishops. Other decisions of the bishops also validated Bohachevsky's policies. The conference stressed the responsibilities of the bishops over religious and fiscal lay Catholic organizations: "The bishops' conference calls attention to the rights of the eparch over all clerical organizations in his territory and resolves that actions of such organizations can be undertaken only with the express permission of the bishop, which needs to be received for each occasion."[2] The bishops at the meeting encouraged outreach to counter radicalism: "The bishops' conference resolves to prepare a joint pastoral letter warning about Bolshevik and other enemy elements, about how they behave; and [we should] provide a list of ways of countering their actions. The clergy should focus on organizing church brotherhoods and the Apostleship of Prayer to attract the devout faithful to these organizations."[3]

Bohachevsky was so disappointed that he missed the conference that uncharacteristically he complained about it to Bishop Kotsylovsky. Kotsylovsky comforted him by describing the unpleasant moments of such meetings.[4] Still Bohachevsky would have liked to present his proposal for the expansion of the bishops' conferences in person.

While in Rome in 1927, Bohachevsky prepared a five-page, neatly hand-

1. Vashchyshyn to Bohachevsky, March 11, 1927, and March 24, 1927, UMAS, Chancery-Archive.
2. PKEL, April 30, 1927.
3. Ibid.
4. Galadza, The Theology and Liturgical Work of Andrei Sheptyts'kyi, 312.

written report in Latin providing the Vatican with a clear picture of the situation of the Ukrainian Catholic Church in America. He estimated that of the 250,000 Ukrainians in the United States at the time, 150,000 were Catholics. He explained that it was the wealth and its potential for growth that made the Ukrainian Catholic Church attractive to outsiders, who cared little about its spiritual value. Bohachevsky described the difficulties, but did not dwell on them. The bishop stressed the size of America, his need to assert greater authority, and to have an auxiliary bishop. He built the first case in his more-than-a-decade-long argument for an auxiliary by noting that bishops in Halychyna had auxiliary bishops, although the size of their jurisdictions covered a fraction of some American states.

Bohachevsky returned from Rome to Philadelphia in April 1927, tense and frustrated. In contrast to the excitement of his arrival in America in 1924, he now knew that the road ahead would be lonelier than he had originally imagined. Then he had thought his vision would rally the immigrant society; now he knew that rallies and visions would not build the church. He realized that his most reliable local support came from his small circle of clergy and growing group of committed churchgoers, many of them illiterate but clearheaded. Every visitation highlighted anew the needs of the local congregations. At the same time, the daily opposition to him was immediate and ubiquitous. In the words of Mother Maria Dolzhytska, OSBM: "God alone and maybe a few of us know what Golgotha the bishop survived. They beat him, and spit at him, slammed the doors in his face, called him a traitor and a Pole."[5] Bohachevsky sought respite in prayer. Nazaruk lamented: "[he now] says 'we must live an internal life' (as if he were a monk!)."[6] The few informal notes that survive from clergy meetings during these two years (1927–29) illustrate that many priests saw eye-to-eye with the bishop. Judging by the correspondence among the priests, their interest in pastoral work revived, and they encouraged each other to publish popular articles and to develop friendlier relations among themselves.

There were two developments favorable to Bohachevsky's side. Luka Myshuha was forced to disband the Alliance (Obyednannia) for lack of funding and support. Formally, he fused it into the Ukrainian Nation-

<hr />

5. Quoted in "Vivat Academia," *Svoboda*, May 9, 1968, from a speech she delivered; repeated by Danylo Bohachevsky, *Mytropolyt Konstantyn*, 38.

6. Nazaruk to Lypynsky, April 4, 1927, in Lypynsky, *Collected Works*, 411.

al Association. That step destroyed the fiction that the Alliance unified the community. The clergy now found it easier to support the bishop's interpretation of what was good for the people. Second, a large part of the clergy met Bohachevsky more than halfway. The priests cooperated with the chancery once Bohachevsky demonstrated that he would not tolerate fiscal irresponsibility and that pastors at smaller parishes would receive an equitable stipend. Many priests worked with the bishop to smooth the return of the breakaway parishes.

The bishop's loyal priests disagreed among themselves on the course to take with the priests who had been officially suspended from office. Some argued for an overall and unconditional amnesty for all priests who wished to return to the diocese. They maintained that in the interim these would-be dissident priests had provided a service to many otherwise loyal Catholic Ukrainians. Now these faithful were concerned as to whether the offices performed by suspended clergy were canonically valid. Ukrainian immigrants in industrialized America faced a problem that troubled Central Europe in the late Middle Ages—can unworthy or invalidly consecrated priests perform valid sacraments? Others, however, objected to an amnesty. Initially some priests even considered publicizing damning behaviors of the dissident priests, to the effect that many were in violation of canon law or were even criminals who should not have been priests. In effect, they wanted a public purge. Bohachevsky objected to making such information public, maintaining that it would be injurious to the dignity of the whole church.[7]

The apostolic delegate, Pietro Fumasoni-Biondi, put an end to the debate. He insisted that the dissident clergy who wished to return to the eparchy offer individual public apologies to compensate for offending the faithful and to establish a sense of administrative responsibility. Bohachevsky ultimately concluded that the dignity of the office demanded such a procedure.[8] He expected each repentant priest to announce publicly his return to the diocese, usually in a paid newspaper advertisement. Each priest devised his own text—stressing faulty judgment, regret at mislead-

7. A handwritten and edited version of a communiqué the priests were preparing is in UMAS, Chancery Archive.
8. Handwritten notes of the meeting, unsigned, in the correspondence and notes of the clergy, UMAS.

ing the public, and, wittingly or unwittingly, undermining the Catholic Church. Most ended with a promise to work for the salvation of the souls of the Ukrainian people in the Catholic Church. Often, this was followed by a call for others to do the same.

Relations with the American Catholic Church normalized. As the Latin clergy became more aware of the global varieties of Catholicism, collegial encounters with Ukrainian priests replaced sharp clashes, but we have few records of these. Difficulties between the Latin and Ukrainian Catholic clergy tended to be recorded, while the more positive experiences were remembered only locally. From his vantage point Bohachevsky realized that the Ukrainian Catholic Church in the United States was much too weak to challenge the American Latin-rite Catholic Church hierarchy and still hope to remain within the Catholic *Ecclesia*. His chancery did not have the resources to prove the justice of the Ukrainian Church's claims in each confrontation of individual priests with higher Roman Catholic clergy, even if decisions made by these clergy were injurious to the Ukrainian Church. During the 1927–29 period, the temptation for Ukrainians to join a less strict denomination was still strong. However, an open confrontation with the American Catholic Church was too risky for the weakened Ukrainian-American Catholic Church. Bohachevsky tried to maintain good and stable relations with the Latin Catholics despite genuine or perceived slights of Ukrainian priests by Latin prelates. This approach angered some Ukrainian clergy.

THE VATICAN REVIEW OF THE UKRAINIAN CATHOLIC CHURCH IN THE UNITED STATES

The bishop moved slowly with quiet determination to build the church. He felt that he had a chance to hold the eparchy together. The only tool he had was work by example, and he hoped that his example would carry others along despite the persistent criticism of all his actions. The lay congregations, at times even sooner than the clergy, recognized the bishop's goal and his strategy—the church is in the people, not in the grand cathedrals, its value is internal and not reliant on outside recognition.

The speed and the number of clergy and congregants who returned to the Ukrainian Catholic Church, however, surprised the Vatican. Moreover, although dissident priests were returning to the Ukrainian Catholic

Church, complaints about Bishop Bohachevsky, some from highly placed priests, still trickled in to the Congregation for the Eastern Church. Particularly troubling was that Rev. Volodymyr Petrivsky, the erstwhile secretary to Bishop Ortynsky, objected to Bohachevsky's policies. He had made two specific complaints about Bohachevsky to Luigi Cardinal Sincero, the secretary of the Congregation. First, the bishop had not publicly challenged the Latin-rite Catholic bishop who had allegedly said at the Chicago Eucharistic congress that "it is high time to liquidate the Greek Slavonic rite in the Catholic Church." Second, Bohachevsky had erred in treating the assassinated Rev. Vasyl Stetsiuk as a martyr, because in Petrivsky's opinion Stetsiuk was responsible for Ortynsky's death.[9] Additional complaints from others included Bohachevsky's unwillingness to address certain local issues and the chancery's slow or inadequate responses to others. Other priests accused the bishop of being too much of a disciplinarian, whereas others thought him too lenient.

Back in 1927, while Bohachevsky was still in Rome, both his supporters and his detractors had filed petitions to the congregation through the papal nuncio. Vashchyshyn also circulated a petition, signed by fifty-six priests, to assure the papacy that Bishop Bohachevsky had strong support.[10] The apostolic delegate, Fumasoni-Biondi, did not put much credence in the criticism; nevertheless he felt that the complaints needed to be officially investigated in Rome.[11] Privately, he assured Bohachevsky that the investigation was a formality and there was no cause for concern. Still, the Vatican investigation must have made Bohachevsky feel vulnerable.[12] None of his superiors had questioned his judgment or good faith, and only the hostile Polish police had investigated him.

9. Petrivsky to Fumasoni Biondi, April 1, 1927, in Rigotti, 784.

10. CEC, Prot. 566/1928. The letter was printed and hand signed.

11. Hand copied version of the petition in ASV, America, Prot. 6/9, pp. 605–6; see also *Svoboda*, February 25, 1927; and Kuropas, *Ukrainian Americans*, 309. The following year, on June 23, 1928, another priest, Rev. Josef Dzendzera also complained to the congregation about Bohachevsky's alleged cruelty: the bishop refused to give the priest medical leave to go to Canada. CEC, Prot. 466/ 28 [Rigotti, 786, 796–800]. Petrivsky's April 13, 1927, complaint, written in Washington, D.C., had to be addressed because he had been Ortynsky's right hand, CEC, Prot. 466/28 [Rigotti, 784]. Petrivsky faulted Bohachevsky for not defending the Ukrainian Church and for supporting the suspension of Rev. Joseph Zuk.

12. Along with Bohachevsky's report for 1931, on December 9, 1932, Fumasoni-Biondi sent Cardinal Sincero a letter in which he characterized Bohachevsky as "the best bishop for

The cardinals at the Vatican who reevaluated the complaints against Bohachevsky were not very concerned about the lay protests. The Vatican clergy had become inured to the unrest in the Ukrainian Catholic Church in America—there was a whole drawer at the Congregation for the Eastern Church marked "*Lamenti Rutheni.*" What most concerned the congregation were the activities of the Ukrainian Catholic clergy—the fear that those validly consecrated priests who so readily questioned the bishop might just as easily join the Eastern schism against the papacy. The protest meeting that the Ukrainian Catholic clergy had held in February 1927 still caused sharp consternation at the Vatican because of Rev. Joseph Zhuk's eminence within the Catholic hierarchy. Regardless of how he viewed his own role, the Congregation for the Eastern Church recognized Zhuk as the leader of the protest. The cardinals did not care if Zhuk had been used by outside political forces. What mattered to them was that Zhuk held formal positions of authority. As a priest of the Lviv metropolitanate, he was subject to that discipline. Sheptytsky's office had not formally recalled Rev. Zhuk, who continually used his alleged connection with the metropolitan to bolster his credibility.

A special investigator, Rev. Placido de Meestr, was charged with providing a detailed analysis to the Holy See of the work of both Bishops Bohachevsky and Takach. De Meestr presented his report in October 1927, concluding that Bohachevsky's work was exemplary, especially in carrying out visitations and in struggling to reduce the exarchy's considerable debts. As an aside, de Meestr bemoaned the defection of so many Ruthenians to Orthodoxy, but explained that the Ruthenian clergy were not the best representatives of the profession. He praised Bohachevsky for understanding that the very freedom that Americans enjoy necessitated the counterbalance of Catholic education for the faith to survive in the New World. De Meestr's report was added to the growing file that the congregation had assembled to review the Ukrainian-American situation.

Seven cardinals studied de Meestr's report and all other pertinent materials on the two Ukrainian bishops in America. The summary report prepared for Pope Pius XI pointed out that both Ukrainian bishops had

the Halychyna Ruthenians and Ukrainians." Fumasoni-Biondi stressed that Bohachevsky was easy to work with and "a man of God, animated and always ready to perform his tasks." CEC, Prot. 566/28.

performed admirably under very difficult conditions. It encouraged both bishops to raise the level of their clergy and to establish a joint seminary. The cardinals upheld clerical celibacy, understanding that the American Latin-rite faithful were shocked by the notion of married Catholic clergy. They hoped that the tensions between the Ruthenians and the Ukrainians would subside and the two branches could reunite into one diocese. The highly placed Raffaele Cardinal Scapinelli, who had earlier served as the nuncio to the Habsburg Monarchy, also hoped that the common use of Church Slavonic in their services would help bring Ukrainians and Ruthenians closer together.[13] This was by no means a novel idea. Early in 1927, Bishop Takach had petitioned the congregation for permission to hold a synod of his clergy to discuss and treat current problems. Luigi Cardinal Sincero, the secretary of the Congregation for the Eastern Church, had countered that such a synod should be postponed to give priority to establishing a seminary. Moreover, he commented, it would be a good idea for the two exarchates to hold a joint synod.

The Congregation for the Eastern Church repeatedly reminded Takach and Bohachevsky of the key importance of the office of bishop. The cardinals were worried that the new bishops, working on their own, did not have models for episcopal behavior and might not recognize the full scope of the power they could exercise. Sincero in his summation of the discussions, focused much attention on the bishops' fiscal responsibility. It was imperative, he emphasized, that the bishop centralize all the holdings of the eparchy and control of all financial matters of their dioceses. In the end, the cardinals agreed that both bishops had performed admirably, but pointed out that the issues confronting Bohachevsky were particularly difficult. After the whole set of pertinent papers made its rounds, on February 11, 1928 the seven cardinals finally met to answer two questions: How should Bohachevsky's report be acknowledged and what directions should be given to the bishops? Thus, almost a year after Bohachevsky's first official trip to Rome as bishop, the worthies at the Vatican concluded that he and Bishop Takach were effective churchmen working under very difficult circumstances:

13. CEC, Prot. 576/1927 [Rigotti, 673–700]; and 576/1928 [Rigotti, 697, 701]; printed version marked Prot. 3316 [Rigotti, 684–710].

1. A letter of praise should be sent to Bishop Bohachevsky commending the apostolic spirit which [Bohachevsky] exhibits through the work he managed to perform in the difficult circumstances in which he finds himself.

2. [Both] bishops should be encouraged to develop welfare programs, good [Catholic] periodical publications, and parochial schools, ensure the continued visitations of parishes and attendant missionary work, foster vocations, oversee the education and discipline of the clergy, assure that the eparchial finances are properly handled and that the bishop plays a leading role in these matters.[14]

Congratulatory letters were sent to both bishops.

The cardinals had barely finished their deliberations about the Ukrainian Catholic Church when the next complaint from the Ukrainians reached the Vatican. On the eve of the expanded conference of Ukrainian bishops, which Bohachevsky was to attend but could not, the dissident priests from America still hoped that their complaints about the bishop would sway the congregation and Metropolitan Sheptytsky to censure, if not dismiss, Bohachevsky. This time the petition was also signed by priests who had supported the bishop, among them Revs. Onufriy Koval-sky (Onufry/Humphrey; Kowalsky), Oleksa Prystay, and Maksym Kinash, the last signing himself Maximillian for purposes of the Latin text. These priests charged that Bohachevsky's administrative innovations Latinized the Byzantine rite.

The Congregation for the Eastern Church, occupied with editing the papal bull on all the Eastern churches, almost dismissed the last complaint against Bohachevsky out of hand because the dissident priests were known troublemakers.[15] Fumasoni-Biondi summed up this petition by noting that "the charges come from unworthy priests, who are not ashamed to fan the fires of discontent with the bishop, instead of joining him [the bishop] in reestablishing order in their unfortunate diocese."[16] Nonetheless, the cardinals decided to share the letter with Bohachevsky so that he would be well informed about the views of his clergy. They asked him to comment on the new charges. Bohachevsky received a copy

---

14. CEC, Prot. 576/1928 [Rigotti, 697].

15. CEC, Prot. 526/28, a final discussion prior to the papal audience of February 11, 1929.

16. CEC, Prot. 566/28 [Rigotti, 813]. The typewritten complaint is in Latin, CEC, Prot. 526/18; Bohachevsky's correspondence with Sheptytsky and Kostelnyk is in UMAS, Chancery Archive.

of the eight-page criticism on June 29, 1929, as he prepared for a trip to Canada to consecrate Basil Ladyka, a Basilian, as bishop.

In Halychyna, the laity had become increasingly interested in replacing Old Church Slavonic with the vernacular Ukrainian popularized by the Ukrainian Autocephalous Orthodox Church. Havryil Kostelnyk and his journal, *Nyva*, primarily championed the movement to return to the Eastern roots of the church as well as the decentralization of the church's hierarchic structure. Bohachevsky feared that such discussions could destabilize the still-shaky American eparchy, and he complained to Sheptytsky. The metropolitan countered that these discussions were welcome in Lviv, and suggested that Bohachevsky join them. Bohachevsky, faced with daily crises, did not have the time for essay writing. Bohachevsky felt he needed to respond firmly to the charges of these activist priests to maintain his authority.

The more active Ukrainian Catholic priests inevitably ran into problems with Catholic bishops of both rites. Bohachevsky seemed unwilling or was unable to confront the Latin-rite Catholic Church bishops in cases when the interests of the Ukrainian churches clashed with those of the Latin Catholics. The career of Rev. Humphrey (Onophrius or Onufriy) Kovalsky epitomizes the challenges of being a Ukrainian Catholic priest in the United States. He was an energetic activist and a great self-starter—at one point he studied at Columbia University's General Studies College and claimed to have introduced Clarence Manning to the works of Taras Shevchenko, thus launching Manning's long cooperation with the Ukrainian-American community. Kovalsky ran afoul of authority, including Boston's Archbishop (soon to be made cardinal) William H. O'Connell, in the spring of 1928 when he was fundraising in Roman Catholic churches and schools without having first cleared the campaign with the Latin archdiocese. O'Connell also objected to the practice of married Ukrainian clergy officiating in Roman Catholic churches. Faced with extended internal community unrest in his parish, Kovalsky acquired property on Beacon Street in Boston to use for Ukrainian church services; and O'Connell, working on gentrifying his own church, felt that the contentious immigrant churches did not belong on Beacon Street. The Ukrainian Catholics, meanwhile, had already split into two publicly warring groups over Kovalsky's appointment; and the Orthodox were making heavy inroads into the split community. O'Connell felt that Kovalsky had overstepped the bounds of propriety and demanded an apology, informing Bishop Bohachevsky of that demand. Bohachevsky then asked Kovalsky to apologize. Kovalsky wrote a letter asking O'Connell to tell him for what exactly he should apologize. The archbishop, who broke an appointment with Kovalsky only to run into him on his way to a waiting car, stuffed that letter into his trouser pocket without reading it. When he read the letter later that evening, he immediately demanded satisfaction from Bohachevsky for what he considered Kovalsky's inappropriate behavior. In an attempt to placate Archbishop O'Connell, Bohachevsky and his chancellor, Rev. Pyk, both writing in Italian, transferred Kovalsky from Boston to Nanticoke, Pennsylvania, and threatened him with suspension if he refused. They sent copies of their letters to O'Connell, in another placating gesture.

Humphrey Kovalsky had supported Bohachevsky in his hour of need and felt that the bishop should have defended him in an incident involving Boston's Roman Catholic archbishop, even at the cost of alienating the American Latin-rite Catholic establishment. Rev. Prystay seconded Kovalsky, who, convinced of the justice of his cause and of his bishop's servile negligence in not defending him before the Latin-rite Catholic archbishop, disregarded the transfer. Bohachevsky suspended Kovalsky, who quickly borrowed money and went off to Rome to prepare his petition against "the Lord Cardinal's grossly sinful abuse of me and of my parish."[17] Along the way, Kovalsky contacted Metropolitan Sheptytsky, complaining "my bishop won't help me in Rome, although the matter deals directly with our diocese [sic]."[18] Sheptytsky penned a brief note to Cardinal Pietro Gas-

17. Kovalsky's complaints surface in multiple versions; see CEC, Prot. 564/28, Kovalsky to the apostolic representative (Pietro Fumasoni-Biondi), July 12, 1928, p. 2. In a private letter to an unnamed friend, Kovalsky characterized Bohachevsky as "an unformed fetus [nedoliudok] who is destroying our diocese," TsDIA, Lviv, f. 358, op. 1, spr. 368, stamped #28453, p. 83. In a letter to Sheptytsky, dated October 13, 1927, Kovalsky complained that Bohachevsky is "a passive mannequin," ibid., 181; and in f. 538, spr. 273. He was an independent risk taker, as determined as Bohachevsky, and as representative of Ukrainian Catholic clergy as Bohachevsky. For a recent illustrated history of the Ukrainian Catholic parish in Boston, in which Kovalsky served for a time, see Anna Chopek, "Recollections of Anna Chopek Regarding the Trials and Tribulations of the Ukrainian Catholic Church in Boston and Its Parishioners," in *Christ the King Church: History of the Ukrainian Catholic Community in Boston 1907–2007* (Boston: Christ the King Ukrainian Catholic Church, 2007), 75–103.

18. Kovalsky to Sheptytsky, October 13, 1927, TsDIA, Lviv, f. 358, op. 1, spr. 368, pp. 119–20.

parri attesting to Kovalsky's probity and ecclesiastical service and asking that his case be studied. But no one at the Vatican wanted to challenge the newly nominated American Cardinal O'Connell nor to make life more difficult for the valiant Bohachevsky. Kovalsky duly documented his futile travels through Europe, presenting his version of the story. He wanted the Catholic authorities to know that Cardinal O'Connell in effect was objecting to a Ukrainian-Catholic presence in the better part of Boston, a point O'Connell had apparently once openly made to Kovalsky. O'Connell later challenged the priest's veracity. Bohachevsky, still in a precarious position, did not feel strong enough to take on the Boston Latin-rite archdiocese. Within a year, Kovalsky saw the impossibility of his cause and returned to the fold. Prystay and Kinash, his fellow critics of the bishop, joined him in the return journey to the ecclesiastical fold.

Prystay's problems were with the new Orthodox priests, consecrated by erstwhile Catholics now Orthodox of episcopal rank who repeatedly pushed Prystay out of the parishes that Prystay claimed as his. Prystay again accused Bohachevsky of cowardice for not coming to his defense. At the other side of the pendulum, Rev. Khlystun voiced disappointment that the bishop accommodated the politicized Ukrainian society at the cost spirituality. He charged that the bishop surrounded himself by yes-men who had no new ideas. "To all demands and signs of life, he [the bishop] has one answer—work, do what you can, and we'll see how it goes."[19]

Bohachevsky's response to the Vatican about these newer charges, as to the previous ones, was measured and to the point. He briefly reiterated the difficulties in the eparchy and charted the means he had used to overcome them. He stressed that steadfastness, discipline, and evenhandedness brought effective results in the bishop's relations with the

19. Rev. Andriy Khlystun to Nazaruk, June 25, 1936, TsDIA, Lviv, f. 406, op. 1, spr. 22, p. 43. In an earlier letter (February 28, 1935), Khlystun also objected to Bohachevsky's support of *America* and of the Providence Association, because neither propagated active religious life among the laity. TsDIA, Lviv, f. 406, op. 1, spr. 22, pp. 31–37. Khlystun, then pastor of Watervliet, N.Y., had been involved in the Hetman movement, so his criticism of Bohachevsky was also colored by the bishop's unwillingness to go on record publicly to support the conservative Hetman cause. Protsko to Nazaruk, April 14, 1937, TsDIA, Lviv, f. 359, op. 1, spr. 305, ark. 15–18. Khlystun resented that the bishop established contacts with representatives of the Ukrainian National Association and *Svoboda*, "because they are people without honor or faith." Khlystun to Nazaruk, March 29, 1937, UMAS.

clergy. The bishop felt that even if some clergy had fallen by the wayside, the strength of those who stayed and the recommitment of those who formally returned to the fold had offset the losses. The bishop was sorry that some clergy left, but he was certain that those men were unsuited for priesthood. He could say with a clear conscience that his church was stronger, even though slightly smaller in numbers.[20]

Moved by Bohachevsky's direct style and unassuming demeanor, the cardinals at Rome again praised his tactics in trying times and strongly encouraged him to continue working as he saw fit. The bishop refused to draw himself into another public polemic in the Ukrainian press, even as the congregation carried out two formal investigations of him. He took these proceedings in stride. There is no evidence that Bohachevsky shared information about the high regard in which he was held in Rome, but the cardinals' support must have been a balm to his battered ego.

Bohachevsky succeeded in achieving his first goal—he saved the Ukrainian Catholic eparchy in the United States from becoming a pawn in the hands of competing political groupings. In a contemporary analysis of at least one old-time priest, Bohachevsky also saved the eparchy from likely communist inroads.[21] Ensuring the continued independent existence of the Ukrainian Catholic Church in the United States within the universal Catholic Church, Bohachevsky had also fostered conditions for its growth. The first sign of the bishop's success came as parish after parish returned to the diocese and parishioners paid their parish dues. The bitter period was over.

STRENGTHENING THE CHURCH

Bohachevsky asserted his authority while winning the active support of his faithful. The solid core of the church-going public and the trustees whom they elected saw through the rhetoric of the opposition. Throughout the 1920s and early 1930s, these American immigrants, semiliterate in Ukrainian and rudimentary in English, managed to send enough letters of

20. CEC, Prot. 566/28 [Rigotti, 810–19; 820–21].
21. Rev. Vasyl Maniovsky to Rev. Mykhaylo Lysiak, November 12, 1926, UMAS, Chancery Archive.

support to the bishop to prove his worth. The letters may have been grammatically incorrect, but they provide information and attest to the keen perception of the writers in their assessment of social and community affairs.[22] These parishioners recognized the value of combining church and educational institutions, they saw proof of the bishop's commitment, and they gave him their support.

Several major problems claimed Bohachevsky's immediate attention. The diocesan structure had to be perfected, and parishes organized within the legal framework. Not all parishes accepted the bishop as the legal owner of church property. Furthermore, the bishop had no money—what he collected went for the upkeep of the church and its institutions in the United States, or to support orphans and handicapped veterans in Ukraine. He had difficulty justifying the need for the administrative expenses of the chancery, as well as the publication of the eparchial monthly newsletter, the *Eparchial News*, even to his own priests. Hence he welcomed Epiphanius Theodorovych, a Basilian monk, and his bi-monthly newspaper *Katolyts'ky Provid (Catholic Leadership)*, which served as a semi-official eparchial publication until the exarchate had enough funds to renew the *Eparchial News* four years later, in 1933. The editor had a free hand in the choice of collaborators, but Bohachevsky took a personal interest in the paper and readily excused the editor for all shortcomings.[23] The information in *Catholic Leadership* was basic; for example, one article provided practical information on how to form a parish. Explaining that it was not enough for a few good men to get together to establish a parish, the writer underscored that a parish must be attached to a larger entity, the eparchy. The reality of a larger community—the Ukrainian Catholic Church as a physical entity—had to be drummed in repeatedly.[24] The newspaper reminded its readers of the date of Ortynsky's death, and it documented donations made to various causes. Theodorovych sought to expand the readers' interest by including articles on a variety of subjects, such as how

22. For instance, Oleksander Kudla from Philadelphia offered his services to the bishop, were the bishop in need of them, Kudla to Bohachevsky, October 24, 1926, UMAS.

23. Bohachevsky wrote a very pleasant letter to an irate Nazaruk, assuring his erstwhile editor that he would be paid for a recent article, Bohachevsky to Nazaruk, October 13, 1928, Nazaruk file, TsDIA, Lviv, f. 359, op. 1, spr. 305, p. 49.

24. *Katolyts'ky Provid*, January 20, 1928.

FIGURE 8. CONSTANTINE BOHACHEVSKY IN VESTMENTS
MADE BY ORPHANS, 1931

to behave in public.[25] To stress the relevance of the church to daily activities, the paper included pointers on proper table manners and appropriate dress. Such advice was welcome for a population that was seeking to better itself without losing its own culture. Outside of Ukrainian territories, the church more than ever became the primary link to ancestral identity. Simply put, the church made it possible for those who identified with American society, rather than with a Halychyna they had never seen, to preserve their Ukrainian identity while acting like Americans.[26] Later, when the *Eparchial News* resumed publication, I suspect it was Bohachevsky who snuck in small articles similar to those that had turned up in *Catholic Leadership*, such as how to be thriftier in the kitchen by using leftovers creatively, not just throwing them out.

Meanwhile, property issues had to be settled, usually through onerous and costly court proceedings, even when lawyers charged minimal fees. Some church communities tried to build churches they could not afford; others refused to pay for work already completed. Ugly court cases continued, though decreasing in volume, until 1938. There were problems with church committees who saw no reason why their membership needed to be formally approved by the chancery.[27] Problems with individual priests continued sporadically until 1931.

As if to stress God's protection of Bohachevsky in 1929—the black year of economic collapse in the United States—three significant actions helped to consolidate the bishop's episcopal authority: the papacy openly defended the legitimacy of the Eastern churches in territories presumed to be Western; the Ukrainian-American clergy pledged their support for the bishop; and the Ukrainian Catholic bishops worldwide established a coordinating committee which Bohachevsky would support financially until the Soviet-Nazi cooperation agreement in 1939 and the outbreak of the Second World War.

In September 1928, Pope Pius XI called for greater understanding of

25. Among the more interesting pieces was his description of a Catholic parish on 12th and Lombard Streets, in Philadelphia, which was almost wholly composed of African-American migrants from the South. No one drew a parallel between the two rural societies, Ukrainian and Southern African Americans, thrown into common city life. Race was too new a factor for the Eastern Europeans to see similarities in the two societies.

26. *Katolyts'ky Provid*, July 15, 1930.

27. Rev. Dovhovych to unknown friend, August 21, 1927, UMAS.

the non-Latin rites within the Catholic Church and "voiced his desire that 'the first elements of the Oriental questions' be taught in all Roman Catholic theological seminaries."[28] It was helpful that Pope Pius XI had issued (in the previous year) an encyclical encouraging Roman Catholics to learn more about their Eastern brethren. In March 1929, the pope promulgated *Cum data fuerit*, a decree that expanded the power of the Ukrainian bishops in the United States, although predictably it repeated the stipulation that only celibate priests serve there. The celibacy requirement for Ukrainian-American clergy sparked a major clergy revolt among the Ruthenians, but caused little more than grumbling among the priests from Halychyna.

Bohachevsky deliberately stressed the positive aspects of *Cum data fuerit*: it strengthened the position of the Eastern-rite bishop and modified earlier papal pronouncements limiting the powers of the Eastern exarchates in the United States. To offset a renewal of anti-Vatican demonstrations, he held a special meeting of the clergy on March 1, 1929, at which a free-ranging discussion among the clergy focused on the papal decree. That summer, on August 1, 1929, Bohachevsky convened the clergy again, a meeting that the editor of *Catholic Leadership*, in his zeal, elevated to a congress.[29] During this meeting, the Ukrainian-American clergy—its ranks already diminished and its emotional resources depleted—again looked for the positive aspects of the papal decree. Among other things, *Cum data fuerit* specifically enjoined Ukrainian Catholics to establish seminaries in the United States and permitted Ukrainian-American bishops to petition formally for additional clergy from the home country. Bohachevsky again stressed the decree's positive aspects: It strengthened the legal position of the Ukrainian Catholic Church within the context of the whole Catholic *Ecclesia*.

At the March 1929 meeting, the Ukrainian-American priests resuscitated a plan for a mutual-aid society exclusively for the clergy. The plan was to have a clergy organization whose dues would create a reserve fund for members in need and in retirement. The organizers wanted all Ukrainian Catholic priests in the United States to become members. The bishop

28. Procko, *Ukrainian Catholics in America*, 67. The encyclical, titled *Rerum Orientalium*, was issued on September 8, 1928.

29. *Katolyts'ky Provid*, August 30, 1929.

readily agreed, although he doubted that the priests would persevere in paying their self-determined dues. The motion was approved with thirty-three of the fifty-six priests at the meeting in favor, but there is no evidence of any related follow up.

Bohachevsky used the clergy meeting as a venue to clarify other issues, beginning with the continued use of the term "Ruthenian" alongside "Ukrainian" in official correspondence. He explained that as long as the mother church in Halychyna used the term Ruthenian, the American Ukrainian Church did not want to introduce changes in common terminology that would separate the American eparchy from the home country. He further posited that the American eparchy could not issue its own set of diocesan rules without seeming to disassociate itself from the home country. The bishop urged the clergy to contribute articles to the monthly newsletter, *Eparchial News*, on parish activities or on their views on controversial topics so that others would learn about Ukrainian Catholic life in America. Bohachevsky asked for suggestions for nominations for the diocesan consultors, and for understanding the celibacy requirement as well as the difficulty of granting vacations that would leave a parish temporarily without a pastor. The bishop also raised the problem of staffing deaneries in areas where parishes were widely scattered. Finally, he felt that it was important to explain once again that the monthly parish dues to the chancery were not for the bishop's personal use but for administrative purposes.

With canon law firmly on his side, Bohachevsky was better positioned to speak with authority to all Catholics, not just the Ukrainians.[30] The parallel episcopal jurisdiction of the Eastern-rite bishops could no longer be questioned by the Latin-rite Catholic clerics in the United States. Bohachevsky's relations with the Roman Catholic clergy, while not entirely devoid of misunderstandings, became more cordial.

Meanwhile, the ranks of the pro-bishop stalwarts had swelled so dramatically that Vatican officials again thought that the rate of return of the Ukrainian dissident clergy and faithful to the exarchy was suspect. On August 1, 1929, thirty influential priests in Bohachevsky's diocese publicly reconfirmed their loyalty to the pope and to the bishop, pledging their

---

30. Procko, *Ukrainian Catholics in America*, 61; *Katolyts'ky Provid*, August 30, 1928.

"full solidarity and allegiance as well as their loyalty." They also hoped that the bishop would accept these sentiments "as retribution for all the unpleasantness and difficulties he had suffered.[31] During the next two years, 1928 to 1930, the pages of *America* printed formal statements of apology to the bishop and to the church by priests who admitted either faulty judgment or unfortunate actions and requested to be reunited with the church.[32] The nuncio assured the congregation that he had personally looked into the matter and found that, indeed, dissident Ukrainian priests were returning to the diocesan fold rapidly and in large numbers. A few years later, in 1933, when the new apostolic delegate, Amleto Cicognani, arrived in Washington, he too suspected that the reports were inflated. He looked carefully into the exarchy's work, and especially at the work of Bohachevsky, and finally reported that "in the last two years one notices a distinct progress, which, in the words of the bishop himself, is the result of [his] strict adherence to principles." The nuncio continued:

He has no fear of the priests who threaten to turn Orthodox or who indeed join the Orthodox; . . . he treats them all without exception as troublemaking schismatics; he [is aware] that a [political] nationalist subtext permeates the struggle against [clerical] celibacy for the sole purpose [that others might] fish in the muddy waters, and he clearly let it be known that there would be no exceptions in this matter.[33]

THE 1929 UKRAINIAN BISHOPS'
CONFERENCE AT ROME

Bohachevsky was formally responsible directly to the pope, with the Congregation for the Eastern Church serving as his official conduit. He was concerned, however, that there was no institutional mechanism for cooperation with Lviv other than his direct communication with Metropolitan Sheptytsky. For him this connection was personal but he also wanted an

31. *Katolyts'ky Provid*, August 30, 1929; before his trip to Europe, in July 1929 Bohachevsky participated in the consecration of Bishop Basil Ladyka in Canada, establishing closer relations between the two churches.

32. Kinash published an apology for participating in "the movement that should be denounced [*nahany hidnomu rusi*]," in *Katolyts'ky Provid*, November 13, 1927; Mykhailo Lysiak followed on December 15.

33. Amleto Cicognani to Sincero, March 31, 1934, AES, America, pos. 713, fasc. 7783-I.

institutional one. Bohachevsky was aware that his successors would not have the personal connection with the Lviv metropolitan that he enjoyed. Formally, there was no institutional channel to communicate with Lviv. Bohachevsky looked forward to attending the next bishops' conference scheduled for 1929 in Rome to establish an institutional framework for the Ukrainian bishops' conferences such as Njaradi had proposed at his behest in 1927.

In the late 1920s, the Ukrainian Catholic Church in Halychyna was under double fire: defending itself from growing encroachments of Polish administrative power, which moved toward authoritarianism, while battling the radicalization of Ukrainian society, especially its youth. A united position of the bishops on ecclesiastical and community issues was obviously welcome.[34] I suspect—although Bohachevsky never even hinted at it—that he expected some expression of support from his metropolitan, Sheptytsky. He wanted to maintain ties with the mother church in Lviv. The joint meeting of the Ukrainian bishops could serve this purpose. Bishop Dionysius Njaradi, whose churches found themselves in multiple states after the Versailles settlement and had to deal with demands, had encouraged Metropolitan Sheptytsky to hold an expanded meeting of Ukrainian bishops to work on reaching a consensus about the specifics of their rite and about administrative practices. Today we would say that the global nature of the 1929 conference is illustrated by the fact that it was not recorded in the standard minutes of the Halychyna bishops' conferences.[35] Vasyl Lakota, Bohachevsky's erstwhile confrere from Peremyshl

---

34. That commission (Komisiia Sprav Uriadovykh) was headed by the venerable Isidore Dolnytsky.

35. The minutes of the meetings of the Ukrainian bishops are quite terse, and it is difficult to detect the tone of the discussion. We know that the bishops of Peremyshl and especially of Stanislaviv were pushing hard for a more actively practiced Catholicism. Bishop Khomyshyn of Stanislaviv, perhaps the only Ukrainian Catholic bishop whose parents were peasants, was in the forefront of the movement to modernize the church and have its laity play an active role in promoting Christian politics. But the politically conscious Ukrainian intelligentsia opposed him as well as Kotsylovsky because of the bishops' support of clerical celibacy and their alleged cooperation with the Polish regime. Bohachevsky sided with the younger two bishops in their view that the proper role of the church is spiritual and social, but not political. The official statements of loyalty to the papacy and the brief final document from the conference were published in the December 15, 1929, issue of *Katolyts'ky*

and now Bishop Kotsylovsky's vicar, was charged with preparing parts of the agenda for the gathering.[36] Bohachevsky welcomed the plan enthusiastically.[37] It is telling that later writers tend to credit Sheptytsky rather than Njaradi with the plan to assemble all Ukrainian bishops.[38] The difficulties in organizing the conference are best illustrated by the fact that Takach and Bohachevsky replied to the preliminary letters about when to organize the meeting with differing responses, one replying in the fall, the other in the spring.[39]

The conference took place at Rome between October 21 and 29, 1929. It brought together the largest number of Ukrainian Catholic bishops to date with the goal of facilitating and bringing into conformity liturgical texts and traditions of worship in the Ukrainian Catholic tradition. The bishops were encouraged to reach a consensus on the most pressing issues of worship. They hoped to help each other through frank discussions about the increasing challenges that the church faced in the various countries in which its faithful now found themselves.

Provid. See also correspondence of Bishop Ivan Buchko with Bohachevsky, TsDIA, Lviv, f. 201, op. 1, spr. 5952. Rev. P. Khomyn, in his report on the 1929 conference ("Konferentsiia ukraiins'koho hr.-kat. Epyskopatu v Rymi," Nyva [November 1929], 434–39) considers the 1927 conference that Bohachevsky missed and the 1929 one as initiating Ukrainian bishops' conferences.

36. Eastern church usage refers to the formal gathering of clerics as council or *sobor*. Within the Ukrainian Catholic Church an informal diminutive of this term—*soborchyk*— was used to refer to the periodic meetings of priests that the bishops convened either for spiritual exercises or to discuss administrative issues. The 1920s and 1930s meetings of the Ukrainian Catholic bishops are documented as "conferences," using the Ukrainianized Latin form—*konferentsii*. Latinized terms peppered the speech of the Ukrainian educated class at the time, in the home country and abroad. In the usage of the time, *konferentsia* connotes more of a meeting convened for discussion rather than decision purposes. Another Latin term—*konzilium*—was used for gatherings that were expected to deal with specific, generally pressing issues, often of a juridical nature.

37. The preliminary correspondence focused on the potential participants—should vicars-general be part of the meeting? Bishop Takach said yes; Bohachevsky, no. The latter seems to have been the majority position.

38. Cyrille Korolevskij, *Metropolite Andre Szeptyckyj, 1865–1944* (Rome: Ukrainian Theological Society, 1964), 52–53, erroneously credits Sheptytsky with this initiative.

39. In preparing the conference, Sheptytsky, in a letter to Kotsylovsky, July 29, 1927 (Archiwum Panstwowe w Przemyslu, zespol 142, f. 9485, p. 152), replied that Takach, the Carpatho-Ruthenian bishop and Bohachevsky needed to decide between themselves on the specific time of the year when they would like the conference to be held.

Religious discussions among the Ukrainian Catholic laity often focused on ritual. Among the clergy, the specifics of ritual, vestments, as well as the texts of canonical books for Ukrainian Catholics had not been reviewed in more than a century. Prior discussions on such matters had lasted for decades: some dealing with erudite textual interpretations, others focusing on such seemingly incidental issues as clerical head coverings, the use of flowers in church, and specifics about candles. As far back as 1904, Metropolitan Sheptytsky had created a core commission to study textual issues. In 1914, the 1904 commission was reorganized as a liturgical commission and tasked to prepare an archeparchial synod. The commission emphasized the need to establish a common standard in the mode of worship and textual usage, and slowly continued its work until the outbreak of World War II. It was deeply immersed in scholarly and doctrinal issues through the detailed analysis of the various texts used before and after the Union of Brest. Many saw the key to the reconciliation of the Orthodox and Catholic Churches in these documents. The commission worked behind closed doors, but rumors of its work generated a public discussion on issues of religious worship. Sheptytsky had appointed Bohachevsky to the liturgical commission in 1914, Bohachevsky found it difficult to study liturgical issues when he was dealing with organizational and disciplinary matters in the United States. The Ukrainian community in the United States did not have clergy, let alone laity, well enough versed in liturgical and doctrinal matters to engage in a constructive debate on these issues. Therefore, the bishop focused on putting the diocese in order.

The agenda for the Rome conference was ambitious. All bishops agreed that secularism and materialism were undermining the foundations of their church, and all vowed to present a united front before the faithful. They acknowledged that the conversion of the East was a major goal of the Ukrainian Catholic Church, but they did not elaborate on how this goal was to be pursued. They agreed on the revised text of the Liturgy of St. John Chrysostom. There was a lengthy discussion on the appropriateness and validity of the *Sluzhebnyk*, a fundamental Eastern prayer book, that the commission published under Sheptytsky's aegis. Bishop Khomyshyn, supported by Kotsylovsky and Bohachevsky, objected to the edition but were outvoted by Sheptytsky and Njaradi. Other issues on the agenda covered the divisive topics that split the Ukrainian Catholic community: celibate ordination for priests, the use of the vernacular in worship, the services honoring the Virgin in May and the Sacred Heart in June, the texts of prayers for Ukraine (which did not have a formal legal status) and the like.[40] The actual hierarchical structure of the bishops was not yet settled, and the bishops could not agree on the dating of some critical texts, but those attending the conference were able to agree on the basic text of the liturgy.

The most concrete result of the 1929 Ukrainian bishops' conference was the creation of a permanent office for the conference. Bohachevsky was its most active supporter, both morally and especially financially. Having seen what Latin-rite American bishops could accomplish by discussion, Bohachevsky had great hopes for a permanent conference or commission of Ukrainian Catholic bishops, despite the obvious and even public disagreements among the bishops of the Ukrainian Church. He provided financial support for the Lviv office until the outbreak of the Second World War. Bohachevsky hoped to preserve structural ties among Ukrainian Catholic churches worldwide, realizing that his successors raised in the United States would not have the same emotional, let alone, personal ties that bound him to the Lviv metropolitanate. Institutional ties were more likely to endure than mere attachment to a local tradition. The bishop actively supported the office that was to facilitate cooperation, or at least communication, among the Ukrainian bishops. He set great store on this work, consistently sought to expand it, and tried to involve Bishop Takach's Ruthenian eparchy in its activities.

For all the beautiful ceremonies and pleasant words, the conference demonstrated that the Ukrainian Catholic Church, like the Ukrainian community at home, was divided and at odds with itself. In Halychyna,

40. Lakota noted the following agenda: draft suitable letters to the Holy Father and the congregation; discuss and resolve: publication of the edited texts; address the use of vernacular in church services, as well as ways of dealing with schismatic propaganda, approaches toward fostering conversion of the East, priestly celibacy and codes of behavior, monastic rules, episcopal rights, and innovative religious worship, such as "moleben" to the Sacred Heart of Christ. Letter in Archiwum Panstwowe w Przemyslu, zespol 142, f. 9485, p. 154. See also correspondence of Bishop Ivan Buchko with Bohachevsky from 1924 through 1939, TsDIA, Lviv, f. 201, op. 1, spr. 5952, 194; and correspondence until 1959 at UMAS. Previous eparchial synods had been held at Lviv in 1891, in which the papal suggestion for celibacy was defeated, and in 1897. Przemysl hosted a synod in 1898 at which consensus was also not reached. On the synod of 1891, see Himka, *Religion and Nationality in Western Ukraine*.

Rev. Kostelnyk joined forces with the emergent Ukrainian Catholic Action to encourage public discussions "to defend the spiritual and material priorities of the clergy. We will take a stand on all pressing issues of church-religious life . . . to reduce to a common denominator the ideological differences among the clergy which in the last years have become downright chaotic."[41] Bohachevsky was not keen on having more "chaos" in his diocese, but he did encourage the activities of Catholic Action as much as he could with the meager manpower resources available in his congregation and in light of the growing economic crisis.

The conference coincided with the fiftieth anniversary of Pope Pius XI as priest and served as a background for the elevation of Ivan Buchko, Bohachevsky's close friend, to bishop. The pope chose one of the conference days to bless the laying of the foundation for the St. Josaphat Ukrainian Seminary on the hills of Rome, an institution that the pope personally financed for the benefit of Ukrainian Catholics. Bohachevsky participated in all ceremonies related to this. In a photograph taken at an audience with the pope on October 29, 1930, he appears gaunt, showing signs of the strain of the previous few years.

A RETURN TO HALYCHYNA

The 1929 Rome meeting was also important for Bohachevsky because he saw that other bishops attending were having administrative problems similar to his. The very lively debate between Metropolitan Sheptytsky and Bishop Kotsylovsky over technicalities in editing of the liturgical books was a painful reminder of the tension within the Ukrainian Catholic Church. Also at issue was the extent of authority that the metropolitan exercised vis-à-vis matters that the bishops felt were common provenance. Bohachevsky sided with Kotsylovsky and Khomyshyn, but realized how removed he was from the internal life of the Halychyna church province. Bohachevsky saw the need for consolidation and study. Despite the disagreements, the exchanges invigorated him for the tasks in America. This trip, which would prove to be his first and last visit to his homeland and

---

41. *Nyva* (November 1929): 424–25; Rev. Prof. Josef Slipyj, Very Rev. Vasyl Lytsyniak, and Rev. Petro Khomyn signed the joint statement of *Nyva* and Catholic Action.

the last time he was to see his mother, also provided evidence that the outlook for Ukrainian statehood was grim. It confirmed Bohachevsky's view that the Ukrainian Catholic Church in the United States would have to draw upon its own resources. After the formalities in Rome, Bohachevsky made his way east to Halychyna. He spent most of his time on church matters, visiting bishops and monasteries. He had a long talk with Bishop Khomyshyn and made sure to visit the priests he knew. He stayed two days in a Basilian monastery, enchanting the young monks with his accessibility. They liked the friendly and approachable bishop from America, so different from their own formal higher clergy. A seminarian detailed to attend the bishop was pleasantly shocked when the bishop asked him to accompany him on a long hike in the countryside.[42] If Bohachevsky visited Sheptytsky, the encounter was not documented.

Bohachevsky had scheduled only one afternoon with his mother and brothers, who at the time lived in Sokal, some seventy miles north of Lviv. There was no longer any central Bohachevsky family home for this branch of the family. None of the brothers had managed to do well financially. The bishop's mother was living with Danylo in a very cramped apartment. Half a century later, in a brief paragraph dedicated to this family visit, Danylo noted that the announced afternoon visit was shortened to a few hours, because the bishop had to make formal calls on all the priests in the area. Bishop Bohachevsky spent the night in a neighboring monastery in Krystynopol (now Chervonohrad), where the family visited him the following morning. Even if the bishop had wanted to stay with his mother, there was no room in the apartment, as his brother Omelian lived there with his wife and child. Danylo, who had just started practicing law, was the only one to have an income.[43] The bishop did not discuss America

42. A Rev. Boychuk to Rev. Theodosius Halushchynsky, no date but 1929 file, in "Lysty Ihumena Theodosiia Halushchynskoho," vol. 1, TsDIA, Lviv, 584, t. 2, pp. 21–22. Bohachevsky spent two nights at the monastery, where the young Rev. Boychuk showed him "everything there was to see. . . . We also spent a day in Mykulynychi, where we took a four-hour hike into the mountains, talking about everything—[he is] a nice bishop." The bishop spent two evenings in long conversation with Khomyshyn, who promised to send eight priests to America.

43. The bishop's help was limited to $5 monthly that his mother used to supplement the family's income and separate support of the younger brothers, Ivan and Omelian. Danylo's oral reminiscences were confirmed by my mother, Rostyslava, who lived with the elder

with the family, and if the mother corresponded with the eldest son Volodymyr, no one knew about it.

Bohachevsky's month-long trip to Rome and to his homeland made him painfully aware that the mother church in Lviv could not help the embattled Ukrainian-American Catholic Church. The church in Ukraine was under increased pressure from the Polish government and the rising political extremism of Ukrainian nationalist movements. These pressures reverberated in the American Ukrainian milieu. Toward the mid-1930s, the church in America felt a nationalist tug or two, but the bishop was able, for the most part, to keep an independent course. Realizing that the times were not auspicious for the Ukrainian clergy to organize a worldwide network, he focused on strengthening the church in America, providing financial support for the Ukrainian Church in Halychyna when possible, and supporting the fledgling bishops' conference. To save money to promote these three goals, Bohachevsky denied himself trips abroad, even to mark an anniversary of his seminary in Lviv. By this time, the Polish government had instituted a veritable reign of terror against Ukrainian activists, including priests, a policy that went under the cynical name of "pacification" and left little room or hope for change.

HOME TO AMERICA

Bohachevsky returned to Philadelphia even more determined to build up the structure of the diocese for the benefit of the Ukrainian settlers—otherwise they all would melt into the materialistic gray mass of modern America and be of no use to the embattled society in Europe. He reminded the American Ukrainian community that economic conditions even in the worst of times were much more favorable in America than in Halychyna.[44] On January 15, 1930, he used the occasion of the blessing of the episcopal garments embroidered in a folk motif which he had brought from Halychyna to remind his faithful that "Despite the misery I saw wherever

---

Mrs. Bohachevsky until 1944. Danylo Bohachevsky's account of the bishop's family visit is in his *Na vozi i pid vozom*. Danylo gives his brother's visit to Sokal eleven lines, in which he notes that the bishop did not say a word about the difficulties he was having in his eparchy (91). There is no mention of the visit in Danylo Bohachevsky's *Vladyka Konstantyn Bohachevsky*.

44. *Katolyts'ky Provid*, January 15, 1930.

I went, the people [in Halychyna] do not lose faith. And what do we do here [in the United States]? Money is easier [to get] here! It's easier for us to build. [Our] community [should be] an example to others."[45]

Nevertheless, the economic depression in their new homeland hit the immigrants hard; many lost the little they had and faced poverty that was worse than that of their old villages. Times were very difficult, money was scarce, and the demands of the church to support new schools were not easy to accept. Slowly, however, the congregations rallied to support their church and its goals. The bishop's oft-repeated argument—generosity breeds generosity—over time proved to be true. Yet within a year of his return, the bishop would have to fight another bitter battle to keep his churches. This time, the struggle would entail foreclosure rather than insurrection among the clergy.

In September 1930, Bohachevsky made a formal visit as the papal legate to the Ukrainians in Brazil. There he saw with what determination Ukrainian Catholic immigrants worked to build a city of God on earth. In Brazilian Ukrainians he saw the proverbial level-headed, hardworking Ukrainian peasant, uncorrupted by materialistic society and its false prophets. On one leg of his visitations between cities, his car broke down and he had to continue the trip the following day on horseback, an inconvenience that invigorated the bishop. While in Brazil, Bohachevsky also met with Rev. Josaphat Ananevych, who had established a lay religious order for women. Years later, in 1939, he persuaded Ananevych to come to the United States to help set up the long-awaited seminary.

The existence and use of many of the visible accouterments of the Ukrainian rite were not codified; some most likely will always reflect a personal preference. We have noted that many liturgical texts had not been reviewed in a century or more—hence discussions on these topics flourished among Ukrainians with varying degrees of knowledge and vehemence. In dealing with these problems Bohachevsky exhibited tolerance and understanding—precisely the qualities he was accused of lacking in his interactions with the faithful. He ordered the gradual removal of statues, which were then replaced with icons. He lobbied for the construction of

45. Ibid.

iconostases, the screen of icons that separates the nave of the church from the holy of holies, but did not insist on the floor to ceiling ideal, with the predetermined order of icons. He limited the use of flowers in churches because they were not part of the Eastern ascetic tradition. At the same time, however, he admonished priests to consider the sentiments of the public.

There was a threat of another bout of unrest over confessionals, the specific enclosed spaces with a physical barrier between the priest and the penitent that were common in Latin churches. In the Eastern tradition the priest covers the penitent with his stole during the whole exchange in whatever part of the church is considered customary. The specific location could vary. But by the 1920s separate confessionals were growing in popularity in Ukraine, although some considered them a sign of Latin influence.[46] In keeping with this trend in Ukraine and with his allegiance to the universal church, Bohachevsky actively supported the introduction of confessionals. He specifically reminded his priests that hearing confessions in the area behind the altar or in the robing room should be limited to the hard-of-hearing and other exceptional cases. While urging the use of confessionals, a tradition clearly borrowed from Western Catholicism, Bohachevsky also reminded his flock of the value of Eastern principles in fasting and in prayer, which were stricter than Western practices. Fasting regulations, however, did not capture the public imagination.

The stability of the Ukrainian Catholic Church in the United States was all the more important in view of the attacks upon the mother church in Lviv, from both the Polish regime and the growing Ukrainian anticlericalism, which emerged from the left and the right. The Congregation for the Eastern Church, meanwhile, feared what it considered to be growing Russophilism in the Carpathian region where some of the émigrés from the Russian Empire had settled.[47] The protest movement within the Ruthenian Church in the United States echoed this development. Bohachevsky published the pastoral letters of the now embattled Bishop Takach, but whatever conversations the two bishops may have had seem not to have been recorded.

46. *Eparkhiial'ni Visti*, April 1925, 3–4.
47. The movement was partly fueled by the Hungarian government, largely with the help of the Russian émigrés, CEC, Prot. 206/31, especially fascicle II.

Struggling against Polish repression and economic stagnation as well as the growth of the anti-intellectual Organization of Ukrainian Nationalists, the mother church in Lviv could pay scant attention to its emigrants in America, limiting its input to short thank-you notes for Bohachevsky's frequent financial contributions. An additional complication came from the Halychyna laity's involvement in Catholic Action societies. Some of the leaders of that movement (many of whom were the first male lay descendants of generations of priests) tried to influence the church in ways that the bishops thought extreme. In an attempt to dissipate the charged political climate among the Ukrainians and demonstrate the unity of the church and the people, the Ukrainian prelates declined to take part in the state-wide All-Polish Eucharistic Congress; instead, in 1933, they held a major Ukrainian Catholic public rally—"Ukrainian Youth for Christ"—to mark the two thousand years since Christ's death. (The Ukrainian Catholic Church in Halychyna was trying to staunch the growth of right radicalism without overtly becoming politically involved, and at the same time opposing the much stronger Polish right-wing radical nationalism.) The American Ukrainian press featured stories and articles about Polish repression, but printed nothing about the danger of nascent right radicalism that the higher Ukrainian clergy in Halychyna sought to contain. The newspaper America covered Ukrainian and world affairs as well as its staff could manage. It also covered major community affairs, such as the preparations for the World's Fair in Chicago, but it avoided political polemics. The bishop kept his focus on education and the church organizations.[48]

America seemed to have no borders. The Ukrainian Catholic Church was always short of priests. Bohachevsky continued asking Halychyna to send additional religious men and women to serve Ukrainian Catholics in America. The Basilian order was especially important. With Bohachevsky's agreement, Basilian priests took over parishes in Chicago and in New York. One Basilian priest, Andriy Trukh, with the help of Reverends Tarnawsky and Khlystun, speeded up the organization of the

---

48. Prystay in an America article on January 2, 1933, complained that the Ukrainian public did not support the participation of the church in the World's Fair. The churches were asked not to take part in the fair, to avoid conflicts.

Ukrainian Catholic Youth League in 1933.[49] Other priests sought to activate a temperance society, an apostleship of prayer, and other religious organizations for the laity. Bohachevsky wanted practicing believers, held regional clergy meetings centered on a strong spiritual component, and personally ran lengthy retreats.[50]

Innovative and traditional issues involving church rites could not be resolved by the American church alone. Earlier émigrés sought to preserve the life and rituals they had known, but the life of the home community had changed. Present-day, common, household traditions, such as bringing a Christmas tree into the home, had not been practiced in Halychyna villages in the 1920s. Innovations appeared in the United States more quickly than in the home church. New feast days, like the proclamation of Christ the King in October 1928, were incorporated into the Ukrainian Church calendar simply by quoting parts of the liturgical ritual that referred to "Christ, our King and God," thus showing Latin Catholics that it was also part of the Eastern tradition.[51] The new practice of formal First Holy Communion caused some consternation, but its popularity among Latin-rite immigrants quickly made the attendant ceremonies equally popular among Ukrainians. The bishop reminded the parishes that the tradition was to hold the ceremony at the end of the school year, that it should be festive, and that it should include the whole parish and not only the families involved. Novenas to the Virgin in May and to the Sacred Heart in June, which Metropolitan Sheptytsky promoted in Lviv, were new to the immigrants. Priests were encouraged to support them. A ritual symbiosis emerged—an Eastern akaphist, better-known at the time as a molebem—would end with the literal crowning of a statue of the Virgin by a young girl. The exarchy did not have the resources to analyze the ritual incompatibility; priests were busy with running the parishes.

Priests complained of the hardship of manning two parishes, and the faithful asked for priests to cover the expanding area of Ukrainian settle-

49. *America*, February 4, 1936. The Ukrainian Catholic Youth passed a resolution calling for a change in the calendar.

50. Bohachevsky combined as many tasks as he could during his travels: *Katolyts'ky Provid*, January 3, 1929, reported that Bohachevsky ran a three-day retreat in conjunction with the blessing of the Chicago church. He preached an eight-day retreat prior to the blessing of the church in Watervliet. *America*, August 23, 1932; *Katolyts'ky Provid*, January 15, 1930.

51. *Katolyts'ky Provid*, October 28, 1928.

ment. Judging from the correspondence of the priests among themselves, a posting "west" was considered a punishment. A mission parish—that is, one that did not have a large enough community to establish a school and a church—meant constant travel and low pay. Bohachevsky was relieved, however, that the chancery could afford to place priests on salaries to somewhat equalize the hardships. The bishop expected his priests to be soldiers of Christ, while the priests hoped to be settled pastors with some worldly comforts for their families. Bohachevsky ran a tight office, and his decisions held. The bishop was all business from his first days in America, and now he had helpers to make things even more efficient. His advisory body rotated regularly. He trained young seminarians to become his secretaries, by all accounts a difficult but satisfying task. Parishes and missions grew, and there were requests for more priests as the Ukrainian Catholic population followed jobs into other cities. By 1931, Bohachevsky had restructured his exarchy into six deaneries. These covered the industrial centers of the time: Philadelphia, New York, Chicago, Pittsburgh, Buffalo, and Wilkes-Barre for the mining districts in western Pennsylvania. The rest of the United States remained mission territories for the Ukrainian Catholic clergy. The bishop met monthly with his five advisers and less frequently with the deans.

As the Ukrainian political movements increasingly turned against each other, Bohachevsky remained firm in his contention that engaging in Ukrainian émigré politics was futile. He placed his hopes on the efficacy of his educational policies and, naturally, on God's grace. With the growing success of his policies, he did not need to be so rigid in the defense of Catholic principles of faith. Subtle changes in his behavior revealed that Sheptytsky's lessons had borne fruit: Bohachevsky even began quoting the poet Ivan Franko in his official statements.

A distinctive difference between the Latin and Eastern rites lay in the language and nature of worship. Ukrainian Catholics used Old Church Slavonic, eschewing Latin, which had been the norm in all Latin-rite churches. Speakers of Ukrainian could understand Old Church Slavonic, albeit with increasing difficulty. Its exclusive use in church ritual gave the language its sacred patina. Church ritual, moreover, envisaged the active participation of the congregation, ideally by chanting the service, making the congregation as active a participant in the services as the priest. In practice, however, the cantor became the chief counterpoint to the priest, and the choir took the place of the chanting congregation. On weekday liturgies, women often chanted the responses, but that daily practice was always viewed as an exception. In September 1925, the *Eparchial News* reprinted an article from the Stanislaviv diocese, explaining that the introduction of the vernacular would bring the church down to the level of a community organization and deprive it of one of its sacred markers. Some clergy warned that the "liberal intelligentsia" sought to reduce the church to just another organization, robbing it of its sacred character.[52] Bohachevsky, throughout his whole life, remained a proponent of Old Church Slavonic in worship. He worried that the introduction of the vernacular into the body of textual worship (prayers, liturgies, and other sacred activities) would create further dissention among the faithful. His opposition to the vernacular in liturgy was pragmatic, for many members of the Ukrainian Catholic Church did not speak Ukrainian.

Another, and arguably thornier, issue for the Ukrainian public was to determine what constituted Ukrainian style in churches: their interiors, architecture, implements, and vestments. Few churches in the United States exhibited what could truly be characterized as "traditional Ukrainian style." Some churches reflected the peculiarities of a home village; others, an eclectic collection of many different styles and characteristics. A golden dome and a belfry were among the most desired features. In truth, that style is difficult to define, given the varieties of traditional churches throughout the large home country. Ukrainian churches in the United States were modest, many still supported by the bake sales of *pyrohy* (that ironically were known by the Polish term *pierogi*) on Friday evenings.

Many churches sported Latin-rite accretions—Stations of the Cross, statues (especially of the Immaculate Conception and the Sacred Heart), monstrances, flowers on the altar, inappropriately placed icons on the iconostasis, or at times the absence of an iconostasis. Vestments also reflected so-called Latin influences: tatting and lace work on the priestly undergarment (*stykhar*), a shortened stole (*epitrakhyl*), the absence of head coverings (*kolpaky*) for the priests, the use of improperly made cinctures

---

52. "Rezonne Slovo, Iz vistnyka stanyslavivs'koyi eparkhiii," *Eparkhiial'ni Visti*, September, 1925, 8–10.

for the higher priests. Head coverings for priests were to be in a distinctively Eastern format, and in his first years as bishop for the Ukrainian-American faithful Bohachevsky tried to get the clergy to adhere to that tradition. The Basilian nuns in Philadelphia even opened a shop that made *kolpaky*. But the tradition was not kept up, and it eventually faded, to be resurrected in the new millennium.

Bohachevsky's strong conviction of the national importance of the Ukrainian Catholic Church for all of Ukraine was strengthened during his time of troubles. The bishop was quick to draw lessons for the community from his experiences. Discipline enabled the church to prevail against the growing chaos in Ukrainian communities:

We can see how this destructive chaos bored through the national [narodny] organism, that, unprecedented in all of history, in just one year under Bolshevik power, millions of souls in Great Ukraine starved to death. [Yet even that tragedy the famine of 1921] could not unite us and force us to protest and [effectively] provide the kind of defense that our great people deserve and which the whole world expected.[53]

Bohachevsky believed that "the Greek Catholic Church is the bulwark of the authentic faith, the bulwark of Ukrainian culture and independence." He remained firmly convinced that Ukraine could become independent and strong only if it joined its Eastern spirituality with a Western cultural framework. His firm belief in the efficacy of a rational structure strengthened his resolve to forge the church as a centralized, disciplined, solvent, and self-replenishing organization. The modern scaffolding was essential, because otherwise the embattled church, which was a fusion of East and West, would not be able to rejuvenate itself.

The bishop was very conservative with money and distrusted the bond market. The experiences of his older brother, magnified through the Great Depression, made him self-reliant. As bishop, he did not have a separate account for himself until the end of the 1950s. His needs remained not just modest but minimal. One suit for public appearances, and a worn one for work. He had no other clothes. He took no vacations. He did not even go

53. Bohachevsky, Lenten pastoral letter in preparation for the Resurrection, Eparkhiial'ni Visti, February 1934.

to the anniversary celebration of his alma mater, although Slipyj wrote to him twice, in disbelief that this bishop would not make the trip.[54] He published by name all contributions made to him and to the church, beginning with the contributions welcoming him to America. From that sum, Bohachevsky immediately earmarked money for the upkeep of the seminarians.[55]

The bishop was very conscientious about visiting even the smallest parishes and missions. He participated in the services, heard confessions, perused the church books, met with parishioners, and talked with the pastor and other priests. He wrote extensive reviews of his visit, addressed only to the pastor. The letters reveal a very thoughtful and respectful supervisor, one who offers helpful suggestions after pointing out either missteps or drawbacks. The bishop covered both the material and spiritual aspects of the business of running a parish. He paid attention to work with youths, to outreach activities, to the ability to establish schools or at least to encourage young people to study their faith and their heritage. Given Bohachevsky's reputation as a strict martinet, these weekly letters were surprisingly mild and respectful. They remain closely guarded because of their personal nature.

The bishop's main concern was the spiritual welfare of the people. But given his view of the church as a hierarchic structure and of the critical role that the priests played in it, he could not care for the people without the clergy. Not only were there never enough priests. The priests he had were overworked and underpaid, many of them aging and most of them poor. The bishop had no replacement priests and felt he could not leave parishes empty. An empty parish was in danger of losing both people and property. Only one priest who knew Bohachevsky mentioned seeing the bishop cry: Rev. Stephan Hryniokh told me the bishop broke down in tears in front of him, a young priest, because the faithful were begging him for

54. Slipyj to Bohachevsky, January 23, 1932, TsDIA, f. 451, op. 2, spr. 221, p. 14; in a letter dated February 3, 1934, Slipyj reminded Bohachevsky of the upcoming 150th anniversary of Lviv Seminary: "I'm hurt I have no answer to that letter." TsDIA, f. 451, op. 2, spr. 221, p. 22. Bohachevsky did write—a personally handwritten letter to Rector Slypyj—that Mr. Ivan Khomiak, whom Slipyj recommended for the seminary in the United States, could not be accepted because he had failed to submit the required documentation. October 25, 1934, TsDIA, f. 451, op. 2, spr. 221, p. 27.

55. Eparkhiial'ni Visti, October 1924.

priests, and he had none. Yet the young Hryniokh preferred a posting to the most distant parish over an offer to be the bishop's secretary. There was no rest for the holder of that position.[56]

One can argue that the bishop's firm stand on the issues that he thought most important dampened the clergy's initiative. Judging by their correspondence, some priests feared the bishop and were loath to take risks. Some complained that the bishop did not give specific orders on how to go about organizing a youth group or a school. Others objected that Bohachevsky focused on his educational projects and did not give enough attention to youth and religious organizations. The bishop took it for granted that these functions belonged to the clergy and continued to expect them to show initiative. He exhorted his parish priests to branch out and help organize the laity, especially the youth. He believed in the organic growth of community undertakings.

The most active of the bishop's supporters misread the man in the same way his opponents had done. The Ukrainian-American community activists who supported the bishop because of the social and political influence that the church had in undercutting radicalism, now thought—as the opposition had done earlier—that the bishop was no longer interested in community affairs. Nazaruk, as we have seen, was crestfallen. Even a decade later, one of the priests complained that the bishop changed: "Initially he was very principled . . . but now he is willing to work with those who opposed him.[57]

The bishop was not a changed man, however. He was merely more secure in pursuing the long-term goals that he had set out to accomplish when he first arrived in America. What sustained Bohachevsky and en-

56. Rev. Stephan Hryniokh, in telephone conversations with the author, April 28 and 29, 2009.

57. Andrii Khlystun to Nazaruk, June 25, 1936, TsDIA, Lviv, f. 406, op. 1, spr. 22; TsDIA, Lviv, f. 406, op. 1, spr. 22, pp. 2–3. The writer, Rev. Andriy Khlystun, pastor of Watervliet, N.Y., in June 1936 also complained in two letters to Nazaruk, then the editor of the Catholic *Nova Zoria*, that the bishop had changed markedly, now paid attention to those who praised him, and put culture and education above all other interests. Granting that the bishop was in contact with him, this priest fretted that the bishop did not have an overarching plan but rather asked each priest to do what they could in their own parishes. He accused Bohachevsky of being openly ambitious to build a grand seminary, when a more modest and a more modern one could have been had for less money. Khlystun had worked closely with Nazaruk in building up the conservative Hetman movement in the United States.

abled him to perform his work day in and day out was his vision of the task that God had set out for him—to build the schools that would ensure the life of the Ukrainian Catholic Church in the United States. That vision directed his sights high above daily frustrations. It was a measure of the man that he deferred the goal until he was certain that the diocese that he headed was firmly entrenched. He continued to build the diocese as he strove to create an educational system that would ensure the existence of the diocese itself. Gradually his people accepted his vision and made it their own. Halychyna was in no condition to pay attention to what the Ukrainian Catholic Church in the United States was doing. The only things that Bohachevsky received from home were reports on the political and economic difficulties that the home country faced. Their requests for help showed no awareness of either the bishop's successes or his difficulties. But Rome had time for its distant and small exarchate. In 1929, when Bohachevsky sent the Vatican the report on his first five years as the Ukrainian ordinary, Nuncio Fumasoni-Biondi referred to him as "the best of bishops for the Halychyna Ruthenians."[58]

Bohachevsky dismissed the difficulties confronting him as another testing of his faith. The *fayt* did not embitter him, but it did make him more self-reliant and self-sufficient. He was not a risk-taker, and the harrowing experiences of 1926 and 1927 made him even more cautious in dealing with the Ukrainian and the broader Roman Catholic communities in America. A few perceptive priests realized that the experience had made the bishop less venturesome, more reliant on the clergy from the American East-Coast communities, and less willing to explore the broader vistas of the American heartland.

58. Fumasoni-Biondi forwarded Bohachevsky's report to the Congregation for the Eastern Church on November 21, 1931; CEC, Prot. 576/28.

CHAPTER 9

Stable Development in
Unstable Times

Bishop Bohachevsky knew that Ukrainians in the United States would be heard only if they established a strong community of successful and educated individuals. He tried to fashion such an ideal community—one that melded progressive social policies with traditional family values to create conditions for a good and productive life that would also promote spiritual development. He wanted a public debate on his view, just as he had wanted a hearing for his educational policies. He had a hard time relinquishing his attempts at provoking a cathartic discussion within the Ukrainian Catholic community. He tried to involve the clergy and encourage the faithful to take a hard look at their situation and recognize the irrelevance of the ideological considerations of European politics for the immigrant community. He thought that a discussion within the Ukrainian-American community would help people recognize that the expansion of Ukrainian institutions in the United States was the most appropriate and effective form of patriotic action for them.

His February 1931 Lenten pastoral letter, prominently featured in *Catholic Leadership*, openly challenged Ukrainian society to use the liberty that its members enjoyed in the United States to strengthen their own schools and institutions rather than engage in Ukraine-centric rhetoric, which had little, if any, practical impact. In his 1932 pastoral letter, aimed exclusively at the clergy, he tried to present his case more fully, but that did not provoke an open debate even among the clergy, and he was dissuaded from publishing the text. He continued to repeat the argument that Catholic education would reconcile the two seemingly contradictory pressures on the immigrants: to know and honor their heritage and to become Americans. Rather than political action, the bishop stressed the value of cultural and spiritual riches that could be institutionalized and popularized freely in the United States. He saw America not as a melting pot, but as a mosaic. Although his approach resonated with the churchgoing community, it did not yet appeal to the Ukrainian political activists. They did their work for Ukraine, while the bishop and his church worked for Ukrainians. Both had right on their side.

The church survived on donations that came from poor immigrants and therefore could not develop as quickly as the bishop would have liked. Ukrainian immigrants—still impoverished and uneducated—were slow to learn from other immigrant groups how to enrich their lives. Hence, the immediate task of the Ukrainian-American leadership, as far as Bohachevsky was concerned, was to help the community recognize the opportunities that the American model of separation of church and state offered. In his vision the ideal Ukrainian Catholic bourgeois family would support the church and a Ukrainian Catholic school and would still have money left over to help poor people in Ukraine.

To achieve his goals, the bishop even resorted to intra-Ukrainian rivalry to jolt his public. He praised the Carpathian Ukrainians for creating strong church and civic organizations, contrasting them to the Halychyna Ukrainians who often managed to destroy the institutions that they built. His praise for the probity of the Carpathians was premature, however. The flare-up of opposition to Bishop Takach who, in line with the Vatican directive, began enforcing clerical celibacy in the 1930s, again stirred Vatican fears of "Russophilism," which meant defection to Orthodoxy.[1] Bohachevsky even published Takach's pastoral letter, retaining his Rusyn-style orthography when the Rusyn dissidents blocked his access to the press.[2] This collegial act was criticized—Bohachevsky should not popularize variants of the Ukrainian language.

The 1930s were characterized by economic collapse, the rise of inte-

1. CEC, Prot. 163/31 [Rigotti, 754–62].
2. Eparkhiial'ni Visti, February 1933, 5–10.

FIGURE 9. UKRAINIAN BISHOPS IN ROME, 1929

gral nationalism, the spread of totalitarianism in Europe, and the growing threats of a new world war. For Ukrainians in the United States, as in Europe, the hardships of the Depression were just one more aspect of the difficult 1930s. There were additional tragedies in Europe—the flare-up of Polish brutality in the so-called pacification in Halychyna, quickly followed by the Soviet, man-made famine of 1932–33 in Eastern Ukraine. The Ukrainian community felt that these events needed to be protested in America, where protest was possible. Bohachevsky offered as much financial support as the eparchy could to help widows, orphans, and veterans in Ukraine.

The bishop remained steadfast and focused on his duties. His powers of concentration and especially his ability to find solace in prayer continued to steel him. Unlike the leadership of the Ukrainian-American political groupings, who felt that their main duty lay in broadly conceived actions in support of Ukraine, Bohachevsky realized that the Ukrainian Catholics in America could do little to influence events in Europe or in the United States. The cornerstone of his political credo remained the school system. As the Ukrainian Catholic eparchy in the United States expanded with the growing mobility of the congregation, the bishop eagerly awaited the emergence of young, American-born, Ukrainian clergy. Meanwhile, he continued his ascetic life style. He had two suits, the new one to wear in public, and the worn one for the office. He used the cassock for formal religious occasions, and travelled in suit, hat, and coat. He had no servants, but relied on the nuns for food and housekeeping.

STRENGTHENING THE EXARCHY

Bohachevsky spent the first half of the economically difficult 1930s refining the structure of the exarchy and working with the clergy to encourage their spiritual growth. At the end of December 1931, Bohachevsky sent the Congregation for the Eastern Church a handwritten register of the 140 churches under his jurisdiction. He immediately began working to ensure that his next report would be more professional. Most of the Ukrainian clergy in the United States, under the bishop's rigid code of behavior, settled down to running their parishes. Celebratory accounts of parish jubilees and coverage in the still-vibrant Ukrainian-language press provide some information about the daily life of parish priests as the immigrants' living conditions changed. Without the extended family that was a constant feature of parishes in Halychyna, life of priests in the United States was difficult and often drab. Even the bishop complained that compared to the Irish who invited their pastors to their homes, Ukrainians treated their priests poorly. The American middle class with its work ethic and urban living did not replicate the pastoral living of rural Halychyna in which the multi-generational family of the village priest ideally, if not in fact, provided the model for cultured living. In the United States the parish held social gatherings and community picnics as best it could to build a sense of togetherness. Some priests built up the bishop's visitations into massive public functions. For one such event, Stephen Pobutsky arranged special trains to bring congregants to Syracuse to take part in the activities connected with Bohachevsky's visitation, which after religious ceremonies and a formal banquet with local dignitaries, ended in a dance.[3]

In 1931, Bohachevsky restructured his exarchy into six deaneries. These covered the industrial centers of the time: Philadelphia, New York, Chicago, Pittsburgh, Buffalo, and Wilkes Barre. The parishes outside the deaneries were treated as missionary churches and were administered directly by the chancery through the missionary priests. He held regular administrative meetings with these priests and exhorted them to become more proactive missionaries in their parishes. He met monthly with his five advisers and a few times a year with the deans. For him, the good life meant efficient, daily work, and this included the company of his priests. His brutal schedule demanded much of those who worked with him daily, and some priests opted for assignment to far-flung parishes rather than work in the chancery. The bishop turned again and again to the clergy with renewed exhortations to put their initiatives to good use in the church and within the community. He advised them to begin small, believing that effective projects would grow in popularity. He sought to whip up the flagging energies of his flock with appropriate quotations, learned or literary. He reminded his priests that the reaper endures the blazing sun for the comfort that the harvest eventually ensures.[4]

3. "Thousands to Take Part in Ukrainian Day Celebration," *Citizen-Adventurer* (Auburn, N.Y.), August 14, 1934.

4. Bohachevsky, "Letter to the priests and the faithful," *Katolyts'ky Provid*, September 3,

By the second half of the 1930s, Bohachevsky had fashioned clergy committees to help him administer the diocese. He controlled the finances scrupulously, permitting himself no luxuries. At the same time, he expected his priests to keep the good of the church community in mind. He continually adjusted salaries so that priests in smaller parishes would not suffer privation. By the end of the decade, he again restructured the deaneries, extending them throughout the territories of the United States where the Ukrainian Catholic Church had a presence. The seven deaneries now comprised Scranton, Pittsburgh, New York, Hartford, Chicago, Buffalo, and Philadelphia.[5] Areas beyond these cities were considered mission territories, responsible to the chancery. There was always a demand for more priests.

By the mid-1930s, despite persistent economic difficulties, several factors were working in Bohachevsky's favor. First among these was the importance of education to American society. Contrary to the intelligentsia's lament about anti-intellectualism in America, Ukrainian immigrants recognized the importance of basic education, if for no other reason than because it fostered upward mobility. That generation of immigrants, all too aware of their own disadvantages, appreciated the bishop's educational program for their children.

Another factor that aided Bohachevsky was the Ukrainian immigrant society's revulsion to the so-called flapper culture. Evidence of this could be found in émigré newspapers of all persuasions. The growing financial crisis in the United States also made Bohachevsky's call for moderation more attractive. After the disorder in the Ukrainian Catholic Church calmed down, the Ukrainian Autocephalous Orthodox Church stopped gaining many converts from disgruntled Catholics. With the end of tsarist financial support and the decline of any interest in the creation of a Ukrainian, national, communist state, Orthodoxy and communism both lost their edge.

Public opinion shifted to the right. The pope was anti-Soviet, which made him popular in the Ukrainian immigrant community.[6] The pet-

---

1931. Bohachevsky ended with Psalm 125, v. 6: "Weeping we sow the seeds, while the coming generations will accept the harvest joyfully."

5. Procko, *Ukrainian Catholics in America*, 70.

6. Pope Pius XI exhibited his anti-Communism in his March 19, 1937, encyclical *Divini*

tiness of émigré bickering about ideological and financial issues steered some Ukrainian families back to the church and its frugal bishop. Often it was the family elder who made the decision to return to the traditional Catholic fold. The elders saw the bishop as a righteous man. Bohachevsky's clergy complained of the faithful's parsimony, but the bishop continued to travel through his extensive eparchy, proclaiming the value of a Ukrainian-Catholic education. In this respect, Bohachevsky had read American society better than his intelligentsia opponents had. He understood that faithful churchgoers wanted schools where their children would not have to choose between what they were taught and what their parents believed. Catholic education bridged that divide. With time, the Ukrainian immigrants came to support the bishop's vision because it reflected their own aspirations.

Finally, the Ukrainian community was not merely settling down, it was—in as much as was possible at the time—even prospering. Increasingly, the community produced modest but effective entrepreneurs, people who went into business for themselves, opening restaurants, bakeries, tool shops, moving services, and so forth. Some Ukrainians entered the professions, becoming morticians, insurance and real estate agents, and even lawyers and physicians. If not a real middle class, at least an upwardly mobile working class was evolving from the ranks of the immigrant community. As trite as it may sound, the bankruptcy of the upper classes, who still lived in physical proximity with the working folk, gave the immigrants opportunities to acquire good furniture cheaply, even an occasional piano.

The Ukrainian Catholic daily *America* became in fact, as well as in name, a Catholic newspaper that openly supported Bohachevsky's policies. The newspaper now published articles such as Lonhyn Tsehelsky's memoir of the Ukrainian revolution of 1918, a first-person account that laid the failure of the Ukrainian revolution on the shoulders of the Ukrai-

---

Redemptoris. An earlier dramatic example of that policy was the Vatican papal liturgy held on March 19, 1930, for the Christians persecuted in Russia and Ukraine. In protest, the Soviets closed the Orthodox churches in Chelabinsk, Samara, Kazan, Vitebsk, Smolesk, and Nizhni Novgorod, *Katolyts'ky Provid*, August 30, 1930. Rev. Sergei Sypiagin, who had briefly attended the Canisianum with Bohachevsky, and Sergei Verygin, another Russian, were in attendance. These two Russian priests were close to Metropolitan Sheptytsky.

nians. It provided historical proof backing the bishop's argument that lack of self-discipline and failure to organize in a timely and efficient manner were the underlying reasons for Ukraine's repeated political failures.

Complaints about Bohachevsky, nevertheless, continued to reach the Vatican. The bishop's embrace of clerical celibacy and his unwillingness to provide resources for public activism were reasons for criticizing the church and its bishop. Bohachevsky's willingness to let parishes change to the Gregorian calendar continued to be seen as a sign of Latinization. The parishioners of Sts. Peter and Paul Ukrainian Church in Cleveland, for example, petitioned the pope to recall Bohachevsky because "his God is not the Lord but a dollar . . . because the many things and scandals which have been attributed to Bishop Bohachevsky are extremely detrimental to our Catholic Church." The signatories informed the pope that "the Roman Catholic Churches and its eparchies severed every connection with Bishop Bohachevsky, because his person is considered highly dangerous to the Catholic Church. . . . Bishop Bohachevsky is morally, and in every other way, guilty of all the problems that caused the chaos in our Greek Catholic Church of America."[7] At a memorial concert for the fallen Ukrainian soldiers of the national liberation struggle, a flyer was circulated accusing the bishop of destroying the church, working for the Poles, and using money to build schools in America rather than support worthier causes in Ukraine.[8] The Vatican remained sensitive to the potential spread of Orthodoxy among Ukrainian Catholics in the United States, and the Congregation for the Eastern Church also reacted strongly to that danger, but the ban on ordaining married men in the Ukrainian Catholic Church in the United States remained, apparently swaying a few young men into Orthodoxy.[9] The clergy also complained to the bishop, usually about the shortcomings of their parishes. Some priests asked for transfer to other parishes, or objected to the way in which their church committees treated them.

7. ASV, Poland, 1930–33, Pos. 132, P.O. fasc. 159, p. 5.

8. Nazaruk file, TsDIA, Lviv, f. 406, op. 1, spr. 108, ark. 52. The speakers at the concert included Myshuha, Galan, Teofil Swystun, and Stefan Musiychuk, while the featured choir was from the Ukrainian Autocephalous Orthodox Church.

9. Rev. Oleksander Ulytsky, who had had his disagreements with Bohachevsky but never considered himself separated from the diocese, periodically wrote letters to the congregation, to other clergy, and to the bishop arguing that the insistence on celibacy was both unwise and uncanonical. Correspondence at UMAS.

Whereas during the pioneer days the transfer of parish priests was carried out rather informally, Bohachevsky insisted that detailed inventories be drawn up at each change and that both the incoming and outgoing priest acknowledge the formal parish books. The bishop insisted that the pastor be present in the parish daily, which limited the already circumscribed social life of the clergy. The clergy complained about money, about having to pay dues to the chancery, and especially about the extra levies for schools. They found the bishop's insistence that each parish submit the names of its parish trustees and committee members for approval by March of every year onerous. In private correspondence, the clergy compared notes with each other on running parishes and bemoaned their loneliness.

Bohachevsky relied on Rev. Tarnawsky to handle complicated issues that required more guidance. With Tarnawsky's patient prodding a number of older parishes returned to the fold *en masse*. The situation in McKees Rocks, Pennsylvania, provides an interesting example. Denys Kulmanytsky, a Basilian priest, at the time pastor of St. George's parish in New York City, admitted to Rev. Tarnawsky in 1935, several years after the fact, that between 1929 and 1932, his previous parish at McKees Rocks in Pennsylvania had considered itself Orthodox. The modest monk had been swept up by Rev. Joseph Zhuk's claim that Metropolitan Sheptytsky supported Zhuk to be bishop of all Ukrainian Catholics in the United States. Kulmanytsky broke with the Catholic Church, but quickly realized his error. By that time, the parish had voted to cut ties with Bohachevsky. Kulmanytsky played along with the congregation while initiating secret moves to return to the Catholic fold. Tarnawsky understood the need for slow diplomacy, made no decision about the parish, and waited three years for the entire parish to announce that it was rejoining the diocese. Bishop Bohachevsky still insisted that Kulmanytsky renounce his error publicly.[10]

Nevertheless, where in the 1920s the chief problem had been finding ways to hold on to the parishes, in the 1930s the goal was ensuring the return of the dissident communities that had caused administrative difficulties. At times, non-Catholic Ukrainians turned to the chancery to help shore up the local Catholic parish because the parish was the outward sign of a Ukrainian presence. For example, Ivan Petrushevych, who happened

10. Bohachevsky to Tarnawsky, March 23, 1935, UMAS.

to be Orthodox and who worked as a translator and film writer in Los Angeles, pleaded in a letter dated June 10, 1935, to send a Catholic priest to organize a Ukrainian parish to offset the Russians, who under the guise of setting up an Orthodox parish, absorbed the Ukrainian community. The bishop did not have a priest to spare to work in a community that showed little interest in having a parish, let alone supporting one. As usual, the bishop was short of priests.

The chancery also felt the pressure of the day-to-day administrative tasks that the bishop supervised, which suffered from the lack of trained help. Even such a luminary as Petro Poniatyshyn was sloppy in the way he handled parish finances.[11] Despite difficulties, the eparchy and the bishop weathered the Great Depression with dogged patience and remarkable resilience. The priests called for greater faith and personal sacrifice "because only your life and your actions can give meaning to the traditional Merry Christmas greeting, and not the availability or lack of material goods."[12] Perhaps the hardships of the time coaxed many who had no prior interest to join the church. The Ukrainian immigrant population, not yet conditioned to an economy of spending, tightened its collective belt and shared the little they had with the projects that their church had undertaken.

A dramatic demonstration of the growing support for Bohachevsky's policies took place at Perth Amboy in May 1935. The tug of war within different factions had finally exhausted this contentious anti-Bohachevsky community, and on May 26, 1935, a committee proposed that the Catholic and the Orthodox priests should celebrate jointly, with the aim of establishing one church. However, the full community meeting overturned the committee and voted to rejoin the Philadelphia eparchy, placing this industrial town squarely in the bishop's camp.

The Ukrainian Catholic Church in the United States steadily settled into a stable routine. And because the bishop's actions were predictable,

11. Among other things, he had even failed to establish a separate parish account, married a couple without the necessary documentation and permitted nonsanctioned collections in the church to the detriment of officially mandated ones; Bohachevsky to Kinash, March 24, 1937, UMAS, Chancery Archive. As often in touchy cases, Bohachevsky asked Tarnawsky to handle the matter.

12. Editorial, *Katolyts'ky Provid*, December 22, 1932.

the priests knew where they stood. The nuns ran the growing number of day schools, and things seemed to move along. Although property court cases continued until 1951, and the bishop was unable to avoid personal involvement in the litigation, even that painful procedure assumed a routine course. Bohachevsky was increasingly able to use his visitations to assess the work of the priests. Indeed, the bishop provided a lengthy written evaluation after each visitation in which he balanced praise and criticism, suggesting means of improving this or that aspect of the parish. He was circumspect in his public praise of the clergy, and that praise came to be appreciated.

Bohachevsky adhered closely to the regulations of the eparchy even if a slight deviation would be advantageous to the church in the long run. He was particularly strict when an ethical consideration was at stake. Thus, he refused to accept the Orthodox Rev. Semensky into the Catholic Church because although Semensky was ready to join the Catholic Church quietly, he would not publicly renounce his Orthodox affiliation.[13] This decision cost the eparchy a debt-free church in Muskegon, Michigan. Some of the changes implemented to improve things created their own problems. Tighter administrative control in the parishes and the establishment of full-time schools, which replaced the evening and Saturday courses, left many cantors without jobs. The chancery warned pastors to be circumspect in hiring cantors.[14]

In 1932 and 1933 the Ukrainian-American community leadership had a more immediate concern than church policies and was to make a good showing at the Chicago World's Fair by building a Ukrainian-American Pavilion. To prevent a potential outbreak of religious conflict, the organizers of the Chicago World's Fair asked all Ukrainian churches not to take part in the fair. Bishop Bohachevsky not only honored the decision, but even abandoned his attempts at redirecting the community conversation. He gave up the idea of stimulating a discussion within the community, and limited himself to the pulpit. After the World's Fair, however, Bohachevsky helped the broader community by buying the ethnographic collection that Mother Maria Dolzhytska, had brought to Chicago. In addition, he per-

13. Kowalsky to Tarnawsky, March 26, 1935, followed by a May 21, 1935, petition of Chicago faithful, UMAS, Chancery Archive.

14. *Eparkhiial'ni Visti*, April 1934, 20.

suaded her to remain in the United States to strengthen the academic potential of the Basilian sisters who had established the St. Basil Academy, a high school for girls, at Fox Chase in northeast Philadelphia.

Occasional problems emerged between the lay community and the church, but none were of the scope of the earlier decade. Osyp Nazaruk, writing from Halychyna, warned that the nationalist camp was sowing political chaos in the bishop's diocese.[15] As an antidote, Nazaruk offered to prepare a booklet highlighting the achievements of the eparchy at the cost of about $100.[16] Bohachevsky did not consider such publications necessary. Nazaruk, nevertheless, remained concerned about "the strange bifurcation of [former enemies of the bishop] who privately court the bishop, or rather the bishop's entourage, while in their publications they attack the church."[17] He would have preferred Bohachevsky to take a more openly political stand, but he refrained from saying this publicly.

THE GOLDEN ANNIVERSARY OF
THE UKRAINIAN CHURCH IN
THE UNITED STATES

The year 1934 marked the fiftieth anniversary of the celebration of the first Ukrainian Catholic liturgy in the United States in an administratively recognized Ukrainian Catholic Church. Bohachevsky prepared for the event two years in advance. He wanted to mark the anniversary by documenting an organized Ukrainian Catholic presence in the United States, so he commissioned Rev. Volodymyr Lotovych to canvass parishes about their history, makeup and all religious organizations. Lotovych prepared a questionnaire, and followed up the first with three additional ones. This

15. Correspondence between Nazaruk and Rev. Pavlo Protsko. Nazaruk accused the Ukrainian nationalists of demagoguery against the church. He again mentioned the bishop's small and unheated room, TsDIA, Lviv, f. 406, 1, spr. 56, pp. 342–45.

16. Nazaruk to Rev. Protsko, December 5, 1933, and May 18, 1935, ibid., pp. 59–60.

17. Nazaruk to Tarnawsky (most likely) March 13, 1937. Nazaruk had received an anonymous letter, in which the bishop was criticized for not reacting adequately to "neo-pagan youth, sectarianism, false nationalism, communism, and liberal tendencies" in Ukrainian society. Nazaruk suggested that the correspondent write a fuller article and be willing to sign it; meanwhile, he sent the letter, anonymously, to Protsko. I have not been able to ascertain the author of the letter, TsDIA, Lviv, f. 359, op. 1, spr. 204, and p. 33.

information formed the basis for the first published listing of all Ukrainian Catholic parishes in the United States, an expanded historical schemata of the parishes, and the pastors who served in them. There were two other anniversaries in 1934 that encouraged Bohachevsky to take stock: the tenth anniversary of the bishop's arrival in the United States as well as his fiftieth birthday. To mark the half-century of organized Ukrainian Catholic presence in the United States public festivities were held in the newly acquired site of the diocesan high school and proposed college in Stamford, Connecticut. Bohachevsky wanted to show off the campus. By holding the event (which included a liturgy, procession, rally, and concert) on the grounds of his future cultural institutions, the bishop underlined the intimate connection between the church and the fostering of Ukrainian culture in America.

Some of the clergy complained that the bishop missed a major opportunity to stage a more effective public event. Lev Sembratovych, one of the priests who had arrived with Bishop Ortynsky back in 1907, summarized the criticism. Bohachevsky did not heed his advice to organize a grander event in the Midwest, where there would have been a bigger audience. Sembratovych worried that "some of the bishop's advisers are very provincial and do not realize what is at stake. They reduce major issues to minor matters."[18] He argued that the exarchy should use the 1934 anniversaries to manifest the Ukrainian presence on the broad American arena and hold a major, as he referred to it by an old-fashioned name, "pageant." If the bishop did not want to celebrate the occasion in the Midwest, then it should be held either in Philadelphia or in Shenandoah, the site of the first Ukrainian Catholic liturgy. Sembratovych envisioned the celebrations as a major American (not only Ukrainian immigrant) affair, and offered to organize it. The elderly priest did not consider the cost of his proposal nor the changed interest of the public.

Offending Sembratovych was not a particularly wise move, since the older priest supported many of Bohachevsky's ideas. He had served as the pastor of the Detroit area from 1922 and had managed to preserve peace there despite numerous attempts of takeovers of church properties in the area.[19] He was also one of the few Ukrainian priests who realized that

18. Sembratovych to Tarnawsky, April 4, 1934, UMAS.
19. Some of these attempts, as in Muskegon Heights, led to court cases. Letter to Tarnawsky, March 26, 1934, UMAS.

increased participation of Ukrainian immigrants in American public life would be to their benefit and not, as the conventional wisdom had it, threaten their Ukrainian identity. Nonetheless, Bohachevsky disregarded Sembratovych's advice. Although cost was a factor, Bohachevsky also feared potentially uncontrolled crowds. In his opinion, a Ukrainian immigrant crowd in a large industrial city could easily and quickly be manipulated by any number of real or imagined foes of the church. On the other hand, failure to garner a large crowd after making grandiose earlier pronouncements would be equally embarrassing. So Bohachevsky decided to play it safe and showcase his two tangible achievements: an organized exarchy with functioning parishes and the cultural complex at Stamford.

The Jubilee Almanac of the Ukrainian Greek-Catholic Church in the United States on the Occasion of the Fiftieth Anniversary of Its Existence, prepared by Rev. Volodymyr Lotovych, Rev. Lev Chapelsky, and Dr. Semen Demydchuk, was the official Ukrainian language publication that charted the growth of the Ukrainian Catholic Church community.[20] The almanac was mostly free of the flowery oratory and self-congratulations that generally accompanied such publications.[21] Instead, it provided the fullest listing of Ukrainian Catholic "churches, parishes, clergy, missions, schools, church properties, etc." in the United States.[22] It was Bohachevsky's report on the ten years of his episcopal tenure and the first detailed listing—a schematism, in clerical terminology—of all Ukrainian Catholic parishes and missions in the United States.

To stress that the Philadelphia exarchate was not merely an isolated small church, the first pages of the publication featured, in addition to a photograph of Pope Pius XI, a brief description of the competencies of the Congregation for the Eastern Church in Rome, information on the new apostolic delegate to the United States, Bishop Amleto Cicognani, and a list of all the "Bishoprics belonging to the Halych Metropolitanate." These included Peremyshl, Stanislaviv, Kryzhovic, and Volyn. To stress the unity of the Ukrainian Church the Carpathian province was listed on the same

20. Lev Chapelsky (1887–1953) had come to the United States in 1914.
21. Sembratovych, "Yak pryyshlo do imenuvannia nashoho pershoho epyskopa v Amerytsi" [How the Nomination of the First [Ukrainian] Bishop to America Came About], 103–7.
22. Iuvyleyny Al'manakh Ukraiins'koii Hreko-Katolyts'koii Tserkvy, 17.

level as Halych and included Mukachiv and Priashiv (then in Czechoslovakia). To emphasize the reach of the Ukrainian Catholic Church, the bishopric of Canada in Winnipeg and the Brazilian mission in Prudentopolis were also listed.

The photograph of Sheptytsky in the almanac is a rare one—a profile of an intense man, revealing the early onset of gray and an untended beard, a full head of longish wavy hair, a plain overcoat with a hint of a hood. The metropolitan is not wearing any head covering; his forehead is tightly drawn, and his eyes are narrowed in thought. The mouth is not visible. The photographs of Bohachevsky, Takach, Bishop Ladyka of Canada, and the late Ortynsky show all in skullcaps, without miters. A large photograph of Petro Poniatyshyn, the erstwhile administrator of the eparchy, completes this section. The photographs of the priests and cantors, as well as churches and choirs, vary in size, angle, and quality and seem to dictate the layout. Although the book was essentially an illustrated address book that included a detailed calendar for 1935–36, the editors also presented Bohachevsky's educational vision. A two-page article, "On the Tenth Anniversary of Ceaseless Labor: 1924–34," describes the bishop's achievements. The editors contrasted the difficulties that Bohachevsky faced with those of his predecessors, Rev. Voliansky and Bishop Ortynsky. The latter were focused on building churches, which always garnered popular support. Bohachevsky's course, as the article explained, was more difficult:

In contrast, the attempts of the present bishop to establish a higher Ukrainian school were met with indifference. . . . There were those who predicted failure from the very beginning. They said that there are no pupils [in existing evening schools], so there will be no students [to enroll in the new ones]. . . . [We] still feel the weight of the terrible burden that lay heavy on him and on those who supported him.[23]

Two group photographs of the ceremony of Bohachevsky's first appearance in the cathedral, a brief note about his arrival in the United States (written by a Lithuanian civic activist), and a note on the difficulties of preparing the almanac rounded off this part of the book. In both group photographs, the bishop's face is fully obscured by his crozier.

23. Ibid., 15.

A longer narrative section focuses on the achievements of the early Ukrainian priests in the United States. Reverend Poniatyshyn briefly describes the difficulties that he faced during the episcopal inter-regnum and focuses on the life of the church, leaving politics aside. None of the financial scandals in the cathedral parish or in any other parishes are mentioned, and there is no mention of the priests who opposed the bishop. All priests, regardless of whether they had left the church or not, are included in lists of those who served in the parishes. The goal was to have an inclusive listing of the Ukrainian Catholic Church in the United States as it was in 1934, not to delve into its stormy period and to not erase the work of those who chose to leave the eparchy. The focus is on the church, its people, its parishes, clergy, and choirs. Photographs of individual churches, parish priests, and choirs are included for many of the churches.

By documenting all Ukrainian Catholic churches, religious orders, and affiliated organizations in the United States, the publication provides a realistic picture of the Ukrainian Catholic Church in America. The *Jubilee Almanac* listed parishes by state in alphabetical order in Ukrainian, adding addresses for each in English. The presumption was that anyone who needed specific information, other than the address, would know Ukrainian. Each parish provided as much information as it could on its founding, the monetary value of the church property and its description, the number of parishioners, a list of previous pastors, and the marital status of its current pastor. The availability of information varied from parish to parish.

The complete work was inclusive. To emphasize the unity of all Ukrainian Catholic churches, the *Jubilee Almanac* provided basic information on all existing Ukrainian Catholic dioceses worldwide. The emphasis on the institution of the church contrasted with the almost complete exclusion of the person of the bishop, which reflected not only Bohachevsky's unwillingness to claim the limelight but also his unwavering commitment to the established presence of the Ukrainian Catholic Church in the United States. The almanac provided closure for Bohachevsky—a fitting end to a decade of bitter questioning of his Ukrainian patriotism, of his reliance on the support of the papacy, and of his administrative style. The publication was a symbol of achievement, visible proof of the growth and stabilization of the Ukrainian Church. In the words of Reverend Lev Sembratovych—"[the church's] ship was out of the muddy shallows of that widespread fairy tale, of Moscophile origin, that Rome (that is the Apostolic See) was pro-Polish and anti-Ukrainian."[24] The anniversary book was prepared at the time of the 1932–33 Great Famine (known as the Holodomor) in Ukraine and coincided with U.S. recognition of the USSR, a bitter time for Ukrainians. But it was also the year that Amleto Cicognani was appointed as the apostolic delegate to Washington, D.C. Cicognani proved to be a great supporter of the Ukrainian Catholic Church in the United States.[25]

Bohachevsky's report to the Vatican (transmitted by the nuncio along with a copy of the Jubilee Almanac) was well received, and Cicognani conveyed the pope's praise to the battle-scarred Bohachevsky. In his communiqué to the bishop, Cicognani quoted Cardinal Sincero, secretary of the Congregation for the Eastern Church:

The Holy Father . . . was extremely pleased with the report, and deigned to delegate me, through your Excellency to extend to Mons. Constantine Bohachevsky his praise for all the good he has accomplished, and above all for his diligent observance of the decrees emanating from the Sacred Oriental Congregation. His Holiness graciously wishes to bestow upon Mons. Bohachevsky, as well as upon the clergy and laity of the Ruthenian Eparchy under his jurisdiction, his wholehearted and paternal Apostolic Benediction.[26]

Cicognani added his own congratulations "upon this gracious and encouraging message from the Holy Father, which of course may be published." The new Vatican representative to Washington, D.C., valued highly "the good you have accomplished in the diocese." Bohachevsky appreciated the

24. Rev. Lev Sembratovych, in his recounting of the formation of the diocese, suggested that his co-patriots suffer from a persecution complex about Rome, because "they do not realize that by establishing the Ukrainian Greek-Catholic dioceses on territories with existing Catholic dioceses, Rome broke its own tradition—[in favor of] all for us, Ukrainians" in The Jubilee Almanac of the Ukrainian Greek-Catholic Church, 103. His frame of reference for Ukrainian community was still that of the rise of the democratic national movement against the conservative Moscophiles, who by this time in the home country were a fringe movement at best. Sembratovych to Tarnawsky, March 26, 1934; April 4, 1934, UMAS.

25. Cicognani was elevated to cardinal in 1958, the year that the Ukrainian Catholic Church in the United States became a fully formed archbishopric.

26. Copy of the letter, as well as the rough draft of Bohachevsky's reply, UMAS, Chancery Archive.

praise and the support. The papacy, in fact, offered Bohachevsky the most consistent support, exceeding anything which Lviv, itself under constant pressure, could provide.

Within the ecclesiastical structure, the Philadelphia exarchate was under the jurisdiction of the pope through the Congregation for the Eastern Church. Emotionally, however, Bohachevsky felt a filial bond with the metropolitanate of Lviv and considered America part of the Halychyna church. He tried to foster the bond in his first years in America by explaining his actions in detail to Metropolitan Sheptytsky. But Sheptytsky, relieved that the American church was functioning, seemed to pay little attention to it. The metropolitan was far more preoccupied with the domestic situation in Europe, which bred crisis upon crisis, and he was also concerned about the church's diminishing resources. On the other hand, Bohachevsky, considering it inappropriate to call attention to himself and his exarchate, gave little incentive for others to notice the growth of the church in America. Bohachevsky was famous for not answering correspondence that did not demand an immediate answer, yet he was affected by the silence of his Ukrainian peers about the developments in the American exarchate.[27]

Bohachevsky expected to be included in the Ukrainian Catholic episcopal fraternity and was hurt by the perception that the European upper clergy seemed to dismiss the concerns of its far-flung branches. He had been particularly keen to attend the 1932 bishops' meeting in Rome, during which the bishops were to thank the pope for funding St. Josaphat Seminary in Rome.[28] Bohachevsky expressed his bitter disappointment to Kotsylovsky at not being apprised of the date of the meeting, presuming that the meeting had been moved to the following year. When the invitation for the November 10 gathering finally arrived (on September 6), Bo-

27. Slipyj called Bohachevsky out: "Although I know that Your Excellency does not answer letter [sic]." Letter reminding Bohachevsky of the upcoming anniversary of Lviv Seminary, February 3, 1934, TsDIA, f. 451, op. 2, spr. 221, p. 22. The thank-you letters Bohachevsky received from the donations he sent tended to be formal, followed by requests for more help.

28. Bishop Kotsylovsky wrote to Bohachevsky, apologizing for not thanking him earlier for various donations Bohachevsky had sent to Peremyshl, because he had just attended one of the Velyhrad Christian Unity conferences that Sheptytsky favored. He told Bohachevsky that Metropolitan Andrei invited the bishops for a conference in Rome on November 10, and Kotsylovsky offered to meet Bohachevsky a few days before the gathering. Kotsylovsky to Bohachevsky, August 25, 1932, a three-page, handwritten letter, UMAS, Chancery Archive.

hachevsky would not reschedule or cancel the visitations. Thus he missed another episcopal meeting. His absence was barely noticed. In view of the economic crisis in America, no one thought that there was anything strange about the bishop's failure to make a costly transatlantic journey.

Given the strained relations between Sheptytsky and Kotsylovsky, and Bohachevsky's support of the latter, it is easy to see why Bohachevsky's presence at such meetings was easily overlooked. Bohachevsky, nevertheless, strengthened the institutional ties within the Ukrainian Catholic Church. He was concerned that the American church would be cut off even from personal, tenuous ties with the home country once church leadership devolved onto American-born men. Hence, Bohachevsky financially supported an office in Lviv for the conference of bishops. For understandable reasons the mother church at best treated these attempts with benign neglect.

Bishop Kotsylovsky tried to keep his erstwhile helper up to date about episcopal relations back home. He also asked Bohachevsky for more detailed information about events in his diocese, advising him that Njaradi thought that things were still as bad in Bohachevsky's eparchy as in Bishop Takach's. Bohachevsky stressed that his eparchy was indeed finally peaceful, and Kotsylovsky was happy that he had evidence to prove that Philadelphia was on the mend.[29]

For his part, Bohachevsky presumed (now that the worst internal strife was over) that the priests would initiate individual policies which they considered to be effective. The bishop now had the visible support of the Congregation for the Eastern Church in his continuous quest to transform a parish pastor into a fiery missionary.[30] He took pride in the professionalism of the eparchy and liked to see a well-run parish with an active congregation. His firm belief in the efficacy of a rational structure strengthened the bishop's resolve to forge the church as a centralized, disciplined,

29. Draft of Bohachevsky's letter to Kotsylovsky, September 7, 1932, UMAS, Chancery Archive. The Vatican was very concerned with this repeated threat of defection to Orthodoxy, since this movement was covered in the local American press; for instance, the *Standard-Sentinel* (Hazelton, Penn.), August 5, 1933, wrote about Rev. Ulytsky's demand for the abolition of the celibacy requirement. See also CEC, Prot. 59/35 [Rigotti, 323–27].

30. The congregation provided Bohachevsky with recommendations on the catechization of the faithful and strengthening the role of the bishop. *Eparkhiial'ni Visti*, August 1935, 25–31.

solvent, and self-replenishing organization. The modern scaffolding was necessary to preserve the embattled organic fusion of East and West that was the uniate church. With this in mind, Bohachevsky remained focused on his visitations and regional retreats for the priests.

The bishop continued to expect much from his priests, repeatedly stressing their high calling. He considered his priests capable of the highest dedication. A priest, in his view, was first and foremost a servant of God and served as an example to the other servants of God, the faithful. Throughout his episcopate, Bohachevsky sought to guide his priests to adhere to this principle. He often drew upon the parable of the lazy servant who did not use the money/talent given him to increase the wealth of the master. He particularly focused on service and sacrifice as the most critical duty of priests, always stressing the virtues of active service over passivity. He remained a supporter of celibacy. Perhaps because of the antics of his older brother, he noted that the family, while blessed by God, could also be an impediment to one's service to God. Because part of the agreement with Rome for a distinct Ukrainian eparchy was the consecration of celibates only, there was little substantive discussion on the issue in the United States.

Bohachevsky happily welcomed church involvement in rating motion pictures, including support of the Legion of Decency.[31] The bishop wrote a special pastoral letter in November 1936 in support of Edgar Hoover's anticrime speech. He worked this approach into the broader theme of the need for Catholic education, which he considered to be the sure-fire way of preventing the youth in his congregation from going astray.[32] In his Christmas pastoral letter of 1938, Bishop Constantine argued that small and poor Ireland had won its independence from mighty Britain because of Ireland's unwavering loyalty to the Holy Catholic Church.[33] He continued, albeit with little success, to raise interest in the celebration of Markian Shashkevych, to mark the centenary of the publication of *Rusalka Dnistrova*, one of the first publications in the vernacular in Western Ukraine.[34]

31. *Eparkhiial'ni Visti*, November 1935, 50–51.
32. *Eparkhiial'ni Visti*, November 1936, 65.
33. *Eparkhiial'ni Visti*, November 1938, 40–41.
34. "Zdvyhnem pamiatnyk Markiianovy Shashkevychevy," *Eparkhiial'ni Visti*, November 1935, 50–51.

Bohachevsky also urged a war on alcoholism and wasteful living, counselling rational housekeeping and thrifty cooking and warning against moral degradation. He was overjoyed that the Sister Servants opened an old-age home and small clinic in Philadelphia, which he blessed on October 10, 1937. Soon after, the Order established a residence for young women employed in Philadelphia factories.[35] A three-day retreat for women was held at Stamford in 1936.[36] As the faithful became settled and more at ease within the broader American community, the church held more joint functions with the Latin-rite Catholics. This started with increasingly larger Eucharistic congresses and included smaller church-unity celebrations that will be discussed in a later chapter. Church activities, and even fundraising, increasingly began to meld into social functions. Open-air activities, festivals, and picnics, became especially popular.[37]

OUTREACH

The bishop became even more effective in his visitations, and the congregations now approved his direct style. In private moments Bohachevsky was friendly and forthright. He still drew on his repertoire of old jokes, and his genuine nostalgia for the settled ways of the old country resonated with the community elders. Neither his living conditions nor his simple tastes changed. He had no personal life beyond the church, and the few vacations he took were car trips that included a visitation.

In the early 1930s several Ukrainian-Catholic youth groups were organized by individual priests. The indomitable Rev. Tarnawsky and Rev. Stephen Knapp are usually credited with initiating the first Ukrainian-Catholic youth organizations. Some of Bohachevsky's strongest supporters, nevertheless, were concerned that the bishop was expecting miracles while not providing sufficient leadership or money in this vital area. In an

35. "Dim startsiv i klinika," Eparkhiial'ni Visti, November 1937, 40; and Eparkhiial'ni Visti, August 1939, 47.

36. Eparkhiial'ni Visti, February 1936.

37. For instance on July 22, 1934, Rev. Oleksander Pavliak, with the help of parishioners Antin Pashuk, Ivan Borysevych and Stefan Oles, organized a Ukrainian Day for the Seminary in Philadelphia's Schuetzen Park. Bohachevsky permitted an outdoor liturgy. This type of fund-raising event, which combined prayer with games and dancing, was particularly popular from 1935 through 1938.

October 7, 1935, letter to Joseph Chaplynsky, Rev. Andriy Khlystun (usually a zealous supporter of the bishop) was very critical of the "proud bishop" who does not understand the importance of working with the youth and only keeps repeating "just start working, Father, and then we'll see."[38] Khlystun organized the first East Coast Catholic Youth Rally (in Springfield, New Jersey), which *America* detailed lovingly so that other pastors would be encouraged to follow suit. The rally included an open-air liturgy, which at the time was a rare and welcome event, followed by baseball, races, games, singing, and an outdoor buffet of traditional Ukrainian food.[39] Such events were very popular with the participants in the years immediately preceding the Second World War. They led to the creation, in 1933 of the Ukrainian Catholic Youth League.[40] Judging by the correspondence of its first three recording secretaries (Rose Lishak, Eva Piddubcheshen, and Julia Prokopik), the Catholic Youth League aimed to bring together different local parish youth groups for periodic common activities. In general, its aim was to propagate the Catholic Action agenda. More specifically, the league held conferences and even planned a trip to Europe, including Halychyna.[41] At its height, the Catholic Youth League numbered over sixty branches countrywide and published the *Ukrainian Youth: Official Organ of the Ukrainian Catholic Youth League* from 1934 to 1938, and then again in 1942.[42] Of course, the more active the youth, the greater were demands for a change in the church calendar. These demands, however, were civilly presented, periodically discussed, and duly voted upon in individual parishes. In turn, the youth organizations occasionally hosted Ukrainian

38. Rev. Andriy Khlystun quoted the bishop's frequently used phrase when he complained to Nazaruk, at the time editor of *Nova Zoria*, that the bishop did not offer specific instructions on how to establish organizations, see Khlystun to Nazaruk, February 28, 1935, in Nazaruk correspondence, TsDIA, Lviv, f. 406, op. 1, spr. 22, pp. 31–37.

39. *America*, June 12, 1937. When, after WWII, Plast (Ukrainian "scouting"), was organized in the United States, Bohachevsky funded some of their ventures in Philadelphia.

40. For a discussion of the overall Ukrainian-American youth movement, see Kuropas, *Ukrainian Americans*, 361–75.

41. Rose Lishak, replying to Mary Shwed of Scranton, explained that the purpose of the youth league was to organize all Ukrainian societies, clubs, and youth organizations into one strong Catholic body. It was to be directly supervised by Bohachevsky to help propagate Catholic Action. On May 29, 1936, Eva Piddubcheshen wrote Bohachevsky that the Ukrainian youth needed a summer camp. Julie Prokopik, later Mother Emellia, OSBM, continued the copious correspondence of the group. UMAS.

42. Khlystun to Nazaruk, June 25, 1939, TsDIA, Lviv, f. 406, op. 1, spr. 22, pp. 42–50.

concerts, which allayed the fears of the older generation that the young people were becoming too Americanized.[43]

For some priests, however, the league and the focus on youth was simply another demand of the bishop that meant more work for them.[44] Their reluctance (or sheer inability) to be actively involved in promoting youth-centered activities and events made it difficult for some young people to find a group to join or information about youth-oriented activities. In a letter to a young man, Bohdan Katamay, who wanted more information on an existing youth organization, Rev. Volodymyr Lotovych explained that the chancery divided its work into areas of interest and that he (Katamay) should address his request to the proper office.[45]

For the most part, Bohachevsky left the youth field to the initiative of individual priests. The young Rev. Stephen Tykhansky consolidated various parish youth groups into the Ukrainian Catholic Youth League. This organization still awaits its historian. Among other things, Tykhansky organized a meeting of Bohachevsky with the clergy at the Jermyn Hotel in Scranton on June 10, 1936, to plan for a large youth conference. Towards the end of the decade the eparchy held another successful Eucharistic congress, this time in New York.[46]

These developments were welcome, yet as far as the bishop was concerned nothing was as critical as the creation of a full-scale seminary for the training of Ukrainian-American priests. Bohachevsky could not even conceive of any other more immediate and pressing goal than the seminary and its attendant schools. But achieving this end required money and support. As described in more detail in the next chapter, in 1938 Bohachevsky finally got the approval of his closest advisers to found a college in Stamford.[47] The following spring, the state of Connecticut recognized St. Basil

43. For instance, *America*, March 15, 1935, carried a report on a particularly successful Shevchenko concert organized by the "youth."

44. Rev. Roman Krupa in a letter dated only June 1933, complained that the bishop asked him to organize a "Ukrainian Catholic Youth of Philadelphia Day," but provided no money, UMAS.

45. Lotovych to Katamay, June 1935, archival material on the work of the Ukrainian Catholic Youth League, UMAS.

46. *Eparkhiial'ni Visti*, May 1937, reporting on the November 22–25, 1936, congress.

47. *Eparkhiial'ni Visti*, November 1938, 42, reporting on the Ukrainian Catholic College at Stamford.

College, Stamford, Connecticut, as a degree-granting institution.[48] Thus, at the age of fifty-five, fifteen years after arriving in the United States, Bishop Bohachevsky could finally breathe a sigh of relief: There were schools in the country able to develop an American-Ukrainian educated elite. These young people, unsullied by Old World pettiness and acrimonies, would develop the society and its church. The bishop finally felt that he had the people behind his efforts to assure a proper education for the young Ukrainian Americans who would become the productive elite for America's Ukrainian community.

A PUBLIC ROLE, RELUCTANTLY

Bohachevsky was not one to articulate identities. For him, identity was such a natural ingrained personal matter that it needed no public definition. He simply presumed that the well-educated, sensitive, and empathetic graduates of Ukrainian Catholic schools would be able to recognize themselves as American citizens who were also descendants of a culturally rich people. He never tired of praising Ukrainian cultural values, on occasion identifying these values with true wealth.

At the same time, Bohachevsky valued Europe because Europe had become the repository of the Catholic Church, the vessel of the salvation of humanity. In a February 1937 pastoral letter on the need to develop one's God-given talents, the bishop noted: "It is this little Europe . . . that controlled the whole earthen globe. And the reason for its predominance is its spiritual culture, which this race built grounded in the holy faith."[49] He repeated the importance of the "holy faith" that autumn as the only means through which Ukrainians could gain any sense of national unity.[50] Again he encouraged his faithful to cherish their culture and its language as the only solid valuables in life. Although a museum had not been planned, he collected whatever Ukrainian valuables he could to offer tangible proof of Ukraine's glory to young American Ukrainians.[51]

48. See Procko, *Ukrainian Catholics in America*, 70 and 153, quoting Connecticut Special Laws (1939) XXIII, Part 1, 300.
49. *Eparkhiial'ni Visti*, February 1937, 2.
50. Christmas pastoral letter, *Eparkhiial'ni Visti*, November 1937, 35.
51. In addition to the ethnographic material which he purchased from the Ukrainian

The bishop was not involved in American politics, either nationally or locally. With few exceptions, he was not active in émigré politics either. Such politically reticent behavior was in line with the directives of Rome and Lviv. Bohachevsky was, however, outspokenly anti-Communist, since that political group openly persecuted believers. He continued to stress the role of the Catholic Church in leading souls to salvation, and he often brought up the practical advantages of the Vatican connection for Ukraine.

In the pre–World War II years, most Ukrainian immigrants in the United States voted, if they voted at all, for Democratic candidates. For the activists, politics meant ward affairs. It can be assumed, judging from the bishop's later conversations on politics, that he simply realized that his voice did not matter in the broader political configurations. For Bohachevsky, all public positions were a matter of principle. In his mind, there was no difference between the private and the public as far as values were concerned. One simply had to perform one's duty wisely and rationally.

Bohachevsky's unwillingness to play a more active public role was his major weakness, as far as the activists in the Ukrainian community were concerned. A man in his position, they felt, should use his pulpit for the common cause. The community continued its efforts to force the bishop's hand to use his Vatican connection for the Ukrainian cause. At a meeting of some four hundred people in the Philadelphia Community Hall, the organizers wrote to Eugenio Cardinal Pacelli (soon to be Pope Pius XII) that they, the faithful in the United States, supported those bishops who opposed Polish oppression of the Ukrainians. Participants at another gathering, this one held on April 10, 1938, wrote to Rome to protest the policies of Bishop Khomyshyn of Stanyslaviv in Halychyna.[52]

As a Ukrainian, Bohachevsky was expected to be a promoter of a Ukrainian state—that is, a nationalist. Thankfully, Ukrainian nationalism in the United States did not develop into its most extreme form, even in its most fervent practitioners. Nonetheless, Bohachevsky had neither the

---

National Women's League of America in 1933, he laid the groundwork for a museum by acquiring a document signed by Hetman Ivan Mazepa. He also found a manuscript sheet of his personal hero, Markian Shashkevych. Bohachevsky also supported contemporary artists, such as the sculptor Alexander Archipenko.

52. CEC, Prot. 226/35 [Rigotti, 188–226]. The protesters targeted the Polish Parliament for publicly mocking Sheptytsky and the papacy for commending Khomyshyn.

time nor (especially by the 1930s) the inclination to follow the ideological debates closely. For him true nationalism was inextricably fused with a selfless love of God who bestowed on every person a specific goal in life. In spite of this, the personal duty of service to the people/nation was so deeply ingrained in the bishop that he could never entirely disregard it. He did his best to reorient the cult of heroism from the glorification of a noble death to life-long service for an entity greater than the self. In many pastoral letters he stressed the nobility of life lived in practical service to the common good, for God and Country, rather than dramatic assertions of readiness to die for the cause. "It is because of the sacrifice of individuals that nations live," he exhorted in his pastoral letter of May 1936.[53]

Sacrificial death, in Bohachevsky's view, was not enough; individuals must be ready to live hard lives of sacrifice. He argued that to die for one's ideals is a noble but quick death, whereas true nobility demands enduring efforts to live a life that could help bring those national ideals to fruition. He consistently stressed the church's responsibility to prevent the spread of ideas repellent to God's will. For him, both fascism and integral nationalism fell into that category. Again and again Bohachevsky raised Shashkevych's patriotism as an example for all to emulate, and specifically Shashkevych's emphasis that what mattered was not so much dying for the cause as living for it.[54]

Bohachevsky remained a conservative, and as the decade progressed, he was increasingly willing to publicize his political sympathies. This became especially evident in 1937, when the heir-apparent of the Ukrainian monarchist movement, Danylo Skoropadsky, visited the United States on behalf of the Hetman party. Bohachevsky personally provided the young man with hospitality at the new campus complex in Stamford.[55] The bishop officiated at a festive liturgy, assisted by eight priests, at which the

<hr>

53. *Eparkhiial'ni Visti*, May 1936.

54. *Eparkhiial'ni Visti*, November 1939, 58. On this topic, Rev. Chapelsky collected funds for a statue of the poet-priest Markian Shashkevych in Stamford, *America*, January 25, 1936.

55. He may have been sufficiently impressed by the young man to treat him formally as a representative of a government. I base this on the admittedly skimpy evidence that when I was in my very early teens, one of the Basilian nuns in the Philadelphia school told me that the bishop had come down to the nave of the cathedral and blessed the Hetmanych with the still unconsecrated host during a solemn liturgy. I have found no corroboration of this gesture.

Hetmanych, an Orthodox, was present. Later Bohachevsky participated in other public activities with Skoropadsky, and did not protest the inclusion of his own speeches and photographs in the Hetmanate publications connected to the visit. Nor did the bishop oppose the action of some of his senior clergy, who blessed a plane in the Hetman's presence.[56] In his personal correspondence to Rev. Chapelsky, then director of the Stamford Museum, Bohachevsky referred to the young man as "Pan Hetmanych," an informal honorific meaning "the son of the Hetman."[57]

Nazaruk, who at the time was at odds with Viacheslav Lypynsky, the philosopher of the Ukrainian conservative movement, thought Bohachevsky's hospitality to the Hetmanych was a sign of his support for the whole monarchist movement.[58] But hospitality for the young Skoropadsky was as far as the bishop was willing to involve himself in the intricacies of Ukrainian émigré politics. The bishop scrupulously avoided contact with openly nationalist parties, and he condemned all violence. At the same time, he did not hide his conservative predilections: he deplored materialism and the various plagues of modernity, from cards to movies to the breakdown of family life. And he used every opportunity to bring a religious understanding to daily life. Thus, in his 1934 Lenten pastoral letter, Bohachevsky stressed the physical as well as the spiritual benefits of moderate fasting. The final benefit of fasting, he claimed, is that it "helps us raise people physically and morally to be healthy and thus ready to fulfill their duties in church and in society."[59]

Bohachevsky's strong convictions about the importance of the Ukrainian Catholic Church for all of Ukraine had grown stronger during his time of troubles, and he was quick to draw lessons for the communi-

56. The Hetman party bought the plane as part of their civilian military preparedness program. The aged Rev. Nykolai Simenovych assisted by Rev. Epiphanius Theodorovych, the abbot of the Basilians, and the Reverends Sylvester Kollar and Mykhaylo Oleksiv officiated at the ceremonies. Information in a communique of the Press Section of the Hetman movement, Nazaruk file, TsDIA, Lviv, f. 406, op. 1, spr. 22, pp. 120–21.

57. In the same letter, dated October 1, Bohachevsky informed Chapelsky, that the Hetmanych would stay a few days in Philadelphia, arriving in Stamford around October 20, then most likely would head to Washington, New York, and back to Stamford. Bohachevsky to Chapelsky, October 1, 1937, UMAS.

58. Nazaruk to Ludvyg Sidletsky (who wrote as Sava Krylach), October 14, 1937, TsDIA, f. 406, op. 1, spr. 21, pp. 99–100.

59. Eparkhiial'ni Visti, February 1934, 3.

ty from the experiences of the church. Discipline had made the church strong so it could prevail even amidst the chaos that was continuously destroying Ukrainian communities; the community, however, had not learned from the church's example and should be chastised for its errant ways: "We can see how this destructive chaos drilled through the national organism, unprecedented in all of history; in just one year under Bolshevik power millions of souls in Great Ukraine starved to death. [Yet even that tragedy] could not unite us and force us to protest and [effectively] provide the kind of defense that our great [velyky] people deserve and which the whole world expected."[60] Bohachevsky became convinced that all the calamities that befell Ukraine stemmed from the failure of the 1596 Union of Brest to encompass all of Ukraine. Because Ukraine did not become Catholic on its own terms, parts of the country were left outside of the Western cultural framework. "All failures of the [church] union reflected the failures, some even catastrophic, of the nation. . . . . Ukrainian history in its thousand-year existence does not provide a single example where any religio-cultural break with the West has [resulted in] any durable national advantage."[61] An awkward, but very diplomatic, way of stressing that Ukraine gains from Catholicism.

Bohachevsky's unshaken trust in God's Providence would never permit him to doubt that Ukraine would achieve liberty and statehood. Each crisis strengthened his faith—at least publicly. There was one thing he feared constantly, however—the absence of a Ukrainian bishop in the United States who could step up and take over should he, Bishop Bohachevsky, die.

HOW TO SECURE AN INCOMPLETE LEGACY?

As Bishop Bohachevsky inched toward his sixth decade of life, he was keenly aware that the men of his family were predisposed to heart trouble. Recent history fanned the bishop's concern about the need for a trained

60. Ibid. In the Christmas pastoral letter of 1939 (*Eparkhiial'ni Visti*, November 1938, 40–41), Bohachevsky stressed that small and poor Ireland was able to win independence from mighty Great Britain because the Irish had faith in the Holy Catholic Church.

61. A quotation from Stefan Tomashivsky's *Vstup do istoriyi Tserkvy na Ukrayini* that Bohachevsky used in his Lenten pastoral letter, *Eparkhiial'ni Visti*, February 1933, 3. In much the same vein, Bohachevsky held Luther responsible for the failure of Germany to live up to its Christian potential, although he did not specifically blame Luther for Hitler.

successor waiting in the wings, were the bishop to die. He had seen the ru-
inous effects of World War I on the otherwise stable dioceses in Halychyna, and he had never forgotten his first tumultuous years in the American
eparchy, which was still an exarchate. More than many other American
bishops, he realized that even if the United States did not involve itself
in any European politics, the repercussions of European conflict would
have a direct negative impact on his church. He had to secure his eparchy
against the most palpable danger he knew—an episcopal interregnum.
The Ukrainian Catholic Church in the United States could not again be
left without a bishop. In February 1937, Bohachevsky drafted a letter to the
Congregation for the Eastern Church, uncharacteristically detailing his
successes, to make another request for a possible successor:

What in our circumstances could be done, I tried to do. I know that much work
remains to be done. Religious indifference of many, extreme nationalism, lack
of Catholic schools and education, these are the weaknesses that remain to be
remedied. . . . [But] after the crisis of 1927 subsided, I have not [had] a [single]
case of a[n] apostasy of a parish or a priest. . . . Most of the apostatized parishes
came back, the others are very near conversion. The priests all returned, except
for a few of those who have married after their ordination. The following are the
numbers, which show the growth of our eparchy during my bishopric: [we have]
thirteen newly established parishes with resident priests, eight newly established mission churches, twenty-five new priests since 1924, fifteen new church
buildings, ten new school buildings. . . .

I ask . . . for the appointment of an auxiliary bishop *cum jure successionis*. The
candidate must have a spirit of sacrifice and be familiar with the Ukrainian and
English languages. I don't have a priest in my eparchy that I could present as a
candidate or a priest possessing the required qualities, sufficient age, and experience.[62]

Bohachevsky wrote the letter in Ukrainian, and a priest who had been educated in Europe (judging by the handwriting) translated it into English on
February 28, trying to keep as close to the original as possible. The bishop
pondered the translation for a day or so, and on March 2, 1937, he sent the
letter to the congregation via Cicognani, the papal nuncio.

62. Rough draft of letter at the UMAS. The bishop made a handwritten list in columns
of the new parishes and new missions, and of the fifteen new churches built and the ten new
schools organized. He listed twenty-five new priests, although three appear to be priests
who returned to the exarchy after a year or so of dissent. Both documents at UMAS.

Six months later, on October 26, 1938, the Congregation for the Eastern Church offered the position of vicar to Rev. Joseph Slipyj, who at the time was serving as rector of the Lviv seminary as well as of the Lviv Theological Academy that had been established in 1927.[63] The nomination letter stressed that the position ensured the right of succession to the Philadelphia See.[64] Slipyj, an outspoken adherent of mandatory celibacy for Ukrainian Catholic priests and an open opponent of the rising clandestine Ukrainian nationalist movement, was a logical choice for the position. The younger cleric shared Bohachevsky's views on celibacy, the essential role of Catholic education for the success of the Catholic mission, and the noninvolvement of the church in political squabbles. But Rector Slipyj had his heart set on remaining in Lviv and declined the offer immediately, pleading the importance of the seminary and the Theological Academy. Slipyj recommended two candidates, Rev. Petro Werhun and Bishop Ivan Buchko, for the American position.[65] His recommendation of Buchko, who was then serving as Metropolitan Sheptytsky's auxiliary and was thus a strong contender to succeed him, was the stronger of the two. There seems to have been no follow-up to this proposal at the Vatican, and it is likely that further action on the entire matter was precluded by the political crises that led to the outbreak of World War II.

There is little documentation of discussions at Lviv regarding the development of the Philadelphia exarchate and Bohachevsky's request for help. However, Metropolitan Sheptytsky became particularly interested in the growth of the Ukrainian Catholic seminary in the United States. The metropolitan often relied on information from priests in the diocese rather than on the bishops. The metropolitan wrote to his fellow Basilian, Rev. Volodymyr Andrushkiw, asking how the Ukrainian schools in America

63. The Western Ukrainians for more than fifty years had vainly sought to establish a Ukrainian language university in Halychyna. The Polish administration limited the number of Ukrainian students that could attend the Lviv University. When the Ukrainian students announced a boycott of the university, Sheptytsky turned a blind eye to the functioning of the Clandestine Ukrainian University classes on the territories of the metropolia. Sheptytsky also established a theological academy that could serve as a nucleus for the future Ukrainian university.

64. TsDIA, Lviv, f. 451, op. 2, spr. 157, p. 8. The correspondence went through the papal nuncio in Warsaw. It was not until 1940 that Rome (with the help of Eugenio Cardinal Tisserant) agreed to raise the Lviv Academy to a university.

65. Ibid, 9–14.

were getting along. After offering apologies for not having written more frequently, the priest focused on the expansion of Catholic Ukrainian schools and cultural institutions in America. The subtext of the letter was a defense of Bohachevsky's policies; the writer enumerated the success of the Ukrainian-American schools, especially the Stamford complex. Andrushkiw described the beautiful setting and the modern conditions, the laboratory and other appurtenances available to the almost one hundred high school students. He offered his own assessment of Bohachevsky's tenure:

Permit me to say a few words about Ukrainians . . . in America. As pastor in Nanticoke, Pennsylvania, I had a chance to get to know my nation [narod] in real life, as it really is. It pains me that the nation does not follow its pastor but seeks out charlatans and believes them more [than the legitimate powers]. That is the reason for the dissention. Bishop Constantine asked me to be the prefect at Stamford, Connecticut. Hence I am educating youth to be good priests. . . . We also have a type of a gymnasium/high school with ninety-four students and five faculty that is well received in the neighborhood. . . . Bishop Constantine put forth the slogan to "build schools!" and for that he indeed can be called "the builder of Ukrainian schools in America."[66]

The matter of succession was again put on hold as more weighty issues claimed public attention in Europe, especially on its Eastern flank—issues that were more pressing than the needs of a small exarchate in the distant and peaceful United States. Succession in the Philadelphia eparchy, with its still youthful and vigorous-looking bishop, was not considered a top priority either at Rome or at Lviv.

THE BRIEF HOPE OF CARPATHIAN UKRAINE

The intelligentsia leadership of the Ukrainian community in America, largely shaped in and by the old country, viewed cultural nationalism clad in romantic rhetoric as the most attractive political movement of the 1930s. These leaders implemented and practiced their views in the United States through a variety of ethno-cultural organizations, as well as through some youth groups. There were also a few semi-military clubs and

66. Rev. Volodymyr Andrushkiw hoped that his new position would give him more opportunities to correspond. TsDIA, Lviv, f. 201 (Hreko-katolytska konsystoria), op. 4b, spr. 2528, pp. 79–80.

an airborne club that drilled, built, and flew small airplanes. Their members sang patriotic songs that expressed their yearning for the freedom-loving fatherland that fewer and fewer of them had seen or would ever see. Even the leadership of the Ukrainian National Association sought to moderate the extreme nationalism that became popular in the years immediately preceding the outbreak of the war in 1939.[67] The paramilitary organizations disintegrated mostly because the younger, American-born population within the Ukrainian community simply lost interest. The leadership of the Ukrainian-American organizations, including the clergy, followed the events in Europe more closely than average American citizens did. By the beginning of 1938, some maintained that war in Europe was inevitable; others were convinced that Europe would not repeat the bloody horrors of the past. The looming possibility of war evoked the grim hope that the defeat of all major contenders would give Ukraine an opportunity to try yet again for independence. Bohachevsky had been critical of extreme nationalism earlier and now reprinted the L'Osservatore Romano article in the Eparchial News that condemned Nazism. The bishop had served on the Italian front as a chaplain and knew about war from first-hand experience. As much as he supported the cause of Ukrainian independence, he could not idealize war as a means to gain it. War for him was a result of moral weakness, proof of the reality of evil and of human stupidity. Instead, Bohachevsky promoted service. In his Easter pastoral letter, Bishop Constantine tried to shore up the faithful by reminding them that all work is equally important in the eyes of God. He wanted to keep members of his flock focused on tasks in which they could participate meaningfully instead of getting carried away by visions of heroic death on the vast steppes of Ukraine: "Each century, each year even has its program, its own concrete goal in God's strategy. For us now it is the founding of schools.... Most importantly, we cannot despair in the face of danger; we must stand firm as the soldiers of Christ's Kingdom. We do not need to see triumph and victory, but we must stand our ground."[68]

67. "By 1939 the Nationalists were the largest Ukrainian political faction in the anti-Communist camp and in firm control of the largest Ukrainian fraternal organization, the UNA." Kuropas, Ukrainian Americans, 253. The nationalist wing in the United States was concerned enough to send Luka Myshuha to Halychyna to moderate both the rhetoric and the tactics of the clandestine Organization of Ukrainian Nationalists.

68. Eparkhiial'ni Visti, February 1938, 3.

Soon Bohachevsky's views were put to test. How would he defend Ukraine, given the chance to act? In November 1938, Ukraine was an unstable region in the shadow of expanding Nazi Germany and under constant threat from the USSR. Austria had joined Germany, ostensibly voluntarily, but Czechoslovakia was a clear victim. Nonetheless, the Ukrainians in Transcarpathian lands saw a sliver of opportunity to declare their claim for an independent existence, as Czechoslovakia fell to German and Hungarian expansionism. They demanded autonomy and proclaimed the establishment of a Carpathian Ukrainian State. Headed by a Catholic priest, Augustine Voloshyn, the new entity was supported militarily by untrained and idealistic youthful volunteers who in a few months would be bloodily defeated by the Hungarian military.

In honor of the Carpathian Ukrainians, Bishop Bohachevsky proclaimed November 27, 1938, as the "Day of Prayer for the Welfare and Happiness of the Ukrainian People."[69] Sometime earlier, he had written to Bishop Njaradi asking for Voloshyn's address.[70] He then duly sent a personal note and money to Rev. Dr. Voloshyn, the premier of the short-lived Carpathian Ukrainian Republic. Addressing Voloshyn as "Your Excellency, the Highly Esteemed Reverend Premier," Bohachevsky noted that "God's Providence leaves visible signs of the dawn of Ukrainian statehood. We are glad that God's Providence chose the most forgotten part of the Ukrainian land to show His love. . . . May we live for the moment when the blue and yellow standards of Christ the King wave in all cities of Ukraine. May God bless your work."[71]

This letter reflects the hope that the impending crisis in Europe would provide a new chance (as did that of 1918–19) for the establishment of a Ukrainian state. It revealed as well an extremely rare example of the bishop's emotional patriotism, a sentiment Bohachevsky usually kept on a tight rein. Voloshyn replied on March 3, 1939, thanking Bohachevsky "for your warm words of fatherly greeting and your royal gift for the development of our small young Ukraine."[72] Voloshyn stressed that Bohachevsky

69. "Den' molytvy za dobro i shchastia ukraiins'koho narodu." *Eparkhiial'ni Visti*, November 1938, 43.

70. Bohachevsky to Njaradi, July 10, 1938, UMAS, Chancery Archive.

71. Bohachevsky to Voloshyn, November 13, 1938, UMAS, Chancery Archive, carbon copy of letter.

72. Voloshyn to Bohachevsky, March 3, 1939, UMAS, Chancery Archive, a handwritten

was one of the miniscule few who had "offered princely material help for the development of our small and young Ukraine."[73] Both money and correspondence with Voloshyn went through a go-between—Rev. Paul Protsko, then serving at Stamford as rector of the seminary—rather than through the Philadelphia chancery.[74]

Bohachevsky welcomed the creation of the Carpathian Ukrainian Republic, although it was only an autonomous region within a dying Czechoslovakia. He prepared a statement on the new republic (dated December 5, 1938) and ordered that it be read at all liturgies on December 25, at which time a collection would be made. The one-page declaration was titled, without much concern for political niceties, "Carpathian Ukraine." Its tone was simple: "God's Providence directs the fate of nations. And for the Ukrainian people unexpectedly a self-governing Carpathian Ukraine was born in the Carpathian Mountains."[75] The bishop urged that the faithful support and bolster this hopeful event as much as they could and requested that all monies collected were to be sent to his chancery immediately. By the time Rev. Voloshyn thanked Bohachevsky, not only Carpathian Ukraine but an independent Czechoslovakia had disappeared from the European map.

The echo of the war became more audible in America. The U.S. government investigation of organizations that may have had a connection with German agencies also put a damper on nationalist organizations. The so-called Ukrainian nationalist milieu in America welcomed the formation of a special investigating commission, the House Committee on Un-American Activities, because the interrogation was directed against the leftists and fascist subversives. But soon, ironically, the nationalist rhetoric of the Ukrainian émigré organizations began attracting the com-

---

note on the original documents that a check for $3,669.43 had been sent on February 11, 1939.

73. Ibid. The letter is signed by Dr. Augustine Voloshyn, Premier-Minister. Voloshyn's son thanked Bohachevsky, noting that the donation was a rare one, and much appreciated.

74. UMAS. Rev. Paul Protsko (1889–1949) was one of the first priests Bohachevsky invited to the exarchy. Through the years he served in various capacities and was especially effective as rector of St. Basil Seminary at Stamford, 1933–1941.

75. From the text of a one-paragraph leaflet on Carpatho-Ukraine published under the bishop's signature with no further documentation. It is dated Philadelphia, December 5, 1938, and headlined "Carpathian Ukraine." The text was to be read on Sunday, December 25, and a collection taken for the needs of the Carpathian Ukrainians. UMAS.

mittee's attention. Some of the church's open "enemies," including the newspaper *Svoboda*, were somewhat discredited during the investigation by testimony of their own members.

The extent of Bohachevsky's financial support of Rev. Voloshyn, the premier of the Carpathian "state," was not known; and Bohachevsky's support of the undertaking was not viewed as a political act. Neither the Ukrainian Catholic Church nor any of its clergy fell under suspicion of engaging in activities inimical to American security. Unlike some of the secular Ukrainian-American organizations whose American patriotism was questioned, Bohachevsky's conservatism served the church well. The Ukrainian Catholic Church in America did not draw any untoward attention to itself, in part because Bishop Bohachevsky's stewardship had ensured a secure place for the church in the country. Relations with the Latin-rite, Catholic upper clergy were, for the most part, not only cordial, but even friendly, and the Congregation for the Eastern Church helped resolve the problems that did arise.

CHAPTER 10

Salvation through Education

Bishop Bohachevsky came to be known as the builder of Ukrainian-Catholic schools in the United States—parochial grammar schools, Sunday schools, high schools, residential academies, two colleges, a full-scale undergraduate, and a graduate seminary. To the end of his days, Catholic schooling on all levels remained at the heart of his interests. Even his enemies recognized his success in this field. The schools speeded up the growth of a native Ukrainian-American elite, nurtured the Catholic faith, and fostered knowledge of Ukrainian culture and religious values in its students. They raised American awareness of Ukrainians and of the Eastern rite within the American community.

TO BREAK OUT OF *DAVNTAVN*

Bohachevsky's educational achievement should be seen within the context of the United States and Halychyna. In the 1930s an American high-school education was considered a "higher education," and few immigrants set more ambitious goals. In Halychyna economic and, more importantly, political impediments blocked access to higher education for Ukrainians. As a result, throughout the twentieth century, Ukrainian political and educational goals coalesced, especially within Western Ukraine.[1] The demand

---

1. For an overview on clerical education, see Kaszczak, *The Education of Ukrainian Greek-Catholic Clergy*. First-hand stories about the most egregious unschooled village priests

for a university that offered lectures and instruction in the Ukrainian language remained a political goal, one that World War II émigrés would bring to the West. The Lviv Theological Academy was not established as a separate academic entity until 1928, mostly through the efforts of Metropolitan Sheptytsky.[2] In Rome, it was owing to the personal funds of Pope Pius XI that a Ukrainian seminary collegium was built on the Janiculum hill in 1929.[3] Therefore, the very idea of a seminary and college for the benefit of Ukrainian Americans, few of whom had even a high-school education, seemed unrealistic, if not pretentious, for many. Nor can we discount that there was a certain amount of jealousy in the home country for the upstart American immigrants who were presumptuous enough to think about their own seminary and college.

The bishop had no such misgivings. He was confident that Ukrainian-Catholic schools would be the moorings in the New World, which would enable Ukrainians to keep a Ukrainian-Catholic identity while flourishing as successful Americans. His original vision, which he shared back in January 1925 with a colleague from Innsbruck, was to establish a Ukrainian-Catholic seminary with a strong academic component that would not only properly educate the Eastern clergy but also give Latin-rite

---

were still common during Bohachevsky's youth. For a brief but telling account, see an essay by Rev. Fylymon Tarnawsky, "Z Temnoii Doby Halychyny" [From Halychyna's Dark Period], in *Propamiatna Knyha iz sviatochnoho obkhodu Ukraiins'koho Katolyts'koho Kaledzha, 24 Lystopada, 1940, u Filadelfiii* [*The Commemorative Book of the Festive Celebration of the Ukrainian Catholic College*] (Philadelphia: America, 1941), 103–5.

2. The Ukrainian Catholic Seminary in Lviv was established in 1783. The theological academy was planned in 1923 as a preliminary step toward the establishment of a Catholic university in Lviv. Initially only theology was taught; a philosophy department was established in 1932, and plans were drawn for schools of law and medicine. Metropolitan Sheptytsky could not get Rome's permission to form a university until Cardinal Tisserant acceded to the request in 1939. (The congregation declined Sheptytsky's requests in 1932, ASV, Poland, Pos. 178–79, fasc. 201.) The university opened with six full and six associate professors, four lecturers, and ten assistants. Mykola Chubaty, "Hreko-Katolyts'ka Bohoslovs'ka Akademia u Lvovi" [Greek-Catholic Theological Academy in Lviv], in *Propamyatna Khyha iz sviatochnoho obkhodu Ukrayins'koho Katolyts'koho Kaledzha* (Philadelphia: America, n.d.), 131. During the 1930s, with or without Sheptytsky's knowledge, the facilities were used by an informal "Ukrainian free university," to hold classes for expelled Ukrainian students, Martha Bohachevsky-Chomiak, "The Ukrainian University in Galicia: A Pervasive Issue," *Harvard Ukrainian Studies* 5, no. 4 (December 1981): 497–545.

3. Ivan Buchko, "Ukrayins'ka Kolehiia v Rymi" [The Ukrainian Collegium in Rome], in *Propamiatna Knyha iz sviatochnoho*, 114.

students an opportunity to understand Eastern Christianity. Through this path Bohachevsky hoped to serve the underlying *raison d'être* of the Ukrainian Catholic Church—the reunification of Christendom. The union of Western and Eastern churches was a major goal of activist Catholic Ukrainians, and was most effectively enunciated by Metropolitan Sheptytsky. The message was generally directed toward the Eastern Orthodox, but Bohachevsky saw that the West—"the Latins"—also needed to be informed about Eastern Christendom. For the Ukrainian Catholic Church and its traditions to be taken seriously, the church as an institution needed to present itself in its entirety, not merely through the physical distinctiveness of its buildings and its icons. To achieve this end, Bohachevsky had to do in the United States what Sheptytsky was doing in Europe—excavate the spiritual underpinnings from the traditional, agrarian, ritual culture and adapt them to a different age.

The conventional view of the Ukrainian immigrant population was that they were primarily interested in making money. Bohachevsky rejected that premise. The bishop foresaw a developed Ukrainian-American society, with its own professional and intellectual elites. He also hoped that the Ukrainian Catholic institutions of higher learning would draw the Halychanyns and the Carpathians closer together. The bishop saw that his American flock appreciated the spiritual benefits of the traditional rite, and he also saw they were unable to convey that spiritual response to their own children, let alone their non-Ukrainian neighbors. They needed to know more about the Ukrainian Church to be able to present it to their Western counterparts. Bohachevsky wanted to ensure that the Ukrainian Catholic Church would be seen not as a small transplanted church operating under the broad auspices of the Latin-rite Catholic ecclesia, but as what it actually was—part of the ecumenical Catholic Church that was also an integral part of its people, wherever those people might be. Thus, the small Ukrainian Catholic mission church in America would not only expand its reach geographically, but would also fulfill its integrative function as a bridge between Eastern and Western Christendom. The bishop remained convinced that only a well-educated elite could convey that vision to the generations of Ukrainians and Americans born in the United States. As his immediate ancestor-priests, he envisaged the young Ukrainian-American women and men as being well-educated, confident,

FIGURE 10. ICONOSTASIS OF THE OLD CATHEDRAL

dedicated practitioners of an active Christianity, unhemmed by hostile restrictions and endemic poverty that had plagued their ancestors. They would embody his optimism and his drive. Foremost among them would be a cadre of well-educated, Ukrainian-American, women religious and of course, priests.

Bohachevsky never lost sight of the importance of full-time, Ukrainian-Catholic grammar and high schools in the United States. They were the foundation for higher learning, the guarantee of the existence of the Ukrainian people and their church. The afternoon community schools, usually staffed by a single cantor, were not very effective, and the children considered them second-rate. The bishop focused on establishing full-time grammar and secondary schools accredited by the states, and staffed at least in part by people who could transmit the Catholic faith as well as knowledge about Ukraine and its culture. He gradually managed to set up these schools—a feat accomplished by his hard work, visitations, wise and convincing sermons, and especially through the selfless dedication of the women religious. The women who entered the convent to serve God served the children of their fellows. They studied to earn professional teaching degrees, understanding that knowledge and faith were not at cross-purposes. Like their bishop, the nuns lived a life of service and prayer.

The working-class immigrants who financed the schools which their children attended eventually realized the necessity of supporting the establishment of a college and seminary as a way to preserve their traditions and to avail their families of the opportunities which America offered. As he worked on organizing teachers for the Ukrainian Catholic schools, Bohachevsky had the rich reservoir of the women religious, especially those of the Order of St. Basil the Great with whom he had worked in the first years of his episcopate. He pressured the order to promote the education of its novices and nuns. He relied heavily on women, in the home and in the school, for the proper formation of the Catholic child. The bishop encouraged the education of women, of course with the usual caveat that the child not be cheated of maternal care.

A TRINITY OF DOERS

Within the American context Constantine Bohachevsky saw himself as the third member of the clerical trinity instrumental in building up the Ukrainian Catholic community in the United States: Reverend Voliansky had established the first church, Bishop Ortynsky had laid the foundations for the eparchy, and he, Bishop Bohachevsky, would ensure its continued existence through a network of Ukrainian Catholic schools, crowned by its own college. These schools would produce a dedicated Ukrainian-American elite, a cadre of dynamic, American-born priests and professionals who would enrich the universal Catholic Church both in the United States and Europe. Bohachevsky quickly realized that only American-born, Ukrainian clergy could reach the youth in his diocese. He saw the development of educational opportunities for his faithful as a major part of his duty before God and nation. Catholic education—which the bishop considered to be modern education—would break the cycle of poverty, promote self-awareness, steer the community toward concrete work, and foster the growth of an upwardly mobile society. At the same time, Ukrainian schools would validate Ukrainian culture for the youth now being attracted by the materialism of modern America. The schools would also educate the American public, including its Roman Catholics, about the Eastern Catholic rite and the Ukrainian people. Eastern mystics experienced the Wisdom of God, Sophia, through spiritual exercise; Bohachevsky's Sophia/Logos was grounded in education. He was so convinced of the rectitude of this vision that he was willing to risk chronic community opposition in order to implement it. And, in time, despite the opposition of the large cadre of cantors and some priests, the community began to support the bishop's vision. Bohachevsky's tireless efforts to build Ukrainian-Catholic high schools and a seminary and then to crown his academic edifice with two colleges finally won him the respect of the Ukrainian-American community that had eluded him for almost a decade.

Bohachevsky believed in the intimate relationship of religion and culture. By "religion" he meant the Ukrainian Catholic Church, with its specific rite, which was being studied and codified by the textual commission at Lviv and Rome.[4] By "culture" he meant the study and appreciation of literature, language, history, art, and, above all, everything connected with the church and the chiseling of a refined spirit. Although spiritually embedded in the Eastern ritual as manifested in the Ukrainian Catholic Church, Bohachevsky was a cultural westernizer who saw no tension between Western cultural values and the Eastern church. The bishop had an idealized picture of European civilization, perceiving it to be based on virtue, order, discipline, and above all the innate striving of humanity for the good. He was culturally very old-World European, at one point pro-

4. In the introduction to *Nasha Shkola, Nasha Peremoha* [Our School, Our Victory], ed. Petro Oleksiv (Philadelphia: n.p., 1940), a selection of informative articles on the diocesan educational projects, Rev. Petro Oleksiv summarized Bohachevsky's view: "The only authentic and firm basis on which we can build our Ukrainian life in America—is our church and our rite" (1). Bohachevsky insisted on teachers schooled in the Ukrainian-Catholic rite. When Nazaruk had suggested that German nuns organize the grammar schools, Bohachevsky protested "vehemently, flailing both his arms," Nazauk to Lypynsky, October 15, 1924, Lypynsky, *Collected Works*, 224.

claiming: "this little Europe . . . which seems only a sliver-peninsula of the Asian continent, gained political prominence over the whole globe . . . because its spiritual culture is built on the holy faith."[5] Yet unlike many of his European colleagues, the bishop saw advantages in the American system of education because it forced the church to be autonomous from the state.[6] Thoroughly convinced that the Catholic system of education had made the American Catholic Church strong, he considered it imperative to craft a grand design that would likewise enable the Ukrainian community to not only grow, but prosper: "In the last nine years our community lived through a great spiritual and intellectual crisis. It became clear that the periodic outbreaks of conflicts, of everybody against everybody, among our immigrants arise because we lack our own schools to promote our culture."[7]

Time and time again, Bohachevsky stressed that God had given the Ukrainian people many talents, the first of which was "the Holy Church, the source of culture." That was immediately followed by "our native rite, which we received from the Lord God." Language and music were also gifts from God that needed to be nurtured and expanded. Even "our own history is a talent from God."[8] In his repeated calls for the active practice of Greek-Catholic-rite Christianity, the bishop pointed out that in the changing whirlwind that characterized the political world stability was found only in God: "Laws of states change, constitutions are changed, but God's law is eternal, immutable."[9]

Bohachevsky sought to prove how integral the fostering of education was to the whole Catholic worldview, and especially to Catholic Ukraine. In February 1934, the year he turned fifty and the diocese celebrated its golden anniversary, Bohachevsky wrote an unusual Lenten pastoral let-

---

5. Eparkhiial'ni Visti, February 1937, 2.

6. Rev. Fylymon Tarnawsky suggested that priests preparing to serve in Ukraine (Halychyna) should study at U.S. seminaries: "it is essential for Ukrainian seminarians to learn not only English, but the American organization of the Catholic Church, which is separated from the state and therefore independent of it. That makes her the strongest part of the universal Catholic Church." This quotation is taken from Danylo Bohachevsky's transcription of parts of Tarnawsky's memoirs, Spomyny, 159.

7. Eparkhiial'ni Visti, May 1933, 19, also quoted in Procko, Ukrainian Catholics in America, 63.

8. Lenten message, Eparkhiial'ni Visti, February 1937, 2.

9. Eparkhiial'ni Visti, November 1938, 40–41.

ter.[10] The eleven-page document (most of his pastoral letters did not exceed three pages) presented the bishop's view on life. He considered it axiomatic that the goal of life was happiness in union with God. That happiness, he argued, can be achieved only within the church and only through the conscious actions of the self toward the ideal, that is, God. Christian charity, the study and practice of asceticism, fasting and penance were only some of the means to achieve ultimate happiness. It was equally necessary to care for one's body and lead a healthy life, thereby conditioning the will toward the good. Promotion of learning led to a better understanding of authentic value, and that could best be achieved through Catholic education. A good Catholic press should encourage and enable adults to continue their intellectual development.

One can fault the bishop for the optimistic simplicity of his views on human nature. But even within this optimism, he struggled with the concept of Christian obedience. Early on he had concluded that Christianity had triumphed not only because of the truth of God's word, but also because it was a force able to structure the unruly barbaric masses. Analogously, the body with its unstructured emotions also had to be consciously organized in accordance with God's principles. At the same time, Bohachevsky was certain that the church could not have relied on force alone to build up its power while still remaining true to Christ's gospel of love. As he wrote:

Christ insistently demands that we bring Him useful fruits, that is—good deeds. Good deeds constitute the only use Christ can have of us, because they belong solely to Him. "We are created in the good deeds in Jesus." As [Christ] cursed the barren tree, so He judged the lazy servant guilty. Hence, within Christ's Church there is only one way of being His obedient servants and that is *obedience, as willing service from love.*[11]

This understanding of willing submission to the will of God, which by definition is always good even if we do not recognize it at the time, enabled Bohachevsky's Christianity to be vibrant and goal-oriented. He was convinced that such action promoted authentic happiness, and he found it difficult to accept passivity. It pained him that a country as large as Ukraine could not

10. *Eparkhiial'ni Visti*, February 1934.
11. *Eparkhiial'ni Visti*, November 1934, 7.

fare better in this world—obviously because Ukrainians had failed to understand and live up to the time-tested, effective Christian principles that had helped other nations achieve independence and well-being:

What we read in the pages of responsible newspapers and what we heard for years upon years at public meetings, rallies, conventions, and congresses were sermons of disobedience, the flouting of church and community authority. The limitless egotism of certain individuals, their unbridled politicking, lack of discipline and of public responsibility dissipated the unity and strength of our church and of our nation. Mutual distrust and hatred among political groups reached such levels that none of the major Ukrainian organizations is certain about its future. Now the firm land is slipping from under the feet of even those leaders whose wide-ranging demagoguery destroyed all legitimate power, and especially the respect for our native church, and they themselves are becoming the victims of the dark, ignorant, and senseless mass in which they had previously turned upon others . . . . We can safely say that many among our people in this emigration are led astray by the Bolshevik, fog-inducing weed [durman]. But even that part of the Ukrainians, which still hold on to their [Ukrainian] organizations are so confused by the many contradictory slogans that they are incapable of concerted action. As long as nothing is being done, everything seems peaceful. But if you only begin a useful undertaking, the ever-present dormant destructive forces spring into action. Just initiate any community action, such as the establishment of a full-day, Ukrainian parochial school, and immediately you will be confronted by all shades of opposition—perfidy, corruption, revolt, narrow party politicking that will resound from the lowest instincts of the untutored mass and kill the good deed before it is even begun.[12]

Bohachevsky wrote this in the aftermath of two tragedies visited upon Ukrainians in the homeland. In 1930 the Polish regime in Halychyna unleashed a brutal pogrom on Ukrainian leaders and institutions, including the clergy. There were mass beatings, looting, and public humiliations, as well as arrests that went into history books under an Orwellian name—"pacification." The goal was to terrorize Ukrainians into submission, but the reaction led to the growth of left- and right-wing extremism. The years 1932–33 brought the unprecedented Soviet-engineered famine/ Holodomor, which graphically demonstrated Ukraine's weakness. The inability of Ukrainians beyond the borders of the Ukrainian Soviet Socialist

12. Ibid., 8.

Republic to persuade the rest of the world that a devastating famine was decimating the population was a great blow. Bohachevsky proclaimed Sunday, December 24, 1933, as a Day of Compassion for the starving masses in Ukraine, and sent money for the victims directly to Sheptytsky.[13] The rest of the Ukrainian-American community organized a relief committee only after Bohachevsky had sent the diocesan contribution.[14] Of course, the America of the Great Depression was hardly a land of plenty for Ukrainian immigrants, and donations were generally modest. The counterproductive squabbling within the community continued. In a pastoral letter, Bohachevsky again expressed his sorrow about the condition of Ukrainian society:

Satan with his entire hell is hard at work to erase the Ukrainian people from the face of the world. And our reaction? Discord among Ukrainians in America completely weakened us and destroyed almost all our means of defense [we could have used] against those determined to eradicate our people in Greater Ukraine completely. Today, at a time of the greatest need in the national history of our people, we immigrants find ourselves in such [desperate] straits that much as we want to, we cannot provide the needed help for desolate Ukraine . . . as we might have been able to had it not been for the earlier and ever present rifts amongst us. The worst of enemies have not harmed us as much as the long-standing litany of irreverence, revolt, and distrust of our own pseudo-leaders.[15]

In Halychyna the bishops promoted a more active Christian way of life among the faithful, trying to draw the laity into combating materialism and to keep the priests from becoming directly involved in politics.[16] All

13. *Eparkhiial'ni Visti*, December 1933, 45–46.

14. In a letter to the Ukrainian National Women's League of America, dated February 6, 1934, Bohachevsky informed the women that the church had completed its campaign the previous year, and therefore could not participate in their campaign for the same cause; Bohachevsky to the Ukrainian National Women's League of America, February 6, 1934, UNWLA Archives, New York, uncatalogued. UNWLA is the oldest functioning Ukrainian women's organization in the United States. Some of the archival holdings have been sent to the University of Minnesota. The organization continues to be active and actively cooperates with related organizations worldwide.

15. *Eparkhiial'ni Visti*, February 1935, 9.

16. See Bohdan Budurowycz, "The Greek Catholic Church in Galicia, 1914–1944," *Harvard Ukrainian Studies* 26, nos. 1–4 (2002–3): 291–353; and Andrew Sorokowsky, "The Lay and Clerical Intelligentsia in Greek Catholic Galicia: Competition, Conflict, Cooperation, 1900–1939," *Harvard Ukrainian Studies* 26, nos. 1–4 (2002–3): 261–90.

Ukrainian Catholic bishops had agreed to promote religious education as an important element in forestalling further national catastrophes, but they failed to establish a united political agenda.[17] Some bishops tried to establish a Christian political party to undercut the popularity of modern political movements. Bohachevsky shared these views, but he must have realized that within the American context hopes for any type of Ukrainian Catholic politics would not have mass support. He kept his political expression to comments in his pastoral letters on legality, decency, fidelity to God, and the Ukrainian heritage[18]

Bohachevsky felt he had enough lay support to proceed with a slow implementation of his ambitious vision, but he had a difficult time persuading many of his priests to prioritize his educational agenda. Some of the old timers complained about the scarcity (and even lack) of primers and introductory children's books in Ukrainian; in the absence of these, what was the sense of talking of high schools and even a college? Such talk depressed Bohachevsky. Indeed, the one known instance that the bishop shed tears in public was documented during this time, specifically when he tried to draw the young, Philadelphia-born Father Stephan Hryniokh, who had been educated in both the United States and Europe, to become his close helper, to relieve him of some of the administrative duties, to take over the structuring of the seminary.[19] Hryniokh turned down the bishop's request, preferring to pursue his parish work in the Dakotas instead of engaging in administrative and fund-raising duties.

The intelligentsia deplored the Americanization of Ukrainian immigrants. Bohachevsky worked to adapt the church so that it would survive

17. At their meeting at Lviv, May 9, 1925, the bishops' conference agreed to establish a Ukrainian-Catholic university to combat antireligious views.

18. In 1924 Sheptytsky appointed Rev. Tyt Halushchynsky to set up a secular Ukrainian Christian Organization that would promote Christian politics, Halushchynsky sent out preliminary fliers, but there does not appear to have been much follow up. See Halushchynsky's report to Sheptytsky, TsDIA, Lviv, f. 358 (Sheptytsky), op. 1, spr. 42, pp. 1–2.

19. Rev. Hryniokh, in telephone conversations with the author, April 28 and 29, 2009. Bohachevsky repeatedly offered him more responsible positions after he completed his education at Fordham University, but Rev. Hryniokh (Hrynuck) preferred parish work. At age 100, the reverend father reluctantly gave up his weekly service of the novena. He died in 2012 at the age of 102. One reason for his withdrawal from the limelight may have been that his brother Ivan, also a priest, was very active in the Ukrainian underground in Europe during and after World War II.

acculturalization in the United States. Education would arm his people with the power and ability to preserve the essence of the Ukrainian Catholic faith as well as the church.[20] Conversational Ukrainian might disappear, but the language of worship would remain, preserving a Ukrainian cultural identity.[21] With the help of the Basilian nuns and some of the clergy, the bishop expanded the small, part-time Ukrainian classes, held either through or in cooperation with the church, into full-time accredited schools. By the 1930s Bohachevsky had created a new office at the chancery—coordinator of diocesan schools.[22]

The bishop, despite his "keen eye and quick understanding of the Ukrainian community in the United States,"[23] could not convince the immigrant intelligentsia that his vision was as progressive as theirs. But he persuaded the mass of Catholic Ukrainian immigrants that they could become educated, financially successful American citizens and still remain practicing Ukrainian Catholics.

HIGHER EDUCATION FOR UKRAINIANS

During the messy 1920s, many Ukrainian-Catholic clergy in America forgot that they had been discussing the need for a Ukrainian-Catholic seminary since at least 1907. Bohachevsky's predecessor, Soter Ortynsky, risked his life on the eve of the First World War, to carry out personal negotiations with the local Hungarian government for funding the American project.[24] Given this historical precedent, Bohachevsky did not see the point of further postponing the planning. Immediately upon his arrival in

20. Pastoral letter, February 1938, *Eparkhiial'ni Visti*, 3. In his second pastoral letter to the faithful Bohachevsky provided scriptural support for establishing schools: "Value learning and wisdom, for the Holy Ghost says (Prov 18:16) 'Man's learning widens his path,' but remember that learning is not happiness, only the light that points the way to eternal happiness." *Eparkhiial'ni Visti*, November 1924, 2, 3.

21. Pastoral letters, *Eparkhiial'ni Visti*, June 1925; and again in November 1926.

22. *Propamiatna Knyha iz sviatochnoho*, 45.

23. Rev. Petro Oleksiv, "Teper cherha na dukhovny semynar" [Now Is the Turn for the Spiritual Seminary], in Oleksiv, *Nasha Shkola, Nasha Peremoha*, 24.

24. During his first visit to America in 1910, Sheptytsky blessed the foundations of what was to have been a seminary in Philadelphia. Rev. Isidore Sochotsky, "Ukraiins'ka Katolyts'ka Tserkva vizantiys'ko-slovians'koho obriadu, The Ukrainian Catholic Church of the Byzantine-Slavonic Rite in the USA", 265.

the United States, he initiated mandatory contributions for the seminary. He held the first collection on December 24, 1924. Most Ukrainian Catholics in the United States were not yet celebrating Christmas at the end of December, continuing their adherence to the Julian calendar and celebrating Christmas on January 7. The faithful, surprised by Bohachevsky's request, were not generous; some thought the collection was for a private school in Halychyna. The bishop broached the need to raise funds for the seminary again at the beginning of his second year in the United States (in September 1925), as he would again and again. Indeed, he proclaimed 1926 to be the "year of the seminary."[25]

The first offering Bohachevsky made to the students was to donate the bishop's residence to serve as a dormitory for the high-school boys. By repurposing the bishop's residence into a dormitory, he could establish the minor seminary, the former Institute of St. Paul, as early as December 1924, despite the lack of money and threat of foreclosure. The significance and, I suppose, nobility, of the act was not recognized by the populace. Bohachevsky saw it as the only available means at the time to accommodate future priests. As he explained to the classmate from Innsbruck who wanted a photograph of the seminary, the bishop's residence would temporarily serve as a dormitory for boys who attended local Catholic high schools during the day and studied Ukrainian subjects in the evenings.[26] Willing and worthy graduates of St. Paul's were chosen for theological studies in Baltimore, Rome, Innsbruck, Lviv, Stanislaviv, or the Catholic University of America in Washington, D.C. The American candidates for priesthood sent to Europe had a double burden—dealing with a foreign language as well as speaking nonnative Ukrainian. They also faced a different style of academic presentation and preparation.[27]

At first, Bohachevsky and Takach planned to pool resources, but they, as well as the Vatican, realized that the tension between the Ruthenians

25. Eparkhiial'ni Visti, no. 4, February 1926, 5.

26. The cost was $25 per month for schooling and upkeep, and the boys were responsible for their own linen, clothing, and books, as described in a flyer published by America found at UMAS.

27. A Lviv seminarian studying at Innsbruck wrote to Slipyj on December 12, 1937, that the "five students sent by Dr. Bohachevsky are not well versed in our rite, language, etc. . . . Rev. Stetsiuk spends an hour a week with them for extra lessons." Lystuvannia rektora Slipoho, TsDIA, Lviv, f. 451, op. 2, spr. 213, p. 69.

and Ukrainians was still too raw for collaborative moves. Instead, Bohachevsky began working with the more open-minded Latin-rite Catholic clergy at Catholic schools, developing *ad hoc* programs to serve the special needs of Ukrainians at Latin-rite institutions. With the blessing of the Vatican, the president of the Catholic Union Seminary in Philadelphia at the time, Reverend Augustine Galen, encouraged both new Ukrainian bishops, Bohachevsky and Takach, to partner with this institution. Galen hoped the experience would "weld all racial elements closer together, and, as they go forth, they will bring their own people into more intimate touch with American life and thought."[28] Most likely, however, neither Takach nor Bohachevsky at this time were very much interested in melding rites. They were busy fighting for their own churches. There was little funding for the project, and the experience left a bitter taste in Bohachevsky's mouth. According to Rev. Khlystun, Bohachevsky did not want to initiate direct contact with the Catholic University of America in Washington because he felt that such a move would belittle the Ukrainian Church.[29] I have not come across any evidence to that effect. Eventually, this contact would be established and St. Josaphat Ukrainian Catholic Seminary would be built on grounds near the Catholic University of America.

The institutional base for Bohachevsky's academic program was meager. He began his educational plan modestly, building on existing institutions, paying due homage to all who labored in the field, and hiring from within the community. But most cantors who ran the part-time church schools could not be certified as teachers within the American educational system. Some were more interested in politics, art, and music, than in education. It is also safe to presume that most opposed the celibate requirement for the clergy. Thus, they became the primary opponents of the full-time parochial schools that the bishop wanted to establish and parishioners came to support.

The bishop insisted that the pastors establish schools for the parish children and put off the construction of churches until later. He maintained that without effective schools and a vibrant seminary the beautiful Ukrainian Catholic churches would soon be empty. He personally engaged in fundraising, traveling to raise money for the seminary. He even used

28. Augustine Galen, "A Forward Step in Reunion," *Commonweal* (March 31, 1926), 567.
29. Rev. A. Khlystun to Nazaruk, February 28, 1935, in TsDIA, Lviv, f. 406, op. 1, spr. 22.

the little money he paid himself monthly to supplement the needs of the seminary. To save money he stayed in the residences of the churches he visited, often to the discomfort of the local priests. Even if contributions were only a pittance, even if only coins (pennies on one occasion), the bishop dutifully and humbly put penny to penny, refusing to become discouraged.[30] He taxed each parish a specific sum for the seminary, later for the college, and, of course, for the parish school. He made the same argument for the need for all levels of education: because that was how nations became great—through the steady filter of the learning of God's wisdom by means of human understanding, however faulty, generation after generation.[31] Schools and churches, working jointly, would assure the perpetuation of successive generations. Neither could survive singly. As bishop, Bohachevsky needed priests who would function effectively in the United States, and that essentially meant American-born priests who could reach out to the American-born. Bohachevsky realized that there would be no outside support to build up his church, so he would have to rely on his own resources and on the resources of the faithful to create Ukrainian institutions for the training of the Ukrainian-Catholic clergy so sorely needed in the United States.

The opposition to a seminary remained vociferous, however. Many educated Ukrainians in the United States, and even more in Halychyna, did not see any need for a facility to train Ukrainian-Catholic priests in the United States. Indeed, friends and foes alike questioned the need for a Ukrainian seminary in America.[32] Critics, albeit fewer and less fervent than those who had challenged the bishop in the previous decade, argued that Bohachevsky's dedication to the development of educational and cultural institutions clouded his judgment in matters related to running the

30. Danylo Bohachevsky, *Vladyka Konstantyn Bohachevsky*, 50.

31. *Eparkhiial'ni Visti*, September 1925, 6.

32. Here are two examples of the difficulties which the clergy had collecting money for the planned seminary: Rev. Vasyl Turula from Rochester, in letters dated November 12, 1926, and February 9, 1927, reported that the trustees at the his parish did not approve the increase of chancery dues and the mandatory collection for seminary. They would, however, discuss the issue at the annual parish meeting. The pastor was not optimistic about the outcome. In the same vein, Rev. Myron Zalitach of Scranton wrote in February 1928, that he supported the bishop, but had no funds to offer for the seminary. The parish would not levy extra funds until the next regular parish meeting. UMAS, Chancery Archive.

church. Even Rev. Lev Sembratovych, who had come to the United States with Ortynsky and was one of the few Ukrainian priests who sought to gain greater visibility for the Ukrainian Church in the Midwest, questioned the feasibility of organizing a seminary when there was a lack of simple prayer book.[33]

There were two different approaches to building Ukrainian educational institutions. One group wanted the system to be created from the bottom up; the other argued that upper-level schools should be the top priority in order to expand the class of educated Ukrainians. Both groups in America thought in terms of supplementary, Ukrainian-language programs. Bohachevsky sided with both groups, because both types of school were essential. The bishop thus began a two-pronged educational program—building local Catholic grammar schools while at the same time working toward the creation of a seminary and a college. The schools would teach most subjects in English. They would provide the same course of study as the public schools did but would also offer courses on the history and literature of Ukraine, as well as the Ukrainian language, and religious instruction in Ukrainian.

The bishop built on what little there was and delegated priests to coordinate educational programs, which some simply refused to do.[34] Bohachevsky then turned to the unsung source of Ukrainian-Catholic education in the United States—the young, American-born, Ukrainian girls entering the Basilian monastery. During the years of turmoil, the bishop's work with the Basilian women novices had given him solace and hope, although it had also served as grist for juicy, albeit primitive and spurious, attacks. As Bohachevsky began implementing his educational agenda, the Basilian Sisters again became the bishop's first and major allies, his assurance that there would be a pedagogical staff for the yet-to-be-created schools. Most significantly, the nuns staffed the primary and secondary Ukrainian-Catholic schools and thus prepared candidates for the seminary and the college that were to become the bishop's crowning achievements.[35] The bishop relied on the nuns to build up a teacher

33. Sembratovych to Tarnawsky, March 26, 1934, UMAS, Chancery Archive.

34. "Ukrayinski pochatkovi shkoly v Zluchenykh Derzhavakh" [Ukrainian Grammar Schools in the United States], in *Propamiatna Knyha iz sviatochnoho*, 41–47.

35. Through the decades I profited from long, personal discussions with Mother

corps for the secular schools as well as for the parish schools. With this far-reaching intent, he helped the nuns establish themselves both materially and intellectually. Seeking adherents who would help him achieve his grand dream, the bishop then persuaded the Latin-rite Catholic prelates to permit the Sisters of St. Basil to collect money for the Ukrainian-Catholic schools and their orphanage in Roman Catholic dioceses. As early as 1925, the Basilian nuns transformed the orphanage in Philadelphia into the first full-time, Ukrainian-Catholic grammar school in the United States. The Sisters began with the basics—grade one—adding a grade each year. It was from such humble beginnings that St. Basil Academy, a secondary school for girls, gradually emerged, opening in 1931 as a day and residential high school in the Fox Chase area of Philadelphia. In 1929, Mother Maria Dolzhycka came to the United States to raise money for an orphanage in Halychyna. Recognizing that she had the formal qualifications necessary to administer and elevate the standards of the Fox Chase School for girls, Bohachevsky encouraged her to remain in America. In 1933, the Academy of St. Basil the Great for girls moved into modern boarding facilities adjacent to the motherhouse at Fox Chase.[36] The school's amenities included a science laboratory, a gymnasium, a library, and landscaped grounds—a far cry from the original cramped orphanage in downtown industrial Philadelphia. St. Basil's offered a choice for its students: an academic degree that prepared them for college and a business degree that opened the door to immediate good employment.[37] Given the economic necessity of Ukrainian women in the United States to work, the residential school was a godsend to many Ukrainian families. The official history of the Basilian nuns attests that: "Bishop Constantine Bohachevsky was untiring in his efforts to raise

Emellia Prokopik and Mother Bohdanna Podney, both religious of the Basilian Order, who were among the novices under Bohachevsky's religious tutelage. In a letter to Nazaruk, April 14, 1937, Rev. Protsko reminded the journalist that "during the awful struggle . . . the bishop worked assiduously in raising the spiritual and material position of the Basilian nuns, because he wanted teachers to work with the people, wanted teachers for the Catholic full-time schools." TsDIA, Lviv, f. 406, op. 1, spr. 25, pp. 3–5.

36. Mother Maria Dolzhycka recounted the flavor of the time in a speech delivered at the St. Basil Academy on April 28, 1968, published as "Vivat Academiya," Svoboda, May 9 and 10, 1968. She bemoaned the failure of the post-World War II immigrants to attend these schools.

37. Eparkhiial'ni Visti, November 1936, 69. The article singled out Rev. Andriy Khlystun for his support of the Basilian "business college for girls."

the intellectual and educational status of the American Ukrainians, and so initiated the Ukrainian-Catholic parochial school system, established mission churches, and expanded the schools now staffed by the Sisters of St. Basil the Great. . . . [He] was instrumental in helping the nuns purchase a farm and surrounding land in Fox Chase, Philadelphia."[38]

Initially, the intelligentsia opposed the bishop's ambitious educational program; many felt that there were more than enough priests who could come from the old country. Nor was Ukrainian-Catholic education a priority for the overworked parish priests who dealt with the daily travails of parish life. The cantors, who represented the actively patriotic Ukrainians, resisted the full-time schools as an unnecessary luxury that would reduce donations to the home country as well as their own salaries. But the primary resistance came from Ukrainian community activists who were more interested in collecting funds for political prisoners or other immediate causes. Money for Ukrainian-Catholic schools was a secondary consideration, if it was considered at all. The consensus among the Ukrainian-American intelligentsia was that Ukrainians in the United States could acquire an adequate education in American educational systems. The establishment of Ukrainian-Catholic schools as a community goal simply lacked patriotic panache. As Chancellor Paul Protsko informed Nazaruk some years later: "This work of the bishop appeared rather local, so that the enemies of the Catholic Church could easily attack him in the press and incite the people against him."[39]

In the long run, however, Bohachevsky read the Ukrainian immigrant public better than his critics did. He was aided by the U.S. Board of Education, which broke whatever residual opposition to schooling may have existed among the Ukrainian immigrants by mandating compulsory education for all children. In addition, immigrants who had shown little interest in having their children educated now began to worry about the moral well-being of those children—the old specter of communism was being replaced by the threat of the free and easy flapper. They want-

---

38. Sisters of the Order of St. Basil the Great, "History of the Province of the Sacred Heart Philadelphia, PA, USA," in *Vessels of Election: Sixteenth Centenary of St. Basil the Great; A Historical Sketch of the Sisters of St. Basil the Great, 1037 to 1979* (Philadelphia: Sisters of St. Basil, 1979), 58–59.

39. Pavlo Protsko to Nazaruk, April 14, 1937, TsDIA, Lviv, f. 359, op. 1, spr. 305, pp. 15–18.

ed their children schooled but not corrupted. The faithful supported the schools organized by the church. That was the American way to secure and preserve the viability of the Ukrainian heritage. As support for the parish schools, a high school, and a seminary grew, so did the variety of fundraising efforts. Church picnics grew into large-scale affairs held on farms outside city limits. By the mid-1930s, Ukrainian Seminary Days were held regionally. The bishop enthusiastically participated in these events, raising consciousness of the need for institutions of higher learning as he raised funds for the cause.[40]

Bohachevsky's extremely modest living arrangement, which continued until the last decade of his life, was yet another way in which he demonstrated the primacy of his educational goal over other considerations. Neither the prestige associated with a modestly comfortable residence nor the most beautiful church would ensure the continued existence of the rite. Only the dedicated service of the faithful, under the guidance of God and the church could accomplish the task. The seminary remained a paramount goal: How was the rite to survive without priests? The bishop continued collecting funds and searching for a suitable location for a preparatory high school, the seminary, and eventually a college. The place to be selected had to promote the proper upbringing of boys and demonstrate the full worth of the Ukrainian Catholic Church, and hence of Ukraine. There was a consensus that such an educational ensemble should be situated near a large concentration of Ukrainians living in the United States. The worsening Depression only bolstered the bishop's resolve to push through his educational project. Attempts to acquire land in New York City failed, but the Great Depression, which wreaked havoc on the haves and the Ukrainian have-nots, made the purchase of formerly unreachable property possible. Bohachevsky, through his visitations, thrift, and fundraising efforts, had managed to save money and safeguard these savings from the vicissitudes of the markets. His success in building up the school system and stabilizing the eparchy kept Bohachevsky on an even keel during the Depression.

40. These events were advertised and sometimes even covered in the Ukrainian-American press. Thus on July 22, 1934, Rev. Oleksander Pavliak, with Antin Pashuk, Ivan Borysevych, and Stefan Oles, organized a gala event at the Schuetzen Park in Philadelphia that brought parishioners of different parishes together.

Bohachevsky tried to infuse scholarly content into the eparchy. He created the Scholarly Theological Society (*Naukove Bohoslovske Tovarystvo*) and included short reviews of new Ukrainian-Catholic publications in the *Eparchial News*.[41] He relied on the Basilian printing press to help with diocesan publications. Mandatory retreats were held for the clergy, and the bishop insisted that the priests undergo formal periodic examinations on theological issues and how they affected their pastoral tasks. He repeatedly sought to raise the educational level of the cantors. An attempt was even made to set up a two-year program for cantors that would stress religious chanting as well as a music school.[42] As with many projects that were not directly related to his primary interest, Bohachevsky presumed that someone would take over and bring them to fruition.

THE SEARCH FOR PLACE

The bishop asked everyone to look for a suitable location for sites for schools. The search was complicated by traces of opposition from some of the Latin-rite Catholic clergy to what they considered a useless perpetuation of separate rites within the universal Catholic Church. Catholic bishops, expanding their innovative Catholic University of America in Washington, D.C., questioned the validity of the Ukrainian Catholics' graduate seminary, since the Catholic University of America was to serve all Catholic bishoprics. Bohachevsky sought to calm Latin-rite fears that his educational plans would undermine those of the Roman Catholic Church in the United States. As late as 1941, Bohachevsky felt obliged to write a formal letter to Archbishop Michael J. Curley of Baltimore assuring him that Ukrainians were not trying to undermine the Latin-rite Catholics by establishing their own schools.[43]

41. Announced in the lead article of *Eparkhiial'ni Visti*, March 1926, 1. The society was patterned on the Lviv model, which Rev. Tyt Halushchynsky had established in 1921.

42. *Eparkhiial'ni Visti*, August 1941, 33, enjoined priests "to encourage and insist that cantor-teachers take part in the retreats." *Eparkhiial'ni Visti*, May, 1, 27; and then again in August 1937, on the establishment of the Ukrainian Catholic Music Institute for the training of cantors in the Ukrainian-Catholic tradition, put in a caveat: "if there will be a suitable number of candidates." There is no follow up and no further documentation, so I presume it remained unrealized. The two-year program advertised a $300 annual tuition.

43. "[The Vatican] instructed me to establish a diocesan major seminary in order to

A number of locations were being considered, among them one in Baltimore, one in upstate New York, and another in Philadelphia. Bohachevsky preferred a country location to an urban one, presumably to shield the young seminarians from worldly temptations and to make them physically fit, something easier to accomplish in a rural environment. It is important to remember that most of the Ukrainians in the United States in the 1930s and 1940s were raised in inner cities with few opportunities to enjoy the healthy benefits of "the great outdoors."

In the latter half of 1932 Bohachevsky intensified the search for property suitable for a preparatory seminary and college. He returned to the sites in Philadelphia that his predecessor Ortynsky had considered. He then considered Baltimore, the oldest of the Roman Catholic archbishoprics in the United States. He asked Rev. Vasyl Maniovsky, the pastor of the Ukrainian-Catholic church in Baltimore, to check out the feasibility of buying the buildings of the old St. Joseph's Latin-rite Catholic seminary and an adjoining hotel. The property, dating from the 1890s, would accommodate fifty boys. It seemed to be in good shape. After making inquiries, Maniovsky wrote to Bohachevsky ending his letter with the query posed to him by the Roman Catholic Monsignor Pastorelli, a query that seemed to reflect the old cleric's skepticism: "Where will you get the students?!"[44] But the bishop's trust in God was unwavering: If he built a school, the students would come, Depression or no Depression.

Meanwhile, Bohachevsky gravitated north in his search for a home for

---

assure for the students a proper education [and] to give them a knowledge of our rite." Bohachevsky to His Grace Most Reverend Michael J. Curley, D.D., September 17, 1941, in the Archives of the Archdiocese of Baltimore, B1157. Bohachevsky himself most likely typed the letter, no. 2553, from the bishop's Chancery Office: "repeatedly" is misspelled and mistyped, and the sentences do not have internal punctuation.

44. The handwritten letter is dated November 14, 1932, and addressed simply to the episcopal "ordinariate." UMAS. Rev. Vasyl Maniovsky was born in 1871, and served in the United States since 1915. He died in 1956 and is buried in Baltimore. But it turns out, according to a letter of Rev. Stephen Chechansky (also transliterated as Tychansky) to Tarnawsky dated December 3, 1932, it was Chechansky, in the company of the Rt. Rev. Mons. Pastorelli, who visited and studied the buildings. Chechansky asked Maniovsky to draft the report to the chancery because the younger priest did not trust his written Ukrainian. It seems odd that Maniovsky would take almost a year to draft the letter, so one of these letters has the wrong date. Chechansky asked Tarnawsky to talk the bishop out of founding the seminary in Baltimore: the buildings were in disrepair and the area seemed to be declining in value. Chechansky (1905–1985) was the first American-born man to be ordained a Ukrainian priest.

the seminary. He tried New York again, investigated Yonkers, and looked at potential property further upstate. Ukrainian Church members and Latin clergy offered advice and concrete suggestions. A settlement case in Stamford, Connecticut, an hour's distance from Manhattan looked promising. In his excitement, Bohachevsky confidentially informed Bishop Buchko in Lviv at the end of December 1932, that he might succeed in buying land near New York City for the school and that he had the necessary $50,000—in hand and in cash.[45] In April 1933, Bohachevsky, carrying the $50,000 in cash in his trusty small black suitcase, took the train from Philadelphia to Stamford and bought the property where he would build his cultural center.[46] The Ukrainian Catholic Church thus acquired a site in Stamford, Connecticut, for the preparatory seminary. The Institute of St. Paul was moved there, and a high school was established. The first step to creating the seminary had been taken.

Stamford, Connecticut, bridged two worlds. The town, within commuting distance of New York, had some of the panache of America's upper class, but it was also the site of a Ukrainian-Catholic parish established in 1916, a poor parish whose parishioners worked in the textile and other manufacturing industries that dotted communities to its north. The estate which Bohachevsky purchased for his grand educational and cultural complex stood on land that had been purchased directly from Rippowam Indians back in 1640. The imposing French Second Empire mansion, nestled on eight and a half acres of parkland, was built in 1867 and was later expanded in a French Renaissance style. Eventually the property was adapted for a girls' finishing school, grooming America's young ladies for study at prestigious women's colleges. The school closed as women's schooling changed, but the nativist, high-class pedigree of the estate was important for Bohachevsky, who wanted his Ukrainian Church to be recognized as an important cultural institution. He was proud of the property, and loved its serenity and its old trees. Yet he rarely stayed there and never lived in the impeccably restored building, with its Tiffany lamps, beveled windows, and semi-circular porch that reminded him of his Car-

45. Bohachevsky to Buchko, December 22, 1932, TsDIA, Lviv, f. 201, op. 1, spr. 5952, p. 13.
46. I do not know who accompanied him. Lore has it that he personally brought in his suitcase the $50,000 in the small bills in which the funds had been collected through the years. The money had to be counted a number of times.

pathian home. It was almost as if he were consciously denying himself the pleasures of the place he found and loved, as part of ascetic self-discipline.

It is not clear at which point Bohachevsky's educational project grew to encompass a whole "Ukrainian cultural center."[47] There had not been much local opposition to the establishment of the St. Basil High School and Minor Seminary at Stamford. These were, after all, the first higher learning institutions in Connecticut's rising Fairfield County. Bohachevsky stressed that the Congregation for the Eastern Church had instructed him to establish a seminary. Between 1933 and 1939 the center became a reality as the Stamford campus saw the construction of a boys' high school, a college, a preparatory seminary, a library, and a museum.[48] For good measure, the bishop helped found a Ukrainian-Catholic girls' high school nearby. The Stamford project was costly, and the construction of new buildings drained the treasury. Bohachevsky sent personal checks almost monthly to cover the shortfall. The bishop loved the area.

Bohachevsky immediately opened a high school for boys on the Stamford grounds. The old St. Paul Institute, transferred from Philadelphia, became a full-fledged high school and pro-seminary, accredited by the Catholic University of America. Half of the students were in early stages of clerical preparation and lived in the dormitory; the other half consisted of boys in the regular high-school program. St. Basil's Preparatory School began with an enrollment of twenty-two that doubled within a year. As enrollment grew, the campus expanded, and new classrooms and dormitory buildings were built. Bohachevsky turned to Rev. Stephan Pobutsky and Rev. Petro Oleksiv to mount a collection of the additional funds for the college and seminary. By 1938 the bishop had launched a major drive for a college, and a year later St. Basil's College, accredited by the State of Connecticut and the Catholic University of America, opened its doors to thirty-one students. Bohachevsky fully expected that the college would develop

47. The anonymous author of the brochure *Yak Tvoryt'sia Ukraiins'ky Kul'turny Tsentr v Stamfordi* (Philadelphia: n.p., 1937) wrote grandiloquently: "In the few lonely hours free from the interminable travels to parishes that covered territories as [as large as] the distance from Madrid to the Urals, the bishop nurtured plans of creating a center of Ukrainian culture in America." (8).

48. Opponents snickered that the bishop even planned an academy of sciences. Bishop Buchko, in his greeting in the *Propamiatna Knyha iz sviatochnoho*, expressed hope in the creation of an academy of sciences, and there are little hints of other such comments.

into "a university patterned on the American Catholic colleges and universities."[49] Within two years, with the new buildings completed, the original mansion became the Ukrainian Museum—a critical component of Bohachevsky's dream and the result of his own collection.[50] The museum, though formally opened in 1935, had functioned since 1933, with Rev. Lev Chapelsky as its head. The initial collection included folk costumes, embroidery, handiwork, and *pysanky*, the traditional Ukrainian batiked Easter eggs. Of even greater importance was Bohachevsky's purchase of historical documents, including the proclamations—known as universals—of Cossack hetman Ivan Mazepa (dated January 15, 1704) and Ivan Skoropadsky (February 12, 1712), as well as a sheet of an original poem in Markian Shashkevych's hand.[51] In selecting these and other acquisitions for the museum, Bohachevsky sought the advice of Ilarion Sventsitsky, the director of the Lviv Museum founded by Sheptytsky, and of the archeologist Yaroslav Pasternak. Bohachevsky had worked on the Sheptytsky collection at Lviv before that museum was established. Sheptytsky, sending his portrait to be hung in the new museum, wanted to know what the museum's specialty would be. Chapelsky explained that since there was no other Ukrainian museum in the United States, the Stamford center would try to reflect as best it could the breadth of Ukraine's cultural heritage. He commissioned the premier Ukrainian sculptor of the time, Serhiy Lytvynenko, to create display versions of St. Sophia Cathedral, Kyiv's Golden Gate, the tomb of Yaroslav the Wise, the cross on Taras Shevchenko's grave, and the tower on Shashkevych's Bright Mountain as visual examples of their heritage for Ukrainian Americans.

A fund-raising booklet published in 1937 provided a lyrical description of the buildings and how they were acquired or built. It thoroughly detailed every aspect of the buildings and the staff. Rev. Paul Protsko

49. Rev. Stephan Pobutsky, "Pershy ukraiiiinsky katolytsky diyatsezalny kaledzh v Zluchenykh Derzhavakh Pivnichnoii Ameryky," in Oleksiv, *Nasha Shkola, Nasha Peremoha*, 38.

50. *Iak Tvorytsia Ukrayinsk'y Kul'turny Tsentr*, 15. Bohachevsky's initial seven hundred acquisitions for the museum included Hutsul ethnographic items, incunabula, and manuscripts.

51. *Eparkhiial'ni Visti*, November 1937, 4. Some decades later, Dr. Vasyl Lencyk, the director of the museum and library at Stamford, wrote to my father that the universals are lost, although documentation and photographs of them exist. He presumed that other items had been lost also. Lencyk to Danylo Bohachevsky, April 5, 1973, in author's possession.

ran the whole complex, and Rev. Lev Chapelsky oversaw the library and manuscript division. The campus was elegant. Its total cost was about $189,000, all but $20,000 raised by the bishop himself.[52] Bohachevsky travelled incessantly to raise the funds, arguing, and badgering his impecunious faithful to disregard the Depression and unemployment and support his grand educational venture.[53] He gave his whole to the Stamford complex. He wanted to know all the details, and he handwrote specific instructions to Rector Protsko, as he adamantly resisted burdening the chancery priests with that work. Since he considered the use of personal printed stationery an unnecessary expense, he had a stamp made for the Ukrainian-Catholic seminary at Stamford for correspondence. He attended to all details concerning the campus and those living and working there. He wanted to know what was being done with the seminarians who were caught smoking and how the construction of the fence was coming along.

Oddly enough, the bishop was careful to maintain a separation between his support of the physical complex and the content of the academic program. Although he was outspoken about the students' moral development, he refrained from interfering in the program's academic content. He left that to the specialists. He did offer lectures, but judging from the notes for one such event, they seem to have been more spiritually uplifting than academic in tone. The vicissitudes of the long years of administration had left him no opportunity to pursue his own scholarly interests.

Once there was a building, land, a preparatory school, and operating funds for the college—or as some hopefully referred to it, the Ukrainian university—community support grew. Parishes and the growing Ukrainian-Catholic youth organization held more fundraising activities. All-day picnics in parks or on the outskirts of the cities were very popular, as were dances and door-to-door sales of homemade lottery tickets.

The college formally opened in the fall of 1939. Its goal was to educate a new male elite for the Ukrainian community in the United States. The students included candidates for priesthood in the Ukrainian Catholic Church as well as Ukrainian American-born and local American youths

52. *Yak Tvoryt'sia Ukraiins'ky Kul'turny Tsentr*, 9.
53. Immediate renovations and rebuilding cost an additional $31,000. An additional $89,000 was needed to outfit the college.

who it was hoped would in time become professionals and effective leaders of the community. The Stamford cultural center was meant to serve the entire Ukrainian immigrant community, not only candidates for priesthood.[54] Bohachevsky tried to get as much Ukrainian academic talent as was available to teach at the high school and the college. He did not pay too much attention to the political persuasions of those he recruited. The first teachers were Americans—Oleksa Tykhansky, a native of Olyphant, Pennsylvania, and a graduate of Pennsylvania State University, taught mathematics and physics; and Michael Nagurney, of Jessup, Pennsylvania, and a graduate of St. Thomas College at Syracuse, taught French and English. Other teachers included the composer Antin Rudnytsky and Andriy Mykytiak, an organizer of community schools, both of whom were considered leftists,[55] as well as Mykola Chubaty, from the opposite end of the political spectrum. The bishop appointed Luka Lukiv, a veteran of the Ukrainian Army detachment of 1919, as head of security.

The high school opened with twenty students, and by 1941 had over one hundred. The college was accredited in 1939, and like the high school, attracted lay students as well as those who were considering priesthood. It offered the standard liberal arts college program, including basic sciences. And it also offered additional courses in Ukrainian studies and on aspects of Eastern Catholicism that were not taught elsewhere in the United States.[56]

A special argument had to be made to justify the expense of the library. Bohachevsky enlisted two New York-based, American scholars who were interested in Ukrainian issues, Percival Coleman and Clarence Manning. The latter became interested in Ukrainian subjects after meeting Rev. Humphrey [Onufriy] Kovalsky, a classmate at the Columbia University evening extension courses. They helped build the Stamford library through donations of private collections, which often were in danger of being thrown out as their owners passed away. The bishop periodically bought books for the library, including classics of German philosophy. He also liked John Ruskin, who had argued that one needed to believe in God

54. *Yak Tvoryt'sia Ukraiins'ky Kul'turny Tsentr*, 16.
55. Rev. Khlystun was especially incensed with this appointment because Mykytiak had worked for a time in the Ukrainian Soviet Republic and was considered to be a leftist.
56. Procko, *Ukrainian Catholics in America*, 70, 153.

in order to love one's fellow men and had been credited with saying that "to practice democracy, one must sacrifice oneself," sentiments the bishop gladly embraced.[57]

The dedication of the Stamford property on September 4, 1933, provided a public vindication of Bohachevsky's policies. It was a truly magnificent event, attended by over four thousand people. Finally, a decade after disembarking in New York, Bishop Bohachevsky was hailed by the Ukrainians in the United States as a community leader, a true prince of the church. The Stamford Ukrainian Cultural Center was seen as the apogee of the Ukrainian school system in the United States. For Ukrainian Catholics of that time it meant that awareness of their heritage was ensured. Historian Bohdan Procko described the dedication of the Stamford complex as an event "ushering in a new and brighter era in the history of the Ukrainian Catholics in the United States. It marked the beginning of the end of that non-history of struggles, of doubts concerning the future of the Byzantine rite in America. The American-Ukrainian Catholics could now look boldly to the future."[58]

On September 5, 1937, another major function was held to dedicate the newly built dormitories and classrooms of the St. Basil Preparatory School and the seminary in the presence of thousands of faithful and again to the sound of the united choirs under the direction of Theodosius Kaskiw. In a special pastoral letter Bohachevsky stressed the richness of Ukrainian culture, with its ancient pedigree that antedated the U.S. Constitution. The bishop exhorted all Ukrainians to the unity that only the Christian faith could provide. He used a patriotic simile for the study of Ukrainian—comparing the language to blood in the national organism without which the nation would die. He extolled music and the arts. He wanted to impress the American-born youth with the richness of their Ukrainian culture: Cossack documents, Oleksander Archipenko's statues, exquisite folk arts.

57. John Ruskin (1819–1900), British art critic and social thinker, was pretty much a household name in European conservative circles. From Bohachevsky's handwritten notes in preparation for a meeting at which he proposed mounting an exposition in the library to mark the 1,000th anniversary of Prince Yaroslav the Wise founding of a library in Kyiv. UMAS, Chancery Archives.

58. Procko, Ukrainian Catholics in America, 64. America noted the presence of Bishop Takach from the Pittsburgh eparchy and Bishop Ladyka from Canada; Mykola Murashko represented UNA, which had made a contribution to the building fund.

He drew in his faithful by asking them to pray for the success of their common work.[59]

Bohachevsky's early work with the Basilian nuns—in Peremyshl and in Philadelphia—paid off in the essential role of the nuns in developing Catholic schools.[60] By the end of the 1930s, criticism that the nuns were not adequately educated no longer carried weight. By the outbreak of the Second World War, there were sixteen full-time Ukrainian-Catholic, eight-year grammar schools run by fifty-two nuns. Nuns also ran about twenty afternoon schools in smaller parishes. The Basilian rule of chastity, poverty, and obedience implied humility; and perhaps the broader Ukrainian-American community never fully appreciated the extent of the nuns' sacrifice during the decades in which even the use of the term "Ukrainian" had to be asserted, explained, and often defended. The nuns created a balance between an understanding of America and reverence for Ukrainian traditions.

In 1935 the order of the Sister Servants of Mary Immaculate from Canada also established a number of schools in the United States, including a residential high school for girls at Stamford, and another at Sloatsburg, New York. From 1925, the year the Basilian Sisters had established the first accredited, full-time school on the grounds of the Philadelphia orphanage, the nuns became the teachers who provided Ukrainian-American youth with the skills they needed to become upstanding members of the church and leading members of Ukrainian society.[61]

By 1947 the Basilian nuns, upon the initiative of Bishop Bohachevsky, had also established Manor Junior College for young women, an institu-

59. *Eparkhiial'ni Visti*, November 1937, 35–37.

60. In 1941 with the help of Rev. Ananevych, Bohachevsky brought a few Ukrainian Franciscan sisters to the United States. His vicar, Ambrose Senyshyn, suggested the name of the order be changed to Missionary Sisters of the Immaculate Conception. This order worked in parish churches and established an academy/high school for girls at Sloatsburg, New York.

61. In 1940, the Basilian nuns ran 9 full time grammar schools for 634 children and 12 afternoon programs for 580 children; the Sister Servants of Mary ran 7 full-time schools (449 pupils) and 7 evening schools for 480 children. *Propamiatna Knyha iz sviatochnoho*, 52–54.

tion adjoining the St. Basil Academy for Girls at Fox Chase, a growing area that skirted Philadelphia. Mother Dolzhycka persuaded the Pennsylvania Board of Education that the college would stress Slavic studies, which were not well covered in the state. Despite the best efforts of the teaching staff, however, the interests of the students lay elsewhere. Focusing heavily on business education, the school profited from its location to become a flourishing institution that offers professional training and transfer opportunities. While the Order did all it could to preserve the school's Ukrainian character, most of its student body, like that of the high school, was drawn from the local Latin-rite Catholic population.[62]

The bishop's reliance on the Basilian nuns was vindicated. He wrote to his colleague, Bishop Buchko, on August 3, 1937, that the exarchy was blessed by vocations, but the country was so large that it needed more priests for the growing Ukrainian population: "Last year we had eleven new candidates for theology, [that is,] in only one year eleven seminarians compared to the one hundred priests in the whole exarchate. And it seems we will have a good year again this year. But for now I ardently ask for priests to come here as soon as possible."[63]

In 1940, a year before the United States entered World War II, Reverend Petro Oleksiv edited another fundraising booklet about the Stamford complex. First and foremost, Oleksiv stressed the importance of Catholic education within a Ukrainian cultural context. Without it the community would wither. Professor Mykola Chubaty, a newcomer to America, in an article on Metropolitan Sheptytsky, took special care to stress the importance of the distinctive Ukrainian Catholic Church in the metropolitan's global plans for unity with the Orthodox Church. That underscored Oleksiv's argument on the importance of Catholic Ukrainian schools in America in developing a native Ukrainian-American intelligentsia:

We have to nurture our own conscious Americo-Ukrainian intelligentsia, particularly our own Ukrainian clergy that is aware of its roots. And for that we need to nurture the boys in their own school in their own cultural environment, and in their native atmosphere. This is the platform from which Bishop [Bohachevsky] began his hard labor. He dedicated himself fully to the upbringing

62. Mother Maria Dolzhycka, speech at the Manor College jubilee banquet, *America*, November 19, 1979.

63. Bohachevsky to Buchko, August 3, 1937, TsDIA, Lviv, f. 201, op. 1, spr. 5952.

of Ukrainian youth through the creation of parish schools, the creation of the Ukrainian Cultural Center at Stamford—its high school, library, museum, and the first Ukrainian College in the land of George Washington. And he achieved this goal in a relatively short time.[64]

The continued development of Bohachevsky's educational program was closely intertwined with the repercussions of the Second World War. The bishop's trust in God's providence was justified—some of the repercussions served the eparchy well.

THE WAR BRINGS A HELPER

A few months before the outbreak of hostilities, Metropolitan Sheptytsky had asked Bishop Ivan Buchko, his close collaborator in Lviv, to make a formal visit to the Ukrainian-Catholic parishes in Argentina and Brazil. There may have been other reasons for Sheptytsky's decision, but at least one was political in nature. As a close collaborator and even possible heir to Metropolitan Sheptytsky, Bishop Buchko dealt with the growing interest of Ukrainian youth in Halychyna in the organized nationalist underground movement. Although Buchko was not a supporter of the Organization of Ukrainian Nationalists (OUN), he understood the frustrations of the young Ukrainians, including the seminarians among them, with the growing persecution of Ukrainians in Halychyna. For those who ran afoul of regulations, Buchko offered comfort and help, thus earning a reputation of being an OUN sympathizer. This placed him in a very awkward political position and was one of the factors that made Sheptytsky choose him, rather any other bishop, to embark on the visitation to South America.[65] And that is where, on September 1, 1939, the outbreak of World War II caught Buchko.

Bohachevsky used the opportunity to have Buchko appointed as his vicar. The appointment could be viewed as a demotion, were it not for political exigencies and the matter-of-fact approach of both bishops. Bohachevsky even shared with Buchko the few open complaints he permitted

64. Oleksiv, *Nasha Shkola, Nasha Peremoha*, 1.
65. The disagreements within the close collaborators of Metropolitan Sheptytsky were so open that they not only became public, but were embarrassing. Metropolitan Sheptytsky tried to put some distance between feuding parties.

himself about how Lviv disregards the American flock.[66] Buchko agreed to serve as Bohachevsky's vicar until a permanent suitable candidate could be found, and Bohachevsky viewed Buchko's appointment as a sign of God's grace on the Ukrainian Church:

These evil times again demand we sacrifice and toil for our people in the New World . . . Some of our immigrants have become dejected, even saying that Bishop Bohachevsky is the last bishop [Ukrainians in America will have]. . . . but at this time of despair . . . Christ's Successor lifts us up . . . [by nominating a helper] proving that the Catholic Church wants our people and our church to live on, so that our rite, our inheritance prosper in the New World. So away with all this depression, laziness, lack of idealism![67]

Bohachevsky installed Buchko at St. George Parish in New York City, which was handily administered by the Basilian order. He was very deliberate in ensuring that the clergy add the appropriate episcopal reference, the Greek kyr, to Bishop John [Ivan] in the requisite prayers: "Let us pray for our God-loving Bishops, Kyr Constantine and Kyr John."[68] Buchko relieved some of the administrative pressure on Bohachevsky, and importantly, gave the bishop the comfort of a collegial presence. Most importantly, Buchko made the Ukrainian-American community aware of their bishop's extraordinary achievements.

The Ukrainian Americans in New York gave Buchko a royal welcome because, as an editorial in Svoboda noted, it was quite some time since the United States had had a chance to welcome a "bishop-patriot" such as Buchko. Buchko became as a visible symbol of the vitality of the Ukrainian people. He touched the hearts of the faithful as no other before him, and many of those welcoming him wept openly.[69] But Buchko deftly cut off unwelcome political speeches by intoning the hymn, "Oh Mighty and Sole God, Save Our Ukraine for Us."

The silver anniversary of Buchko's priestly ordination, a month after his arrival in the United States, provided another opportunity to celebrate "the well-known community activist, His Excellency Ivan Buchko." The

66. Ivan Buchko (October 1, 1891–September 21, 1974) was among those considered to be a likely successor to Metropolitan Sheptytsky.

67. Eparkhiial'ni Visti, May 1940, 17.

68. Ibid.

69. Svoboda, May 14, 1940.

tactics, aimed at portraying Buchko as a different type of bishop from Bohachevsky to sow discord between them, failed. Buchko was as wary of politicizing the church, as Bohachevsky. Neither bishop permitted himself to be provoked into this mode. Buchko let the intelligentsia's hosannas slide. Bohachevsky sympathized with the position in which Buchko found himself—after all, Bohachevsky himself had recently been considered a supporter of the Hetmanate even though he was simply extending a friendly hand to Danylo Skoropadsky, a fellow Ukrainian who happened to be an authentic Orthodox, one whose faith he admired. Instead of being politically active, as the Ukrainian intelligentsia wrongly presumed, Buchko worked to ease the residual tension between the intelligentsia leadership and Bohachevsky.[70]

During the first years of the war in Europe, Bohachevsky tried to maintain the momentum for the support of his educational institutions. He stressed that St. Basil College at Stamford was for all boys, not solely for those preparing for priesthood. He used the blessings of the building grounds and the completion of buildings as opportune means of rallying the faithful. But the crowd at the blessing of the college at Stamford in 1940 on Labor Day weekend was relatively small; the Ukrainian-American community was responding to the tension in Europe, rather than to their own needs.[71]

Buchko encouraged the community leadership to see that Bohachevsky's achievements lay not only in the religious but also in the national sphere. He worked with Tarnawsky to achieve what Tarnawsky gauged as a miracle: and the two men persuaded the leadership of the immigrant organizations, including the major fraternal organizations to show support for the cultural center in Stamford and for its founder, Bohachevsky. A committee under the patronage of Bishop Buchko and headed by Rev. Tarnawsky brought together representatives of most of the major Ukrainian community organizations: the Ukrainian National Association, the Providence Association, the Ukrainian National Women's League of America,

---

70. In contrast to Slipyj who expelled any young man believed to be a member of the OUN, Buchko offered both help and advice to the politically active seminarians, and asylum from the Polish police.

71. Rev. Petro Oleksiv edited *Nasha Shkola, Nasha Peremoha*, a booklet to commemorate this event.

the Association for a Hetman State, as well as various church brother-hoods. Local community organizations pooled their resources to carry out a grand and ceremonious day of prayer in Philadelphia, an event which included a concert and culminated in a dinner and dance held on November 24, 1940, all with the aim of raising more funds and calling attention to the projected cultural center. The event was very successful, prompting the untiring Tarnawsky to give at least speculative credit to divine intervention:

We achieved a real miracle—all Ukrainians, be they Catholics or non-Catholics, UNA members or Providence supporters, nationalists, hetmanists, or socialists sat down at the same table. They were all linked by one idea . . . work for their Ukrainian cathedral of learning. . . . For once Ukrainian Americans felt to be one body, one heart, and one soul. . . . We demonstrated that a creative project gathers and strengthens all national forces.[72]

Representatives of these diverse groups carried out a major full-day celebration in Philadelphia on November 24, 1940 (coinciding with the Thanksgiving holiday), of the Ukrainian Catholic College.

For the first time since Bohachevsky's arrival in America, almost the whole community rallied to support him. The committee concluded its fundraising with the publication of a three hundred-page, Ukrainian-language almanac edited by Lonhyn Tsehelsky: *Propamiatna knyha iz sviatochnoho obkhodu Ukraiinsk'koho Katolyts'koho Kaledzha* [A Book of Remembrance on the Occasion of the Festivities of the Ukrainian Catholic College].[73] Bohachevsky's contribution to this almanac consisted of two brief citations from Paul (published in Old Slavonic script): "Where the Spirit of the Lord resides, there is liberty" (2 Cor 3:17), and "Those who dwell in the house of the Lord are the sons of God" (Rom 8:4). The choice was doubtless prompted by the ongoing war in Europe where the two godless tyrannies continued to ravage and abuse his homeland. Most likely plagued by memories of his

72. "Den' Ukraiinsk'koho Katolyts'koho Kaledzha" [Day of the Ukrainian Catholic College], in *Propamiatna knyha iz sviatochnoho*, 11–13.

73. This publication does not have an English title. There is one title on the outside binding, translating as *Commemorative Book on the Ukrainian College Day*, and another inside on the title page, as *The Commemorative Book of the Festive Celebration of the Ukrainian Catholic College*. *Propamiatna Knyha iz sviatochnoho obkhodu Ukraiins'koho Katolyts'koho Kaledzha, 24 Lystopada, 1940, u Filadelfiii* (Philadelphia: America, 1941).

pastoral service on the front, Bohachevsky sought comfort in the words of Paul the Apostle, who also had known the horrors of combat.

In addition to a detailed report on the Stamford school, a large segment provided information on the various Ukrainian part-time schools in the United States and overviews of the "history of Ukrainian educational aspirations and achievements from the beginning to the present."[74] In his postscript, Tsehelsky stressed that the bishop wanted a historical exegesis to prove to American Ukrainians that they could build their own schools.[75] This publication described what must have been one of the most satisfying days of Bohachevsky's highly structured and laborious life. Bohachevsky's speech at the end of the festive banquet brought him a standing ovation. Rev. Tarnawsky, who was not given to panegyrics even about his bishop, nevertheless felt obligated to note that "the torrent of applause that greeted the bishop demonstrated that Bohachevsky was not only the head of the church but also the spiritual-national leader of American Ukrainians."[76] Bishop Constantine's seven-paragraph speech succinctly reflected not his vision of what Ukrainian-American society was or had done but his directive on what the Ukrainian-American community could do. He extolled the superiority of culture over politics, offering as proof the continued popularity of German music and literature in the United States even as Germany was becoming an enemy. Ukrainians, he asserted, also had their own culture in all facets of life and thought, beginning with the "the faith of Volodymyr" which needed to be studied and thus required schools that would engender "love of our heritage. "We need," he stated, "parochial schools for elementary preparation, we need our very own high schools and academies to ground that knowledge, and we need our own college, that is the pinnacle and crown of our scholarship."[77] Bohachevsky focused on the sacrifices that Ukraine and its people had made through the ages while defending "Christ's faith and civilization against the Asiatic hordes." He pointed out the genuine heroism

74. Ibid., 215.

75. Ibid., 140.

76. Titled just "Slovo Preosv. Kyr Konstantyna [Statement of His Excellency Kyr Constantine]," in ibid., 19.

77. *Propamiatna Knyha iz sviatochnoho*, 9. Buchko, in a simultaneous celebration in the lower level hall of the Ukrainian Citizens' Home in Philadelphia, went a step further and called for the creation of a Ukrainian academy of sciences in the United States.

of everyday activity. Speaking to a society known for glorifying its dead heroes, he pointed out the need for another type of heroism:

Their suffering was brief and their death glorious. Our heroic challenge has to be directed against ignorance, sloppiness, lassitude, demagoguery, greed, crudeness, discrimination, ignorance. This is a protracted battle. We will have to toil whole lifetimes, chipping the dense boulders [a reference to the Franko's best known poem], breaking through barriers built not by the enemy, but by our own dear brothers, not by foreigners, but by ourselves, us Ukrainians. Sloppiness in parishes, intransigence of committees, apathy of the intelligentsia—these are the boulders [we have to move].[78]

Bohachevsky ended his speech at the festive banquet on a positive note, adding that the work must continue: "the day calls for people of action and deeds."[79]

ST. JOSAPHAT SEMINARY

With the outbreak of the Second World War, which left Ukrainian territories struggling under Soviet and Nazi occupations, Bohachevsky was forced both to speed up and to modify his plans to open a graduate-level seminary, the crown jewel of his schools. The ten American seminarians who were sent for further study to Innsbruck and Rome at the end of August 1939 had to be brought back to the United States at considerable cost, along with some twenty other seminarians who had been studying in Europe. The students from Innsbruck were transferred to Switzerland, to the Jesuit residence in Sion.[80] These costs depleted the funds which Bohachevsky had

78. Ibid., 18.

79. Ibid., 18–19. Bohachevsky pointed to the British example for belt tightening, reminded his hearers of the erstwhile action in Halychyna to refrain from tobacco and alcohol (Polish government monopolies) and giving the savings to the schools. He reminded all about tithing.

80. St. Basil College File, Stamford, contains the letters from 1940–41 in which Michal Hoffman, the head of Canisianum, conveys expressions of high praise for Bohachevsky from his old colleagues, but also points out that the candidates need to grow more in piety and scholarship. "Pity that Poles won't let them go to Poland where there are all possibilities to study language and liturgy," Hoffman commented. Detailed expenditures connected with the return of the sixteen students (among them John Stock, Antin Ostap, Stefan Khrepta, Mykola Babak, Pavlo Greskiv, and Volodymyr Kachmar) are carefully documented. UMAS, Chancery Archive.

set aside for a full-scale seminary in Philadelphia. He then explored a less expensive alternative and sent the pastor of the Ukrainian church in Baltimore to look at the Latin-rite seminary there. He began studying property near the Catholic University of America in Washington, D.C., and became convinced that the nation's capital would be the most appropriate venue for the seminary of his growing church.[81] Bohachevsky continued to persuade his flock that support for the schools, and especially of the seminary, was more pleasing to God than the funding of additional painting of churches or buying more candlesticks or an elaborate binding for the Gospels or even a golden chalice. Even Luka Myshuha felt it necessary to take out a half-page greeting in the publication that marked the next step in the implementation of Bohachevsky's educational program.[82]

In September 1941 Bohachevsky rented an apartment near the Catholic University of America in Washington, D.C., to house the Ukrainian seminarians studying there.[83] This marked the beginning of St. Josaphat Seminary. Its first rector was Rev. Omelian Ananevych. Within a year, the seminary moved into a rented building in the same vicinity.[84] In 1942 the eparchy purchased land adjoining the campus of the Catholic University of America. Groundbreaking for the building that would become St. Josaphat Seminary began in 1950. The institution formally opened its doors to students on May 31, 1952.[85]

Bohachevsky established the St. Josaphat Ukrainian Catholic Seminary in 1941 by bringing in the first students, although building of the seminary was postponed until construction prices fell, a few years after the war. This delay was similar to that experienced in Peremyshl after World War I. Now, as the Second World War raged, Bohachevsky pushed

81. Procko, *Ukrainian Catholics in America*, 70–71.

82. Dr. Luka Myshuha, in *Propamiatna Knyha iz sviatochnoho*, 215: "I wish that this undertaking succeed and bring glory and honor to the Ukrainian name."

83. Initially Bohachevsky rented apartments for the seminarians at 2315 Lincoln Rd. SE, then a building at 714 Monroe St.; and finally on April 21, 1943, the diocese bought a little more than an acre of land from the Franciscan Society of the Atonement that became 201 Taylor St. NE, the site of the soon to be constructed St. Josaphat Seminary.

84. Athanasius Chimy, OSBM, became the rector in 1941.

85. Procko, *Ukrainian Catholics in America*, 77, summed up the bishop's educational achievements: "by 1949 ... the exarchy was to contain a very impressive list of institutions ... St. Basil College in Stamford. Manor Junior College ... five high-schools ... and twenty-five parochial schools."

relentlessly for the construction of the seminary. "It is time to build a national monument, a living monument: a representative seminary in the nation's capitol, in Washington."[86] It was tough going, but Bohachevsky soldiered on, calling for continued dedication and service from his hard-working priests and generous faithful. He negotiated with the architect, Julian Jastremsky, and put out a request for bids "which do not tie down anybody to anything" because "we need to build quickly to be able to house the students in September."[87]

The bishop made certain that the Washington seminary was well staffed, and it was definitely a matter of pride to him that the Ukrainian Catholic Church had a seminary within sight of the prestigious Catholic University of America. He tried to staff the institution with the best people he could find: Rev. Ananevych; Rev. Athanasius Chimy, OSBM; Rev. Jacob de Boer of the Congregation of the Most Holy Redeemer; and Stephan Hryniokh and Rev. Roman Lobodych, who had represented Ukraine in the Polish Senate, were the first rectors of the institution.

Opposition to Bohachevsky's attempts to establish a full seminary/college for Ukrainian men in the United States subsided, so much so that few even remember that there had been any opposition at all to the undertaking. The ravages of the Depression had removed the person of the bishop from the center of discussion in the Ukrainian press. As a result of his work—the functioning schools, the return of the faithful to the Catholic Church, the disciplined service of the priests—he came to be seen for what he was, a dedicated servant of his church. The growth of the Stamford campus had marked a real change in the role Bohachevsky played in the Ukrainian community in the United States. The community now had visible, tangible proof that the bishop meant to carry through what he planned.[88] He had ensured the means by which the young generation of Ukrainian Americans could be raised in a way that would benefit the Ukrainian nation and the Catholic Church. He had become a pastor for generations.[89]

86. Lenten pastoral letter, *Eparkhiial'ni Visti*, February 1949. He proudly continued: "Land has already been bought on the hills near [the] Catholic University [of America]" (8).

87. Bohachevsky to Protsko, April 14, 1941, UMAS.

88. Each of the publications supporting the Stamford Cultural Center garnered supporters especially from the small businesses which the Ukrainian immigrants still had.

89. "Vidozva," *Eparkhiial'ni Visti*, November 1939, 39.

The world was in turmoil; the fate of Ukraine tragic. But between 1933 and 1939, in a most difficult period for Ukrainians everywhere, Bohachevsky managed to establish grammar schools and high schools, a college, library, and museum, and a graduate seminary. More than ever Bohachevsky realized the importance of his seemingly marginal diocese to the existence of the whole Ukrainian Catholic Church. The church in the United States had not only to survive; it had to help the universal church endure. "Individuals and nations survive only because individuals selflessly dedicate themselves and their wealth. [In contrast] egotism, ideological nihilism, disobedience, a search for comfort and tranquility, and [above all] avarice bring destruction and death. These traits . . . have led many . . . prominent individuals in our nation to a catastrophic end. They lacked the faith and the life drawn from faith."[90]

A fitting sequel to this segment of the story is to mention a letter that Bohachevsky received in 1948 from a recent high-school graduate in a displaced persons camp in Salzburg, Austria. On July 6, 1948, Lubomyr Husar requested entry into the seminary in Stamford. He noted he had just graduated with honors from a Salzburg gymnasium and felt a vocation to the priesthood. Bohachevsky replied immediately that the young man should inform him as soon as he arrived in the United States.[91] In half a century Lubomyr Cardinal Husar would become the archbishop-major of the Ukrainian Catholic Church in independent Ukraine.

90. *Eparkhiial'ni Visti*, August 1941, 33.
91. Husar to Bohachevsky, July 6, 1948; Bohachevsky to Husar, July 29, 1948, UMAS, Chancery Archive.

CHAPTER 11

The Second World War

A DISTANT WAR, YET SO CLOSE BY

Pope Pius XI, who had named Bishop Bohachevsky to his post in America and who had supported him through the most difficult period of his tenure, died on February 10, 1939.[1] The pope's death was a personal loss for the bishop and a reminder of his own advancing age. The College of Cardinals quickly elected Eugenio Pacelli as Pius XI's successor. He was duly enthroned on March 2, 1939, as Pope Pius XII. Pacelli was an experienced churchman, well informed about the Ukrainian Catholic Church. He had good relations with the Ukrainian bishops, including Bohachevsky, but the intimate spark of shared experience between Bohachevsky and the previous pope was missing.[2]

Soon after the death of Pope Pius XI, Germany and the USSR invaded Poland. Bohachevsky's father had died on the eve of World War I in 1914,

---

1. Mother Emellia Prokopik reminisced that Cardinal Pacelli during his two-day stay in 1936 in Philadelphia (at Villanova University) mentioned that Pius XI cherished and valued Bohachevsky greatly. I have not come across that information elsewhere. Prokopik, conversation with the author, March 25, 2011, at the Jenkintown, Penn., motherhouse.

2. Pope Pius XII, more than his predecessors, saw the importance of the American Latin-rite Catholic Church. Where Pius XI saw U.S. Catholics reflecting European identities, the new pope recognized the new modern America with its homogenizing tendencies. His support of Francis Cardinal Spellman gave the American Catholic Church a new recognition in Rome. Spellman was the first American to have been elevated to bishop in the Holy City (1932). Pius XII even lent him his own vestments for the ordination.

FIGURE 11. THREE BISHOPS AT THE HOLY GATES

and Pope Pius XI's death affected Bohachevsky again when war broke out that September 1939. The derisive term that the Axis powers used to designate the period between this date and the disintegration of the Soviet-Nazi collaboration on June 22, 1941, was "Sitting War"—*Sitzkrieg*. In the West the term was the "Phony War." There was nothing phony for the Western Ukrainians, who were immediately incorporated into the Ukrainian Socialist Soviet Republic or used as a forced labor source by the Nazis on the German demarcation line.

The Second World War had additional layers of meaning for the Ukrainian immigrants in the United States than for the average American citizen. For Ukrainians in the New World, the USSR was equivalent to Russia, and the nominal Ukrainian Soviet Socialist Republic was, at best, a shell of a state, and more accurately, a colony. This godless USSR, among its other crimes, persecuted all religions, but it had singled out the Ukrainian Catholic Church for complete destruction. The relationship with Germany was more difficult. What the Western Ukrainian knew about Germany came mainly from years of living under the Austrian Habsburg administration. Moreover, many educated Ukrainians knew Western culture through German literature and translations. Compared to the Soviet Union, the Nazi Reich, at least for a while, seemed the lesser of the two evils, but an evil nevertheless. The brutal policies of the German Nazis against Ukrainians and others quickly disabused Ukrainians of any hopes that they might have had that Germany would free them from Communist control and the oppressive collective farm system. Unlimited war, violence, and political unpredictability in Ukraine would last until well into 1952. For many Ukrainians, Soviet brutality ended only with the end of the regime toward the end of the twentieth century.[3] If the Ukrainian Church were to survive, it had to survive in the West. The American church was the last bulwark.

In his utterances, Bohachevsky deliberately avoided the term "war," since the United States was not a combatant. Instead, he wrote: "Unexpectedly our native land finds itself in a difficult situation." He wanted his faithful in America to recognize the full burden that devolved upon them because of the war: "We must preserve our faith, our rite, our church, our cultural heritage."[4] Bohachevsky reacted to events in America as well as those in Ukraine. He remembered how important the role of the priest was in any crisis. He reviewed the 1935 encyclical of Pius XI, *Ad Catholici Sacerdotii* (*On the Catholic Priesthood*), which highlighted the importance of an active, well-educated, and effective clergy: "A priest has to be a modern man . . . as the Church is modern in that it pervades and encompasses all humanity."[5] He was concerned that the Ukrainian Church would not keep pace with an increasingly mobile American congregation. Now that all contact with the home metropolitanate was broken, there was even greater pressure on Bishop Bohachevsky to ensure the adequate function-

3. For a recent formulation of the argument, see George O. Liber, *Total Wars and the Making of Modern Ukraine, 1914–1954* (Toronto: University of Toronto Press, 2016).

4. Pastoral letter read on the last week of November 1939 at all parishes, *Eparkhiial'ni Visti*, November 1939, 58.

5. "From the Office of the Ordinary," *Eparkhiial'ni Visti*, May 1943, 22. The text was timed before the collection for the support of the papacy, the so-called Peter's Pence. A list of specific instructions on bookkeeping and assorted office procedures followed.

ing of the church in America. The Soviet threat to the Ukrainian Catholic Church in Western Ukraine highlighted the importance of the Ukrainian Catholic Church in the United States.

Both Bishops Buchko and Bohachevsky had known that Buchko's stay in America would be short. His undeserved reputation as a supporter of the radical Organization of Ukrainian Nationalists made him a darling of Ukrainian-American activist émigrés. At the same time it made him an unwelcome guest of the United States, which was slowly but inexorably moving toward an active anti-Nazi stance. After September 1, 1939, the date that the Soviets took control of Halychyna, Buchko was the only European Ukrainian-Catholic bishop in a territory outside Soviet or Nazi control. When the United States entered the war after the Japanese attack on Pearl Harbor in December 1941, Buchko (whose Polish passport showed Austria as his country of birth) had to leave the United States.[6] He headed to Rome early in January 1942.[7]

Bohachevsky was again left without an heir apparent, a fellow bishop who could step into his place were he to die. The expansion of the war made it unlikely that any European candidate would be available in the foreseeable future, so Bohachevsky had to settle for a priest already in the United States. He was determined not to take any chances, adamant in his belief that an episcopal vacancy in the Ukrainian Catholic Church would undermine its existence. He considered not only the growing possibility of his death but also the possibility that the Vatican could be overrun by Fascists or Communists—neither contingency seemed far-fetched to him at the time.

---

6. Immigration gave him ten days to leave the country. Roman Ferencevych to the author, January 20, 2011. For a brief analysis of Buchko's political views see Sorokowsky, "The Lay and Clerical Intelligentsia in Greek Catholic Galicia," 276.

7. The *Modesto Bee and Herald*, December 9, 1941, carried a small item falsely accusing Buchko of being a fascist sympathizer. In Rome Buchko organized an aid committee, and in 1946 he was appointed the official visitator/papal representative to Ukrainian Catholics in Western Europe. Buchko was elevated to archbishop in 1953. He died on September 21, 1974, his important role eclipsed by the drama of Metropolitan Slipyj's release from Siberia and his resumption of activity within the Ukrainian Catholic Church.

Rome concurred. On July 6, 1942, Ambrose Senyshyn, OSBM, was appointed Bohachevsky's auxiliary bishop.[8] Senyshyn was the product of the Order of St. Basil the Great that Sheptytsky had been so instrumental in rejuvenating. He was also a "new" priest—the first cleric in a family of small merchants. His family background made him more attuned with the American-Ukrainian community than were priests who came from the hereditary clergy. He had entered the order in 1923, when he was barely twenty years old. After being ordained by Bishop Kotsylovsky in 1931, he served for two years as an assistant pastor at the Basilian church in Warsaw, arriving at Chicago's St. Nicholas parish in 1933 to minister to one of the largest Ukrainian-American congregations. His nearly fifteen-year service in the priesthood in the United States gave him intimate knowledge of life here on the parish level. The American-born, Ukrainian faithful saw Senyshyn as one of their own. He mixed with people, had a sense of camaraderie with his American neighbors, got along well with the Irish clergy, spoke colloquial English, and even used the informal "you" (ty) liberally in Ukrainian. (The old-fashioned Bohachevsky hardly used the pronoun for anyone over eighteen.)

Thus, this monk, who was born in Ukraine but who had spent most of his life in Chicago, became the first Ukrainian Catholic to be formally ordained a bishop in the United States. The ceremony took place in Chicago on October 22, 1942. Bohachevsky, Takach, and Canada's Bishop Vasyl Ladyka officiated. Finally, Bohachevsky had a successor who was vested with the necessary ecclesiastical powers to take up the reins in an emergency. The appointment and consecration of Ambrose Senyshyn as auxiliary bishop marked a major change in Bohachevsky's administration. Even Bohachevsky's routine changed: To keep his vicar apprised of all that was happening, the bishop now had the texts of his most important correspondence copied into Ukrainian language letters which he sent to Bishop Ambrose almost daily. Each letter either posed a problem that needed to be solved or suggested a course of action, generally accompanied by a re-

8. Bohachevsky provided a brief biography of the nominee in the *Eparkhiial'ni Visti*, August 1942, 24–25. It was headlined "From the Bishop's Ordinariate." Senyshyn was born at Stary Sambir, near Kalush, on February 23, 1903. For a recent biography, see Basil H. Losten, *Archbishop Ambrose Senyshyn and His Vision of the Ukrainian Catholic Church in America* (Toronto: Basilian Press, 2016).

quest for the younger bishop's opinion. This approach was pragmatic rather than social in nature: The bishop's finely honed conscience demanded assurance that, were he to die suddenly, his legacy would not cause any surprises for his successor. It also sharpened the chancery's younger priests' Ukrainian language skills.

Senyshyn helped Bohachevsky expand contacts with Roman Catholics and disseminate information about the Ukrainian Catholic Church. He understood the value of outreach, readily wrote short informative brochures, and felt comfortable among crowds. He was the chief organizer of the First Eucharistic Council of the Eastern Churches in 1941, which was held on June 29, 1941, a few days after the 1941 Chicago Eucharistic Congress, and which featured Bishop Cicognani as the major speaker.[9]

Senyshyn's appointment in August 1942 as Bohachevsky's vicar ensured an orderly transition and further stabilized the exarchy. Bohachevsky had been concerned that the death of his patron Pope Pius XI in February 1939 might be used to review the autonomy of the Ukrainian exarchate. There was always the fear that the Latin-rite Catholic clergy who opposed a separate Ukrainian Catholic Church in the United States might sway the Vatican to its point of view. Bohachevsky used the occasion of Senyshyn's appointment to express his loyalty to the new pope, Pius XII.

Ortynsky built the foundations of our diocese. His achievements came at a great price. . . . A catastrophe threatened because Ortynsky's death removed the heart and brain of the eparchy. The present appointment is critical, in view [of what happened to Ortynsky's] legacy. I am grateful to the Holy Apostolic See for this new proof of its gracious solicitude, and I express my homage to His Holiness Pope Pius XII.[10]

Bohachevsky had the new auxiliary bishop reside at the spot Constantine loved most in the United States—the cultural center in Stamford,

---

9. The Latin-rite Catholic congress was held on June 24; five days later the First Eucharistic Congress of the Eastern Rites featured the nuncio, Amleto Cicognani. Characteristically, *Svoboda* limited itself to a small, front-page item under the headline "Sluzhba Bozha v Katolyts'ko Slovians'kim Obriadi" [Liturgy in the Catholic Slavonic Rite], on June 28, 1941, p. 1, that Bishop Takach celebrated a Byzantine-rite Mass and that the service had been transmitted by radio.

10. Cicognani'a assurances that the papacy would acknowledge the best wishes of the eparchy was duly published in the *Eparkhiial'ni Visti*, August 1942, 24.

Connecticut, where the new bishop could study firsthand the rich cultural heritage of the Ukraine he had left behind as a very young man. This residence isolated Senyshyn from the hassle of daily community life, with its crises and interminable policy discussions.

Senyshyn had proven his political skill by organizing a very successful Eucharistic congress in Chicago in June 1941. He was able to move more resolutely into helping young people organize and was instrumental in expanding the activities of the altar boys. But most importantly, Senyshyn actively reached out to the American world. He published a seventy-one-page brochure in English, titled *The Living Twig of God's Tree*, about the Ukrainian rite. Four years later, he followed with a description of the Byzantine Catholics. He used the radio whenever offered a chance. In November 1946, Bohachevsky demonstrated his reliance on Senyshyn by appointing him president of the seminary and college, as well as of the high school that housed and educated Bohachevsky's beloved second-generation immigrant children.

THE EFFECTS OF THE WAR

The war shattered the lives of Ukrainians in the homeland in Eastern Europe and intensified feelings of helplessness among the Ukrainian-American settlers, most of whom had family back home. For Ukrainian immigrants, the first and foremost enemy (even before the United States contemplated direct entry into the hostilities) was the Soviet Union, viewed as a godless tyranny whose crimes were beyond human imagining.

American entry into the war placed additional burdens on the American Ukrainians. Bohdan Procko counted some 28,000 men and women, out of a church membership of 303,069, who were actively serving in the U.S. military. The Ukrainian parishes were financially strapped. Donations dwindled. All church construction had to be stopped, including work in churches that had already set money aside for this purpose. Bohachevsky stressed unity, and the need for public support of the educational institutions that would assure that goal. The fall of Halychyna to the Bolsheviks and of France, among others, to the Nazis, Bishop Constantine pointed out to his priests, meant that there would be no clergy or intelligentsia coming from Europe. Ukrainians in America would have to rely on their own resources, on their Ukrainian Catholic schools. Bohachevsky worried that unrest in Europe could have direct repercussions on Ukrainian-American society and worked to maintain peace in the parishes. In February 1939, the bishop's office reminded the priests that collections at all functions held on church properties were to be sent to the chancery, which would then forward funds to designated recipients or institutions. "This will foster a sense of solidarity among the clergy and a sense of duty among the faithful and will highlight the charitable and patriotic work of the church."[11] No wartime shortages could deter Bohachevsky from preparing for the future—establishing the graduate seminary. He issued direct instructions to Rev. Paul Protsko: "I want to be absolutely clear. I want to prepare everything to be ready to build [the seminary in Washington], so we should provide specifications to the contractors and solicit . . . bids from them."[12] By the end of the war, Bohachevsky had bought land in Washington for the seminary. In keeping with this plan, the bishop set up a committee for the building of the seminary in the nation's capital.

Bishop Bohachevsky had firsthand information on what was happening in his native lands during the first two years of the war. One of his American-born students, Bohdan Olesh, was a student at the Lviv seminary when the Germans invaded Poland on September 1, 1939, and most of Halychyna fell to the Soviets. The young seminarian was finally able to leave the USSR only in February. After his return to America, he provided an account of his activities in the newly expanded USSR. The bishop kept the account, signed by the transparent pseudonym Oles Bohdan, marking it "keep confidential."[13] It could have made an immediate best seller, but at the cost of the people described. The Youngstown-born seminarian recounted his saga with no embellishment, beginning with the execution of Ukrainians by Polish authorities as the Polish Republic fell, followed by

11. *Eparkhiial'ni Visti*, February 1939, 1. That year the May issue of *Eparkhiial'ni Visti* also reprinted Khomyshyn's lengthy pastoral letter on the importance of the independence of the church. The papal letter appealing for world peace was duly published in the May issue of the *Eparkhiial'ni Visti*.

12. Bohachevsky to Protsko, April 14, 1941, UMAS.

13. The typed copy of the report, headlined "Halychyna, 1 September 1939–28 January 1941," is marked in Bohachevsky's hand "Attention. Very Confidential. +Constantine, Epp." UMAS, Chancery Archives.

even more brutal terror by the Soviets. Stranded without money and under pressure to accept Soviet citizenship, Olesh nevertheless contacted the clergy in Stanislaviv, Lviv, and Peremyshl, as well as in border villages in Halychyna. He travelled twice to Moscow to reaffirm his American citizenship before he was permitted to leave for the United States via Japan. Olesh, as his superiors, did not want to place the clergy and the faithful in Ukraine under greater risk by publicizing their bitter plight. That self-censorship continued to guide the community in the United States for the next fifty years.

Bohachevsky had received an earlier confidential report from a Belgian Dominican priest who had made his way to Warsaw from Lviv via Peremyshl. He reported that by 1941 over four hundred priests had been arrested, a dozen Basilian monasteries closed, and scores of nuns raped. The Belgian confirmed the arrests, including that of Bishop Kotsylovsky, and provided the text of the statement that Ukrainian Catholic priests had to sign if they did not wish to be exiled to Siberia: "I, so & so, and my whole parish, without any pressure, request the lay delegate of the Religious Department to kindly accept us into the Russian-Orthodox Church." If the priest refused to sign the document, he would be arrested. Since there were not enough Orthodox priests to staff all Ukrainian Catholic parishes, the exiled Catholic priest was often replaced by an approved functionary who had undergone three to six weeks of training in what the people called "the Stalinist course in theology." The Belgian ended his account with what he, a foreigner who had accepted the Eastern rite to work among Ukrainians, found most important:

Barely a month after the arrival of the Bolsheviks, the people drastically changed their relationship to the clergy. From 1940 on the faith grew in the people. There were huge manifestations [of faith]. More people receive the Host, even on workdays. They come to help the clergy, even in real estate matters. The whole people rise against Bolshevik propaganda. Large numbers join underground partisan organizations motivated by their national and religious convictions. The partisan movement is very strong in these lands, and it has a religious flavor and even lives up to some basic religious principles.[14]

14. Memorandum of Rev. Papp given to a Basilian priest in Warsaw, translated into Ukrainian by Rev. M. Gniesco. UMAS, Chancery Archive.

The terror of the war, the indiscriminate killings, and the internecine bloody feuds within the Ukrainian nationalist party (the Organization of Ukrainian Nationalists) provided confirmation to Bohachevsky of the complete failure of materialism. Were he ever in need of validation of his convictions, the two world wars in the life of his generation more than provided it. In his sermons and writings, the bishop tried to impose his moral authority on his flock, convinced that this was the only way to make a lasting impact on society. He focused on realistic goals, and especially on those that strengthen the church and its organizations. He had neither the ambition, nor the talent, to venture into a leadership role beyond the structure of the church. His forays into "bigger politics"—mostly limited to sporadic contacts with Ukrainian monarchists and some long-range ideas on the short-lived Carpathian Republic—were emotionally satisfying, but politically barren. Moreover, the levelheaded bishop expected no miracles within the limited public sphere of the Ukrainian-American community.

The bishop had to maintain stability and project an image of strength amid the terrible news from the homeland. His own experience at the front lines in the previous world war made him realize how little could be done to influence either the course of the war or its randomness toward any individual. He recognized that Ukrainians were victims of forces beyond their control and even beyond their comprehension. They would be crushed between two totalitarian states, the USSR and Germany. When the United States entered the fray at the end of 1941, Ukrainian-American immigrants were as lost in great power shifts and small state shenanigans as any of their average American neighbors. A sense of anxiety for their own safety pervaded the Ukrainian-American community. Would Ukrainian Americans, whose place of birth was the former Habsburg Austria, be seen as enemy aliens?

As always, the aged but untiring Rev. Fylymon Tarnawsky managed to provide a reason for a joyful celebration. In August 1941, thanks largely to his efforts, the renovation of the Philadelphia cathedral was completed in time to mark the thirtieth anniversary of Metropolitan Sheptytsky's blessing of the structure. The interior of the Protestant building had been transformed into a gold-bedecked Byzantine church, with a new iconostasis, hidden confessionals, and traditional icons. Bishop Bohachevsky saw signs of renewal and hope in the renovation. He singled out Pavlo Protsko,

Oleksa Pyk, and Fylymon Tarnawsky for their work in assuring that the cathedral remained in Catholic hands and launched into a small historical exegesis. He focused on Sheptytsky's blessing of the Philadelphia cathedral back in 1910, and then surprisingly reminded his public: "[then] came 1926, the year of the [so-called] 'congress,' [whose] commandment [was to] fight."[15] This is the closest that Bohachevsky came to an emotional outburst, he dropped the subject immediately, reverting to an upbeat praise of the renovation, which was important "because all the faithful, especially foreigners, measure our faith and our culture by the beauty of the cathedral."[16]

The initial émigré war efforts focused primarily on extra prayers for the homeland, for America, and for the church. Homebred politicians developed their analyses in the émigré press. The bishop and the clergy condemned violence and spoke out against the persecution, but they continued to refrain from direct political involvement. During the first years of the war, the bishop put greater stress than ever on the argument that the structure of the Ukrainian Catholic Church had saved the nation in times of dire need: "The whole life of our nation developed and continues to develop around our churches."[17] To extend the church's reach, the eparchy launched a new weekly newspaper, The Way (Shliakh). It was published in two languages (English and Ukrainian) under the auspices of the lay apostolate and was financed by the eparchy. The newspaper was: "to unite all diocesan organizations under the leadership of the clergy into one entity of faith and the works of faith with the bishop in unity with the Holy Catholic Church, founded on St. Peter and his successors, the Roman pontiffs."[18]

The Way encouraged the Ukrainian immigrant community in the United States to engage in constructive social and economic work. The Way "fostered the [intellectual] growth of the faithful, re-educating them, reforming the parish."[19] Irene Tarnawsky, the American-educated daughter

15. "Blessing of the Renovated Cathedral," Eparkhiial'ni Visti, August 1941, 32.
16. Ibid.
17. Christmas pastoral letter, Eparkhiial'ni Visti, November 1942, 36–37.
18. From the lead article of the first issue of The Way. On January 5, 1940, the bishop handwrote a letter of thanks to one of the elder priests, Volodymyr Obushkevych, for "being the first to support . . . our own newspapers." UMAS.
19. "Our Eparchial Newspaper," Eparkhiial'ni Visti, May 1940, 20.

of Rev. Fylymon, managed the newspaper and recruited younger contributors. Bohachevsky was so pleased with the newspaper that he wanted to increase its run, but the wartime paper shortage prevented him.[20] Each pastor had to sell a specified number of issues of the bilingual newspaper, or pay for them himself. Some priests complained that the requirement to buy both the English and Ukrainian versions of the paper was burdensome.[21]

THE SEMINARY, CONTINUED

The longer the war lasted, the more Bohachevsky feared for the fate of the Ukrainian Catholic Church. The functioning of the church in the United States as an exarchate did not automatically assure its continued existence, and the United States was an ally of the Soviet Union, an open and persistent challenger to the very existence of the Ukrainian Catholic Church. The Ukrainian Catholic Church in America had to prove its viability repeatedly. Bohachevsky was convinced that only a well-run, full-scale seminary would offer Rome irrefutable proof of the Ukrainian Catholic Church's long-range future in the United States. The seminary would not only provide a clergy; it would evidence the exarchate's readiness to be recognized as a diocese.

Bohachevsky knew that the war in Europe would end with Germany's defeat—that much was clear to the former Austrian chaplain from the very beginning of the war. It was the Soviet Union that was the great unknown and the threat that made timely action imperative. Were (as many hoped) the USSR to crumble, the vast Eurasian plain would need spiritual sustenance; at a minimum, Ukraine would need Catholic priests. That made the need for the seminary more urgent. The seminary would produce the clergy who would ensure the continuation of the all-but-destroyed church in Ukraine and minister to the church in America as it grew and changed.

20. Letters of March 14, 1945; and Bohachevsky to Protsko, January 8, 1940, UMAS, Chancery Archive.

21. Rev. Volodymyr Dovhovych, from Elmira Heights, New York, in a letter dated May 8, 1946, wrote that there were few takers for the Ukrainian edition of The Way. He also complained that the Ukrainian Catholic Church did not pay adequate attention to converting Protestants to Catholicism. UMAS.

Where others dreamt of peace, Bohachevsky saw a grand seminary ready to prepare God's cohorts. Even as the war stretched the resources of the Ukrainian Catholic faithful, it did not dampen the bishop's drive to complete the construction of the seminary in Washington, D.C. He argued the point in a statement prepared in November 1939 and scheduled to be read on Christmas Day: "Our Ukraine has fallen into the hands of the Godless communists. They are destroying our whole inheritance for which we toiled hundreds of years. They are destroying our church as they had destroyed it in Eastern Ukraine. We have freedom here in America. We can educate priests for ourselves and for them [in Ukraine]. Do not skimp on your donations for Stamford."[22]

Bohachevsky did not bother to explain the connection between the imminent danger to the Ukrainian Catholic Church at home and the need to expand Ukrainian Catholic schools in the United States. He had made this connection many times. He simply informed the clergy that the blessing of St. Basil College in Stamford was set for Labor Day weekend of 1940. The bishop's feverish pursuit of the founding of a uniquely Ukrainian seminary in the United States suggests that he realized that his diocese would confront its greatest challenge after the war: the destruction of the Ukrainian Catholic Church in Ukraine and the influx of a new wave of immigrants. Between 1939 and 1941, Bohachevsky had feverishly sought to find a home for the graduate seminary. Regardless of what happened between the warring parties in Europe, the fate of the Ukrainian Catholic Church was paramount.

Nevertheless, the proposed seminary in Washington became the first Ukrainian-American casualty of the war. In 1938 and 1939 the bishop, unwilling to accept that war was imminent, sent some twenty seminarians off to study at the Pontifical College Canisianum at Innsbruck, Austria, and at the seminary at Lviv. By the summer of 1940 these young men, as well as about another ten who were studying in Europe, had to be brought back to the United States, at great financial, not to mention emotional cost. The largest group of seminarians, those studying at Innsbruck, in-

22. *Eparkhiial'ni Visti*, November 1939, 59. November 1 had been a traditional day to mark the establishment of the Western Ukrainian Republic in 1918 and to commemorate Ukraine's fallen. Bohachevsky marked that day.

curred the highest costs because the Jesuits brought them to Switzerland after Hitler closed the Catholic institution.[23] All American seminarians had to be brought back to the United States, and the bishop had to cover the cost of their return.[24] The expense caused a major dent in the diocesan finances.

To maintain schools with a uniquely Ukrainian academic component, Bohachevsky needed help from religious orders. They were willing to work for a pittance and work selflessly at that. In 1944, with the help of Bishop Senyshyn, Bohachevsky founded a new order of women, the Missionary Sisters of the Mother of God. These women dedicated themselves to service for others as a means of venerating the Blessed Virgin of the Immaculate Conception. The new order established the Mother of God Academy, a high school for girls, at Stamford, Connecticut, and managed the households of both bishops. An order from Halychyna, the Sisters Servants of Mary, founded another residential high school for girls at Sloatsburg, New York, and later, a home for the elderly. While in Brazil, Father Ananevych helped establish the Franciscan nuns in that country in 1933. Some member of the order came to the United States for a brief stay in 1939. Yet another order, the Servant Sisters of the Sacred Hearts (a distinct order from the French-founded Order of the Sacred Heart) were brought in from Italy in 1948. At the request of Pope Pius XII, in 1945 Bohachevsky welcomed the Byzantine-Slavic rite Franciscans to the United States—Roman Catholic clergy who were prepared to minister to Eastern Christians. Another order, the Redemptorist monks, took over the Newark-based St. John the Baptist School and parish in 1946. Bohachevsky prayed that all monastic orders would flourish, and his prayers seemed to be answered. He expanded the teaching and museum staff at the Stamford campus and turned to the activists in the Ukrainian Catholic Youth League for further assistance. He was happy to hire new talent from this pool, especially Eva Piddubcheshen, an activist from the Catholic Youth Organization, and Maria Klachko, a historian who arrived from Western Ukraine to join her immigrant father. Bohachevsky considered hiring Volodymyr Dushnyck

23. Most seminarians were well taken care of by the Jesuits; some however, had to pawn their valuables to get by.

24. Using the experience as a teaching tool, the bishop expected the seminarians to provide detailed accounting of their expenses.

who had completed his undergraduate studies at Louvain University in Belgium and had recently acquired a master's in history from Columbia University. The young man, however, was drafted into the army and then chose a political rather than an academic career.

Despite all the shortages and difficulties, Bohachevsky found people to contribute to and produce an almanac honoring the centenary of the death of Rev. Markian Shashkevych (1811–43), the priest who had been the first to preach in vernacular Ukrainian in Halychyna. During the memorial celebration Bohachevsky delivered a tightly structured and highly emotional overview of Shashkevych's short life. Uncharacteristically, he also reminisced about the 1911 celebration of the centenary of Shashkevych's birth. The book was published "with the episcopal blessing and fatherly advice and help of the great supporter of Markian's ideas on the American soil, His Excellency Kyr Constantine." It contained articles by the young Stephen Shumeyko and Bohdan Katamay, later activists in the community.[25]

The bishop's disciplined focus on what he could do, rather than lament his inability to influence what he could not control, served him well during the war years.[26] There was never any doubt in his mind that despite the horrors that his generation had to undergo or witness, the goal of God's Providence was the salvation of His creation. Bohachevsky's reasoning was straightforward, and he vividly expounded on it in the Easter pastoral letter in 1947, a year after the destruction of the Ukrainian Catholic Church in the homeland: "Our faith, our holy faith, active faith, this faith is in itself a victory. This is the faith that achieves, wins. Christ is risen. Faithful, arise."[27]

THE DOMESTIC FRONT

Bohachevsky also had to contend with other, by now familiar, community complications. Luka Myshuha rejoined the church, but did not offer the

25. Quotation from the dedication page of *Propamiatna knyha Amerykan'skykh Ukraiintsiv vydana u stolitniu richnytsiu smerty o. Markiiana Shashkevycha 1843–1943* (Philadelphia: America Publishers, 1943).

26. The bishop's direct involvement in all affairs of the Stamford complex is evident from the increased correspondence, as well as from its tone. At times, the bishop even permitted himself a flippantly friendly joke in a letter.

27. Easter pastoral letter, *Eparkhiial'ni Visti*, February 1947, 3.

bishop the expected formal public apology. Bohachevsky did not insist. But both Myshuha and his colleagues sought ways to partner publicly with Bohachevsky to demonstrate that Myshuha was cooperating with the bishop. In December 1940, Myshuha organized a concert, to be held at New York's Town Hall, in honor of Metropolitan Sheptytsky, which he felt Bohachevsky would not dare to miss. This would put Bohachevsky on the same stage with Myshuha, who was to be the main speaker. While Bohachevsky let the lack of public apology slide, he would not appear with Myshuha. In solidarity with Bohachevsky, none of the clergy attended the concert.[28]

On the other hand, Bohachevsky gladly shared the limelight with Senyshyn, his younger colleague, although that was not without its mis-understandings. Their relationship was cordial—open, but not intimate. From the start, the elder bishop made certain that the younger man be fully drawn into the work of the exarchate. Senyshyn, for his part, tried to lighten Bohachevsky's approach to work and living conditions. He vain-ly suggested vacations or pilgrimages, or at least better public exposure than the elder bishop's visitations, which were too informal, too centered just on the Ukrainian parishes. In direct contradiction to Bohachevsky's wishes, Senyshyn prepared a celebration of the twentieth anniversary of Bohachevsky's episcopate, which fell in 1944. The auxiliary sent invita-tions soliciting donations for a residence for the bishop. Bohachevsky was chagrined, refused to participate, but controlled any public sign of his outrage. The younger bishop argued that canceling the event would un-dermine him and expose the eparchy to ridicule. Bohachevsky gave in to Senyshyn on the condition that the festivities be prayerful and not focus on the bishop's anniversaries. He insisted that they be held at the Stam-ford facilities and not in some commercial hotel.[29] Senyshyn arranged

28. *Svoboda*, December 31, 1940, front-page article, with a comment that the *New York Times* had a note about the concert, at which both Antin Rudnytsky, the composer; and his wife, Maria Sokil, the singer, took part. Rudnytsky's sister, Milena, in her memoirs ("Z my-nuloho rodu Rudnyts'kykh") mentioned that at an earlier meeting with Antin Rudnytsky, Bohachevsky pointed out that one of their indirect ancestors in the sixteenth century was Lev Rudnytsky, bishop of Lutsk. Milena Rudnytska, *Statti, Lysty, Dokumenty*, ed. Martha Bohachevsky-Chomiak, Myroslava Diadiuk, Yaroslaw Pelenski (Lviv: Central State Histor-ical Archive, 1998), 39.

29. The biography of Bohachevsky that was included in the Jubilee program contained serious errors. In it, Bohachevsky is twice made prefect of the seminary at Innsbruck, and

for the Sodalities and the Apostleship of Prayer to meet a few days apart around the anniversary of Bohachevsky's episcopal ordination. Thus, on Sunday, June 11, the bishop met with the Sodality delegates. A few days later, on June 16, a special conference for the clergy was held.[30] On the following Sunday, June 19, 1944, the Apostleship of Prayer convened their gathering. Some forty parishes sent representatives, as did many religious and some public organizations. A concert and dinner were held in honor of the bishop. The speeches were not preserved, but some individual congratulation letters were, and these attest to the linguistic and educational variety among the faithful and the clergy. Rev. Dr. Myroslav Simenovych, characterizing himself as "arch-jubileer," used the occasion to provide a three-page handwritten missive comparing Bohachevsky's educational achievements to those of the sixteenth-century metropolitan, Petro Mohyla. Other greetings, written with varying knowledge of either language, painfully illustrated the strained economic conditions of clergy and faithful alike while stressing the spiritual comfort that the church under Bohachevsky's leadership provided.

COLLATERAL DAMAGE: THE UKRAINIAN DISPLACED PERSONS

The war and the U.S. government's security measures mobilized the Ukrainian-American community even before there was any hint of the tectonic changes that would come after the war with the influx of new immigrants into the United States. The fraternal organizations managed to bury their differences, bring together the nonsocialist émigré groups, and establish (in May 1940) a new coordinating organization, the Ukrainian Congress Committee of America (UCCA). The Providence Association hesitated to join, concerned about the worldviews and politics of some of

---

the name of Rev. Eugene Husar is presented as Huzarevich. The letters, although many are pro-forma, nevertheless provide a rare, less formal look at the clergy. The booklet also featured articles on and photographs of the Stamford complex and the summer camp at Stratford, N.Y.

30. In addition to schools, homes for the elderly (including a residence for retired clergy) was a popular topic. Bohachevsky had tried vainly to impose mandatory insurance for the clergy to ensure that they have a retirement fund. The priests were pastors of their flock, but each one was an individualist in private finances, and few agreed on a pension plan.

the constituent groups. Bishop Bohachevsky waited to see what this new organization would accomplish on its own as he and his vicar pursued different venues through which to help the European needy.

Predictably, without the active participation of the Catholic faithful, the UCCA was mostly dormant. Bohachevsky remained wary of political activists and their overarching rhetoric. Finally, in 1944, the Providence Association leadership overcame Bishop Bohachevsky's ambivalence toward the UCCA, convincing him that the new organization's focus on humanitarian and cultural issues would not embroil the church in party politics or compromise it by non-Christian acts and extremist ideologies. The Providence Association began to play a leading role in the UCCA and became one of its strongest pillars.[31] The UCCA, as the organization continues to be known, sought to represent the entire Ukrainian-American community, excluding its communist faction. Its leaders made no open demands on the churches, other than to request prayers at public events. They collected funds at a discreet distance from church grounds, and the pastors pretended not to notice any infringement against eparchial policy.

As the war ended, so did the wan hope that the anti-Soviet and anti-Russian insurgencies in Eastern Europe could succeed. Eastern Europe fell to the Soviet bloc. The war created what seemed to be a mass of displaced humanity that flooded Western Europe. Ukrainians who had been forced into agricultural labor in Germany or into labor camps, those arrested by the Germans, and all those faced with the inevitable Soviet control of Eastern Europe, fled as far west as they could, joined as well by others who, for whatever reasons or exigencies, had survived the Nazi camps. These people became known as the "displaced persons," or DPs.[32] Some had been forcibly indentured into the Nazi economy. Others had fled as the Soviet troops advanced. They had no legal standing, most had no money in any currency, and there were no economic or legal structures in the bombed-out landscape to help them. Their misery was palpable across the ocean but especially to the Allied troops. Moreover, in line with the terms of an

31. Kuropas, *Ukrainian Americans*, 285, relates that 805 delegates from 168 communities met in Washington, D.C., on May 24, 1940, to establish the UCCA.

32. For an overview, see *The Refugee Experience: Ukrainian Displaced Persons after World War II*, ed. Wsevolod Isajiw, Yury Boshyk, and Roman Senkus (Edmonton: Canadian Institute of Ukrainian Studies, 1992).

international agreement and to bring back the Allied pilots who landed or were shot down over Soviet territories, Great Britain and the United States began to repatriate the refugees forcibly to the lands that became part of the Soviet Union. Faced with violent opposition (including mass suicides), the Allies devised a system of categorizing displaced persons. Those who had collaborated openly with the Nazis were either arrested or evicted from the camps with no hope of any aid. The rest were placed in camps where they received temporary housing, food, and some training. The question remained what to do with them in the long run and where to put them while this was being decided. Time and resources were limited. The post-war reconstruction, which began with care for the displaced population, is one of the most uplifting stories of the century that played out as the Soviets insisted that all residents of lands that were now incorporated into the Union of the Soviet Socialist Republic be transported to the USSR, regardless of their wishes.

There were about three million Ukrainian refugees in Western Europe after the war. Among them were some three hundred Ukrainian Catholic priests, most with families. They were Bohachevsky's first concern. It is impossible to determine whether he was surprised by the number of clergy who had left their parishes in Ukraine with permission or under fear of persecution. Instead, pragmatist that he was, he tried to work out a way to bring as many priests to his diocese as he could, even if he had to bend the rules. Bohachevsky worked with Bishop Buchko, Cardinal Tisserant of the Congregation for the Eastern Church, and the American government and military authorities to bring the priests and their families to the United States. But the critical element was the readiness with which the Ukrainian-American community responded to their people in need.

To justify the immigration of so many Ukrainian Catholic priests into the United States, Bohachevsky needed to prove to the Department of Immigration and Naturalization that there was a request for their services. The legalist Bohachevsky confided to Tarnawsky what had to be done to satisfy this condition. The letter, dated November 1, 1945, and marked "Confidential" reads:

> For some time now, the chancery has been getting requests from our refugee priests for inclusion into our diocese. You know well the reasons for such heart-wrenching requests. The bishop's ordinariate has been trying and con-

tinues to strive to get permission to bring the reverend fathers to the United States. I still do not know what the result of these attempts will be. There is some likelihood that these attempts could have some success. There is one thing certain, however. It will be necessary to provide individual affidavits for each priest separately, with proof of where and in which parish there is a need for a priest and that the priest will receive full and suitable support from the parish community. Should the Immigration authorities check on the information it will be necessary to provide full proof. To prepare such a list that there indeed is a need for [more] priests, please let us know confidentially as soon as possible if your parish needs an assistant priest and if—as well as how—will a suitable livelihood of that priest be ensured. Many of these refugee priests are married and have families. Write to us confidentially and do not talk about this with anybody, or promise anyone anything, because we cannot know if we will receive the needed permission [from Immigration] nor if we [the chancery] would be able to provide you with material support. For the time being, we [the chancery] need to demonstrate that there are pastors who can prove such a need and prove as well that they would be able to provide the necessary material support for the refugee priests from their parish.

I ask you for a quick reply. Constantine, epp.[33]

The American Ukrainian clergy, hardly enjoying a comfortable life themselves, rose to the challenge. Parish communities, in an unprecedented show of support, sponsored not only the clergy but other refugee families.

The Ukrainian community in the United States worked on two fronts. It kept up its defense of the right of Ukraine to be a sovereign country, although the emergent United Nations complicated this point with the nominal recognition of the independence of the Ukrainian Socialist Soviet Republic. It also began to organize a relief effort for the refugees in Europe. The first battle was to establish some legal standing for the "displaced persons." This was achieved in 1948 through the passage of legislation that cleared the arrival of Ukrainian immigrant displaced persons to the United States. The second front was to speed up the relief effort; for this the community came together and demonstrated an unprecedented outpouring of genuine charity. Concern that Ukrainians in Western Europe were being forcibly repatriated to the expanded USSR pushed the Ukrainian Catholic Church in America into what could be perceived as po-

33. Bohachevsky to Tarnawsky, November 1, 1945, UMAS, Chancery Archive.

litical action: lobbying U.S. government authorities to prevent the forcible repatriation of Ukrainian laborers and other émigrés to what had become Soviet lands.

Bohachevsky again postponed construction of the seminary. The plight of refugees was more pressing. They needed the basics—food, clothes, and shelter. Some provision for their resettlement had to be addressed. The effort would have to involve the whole Ukrainian Catholic Church in America—clergy and the faithful. The exarchy did not have funds to spare to make this commitment for the numbers of people involved. Bohachevsky needed to know that he had the faithful behind him. This was not a decision he could make alone.

Bohachevsky suggested that Bishop Ambrose Senyshyn convene a meeting of the chief clergy advisers to discuss how best the Ukrainian Catholic Church in America could proceed. In his letter of invitation to this meeting, Bishop Ambrose stressed that the proposed goal of the assembly was "to discuss how the clergy will raise Ukrainian concerns on the American forum in the name of divine and human rights to life."[34] The priests (Tarnawsky, Anton Lototsky, Rev. Vasyl Fedash, editor of *The Way*, along with Reverends Lev Chapelsky, Stephan Pobutsky, Stefan Balandiuk, Pavlo Protsko, and Stephan Hryniokh) met at Stamford on May 9, 1945. The ensuing discussion was broad, ranging from concerns about whether the church in the United States had the right to speak on behalf of the mother church and the forty-five million citizens of the Ukrainian nation to concerns about a lack of consensus among Ukrainian Americans on a vast array of political matters. Senyshyn carefully steered the meeting away from a discussion of the minutiae of aid (for example, should we collect money or useful items?). But even this small group could not agree on a draft that Bishop Bohachevsky needed in his negotiations to bring the refugee Catholic Ukrainian clergy into the United States. There was also some concern about whether any Ukrainian-American involvement with Ukrainian refugees would not backfire in more reprisals for believers in the home country.

Consensus was finally reached on essentials: the need for the church in America to speak up on behalf of the Ukrainian Catholic Church and

34. Senyshyn to the clergy advisers, May 1, 1945, UMAS, Chancery Archive.

the fate of Ukrainians in general and the feasibility of organizing a separate Ukrainian-Catholic committee to aid the refugees that would supplement UCCA activities. The priests were united in their views on the importance of the Ukrainian Catholic Church's ability to draw on the help of the universal church and especially of American Roman Catholics. The majority of the priests argued that a separate Ukrainian Catholic relief organization, ready to cooperate with the Roman Catholic Americans was clearly needed; they pointed out that congregations were already accusing the church of inaction. The minority, especially the venerable Lev Chapelsky, maintained that the church should simply work through the existing community aid organization—he held that some faithful would think that a Catholic committee would undercut the community effort. The decision to create or not create a Catholic relief committee was ultimately left to Bishop Bohachevsky, but Father Stefan Hryniokh added that such a committee, if established, should limit itself to accepting monetary donations—his parish hall could hardly handle clothing donations for the community effort.

A lively discussion then developed on what kind of memorandum the Ukrainian Catholic Church in the United States should craft and under whose name it should appear. That discussion was wide-ranging—from expressions of support for all measures that would bring about peace to concern about the Soviet propaganda emanating from the San Francisco United Nations discussions. The attendees finally concluded that the chancery of the Ukrainian Catholic Church in America should compose a memorandum in defense of the Eastern Church and its people on a broad platform of religious freedom, human rights, and shared values. It was up to the bishops and the chancery to draft such a document.

Bohachevsky, Senyshyn, and the Philadelphia clergy submitted a petition to General George C. Marshall. In their letter of August 25, 1945, they cited "reports from semi-official and private sources revealing tales of relentless and barbaric religious, social, and political persecutions, imprisonments, and executions of Ukrainians, especially the intellectuals, clergymen, etc., by the Soviet authorities."[35] They asked that Ukrainian refugees should not be forcibly deported to the USSR. The petition focused

35. Chancery to General George C. Marshall, August 25, 1945, UMAS, Chancery Archive.

on the argument that Ukrainians should not be considered either Poles or Soviet Russians, and asked that the Ukrainians in the American zones of occupation be given asylum, permission to organize for self-help ventures, and assistance through the Red Cross and the United Nations Relief and Rehabilitation Administration (UNRRA). On the advice of Msgr. William Cleary, the petition was submitted to General Marshall through the U.S. Chaplain James H. O'Neil at the headquarters of the Third Army.[36]

The Roman Catholic bishops reacted quickly, some with tangible help, all with encouragement. They invited the Ukrainian bishops to address the next session of the bishops' meeting, which Bishop Senyshyn did.[37] They addressed the State Department directly to help Ukrainian refugees living in the American zones in Europe. Lest the American bishops be accused of preferential treatment of the Ukrainian Catholic Church, Bishop William A. Griffin of Trenton, New Jersey, asked for "a wide and thorough discussion, not merely on the sufferings of the people of the Ukraine but of others as well because of religious persecution."[38] The Catholic Near-East Welfare Association (headed by Francis Cardinal Spellman), at the urging of Eugene Cardinal Tisserant, the head of the Congregation for the Eastern Church, began a campaign to clothe the refugee Ukrainian priests in Western Europe. Tisserant sent $5,000 of "liturgical stipends" to the needy priests.[39]

Meanwhile, UCCA publicly called upon the clergy and other activists to work not only for welfare support, but also to assert the right of Ukraine to

---

36. Both bishops drafted the text of the petition, dated August 25, 1945. Bohachevsky gave very specific in his handwritten instructions that a full copy of the text—retyped—be also submitted to Msgr. L. Raimondi. They dated August 25, 1945, UMAS, Chancery Archive.

37. Bohachevsky to Senyshyn, November 10, 1945, sent special delivery, UMAS, Chancery Archive.

38. Among the letters from other Roman Catholic bishops to Bohachevsky, UMAS, Chancery Archive.

39. Tisserant informed Thomas McMahon, the secretary of the Catholic Near-East Welfare Association, who in turn wrote to Senyshyn on November 29, 1946, promising help, including financial support for fifty refugee students at St. Josaphat Seminary in Rome, and for another sixty-eight studying for the priesthood at Hirschberg in Germany. "I am writing you these things so that you will know how much is being done by the Oriental Congregation for your dear people. You may be sure that I shall continue to do everything in my power." McMahon to Senyshyn, November 29, 1946, UMAS.

exist as a separate country.[40] In August 1946, the UCCA—working with the Red Cross, United Nations Relief and Rehabilitation Agency, and other volunteer organizations—cranked up the relief effort. The organization called upon all clergy, activists, and social organizations to collect funds for causes that would support the displaced persons and would defend the cause of Ukraine in the West. Under the aegis of the UCCA, the Ukrainian-American Relief Committee (UARC), headed by Walter Galan, was established in Philadelphia. Eventually it was to serve as an umbrella organization that included all the other smaller Ukrainian relief organizations, including one founded in Michigan by John Panchuk.[41] The heart-wrenching stories of devastation in Europe and especially of Soviet enforcement of repatriation pushed the community into spontaneous cooperative actions that quickly strengthened both UCCA and UARC. Neither of the two organizations had yet developed a mechanism for the disbursement of the collected funds. Both needed Bohachevsky's express blessing, because only that ensured full financial support of the community. Bishop Bohachevsky and some of his advisers were still wary of close cooperation with community efforts, especially those involving finances. They feared that the funds could be misused and the good name of the church compromised. As a young man Dr. Galan had been critical of the bishop. Now, as the UARC chairman, he explained that he needed Bohachevsky's participation because without the bishop's express participation people mistrusted the committee and did not support it financially: "We ask your Excellency to become of a member of the Relief Committee and provide us with a brief letter to that effect, which we could publish. This [action] will be of tremendous consequence to the whole relief effort; it will [moreover] negate the rumors that evil spirits are disseminating in the community."[42] Bohachevsky acceded to the request, which in time brought other obligations.

As the Ukrainian Congress Committee of America developed, it became not so much a lobby in the American political sense, as a voice of Ukrainian-Americans. Its leadership asked Bohachevsky to delegate a

40. Flyer dated August 29, 1945, UMAS.
41. There is a conveniently concise introduction to the subject in Kuropas, *Ukrainian Americans*, 390–405.
42. Dr. Walter Galan to Bohachevsky on the United Ukrainian Relief Committee, Inc., letterhead, June 9, 1945, UMAS.

cleric as a formal representative to the organization to provide it with a stamp of approval. In a letter dated December 15, 1955, Leo Dobriansky and Dmytro Halychyn, the UCCA leaders, cited "the unparalleled heroism of the bishops and clergy, their continued martyrdom in prisons and camps" in the defense of the Ukrainian Catholic Church in Europe against "the relentless attacks of Moscow." They argued that it would be politic for the Ukrainian Church in America to take an active part in the work of the Ukrainian Congress Committee of America: "in view of the integral connection of our civic life with that of the church community in the United States, its mutual inter-dependence in the joint service to the Great Cause of God and Country, as well as the traditional conjoining of the fate of the Ukrainian people with that of its church."[43] Claiming to be "the sole, only, and central representative of civic life among American organizations," the leaders pointed out that they had been called upon to voice not only the needs of Ukrainians in the United States of America, but also to call attention to the plight of Ukrainians in the homeland. They reminded the bishop that the organization in its past conventions had called upon the government and the people of the United States to speak up on behalf of "the Church of Christ . . . under the tyrannical rule of Moscow."[44]

Bohachevsky remained hesitant. The reminder that UCCA spoke up on behalf of the oppressed church appeared gratuitous. He brought the matter to the attention of his consultors. Two of them (one a recent émigré, the other a U.S. citizen) summed up all the arguments for delegating a formal representative of the church to the UCCA. That person, they posited, would not only defend the interests of the church, but would be able "to defend the interest of religion in general and of our church by tactfully blocking influences of communists, ultranationalists, party hacks, or other sundry persons opposed to the church and to religion."[45] The consistory and the Catholic scholarly organization Obnova, with Rev. Platon

43. Leo Dobriansky and Dmytro Halychyn to Bohachevsky, December 15, 1955, UMAS. It is a two-page, single-spaced letter, with an attached list of the UCCA membership.

44. Ibid.

45. Rev. Oleksander Krokhmalny, pastor of Ambridge, PA, to Bohachevsky, received at the chancery on February 4, 1956. Father Krokhmalny came to the United States in 1937, and remained pastor of Ambridge from 1937 to 1977. The second letter making the same point was from Rev. Roman Bodnar, written January 30, 1956, from his parish in Elizabeth, N.J. He arrived in the United States in 1949. UMAS.

Kornyliak; as well as Ihnat Bilynsky, the editor of *America*, also spoke out in favor of the proposal. The church's participation in the UCCA, which had already existed informally, now became formally sanctioned.

Meanwhile, the Ukrainian Catholic (Relief) Committee for Refugees, headquartered at Stamford under the leadership of Bishop Senyshyn, worked since its founding (in 1946) with the National Catholic Welfare Committee to bring some sixty thousand Ukrainian immigrants to America. This constituted more than half of the one hundred thousand Ukrainians who emigrated to the United States.[46] That August the bishops dispatched Rev. John Stock to minister first-hand to the displaced Ukrainians. The young priest labored selflessly for six years, crisscrossing Western Europe and personally dealing with thousands of anxious refugees.[47] Modest, likeable, outgoing, and completely selfless, the priest from St. Clair, Pennsylvania, had served as a chaplain in the U.S. Army. He did not limit himself to fact-finding but personally helped everyone he could and comforted those he could not help.

Not all refugees, it must be conceded, realized the true depth of the sacrifice made by Ukrainian Americans because even American slums looked better than bombed-out Europe. It did not occur to many of the postwar refugees that their American hosts themselves were still barely making ends meet.

Ukrainian-Catholic refugees were but one small part of the vast relief effort that gave rise to the United Nations Relief and Rehabilitation Administration, and later, to the International Relief Organization. The broader story is dramatic and panoramic, and illustrates how Allied resources, civilian as well as military, resolved a potential postwar catastro-

46. According to Procko, *Ukrainian Catholics in America*, 74, the National Catholic Welfare Committee brought about one hundred thousand Ukrainian Catholic families to the United States through its programs. See also Kuropas, *Ukrainian Americans*, 404, who cites a report by Bishop Senyshyn that his committee sponsored some forty-five thousand displaced persons, in addition to bringing over 175 priests and their families, as well as three hundred orphans.

47. John Stock was born on July 5, 1918, at Blackwood, Pennsylvania. Bohachevsky ordained him on December 4, 1943. He was one of the seminarians stranded in Switzerland; his ship to the United States survived a torpedo attack. He became bishop in 1971, but died in an automobile accident a year later. Vasyl Lencyk prepared a bibliography of Bishop Stock's post–World War II correspondence and a brief biography published in Ukrainian as *Tireless Worker: Biography of Bishop John Stock* (Lviv: Svichado, 2006).

phe. Bohachevsky and his American church played a significant role in the whole post-1945 world arena. However one might judge Bishop Bohachevsky, the faithful he led lived the Sermon of the Mount in post-World War II America. As a Christian pastor he had done his duty.

THE SOVIETS AND THE UKRAINIAN CHURCH

During the Second World War and its immediate aftermath, the Ukrainian-Catholic churches tried to survive Soviet persecution, various insurgencies, and overall instability. On behalf of Metropolitan Sheptytsky, Rev. Slipyj negotiated with the Soviets in Moscow about the Ukrainian Catholic Church. The Soviets tried to talk the Ukrainian clergy into joining the Russian Orthodox Church, which Stalin had reinstituted. Stalin did not touch Sheptytsky. Even after Sheptytsky died on November 1, 1944, the Ukrainian Catholic Church was left in relative peace for a month in the hopes that the Orthodox Church could persuade Ukrainian Catholics to join them after all. When this failed to happen, the Soviets began a brutal campaign against the Ukrainian Church on December 15, 1945. All Ukrainian Catholic bishops were arrested to shock the priests into participating in a *sobor* (an official church council) that was convened in March 1946. The overarching mission of the *sobor* was to officially abrogate the 1596 union of the Ukrainian Catholic Church with Rome, which it formally did.

Bishop Bohachevsky learned about the Lviv *sobor* from a letter that Amleto Cicognani, the apostolic delegate, wrote to him on April 4, 1946. The delegate informed Bohachevsky that Bishop Khomyshyn was killed and that "all the other bishops were arrested, while the death of Archbishop- Metropolitan Slipyj has not yet been confirmed."[48] Eugene Cardinal Tisserant, reflecting the Vatican's view, was most concerned that there might be another flurry of pro-Orthodox activism among Ukrainians in the United States if they believed that the faithful in Halychyna had willingly turned to Orthodoxy. The Vatican was relieved that none of the Ukrainian bishops had taken the bait to join even *pro forma* with the Orthodox and that in Ukraine Catholics joined Orthodoxy only under duress. Nor was there any movement in America for Catholics to join Orthodoxy.

48. Cicognani to Bohachevsky, April 4, 1946, UMAS, Chancery Archive.

Cicognani, who was focused on the American scene, referred to the chief architect of the unification scheme in Ukraine (that is, Rev. Kostelnyk) merely as someone who campaigned against celibacy. The other two major signatories of the "new order," Rev. Melnyk (the vicar at Peremyshl) and Rev. Pelvetsky (vicar of Stanislaviv), were unknown beyond Ukrainian circles. The Ukrainian Catholic Church had overwhelmingly proven its loyalty to Catholicism.

When receiving the news of the Lviv pseudo-sobor, which unilaterally abolished the Ukrainian Catholic Church by fusing it with Russian Orthodoxy, Bohachevsky must have experienced both horror and relief: horror at the destruction of the underpinnings of the church and relief that the bishops had stood their ground. Then came the death or arrest of all Ukrainian Catholic bishops, including Slipyj, the new metropolitan. To the beleaguered faithful, this became a matter of pride for their martyrdom and suffering. Bohachevsky provided his own reading of the Lviv *sobor* to the papacy early in the spring of 1946, but the relevant document cannot be located.

Sheptytsky's death in November 1944 and the liquidation of the Ukrainian Catholic Church in 1946 were two devastating blows that severed the already tenuous ties between the mother church and the American diocese. Although Lviv had generally paid scant attention to its émigré churches and did not even seem to acknowledge Bohachevsky's financial support of the office of the Conference of Ukrainian Bishops, the Lviv metropolitanate had been a source of strength for the bishop. Now nearly all his confreres were dead or exiled, and all normal channels of communication had been severed. This meant that it was up to the Ukrainian Catholic Church in the United States to foster its own growth in the hopes that it would eventually be able to bolster and revitalize the persecuted church in the home country. The correspondence of the time painfully illustrates the isolation of the Ukrainian Catholic Church in Ukraine at the war's end. Even the Vatican was affected, fearing apostasy in the face of Soviet pressure and the attractiveness of an Orthodox solution to preserve at least a framework for the Ukrainian Catholic Church.

The Ukrainian Catholic Church in the home country had been destroyed, pushed underground, its clergy killed or scattered east and west. None of the Ukrainian Catholic bishops collaborated with the Soviets, and the priests that accepted Orthodoxy, did so with reservations.[49] There were a few attempts at negotiating with the Soviet government to assure some safety for the church, but these were essentially futile.[50] As the Soviets gained control over greater and greater swaths of Eastern Europe, Bohachevsky (like the Vatican) was most fearful that the Ukrainian Catholic Church in the home country would reject Catholicism and embrace Orthodoxy. All direct contact with Halychyna remained cut off.

These events, painful to Bishop Bohachevsky, the devout man of the cloth, were also painful to him on a personal level. On September 21, 1947, Kotsylovsky, Bohachevsky's last mentor, was executed in the Kyiv jail—a stone's throw from the ancient St. Sophia Cathedral.[51] Perhaps even more painful was the fact that Havryil Kostelnyk had served as head of the pseudo-sobor of Lviv that abrogated the 1596 Union of Brest and officially joined the Ukrainian Catholic Church to the Russian Orthodox Church.[52] Kostelnyk had been one of the chief proponents of an idealized Eastern Christianity that antedated the future liberalization of the Catholic Church and combined it with a return to an Eastern ritualism. In view of the inevitable destruction of the Ukrainian Catholic Church, Kostelnyk had sought to save the congregation from more bloodshed. He was killed soon after the Lviv council, having saved the Soviets the embarrassment of formally banning the Ukrainian Catholic Church.[53]

49. According to Luzhnytsky, *Ukraïinska Tserkva mizh Skhodom i Zakhodom*, 582, about two hundred priests, most married and with families, had been given permission by their bishops to flee the country before the oncoming Soviets. Luzhnytsky does not substantiate the claim.

50. Slipyj even headed a formal delegation to Moscow that predictably returned empty handed. For fuller discussion, see Bociurkiw, *The Ukrainian Greek Catholic Church and the Soviet State (1939–1950)*.

51. While the fates of all the Ukrainian Catholic bishops in Ukraine at the time are both heart-wrenching and morally uplifting, Kotsylovsky's story has the most drama. He physically fought the detail that came to arrest him in 1945. Freed from a prison in Riashiv, Kotsylovsky walked the fifty miles to Peremyshl. When he again refused to participate in the denunciation of the Union of Brest of the Ukrainian Catholic Church he was arrested again, and this time transported to Kyiv, where he was executed.

52. See *Likvidatsiia Ukraïins'koï Hreko-Katolyts'koï Tserkvy*, vol. 1 (Kyiv: Shevchenko Ukrainian National University, 2006), for a selection of primary source materials on the process.

53. The official cause of death was a road accident, but there is proof that the truck ran him over on purpose.

The shock of the church's suppression, the dismal fate of Ukrainians, and the realization that his mother—the mother of seven sons—had died alone, abandoned in a village at the crossroads of two armies and three insurgencies, did not break Bohachevsky. All wars, in Bishop Bohachevsky's mind, were products of human ineptitude. They underscored the need for an organized church that depended on a legion of well-educated and well-trained priests. His job was to ensure that his diocese was duly prepared to fulfill its part of the mission to reclaim a better world, one that better reflected the original design of the Creator.[54]

Sheptytsky's death and the liquidation of the church in Ukraine, the persecution of its clergy and faithful by a regime whose antecedent on occasion called itself the Third Rome,[55] changed the American church from an immigrant church to caretaker and preserver of the whole Ukrainian Catholic tradition. Not surprisingly, Bohachevsky readily accepted the responsibility that devolved on him and the other Ukrainian bishops of the Catholic Church outside Ukrainian territories to maintain the organization of the whole church and keep it functioning. And now that Lviv was no longer capable of convening the Ukrainian Catholic bishops, it would be up to the American churches to take on this function.

54. In a pastoral letter on November 1947 (*Eparkhiial'ni Visti*, 41–43), Bohachevsky called upon the faithful to "live the lives of faith, prayer, and good works . . . [so that] the old glory of our forefather, the holy martyrs, live on in us, their descendants. . . . The time will come when the Bolshevik prison shall crumble. At what hour, at what time? Christ, God alone knows . . . [but] we can hasten this hour of victory by our prayers, good deeds, and generous charities."

55. The Romanovs accepted a theory, which was articulated roughly a century after the fall of Constantinople to the Turks, that Moscow was the Third Rome, the defender of Christianity after the fall of Christian Rome and of Constantinople, the second Rome. Vladimir Putin revived the myth.

CHAPTER 12

Growth through Tragedy

The Second World War had a triple impact on the Ukrainian Catholic Church in the United States. First (and most direct) was the participation of almost thirty thousand young men and women of the diocese in the American Armed Forces.[1] Bishop Bohachevsky appointed Rev. Volodymyr Lotovych of Jersey City to coordinate care for the wounded with the veterans' groups.[2] The second impact was demographic: European emigration during and after the war more than doubled the number of Ukrainian Catholic priests in the United States and increased the Ukrainian Catholic faithful in the United States by some seventy thousand, forty thousand of them coming through Catholic charities. Third, the brutal Soviet destruction of the mother church at Lviv in 1946 made the survival of the church in the United States imperative for the papacy, if Rome were to prove its commitment to the Eastern Catholic churches.

The war took a heavy toll on all Ukrainians. Toward its end the anti-Soviet Poles and anti-Soviet Ukrainians fought each other while simultaneously carrying out guerrilla warfare against the Nazis, the Communist Poles, and the USSR. Organized resistance to the Soviet regime continued

1. "Orhanizuvannia Ukraiins'kykh Hreko-Katolytskykh Voiennykh Veteraniv v Nashiy Diietsezii," *Eparkhiial'ni Visti*, August 1944, 34. By the time the war ended, the number reached thirty-eight thousand serving in various capacities, Procko, *Ukrainian Catholics in America*, 73.

2. *Eparkhiial'ni Visti*, February 1945, 8–9; *Eparkhiial'ni Visti*, May 1946, 20; and *Eparkhiial'ni Visti*, May 1947, 19.

until as late as 1952, combined with mass arrests and deportations to Siberia. Vast, forced shifts in population in Eastern Europe brought further suffering. Ukrainians lost a large part of Western Ukrainian ethnic territory, including Peremyshl and a part of the Carpathians. Outside the borders of the USSR, fear of persecution by the Soviets, whether experienced or anticipated, flooded Western Europe with immigrants that came to be known as the "displaced persons." They sought refuge in a war-torn Europe that was in no position to offer aid. Western Europeans needed help themselves and resented all foreigners. The war plunked the plight of the "old country" at the feet of American Ukrainians in the physical reality of the tens of thousands of uprooted people. Ukrainian-Americans had to work through all channels to prevent Soviet efforts at "repatriating" Ukrainian refugees to the USSR and offer what material aid they could.

The devastating news from the homeland only increased Bishop Bohachevsky's sense of responsibility for his church. The brutal reality did not reduce his public expressions of hope for the future. The legacy of his martyred colleagues and mentors had to be preserved, even as they were lost. He focused on what could be done. Bohachevsky wanted the American Ukrainian Catholic Church to be ready, when the time came, to help the mother church emerge from the scattered pieces. He had God, Rome, and a loyal church on his side to make him strong.

A VISITOR FROM ROME

The repression against the Ukrainian Catholic Church and the beginning of its forced underground existence roughly coincided with the 350th anniversary of the Treaty of Brest. In Rome, *L'Osservatore Romano* published an informative article on the union, which the Soviet regime had just abolished. The Vatican radio aired broadcasts on the suppression of the Ukrainian Catholic Church. A concerned Vatican, availing itself of Cardinal Spellman's hospitality, dispatched the head of the Congregation for the Eastern Church, Eugenio Cardinal Tisserant, to the United States to personally check how the Ukrainian exarchate weathered the tragedies that befell its mother church. Tisserant surprised Bohachevsky when he wrote directly to him on March 14, 1947, to announce his impending visit specifically to the Philadelphia Ukrainian Catholic Exarchate and to ask

Bohachevsky to inform the Philadelphia Latin-rite Catholic archbishop, Cardinal Dougherty, of the forthcoming visit.[3] That made the visit of the secretary of the Congregation for the Eastern Church specifically to the Philadelphia Ukrainian Catholic Exarchate unprecedented. Bohachevsky viewed it as special recognition for his church.

The announcement of the visit caused such a flurry of activity that, as stories would have it, the bishop was finally plucked out of his Spartan living quarters. His clergy convinced Bohachevsky that it would be inappropriate to host the cardinal in the humble chancery. This compelled the bishop to purchase a modest two-story house located at 705 Medary Avenue, in a new development in northern Philadelphia. Surrounded by a garden, the bishop's colonial appeared palatial to those who had spent their lives on Philadelphia's narrow, historic, but dirty and crowded streets, unadorned by the flourishing maples on Medary Avenue.

The move did little to change the bishop's life style. He kept up his old schedule and simple routine, adding a commute and changing the housekeeping arrangements. Instead of relying on the Basilian nuns from the monastery down the block, the bishop now had two resident housekeepers: Missionary Sisters Rita and Maria. Energetic, outgoing, and friendly, the two nuns created a comfortable home for the aging bishop. The only item of luxury he permitted himself was a chapel (constructed out of the garage), or, to be even more precise, an elaborate, silver-encrusted iconostasis in that chapel. But even this concession is debatable, as Archbishop Stefan Sulyk later wrote that the real reason for the elaborate iconostasis was because the bishop wanted to help a recently arrived artist, Mykola Mukhyn.[4]

Cardinal Tisserant, an eminent and well-travelled scholar of the Eastern churches and antiquities, was the highest-ranking Vatican cleric to visit the Ukrainian diocese. He arrived in Philadelphia on Saturday, May 17, 1947, and was driven to the bishop's new residence, about half an hour's drive from the cathedral, by a Ukrainian parishioner, Eugene Rohach, who owned a Buick that was judged suitable enough to transport the esteemed

3. Tisserant to Bohachevsky, March 14, 1947, UMAS, Chancery Archive.

4. Metropolitan Stefan Sulyk, *Yak Stefan stav mytropolytom* (Lviv: n.p., 2001), 325, Bohachevsky commissioned refugee artists Mykola Mukhyn and Christine Dochwat to design a chapel with an elaborate iconostasis for the house.

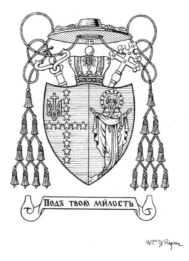

FIGURE 12. BISHOP BOHACHEVSKY'S SHIELD

visitor. The tone of the visit between Bohachevsky and Tisserant was quite collegial. The two celebrated a liturgy in the Ukrainian cathedral, met with the clergy, and attended a concert at the Basilian orphanage. They had the evening to exchange views.

There are few details about the conversations between Bishop Bo-hachevsky and Cardinal Tisserant, but it seems the talk centered on the strength of the Ukrainian Catholic Church outside Ukraine. The Congre-gation for the Eastern Church worried about what some at the Vatican thought to be a magnetic pull of the Ukrainian Orthodox Church, espe-cially of the patriotically Ukrainian Autocephaly on Catholics. Because the settlement camps for displaced persons mixed people of different na-tionalities and religions, Ukrainian Catholics, for the first time on such a large scale, came into direct contact with Ukrainian Orthodox. The dislocation of populations after the war and the imminent immigration to the United States challenged the readiness of the Ukrainian Catholic Church in America to assimilate a potentially disruptive influx. Tisserant openly asked about Catholics joining the Ukrainian Orthodox Church, which seemed to have been rumored around the Vatican. Bohachevsky, whose church was still welcoming dissidents from the 1930s, provided matter-of-fact information on the divisions within the Ukrainian Orthodox, as well as information on some of the Protestant denominations that attracted new immigrants. Bohachevsky did not see the Orthodox or Protestant churches as a threat either to the Ukrainian Catholics in America or abroad. He assured the cardinal that the Ukrainian Catholic congregation in the United States was stable, and quite ready to welcome the victims of the last war. The cardinal accepted the bishop's assessment.

Tisserant left for Washington by train later that Sunday, visibly satisfied with what he saw. His visit with Ukrainian Catholics in the United States continued, partly in the company of Senyshyn.[5] On May 4, he took part in another Ukrainian Eastern-rite liturgy at St. Nicholas Cathedral in Chicago. *The Way* described Tisserant's visit and printed a full front-page photograph of him on May 17, 1947. The cardinal met with Bohachevsky and Senyshyn again at Stamford on June 8. Tisserant's visit with Bohachevsky and other Ukrainian Catholics was uplifting for both clerics. The cardinal personally assessed the state of Bohachevsky's eparchy and was thus able to gauge the preparations for the influx of the displaced persons.

At the end of his stay in the United States, Tisserant visited the Catholic Near East Welfare Association in New York, headed by Francis Spellman, who had just become the archbishop of New York. It should be noted that Spellman prided himself on his work with the impoverished Eastern churches and rather resented the independent streak of the Ukrainian Catholic Church in the United States. When Tisserant departed for Rome, it was Cardinal Spellman and a group of Latin-rite Catholic bishops who saw him off at the airport.[6]

Tisserant had only praise for the way the Ukrainian Catholic Church in the United States functioned, but he was troubled that the Women's Order

5. Rev. Onufry Kowalsky, writing on Hotel Diplomat (on Forty-Third Street in New York City) stationery to the chancery, offered himself as a person fluent in French who could best accompany the cardinal on his American travels. UMAS.

6. Tisserant was made cardinal a year before his visit to the United States. In the summer of 1938 he had unofficially visited Sheptytsky's mountain retreat in the Carpathians. He played an important role in the preparations for the Second Vatican Council and was instrumental in facilitating the presence of the Russian Orthodox observers at the Second Vatican Council. The cardinal's send-off in New York was described by a fellow passenger, an Italian scientist en-route home from work on the atom bomb at Los Alamos, in Emilio Segre, *A Mind Always in Motion: The Autobiography of Emilio Segre* (Berkeley: University of California Press, 1993), 213–14.

of St. Basil the Great in the United States had not had an election in twenty years. Their superior had aged. Shortly after Tisserant's visit, the Congregation for the Eastern Church suggested a formal review of the Order, which would have removed the nuns from outside duties for the duration.[7] The Basilian sisters were the lynchpin of the whole Ukrainian Catholic educational structure. Without their army of educated (and extremely underpaid) teaching nuns, the very existence of the Ukrainian Catholic Church in the United States would be jeopardized. The realization that there were serious difficulties in the administration of the American branch of the Basilian women religious came as a painful surprise to Bohachevsky. As Ambrose Senyshyn was a member of the same order, there might have been some tension between the two bishops over this matter. But, as Bishop Bohachevsky wrote to his vicar, "our open conversation stimulated a frank exchange of views" that made the resolution of the problems easier. The congregation agreed that the Ukrainian bishops of America could adequately address the concerns of the Order, which made direct Vatican intervention unnecessary.[8] The Sisters resolved their organizational difficulties and continued caring for the Ukrainian children in day schools without interruptions.

THE NEWCOMERS

As soon as they could, American-Ukrainians began sending parcels of permitted relief items to the refugees. Churches immediately became the action centers for this activity, and priests were drawn into this superhuman effort. The Ukrainian-American faithful were most generous, both in material donations and in the personal help they offered to the new wave of immigrants.[9] The chancery tried to keep up with the various requests for help. Initially, some of these appeals were penciled on scraps of paper because there was a severe paper shortage in Europe. Appeals came from priests asking for asylum and work in America. The bishop,

7. Bohachevsky to Senyshyn, December 4, 1947, UMAS, Chancery Archive.
8. Bohachevsky to Senyshyn, November 5, 1949, UMAS, Chancery Archive.
9. For a fuller discussion, see Kuropas, *Ukrainian-Americans*, 392–93. There are relatively few first-hand accounts of how the immigrants were welcomed; for a particularly perceptive presentation, see the memoirs of Anna Chopek, Esq., *Christ the King Church*, 75–95.

wary by nature, was concerned that the clergy accepted into the diocese be bona fide Catholic priests. Bohachevsky's close contacts with the nuncio in Washington helped to smooth communications on this matter. By late 1947, the lucky immigrants—those who found U.S. citizens willing to assure their upkeep—were beginning to arrive on America's golden shores. Isydor Nahaevsky, Vasyl Seredovych, Platon Kornylak, and Dmytro Blazejowskyj were the first post–World War II Ukrainian Catholic priests to arrive in the United States at Bohachevsky's invitation.[10]

Bohachevsky was willing to take all the priests, whether married, with families, or single. Bohachevsky and Senyshyn personally sponsored about 170 Ukrainian Catholic priests. Among the newly arrived priests were many who were highly educated, a few of whom had held very high administrative positions in the Ukrainian Catholic Church, and many who had administered large parishes. The bishop's only fear was that the priests who had held high positions in the church in the homeland, would find the relative simplicity and directness of the Ukrainian-American Church uncomfortable and would not adapt well to American culture.[11]

President Truman's Displaced Persons Act of April 18, 1948, provided lawful entry to the United States for hundreds of thousands of displaced Europeans, and for the first time facilitated the entry of refugees.[12] It was thanks to this act that the majority of the seventy thousand Ukrainian immigrants came to the United States between 1948 and 1952.[13] About forty thousand of them came through Catholic charitable organizations,

10. From the little information on the finances of the diocese, we know that the bishop himself paid for the passage of the clerics who were the first to arrive (passage about $200 per person). Other priests had to get sponsors or borrow money for passage. Father Paul Ivakhiv borrowed his passage money from the Congregation for the Eastern Church, so the bishop sent a separate check to the congregation for $258 to cover those costs. Bohachevsky to Senyshyn, April 17, 1946, UMAS, Chancery Archive.

11. This was especially the case with Rev. Nicholas Wojiakovsky, who had been the vicar general and apostolic administrator for Ukrainians in Germany. Bohachevsky tried to discourage this worthy from emigrating. As it turned out, Wojiakovsky and the bishop got along very well, since the older priest was very willing to serve the diocese in an advisory capacity. See the pertinent correspondence between Bohachevsky and Wojakowsky (1945–1949) at UMAS.

12. It also did away with quota limitations until 1952, when the McCarran-Walter Act reintroduced them, giving preference to immigrants from Ireland, Germany, and Great Britain.

13. Kuropas, *Ukrainian-Americans*, 404, computed that Ukrainians made up about 15 percent of immigrants who arrived in the United States through the Displaced Persons Act.

especially the National Catholic Welfare Conference. Although there have been no studies on the topic, it seems that most of the post–World War II Ukrainian immigrants from the Transcarpathian (Ruthenian) lands considered themselves Ukrainian. The Catholics among them tended to join the Ukrainian Catholic dioceses.

Once the legalities were taken care of, the chancery found parishes for the priests. Acculturation was still just an anthropological expression, and the émigrés were expected to adjust as well as they could, accepting or not accepting local advice. Despite the wrinkles and occasional misunderstandings, the influx of clergy produced positive results. The refugee priests doubled the number of Ukrainian Catholic clergy in the exarchate. Meanwhile, with the arrival of the displaced persons, the number of Ukrainian Catholic faithful grew by about 20 percent.

There were various demands on the bishop, sometimes by persons who presumed that Catholic bishops in the United States would have the means to be as munificent to intellectuals and artists as Metropolitan Sheptytsky was reputed to have been. Not only did Bohachevsky not have the funds, but unlike Sheptytsky, Bohachevsky mistrusted the slight liberalization of the intellectual climate evident within the metropolitan's small innermost circle. Kostelnyk's willingness to sign the Lviv protocol abrogating the Treaty of Brest made Bohachevsky all the more wary of people and institutions that had even a mildly socialist or liberal tinge. For the bishop, as for many of his flock, "liberal" connoted political radicalism and sexual profligacy. Thus, he refused to accept honorary membership in the oldest Ukrainian scholarly organization, the Shevchenko Scientific Society, because he remembered the anticlerical and socialist views expounded on the pages of some of the society's pre–World War I publications. He was equally wary of accepting honorary membership in the Free Ukrainian Academy of Sciences because its leadership included atheists.[14]

Many of the refugee priests came from families similar to Bohachevsky's, and he may have expected to find some to whom he could become close, either through family or personal connections. Bohachevsky was very careful not to show any preferences, but he did try to accommodate the priests and their families as best as the eparchy could. He was concerned,

14. Bohachevsky to Senyshyn, November 17, 1949, UMAS, Chancery Archive.

however, that the nature of his chancery and the egalitarian social climate would not suit some of the European clergy. He tried to warn them about the lack of formality in America, usually to no avail. Priests such as Rev. Roman Lobodych, a former senator in the Polish Parliament, who during the war was involved in a desperate attempt to create the nucleus of a Ukrainian army, resented what he perceived to be an unduly narrow curriculum in training priests in America. On the other hand, Nykola Wojakowsky, a canon law scholar who served as the apostolic administrator for Ukrainians in postwar Germany, found a niche for himself in helping Bohachevsky craft eparchial regulations. One would have thought that the European priests would connect readily with Bohachevsky, but his presence exuded an air of such authority that all conversations stopped upon his entry into the room.[15] Bohachevsky was unable—perhaps because of his temperament or because he thought it would be inappropriate—to develop a closeness with others, except for the few priests who worked at the chancery. On the other hand, the bishop showed great pride in the young American-born priests trained in his seminary. Those were his "boys." Bohachevsky reconciled American egalitarianism with the Christian social progressivism of his patriarchal upbringing. His one brief foray into his native Halychyna (in 1929), largely limited to the clerical sphere, had not given him a realistic picture of how the Ukrainian village had changed in the interwar period. From his perspective, he believed that the new immigrants would find their home within the society of the Ukrainian Catholic Church and would continue building on the existing, albeit at times skeletal, structures. At the same time, he wanted the immigrants to realize that they too carried some responsibility for the evil in the world. Evil was not limited to communist atheists or the defeated Nazis. He talked of communist leanings within the Ukrainian community in the United States, pointing out that even among Ukrainians, godless views promoted disorder, attacks on the church, disrespect for elders—in short, "Bolshevik materialism" and all that it stood for. "We all still remember the revolt of 1927 in our eparchy. The promotion of atheism brought its consequences. Revolt led to other revolts, to the Bolshevik chasm."[16] In his Lenten pastoral letter of 1947, he hammered at the evils

15. Sulyk, *Yak Stefan stav mytropolytom*, 141–42.

16. He mentioned the attacks on Bishop Ortynsky by the same newspaper that attacked the church and its bishop in 1927, Easter pastoral letter, *Eparkhiial'ni Visti*, February 1947, 3 .

of communism, stressing the irony that "where they forgot God, turning only to the land, where all labor was to be used to make men rich and well endowed, there is want, unhappiness, and hunger." The bishop saw communism as the enemy of God and truth: "in the name of freedom, for thirty years, it has enslaved millions of people in unheard terror; in the name of democracy, it establishes the greatest tyranny; and all that in the name of the truth? Its militant atheism and violence aim to destroy the Fortress God Himself built on Peter's Rock, the Holy Catholic Church." Bohachevsky quoted approvingly Pope Pius XII's invocation in which the pontiff described modern mankind as "cut to pieces by vicious hatreds, enveloped by conflagrations of conflicts, the victim of its own lawlessness."[17]

COLLECTING THE FAMILY

Among the refugees were three of Bohachevsky's younger brothers and their families, as well as other members of the family. The bishop learned about them late in the spring of 1945 through a note that a nephew wrote from a U.S. internment camp. The note was then passed on by an American-born Ukrainian boy named Lev Shchur, who had been stranded in Europe and ended up with the bishop's nephews towards the end of the war. Shchur, claiming his U.S. citizenship, contacted his parents, who let the bishop know that at least two of his nephews were in the American zone in Western Europe. Further inquiries revealed three brothers and their families, three first-cousins and their families, and several other relatives.[18]

How the bishop felt about some one hundred relatives who suddenly turned up in Western Europe we do not know. We do know that he initiated the necessary immigration proceedings. He also needed to prove to the U.S. government that he had ample funds to care for those he sponsored. The brothers did not immediately jump at the opportunity, and it took almost two years from the first "assurance" dated September 27, 1946,

17. "Posviata Neporochnomu Sertsiu Mariii" [Dedication to the Immaculate Heart of Mary], *Eparkhiial'ni Visti*, May 1948, 22–24.

18. My brother Ihor (1927–2010) wrote that at one family gathering the bishop had laughingly pointed him out, saying, "He was the first to be found." Ihor did not remember the particulars of the original letter he sent to the bishop in 1945, except that he titled him "Your Excellency Uncle," having vaguely remembered the term "excellency" from a family photograph. Ihor and a cousin were separated from their parents during World War II.

for Danylo, Omelian, and Ivan, and their families to complete the paperwork. Danylo arrived in New York on April 17, 1948; the others followed in three-month intervals. The delay was not so much due to red tape as to the desire of the brothers to have their older children finish high school and receive their European *matura* (certification of completion of the gymnasium curriculum), even though the attestations came from a gymnasium in a displaced person camp that had no formal recognition beyond the permission to exist granted by the American Army authorities.

A few months earlier, through church connections, the bishop had learned that his mother had died of typhus. Old and weak, she had refused to continue in the family's flight from the Soviets and stopped in the low Carpathians. She died alone in the midst of war and guerrilla fighting. For the bishop's three brothers, the flight from the Soviets ended in a German labor camp. This was an all-too-common story, and Bohachevsky did not hold the brothers responsible for their mother's fate. He helped them get to the United States and helped them get through the first few months in their new country. He treated them kindly, but with controlled emotion. He sponsored the three brothers and three cousins from his own salary and asked Senyshyn to house them at Stamford for a couple of months, one nuclear family at a time. Then, the bishop told all his relatives that they would have to fend for themselves as the rest of the refugees were doing. He explained that all Ukrainian immigrants had a tough time for the first few years in the country, adding that he would pray for them. He told them frankly that they would now have to get by on their own because he, the bishop, needed the resources available to him for the priests and for other helpless immigrants. If he feared that this large family would complicate his life as his older brother had done, he did not let them feel this. From their end, the family made no claims on the bishop once they realized he would not get them jobs.[19] There is abundant anecdotal evidence that the bishop's family did nothing to diminish his standing with the faithful. It was, in fact, clear to everyone that the bishop's relatives were not getting preferential treatment at the cost of the congregation. The bishop's priority

19. From Danylo Bohachevsky's personal files, written in Ukrainian, in my possession. Danylo, a lawyer by training, was interested in history and sociology. He kept notes on the books he read as well as some copies of his correspondence. Except for the texts mentioned here and in his memoirs, none of the material concerns the bishop.

clearly remained the church, which both the family and the congregation understood. The arrival of brothers and cousins changed little in Constantine's regimen. After the initial three-month stay on the seminary grounds, the cousins fended for themselves. A relationship of deferential closeness grew slowly between the bishop and the family members. The bishop hired one brother as his chauffeur/ secretary. It is likely that he asked the Rohach family to lend money to the three brothers for a down payment on a semidetached house in northern Philadelphia. Apart from his assistance to these relatives, the bishop sent a small sum of money to relatives in Europe.

One family story concerns my father, Danylo, the brother closest in age to the bishop (except for the elder brother Volodymyr who by this time was an alcoholic living on Philadelphia's skid row). My father at some point tried to convince Bishop Constantine that no one would consider it amiss if he were to offer him, Danylo, a low-wage job doing something that would permit him to keep his lawyerly dignity while making ends meet. The bishop responded with the following note of December 15, 1948, which warrants quoting in full:

Dear Brother:

Thank you for your letter dated this December.

Granted, your position is difficult. I believe that you will find a way out, as you have done [always] to this day. I am sorry that I do not have the time, nor do my position, health, and age permit me to participate in your family affairs, although you are asking that I do so. Your fate is in your own hands, and your future depends on you.

You are aware that I provided you with first aid, and His Excellency Ambrose has also shown you his good will.

He has given you your first shelter.

Now you must rely on your own strength.

Search for a solution, and you'll find it.

Thank God, you are healthy. The first [Ukrainian] pioneers came here in worse conditions.

Study, pray, make decisions, and the Lord will help [you.]

As always, I will pray for you to the Almighty.

All the best

I remain in Christ

+Constantine

Epp

Thus, calmly but firmly, the bishop provided a dramatic lesson in American self-sufficiency and democracy to his closest family. He did so in his neat handwriting, not in person. Two weeks later the families of Danylo and Emil Bohachevsky moved to Philadelphia. On January 6 they had Christmas Eve supper at the episcopal vicarage. When Ivan Bohachevsky arrived in America, he had a Bohachevsky home to go to. All three brothers immediately began sponsoring other families. Within five years this communal arrangement splintered into smaller family units.

Danylo, the almost sixty-year-old lawyer, went to wash hospital floors; his son, along with other young men in the community, found whatever jobs they could before they were drafted into another war, this time in Korea; Danylo's wife joined the immigrant textile brigade. A younger brother tried to get a job as a custodian in a Ukrainian Catholic summer camp but was turned down and kept his job at the tire factory. In contrast, Danylo's daughter Maria, my older sister, got a scholarship to a girls' college in Indiana after her initial year at the Basilian-run Manor Junior College. Ivan's daughter was the first in a line of the Bohachevsky girls to attend St. Basil's Academy at Fox Chase. None of the boys enrolled at St. Basil's College at Stamford.

The nature of the bishop's relationship with his family was neither advertised nor kept secret. It was just accepted as part of the postwar adjustments. Everyone, as the bishop had noted, had his or her own share of hardship. And this time, the émigré press did not even comment on the bishop's treatment of his relatives. The relatives must have expected some additional consideration beyond the travel to America, but they did not complain publicly when they realized that none would be forthcoming. Nor was there any serious criticism when two of Bohachevsky's brothers, with the financial help of the Rohach family, opened the Bohachevsky-Rohach & Co. Religious Goods store two blocks from the cathedral (on February 1, 1950). The firm went to great lengths to commission the making of religious goods in compliance with Eastern-rite regulations and the advice of specialists. Chalices, censors, and other accouterments became visibly different from those in the Latin rite.[20] The firm tried to expand into supplying building materials for the construction of the seminary, but its service was unsatisfactory.

20. The firm did well, but neither of the families wanted to continue running it, and

During this time, however, the bishop suffered three heart attacks, in June and July 1948. The following year, the bishop sent Bishop Senyshyn to Rome to deliver the expected ad limina report to the pontiff in his place. He did not feel strong enough to risk the journey to see a Europe recently destroyed by yet another war in his lifetime.

ADJUSTING TO AMERICA

The seventy thousand Ukrainian displaced persons who came to the United States in the 1950s differed from the voluntary migrants at the turn of the century. Many, justifiably or not, saw themselves as political émigrés. More importantly, they came not individually but as part of a larger group. It was not a community of its own making, it was divided by political, social, geographical, and educational differences, yet it was coherent enough to be seen as unit. That gave it strength. Many new immigrants, relieved to find a haven, saw their stay in the United States as temporary and did not integrate themselves into the American polity. Beyond public formalities, most made few attempts to fraternize with the so-called old emigration. Two world wars, major industrial developments, complex class differences, as well as perceived reasons for emigration separated the newcomers from the Ukrainian-Americans already settled here. One would think such differences would cause tensions in the operation of the Ukrainian Catholic Church in the United States. And yet there was no dramatic rift, no distinct change between how the church looked or how its clergy functioned between the years 1945 and 1951. There were just more parishes and more to be done.

The church expanded and integrated the newcomers. Bohachevsky tried to use the new clerical and intellectual manpower to strengthen his church. He now finally had the priests, including some of the best Halychyna had to offer. Sometimes, however, the needs of the immigrant ref-

---

in the 1960s it was taken over by the chancery at cost. A few letters from my father to both Bishops Bohachevsky and Senyshyn remain in the UMAS, Chancery Archive. On January 31, 1950, my father handwrote a letter addressed simply to Your Excellency, asking for prayers and blessing for the venture. Later, a March 3rd letter to Senyshyn is typed. It asks for permission to duplicate and sell his photograph. I remember traipsing through the silversmith district in Philadelphia with my father and translating his instructions to the silversmiths as to how this or that religious vessel should be made to reflect the Eastern tradition.

ugees became overwhelming. Scholars from Soviet Ukraine expected the bishop to have funds available for them to continue their scholarly work in the United States. Western Ukrainian scholars hoped for similar support. The bishop sponsored intellectuals whom he could conceivably employ, for example, Prof. Mykhailo Tershakovets. Ukrainian parishes sponsored eighty more clergy, most with families, to come to the United States above those the bishops sponsored. Bohachevsky not only sponsored Lev Mydlovsky, the editor of the four-volume memoirs by Rev. Prystay that were critical of the bishop, he also hired him to edit *America*. The new priests were assigned parishes in the usual fashion. Some continued as they had done in Halychyna, others plunged immediately into an American self-help mode. Rev. Dmytro Blazejowskyj, for example, tasked with building up the Denver, Colorado, parish, encouraged the families to sponsor other immigrants to locate in Colorado to build a whole Ukrainian community there.[21] The system was simple. Bohachevsky informally asked individual priests if they would take on a helper, usually with a family. Most kindly agreed. There were individual difficulties, of course. The Carnegie parish, for instance, was still in the middle of an unsettled property suit, and taking on an additional priest would have unnecessarily complicated the proceedings.[22] Predictably there were a few run-ins between the settled priests and the newcomers; one was nasty enough to involve the intervention of the papal legate.[23]

The small, Western-Ukrainian middle class, of which the clergy was an important part, was thrown into contact not only with the West European working and peasant classes, but also with Eastern Ukrainian immigrants who, by dint of ingenuity or luck, had managed to pass through the Al-

21. Sulyk, *Yak Stefan stav mytropolytom*, 1672-170. Rev. Dmytro Blazejowskyj (1910–2011) was a missionary turned scholar. Metropolitan Sulyk wrote about Blazejowskyj's first years in the United States, when he slept on a park bench after one of his bus trips from Denver to Omaha, so as not to wake Sulyk, then at his first parish. Blazejowskyj encouraged recent immigrants to sponsor and otherwise draw more immigrant families to settle in Denver to build a Ukrainian community.

22. Bohachevsky to Senyshyn, detailing the case, October 15, 1949, UMAS, Chancery Archive.

23. Revs. John Bilanych, Yaroslav Skrotsky, and Vasyl Stebelsky ran into administrative and financial difficulties that necessitated the intervention of the papal legate. Correspondence of Bohachevsky, Cicognani, and Bilanych, September 13–19, 1949, UMAS, Chancery Archive.

lied screening process. The experience of the displaced person camps had socialized the entire group to joined activities. At the same time it also accustomed some to receiving a minimal degree of care, such as housing, food, and basic medical care. In the immediate postwar era these immigrants built their own little states in the camps. Their national liberation struggle against the authoritarian Polish Republic had taught them to build clandestine networks. After the war these networks could function openly, and they took over or created community organizations within and among the various camps. These newly created committees coordinated schools, institutions, training programs, and even civil courts.[24] Community activities, not anchored to a place and its specific needs, took on theoretical approaches to lofty goals.

Arrival on the fabled American shore (for them as well as for generations of earlier immigrants) marked the beginning of a period of hard work. The priests, and especially their wives, were no exception to this rule; and they were held to a higher standard. When for lack of money a priest became a factory worker, the chancery was scandalized. There are no relevant studies or even statistics, but in general the wives of priests did not work, and priests were poorly paid. Lack of English was a major drawback in the adjustment, but loss of status increased the unease. The new immigrant married clergy found life in the United States difficult, but nevertheless better than anything they could hope for elsewhere. America gave them a chance to educate their children, and for that they were grateful. The chancery gave the "new immigration" priests practical information to help them adjust to the new surroundings. A few of the parishes, however, unused to married clergy, refused to accept the proposed pastor's family. Such priests were redirected to other parishes.

Bohachevsky practiced cultural shock therapy with the DP clergy in the same manner he had dealt with his family when they arrived in the United States. In the preliminary correspondence with the priests, the

24. For instance: On June 17, 1949, a recent immigrant, Volodymyr Pushkar sent Ambrose Senyshyn a photo copy of the verdict of the "Highest Community Court of the Ukrainian Emigration [Nayvyshchyj Hromadiansky Sud Ukrayinskoii Emigratsii, file II K 34/48] which exonerated him, Maria Khomyn, and Stefania Pushkar of rumors of cheating the Halychyna folk arts cooperative, Narodne Mystestvo. The two-page, single-spaced decision used human rights antidefamation arguments. Copy of Pushkar to Senyshyn, June 17, 1949, UMAS, Chancery Archive.

bishop clearly explained that the exarchy in the United States was a mission church that did not have administrative facilities to accommodate a special relationship with the higher clergy. The bishop warned high-level clergy from Lviv and Peremyshl that they might find Europe more satisfying than working in a church influenced by American egalitarianism. The relationship of the bishop with the newly arrived priests, at least at the beginning, was purely professional. The priest was expected to make an appointment at the chancery as soon as possible after arrival in the United States. The meeting with the bishop took place in his spartan office, without even an offer of tea. Documents were signed, and pleasantries limited to a minimum. Even the shell-shocked priests with experience on the front were taken aback by the absence of extended conversations about family or geographical connections. Bohachevsky began interviews by clarifying the professional expectations, explaining some of the differences in administrative matters, and setting limits. He made certain that the necessary legal and practical information about running a parish was available to the new priest. He barely gave the émigré priests time to acclimatize themselves to the new surroundings. He welcomed the newcomers and sympathized with their often ghastly or miraculous experiences. But he addressed them as priests whose dedication should know no limits: "All clerics are called not only to work, but to sacrifice. Not just sacrifice, but for the sacrifice of a life filled with labor."[25]

The reaction of the newcomers to the bishop's professionalism was like that of the priests in the late 1920s who traveled miles to meet their new bishop for a touch of old-time Halychyna hospitality but instead found the prototype of the organization man. Then, as in the 1950s, some wrote off the bishop as a hermit, others as a Romanized American, but most priests eventually saw past the bishop's formal demeanor and accepted his approach to running the diocese. Once organizational matters were settled, most priests discovered Bohachevsky's mild congenial side, usually after the bishop's first visitation. The bishop became particularly close to the priests working in the chancery, a fair number of them from the "new emigration."

Both bishops (Bohachevsky and Senyshyn) regularly scheduled vis-

25. Speech at a regional clergy meeting, October 3, 1950, Camden, N.J., in *Eparkhiial'ni Visti*, November 1950, 74–76.

itations to meet with the priests and their congregations. The visiting bishop reviewed the books (both financial and those recording committee minutes), inspected the church, and heard confessions. Bohachevsky always followed up with a lengthy—at least a page or two, single-spaced evaluation letter. The letters began with praise but also pointed out specific shortcomings and suggestions on how those could be overcome. He analyzed the liturgical and the social activities of the pastor and went through the financial records. The bishop was especially interested in the success of the outreach programs for youth.[26] He tried to balance the "American" and the "European" clergy. He shuffled his priests and pushed to build the seminary in Washington, D.C. In contrast to the upheavals of the earlier decades, dissatisfactions were not brought to the public forum, but handled privately. Thus, when Bohachevsky replaced Rev. Stephan Hryniokh (who had long years of experience in the United States, but was singularly unambitious) as president of the Washington seminary by the former senator to the Polish Sejm, Rev. Roman Lobodych, the latter privately complained that he resented heading the seminary and felt isolated in Washington. He had expected some more visible appointment at the chancery. Bohachevsky's administrative positions were working appointments—he had not developed the European honorific clergy positions, perhaps because the eparchy was always short of clergy, but also because Bohachevsky saw each priest as a working one. Despite private grumblings, Bohachevsky's authority went unchallenged. There were disagreements among the priests but, for the most part, two priests chosen by the chancery handled these. They heard the aggrieved party or parties and recommended a solution. Although some priests did not get along with others, no major scandals occurred during the remainder of Bohachevsky's tenure.

The newly arrived clergy did not always adjust easily to their surroundings. The new immigrants brought additional problems for the Ukrainian Catholic Church, beginning with the issue of documentation. Proof of baptism and marriage were not always available; the validity of Orthodox baptisms was not always obvious; and the level of education of seminarians who came from war-time institutions could not be easily tested.

26. I generalize from the evaluation letters in the UMAS, Chancery Archive.

There were problems with communication, and these were not limited to language or even dialect. The two worlds had to be reconciled. The Ukrainian-Americans had already devised ways to function as a Ukrainian community in a changing America; the immigrants had left a destroyed, vanished world that some of them wanted to restore in America. The bishop early on sought to clarify the practices of the American exarchate vis-à-vis public expectations. This was especially critical in the matter of public ceremonies for the dead, which were often attended by non-Catholics. Life in the displaced person camps had broken down some of the barriers between Catholic and Orthodox Ukrainians, especially when it came to holding prayer services for deceased Ukrainian patriots, regardless of their religious affiliations or lack thereof. The post-war informality did not sit well with Bohachevsky. The diocesan regulations were spelled out in the August 1951 issue of the *Eparchial News*. They stressed the religious nature of the relevant ceremony and repeated the Catholic prohibition at the time of taking part in public, non-Catholic religious ceremonies. "Christ's love demands full civic tolerance toward non-Catholics, especially those with whom we share blood and language. But we cannot hold memorial liturgies for non-Catholics, even if they held high public positions in life."[27] There was no public reaction to this religious regulation; the church was no longer the sole public space for Ukrainians in America.

All Ukrainian-Americans had to make adjustments. The "old emigration" as well as the new had to find ways of accommodating themselves to each other and to a changing America. Life in the United States came as a particularly difficult shock to the middle-class immigrants. They had just barely survived the war years and did not expect the degree of physical labor that awaited them in the United States. Most adjusted with more or less grace. They advanced more rapidly in the growing American postwar economy than had been possible for many of the earlier immigrants. America of the 1950s had more opportunities for work and study than had been available in the 1930s and 1940s.

The influx of new priests was a godsend for Bohachevsky. He now had enough priests to do everything that a fully developed exarchate should do. By 1951, for the first time, he had a full listing of priests prepared—the schematism, or survey, that every office regarded as an achievement. The closest

27. "Eparkhiial'ni Statuty" [Eparkhial Statutes], *Eparkhiial'ni Visti*, August 1951, 76.

Bohachevsky had come to this earlier was the list compiled for the 1934 jubilee book. Cardinal Tisserant, the secretary of the Congregation for the Eastern Church at the Vatican thanked Bohachevsky for providing such "clear, professional, and useful information on the structure of the Exarchate."[28]

STEPS TOWARD ECUMENISM

Bohachevsky wanted a well-organized eparchy whose legitimacy could not be questioned as it became increasingly visible in the broader American context. Now more than ever the Ukrainian Catholic Church found itself between two fronts: communism with the now legalized Russian Orthodoxy and the lesser danger of the Ukrainian Orthodox churches. The second front was less obvious, but more dangerous: the slide of Ukrainian-rite faithful to Latin Catholicism through marriage and convenience. Roman Catholic churches were much larger, more openly American, better organized, and more conveniently located. It might have been hard to be a Catholic in America in the 1950s, but it was easier to be a Roman Catholic than to explain one's adherence to the Rutheno-Ukrainian Greek Catholic Church of the Byzantine Rite which was under the jurisdiction of the pope of Rome.

The apostolic delegate, the Congregation for the Eastern Church, and an increasing number of American, Latin-rite religious helped resolve the problems that arose between the rites. As the Ukrainian-American population became more mobile, the establishment of new parishes to accommodate this mobility became an important consideration. Responding to this trend, Latin-rite Catholic hierarchs asked that Ukrainian priests proposing to organize new parishes consult with the local Latin-rite Catholic priest or bishop to prevent any unnecessary conflict of interest. The nuncio, Cardinal Cicognani, seconded the request, while also assuring Bohachevsky that "this is in no way intended as a limitation of the personal protection which your Excellency enjoys over the Ruthenian faithful in the United States, but only as a measure aiming to avoid embarrassment."[29] A bonus to these collegial relations with the American clergy was that they made it more likely

28. "Pro Eparkhialni Statuty" [About the Eparchial Statutes], *Eparkhiial'ni Visti*, February 1951, 2–3.

29. Cicognani to Bohachevsky, March 29, 1942, UMAS, Chancery Archive. Bohachevsky shared the letter with Senyshyn.

that the Ukrainian Catholic Church would be able to draw on the resources of the Americans in organizing help for the victims of the war. Relations with the Catholic upper clergy remained not only cordial but sometimes even friendly. The clergy worked together to pressure Congress to include religious-based schools in federally funded educational support programs. As Bohachevsky wrote: "It is not fair for some children to enjoy privileges others do not have. It is improper for the government, using universal taxation, to fund medical care, transport, free textbooks for children of public schools while denying them to parochial school children."[30]

Another development working in favor of the Ukrainians was the growth of the liturgical movement among American Catholics in the post–World War II period, aimed at making the laity better informed about the liturgy and its meaning. At the time, services were conducted in Latin and without overt congregational participation. A more intimate understanding of the liturgical prayers would make the celebration more meaningful and interactive. The study of religious ritual spilled into an interest in the Ukrainian rite and its liturgy. Because the Ukrainian Catholic Church in Ukraine was by now a "church of the catacombs," Vatican officials took a more active part in Ukrainian Catholic celebrations in the United States. Eucharistic congresses, markings of the centenary of the promulgation of the doctrine of the Immaculate Conception of Mary in 1954, and observances of other holy years, anniversaries, pilgrimages, and conventions of religious societies offered opportunities to showcase the beauty of the Byzantine rite and call attention to the plight of Ukraine. In 1953, the Congregation for the Eastern Church authorized the inclusion into the Eastern liturgy of a prayer for the persecuted: "We also pray for our long-suffering land so that peace and well-being might be established there without violence" and at the Grand Entrance: "We remember . . . our suffering brothers."[31] It was an important addition, reflecting Sheptytsky's earlier informal usage.

These many small steps and overtures (from both sides) meant that

30. Circular letter, titled "Only Those Have Rights Who Care for Them," was sent to all clergy on June 14, 1949, UMAS, Chancery Archive.

31. The chancery provided the texts in Old Church Slavonic, with suitable stress symbols. It is dated January 1, 1953, UMAS, Chancery Archive. The Ukrainian Catholic Church at the time used Church Slavonic with a Western Ukrainian pronunciation.

the Ukrainian clergy now had more direct and meaningful contact with the American, Latin-rite Catholics in the common work of organizing and receiving displaced persons. Rather than just being on the receiving end of Roman Catholic hospitality, the Ukrainians were now active partners in an important enterprise. Unity Weeks, which became popular in America in the 1950s, provided another means to show the variety of Christianity. The practice originated in 1916, during the First World War, when Pope Benedict XV set aside one day a year (a time frame that was gradually expanded into a full week) for joint prayer of Catholics of all rites and all nations to be led by their respective higher clerics. The goal of the prayer days was to make the whole Catholic Church aware of its diverse nationalities and its many rites of worship as a step toward peace. Bohachevsky actively rejuvenated and expanded the celebrations of the Catholic "Unity Week" in the spring of 1939, a few months before the outbreak of the Second World War. He bolstered the campaign in May 1940, by devoting space to a discussion of this practice in the Philadelphia *Eparchial News*.[32] He also published Cardinal Tisserant's call to plan for ecumenical public prayers and activities each January. Bohachevsky initially appointed Rev. Omelian Ananevych as the person in charge of the coordination of these events, which Bishop Senyshyn greatly expanded.[33] The Ukrainian clergy, faithful, and school children used the occasion to visit American, Latin-rite Catholic communities with information about the Byzantine-Ukrainian rite and Ukrainian culture.

Having lost the Ukrainian Catholic Church to the Soviets, the papacy was equally concerned not to lose the American branch of the Ukrainian Church to the cultural pressure of the stronger Latin-rite Catholic Church. Barely giving his unexpectedly expanded congregation any time to catch its breath, the bishop (now buttressed by the expertise of priests from the new émigré group) increased his emphasis on introducing or restoring more visible signs of Eastern practices. The European priests, especially the younger ones, had been schooled to "de-Latinize" the Byzantine Catholic rite, and the recent émigrés, painfully aware of the fate of their loved ones, were more than ready to recreate the Ukrainian churches as they envisaged them. New talent had become available: a veritable army of émi-

32. "Units'ki tyzhni" [Unity Weeks], *Eparkhiial'ni Visti*, May 1940, 15.
33. *Eparkhiial'ni Visti*, May 1940, 15–17.

gré painters, craftsmen, embroiderers, woodcarvers, and others who were grateful for any work they could find. Artists were only too happy to create icons, the mandatory iconostasis, and proper vestments. They also helped to clean up prayer books and otherwise promote a greater understanding of the faith and adherence to its Eastern practices. The movement proceeded at a quick pace, and as the immigrant population grew, new churches sprang up in communities where enough money was collected to satisfy the minimum the chancery demanded of a parish before new construction could begin.

Relations with Latin-rite Catholics stabilized. The few local difficulties with the American Roman Catholic clergy usually stemmed from requests by elderly Ukrainian priests to say mass in the local Latin-rite Catholic church. Some of the Ukrainian priests were shocked that the American, Roman Catholic clergy could not converse freely with them in Latin. Now and again, a few American clerics still tried to dissuade Ukrainian priests from setting up new Ukrainian parishes and instead join the Latin rite, but such cases were rare, and the problem was generally related to the physical proximity of a Latin-rite church and not global opposition; the Americans had no problem with the erection of the proposed Ukrainian church in another part of the city.

THE EXPANSION OF THE COMMUNITY
AND THE LIMITS OF INTEGRATION

The growth and mobility of the Ukrainian-American population raised new challenges. Since many of the refugee clergy were advanced in years and the increase in the size of the clergy did not parallel the growth of the Ukrainian-American population, the eparchy again became short of priests. Bohachevsky faced his usual nightmare: he did not have priests for the people who wanted them. For example, in 1950 Mrs. Basil Leslie, an American-born Ukrainian Catholic living in Phoenix, Arizona, wrote to the Philadelphia chancery offering free room, and board at a minimal cost to any Eastern-rite Catholic priest who would come to minister to "those who do not speak English well enough [and] no doubt are deprived of the Sacrament of Penance because they do not know how to help themselves."[34] She explained that Father Sebastian Dzielski, a Franciscan who spoke some Polish, was the only priest in the rapidly growing city who could communicate with the Eastern Europeans who flocked there for jobs. "In the meantime," Mrs. Leslie continued, "schismatic and dissident Orthodox 'priests' are busy calling on all Eastern-rite Catholics, soliciting funds and presently building 2 Orthodox churches. They advertise in newspapers calling on Ukrainians, Serbians, and Russians to worship there."[35] In Florida, the problem was slightly different. The local Ukrainian-Catholic priest had run afoul of the Latin-rite Catholics by setting up a parish across the street from an existing Latin-rite parish.

Bohachevsky presumed that the newly arrived priests—many of whom had survived the war and its aftermath by miracle or luck—would be imbued with selfless dedication and willing to serve in any capacity wherever their services were most needed. The bishop thought that these priests would understand the need for missionary work. However, some priests, used to a more relaxed administration and a better standard of living, grumbled about their new situation. The clergy was now more ready to ask for adjustment of visitation dates and assorted regulations.[36] In his first *ad limina* report to Pope Pius XI, Bishop Senyshyn commented that newly arrived priests tended to begin their tenure in the New World by criticizing the existing Ukrainian institutions, complaining that more could have been done by the Ukrainian Catholic Church in America given all the advantages that the United States had to offer.

The new immigrants and clergy contributed to the diversification of the Ukrainian-American community and unexpectedly led to the decline of the older Ukrainian-American, Catholic lay organizations. The new immigrants unwittingly undermined existing Ukrainian organizations by creating new ones. Rather than join the existing organizations, the newcomers established church-related organizations similar to those that had existed in Halychyna, and those did not attract the "old timers." One

34. Bohachevsky to Senyshyn, April 21, 1950, UMAS, Chancery Archive.

35. Ibid. Bohachevsky to Senyshyn, April 21, 1950,

36. Thus Rev. Marko Gil, in a letter to the chancery on September 4, 1957, asked that the visitation planned for Friday, February 8, 1958, be moved to a Saturday. The parish was very spread out, and the children could come for religious instruction only on Saturday mornings.

example was the student branch of the Ukrainian Catholic scholarly organization, Obnova (Renewal). Planned as a Catholic student organization connected with the international Pax Romana student movement, it flourished in the 1950s and the early 1960s. But it consisted mostly of recently arrived youth who did not join the existing Ukrainian-American Catholic Youth League. If there were attempts to reach out to the American-born group, they were not successful. Neither organization prospered beyond the 1960s.

The relationship between the two waves of Ukrainian immigration was complex and has been little studied. There were significant differences in self-perception, manner of urbanization, and social expectations that made close interaction between the two difficult. Bohachevsky treated everyone equally, and did not think that social relations could be planned or engineered. The bishop encouraged and sometimes even financially supported the new lay organizations, such as Obnova or Plast, the Ukrainian scouting association, but he did not personally take on an active leadership role in fashioning a broader community. Instead, the bishop's office delegated individual priests to work with those groups, generally leaving their respective activities up to the members. The increase in the number and types of community organizations meant that the churches were no longer the sole manifestation of Ukrainian presence. There was no need to fight for the control of the churches, because other institutions could fulfill personal ambitions and community needs. Nonetheless, the difficulties of accommodation increased as the "new immigrants" acculturated themselves into American life and wanted different things from their church and social organizations. New organizations, unconnected to the original churches sprang up locally. They reflected the overall secularization of society.

Bishop Bohachevsky had difficulty adjusting to the growing irrelevance of religion in public life. Above all, he feared that the Ukrainian Catholic Church might be drawn into political movements that could undermine it. He warned that nationalism without Christian values deteriorates into hatred, though he failed to recognize that much of the nationalist rhetoric was an emotional crutch, not a reasoned attack on the values of Christianity. The bishop reminded his flock repeatedly of Christian ethical values that must imbue all patriotism and nationalism. He stressed that

Ukrainian public organizations stand and fall with the church and most draw their beginnings from the church.[37]

Bohachevsky was not skilled at creating a relaxed atmosphere in large groups, but he worked well with associates. The priests with whom he worked on a daily basis included married and unmarried clergy, some younger and some older. His relationship with the young, American-born priests was more fatherly than intimate. The bishop built the young men's self-confidence. As Rev. Michael Poloway, one of his last chancellors, put it: "he made a man out of me."[38] The bishop was genuinely proud of his young priests.

As an echo of earlier times, some Ukrainian Catholics again spoke of Ukrainian replacing Church Slavonic as the language of worship. They pointed to the popularity of the Ukrainian Autocephalous Church and pressured the bishop to drop the term "Ruthenian" from the full title of their church. Bohachevsky no longer had Sheptytsky to help him defend the use of the term, but he hesitated to change the name for fear of alienating the Ruthenians and diminishing hopes for a unification of the two exarchates into a single archbishopric—the unstated goal of the Vatican and most likely of all the bishops involved.

Bohachevsky continued to urge the clergy to think about organizing and financing a home for aged priests and to devise retirement plans to include priests who needed financial help.[39] Because the clergy had adamantly refused to consider a mandatory clerical insurance policy back in the 1930s, the chancery did not consider it wise to reintroduce it. He paid close attention to the fee schedule, and repeatedly reminded his priests of the special-purpose collections authorized to be taken during church ser-

37. Christmas pastoral letter, *Eparkhiial'ni Visti*, November 1943, 37; and Christmas pastoral letter, *Eparkhiial'ni Visti*, November 1945.

38. Poloway, telephone conversations with the author, July 5–30, 2009. Between 1954 and 1961, Rev. Michael Poloway (1928–2018) served as the bishop's secretary and chancellor. In his conversations with me, he stressed the bishop's high expectations, focus on order, ability to administer, and a willingness to teach. Poloway did not regret the eleven years he served at the chancery, learned from the bishop, who expected much from others, but more from himself. He noted the bishop's organizational skill in detail work and in long-range planning, as well as the orderly atmosphere in the office. The bishop was strict but fair. "The bishop made a man out of me," was a phrase Poloway repeated to me a couple of times.

39. See, for instance, *Eparkhiial'ni Visti*, February 1945, 8–9; *Eparkhiial'ni Visti*, May 1946, 20; and *Eparkhiial'ni Visti*, May 1947, 19.

vices. Nor did he overlook the practical: in his communications with his priests, he called attention to liability insurance, fire hazards in church structures, and the importance of legally drafted wills and testaments.[40] Priests from Europe had to be reminded to register Mass intentions in a separate, hardbound notebook, not keep them as random notes. The bishop continued to document the finances of the diocese carefully, and, toward the end of his life, was aided by an efficient financial administrator, Basil Holovinsky, who provided directions to pastors on how to prepare the necessary financial reports for the bishop's office.[41] In April 1950, the chancery issued a six-page, single-spaced instructional packet for the clergy, with detailed instructions on how the church and its religious implements should look, how to care for them, when to renew the gold plate, and similar information. Some of these regulations were determined by the Apostolic See itself; the episcopal chancery decided on the others. In either case, the chancery's position and purpose was clear: "Careful adherence to regulations in small matters will contribute to the beauty and order of our rite, to the education of the faithful, and toward God's glory."[42] Some of the older priests complained that young priests seldom wore cassocks, were never seen with a prayer book in their hands, and did not show enough concern for the education of the youth.[43] The bishop, instead, saw their enthusiasm, their knowledge, and their readiness to take on the most difficult of parishes.

As the displaced persons settled, the Ukrainian Catholic Church in America expanded, its schools grew, and the number of its publications increased. The parish structure in the church, and the concentrated nature of the arrival of the displaced persons masked the lack of integration between the immigrant waves. After all, the geographical expansion of the church had been on the upswing throughout the 1940s, with new parishes created in the West, including in California in 1949. New religious orders were brought in—the Sisters of the Sacred Heart from Italy in 1948 and the

---

40. *Eparkhiial'ni Visti*, May 1957, 27, on liability insurance; *Eparkhiial'ni Visti*, August 1958, 103, information on building materials.

41. As in *Eparkhiial'ni Visti*, 1960, 87–98.

42. Copy of instruction in the UMAS, Chancery Archive.

43. Rev. V. Andrushkiw to Bohachevsky; copy of letter sent by Bohachevsky to Senyshyn, August 7, 1950, UMAS, Chancery Archive.

Redemptorist Fathers in 1946.[44] The church remained united, although the faithful gravitated to the parishes that suited them, rather than the one in which they lived.

In July 1948, when his younger brothers were arriving in the United States, Bohachevsky suffered three coronaries. None of the brothers even considered the emotional stress and the physical exertion of his postwar tasks as contributing factors to the illness. They instead accepted heart disease almost as a family badge of honor—a challenge the males of the family had to face.

The standard of care at the time was rest, and Constantine's physician, Dr. Emil Harasym, made certain the bishop had that. When Bohachevsky was finally permitted to move back into his new residence at Medary Street, he stopped at the St. Basil Motherhouse at Fox Chase to pray. In the first difficult years of his bishopric, that was where he had taught the young women who were to become teachers in the Ukrainian Catholic schools. In a rare moment of intimacy, he confided to the young Sister Emellia Prokopik that he felt most at home amid the quiet, farm-like surroundings of the campus of the St. Basil Academy for Girls.[45] For Bohachevsky, it was the cradle of the Ukrainian Catholic Church in the United States. He told Sister Emellia that the monastery was the closest place he had to a warm, homey atmosphere. Having survived the heart attacks, Bohachevsky felt blessed again by God to continue His work. Instead of tamping down his schedule, he redoubled his efforts to build the seminary in Washington, D.C. Rather than viewing the illness as a warning to ease up, the bishop saw it as a call to finish the major task for which he was created: the establishment of the graduate seminary.

Bishop Senyshyn, his trusted auxiliary, again felt that it would be appropriate after Bohachevsky's life-threatening illness to celebrate the milestones of his life. January 1949 marked the fortieth anniversary of Bo-

44. Procko, *Ukrainian Catholics in America*, 75. The Sacred Heart Sisters are not to be confused with the Order of the Sacred Heart that originated in France in the eighteenth century with the specific mission of educating young women.

45. Mother Emellia Prokopik, OSBM, conversations with the author, undated.

hachevsky's ordination as a priest—a significant number at a time when male life expectancy was still not much over sixty. Bohachevsky would turn sixty-five that July. Of even greater significance was the twenty-fifth anniversary of his becoming a bishop, an occasion marked on June 15, 1949.

A special issue of the new diocesan weekly, *The Way*, carried articles extolling Bohachevsky's achievements as well as his patriotism.[46] An article detailing his support of the orphanage ended with a sweet poem. Pope Pius XII sent formal greetings, praising Bohachevsky's achievements, especially the establishment of the seminary, and granting the bishop the right to grant a full indulgence on the day of the celebrations. Bishop Senyshyn felt strongly that these milestones should be celebrated publicly. Bohachevsky, his emotions still raw from the fates of his fellow bishops in communist Ukraine and his own illness, grudgingly consented to public prayer services without, however, a public celebration. Bishop Senyshyn supervised the daylong prayers and ceremonies that made full use of the Stamford grounds. But public prayer had different meanings for all who engaged in it.

Bohachevsky envisaged a day of prayer; but the community leaders expected a public exchange of good wishes, attendant patriotic statements, and private meetings with the bishop. Still weak, Bohachevsky ruled out activities beyond church celebrations, and he retired at the end of the prayer services. The community leaders saw the bishop's failure to grant them a private audience as a slap on the public face and proof of Bohachevsky's lack of manners at best, or, most likely, his lack of patriotism. Senyshyn testily replied that the gentlemen had not even bothered to respond to the formal invitation, they were in no position to give deportment lessons. Another outburst was in the making.

Roman Smal-Stocki was among the scholars who tried to draw Bishop Bohachevsky into the elite, scholarly organizations that the new immigrants had transferred from Europe. First among these organizations was the Shevchenko Scientific Society, the oldest of the Ukrainian scholarly

46. The Basilian journal *Kovcheh* (no. 5, 1954, 85–94), published in Stamford, also ran an article on the anniversaries using a title that Rev. Tarnawsky had used in 1934, "Arkheepys-kop Konstantyn i potriyny iuviley" [Archbishop Constantine and the Triple Jubilee], in the Lviv newspaper *Nova Zoria*, August 19, 1934, 4–5.

societies. It had been founded at Halychyna in the 1890s with the financial support of Ukrainian activists from the eastern parts of Ukrainian territories. Before World War I, the society published in its influential journal some articles which questioned traditional Christian beliefs. Although the society was not inherently or specifically anticlerical or antireligious, and although Catholic clergy contributed to its publications, Bohachevsky, still fearing the popularity of post–World War II procommunist and pro-Russian sentiments, refused to acknowledge what the members of the society claimed to be his membership. For good measure, Bohachevsky also declined honorary membership in the Ukrainian Free Academy of Arts and Sciences, claiming abstention from all public societies.

Giving up on the elderly bishop, Smal-Stocki hoped to "begin a new page" in the history of close relations with the church with Senyshyn and the intelligentsia, including Myshuha. Smal-Stocki sent Senyshyn a breezy letter in which he complained, in his usual light-hearted, snappy manner, that "Kyr Konstantyn treats us, the faithful, as [the Polish President Josef] Pilsudski treated his Parliament. . . . He does not want to recognize us at all."[47] Smal-Stocki's attempted levity shocked Senyshyn, who read his comments as "high-handed teachings [poucheniia]." In a three-page, single-spaced letter, Senyshyn lectured the scholar that "the Silver Jubilee of Kyr Constantine had been planned as a prayer of thanks to the Lord God. No banquets had been planned." He reminded Smal-Stocki that he, Senyshyn, organized at the last minute a lunch for the leaders of the organizations who, he reminded him again, had not even bothered to reply to the invitations sent to them and were now angry that they had been slighted. Smal-Stocki had also used this letter to argue that the rift between Bohachevsky and Myshuha should be bridged. To that, Senyshyn added caustically, "[Myshuha] knows full well that he had not fulfilled all the conditions to which he had agreed." Senyshyn concluded the letter: "with a very heavy heart, because I had never expected that some gentlemen would treat the bishop at his Jubilee in such a manner. I am leaving a copy of this letter in the archive for future generations. Let others find out someday how certain individuals treated their spiritual elders."[48]

47. Smal-Stocki to Bishop Senyshyn, undated, UMAS, Chancery Archive.
48. Both letters in UMAS, Chancery Archive.

GROWTH THROUGH TRAGEDY 443

Neither side wanted an overt clash, and a *modus vivendi* was easily found. To prove this point, the leaders of the community (including recently arrived immigrants) organized another, this time public, celebration of the bishop's anniversaries in Philadelphia. The bishop agreed to attend. The celebration of the bishop's three anniversaries—the twenty-fifth of his bishopric, the fortieth of his priesthood, and his sixty-fifth birthday—was held on October 30, 1949, at Philadelphia's Town Hall. The event, which included a concert and several speeches from community representatives, was a concerted attempt to demonstrate that whatever disagreements had existed between the Ukrainian National Association and the Providence Association (that is, between the practicing Catholics in the bishops' camp and the Catholics who identified with a more secular Catholicism) were patched up.[49]

One of the key speakers at the event was the apostolic delegate to the United States, Bishop Amleto G. Cicognani, whose support Bohachevsky valued greatly.[50] Cicognani's background and his moderately conservative views facilitated a closeness between the two that would probably not have developed had the nuncio come from an upper-class, Italian family. Cicognani, a year older than Bohachevsky, had risen to prominence in the shadow of an older brother. Despite his humble origins, he was elevated to bishop in 1933, the year of the Great Famine in Ukraine and the year that the United States established diplomatic relations with the Soviet Union. He was soon appointed the Vatican's representative to the United States and served in that position until the end of the 1959. During his tenure as an informal ambassador, Cicognani developed an interest in the Ukrainian Catholic Church in the United States. Bohachevsky appreciated that interest and supported Cicognani's successful initiative to spur the creation of the Legion of Decency in the United States, which would, like the Index of Forbidden Books, rate films. During the Second

49. Luka Myshuha was not present.

50. Cicognani's widowed, working-class mother put him and his older brother through schooling, and Cicognani rose in the Vatican diplomatic service. Cicognani (1883–1973) became a cardinal in 1958 in a highly unusual move since his brother was also a cardinal and the Vatican sought to avoid the appearance of impropriety by not having two members of a family in highly placed positions. He became the secretary of the Congregation for the Eastern Church in 1959, headed a Vatican post that is equivalent to the secretary of state, and in 1972 headed the College of Cardinals.

World War Cicognani served as a conduit between the Vatican and Italian opposition factions. In this capacity he sought to help Jewish and other victims of Nazism and fascism, including the Ukrainians. Considering that the Ukrainian national cause did not enjoy the support of any states, Cicognani's presence at all the major events of Bohachevsky's church was likely perceived by the Ukrainian émigré community as a form of recognition of Ukraine's aspirations.

Bohachevsky, for his part, remained vigilant that the church not involve itself in politics. When *America* published a plea for donations to the Ukrainian Congress Committee of America for the liberation of Ukraine, the bishop sent a strong rebuke to its editor: "In churches one collects money for God's work. Moneys collected in churches are to serve God's causes. The committee that edited the plea [you published] wants to use church money for political action . . . and wants to collect the funds independently [of church committees]."[51] The writer of the solicitation article, a recent émigré did not lose his job.[52]

As the decade waned, Bohachevsky meditated on the upcoming Holy Year proclaimed by the pope. He prayed for religious vocations and placed his and the nation's hopes on Catholic higher education: "Now, when the enemy of God and mankind is doing everything to complete the ruin, let us, the free people . . . build our Spiritual Fortress, our Graduate Spiritual Seminary in Washington, which will vouchsafe our future and be the sacred gift we bring the Newborn Savior in the 1950 Jubilee year."[53]

51. Bohachevsky to the editor, Ihnat Bilynsky, May 14, 1948, UMAS.

52. Bilynsky immediately responded, explaining that he did not realize that solicitation for unsanctioned public causes was not appropriate in Ukrainian Catholic churches in the United States. Bohachevsky sent Senyshyn a copy of that explanatory letter on March 22, 1952, UMAS, Chancery Archive.

53. Pastoral letter, *Eparkhiial'ni Visti*, November 1949, 73–76.

CHAPTER 13

The Productive 1950s

THE ST. JOSAPHAT SEMINARY IN
THE NATION'S CAPITAL

Neither Bohachevsky's faith in God, nor his vision of a prosperous independent Ukraine faltered under the barrage of personal disappointments and world problems. The bishop combined his deep unquestioning Christian faith with a practical approach to problems at hand that he considered were his responsibility to solve. Through the cataclysmic changes in the world and in his own society, he maintained that it was better to get a small job done than to despair because a larger goal could not be met. The influx of new parishioners and new clergy gave him a renewed spurt of energy. The people shored up the church as it grew stronger with its schools and its expanding network of solid parishes. To make certain that such progress would continue, he as the bishop of the Ukrainian Catholic Church, had to establish a graduate-level seminary to ensure the proper training of its priests, now that the European seminaries were either destroyed or severely cut. His next task would be to prepare timely, clear-cut rules and regulations for the expanded exarchy. That he would see done. The final step, the reason for his nomination as bishop, depended on Rome—the recognition of the exarchy of the Ukrainian Catholic Church of the United States as an eparchy or even a metropolitanate.

After extensive deliberation and travel, in 1941, Bohachevsky decided on Washington, D.C., as the site for the Ukrainian Major Seminary. Several factors influenced that decision. Washington was the nation's capital. It was the seat of the apostolic delegate from the Vatican, the Ukrainian exarch's direct link to the papacy. The Catholic University of America, a central, American, Catholic institution, was growing in importance. That university, established through the joint efforts of the Latin Catholic bishops, was a bold educational experiment. The American Catholic bishops for the most part functioned by consensus, and they also ran the university that way. Thus, in 1941, Bohachevsky sent the graduates of St. Basil's College at Stamford to Washington. For two years the seminarians lived in rented quarters as they attended classes at the Catholic University of America. In 1943 the eparchy bought a little more than an acre of land near the university. The hilly, wooded spot sported a view of the Capitol and was within easy walking distance of the university. The building of the seminary had to wait until the end of the war. He waited restlessly. He had the land surveyed, the plans drawn, and whatever materials could be had, gathered. The architect Julian Jastremsky provided the plans, which were published in the September 10, 1949, issue of *The Way*. Ground was broken on May 28, 1950. Cutting corners and hurrying the builders, Bohachevsky pushed for completion, and St. Josaphat Seminary was ready in two years.

Set on a hill, the three-story, stone building was imposing. Its classrooms, dormitories, library, and chapel were solemnly blessed on May 31, 1952, with the participation of Bishops Nil Savaryn of Edmonton, Andrey Roboretsky of Saskatoon, and Danylo Ivancho of the Ruthenian Eparchy in Pittsburgh. The papal nuncio and Bishop Patrick J. McCormick, president of the Catholic University of America, were distinguished participants. A large crowd joined in the singing led by a united choir.[1] A festive reception for almost a thousand guests followed. The newly consecrated Bishop Havryil Bukatko of Križevci (in war-torn Yugoslavia) sent a personal letter with a note of thanks for Bohachevsky's financial support, providing a tangible, even if tenuous, link with the old world. Long after the opening ceremonies ended, Bohachevsky enjoyed making unannounced visits to

---

1. Metropolitan Stefan Sulyk wrote that there were seven other Latin-rite Catholic bishops at the ceremony. I have not been able to confirm this statement. Sulyk mentioned that the seminarians had not been invited to the luncheon. Sulyk, *Yak Stefan stav mytropolytom*, 147–50.

the seminary.[2] At the time a convenient trolley line ran from Union Station to a stop a few blocks from the property. The bishop would walk up the sloping hill, his pace steady and firm. He sometimes sat in on the oral examinations of the seminarians, carefully listening to the discussion.

Bishop Senyshyn pointed out that it was difficult for St. Basil College in Connecticut to compete with the more established colleges in the area and sought ways to either strengthen or supplement its program. In the late 1940s, at the initiative of Professor Roman Smal-Stocki, Senyshyn suggested the establishment of an institute of Byzantine studies, which not being accredited, would be easier to staff with new immigrants whose academic credentials were not always acknowledged by American boards of education. He even proposed calling it "the Bohachevsky Institute" to get the archbishop on board, but to no avail. Bohachevsky liked the project, but could not offer it any financial support. As far as he was concerned, the seminary had priority, followed by the needs of the college students, such as a better cafeteria. If Bishop Senyshyn and the Ukrainian scholars considered such an institute a priority, he would have to raise the funds.[3] Bohachevsky felt that the network of the parochial schools, high schools, and colleges, and the seminary, funded by the faithful, provided the foundation that the community needed for its development. The community should take the lead on the other projects its spokesmen considered essential.

At the same time, other projects were considered. Bohachevsky studied the possibility of expanding a summer camp for the seminarians in Stratford, New York, to all children from the eparchy. Bishop Senyshyn, however, had been so impressed by the private scout camp in Chatham,

2. There was one unpleasant incident involving a dozen young parishioners of the local Ukrainian parish headed by a recently arrived pastor, Rev. Volodymyr Pylypets. He let the parish youth sell refreshments for the benefit of the parish near the seminary, without first checking with the Franciscan Friars, the owners of that land. The young people raised $120 but ruined the Franciscan lawn. The friars demanded compensation from Bohachevsky, who instituted a formal inquiry into the matter. Rev. Pylypets was upset that the good will of the young people was not only not appreciated, but the parish paid the fine to the friars for the destruction of the lawn. The event reflected some of the difficulties in the adjustment of European clergy to American realities. Correspondence for June 1952, UMAS, Chancery Archive.

3. Most active correspondence on the topic occurred between August and September 1951, UMAS, Chancery Archive.

FIGURE 13. ON THE MOUNTAIN TOP

New York, operated by the Plast Organization that he concluded that the community did not need the church's support for its youth camps. The eparchy did not have the resources to run a lay camp as well as a separate one for the seminarians. The seminarians kept their summer camp.

AN ARCHBISHOP OF AN EXARCHY

In 1952, Pius XII named Bohachevsky an assistant to the papal throne and a Roman count. This was a personal honorific that acknowledged Bohachevsky's standing at the papal court. The community still responded to such signs of distinction. The following year, five Ukrainian Catholic priests, four of them American-born, were named papal chamberlains, an unusual honor for one exarchy.[4] These distinctions were not wide-

4. They were Revs. Nicholas Babak, Joseph Batza, Dmytro Gresko, Joseph Schmondiuk, and John Stock.

ly recognized beyond the upper Ukrainian Catholic clergy. In April 1954 Bohachevsky was elevated to titular archbishop of Beroe. Although this personal title did not reflect the existence of an archbishopric, it was a recognition of the importance of Bohachevsky's work. The new archbishop treated the title for what it was, a personal honor. Bohachevsky turned seventy that June; he had been a priest for forty-five years and a bishop for thirty.[5] As always, the new archbishop downplayed his important dates while highlighting milestones in the history of the exarchy.

The archbishop now pushed more insistently for the formal recognition of the exarchate as an eparchy/diocese, which would transform the Ukrainian Catholic Church in the United States from an *ad hoc* institution serving an ostensibly temporary or even transient community into an established church with a permanent status. Neither age nor the awareness of his heart condition diminished Bohachevsky's devotion to this mission.

In 1956, the Philadelphia exarchate was considered large enough to warrant a second bishopric. The appointment of an auxiliary bishop to serve under Bohachevsky was a further step in the growth of the church. In July 1956, Joseph Schmondiuk, an alumnus of St. Basil Orphanage School, became the first American-born, Ukrainian Catholic to be consecrated as a bishop in the United States. The ceremony concelebrated by Bishops Bohachevsky, Senyshyn, and Elko, who now headed the Ruthenian branch of the church, was held on November 8, 1956. The choice of the Ruthenian bishop (rather than any of the Canadian-Ukrainian Catholic bishops) reflected the ongoing attempts to reconcile the two parts of the original American Ukrainian-Ruthenian diocese.

Almost simultaneously, the Ukrainian Catholic eparchy took the next step in its development with the creation of a second see, which was to be headquartered at Stamford, Connecticut. This reflected the progress that the Ukrainian Catholic Church in the United States had made toward the goal of the establishment of an archdiocese. On August 8, 1956, Bishop Ambrose Senyshyn was raised from the rank of auxiliary to ordinary for the territory that covered New York and the New England states. New Jer-

5. Bishop Senyshyn ran a long article on Bohachevsky's life, in *Kovcheh* (*The Ark*), May 1954, 58–76, as a preliminary to the program for the National Eucharistic Marian Congress of Oriental Rites. Both terms "Oriental" and "Eastern" were used interchangeably, depending on the predilections of the user.

sey remained in the Philadelphia exarchate. Meanwhile, an interdiocesan commission, headed by Rev. Dr. Basil Makuch, detailed the transition of the Philadelphia exarchate into two units. The administrative reshuffling that resulted ran smoothly. The newly established Diocese of Stamford consisted of 53 parishes and 4 missions; it numbered 101 priests and 86,324 faithful. The Philadelphia eparchy retained 122 parishes, 7 missions, and 219,720 faithful.[6] The creation of the second exarchate necessitated the division of diocesan finances. Senyshyn was very hesitant about bringing up the subject, but was forced to do so because he did not have the wherewithal to cover the new exarchate's expenses.[7] The seemingly pedestrian issue of financial redistribution as well as the numerical calculations about the new geographic division in the number of faithful and the number of clergy marked the beginning of a new era. Most significantly, the obvious need for a genuine institutional financial policy and the introduction of related reforms ended the ecclesiastical paternalism of old Halychyna and placed the Ukrainian Catholic Church on a more formal institutional footing.

Meanwhile, even before the exarchate had developed into a fully recognized eparchy, Bohachevsky was very much aware of the need to document the existence and the experience of the Ukrainian Catholic Church at a time when the existence of the Ukrainians as a distinct nationality was overlooked or questioned. During the Second World War, a special committee supported by the bishop had edited a booklet honoring the centenary of the priest, patriot, and poet Markian Shashkevych, who was the first priest to preach in the vernacular at Lviv in the 1830s.[8] A few years later, Bohachevsky supported the writing and publication of Hryhor Luzhnytsky's *Ukrainian Church between East and West: Outline of [the] History of [the] Ukrainian Church (Ukraiins'ka Tserkva mizh Skhodom i Zakhodom)*. This 723-page, glossy, illustrated tome in Ukrainian very much reflected the traditional Old-World style of scholarship. The fact that the author modestly called the weighty volume "an outline" indicates his frustration at being

6. Sochotsky, "The Ukrainian Catholic Church of the Byzantine-Slavonic Rite in the USA," 199–248; and an English-language, condensed version prepared by Rev. Constantine Berdar, in Kharyna, *Ukraiins'ka Katolyts'ka Mytropolia*, 249–87.

7. Senyshyn to Bohachevsky, October 16, 1956, UMAS, Chancery Archive.

8. *Propamiatna Knyha Amerykan'skykh Ukraiintsiv*.

cut off from indispensable sources. The volume was published in 1954. Bohachevsky also provided support to Mykhailo Tershakovets for what was to have been the definitive study on Rev. Shashkevych.

THE FIRST NATIONAL EUCHARISTIC MARIAN
CONGRESS OF THE EASTERN RITES

Bohachevsky supported Bishop Senyshyn's forays into outreach projects, including the latter's participation in the American bishops' conference. Significant among these projects were the pilgrimages that Senyshyn organized in conjunction with the papal Holy Years: one to Rome in 1950 and another to Lourdes in 1958. In the United States, Senyshyn showcased the Ukrainian Church very effectively at the 1941 Chicago Eucharistic Congress, and on its heels, the First Eastern-rite Eucharistic Congress. Although organized on a small scale, that congress merited praise from the Vatican. Buoyed by this success, Bishop Senyshyn began to plan for a larger congress to be held after the diocese successfully absorbed the new immigrants. He proposed a major American National Eucharistic Marian Congress for the Oriental (or Eastern) Rites.

Much as Archbishop Bohachevsky valued and supported Senyshyn, he did not consider this type of activity to be of equal value to pastoral work, the day-to-day administration of the exarchy, the building of the church's infrastructure, or the support of a major publication. Bohachevsky was ambivalent about committing resources needed for one-time public activities. He did not like mass events, and he was not convinced that they brought permanent benefits. Moreover, Bohachevsky was concerned that some of the more popular religious activities, such as *molebens*—special services directed to a saint or a cause—or the adoration of the Host, violated the traditions of the Eastern rite. Holding festivities that popularized such activities would make a return to the original Eastern discipline more difficult. Bishop Senyshyn worked hard to convince Archbishop Bohachevsky that sponsoring a major congress would not be a waste of resources. He involved the apostolic delegate in the planning of the congress, and Cicognani declared that the *molebens* were in accordance with Eastern-rite traditions.[9]

9. Senyshyn to Bohachevsky, January 14, 1954, letter in UMAS, Chancery Archive.

Still hesitant, Bohachevsky sought guidance where he had always found it—in prayer. Long hours of solitary prayer were his solace and inspiration. Appropriately enough it was Mary, in whose honor this Eucharistic congress was being planned, who swayed the archbishop into supporting the congress. The archbishop felt a particular devotion to Mary in all the guises in which she was portrayed. For the archbishop, Mary's enveloping cloak, which had shielded the Cossacks from Asian nomads and Turks, signified his mother, his country, his people, and his path to God. Metropolitan Andrey Sheptytsky had dedicated the American eparchy to the Immaculate Conception back in 1911. The current year, 1954, marked the centenary of the formal proclamation of the doctrine of the Immaculate Conception of Mary, the belief that the Virgin was born without the stain of original sin that was the inescapable proclivity of humankind to deviate from the good. It was an old belief, attested to by icons and texts, but having it announced from the papal throne in 1854 gave it renewed visibility. Its centenary served the same purpose. Moreover, in 1950 Pope Pius XII had defined another aspect of Mary, the Assumption, according to which at the end of her earthly life she was transported in body to meet Christ. If indeed the Ukrainian Catholic Church in the United States had to make itself more public, then the 1954 Marian Year was an auspicious time to mount the National Eucharistic Marian Congress for Eastern Rites. It was originally planned for May 1954, but had to be rescheduled to October because Rome set the canonization of Pope Pius X for that May.

Once the archbishop relented, he threw himself fully into the preparatory activities. His strict adherence to detail was legendary. Senyshyn drew the broad community into the preparatory work. Bohachevsky wanted to know what the thirty-eight committees were doing. All specialized groups performed their circumscribed functions with great care in order to make the whole congress a recognized success—from crowd control during the processions to the functioning of the latest technology allowing for remote control of the microphones on the altars. Bohachevsky's long years of preparatory organizational work led to the successful staging by his diocese of the First Eucharistic Marian Congress of the Eastern Rites. Bishop Senyshyn was the executive chair of the complex event.

The congress exemplified an important early step toward Catholic ecumenism. Media interest and the participation of Latin-rite Catholics in the very visible prayers and ceremonies called the attention of the broader public to the existence of other Catholic rites besides the Latin rite. The congress was formally hosted by the two archbishops of Philadelphia: John F. O'Hara and Constantine Bohachevsky—a novelty for the Latin Catholic Church in America that had previously adamantly adhered to the old principle of one bishop for a city.

The First National Eucharistic Marian Congress of the Eastern Rites was held on October 22, 23, and 24, 1954, with the very visible participation of the elite of the American Latin Catholic Church and the Vatican.[10] The entire year had been dedicated to Mary to mark the centenary of Pius IX's promulgation of the Immaculate Conception. The three-day Eucharistic congress brought together Catholic hierarchs from America, Europe, and the Near East, as well as the exiled archbishop of China, Cardinal Thomas Tien. The papal nuncio, Amleto Cicognani, presided. Catholicism in the United States was no longer exclusively Latin. Other Catholic rites were placed on equal public footing. The papacy and the Latin-rite Catholics had recognized the equality of Eastern rites earlier, of course; many Roman Catholic priests and even more Latin Catholic laity actively helped the Ukrainian immigrants and their churches, but this event sought to make a public statement of that equality on the historic streets of Philadelphia. We must remember that this was in 1954, when the Catholic liturgy in the world was primarily celebrated in Latin, the *Baltimore Catechism* defined Catholicism for most American Catholics, and other Americans tended to look askance at Catholics for their veneration of a foreign pope. Few Latin-rite Catholics even knew of the existence of the Eastern rites in their church, since most identified Catholicism with Latin.

The congress turned the tables on the presumptions of Latin universalism. The highlight of the gathering was the dramatic joint celebration of the Divine Liturgy in different languages at nine altars set up on the stage of Philadelphia's huge and secular convention center on Spruce Street in

10. The cardinals were Peter XV Agagianian, Samuel Stritch, and Thomas Tien. The bishops were Peter Chami, Isidor Borecky, Maxym Hermaniuk, Joseph McShea, Andrew Roborecki, and Neil Savaryn. The fullest account of the event is provided in the issues of *The Ark*, beginning with May through December 1954. Due credit was given to all participants—clergy, organizations, choirs and orchestras, and participants of some 144 parishes.

the heart of the city. The boxy Convention Hall was transformed into an Eastern church, with a specially made iconostasis. Different banners added to the scene. The crowd, the religious, and the clergy in their distinctive habits and vestments, the school groups in their uniforms, the sodalities in their capes and veils, the hatted ladies, the somber men, the constantly changing choirs, the incense, and the bells—all transfixed the vast public space into a far-off Eastern cathedral.

The liturgy was sung in the Armenian, Maronite, Chaldean, and Latin rites, as well as variants of the Byzantine rite—Melchite, Ukrainian, Ruthenian (with Slovaks and Hungarians), Romanian, and Russian. The coordinated consecration of the Host highlighted the uniqueness of this service. Although there were nine separate services at separate altars, the celebration was one. In a carefully coordinated manner, each rite had its allotted vocal part, while the most solemn part—the Consecration of the Host—was chanted jointly. The Melchites, headed by a Syrian archbishop, sang in Greek and Arabic. The Maronites used Syro-Arabic. The Chaldeans sang in both Arabic and Chaldean. The Armenians celebrated in Armenian, calling attention to the fact that their Christian faith antedated any East-West split. The Catholic Russians of the Byzantine rite used Church Slavic and the Moscow chant, with responses in a Russian accent. The Romanians of the Byzantine rite used Romanian. The Ruthenians, Hungarians, and Slovaks of the Byzantine rite prayed at a common altar but each used their version of Church Slavonic and contemporary Hungarian, all in the Kyivan chant. The Ukrainians of the Byzantine rite used Church Slavonic with the ecclesiastical chant of Pochayiv. To affirm that this was one liturgy, all celebrants chanted the most solemn part of the liturgy—the Consecration—jointly, though in different languages, uniting in their single most sacred ritual. The reverberations of choir and clergy covered up the fact that the Eastern version of the consecration was a bit longer than the Latin variant, because it included the invocation to the Spirit, the epiclesis, which had been weakened in the Latin rite centuries earlier. Peter XV Cardinal Agagianian, archbishop of Armenians, presided at the liturgy and preached the sermon.[11] The papal nuncio and the two Catholic

11. The Catholic Armenians signed their final document on unity with Rome in Lviv in 1742 and were the most numerous the Catholic Eastern churches in Halychyna, next to

archbishops of Philadelphia were among the worshipers. Thousands who had honored the strict fasting rule received Communion.

The organizers, as well as the majority of the twenty thousand participants of the congress, were members of the Ukrainian Catholic Church of the Byzantine rite in America. This was the most populous religious event they had sponsored in the United States. The congress was large, yet intimately spiritual. A sense of transcendent unity pervaded the crowd. Because there were so many languages, language did not seem to matter— nor did geography, nor the unrelenting tragedy of the Ukrainian Catholic mother church, outlawed in the USSR, but despite brutal persecutions functioning underground. Speaker after speaker invoked its martyrs, living and dead. Their presence, their suffering, was palpably present, rekindling the conviction that Providence would eventually bring down the godless Soviet regime.

The long, solemn procession preceding the liturgy included four hundred priests of different rites, guest bishops, celebrant bishops, archbishops, cardinals, and the apostolic delegate who preached the sermon. Women religious filled a large part of the hall. The Eastern-rite bishops and clerics in the procession that preceded the liturgy greatly outnumbered the Latin-rite clergy, who appeared less resplendent compared to the Eastern-rite clergy in their flowing robes and varied head coverings. For many participants—especially the many Eastern-rite Catholics and those Ukrainian Orthodox who participated—the event and its venue were unprecedented. Here they were in the very heart of Old Philadelphia, chanting their prayers and singing their songs—some even wearing distinctive clothing from the old country.

During the three-day congress, services were also held at the Ukrainian Catholic cathedral as well as at the Latin-rite Catholic cathedral. Confessions were held almost round the clock. There was a midnight liturgy at the Ukrainian cathedral. Sts. Peter and Paul, the elegant Latin-rite Catholic cathedral in Philadelphia, popularly known as St. Paul's, was provided with another specially built iconostasis and icons for the celebration of the first Eastern-rite liturgy at its altar. Ukrainian clergy, whose relations with the

---

the Ukrainian Church. As with the Ukrainians, the majority of Armenians and Romanians are Orthodox.

Latin clergy had not been close, were deeply touched by the participation of high Roman Catholic clergy and even more by the readiness with which the local Latin priests offered the use of their churches to priests of other rites for their daily masses.

Pontifical liturgies were held on different days at the Ukrainian and Latin cathedrals. Archbishop John F. O'Hara of Philadelphia, the nominal co-convener of the congress, presided at the liturgy for the youth, which was celebrated by Maxim Hermaniuk, auxiliary bishop of Manitoba. Samuel Cardinal Stritch, archbishop of Chicago, graced one of the special *molebens* at which two hundred seminarians from St. Basil's Seminary at Stamford served as acolytes. Peter XV Cardinal Agagianian, archbishop of Armenians in Syria, blessed the concluding liturgy, which was celebrated by Archbishop Bohachevsky and Bishop Isidore Boretsky, apostolic exarch for Eastern Canada, and Bishop Hermaniuk.

Following the concluding liturgy, the large crowd of participants and attendees, with their respective banners and orchestras, marched through the center of town to hold "a solemn Pontifical Devotion [*moleben*] to [the] Mother of God" at the Latin-rite Cathedral of Saints Peter and Paul. The day ended with a concert at the Convention Hall, which was also the site of related exhibitions and presentations.

Crowds of onlookers lined up along the avenues of a major procession route, and a large number of frustrated drivers objected to road closures. The result was well worth the trouble, however, especially for the Ukrainians. The fact that an event organized by the Ukrainian Catholic Church in the United States had made a favorable impression on American society in Philadelphia was considered a significant achievement. It demonstrated the maturity of the church, its earned place in society, and the distinct beauty of its mode of worship. The crowds were orderly, solemn but joyful; the organizing committees worked with the city; the guest buses had a place to park; the attendant banquets ran on time; the exhibits and concerts had no glitches. Even the weather cooperated—it was clear and mild.

The apostolic delegate, Cicognani, took an active part in the event as a sign of respect for the church that Bohachevsky had so assiduously built up. There was another reason for Cicognani's participation, however—tacit confirmation that the congress reflected the papacy's active support of ecumenism as a growing movement within the whole of Catholicism.

The mid-1950s were not yet the era of ecumenism, but its rise was already evident. The Marian congress garnered a fair amount of general interest because of its exotic nature and the variety of its participants. As far as Ukrainian Catholics were concerned, the event was a resounding national, not only Catholic success. Its organizers were praised for their religious work, and as leaders of the community, spokesmen for the silent nation. For the participants, all of them either recent immigrants or at most two generations removed, this was the largest Ukrainian communal gathering they had witnessed, let alone participated in. In this pre-ecumenical age signs of ethnicity in the United States were considered exotic, and the congress even drew the interest of the mainstream Philadelphia press, which covered it extensively, rather than relegating it to the religion-slash-local customs pages. The leading Philadelphia dailies ran articles and photographs on the congress—the *Philadelphia Daily News* on October 23 and the *Sunday Bulletin* the next day. The Ukrainian daily *Svoboda* ran a front-page, four-column story on October 26, headlined "Over 20,000 Participants in the Eucharistic-Marian Congress in Philadelphia." That the congress took place in the cradle of American constitutionalism and religious toleration, in the heart of Philadelphia, had deep meaning, especially for the still hyphenated Americans.

The medley of services contributed to the richness of the spiritual experience. Only a few purists noted the "Latinisms" in the proceedings. The Adoration of the Host, as a separate service, was a clear-cut Latinism that had become popular in Western Ukrainian cities as well as in the United States in the early twentieth century. Although Archbishop Bohachevsky was not a proponent of the practice, he did not oppose the inclusion of this service in the program. Moreover, the monstrance, the vessel used for the Adoration of the Host at the Ukrainian Immaculate Conception Cathedral, had been a gift to the eparchy by its first bishop, Soter Ortynsky, whose memory was venerated. A large crowd filled the Ukrainian cathedral for an Eastern service before what was a Latin artifact. If the eclecticism was noted, it was considered a sign of Catholic universality. The inclusion of the *molebens* was another example of the popularity of so-called Latinisms. The *moleben* is a prayer of intercession through the Virgin, or the Sacred Heart of Jesus, or some saint to the Almighty. It is similar to a litany and its repetitive nature makes it easy to involve the congregation in public prayer. *Molebens* are said at certain times or at special occasions, which has made them especially suitable for large gatherings. These short services, to the Virgin in May and to the Sacred Heart in June were especially popular in Ukrainian communities in the 1950s. Even young people attended them, albeit to see members of the opposite gender.

Although Archbishop Bohachevsky played a leading role in the festivities, Bishop Senyshyn was the main organizer of the event, and this was comforting proof for Bohachevsky that the church would be in good hands should he die. For Ukrainians, the event was significant for several reasons: It not only showcased the Ukrainian Catholic Church (at least in the eyes of its participants) but it also promoted the Ukrainian cause and increased knowledge about the Ukrainian people. On a broader scale, it was to affect the entire Catholic Church: Soon after the congress, the Vatican, partly under pressure from the Near Eastern Catholic Churches, began promoting public discussions of Christian unity.[12]

The hosting of a full-scale Eucharistic congress was a coming-out event for Bohachevsky's church. Clearly, the status of the Ukrainian Catholic Church in the United States had changed significantly for the better since 1925, when the American Catholics hosted their first Eucharistic congress in Chicago and in the process had trampled on the sensitivities of the Ukrainian clergy. In 1954 it was the Ukrainians who proudly showcased the Eastern churches. The unprecedented public interest in this event was a testament to Bohachevsky's long years of organizing a functioning, all-American community in the church, proof that his instincts had been correct. The community, meanwhile, saw the Eucharistic congress as a manifestation of the power of the people and their dedication to their church.

Archbishop Bohachevsky had one more goal for the congress. He hoped that the grand symbol of Christian unity that the Marian Eucharistic congress provided would encourage all Ukrainian Catholic bishops beyond the enslaved homeland to follow the example of their American, Latin-rite Catholic brethren-bishops and create a functioning conference of Ukrainian Catholic bishops that would coordinate the actions of their

12. John W. O'Malley, *What Happened at Vatican II* (Cambridge, Mass.: Harvard University Press, 2008), 125, mentions that the Melchites urged John XXIII to establish a secretariat for Christian Unity.

geographically scattered church. Bohachevsky had provided financial support for similar bishops' meetings in Europe before the Second World War. After the Marian congress was over, Archbishop Bohachevsky, with all the Ukrainian bishops and the Canadian archbishop, travelled to the Ukrainian seminary in Washington, D.C., to meet as an episcopal council. The bishops met cordially, but institutional unity eluded them. That continued to be a major disappointment for Bohachevsky.

ADMINISTRATION OF THE CHURCH

Throughout the 1950s the archbishop's chancery worked on several fronts: the codification of rules, laws, by-laws, regulations, and liturgical texts that was to establish a greater unanimity within the church and rid the rite of Latin accretions. At the same time, Bohachevsky and his staff helped the recently arrived European clergy adjust to the discipline of the American diocese and to American state regulations.

The memoirs of Archbishop Stefan Sulyk provide a rare glimpse into Bohachevsky's efforts to encourage the European clergy to engage in missionary work in areas where the Ukrainian population was small. Few were interested in answering this call, and Bohachevsky found that very disappointing. He had thought that people who had survived the hell of the Nazi and Soviet occupations would want to dedicate themselves to do God's work in America. Bohachevsky appreciated the sacrifice of those who embraced the hard missionary lot. Sulyk, who would later become archbishop of Philadelphia, had been ordained in 1952 in Philadelphia. He was posted to help Rev. Dmytro Blazejowskyj set up parishes in Omaha and elsewhere in Nebraska. His salary was $50 a month. At one meeting of the clergy, Bohachevsky lauded his good deeds. None of the other clerics said a word, but it was patently clear that the bishop's special praise for a celibate young whippersnapper discomfited them. Bohachevsky, in turn, was made visibly uncomfortable by their response.[13]

As he aged, Bohachevsky delegated as much work as he could to trusted others. He was particularly keen on expediting the collection and

13. Sulyk also described his demanding schedule when working at the chancery, see *Yak Stefan Stav Mytropolytom*, esp. 173–75; 185–86 189–202.

formulation of laws, regulations, and traditions that were then given to priests who were qualified or willing to do the work. The bishop even resorted to humor to goad reluctant or insecure priests into activity.[14] By this time he had become less rigorous in avoiding the appearance of conflicts of interest. The bishop even set aside an hour each Saturday to meet with his brother Danylo. It seems both brothers kept the meetings completely private.[15]

RETURN TO THE EASTERN ROOTS

Once the bishop saw that the new clergy and parishioners had been peacefully absorbed into the exarchate, he felt strong enough to broaden the campaign to introduce more Eastern elements into the churches. The new immigrant clergy had participated in a similar campaign in the home territories. The Vatican also supported the policy of returning the Ukrainian rite to its Eastern roots, as did the papal representatives in the United States. Clearly, the papacy was favorably disposed to the flourishing of Eastern churches in America. Given these conditions, Bohachevsky thought he could risk modifying certain aspects of the traditions to which the American faithful had become accustomed. After a brief hiatus to recuperate from his heart attacks in 1948, he resumed his visitations through the country, preaching and meeting with the faithful, explaining the changes in ritual and church practice not as innovations but as a return to tradition. The changes were implemented slowly and locally, and for the most part the congregations accepted them.

As we have seen, Bohachevsky did not consider such accidentals as the calendar to be an inherent attribute of the rite. He viewed enclosed confessionals as a useful innovation that was as connected to the rite as electricity or the availability of pews. For him the genuine rite consisted of elements of worship and specifics of the discipline, such as prayers, fasts, and good deeds. He did not feel threatened that the Ukrainian Autocepha-

---

14. The correspondence about and to Rev. Stefan Hryniokh (1935–1955) is especially illustrative. UMAS, Chancery Archive.

15. Bishop Basil Losten, conversation with the author, January 27, 2015. The meetings between Constantine and Danylo were set between 1 and 2 P.M., the two men retired to the conference room. I do not remember my father mentioning any of these sessions.

lous Orthodox Church, which had also grown significantly as the result of the new immigrants, remained firmly committed to the old calendar even as they moved toward the exclusive use of vernacular Ukrainian. Some of the new immigrants warned that the failure to use vernacular Ukrainian in the church services could draw Catholics to the Ukrainian Orthodox Church. Bohachevsky, however, would not budge on this point, insisting that Church Slavonic would remain the language for church services. He argued that the introduction of the vernacular into church usage would encourage the use of English in worship and that this change would split the parishes. He was proven right, but fortunately for him, this practice came to fruition only after his death. However, he continued to allow the parishes to vote on which calendar to use, and as had happened earlier, the recognition of the Gregorian calendar opened Bohachevsky to charges of Americanizing the Ukrainian Church.

Bohachevsky succeeded in removing statues from the naves of the churches, and most priests adhered to his insistence that the tabernacle be small, the altar rectangular and free of clutter, and that at least some semblance of the iconostasis, the screen that separates the nave from the altar, be installed. He continued to remind the clergy not to cut corners with the liturgy, especially the long dismissal prayer that should be said outside the Great Doors of the iconostasis. The churches eventually became prosperous enough to order silver and gold chalices and other religious goods that were manufactured to their specifications, rather than relying on the generic Latin-rite items. Slowly the ornate chalices and monstrances were replaced by simpler chalices and by plain prayer discs that did not, as the monstrance had, hold the Host. Priestly vestments underwent a return to tradition—tatting was dropped, white surplices were replaced with colored ones, and chasubles became longer. Another futile attempt was made to reinstitute head coverings for priests.[16] Bohachevsky suggested that the clergy return to wearing Eastern head coverings, now that the Basilian sisters were manufacturing the kolpaky. But the practice did not take root in the United States, except for formal photographs.

16. An item in Eparkhiial'ni Visti, November 1951, 116, informed the readers that there were factories in the United States that made the traditional clerical head covering—kolpak—so there was no excuse for not acquiring them. A few years later (Eparkhiial'ni Visti, February 1955, 7–8), chasubles (stykhar) in colors other than white were mandated.

A major visible aspect of Eastern-rite Catholicism is the participation of the laity with the priest during liturgy through collectively sung or chanted responses. Throughout the nineteenth and twentieth centuries, at least in the larger city churches, the choir took over this historically lay function. Bohachevsky, although a proponent of the traditional lay responses, did not publicly oppose church choirs, which after all were as much social as religious. He had no singing voice, so his part of the service was always loudly chanted, with the choir left to pick up as best they could. Bohachevsky also promoted active lay participation in the liturgy whenever he could. He encouraged the priests to enlighten the laity on correct Eastern religious practice and the nuns to teach their pupils the specifics of the rite, instructing everyone to keep in mind that it was the spirituality and not the physical practice that made the rite truly meaningful. By January 1959, he and his bishops felt strong enough to mandate the recitation of the liturgy by the priest and the congregation on Sundays and holy days.[17] This mandate was never implemented; almost ironically, a decade later, after the Second Vatican Council, it was the Roman Catholic liturgy that became more interactive.

A PERSONAL APPROACH TO THE CLERGY

The modest diocesan quarterly *Eparchial News*, remained the venue for encouraging the priests to keep up with developments in their field. It continued to educate the priests in the niceties of the rite and in liturgical practice as well as in more worldly affairs. The chancery insisted that pastors were to head church committees.[18] The priests were also counseled to borrow building loans only from reputable institutions rather than private parishioners who could not be held legally responsible for promised, but undelivered, gifts. As part of the restructuring program, Bohachevsky became more rigorous in insisting on periodic examinations of the clergy. Not all priests appreciated the practice. To accommodate the recently arrived clergy, some questions were presented in Latin.[19] The bishop also

17. *Eparkhiial'ni Visti*, January 1959, 31.
18. "Holova doradchoho eparkhiial'noho komitetu," *Eparkhiial'ni Visti*, May 1952, 45.
19. Latin was used in the periodic testing of the clergy in Halychyna. See *Eparkhiial'ni Visti*, August 1952, for sample questions.

held regularly scheduled retreats, and continued to hold all-day meetings of regional clergy. At one point (after he was already elevated to metropolitan), Bohachevsky chided the priests because their responses during these periodic examinations were too concise and did not take important specifics into consideration.[20]

Each deanery held an annual day or even two-day meeting, a little *sobor* (*soborchyk*), often attended by one of the bishops. One or two papers were presented at these events, and other matters were discussed, with more or less vigor. Eparchial publications, supplemented by the Basilian press, were the major source of information for the clergy. The *Eparchial News*, of course, remained the most authoritative voice for the clergy. It reminded the clergy to attend deanery meetings and all other diocesan conferences, engage in greater outreach, and follow diocesan regulations for guest priests. Bohachevsky scrupulously published Vatican regulations relating to the Eastern churches. He paid special attention to the preservation of the Eastern rite in marriages between Ukrainian and Latin-rite Catholics. With the increased availability of trained artisans from the displaced persons community, the bishop could more actively encourage and incorporate Eastern elements into the Ukrainian churches: the iconostasis, murals, mosaics, and icons. Statues and flowers were to be removed. This policy was not popular and generally not followed.

Some new immigrants still used formal titles or old-fashioned forms of address when speaking to high-ranking clergy, a practice that was denounced by critics of the church in the old country a few decades earlier. Bohachevsky did not encourage this practice, nor did he actively oppose it. While he lived, the church structure held its own, and pastors struggled with difficulties as best they could. At times, Bohachevsky threw all caution to the winds, and at one clergy meeting he challenged the clergy to live up to their calling:

You discussed liturgical issues with vigor and genuine understanding. But one could notice your discontent and complaints that ran through the discussion. I sympathize—as the saying goes—life's not a joke or a fairy tale [*zhyttia ne zharty*,

---

20. "Zavvahy do rozviazanykh kazusiv za 1958 rik. Remarks on the Solutions of the 1958 Cases," *Eparkhiial'ni Visti*, February 1960, 11. *Eparkhial'ni Visti* was becoming almost fully bilingual.

ne kazky].[21] It brings us all sorts of difficulties and crosses. But Christ's priest, emulating the Lord Christ, should bear the difficulties and discomforts one meets along the way patiently. Your congregations learn how a genuine follower of Christ behaves not only from your sermons but mainly from your own life and behavior.[22]

By the mid-1950s, American mores were visibly influencing the directives issued for running the parishes. Pastors were warned of the dangers of borrowing large sums of money from a single donor. There was a greater emphasis on outreach, on the importance of meetings, on the need for the priests to be more involved in religious lay organizations such as the Apostleship of Prayer and the Marian Sodality. Archbishop Bohachevsky speeded up his program for making Ukrainian churches venues for the Eastern rite, although any regulation relating to church practice again provoked comment and potential unrest. At the same time the new immigrants brought semi-religious ceremonies that seemed offensive to some of the parishioners. Memorial services for known Orthodox personages were difficult to accept by those who had felt personally slighted by members of that faith. The bishop's chancery had to intervene on a number of such occasions, but over time these issues were resolved.

The heart of Bishop Bohachevsky's administrative approach lay in the follow-up letters he sent to each pastor. Those letters were strictly confidential and very substantial. It is difficult to confirm the year when this approach was introduced because the early diocesan archives that might shed some light on the subject are unavailable. But by the end of the 1940s and certainly throughout the 1950s, the bishop wrote highly personalized analyses after each visitation. The letters were written in the spirit of today's evaluation letters. In tone and composition, Bohachevsky emerges as an understanding and very thorough chief executive officer.

Each letter begins with praise for what the pastor under observation did well, and then moves on to specific matters in need of adjustment or more work. Almost invariably the criticism is directed at a failure to be

21. The phrase is taken from an Eastern Ukrainian poem that became a popular Ukrainian Scout song in the 1930s in the Carpathians areas that were home to the Ruthenians. Bohachevsky paid close attention to the events in all parts of the Ukrainian territory and had a soft spot for the Carpathian mountain areas.
22. Sulyk, *Yak Stefan stav mytropolytom*, 174–75.

more proactive in outreach projects, especially those directed at younger members of the congregation. The tone is very direct. The information presented in each letter was carefully guarded and the privacy of the cleric involved was strictly honored.

Bohachevsky also resorted to letters, often handwritten, in dealing with other problems. This practice ensured permanent documentation, which could minimize or entirely preclude later misunderstandings. Two examples should suffice. The first concerned a priest who in the mid-1950s volunteered information about a sexual dalliance on his part. The bishop (in a written response) thanked him for coming forward and suggested he spend, at a time convenient to him, a week or so at a diocesan monastery of his choice. The second exchange was with a recent émigré priest who was detailed to assist high Roman Catholic clergy during elaborate Marian Day liturgical festivities. The priest was high strung, and to be quick, he threw off his own vestments rather than disrobing properly. Bohachevsky noticed this and sent the cleric a letter chiding him not for his nervousness but for failing to alert him (the bishop) that he does not work well under pressure. The bishop noted that he had been very upset when he saw the vestments thrown off publicly and that this action could have scandalized the faithful, adding that if he had known that the priest was uncomfortable in public, he would not have assigned the task to him.[23] A few months after this letter was posted, the priest in question was offered a high post in the chancery where his service became greatly valued and his nervousness not on public display.

With the influx of the new wave of immigrants, including so many distinguished priests, the aging "pioneer-priests" felt underappreciated. Some, such as Rev. Andrushkiw, felt that the spiritual needs of the congregation were often overwhelmed by Ukrainian community concerns. Others, like Rev. Zabava, resented his secondary status in the parish. The old timers wanted some personal acknowledgment of their service from the archbishop, who remained singularly deaf to these concerns. The lack of care facilities for aged and ill clergy remained a painfully unsolved problem especially as the "downtown villages" dissipated.

Bohachevsky sometimes disregarded a congregation's complaints

23. Bohachevsky to Rev. Vasyl Seredovych, December 22, 1951, handwritten, UMAS, Chancery Archive.

about its pastors. Occasionally, only complaints that found their way to the apostolic delegate led to the requested results.[24] Nevertheless, the archbishop took care to see that pastors did not take advantage of their assistant priests, that they paid them their full monthly salary of $100, and did not give them too much extra work. During his lifetime, Bohachevsky was considered a strict supporter of centralization. For all the talk about his devotion to the hierarchical principle, however, the priests were largely left to fend for themselves. When told to appear in Philadelphia, for example, it was their job to figure out ways and means to get there.[25] There were no provisions for housing visiting clergy.

LITURGICAL TEXTS AND CHURCH REGULATIONS

Bohachevsky was a firm believer in structure, and nothing on this matter was as important to him as canon law and the less sacred but nevertheless binding ecclesiastical regulations that applied both to ritual and to other types of guidance. The availability of trained clergy created conditions that made it possible for Bohachevsky's eparchy to begin a codification of regulations specifically for the Ukrainian Catholic Church in the United States, while the loss of the mother church made the task imperative.

To fully grasp the need for this initiative, it is important to recall that the Ukrainian Greek Catholic Church had begun updating its liturgical texts at the beginning of the twentieth century, mostly to correct centuries of large and small changes generally injected by mistake rather than by intent. In over two hundred years of copying, printing, and reprinting the original texts used in prayer and in the liturgy of the Ukrainian Catholic Church, many different influences had impacted the texts, changing them in myriad ways from the original versions. During Sheptytsky's tenure as the metropolitan of Halych, a committee of priests and liturgical scholars worked to extricate the original Ruthenian/Ukrainian religious texts from

24. For instance, the parish in Frackville, Penn., refused to share all the financial information with a pastor, but his successor found a way to work with the same committee; Sulyk, *Yak Stefan stav mytropolytom*, 194–97.

25. Metropolitan Sulyk details an extreme case of his journey from Omaha via Jersey City (to report to the dean, V. Lotovych) to Brooklyn. Mrs. Lotovych offered no hospitality and sent the young priest with his two heavy suitcases on to find his own way by subway to Brooklyn. Ibid., 170–72.

later, corrupted Greek editions. The process, which involved research into various redactions, was complex and contentious. There were sections and subsections, factions and splinter factions of modernists, Byzantinists, Latinists, traditionalists, and of course predilections of individual bishops and clergy whose discussions dragged on the work longer than the Vatican's liking. Consequently, the Ukrainian hierarchs at their conferences in 1927, 1929, and 1932, decided to move the entire project to Rome in the care of the Congregation for the Eastern Church. In one of the reports on the work of the textual commission, which was published in *Eparchial News* in August 1943, Cardinal Tisserant, who was one of the most vocal supporters of the Ukrainian Church and the Philadelphia exarchy, stressed that the goal of the working group was to eradicate Latin accretions that had corrupted the rite, not to establish new regulations. In 1944, months before the end of the Second World War, Pius XII began the formal publication of the documents that were to guide the Ukrainian Greek Catholic Church in its governance and liturgical procedure. The versions provided by the congregation were based on old Ruthenian texts that antedated the Greek versions that had come into use after the establishment of the Russian Empire.[26]

Throughout the 1950s, the Vatican issued, in the historian Procko's words, "a steady flow of regulations ... which affected the Ukrainian exarchy in America."[27] The topics covered included matrimonial law, regulation of religious orders, and issues concerning church property. In 1958, the Vatican addressed the part of the code "which defines the hierarchical structure of the church according to the traditions of the East."[28] Although numerous and weighty, these regulations still left a significant number of issues within the purview of the individual eparchies, and this gave Bohachevsky leave to formalize the by-laws by which his own diocese would be governed.

The chancery highlighted the most visible changes in public worship: limitation on the use of the censer, the reading of the Gospel as well as the dismissal prayer outside the Royal Gates, and other modifications of

26. *Eparkhiial'ni Visti*, August 1943, 39. The memorandum from the congregation was published in both Italian and Ukrainian.
27. Procko, *Ukrainian Catholics in America*, 78.
28. Ibid.

the service. Archbishop Bohachevsky was very careful in introducing liturgical changes, allowing older priests to continue using their familiar variants. Some of the practices in question were brought from Halychyna (such as May and June devotions, respectively to Mary and the Sacred Heart, which Metropolitan Sheptytsky promoted) and were later viewed as latinizations. Mark M. Morozowich captured the conundrum well:

> Bohachevsky attempted to conform eparchial liturgical practice with the ideals of the home country's liturgical reforms. However, the syncretism of latinization continued . . . [alongside the] Eastern practices Bohachevsky encouraged. . . . [This] mixture of liturgical practice [is a] characteristic of the Ukrainian Catholic Church in the United States [that] often remained to the present.[29]

Through the years, at their deanery meetings, the clergy had raised issues of a practical as well as a liturgical nature. Concomitantly, the exarchate had passed a variety of local regulations, standardized customs, and regulated procedures. The European clergy had brought to America practices introduced by Metropolitan Sheptytsky, and the time was ripe to reconcile discrepancies and compile a set of laws, rules, and regulations to guide the clergy in its work.

Rev. Victor Pospishil was largely responsible for the final preparation of the first volume of the *Temporary Diocesan Statutes of the Byzantine Rite Apostolic Exarchate of Philadelphia, Pa., USA*, which was published in 1954.[30] Pospishil, at this time pastor of Ford City, Pennsylvania, had spent nearly

---

29. Mark M. Morozowich, "The Liturgy and the Ukrainian Catholic Church in the United States: Change through the Decades," *U.S. Catholic Historian* 82, no. 1 (Winter 2014): 55. But Morozowich is not correct in considering Bohachevsky a latinizer.

30. Victor Pospishil, trained both as a lawyer and as a priest, came to Philadelphia with experience in the Vatican institutions. He liked the order of Bohachevsky's chancery, and enjoyed working with the bishop. This is how summed up his work on the first volume of the statutes: "I am a well-organized person and therefore have time for many things. This is the origin of my vocation as a writer. The first such undertaking, still carried out in Chesapeake City was finishing *The Statutes of the Archeparchy of Philadelphia*, an assignment that I had received from Archbishop Constantine Bohachevsky and had worked on for some time. Churches enact many laws over time which, after many years, might be collected into a Code of Law. This also happened in smaller units of the church such as a diocese (eparchy) which produces laws, regulations, norms, etc. This happened to the Ukrainians in the United States. It was the bishop's desire to have them sorted, reviewed, corrected, supplemented with additional laws, and published in a code, at the time called a statute, the first for Eastern Catholics in this country." Pospishil, *Final Tally*, 239.

two years studying Latin-rite Catholic statutes and plowing through fifty years of Ukrainian Catholic regulations. Rev. Wojakowsky also contributed his expertise to the task, as did Rev. Joseph M. Quigley, a professor at the Roman Catholic metropolitan seminary of the Archdiocese of Philadelphia.[31] The 130-page book that resulted from this collaboration included the Vatican regulations governing the Ukrainian Catholic Church, beginning with the 1929 *Cum data fuerit*, and specifics related to the administration of churches and cemeteries, the regulating of marriages, and the charting of appropriate civic activities for the clergy.

The *Temporary Diocesan Statutes* sought to cover the major issues facing the clergy, from the administration of the sacraments to financial reporting. Among other things, the volume provided intricate guidelines on the process of ruling a marriage or a baptism valid (or conversely, invalid). Such decisions were especially relevant in the unsettled post-World War II years, when contacts between the Orthodox and Catholic Ukrainians became more intimate. The document was firmly grounded in a historical setting, stressing the continuity from the days of Ortynsky and underscoring that he had held "the Office of the Exarch and Ordinary for all Greek Catholic Ukrainians of the Byzantine Rite, sometimes known also as Ruthenians, who live in the territory of the United States of North America." The code reflected the minor adjustments that spelled out the increased direct disciplinary powers of the bishop in America over all Greek Catholic priests in his jurisdiction. The *Statutes* reiterated that all church property belonged to the bishop and that the pastor was responsible for the finances of the parish. Most importantly, the *Statutes* provided clear regulations for administering parishes and practicing the faith. It dealt in detail with the formalities of the administration of the sacraments. The dedication of this exhaustive volume was symptomatic of Bohachevsky's special reliance on the intercession of the Virgin: "All for the greater glory of God and the Honor of the God-Bearer Virgin, conceived without the original sin, intercessor for our Apostolic Exarchate"[32] One cannot help but hear

31. Ibid., 212. Pospishil worked in the chancery for two years. Then he requested a transfer: "I was in Philadelphia in a Ukrainian community for two years and sometimes had the feeling that I was not in America at all." Ibid., 221.

32. The bishop received papal permission to consider the Immaculate Conception the patron of the Ukrainian Catholic Church in the United States. Metropolitan Sheptytsky had

the echoes of the Jesuit "Ad majorem Dei gloriam"—all for the greater glory of God.

The publication of the statutes was an extremely important step for Bohachevsky's long-range policy of firmly institutionalizing the church in the United States. The Temporary Eparchial Statutes were aimed at the "God-loving faithful," as well as the priests.[33] In addition to the ecclesiastical regulations, Statutes warned the readers against joining dangerous and dubious organizations and bemoaned the growing practice of violating the sacred space around the church for commercial activities, including the sale of newspapers. The next expanded version of the statutes was solemnly promulgated six years later at the Philadelphia cathedral on October 7, 1959, at the First Eparchial Council (sobor) of the Philadelphia Ukrainian Catholic Archdiocese.[34]

It is relatively easy to see that Bohachevsky was doing everything he could, on multiple fronts, to ensure a smooth transition upon his death. He did not want his successor or his church to be blindsided and jeopardized as he himself had been in the 1920s.

VARIANTS OF INTEGRATION

The postwar economic boom speeded up the integration of the Ukrainian Catholic population into American society. While actively promoting the arrival of the newcomers, Bohachevsky was careful to see that their integration into the immigrant community not jar the sensibilities of the existing congregations. The bishop continued his laissez faire approach to community organizations, even if some of the new ones undercut the activities of the older organizations he promoted. He held the view that it was up to the organizations to ensure their own flourishing.

Bohachevsky had envisioned St. Basil's College at Stamford as a good, albeit modest, four-year college for boys, in the American tradition of the time, even to the inclusion of team sports. He likely presumed that his

dedicated the Ukrainian-American Church and its cathedral to the Immaculate Conception in 1911 to strengthen its Catholic visibility, and Bohachevsky expanded Sheptytsky's choice to the whole bishopric.

33. First published in the bishop's chancery office in Philadelphia in 1953 as vol. 1.
34. Pospishil, Final Tally, 230–39.

opinion was shared by the Ukrainian-American community at large. Yet even his own brothers had not fully grasped the nature of the college and considered it to be a preparatory seminary. None of the Bohachevsky boys attended the college, including the two who had attended a Ukrainian Catholic high school in New York.[35] The archbishop had hoped that the new immigrants would help make the college an intellectual center that would be known for more than just being a religious institution. And indeed, some people volunteered their services to enable his goal. Among these were Professor Bohdan Lonchyna and especially Professor Vasyl Lencyk, who worked for many years to build up the library and the museum, another of the bishop's pet projects. Bohachevsky expanded the ethnic handicrafts collection that he had bought from the Ukrainian National Women's League of America in 1933 with materials brought from Ukraine. He had earlier commissioned the premier Ukrainian sculptor of the time, Serhiy Lytvynenko, to prepare small models of possible future statues that commemorated significant events and persons. He continued buying art, but as Bishop Senyshyn took on more duties, acquisitions to the museum fell into his purview. For the most part, however, the secular intelligentsia, like the Bohachevsky's brothers, presumed that the college was meant primarily for the training of priests and the museum was its adjunct. Nor did the new immigrants realize how financially strapped the Ukrainian Catholic institutions were.

A number of Ukrainian Catholic intellectuals found employment thanks to Bohachevsky's support. The bishop was, in fact, happy that he could staff the college and the museum with Ukrainian speakers. The archbishop continued to support Ukrainian scholars, among them Rev. Isidore Nahaevsky, Dr. Mykola Chubaty, and Professor Roman Smal-Stocki. They returned the favor by focusing on matters important to the bishop. Dr. Chubaty, for example, became involved in active scholarship aimed at making Americans aware of the existence of Ukrainians.

Bishop Bohachevsky supported Dr. Hryhor Luzhnytsky's history of

35. Bohachevsky, as his own father, did not pressure young men into the priesthood. I have a short note he wrote to his brother Danylo in 1949 in which the bishop concluded that Danylo's son should pursue mathematics rather than work for the eparchy, since the young man had no inclination for the priesthood and should not be placed in a situation where that career would be an easy choice, rather than the result of a calling.

the Ukrainian Catholic Church, which appeared in a luxurious Ukrainian-language edition in 1954.[36] Rev. Dr. Isidore Nahaevsky published in English a useful book modestly titled *Outline of the History of the Halychyna Metropolitanate* in 1958. The bishop renewed his efforts to make Markian Shashkevych better known as a national hero, hoping that Prof. Vasyl Tershakovets would finish his study on him.[37] The bishop also continued to work closely with Dr. Victor Pospishil, a scholarly cleric and specialist in Eastern Christianity, who eventually taught at the Catholic Manhattan College in New York City.

Both Bohachevsky and Senyshyn heard many suggestions for projects for schools and programs, all requesting funding. Much as they might have liked these offers (including one to establish a theater that would focus on religious plays, or a school for iconographers, or a full-time school for cantors), the two bishops were fully aware that their resources were too limited to afford such luxuries.

During this period of spiritual and intellectual growth, Bohachevsky stayed his course on keeping the church independent of outside pressure by avoiding direct involvement in community politics. Meanwhile, the Congregation for the Eastern Church again pressured the bishop to build the seminary in Washington. Rome, keeping an eye on the growth of the Orthodox Autocephaly, wanted an effective and educated Ukrainian Catholic clergy in the United States. Bohachevsky never lost sight of the persecution of the church in the Soviet Union, repeating time and again the construct of the Ukrainian Catholic Church as a bridge between the Catholic West and "un-united East."[38] He continued to stress the sanctity of sacrifice and the importance of discipline, all the while grappling with the unjust prolonged suffering of Ukrainians under communism. As the decade proceeded and the Ukrainian Catholic community in America grew, so did Senyshyn's contributions to the pastoral letters, which became wordier and eventually covered two or three subjects each. Both Bohachevsky and Senyshyn stressed papal goodwill toward Ukrainians through the ages. In the call for Peter's Pence in 1954 they pointed out

36. Luzhnytsky, *Ukraiins'ka Tserkva mizh Skhodom I Zakhodom.*
37. See Tershkovets's speech at the installation banquet, in Kharyna, *Ukraiins'ka Katolyts'ka Mytropolia,* 91.
38. Lenten pastoral letter, *Eparkhiial'ni Visti,* February 1954, 3.

that: "Hundreds, even thousands of our people, thrown out by fickle fate into unknown wandering [during the First and the Second World Wars], received first aid from the Holy Father. . . . A great number of our students from Ukraine and the USA were scholarship students in Rome, thanks to His magnanimity."[39]

Intellectually, Bohachevsky was still fighting materialism and secularism, now personified in the victory of the communists. As far as he was concerned, the first steps toward the rule of the communists in Ukraine had been aided—albeit unconsciously—by the radical Ukrainian intelligentsia. This mindset fit in with the growing right-wing politics, anticommunism, and, after the 1945 Yalta Agreement, with American Republicans. There is no written indication that the bishop was concerned about the impact that political activists among the refugees would have on the stable Ukrainian-American Catholic community, but the possibility of a renewed *fayt* could not have escaped him.

As they settled into an economically growing America, the most recent immigrants established organizations that had existed in the home country, forgetting that these organizations would have to be self-supporting and run without the largesse of Metropolitan Sheptytsky or other donors. The laymen among them had no reason to remember that the clergy in Europe had received partial government salaries. In the United States, the parish supported the priest, and the bishop had to assure some parity among the clergy whose parishes were large and generous and those working in small mission outposts. Bohachevsky had presumed that the new émigrés would see and understand that only those organizations that had popular grassroots support would flourish. Increasingly, the lay community and the church parted ways, a pattern that began with small signs of tension that arose and defied amicable resolution. Some priests complained that the bishop was not promoting Catholic youth organizations as fully as he could and that he was focusing too much on the recent immigrants. The Ukrainian Catholic Youth League, which had flourished as a forum for Ukrainian-American youth throughout the thirties and forties, lost much of its influence with the arrival of the postwar immigrants, who established their own organizations. Many immigrants threw themselves

39. Collection for Peter's Pence, *Eparkhiial'ni Visti*, May 1954, 40.

into civic activity within the Ukrainian community to such an extent that Pospishil asked the bishop to transfer him from the cathedral to some place where he could meet real Americans. Young parish members, many of whom were now professionals rather than workers, increasingly pressured the church to use more English in its public utterances and publications. Even Father Dovhovych, one of the older priests, resented having to pay for the diocesan bilingual newspaper, *The Way*, in both Ukrainian and English copies.[40]

A few new immigrants resurrected the dormant discussion on the right of Ukrainians to have married clergy, and that discussion escalated during the following decade. In some parishes there were disagreements about what events and what people deserved to be publicly celebrated or prayed for in the churches. For the time being, most of these issues were handled without major disturbances. The laity made some attempts to gain more control of the parish church administration, but the bishop's office repeatedly stressed the fiscal responsibility of the priest.[41] Bohachevsky did not want a repetition of the financial mess that had characterized the beginning of his tenure as bishop.

As the immigrants settled in, they began to worry that their children were not learning enough Ukrainian subjects. Some felt that the church should do more. By late 1958 some of the recent immigrants created lay committees to defend the church from what they considered Latin influences and the use of English. They resented the fact that not enough attention was being paid to teaching in Ukrainian, and placed the blame for this squarely on the upper clergy and the teaching nuns. The diocesan schools, as far as they were concerned, were Americanizing their children. As an antidote, they began collecting funds to establish an exclusively Ukrainian-language high school in Philadelphia, but this project failed for lack of support. Along with that criticism, which was led by middle-class, European-educated professionals who could not always find suitable employment in America, semi-literate leaflets appeared that questioned the good will of the church leadership in general and of the Ukrainian Catholic Church in particular. Even the Ivan Franko controversy threatened to resurface. Bishop Senyshyn worried about the loyalty of some of the upper

40. Father Dovhovych to Iryna Tarnawska, editor of *The Way*, May 8, 1946, UMAS.
41. "Pozychky u virnykh," *Eparkhiial'ni Visti*, May 1952, 45–46.

clergy, especially with the rise of these contentious committees, but Bohachevsky would not permit himself any expression of doubt in the loyalty of his church and its clergy. The American-born Ukrainian Catholic clergy respected their steely bishop who was not given to emotional speeches and who limited his goals to predictably achievable tasks. Bohachevsky continued his consistent visitation schedule, making certain to get to the smaller and more remote parishes so that the congregations there did not feel slighted.

CHAPTER 14

Task Completed

The last achievements of Constantine Bohachevsky's life came in measured steps of papal honors and community recognition that vindicated the road he had taken. He appreciated the recognition but could not rest, since the titles with which the Vatican showered him were personal. The Ukrainian Church in the United States remained an exarchate, even as Bohachevsky became an archbishop. His main task, to institutionalize the Ukrainian Catholic Church in America as an archbishopric, remained. He turned down proffered community honors for fear of compromising the rigid code of ethics that guided him and his exarchy. All honors were ephemeral until the diocese was fully embedded in the United States as a recognized, self-perpetuating entity within the Catholic Church. Within the broader Catholic Church structure that meant the creation of an archdiocese, or in Eastern terminology, a metropolitanate.

Bohachevsky had two immediate goals: to bring together the two segments of the Greek-Catholic Ruthenian-American diocese on the basis—and that was the second goal—of clearly formulated rules and regulations. The former would create a potent force within the whole Catholic Church, and the latter dovetailed with the large Vatican project of preparing a codex for all Eastern Churches. The reestablishment of one Ukrainian Catholic Church in the United States would strengthen the position of the scattered Ukrainian Catholic Church within the Catholic *Ecclesia*, and amplify its voice at the forthcoming council.

Bohachevsky saw the church in the United States as a model for other Ukrainian churches. In contrast to Europe, America was untrammeled by traditions of state religion, its churches were free to develop as they wished. Bohachevsky wanted his church to grow within a clear set of its own laws. He hoped other Ukrainian churches in the West would follow, making it easier for the respective eparchs to cooperate. The publication, in 1954, of the eparchial by-laws (statutes) affirmed the readiness of the exarchate to gain higher ecclesiastical status. Bohachevsky proved to be prescient, because toward the end of the 1950s, the Vatican instructed its churches to update and codify eparchial regulations in preparation for the ecumenical council.

TO RECLAIM UNITY

Throughout this period both the Holy See and the Ukrainian Church in Lviv used the term Ruthenian when writing in Latin to refer to Ukrainians. The church in Ukraine was formally known as the Ruthenian Catholic Church of the Byzantine Rite, and the Vatican kept the name even after its so-called formal dissolution by the Soviets in 1946. Bohachevsky continued using the term Ruthenian (thus linking it to the Ukrainian mother church) in his formal statements about the Ukrainian Church because this was the terminology Lviv used. The archbishop wanted to emphasize the connection between the Ukrainian Church in America and Lviv. He did not want to independently institutionalize a change that would further alienate the Carpathian Rusyns. At the same time, the use of the old nomenclature angered Ukrainian activists.

Bohachevsky, as his mentor Sheptytsky, always saw the Ukrainian Catholic Church as a large institution unhampered by political borders. As a young man, Constantine Bohachevsky had been raised on the lore of Ukraine beyond the river Zbruch—the Great Ukraine, a shimmering land of golden grain and brave people, as the stories went. Most likely in his early years at the seminary, he and his friends discussed ways of spreading Catholicism in Eastern Ukraine, then part of the Romanov Empire. In America, Bohachevsky felt that the bigger the Eastern Catholic Church, the easier it would be to withstand the comfortable tug of Americanization. In his waning years, as the Vatican released its great plans for a church council, Bohachevsky struggled to convince his fellow Ruthenians to come to an agreement that would enable the establishment of more exarchates that would lead to a metropolitanate for the mutual advantage of both Halychanyns and Ruthenians.

When Bohachevsky and Basil Takach were appointed exarchs to the Ukrainian Halychanyns and the Carpatho-Ruthenians, respectively, the presumption was that once disagreements between the two groups subside, their churches would again be one, as had been the case under the first American bishop, Ortynsky. Although relations between Bohachevsky and Takach were cordial (perhaps even friendly), their respective faithful could not find common ground. For his part, Bishop Senyshyn also did everything he could to foster joint actions with the Ruthenians. It was with this goal in mind that he sought their participation in the First Eucharistic Congress of the Eastern Churches in 1954. But while the Russian and Slovak Eastern Catholic prelates officiated formally, the Ruthenian Church, which was going through a leadership crisis, did not.[1]

Toward the end of 1955, Cicognani, either of his own volition or upon instructions from the Congregation for the Eastern Church, tried his hand at nudging the two Ukrainian Catholic Churches in the United States toward unity. He brought together the Ruthenian bishop, Thomas Elko, and Bishop Senyshyn to discuss common ritual issues, as well as mixed marriages and the increasingly popular formal First Communion ceremonies in Ukrainian churches.[2] Both bishops agreed on possible ways of address-

---

1. Takach's successor, Bishop Daniel Ivancho (1948–54, d. 1972), established a seminary for his diocese in 1950, thereby saying that the St. Basil Ukrainian Catholic Seminary could not fulfill the needs of his church. Four years later, he resigned for personal reasons. (He had been married.) Bishop Thomas Elko (bishop 1955–67, d. 1981) also worked for the recognition of the separate status of the Ruthenian Church. While he took part in Bohachevsky's installation ceremonies, he, as his predecessors, declined to participate in the all-Ukrainian bishops meeting on November 29, 1958, because of the sensibilities of his congregation. The next bishop, Stephen Kocisko, became the first Ruthenian metropolitan in 1967. He noted that Rome supported a "clear and purposeful . . . distinction between the Galicians (Ukrainians) and the Ruthenians of Subcarpathia and their respective descendants." Kocisko to Bohachevsky, UMAS, Chancery Archive.

2. In the Eastern tradition, which tended not to be honored, children under seven may receive the Host without prior confession. In the nineteenth century, however, both in Europe and in the United States, the formal First Communion at age seven was widely practiced.

ing these practical matters, but the follow-up failed.[3] The Ruthenian parish congregations seemed opposed to a restoration of the ecclesiastical unity of the pre-1924 period. The bitterness of the past outweighed the potential of the future.

UKRAINIAN BISHOPS IN AMERICA COOPERATE

Back during the 1930s Bohachevsky had supported the fledgling office in the Lviv metropolitan chancery that arranged the joint meetings of Ukrainian bishops. In the postwar years, with the church in Ukraine off the map, it was the Ukrainian Catholic Church in Canada with its four exarchates that suggested periodic meetings of the Eastern-rite Catholic exarchates. Bohachevsky readily joined and organized a meeting in Washington, D.C., on October 25, 1954, at the new seminary.[4] The proclamation of the first Ukrainian-Canadian metropolitanate in America in 1956, with its seat in Winnipeg, Manitoba, was a tribute to agricultural Canada's large Ukrainian population. The Ukrainian Catholic bishops attending the ceremonies that November convened a permanent Conference of the Ukrainian Episcopate of the Free World and agreed to meet periodically.

That same year, 1956, the Ukrainian Catholic Church in the United States, as Bohdan Procko noted, also "reached a great milestone" with the creation of a second Ukrainian Catholic eparchy at Stamford.[5] This was a major step toward the establishment of an archbishopric. Bishop Senyshyn was named exarch for the new diocese. An equally important highlight of 1956 was the election of Joseph Schmondiuk to be the first American-born, Ukrainian Catholic bishop.[6] Bohachevsky named Schmondiuk his auxiliary bishop and soon promoted the young man to vicar general of the Philadel-

3. Senyshyn to Bohachevsky, December 21, 1955, UMAS, Chancery Archive. Paul R. Magocsi, *Our People: Carpatho-Rusyns and Their Descendants in North America* (Toronto: Multicultural History Society of Ontario, 1984), suggested that the Philadelphia eparchy wanted to take over the Pittsburgh Ruthenian church.

4. Bohachevsky to Senyshyn, January 5, 1954, UMAS, Chancery Archive.

5. Procko, *Ukrainian Catholics*, 80.

6. Joseph Schmondiuk was nominated bishop on July 20 and consecrated November 8, 1956. He was an orphan from age five, raised in the school run by the Basilian Sisters in Philadelphia, studied in Rome, and was ordained there in 1936 by Bishop Alexander Stoyko of the Mukachiv Ukrainian Catholic Diocese. One could read into the choice of consecrator a conscious attempt to minimize the differences between Ruthenians and Ukrainians.

phia diocese.[7] Bohachevsky wanted to show the shy young bishop the great hopes he placed in him. Without going through the chancery, Bohachevsky drew up a formal letter on old stationery, with official filing numeration reinforced with a very old stamp-seal bearing the inscription: "Constantine Bohatschewsky, Bishop of the Rutheno Greek Catholic Church USA." The stamp carefully covered the archbishop's old stationery logo. Bohachevsky wanted to hurry the young bishop along his hierarchic journey and circumvented his own administrative practice. The letter read: "Desiring to fulfill to the highest degree my duties toward the faithful committed to my care, and being unable to perform all those varied duties by myself, I have decided to elect you as an assistant to take part in my pastoral vigilance and solicitude."[8]

The creation of the new diocese necessitated fiscal modernization. Access to the pertinent material is limited, but the testier tones in the correspondence between Bohachevsky and Senyshyn make it clear that the latter needed more money. In private, Senyshyn held his own, but he went out of his way to avoid any public disagreement with Bohachevsky.[9] The Ukrainian Catholic diocesan administration grew, the chancery office expanded, the number of diocesan standing committees increased, as did the ad hoc committees that focused on immediate issues. This vitality forced Bohachevsky to give up his old Halychyna patriarchal style of handling all financial matters.

Correspondence between Bohachevsky and the apostolic delegate reveals that promises were made to create an archbishopric, but nothing was yet certain. Rome still worried whether Bohachevsky would be able to integrate the new Ukrainian immigrants into his congregation. Eugene Cardinal Tisserant, the secretary of the Congregation for the Eastern Church, reported overall progress:

7. Procko, *Ukrainian Catholics in America*, 81; *Eparkhiial'ni Visti*, November 1956, p. 101. Bohachevsky defended his young bishop before the Apostolic Delegate from charges of passivity, suggested that Schmondiuk was just shy and would grow into the job.

8. Bohachevsky to Schmondiuk, August 20, 1956, UMAS, Chancery Archive. Bohachevsky favored Schmondiuk, as can be seen from this note and Bohachevsky's defense of Schmondiuk's work in correspondence with the congregation.

9. Senyshyn to Bohachevsky, January 19, 1956, UMAS, Chancery Archive. Senyshyn thought the clergy Society of St. Joseph was still active, but Bohachevsky believed it had been moribund for years.

the last five years in the history of this apostolic exarchy are a time of growth and strengthening, thanks to the fact that God's Providence increased the cadres of the clergy-refugees whom you accepted and for whom you found positions. The creation of thirty-five new parishes and missions, and an equal number of churches, the acquisition of forty-three parish homes and the construction of the Graduate Seminary of St. Josaphat in Washington, which you opened so grandly, give proof of this unusual development.[10]

Cardinal Tisserant was an ardent promoter of the erection of the Philadelphia metropolitanate. He did not just limit himself to the usual congratulatory acknowledgement of the superior work of the clergy and the dedication of its faithful. To offset potential opposition at the Vatican he enumerated rather specifically the indicators of its growth: the exarchate overcame great difficulties impeding the establishment of Ukrainian-Catholic schools, expanded its periodic press and publications, held annual conferences for youth and other Ukrainian Catholic groups "that strengthen brotherly ties and adherence to common traditions and their native rite." Turning to Bohachevsky, Tisserant wrote: "Accept, Your Excellency, expressions of my total satisfaction in the grand development of the Exarchy under your leadership; I express this pleasure also for the work of His Excellency, Your Vicar for his dedicated and helpful work, to the clergy and all faithful who work for the implementation of the Kingdom of God."[11]

Part of the flowery language was to soothe Bohachevsky's ego, if for no other reason than to assuage any perceived offense that the Canadian metropolitanate had been erected, and the one in America had not. Tisserant and the congregation, in fact and in deed, reflected that part of the Vatican that continued to believe in the special mission of the Ukrainian Catholic Church. Tisserant, like Bohachevsky, presumed that the new immigrants would use and build on the institutions that their predecessors had built so laboriously. In this sanguine view, the new immigrants and the Catholic schools would serve as a tourniquet to stem the flow of immigrant children into the Latin rite. These children, it was hoped, would

10. Tisserant to Bohachevsky, January 26, 1955, translated Ukrainian copy which Bohachevsky sent Senyshyn, UMAS, Chancery Archive. I was not able to determine who did the translation into Ukrainian.
11. Ibid.

populate the seminaries and the convents and would ultimately become the new clergy and religious who would have the wherewithal to preserve the Ukrainian Catholic Church in the United States. Experienced veterans of the traditional Catholic Church, both Tisserant and Bohachevsky put great faith in structures to channel individual efforts.

There was a flare-up of questioning at the Vatican of the wisdom of elevating the Ukrainian exarchate in the United States into an archbishopric. Rome did not want to go against the wishes of the American, Latin-rite clergy. As always, rumors had the Americans opposing the elevation of the Ukrainian Catholic Church. Equally, however, Rome remained interested in Moscow, and an understanding with the potentially vast Russian Orthodoxy always hovered in the background. The East, both the disunited and the not-yet-proselytized, too, was very much in the papal field of vision. In that scenario, the Ukrainian Catholic Church became a hindrance, rather than the historical help. Moreover, Ukrainians in the United States were not as visible as those in Canada and were not actively demanding a metropolitanate. It was clear, however, that the elevation of the Ukrainian Catholic Church in America had to be addressed.

The Ukrainian Catholic Church in America was organized, its members no longer threatening to defect to the Orthodox churches. The *Eparchial News* linked the clergy as they pursued their pastoral and administrative duties: notices were posted about all visitations, about the meetings of committees, about the bishops' meetings with groups and individuals—in short, the duty of the parish priest was to know what was going on in the chancery. The core religious societies for the laity expanded during the 1950s. The Ukrainian Catholic Youth League had the largest membership, but the stalwart lay organizations—Sodality of the Blessed Virgin for the women and the Holy Name Society for the men—were now joined by the Knights of Columbus chapters in Ukrainian parishes.[12] Bohachevsky pushed for the Legion of Decency, but it elicited little public interest.

As the postwar economy prospered, Ukrainian-American society devised ways for the two waves of Ukrainian immigrants to live in peace, and often even to cooperate. With few exceptions, the churches accepted the immigrant priests, and congregations melded together. The language of

12. Although Rev. Zachary Orun (1884–1918) had established a Knights chapter in Philadelphia in 1917, the organization did not take root in Ukrainian parishes until the 1940s.

worship remained Old Church Slavonic, but as the congregations grew, priests also preached in English at different liturgies. Linguistic preferences took on a religious coloring. Pastors dealt the best they could with the increasingly varied expectations of the parishioners. Churches were full of both the young and the old on Sundays. New churches were established, no longer constrained to first build a school. The chancery became less vigilant in insisting upon that provision.

In summing up Bohachevsky's achievements on the eve of the establishment of the archbishopric, the historian Bohdan Procko turned to the November 1, 1957, pastoral letter and the archbishop's staccato enumeration of what Ukrainian Catholics in the United States had accomplished:

We have today 172 parishes and eleven missions, divided between [the] two exarchies [Philadelphia and Stamford], not counting the separate exarchy for our brethren of the Pod-Carpathian regions. We have nearly three hundred priests under the leadership of an archbishop and two bishops; rather than just one church, we have 223 churches and chapels. When we include in this three religious orders for men and the four religious orders and communities for women, two orphanages, three homes for the aged, the summer camp for youth, the major and minor seminaries, two colleges, four high schools, thirty all-day parochial schools, 256 classes of religious and catechetical instruction, the church choirs, the long line of religious brotherhoods and organizations, the Ukrainian Catholic Youth League, "Obnova," the Providence Association, the Catholic press and the publishing houses, then it becomes self-evident that the efforts of our clergy and faithful were not in vain. Our Ukrainian Catholic Church stands with a firm foot upon this land.[13]

The bishop was neither worldly nor particularly eloquent but he did stress that the Ukrainian Catholic Church in America planned to stay. One of the few times that Bohachevsky permitted himself a public display of emotion was in the Christmas pastoral letter of 1957–58, which was devoted to the Virgin and in which he described his own deeply felt joyous experiences during the Lourdes pilgrimage.[14] The chancery did not lose sight of the general concerns of the Catholic Church. Bohachevsky remained very concerned that the Ukrainian Church remain vigilant about the broad moral dangers to the congregation, not only to the loss of tradi-

13. Procko, Ukrainian Catholics in America, 83; Eparkhiial'ni Visti, November 1957, 74.
14. Eparkhiial'ni Visti, November 1958, 168–72.

tion. Thus, the August 1956 issue of the *Eparchial News* carried the "instruc-tion" of the Congregation for the Doctrine of the Faith that explained and denounced "situational ethics." The congregation reminded the clergy that such a flexible approach in matters of faith was downright wrong: "Natural law, which we know through reason and which tells us how to act in any circumstance, forms the basis of human action. This law (norm) is not subjective. It is based on eternal and objective truths."[15] Most of the faithful, however, remained more concerned about the preservation of tradition than dealing with the modern challenges to Christianity. They presumed that their children would inherit their faith if they held onto their Ukrainian patriotism.

THE ESTABLISHMENT OF THE METROPOLITANATE

The announcement of the erection of the Ukrainian Catholic archbishop-ric at Philadelphia came in the middle of work on the local church regu-lations. It came as a surprise to the community, but a relief for the newly nominated archbishop of Philadelphia, Eastern Catholic rite.

To assure the American Ukrainians that they were part of the Catholic *Ecclesia*, the pope had personally requested Bohachevsky to help prepare the planned Second Vatican Council. As part of those overall preparations, Bohachevsky prepared a second volume of the *Eparchial Statutes*. He also put much thought and effort into the planning of clerical meetings—the *sobors*—that the Vatican saw as steps toward the convocation of the ecu-menical council. Bohachevsky was arranging the first of such meetings when he received news of the establishment of the metropolitanate and of his own nomination to serve as metropolitan. He interrupted the prepara-tions for the *sobor* to arrange for the establishment of the archbishopric for the Ukrainian Catholics in America, to prepare to announce that he ful-filled the task that Pope Pius XI set him-to institutionalize the Ukrainian Catholic Church in America.

No substantial documentation is available to chart the story of when and who made the decision to establish Ukrainian metropolitanates out-side the initial territories of the Ukrainian Catholic Church in the first

15. *Eparkhiial'ni Visti*, August 1956, 70–75, my translation from the Ukrainian edition.

place. Nor is there anything in the few open sources touching on this matter to suggest that Bohachevsky was particularly interested in acquiring the title. The whole thrust of his work was directed at the integrated growth of the church from the ground up. The Vatican, despite the wishes of some in Europe and in the United States, had at last recognized the right of Ukrainian Catholics to practice their religion as they wished outside their homeland, which at the time could not practice any religion at all.

It took almost a century for the Ukrainian Catholic Church in the United States to grow into a recognized, separate but equal, ecclesiastical province of the Catholic Church domiciled in America. Many speculated that the Roman Catholic reluctance to fragment and weaken its hierarchical structure by the creation of a separate Eastern-rite Ukrainian Catholic Church province was the main reason for the delay in according the Ukrainian Church in the United States its long-awaited recognition. However, this author believes that an even more important factor in the delay was the desire—at least on Bohachevsky's part, if not on the part of Bishop Elko of the Ruthenian Catholic Church—to come up with a workable plan for reuniting, at least pro forma, the Ruthenian and Ukrainian branches of the church into a larger entity. Unity of the Carpathians and Halychanyns was a sacred quest for Ukrainian patriots, but in practice the community did little to promote it. Nor was there a major public outcry at the exclusion of the Ruthenian Church from the Philadelphia metropolitanate. Only one priest voiced his disappointment on this matter, decrying the "continued bifurcation of the same people here in America," which he considered "painful and not conducive to the welfare of our brothers in Pittsburgh."[16] The suggestion of Mykola Vayda, the publisher of the *Carpathian Voice*, that the new metropolitan should work for the union of the two churches was not at the top of the Ukrainian community's agenda.[17] The official historical overview of the Ukrainian Catholic Church in the United States explained the absence of the Carpatho-Ruthenian Catholic Church in the metropolitanate in this terse paragraph: "The branch of the Ukrainian people stemming from Pidcarpathia, who experienced

16. Letter of Rev. Vasyl Lar, Ansonia, Conn., in Kharyna, *Ukraiins'ka Katolyts'ka Mytropolia*, 129.

17. Mykola Vayda to Bohachevsky, November 1, 1958, in Kharyna, *Ukraiins'ka Katolyts'ka Mytropolia*, 156–57 and 162–63.

many storms and lived a separate life for the past thirty-five years, is not contained in the Philadelphia Metropolitan Province, Byzantine Slavonic Rite."[18]

On July 10, 1958, Pope Pius XII, in the apostolic constitution *Apostolicam hanc*, officially established the new ecclesiastical province comprising the Philadelphia and Stamford exarchates. The act formalized the Province of the Ukrainian Church in America as a fully structured part of the Eternal Church, a recognized province of the universal Catholic Church, and no longer a temporary exarchate.[19]

The Vatican had taken a historic step in 1956 with its decision to elevate the Ukrainian Catholic diocese/exarchate in Canada into an archbishopric, and two years later it did the same for the church in the United States. It is again important to note that the erection of these archbishoprics went against the decisions of the Fourth Lateran Council in 1215. That council had divided Christian Europe into East and West. The Latin rite was recognized as dominant in the West, and non-Latin bishops in that geographic territory could aspire only to the position of vicar general. In the East, on the other hand, multiple rites (and commensurate titles) continued to be recognized within the same territory.[20] The creation of the Ukrainian metropolitanates in the West erased this distinction.

The formal installation of Bohachevsky in the new see occurred three months after the edict issued by Pope Pius XII, at the beginning of the reign of the new pope, John XXIII. Thus, Bohachevsky's installation as archbishop/metropolitan foreshadowed the monumental changes that would affect the entire Catholic Church. Bohachevsky chose November 1 as the date for his installation ceremonies, symbolically reinforcing the connection between his elevation to metropolitan and the death of Metropolitan Sheptytsky (November 1, 1944), as well as Ukraine's steps to establish itself as a body politic on November 1, 1918, when Western Ukrainians proclaimed their independence from the Habsburg Empire. Again, it is noteworthy that

18. Sochotsky, "Ukrainian Catholic Church of the Byzantine-Slavonic Rite in the USA," 286.

19. Procko, *Ukrainian Catholics in America*, 83, quoting *Acta Apostolicae Sedis* 51 (1959): 156–57.

20. Mykola Chubaty, "Ukrainian Metropolitan Sees: Their Formation and Present Status," in Kharyna, *Ukraiins'ka Katolyts'ka Mytropolia*, 293–296; and the Ukrainian version "Naystarsha i naymolodsha Mytropolii Ukraiins'koii Tserkvy," 287–292.

the only power that had at least *de facto* recognized the resulting Western Ukrainian Republic by accepting its ambassador had been the Vatican.[21]

In this papal pronouncement, Bohachevsky became "Constantine, by Divine Mercy and the Grace of the Apostolic See Archbishop of Philadelphia, Metropolitan of the Catholic Ecclesiastical Province of the Byzantine Rite in the United States of America." Bohachevsky showed no surprise at the decision. He felt a sense of relief. He had known from the time he set foot in America that if this church were to survive, it would have to grow institutional roots. Bohachevsky was pleased, despite his advanced age. As he wrote to Bishop Buchko, "individuals pass, the institution endures."[22] Both exarchates—Stamford and Philadelphia—created one metropolitanate, and Bohachevsky was named metropolitan, officially a prince of the church. This was and is still viewed as a major achievement for Ukrainians, a recognition of the importance of the Ukrainian Catholic Church within the broader architecture of the universal church.

The entire Ukrainian-American community rushed to publicly express joy at the establishment of the metropolitanate. The daily organizational tedium, the steadfastness of clergy and faithful, the many daily sacrifices that built the church in America were transformed into this new entity—the metropolitanate in Philadelphia. The community acknowledged its reality. The outpouring of support and throngs of people who wanted to be present at his installation ceremonies surprised Bohachevsky. Busy with daily tasks, he did not notice how much the tide had turned. Support for the church had been steady, but by no means overwhelmingly apparent. Now the entire Ukrainian community put disagreements on hold, and at least for a few months, joyfully worked together to plan the celebration that would provide another affirmation of the existence of Ukraine. The chancery had to give up its exclusive rights to religious celebrations, and the metropolitan-nominee had to acquiesce to civic gatherings in addition to the planned religious ceremonies. Fittingly reflecting this religious-civic bonding, the committee to prepare the celebrations included lay as well as religious representatives. Ukrainians rejoiced that Philadelphia,

21. For the fuller story, see Hentosh, *Vatykan I vyklyky modernosti.*
22. Bohachevsky to Buchko, September 7, 1958, UMAS, Chancery Archive. Buchko's congratulatory letter of August 18, 1958, was published in Kharyna, *Ukraiins'ka Katolyts'ka Mytropolia*, 20.

the cradle of American constitutionalism, had also become the seat of the permanent Ukrainian Catholic Church in the United States. Even those who did not like Bohachevsky on a personal level still recognized the importance of his elevation.

The community immediately acknowledged the secular implications of the decision—the success of the Catholic Church was the success of the Ukrainian people. It was an event of major import to all Ukrainians in America, not only to the Catholics among them. In the absence of other manifestations of Ukraine's independence, the ceremony and attendant prayers served to draw the community together. Maxim Hermaniuk of Canada, the only other Ukrainian Catholic metropolitan in North America, captured the importance of the elevation of the second metropolitanate in North America, noting that the Ukrainian Catholic Church was becoming geographically universal as well as truly catholic (*vselen'ska*). Hermaniuk openly articulated his political goals that placed the creation of the Philadelphia metropolitanate at the cornerstone for the future Kyivan Catholic patriarchate in an independent Ukraine. The Canadian metropolitan stressed the preeminent position of the United States in the world of the 1950s and the powerful light it cast on the Ukrainian community. "Henceforth," he announced, "no one can question the existence or the utility of our rite. America has become for all eternity a land of two or even more rites."[23] Ukraine and its suffering church, headed by Metropolitan Slipyj, were very much on the lips of all involved, but Hermaniuk went one step further—he announced that "a new type of Ukrainian statesman [*derzhavnyk*] is being formed today in our Native Lands."[24] The festivities of the day buried that prescient comment. The community was more inclined to focus on protest and resistance than to study the workings of the closed, hostile USSR, which unbeknownst to itself grew its own opposition. Hermaniuk voiced a desirable possibility. The festive throng muted his prediction.

23. Hermaniuk, "Propovid' Vpro. Kanadiys'koho Mytropolyta Kyr Maksyma Hermaniuka," in Kharyna, *Ukraiins'ka Katolyts'ka Mytropolia*, 82, my translation from Ukrainian. He developed the theme further in the speech at the evening banquet, see ibid., 97–98.

24. "Promova Mytropolyta Kyr Maksyma," in Kharyna, *Ukraiins'ka Katolyts'ka Mytropolia*, 97–98. Hermaniuk's other comment, that "a new type of a Ukrainian is being formed in Ukraine," was quite unusual because the Ukrainian nationalist line in the West was that all Ukrainian communists were traitors of Ukraine.

Those preparing the celebration were so aware of its importance that they decided to prepare the documentation pertinent to the event for immediate publication. Later, the editors supplemented the publication with a historical account of the growth of the scattered churches into one metropolitanate/archbishopric. The history of the whole Ukrainian Church and its people had more than amply proven the ephemera of undocumented traditions. Titled *The Ukrainian Catholic Metropolitan See Byzantine Rite, U.S.A./Ukraiins'ka Katolyts'ka Mytropolia v Zluchenykh Derzhavakh Ameryky*, it was published both in English and mostly in Ukrainian by the Byzantine Rite archeparchy of Philadelphia within a year of the ceremony.[25] The three-hundred-page book was edited by Rev. Myroslav Kharyna. He ended his brief introduction with a justification:

This book is meant to express the faith of the times and of the people who lived then and who witnessed this important event. It is meant to convey for future generations the joy that the contemporaries of the event felt at the establishment of the Philadelphia archbishopric. . . . And even if this book serves no other purpose but to preserve the profound thoughts and eloquent statements expressed in the sermons and speeches, that would be sufficient justification for its publication.[26]

This self-deprecating note was intended to offset whatever criticisms might have been made about the many ceremonies taking place in Philadelphia while the homeland was suffering under the Soviet regime. A more salient criticism might have been that all the pomp was a waste of money—a complaint that the archbishop had often raised in the past. This was different. This ceremony marked not only the installation of an archbishop/metropolitan, but the creation of the archbishopric itself. The publication included, in addition to the documents and descriptions of ceremonies relating to the institution of the see, a brief history of the Ukrainian Catholic Church in the United States and a list of the Ukrainian clergy in the United States at the time the see was established. An even more concise overview of Ukrainian bishops rounded off the historical information. The book included letters of congratulations from religious and political dignitaries and from all segments of the Ukrainian commu-

25. The date of publication of Kharyna, *Ukraiins'ka Katolyts'ka Mytropolia*, was 1959.
26. Kharyna, "Predmova" [preface], to Kharyna, *Ukraiins'ka Katolyts'ka Mytropolia*, 5.

nity organizations, a feat that reflected good staff work on the part of the chancery. Well-wishers stressed the achievements of the new metropolitan and touted the historic significance of his new position. The predictable good wishes and prayers came from Roman Catholic and Ukrainian clergy, organizations, and local politicians. All stressed "the stupendous changes that our church experienced as . . . the result of [Bohachevsky's] thirty-four years of constant and heroic dedication to work."[27] The Shevchenko Scientific Society would not admit defeat and again reminded the new metropolitan that he indeed is their member.[28] The rector of the émigré Ukrainian Free University, Ivan Mirchuk, emphasized Bohachevsky's "achievements in all areas—church, civic, national,"[29] but refrained from making another offer of an honorary doctorate. Among the numerous greetings was one from Dr. Mykola Chubaty, who credited Bohachevsky with establishing a renewed Ukrainian Catholicism.[30]

The Catholic Church at the time consistently drew public attention to the evils of communism. For some Ukrainian Americans, each successful endeavor at promoting public recognition of anything even remotely connected to Ukraine promised to bring the dissolution of the USSR ever closer. No one articulated this as clearly as the Canadian Metropolitan Hermaniuk in his speech at Bohachevsky's installation ceremonies: "We are on our way to a Christian synthesis and to the reinstitution of Ukrainian state sovereignty. Let us pray that this synthesis results in the establishment of a Ukrainian patriarchy in Kyiv. The establishment of the archbishopric in Philadelphia signifies the next step toward this noble goal."[31]

Bishop Buchko, whose service in postwar Europe had made him very aware of the extent of American power, reminded Bohachevsky of the sin-

27. Rev. Stepan Bakhtalovs'ky to Bohachevsky, August 11, 1958, in Kharyna, Ukraiins'ka Katolyts'ka Mytropolia, 140.

28. Volodymyr Yaniv and Volodymyr Kubijowych to Bohachevsky, August 27, 1959, in Kharyna, Ukraiins'ka Katolyts'ka Mytropolia, 142.

29. Mirchuk, letter dated September 22, 1958, in Kharyna, Ukraiins'ka Katolyts'ka Mytropolia, 143.

30. Chubaty to Bohachevsky, August 12, 1958, in Kharyna, Ukraiins'ka Katolyts'ka Mytropolia, 159–60. That phrase already hints at the growing discontent among some of the faithful that the church did not pay enough attention to the retention and strengthening of a Ukrainian cultural content.

31. Hermaniuk in the speech at the evening banquet, in Kharyna, Ukraiins'ka Katolyts'ka Mytropolia, 97.

gular importance of the Ukrainian-American Church (that is, in comparison with Ukrainian Catholic churches elsewhere in the world). In his letter of congratulations to Bohachevsky, which was published in the formal historical record publication, Buchko noted:

I expressed my best wishes upon your appointment as metropolitan in the USA [to God] at the feet of the Blessed Virgin at Lourdes, here on paper I am at a loss of words with which to express my joy on this occasion. I am very aware that the establishment of the Ukrainian Catholic Province in the United States is an even greater achievement than the [similar] establishment in Canada—because the Holy See had to overcome greater difficulties in dealing with the Roman Catholic clergy in the United States than in Canada. I am certain that this is a foretaste of your eventual reward in the Heavenly Kingdom for all your hard work and labor to spread the Kingdom of God on this earth, as well as a palliative for all the crosses and sufferings that you endured from our own people in America.[32]

In addition to Rev. Myroslav Kharyna, who was responsible for the liturgical side of the ceremonies as well as editing the commemorative book, other committee members included the future Bishop Basil Losten, a graduate of St. Basil's, and Reverends Vasyl Holowinsky, Petro Lypyn, and Mykhailo Pyrih, the three post-World-War-II immigrants. Religious services and processions were intertwined with receptions and other festivities, all enriched by sermons, speeches, and solemn song. The events ran like clockwork. Nothing went awry, no one was late, and almost all speakers adhered to the time limits. The crowd of twelve thousand or more, which converged on Philadelphia from all over the United States to witness the installation of the new metropolitan at a Solemn Liturgy, was jubilant but orderly. Like the earlier Eucharistic Marian congress, the event was held at Philadelphia's Convention Center, because no church in the city was large enough to hold the expected crowds. As it was, even that massive building was filled to overflowing. Thirteen hundred received communion. A mixed choir of 150 participants sang the responses. The luncheon for three hundred clergy and the evening banquet for over five hundred guests—were both hosted at Philadelphia's premier hotel, the Warwick.

Cicognani presided in one of his last official religious duties in the

32. Buchko, quoted in Kharyna, *Ukraiins'ka Katolyts'ka Mytropolia*, 20.

United States. In an official photograph of the event, two satin-clad and beplumed pages, pupils of Ukrainian Catholic schools, flank him. The apostolic delegate's sermon reflected his intimate familiarity with the history of the Ukrainian Catholic Church. He stressed that the creation of the American metropolitanate marked "a historic milestone for the church" and expressed his hope that "Metropolitan Joseph Slipyj and other members of the Lviv hierarchy suffering in Siberia" would learn about this glorious event.[33] The list of dignitaries attending the event offers proof that outsiders had at last recognized the importance of the Ukrainian-American community and of historic Ukraine, regardless of its present status. Among the Latin Catholic clergy who took part in the festive procession were John O'Hara, archbishop of Philadelphia (soon thereafter named cardinal); Bishops Jerome Hanna and Henry Klonowski from Scranton, Pennsylvania; Bishop Lawrence Schott of Harrisburg, Pennsylvania; Bishop Vincent Waters of Riley, North Carolina; and Bishop Christopher Weldon of Springfield, Massachusetts.

Headed by Metropolitan Hermaniuk of Winnipeg, almost all Ukrainian Catholic bishops outside the Soviet-controlled East attended the installation. They included Nil Savaryn, OSBM, of Edmonton; Ambrose Senyshyn, OSBM, of Stamford; Andriy Roboretsky of Saskatoon; Bishop Joseph Schmondiuk of Philadelphia; Bishop Joseph Martynetz, OSBM, of Brazil; and Bishop Ivan Prashko of Australia. Bishops Nicholas T. Elko, exarch of the Pittsburgh Ruthenian Exarchy,[34] and Stephen Kocisko of the Pittsburgh diocese also took part in the ceremonies.[35] The Ruthenian bishops, however, would not take part in the bishops' meetings that followed. Bishop Elko explained his decision to maintain a rigid division between the dioceses:

33. Address of Archbishop Amleto Cicognani, delivered at the erection of the Philadelphia Slav-Byzantine Metropolitan See, November 1, 1958, Convention Hall, in Kharyna, *Ukraiins'ka Katolyts'ka Mytropolia*, 104–7.

34. "1200 Faithful Witness Historical Installation Rites," in Kharyna, *Ukraiins'ka Katolyts'ka Mytropolia*, 102. In the Ukrainian version the use of the term "Ruthenian" is avoided by listing both Pittsburgh bishops under a general listing of "Our bishops who took part in the procession," "Mytropolychi torzhestva u Filiadel'fii" [Metropolitan Festivities in Philadelphia], Kharyna, *Ukraiins'ka Katolyts'ka Mytropolia*, 75.

35. The new metropolitan was assisted by Chancellor Platon Kornyliak (eventually bishop for Western Europe), Rector Vasyl Makukh; Oleksandr Treshnevsky, Philadelphia dean; Yaroslav Danylchuk, consultor; Dmytro Laputa, Redemptorist abbot in Newark, N.J.; and Theodore Venek (Vynnyk), abbot of the Franciscan Fathers in Sybertsville, Penn.

"The social, political, and religious backgrounds of these two separate national groups [leads us] to avoid any provocation of our faithful by pursuing an action alien to their thinking."[36]

Representatives of all Ukrainian organizations also attended, along with many of their members. But for the new metropolitan, as well as for many of his priests and faithful, the absentees were more notable. For many participants the popularly sainted Andrey Sheptytsky, the exiled Metropolitan Josyph Slipyj, and the whole suffering church in Ukraine, including all the dead bishops and persecuted priests almost palpably hovered over the altar. It was a ceremony that went beyond the moment and the event. It affirmed that the Ukrainian Catholic Church belonged to the people, and the people responded by imbuing the moment with an interpretation that resonated with them. The ceremony was the tool that drew out the inner meaning, and that meaning was "ours"—a visceral assertion of the communal self that found expression within the church.

For Bohachevsky, however, the ceremonial aspect of his installation was something of a formality; what was truly important was the institutionalization of the Ukrainian Church in the United States. Bohachevsky stressed this point in all his public statements, and followed with a plea to the faithful to continue their Christian lives full of active dedication to God and to their people. At his installment, at the clergy luncheon, Bohachevsky's thoughts focused on the absent guests. Immediately after thanking the pope and remembering the support of the deceased Pius XII, the new metropolitan reminded the audience that:

Behind the iron curtain all our dioceses are liquidated, three bishops assassinated, two apostolic administrators and two apostolic visitators banished, 3,040 parishes suppressed, 2,950 priests jailed or exiled; 1,640 religious and 540 seminarians dispersed or disappeared, 4,600 churches closed or handed to schismatics. All Catholic presses silenced. All Catholic schools closed. All Catholic organizations dissolved. Those still living are compelled to profess their faith in hiding because of the pervasive communist yoke. Their suffering is our suffering. For they and we form one Mystical Body with the Vicar of Christ as its Visible

36. Bishop Nicholas Elko to Hermaniuk, quoted by David Motiuk, *Eastern Christians in the New World: An Historical and Canonical Study of the Ukrainian Catholic Church in Canada* (Ottawa: Saint Paul University, Metropolitan Andrey Sheptytsky Institute of Eastern Christian Studies and Faculty of Canon Law, 2005), 84 note, and 82–87.

Head and Jesus Christ as the Invisible Head. Whenever one member suffers, the whole body suffers.

Bohachevsky singled out Cicognani's contribution in supporting the growth of the Ukrainian Catholic Church abroad: "His Excellency, the apostolic delegate . . . has been an invaluable aid, an inspiration, and a benediction to our hierarchy and faithful alike by [His] exemplary and steadfast devotion to duty, . . . timely and ever wise guidance, counsel, and instructions. From the bottom of my heart, I feel obliged to express publicly to Your Excellency my deeply-felt gratitude and the cordial and tender thanks of [all] of us."[37] This uncharacteristically florid speech was an emotional outburst for Bohachevsky. He ended with a brief toast to the reigning pope, John XXIII.

The new metropolitan made the only public acknowledgement of his family that evening by mentioning "my dear relatives." As was his wont, Bohachevsky used the occasion to remind everybody of the need for work and for prayer to achieve all the noble goals that had been mentioned so profusely during the day:

Sweat and blood gain and preserve one's own state [*derzhava*]. Nations exist [either] through the sacrifices of all or [because of] the sacrifices of a few dedicated individuals. Our [Ukrainian] attempts to gain independence electrified the dedicated part of society. [Now is the time] to replace momentary action by constant work, sudden actions [*zryv*] with universal steady labor. Only then will each one of us not have lived in vain. Remember—one never dies completely. Be worthy of Christ's name, because Christ is Sacrifice, [as is each] Christian—a symbol of sacrifice.[38]

In his speech, Bohachevsky's first altar boy and now his physician, Emil Harasym, described the bishop's brutal schedule: "I have seen our Excellency travel across the United States all-night and return to his chancery in the morning ready for his office work. How many of you would like

37. Address of Metropolitan Bohachevsky, delivered at the hierarchy-clergy banquet, November 1, 1958, at the Hotel Warwick, Philadelphia, in Kharyna, *Ukraiins'ka Katolyts'ka Mytropolia*, 109–10.

38. "Promova Vpr. Mytropolyta Kyr KonstantynaBohachevs'koho skazana pid kinets vechirnoho benketu pislia Intronizatsii" [Speech of Metropolitan Kyr Constantine Bohachevsky delivered at the evening banquet after the Enthronement], in Kharyna, *Ukraiins'ka Katolyts'ka Mytropolia*, 98–99.

to work till late every night, and arise each morning at 4:00 A.M. to start your day?"[39]

The presence of American, Latin-rite Catholic dignitaries at various venues and events comprising the installation ceremonies, along with the written congratulations of many more, underscored the hard-won equality between the rites. The Roman Catholic archbishop of Philadelphia, John F. O'Hara, tried to inject a note of mild levity at the installation banquet by referring to himself as metropolitan-senior. O'Hara found the existence of two archbishops in one city very unusual. So it was most appropriate, he commented, that Philadelphia, the city of brotherly love, should be the site for this extraordinary occurrence.[40]

At the communal luncheon, Rev. Dr. Monsignor Stephen Tykhansky [Chechansky] spoke in Ukrainian on behalf of the American generation of Ukrainian priests and called upon all Ukrainian-Americans to work together to justify the faith that the papacy had placed in them. His understanding of the church's importance was straightforward:

We who have been born here can openly declare that were it not for our church, for our bishops and priests we would not exist as members of our nation, our church, and our rite. We were raised not to be ashamed of our heritage, not to forget our language and our rite. We could do that because no one prevented us from doing it, because a good American can only be one who is an honest and upstanding member of his nation [natsíí]. Therefore the new immigrants should follow the example of those who under the guidance of our church preserved the loyalty to our rite, and to our people [narodu], because only under the guidance of our metropolitan will we be able to crown our work with success.[41]

Following this speech came the reading of the numerous congratulatory greetings from the White House; the governors of New Jersey, New

39. Address of Dr. Emil Harasym delivered at the evening banquet, November 1, 1958, in Kharyna, Ukraïins'ka Katolyts'ka Mytropolia, 113.

40. An anonymous article on "The Festive Banquets," in Kharyna, Ukraïins'ka Katolyts'ka Mytropolia, 85–86, reported on O'Hara's speech at the luncheon for the clergy held at Warwick Hotel after after the Liturgy and installation. O'Hara's phrase —"As archbishop-senior, I welcome and congratulate you and wish you all the best"—issued with a note of levity in English, jarred the sensibilities of some of the Ukrainian priests. In December 1958, Archbishop O'Hara was named cardinal.

41. "Promova Vpr o. Monsiniiora Dr.Stepana Tykhan'skoho vyholoshena pid chas vechirnoho benketu" [Speech of Very Reverend Monsignor Dr. Stephen Tychansky delivered at the evening banquet], in Kharyna, Ukraïins'ka Katolyts'ka Mytropolia, 94–95.

York, and Pennsylvania; some members of the U.S. Congress; the mayor of Philadelphia and the chairman of the city council. In his brief thanks to the clergy at the luncheon, Bohachevsky singled out not only the churches which the congregations had built, but also the organizations they had established: the Sodalities of the Blessed Virgin, the Altar Boy Society, the Apostleship of Prayer, the Societies of the Sacred Heart, Catholic Action, and other organizations.

At the evening banquet, greetings were read from numerous Ukrainian community organizations, youth groups, and the Association of Catholic Presses that had been recently founded in the United States by the new immigrants. On behalf of those immigrants, Mykhailo Tershakovets stressed Bohachevsky's "fusion of lifelong service to God and service to the nation in the tradition of our bishops who lived in our land for almost the thousand-year existence of Christianity on that land."[42]

The publication that documented the event, *The Ukrainian Catholic Metropolitan See Byzantine Rite, U.S.A.*, made its strongest statement in three words, softly and elegantly, on the very first unnumbered page: Українська Католицька Митрополія. There was no English translation of this phrase; the term "Ukrainian Catholic metropolitanate" was not yet widely in use. The publication, as mentioned above, was fashioned as a collection of historic documents that created, described, justified, and celebrated this new and important phenomenon. It focused on the legality and solidity of the establishment of the archdiocese, claiming to be the authorized voice marking the occasion. As if fearing that the existence of the metropolitanate could be challenged at some later point, or that some future generation might not comprehend its full significance, the new book documented the legitimacy of the metropolitancy and accentuated the formalities of the installation of the first metropolitan to make the metropolitanate a tangible reality to its scattered membership. A good third of the publication was devoted to the history of the "Ukrainian Catholic Church of the Byzantine-Slavonic Rite in the U.S.A." The official papal documents were

42. "Promova Prof. Dr. Mykhayla Tershakivtsia vyholoshena pid chas vechirnoho benketu" [Speech of Prof. Dr. Mykhaylo Tershakovets' delivered at the evening banquet], in Kharyna, *Ukraïns'ka Katolyts'ka Mytropolia*, 90–91. He also pointed out that "apostasy of faith leads to apostasy of nation," and discussed Bohachevsky's support of scholarship and education.

included in the original Latin, followed by Ukrainian and English trans-lations. Vatican and Ukrainian clerical officials were featured, including the new apostolic delegate to the United States, Bishop Egidio Vagnozzi, who was assigned to this position by the time the commemorative book was published.[43] The Ukrainian Catholic Metropolitan See Byzantine Rite, U.S.A. again underscored the unity of the Ukrainian Catholic Church by provid-ing photographs of Ukrainian Catholic bishops worldwide, naturally in-cluding the bishops of the "silent church"— Metropolitan Joseph Slipyj; Bishops Mykola Charnetsky of Volyn, Pavlo Hoydych and his vicar, Vasyl Hopko, of Slovakia; and Havryil Bukatko of Yugoslavia.[44] The new met-ropolitan's biography, a bit longer than the usual perfunctory versions, overlooked the difficulties he had endured, as these were no longer rele-vant, and focused, instead, on his accomplishments. In combination, the detailed descriptions of the ceremonies; the publication of the sermons and speeches, telegrams and greetings; and the emphasis on the repre-sentative nature of the unprecedentedly large audience, were a cumulative sign of the rejoicing arising from an achievement worthy of remembering and documenting for posterity.

The above-mentioned documentary publication provided explanatory information on various aspects of the metropolitanate that the editors felt would be useful for the readers. The office of the metropolitan itself had to be explained. This explanation was meticulously presented in a dense, four-page, anonymous article that detailed the historical origins of the position of metropolitan and its dual provenance of exercising full pow-er over his territory (the metropolia) and over other bishops. The historical background touched on the desire of the Ukrainian metropolitans of earlier times to free themselves of excessive patriarchal authority; the explana-tion ended with a justification for the authority of the Roman pontiff. The

43. The editors had to scramble at the last minute to include a photograph of the new papal nuncio. They placed it on the page facing Bohachevsky's formal photograph, thereby sacrificing the short description that identified all other major dignitaries.

44. Bishop Bukatko, in his formal letter of greeting, pointed out that "the wonder-ful news that the Holy See deigned to establish a metropolitanate for Ukrainians in the United States reached even us, albeit after some delay. It filled our souls and hearts with joy and exaltation," ibid., 30. Bishop Joseph Martynetz, OSBM, of Brazil used the occasion to thank Bohachevsky for the generosity that he had shown for his flock, and mentioned Bohachevsky's 1931 visit to Brazil, ibid., 34.

difference between a Roman archbishop and an Eastern metropolitan (the latter has more power) must have struck the average reader as arcane. The nuances in the anonymous interpretation of the significance of the pallium intimated the distant rumblings of a potential storm on the extent of the metropolitan's power. At the time this interpretation was penned, few could predict that within the next fifteen years these issues would again shake the Ukrainian Catholic Church almost to its core.

Bohachevsky's formal insignia, his coat-of-arms, which had featured a simple Virgin as Immaculate Conception, now featured on its left side the permanent heraldic insignia of the archdiocese: an arrangement of stars, stripes, and the Ukrainian trident crowned by the cross. The insignia's designer, Dr. Roman O. Klymkevych, in a bilingual article, explained that he prided himself on blending Ukrainian and American as well as religious and civic elements; the combination reflected the integral relationship of the new metropolitanate to the one in Lviv as well as its independence within the papal structure. Reverend Isidore Sochotsky wrote a comprehensive overview of the history of the Ukrainian Catholic Church in the United States.[45] Presented in Ukrainian with a slightly abridged version in English, the work stressed the developmental growth of the American Ukrainian Church as an organic entity, not merely a transplanted one. The publication also included a listing of the metropolitan's powers and a detailed description of his ceremonial vestments by Rev. Henry Sagan, in English,[46] appended by a slightly different Ukrainian-language article on the same topic by Rev. Myroslav Kharyna.[47]

The pallium, an ancient outer garment worn by shepherds when there were still sheep in Rome, merited a special description. The universal Catholic Church had transformed this cloak into a symbol of special authority delegated by the pope to certain named individuals. Through the years, it had changed in style, eventually evolving into a relatively narrow woolen band worn around the neck and shoulder, and worn only with the

45. Sochotsky, "The Ukrainian Catholic Church of the Byzantine-Slavonic Rite in the USA," in Kharyna, Ukraiins'ka Katolyts'ka Mytropolia, 199–248, in Ukrainian; 249–292, in English.

46. Rev. Henry Sagan, "The Vestments of a Bishop," in Kharyna, Ukraiins'ka Katolyts'ka Mytropolia, 177–84.

47. Rev. Myroslav Kharyna, "The meaning and symbolism of the Archepiscopal Vestments," in Kharyna, Ukraiins'ka Katolyts'ka Mytropolia, 165–76.

express dispensation of the pope. Woven from specially harvested wool, the pallium symbolizes the uninterrupted legitimacy of the apostolic succession by endowing its wearer with some powers generally reserved for the pontiff.[48] For Bohachevsky, the pallium was extremely important—an irrefutable sign of papal recognition of the full power of the Ukrainian-American metropolitan. As Sagan explained:

The use of the pallium is reserved exclusively to the pope and to the metropolitans who have petitioned for it and have received it. The latter may only wear the pallium on appointed days and only in their own see. It symbolizes the archbishop's participation in the supreme pastoral power of the Holy Father. Pallia are solemnly blessed on the feast of SS. Peter and Paul and retained in a silver-gilt casket near the traditional site of St. Peter's tomb in the Vatican basilica. The pallium is not transferable, and upon the death of the metropolitan to whom it was conferred, it is also placed with him in his tomb.[49]

Kharyna's comments on the pallium were different. His own brother was among the hundreds of Catholic priests serving time in Siberia for their Catholic faith, and he wanted to make certain that the Ukrainian Eastern Catholic Church would not in any way be considered subordinate to the Eastern patriarchates. While not diminishing the connection with apostolic papal power, Kharyna stressed the independence from Eastern patriarchs that the pallium gave the metropolitan. He also dated the pallium first from the Near Eastern tradition, and only later incorporated into the Roman garb. For good measure he informed his readers that the archbishop of Canterbury had worn a pallium before the Anglican Church severed its union with Rome. "The pallium that Archbishop-Metropolitan Constantine received is a symbol of unity, authority, power, episcopal virtues and love for the flock entrusted him . . . A patriarch or a metropolitan can . . . consecrate bishops and convene *sobors*. . . . Our Metropolitan Constantine Bohachevsky, independent of all patriarchs, is directly responsible to the Roman pope, from whom he received the symbol of his authority—the pallium."[50] The pallium, least known of all the vestments

48. For a recent study on the uses of the pallium, see Steven A. Schoenig, SJ, *Bonds of Wool: The Pallium and Papal Power in the Middle Ages* (Washington, D.C.: The Catholic University of America Press, 2016).

49. Sagan, "The Vestments of a Bishop," in Kharyna, *Ukraiins'ka Katolyts'ka Mytropolia*, 184.

50. Ibid., 175. A minor note—no one commented, as the *Catholic Encyclopedia* does today,

of the metropolitan, reflected special papal recognition and warranted lavish attention. The documentary publication even presented a sketch of the garment.

For Ukrainians in North America, the establishment of both metropolitanates were glorious moments in Ukrainian-American immigrant history. In Philadelphia the sheer number of participants, including the high Catholic clergy and even some government officials, the multitude of nuns and priests, the various school children in their uniforms, as well as representatives of non-Catholic organizations, was an affirmation of Ukrainian existence. And the fact that all this played out against a dramatic background of multicolored vestments, formal pledges of homage to the metropolitan from the clerical deans, flags and standards, exquisite singing by several united choirs, and the spontaneous singing of hymns by a crowd of twelve thousand moved the community greatly. So did the fact that the American press, which until then had seemed rather unaware of the existence of the Ukrainian community (unless reporting on something unsavory) now featured numerous and detailed accounts of the installation ceremony. This event became even more momentous because of the timing: A little over ten years earlier the church in the home country had been driven underground and all had seemed lost.

The series of festivities, the build-up, the vast throngs of people, the pageantry of the services, and the unprecedented news coverage buoyed the community. Impressed by the popular enthusiasm, committee leaders proposed that the metropolitan visit key cities where suitable festivities would enable those faithful who were unable to attend the ceremonies in Philadelphia to experience a morally uplifting encore.

Bohachevsky would have none of this, however. Such frivolity was simply not in his nature. Moreover, he did not view the establishment of the archeparchy/metropolitanate as a personal achievement but as something far more significant. His role in this was secondary. He saw the girders of the church structure in its institutional underpinnings. The community, on the other hand, had reacted emotionally to the magnificent installation ceremonies, the florid prose of papal honors, and communal prayer. In the United States, the church had provided the rare occasion for thousands of

---

that the pallium was most likely an outgrowth of the omophor, which all Eastern bishops wear. In other words, its origin is both Eastern and Western.

people of Ukrainian origin to publicly assemble and experience a celebratory and morale-boosting sense of community. The new metropolitan's advisers and subordinates wanted to carry that experience to the rest of the community. They wanted to share the joy as far the Dakotas. But the metropolitan had become a girder himself; he could not bring himself to luxuriate in the warmth of what was at the time considered a major success. He saw the fragility of the structure, knew his own days were numbered, and rushed to articulate the laws and regulations that would help keep the structure stable.

On behalf of the community, Schmondiuk's committee wanted to give the metropolitan a new automobile to replace the ten-year-old one he was using. Bohachevsky graciously rejected the gift of a car because it would be bought with community funds, and he, as a public servant, did not consider it proper to accept gifts from the community he served beyond the living wage he drew. The metropolitan explained to the recently elevated Bishop Schmondiuk: "Let's finish [with the celebrations] and get back to our duties. Your Excellency knows full well that we have many of those duties, meetings, pressing and unexpected items. I especially want to state, that I cannot accept a new car, because I always maintained that it is unseemly to profit from one's community position or function."[51]

As might be expected, Bohachevsky was more concerned with conducting the church's business than with ceremonial visits or new cars. Among other things, he was aware that a pressing function of the eparchy was to fulfill the request of the Congregation for the Eastern Church for a review and discussion of the recently published parts of the Law for Oriental Churches. Preparations for the diocesan synod (or as it was increasingly designated in the more Eastern usage, the eparchial *sobor*) had begun in 1957, soon after the establishment of the second exarchate. The episcopal consulters and Rev. Victor Pospishil had already begun the work of studying how responsibility for the church was to be allocated between the bishop and the congregation. This work had been interrupted by preparations for the installation of the metropolitan. It was now to be resumed in earnest. Bohachevsky had to finish studying the church documents that he as a young cleric had worked on editing and that were

---

51. Bohachevsky to Schmondiuk, February 13, 1959, UMAS, Chancery Archive.

now being published by the Vatican. He had to update the administrative structure of both dioceses in the United States and even begin work on the creation of new ones. He congratulated his well-wishers, thanked the community for working successfully toward the establishment of the metropolitanate, and then suggested that they get to work.

THE METROPOLITANATE AS A WORKPLACE

As the Ukrainian community celebrated the achievements of its church few, even among the clergy, were aware of the difficulties in each step in its development that the church had to conquer. The individual parishes functioned as before, but the church was only one element in the growing network of Ukrainian-American organizations. Except for the fraternal insurance societies, the new immigrants preferred their own organizations, most of them nondenominational. These tended to be divided by broad political proclivities as the immediate civic goals of the community proliferated. The transplanted religious and scholarly "renewal [obnova]" of Catholic academic society failed to gain popularity, and an attempt at publishing a philosophical lay journal drew a very limited readership. The new immigrants, like the older wave of immigrants, tried to hold on to an exclusive cultural Ukrainian identity in their homes, while at the same time succumbing to the attractions of superior or simply more convenient non-Ukrainian high schools and colleges. The elders wrote elaborate disputations on identity, which almost no one under the age of twenty read. Some complained that the parish schools did not pay adequate attention to the teaching of Ukrainian, even as the number of non-Ukrainian-speaking students grew.

As the more secularized third wave of Ukrainian immigrants settled into American society, some turned their attention to the church as the keeper of Ukrainian identity. The older laity became interested in the outward signs of the rite, reinventing the discussion of the 1930s as to what outward signs make the church a Ukrainian Church, such as kneeling versus standing at church services, the use of pews in churches, the use of icons rather than paintings, palms rather than pussy willows on Palm Sunday, and of course, the perennial problem of the calendar. The *Eparchial News* was peppered with articles elaborating these issues. Bohachevsky was a proponent of the chanted liturgy and even mandated (in 1958) that all liturgies were to be sung or at least chanted with the participation of the congregation, not just the choir. Chanting increases the length of services and is not as melodious as a good choir, so it tends to have more theoretical supporters than practitioners.

Very few of the new immigrant youth entered the religious professions, even if they had been seminarians in Europe. Bohachevsky and the clergy were disturbed by the number of young people who were leaving the rite because they married into Latin-rite Catholicism or into a different religion. Priests were again encouraged to develop youth programs and pay special attention to mixed-gender socials. Most priests were equally worried about the level of understanding of the faith. They called special clergy meetings. Deanery meetings in 1955 focused on "the means to be used to educate our people in their faith and rite."[52] As the American economy grew, the clergy came under greater pressure to keep pace with the growing social mobility within their parishes, while clergy salaries remained very low. The priests responded by helping each other, holding regional meetings, and honing their rhetorical and organizational skills.[53] As postwar conditions settled, the chancery speeded up retreat programs for priests and refocused energy on the obligatory five-year examinations by clerical authorities. The questions dealt both with theological issues and practical questions that might arise in daily parish life. Because contact with the native land was impossible, locally trained priests were not fluent in Ukrainian. Pastoral letters, signed by both bishops, now appeared in both English and Ukrainian.

Few, however, saw these issues as endangering the structure of the church. The community saw the church as solvent and stable. It took for granted that the church would preserve Ukrainian identity. Few in the community felt a particularly strong obligation to support the church beyond the usual dues and donations.

52. *Eparkhiial'ni Visti*, February 1956, 17–19, provided suggestions on how to run deanery meetings effectively.

53. "Zavvahy do referativ, vyholoshenykh na dekanal'nykh soborchykakh 1956 roku" [Comments on the papers delivered at the deanery meetings during 1956], *Eparkhiial'ni Visti*, February 1957, covered public speaking but also stressed the need to focus on church and eparchial regulations more closely.

Outwardly, Bohachevsky showed few signs of his age. Nor did he modify his pace of work in any significant way. He continued his work—holding weekly visitations, sitting on commissions, remaining personally involved in administrative minutiae. He was eager to see that the Philadelphia archbishopric had all the necessary legal formalities completed before the council convened. While the Vatican continued updating laws pertinent to the Eastern Churches, Pospishil, at Bohachevsky's request, had been busy preparing the second volume of the drafts of laws for the diocese. The bishop felt that having basic church regulations codified, thanks to the earlier work of Pospishil and Wojakowsky and the subsequent updating done between 1953 and 1958, the Ukrainian Catholic Church was secure and ready to hold its own in the universal church. The Ukrainian-American archeparchial synod, convened immediately upon the promulgation of parts of the newly revised Vatican Law for the Oriental Churches, was of less pomp but of equal importance as the establishment of the metropolitanate.

The last major function in which the metropolitan played a key role was the solemn eparchial convocation mandated by Pope John XXIII. This was a two-day gathering held on October 7 and 8, 1959, that sought, in the metropolitan's words, "the help, advice, and counsel of Our clergy" to fulfill the order of the Holy Father that: "In every eparchy an eparchial convocation shall be convened at least every ten years, in which such matters shall be treated as refer to the particular needs and welfare of the clergy and the people of the eparchy."[54]

The gathering of upper clergy and priests was of historical significance for the new metropolitanate. It confirmed the existence of the metropolitanate of Philadelphia.[55] Held formally in the cathedral, the eparchial synod was solemn and rather scripted. It was headed by Rev. Dr. Victor Pospishil and formally chaired by Bishop Schmondiuk. Its task was to deal with all matters not specifically covered by the Vatican documents. At the conclusion of the meeting, Bohachevsky—"Constantine, by Divine Mercy and the Grace of the Apostolic See Archbishop of Philadelphia, Metro-

54. "Eparchial Convocation," *Eparkhiial'ni Visti*, August 1959, 63–65. The meeting was a response to Pope John XXIII's *motu proprio* "*Cleri sanctitati.*"
55. *Statutes of the Archeparchy of Philadelphia* (codification by Victor J. Pospishil J.C.D., J.C.O.M.) (Philadelphia: Archeparchy of Philadelphia, 1959), xxiv and 134.

politan of the Ukrainian Catholic Ecclesiastical Province, of the Byzantine Rite in the United States of America"[56]—formally promulgated the 650 statutes that, "governed the Ukrainian archeparchy of Philadelphia for the next ten years."[57]

In the midst of these successes, Bohachevsky began to see fissures in the grand design. Recent émigrés were not choosing vocations connected to the religious life. St. Basil Academy for Girls at Fox Chase attracted more middle-class Irish and Italian girls than Ukrainians. It was financially difficult to maintain parallel English and Ukrainian religious and language classes even as recent émigrés complained about inadequate Ukrainian-language instruction. The clergy felt constrained in the tight ship that the metropolitan continued to run, among other things they needed money and the right to own cars.

In an undated anonymous letter, a few English-speaking, Ukrainian Catholic priests complained to the apostolic delegate in 1956 that the bishop's taxation policies for the support of the college and seminary made it impossible for them to work for the spiritual welfare of their parishioners. They strenuously objected to the bishop's decision to make parishes buy issues of The Way in bulk. The priests assured the apostolic delegate that they supported Bohachevsky but felt that he demanded too much of the faithful. Bohachevsky shared the letter with Senyshyn, but the establishment of the metropolitanate overshadowed this complaint. The materials I consulted for this work do not clarify whether the priests ever followed up on their initial complaints.[58] What is clear is that some of the European priests did not feel at home in the United States. Few of the highly educated, European clergy adjusted as easily as the venerable Rev. Nykola Wojakowsky. Rev. Ivan Bilanych and even Rev. Victor Pospishil sought

56. "Eparchial Convocation," Eparkhiial'ni Visti, August 1959, 63–65, published in English.

57. Procko, Ukrainian Catholics in America, 84; Pospishil, Final Tally, 239: "It was the bishop's desire to have them [previous laws and regulations] sorted, reviewed, corrected, complemented with additional laws and published in a code, at that time called a statute, the first for Eastern Catholics in this country. It was an arduous task. This work received great acclaim from bishops, clergy, and religious, was extended as an obligatory book of laws to the other dioceses of the Ukrainian Catholic Church in the United States, and is still partially in legal force today."

58. A copy of the three-page, single-spaced letter in UMAS, Chancery Archive.

broader venues than St. Basil's College, which was increasingly losing its secular program and focusing on preparation for the seminary. However, most of the immigrant clergy handled the transition to America gamely. There were a few difficult families, but a timely transfer generally helped.

Appropriately, Bohachevsky made his last overseas pilgrimage to Lourdes, reflecting his lifelong dedication to the Virgin. Bishop Senyshyn, as part of his growing outreach program, organized a Ukrainian Catholic pilgrimage to Lourdes to mark (among other intentions) an anniversary in the Christianization of Rus'-Ukraine by the baptism of Princess St. Olha in Constantinople. Fortuitously Bohachevsky combined what would be his last ad limina trip to Rome with that pilgrimage. As was his custom, the archbishop had a specially bound copy of the latest *schematism* prepared for Pope John XXIII.[59]

Since Bohachevsky's anniversaries clustered together, when he turned down Bishop Schmondiuk's plan to celebrate his seventy-fifth birthday in 1958, Schmondiuk and Senyshyn combined Bohachevsky's fiftieth anniversary in the priesthood with the silver anniversary of St. Basil's High School at Stamford and held what was to be the last celebration for the metropolitan.[60] In connection with this celebration, Bohachevsky permitted himself some jokes about his younger brothers. When the organizers asked him which family members he wanted to invite, he replied that both of his brothers "groan and moan about their health," so he doubted they would come, but added that he had no objection to the committee sending them an invitation.[61] The festivities were held at Stamford on May 17, 1959. The pope sent warm greetings.[62]

The community now treated Bohachevsky with respect and did not protest the increased use of English in Ukrainian Catholic publications. At the end of the 1950s, the bishop allowed himself a few inexpensive and simple vacations. He appeared more often in public and even helped finance a modest vacation on the outskirts of Scranton for the extended family. He joined them for lunch there one day, on his way from one meeting to another. He did not remove either his jacket or his Roman collar,

59. Bohachevsky to Senyshyn, April 26 and 29, 1958. UMAS, Chancery Archive.
60. *The Way*, April 8, 1959, also documentation in the UMAS, Chancery Archive.
61. Letter dated April 9, 1959.
62. Pope John XXIII, "Greetings," *The Way*, April 8, 1959.

and seemed unfazed by a slew of wet, screaming children.[63] Visits with smaller groups of family members became more frequent. He also enjoyed spontaneous meetings with scholars, including those who had different views from his. All in all, he seemed in good spirits and reasonably good health. Nonetheless, his physician, the inimitable Dr. Emil Harasym warned him to slow down. The metropolitan modified his rigorous schedule by getting up at five rather than four in the morning. During the last two years of his life, as he became weaker, he asked Michael Poloway, his erstwhile secretary and a consultor at the chancery, to take up residence at the Medary house.

Archbishop Bohachevsky kept up his regular schedule, saying his daily liturgy, having his morning tea and oatmeal, and enjoying what he considered to be a luxurious forty-five-minute drive from his home on Medary to Franklin Street.

On Old-Style Christmas Eve, January 6, 1961 (Julian calendar), the metropolitan spent most of his day at the office, where he kept a room with a bed for a thirty-minute rest after lunch. Late that afternoon he cancelled his promised attendance at a family Christmas Eve supper at his brother's modest row house in North Philadelphia. He felt tired and needed to rest before the Christmas Liturgy. Because such cancellations occurred frequently, there did not seem to be any cause for alarm. On the drive to his residence between seven and eight in the evening, Bohachevsky complained to Poloway of feeling tired. After a light supper, the metropolitan complained of pain and nausea to Sisters Rita and Maria, the two Missionary nuns who cared for his household. By 10:30 P.M. he was in excruciating pain. The nuns called Dr. Harasym, who arrived at the same time as the ambulance. Halfway to the hospital, the ambulance turned off the sirens. The metropolitan suffered massive heart failure and died half an hour before midnight on January 6, 1961.

Bohachevsky was immediately laid to rest in his own chapel, before the iconostasis he so dearly loved. By the time my father, my uncle, and I arrived, rigor mortis was setting in. The following day, late afternoon on Christmas, Bishop Schmondiuk and the closest clergy held private ser-

63. Michael and Mary Petukh ran a lakeside motel and restaurant at Bally Lake, near Scranton, Pennsylvania.

vices in the metropolitan's small chapel, as did other clergy for the next five days that the body lay in the chapel. Immediate members of the family were in attendance.

The body was transported to the cathedral on January 12, where it lay in state before the final, lengthy services for the sacerdotal dead on January 17th. The metropolitan's wish not to have flowers was honored. The cathedral was solemn as various organizations changed guard at the severe casket. Thousands of faithful came to pay him last respects. The funeral liturgy was held before the Old-Style Epiphany Eve. He was laid to rest in the crypt that held his predecessor, Ortynsky, and would eventually hold the other successive metropolitans of Philadelphia.

The whole Ukrainian community mourned the passing of a prince of the church and a great patriot of his people. Headed by the new apostolic delegate, Egidio Vagnozzi, twenty-one archbishops and bishops, twenty-five monsignors, 160 priests, and numerous religious led the large, respectful crowd of mourners.[64] The leadership of the Ukrainian-American community mourned the passing of a patriot. The Philadelphia Inquirer, as well as The New York Times and The Washington Post published obituary articles on the Ukrainian archbishop on January 8, 1961. Ukrainian émigré newspapers outside the USSR provided lengthier articles, without necessarily going into the less pleasant aspects of his life.

At Rome, Rev. Ireneus Nazarko, OSBM, held a 6 A.M. memorial service at the Collegium of St. Josaphat, the first of a series of memorial liturgies. A family member who happened to be in Rome at the time was surprised at the outpouring of condolences from so many people, most of whom he, of course, did not know.[65] Bohachevsky's death was noted in the popular daily Messagero and in L'Osservatore Romano.

The Ukrainian émigré press in what was then called the Free World mourned the death of the metropolitan. Previously, there had always been only one Ukrainian metropolitan, and most newspapers noted that the

64. Procko, Ukrainian Catholics in America, 86.
65. George Bohachevsky was studying voice in Italy and had come to Rome for Christmas. Rev. Mother Zenobia, OSBM, called him with the news early enough for him to make the 6 A.M. liturgy. He detailed his experiences in a letter, dated January 12, 1961, to his parents, Volodymyr and Tetiana Bohachevsky. Copy in the author's possession. Volodymyr was Bohachevsky's cousin, and is not to be confused with Constantine's elder brother.

very existence of three Ukrainian Catholic metropolitans (in Ukraine, Canada, and the United States) was a major historical breakthrough that manifested the strength of the Ukrainian Catholic Church. Constantine Bohachevsky had been the oldest of the three metropolitans, and the longest serving bishop. His death marked the end of the pioneer period of the Ukrainian presence in the Americas. But the "Americanization and secularization" of even the most traditional Ukrainian émigré organizations was evident in that few of them cancelled their January fund-raising dances to mark the period of mourning for the metropolitan.

The editorial in *Svoboda* on January 11, 1961—titled simply "The Death of the Metropolitan"—struggled with the disagreements and difficulties of the pioneer age that:

etched deep fissures . . . in the soul . . . in the pioneer times, which demanded the greatest effort to conquer and contain wildness [*stykhiu*] and establish laws, only persons of great inner strength, self-control, and strong will, persons conscious of their goal could succeed in those tasks. There is no doubt that the recently departed metropolitan had all characteristics of such a leader of pioneer years, and it makes no sense to search for comparisons [with him], for such individuals set the standards for others.

The editorial ended by giving the whole Ukrainian Catholic Church its due:

The Ukrainian Catholic Church in the Free World has become one of the greatest and most potent forces in support of the Ukrainian cause by making the papal see pay attention to it and by gaining a significant place in the spiritual-religious world of Christianity. That place rests on two foundations—the labor and martyrdom of the Ukrainian Catholic Church in the currently ravaged native land, with its monumental personalities, such as the last two metropolitans—the Servant of God Andrey Sheptytsky and Metropolitan-Confessor of the Faith Yosyp Slipyj; and on the work and achievements of the Ukrainian Catholic Church in the Free World, especially in the United States through such personalities as its first bishop, Soter Ortynsky, the first administrator of the diocese, Petro Poniatyshyn, who died last year, and especially its first metropolitan, Constantine Bohachevsky, over whose open casket we bow our heads.[66]

66. "The Death of the Metropolitan," *Svoboda*, January 11, 1961, 1; The English-language weekly supplement to *Svoboda*, *The Ukrainian Weekly*, carried a front-page article in its January 14, 1961, edition.

Bishop Senyshyn summarized his own litany of Bohachevsky's achievements. As the first in line to become the new metropolitan, he hammered away at the specifics of Bohachevsky's adherence to ritual, daily prayers, and meditation, his untiring energy, and the strength of his personal example that should continue to guide the church that Bohachevsky had just left: "Metropolitan Bohachevsky's death was indeed a shocking loss. Nevertheless, because of the strong ecclesiastical organization for which he was primarily responsible, the administration of the Philadelphia Ukrainian Archeparchy proceeded smoothly."[67]

The editorial in the January 10, 1961, *America*, written by Eugene Zyblykevych, credited the Philadelphia metropolitanate with 293 priests in 222 churches; 29 full time parochial schools, 184 evening schools, 22 daycare centers, four high schools, 4 seminaries, and 2 colleges.[68] The official count of all students in Ukrainian Catholic schools in the United States was fifteen thousand. The number offered for registered Ukrainian Catholic parishioners was three hundred thousand. It was estimated that there were an additional one hundred thousand Ukrainian Catholics in the United States at the time. On July 15, 1961, some six months after Bohachevsky's death, Pope John XXIII created the third eparchy for Ukrainian Catholics in the United States of America in Chicago for which Bohachevsky had long argued.

Reflecting the growing spirit of ecumenism within the Catholic Church, one of Bohachevsky's last acts was to prepare, along with Metropolitan Maxim Hermaniuk and Archbishop Ivan Buchko, a proposal to convene a *sobor* of all Catholic and Orthodox Ukrainian Churches. As part of the broad preparations for the Second Vatican Council of the Catholic Church, the October 1959 Ukrainian Catholic bishops' conference, referring to itself as a synod, issued a joint invitation to the Kyivan Orthodox metropolitan to join them in Rome for common prayer. None of the bishops expected Kyiv to do anything without the approval of Moscow, and Kyiv did nothing.

Bohachevsky's testament, which is not available, left all his possessions to the church and named Bishop Ambrose Senyshyn as his executor. The appointment of Bohachevsky's successor was in the hands of the pope.

67. *The Way*, January 18, 1961; Procko, *Ukrainian Catholics in America*, 86.
68. Eugene Zyblykevych, "Bilia domovyny Mytropolyta" [At the Metropolitan's Bier], *America*, January 10, 1961, 1.

Two years after Bohachevsky's death, on January 23, 1963, Cardinal (since 1949, in *pectore*) Joseph Slipyj was freed from Soviet imprisonment and transported to Rome. His arrival shocked and electrified the community; it also split it. Some sceptics took years to reconcile themselves to the possibility of anyone surviving Soviet imprisonment and remaining morally intact. A new period of unrest, limited mostly to the postwar émigrés but having a very negative impact on the nonimmigrant, Ukrainian-American Catholics, began in the Ukrainian Catholic Church in the West. The issue was the establishment of a patriarchate and the recognition of Cardinal Slipyj in that seat. Cardinal Slipyj, steeled by his eighteen-year imprisonment, had little understanding of the situation in the United States and negligible appreciation of the achievements of the Ukrainian Catholic Church there. He may have presumed the transference of the Lviv see and its direct oversight of the other Ukrainian Catholic Churches, although that had not been the style of Metropolitan Sheptytsky. The Ukrainian Catholic community, now global and differentiated, clustered around the new focus—a patriarchate for Ukrainian Catholics. There were outbursts of violence, split parishes, and continued simmering debate largely carried on by the laity.

Metropolitan-Cardinal Slipyj, at his inaugural appearance during the second session of the Second Vatican Council, on October 11, 1963, put out a proposal that the council should elevate the Ukrainian Catholic Church to the status of a patriarchate. The dramatic call—the Ukrainian Church in Ukraine was not legally in existence and the Soviets were very much in control—rallied the intelligentsia core that saw the church as the currently best available surrogate for a Ukrainian state. The movement was composed mainly of the Catholic lay activists, while originally from Halychyna, now quite settled in America or Western Europe. They saw it as their duty, in the phrasing of a 1969 statement, to "enlighten the laity and the clergy" on the validity and timeliness of establishing a Catholic Halych-Kyiv patriarchate.[69] The movement was supported by ac-

69. See Andrew Sorokowsky, "Narys istorii Ukraiins'koho Patriarkhal'noho Rukhu" [Sketch of the History of the Ukrainian Patriarchal Movement], in *Materiialy do istorii ukraiins'koho patriarkhal'noho rukhu, 1963–2001*, ed. Andrew Sorokowsky (Lviv: Svichado, 2009), 28.

tivists of the type of Nazaruk, neophytes discovering the ancestral faith; by the reform movement that was visibly changing the outward Latin-rite ritual; and by the overall protest climate of the time. The peaceful protest turned ugly and became itself subject to internal splits. There were no death threats, but many demonstrations with egg throwing and vile chanting. The protests, directed at the local upper clergy, varied in each émigré community, and had a very negative impact on the nonimmigrant, Ukrainian-American Catholic community. Some, despairing of yet another cleft in the Ukrainian community, drifted to the Latin rite, which introduced changes in ritual that echoed Eastern practices. In 1971, when two of Bohachevsky's most dedicated clerics—John Stock, "the DP priest," and Basil Losten, who would facilitate the training of Ukrainian priests from Ukraine in Ukrainian institutions in the United States—were ordained bishop, there were violent protests of those who viewed these appointments as a slight to Cardinal Slipyj. The cardinal did not publicly encourage the protest, but he did defer to the "will of the people." The patriarchal movement brought to the fore the three major issues in the Ukrainian Catholic Church: the structure of the Ukrainian Church in its global context, clerical celibacy, and the role of the laity in the administration of the church. Future historians will disengage "the patriarchate" as a rallying cry from the on-going efforts of the Ukrainian Catholic clergy to fashion a global network for their church. In Ukraine, the laity identified religious rights with human rights, and risked their lives to fight for both. From 1985, as the Ukrainian Catholics in Ukraine sought to legalize their church, the discussion on the establishment and nature of the patriarchate in Ukraine shifted more toward the clergy, with the participation of some select laity. The patriarchal movement in the West, claiming that it rekindled spiritual life, contributed to other, more modest, splits among the parishioners. New parishes were created in opposition to the local bishops, opting for the Julian calendar, a temporary return to Church Slavonic, and a haven for married clergy.

The proclamation of Ukraine's independence in 1991 changed the Ukrainian Catholic Church dramatically. As the Ukrainian Catholic Church emerged from the catacombs, it not only reclaimed Western Ukraine, but quickly moved back to its original territories in Kyiv and further east and south. Two priests from the American archdiocese, Myroslav

Lubachivsky and Lubomyr Husar, became the first archbishop-majors in modern independent Ukraine. So, in some sense, the Ukrainian Catholic Church in Ukraine was headed by two American missionaries in the first years of its modern independence. Working in concert with the Ukrainian clergy and Ukrainian Catholic congregations in Rome, Ukrainian Catholics arrived at a *modus vivendi* on their internal, global, ecclesiastical structures, while at the same time seeking a closer understanding with the Eastern churches. As Bohachevsky said: individuals pass, the institution endures. One is tempted to say that it flourishes because of the work of its determined foot soldiers, of the kind of Constantine Bohachevsky—but that would not fit his style.

ARCHIVES AND SELECTED BIBLIOGRAPHY

NOTES ON THE ARCHIVES

I drew most of the material in this book from the sources listed below.

Archives in the United States

The archival holdings of the Ukrainian Museum and Archives at Stamford, Connecticut, house materials critical to the history of the Ukrainian Catholic Church in the United States. In addition to the church archives (correspondence, legal documents, promotional material, photographs, etc.), the library has archives of individual priests and lay activists and an excellent collection of periodic Ukrainian immigrant publications. The holdings are being reorganized. The extremely helpful staff provided me with files and boxes of possibly relevant materials, which often proved to be essential for the topic. The archival materials fall into two categories: those in the regular archive are noted as UMAS; those taken from the limited access holdings are marked as UMAS, Chancery Archive.

St. Josaphat Seminary Library in Washington, D.C., has the most complete collection of the *Eparchial News* (*Eparkhial'ni Visti*), as well as the first edition of the *Eparchial Statutes*.

The Vatican Archives

The holdings of the Sacred Congregation for the Eastern Church (Archivio della Congregazione per le Chiese Orientali) provided the many basic documents for this biography. The materials at the congregation are filed under at times multiple numerations as "*protocolli.*" Some of them are brought together in a file. Some are not paginated. The congregation staff helpfully provided a numbered compact disk of the material that I documented, in brackets under the name of the archivist, J. P. Rigotti. In addition, the congregation published in very limited editions reports, *ponente*, which, in some thirty to forty pages, provided a *précis* of available information on a defined topic for papal consideration. Included are reports, correspondence, supplementary materials on prospective nominations, various complaints, and the like. Since I had access to the archive, in 2009 and 2010, its holdings have undergone reorganization. For an overview of the holdings on Ukraine, see Gianpaolo Rigotti, "Sources Concerning Ukraine in the Archives of the Congregation for the Eastern Churches," in *Ukraine's Re-Integration into Europe: A Historical Historiographical and Politically Urgent Issue*, ed. Giovanna Brogi et al. (Alessandria: Edizioni del Orso, 2005), 109–38.

Materials in the Vatican Archive (*Archivio Segreto Vaticano*) house correspondence, notes, memoranda organized chronologically by place of reference or items of importance. Materials from the Vatican State Archive (*Archivio della Congregazione degli Affari Ecclesiastici Straordinari*) include documents of broader scope, usually on the state level, as well as information on the work of the Vatican departments.

Archives in Ukraine

The first chapters of the study rely heavily on the holdings in the Central State Archive of Ukraine at Lviv (*Tsentralny Derzhavnyy Istorychnyy Arkhiv*) and the Lviv Academic Library of the National Ukrainian Academy of Sciences at Lviv (*Lvivs'ka Naukova Biblioteka Natsional'noii Akademii Nauk Ukraiiny im. Vasylia Stefanyka*) holdings.

Archives in Poland

The Polish State Archive at Warsaw (*Archiwum Akt Nowych*).

The Polish State Archive at Przemysl, *Archiwum Panstwowe w Pzemyslu* (previously known as the *Wojewodske Archiwum Panstwowe*) housed the documentation of the Peremyshl Ukrainian Catholic Eparchy (*Archiwum Grecko-Katolickiego Biskupstwa w Przemyslu*). The latter holdings have been thoroughly reorganized since I had worked in the archives of the Przemysl Greek-Catholic bishopric in 1976–77. In April 2017, Anna Krochmal published a new work on these holdings, *Archiwum historyczne eparchii przemyskiej* (Przemysl: 2017).

Selected Bibliography

Andrukhovych, Konstantyn. *Z zhytia Rusyniv v Amerytsi. Spomyn z rokiv 1889–1892*. Kolomyia: n.p., 1904.

Avvakumov, Yuri, and Oksana Hayova, eds. *Mytropolyt Andrey Sheptyts'ky i Hrekokatolyky v Rosiii*. Vol. 1, *Dokumenty i materialy, 1899–1917*. Lviv: Ukrainian Catholic University Press, 2004.

Babiak, Avhustyn. *Podvyh Mytropolyta Andreia Sheptyts'koho iak Apostol'skoho vizytatora dlia Ukraiintsiv (1920–1923) i ioho vzaiemyny z uriadom Pol'shchi*. Trenton: Socita Scientifica Sevcenko-Ucraina, 2013.

Blazejowskyj, Dmytro, ed. *Ukrainian Catholic Clergy in Diaspora (1751–1988): Annotated List of Priests Who Served Outside of Ukraine*. Rome: Ukrainian Catholic University, 1988.

———. *Miy Zhyttiepys. Pro Vykhovannia i Ukraiins'ki Problemy*. Lviv: Kameniar, 2009.

Bociurkiw, Bohdan. *The Ukrainian Greek Catholic Church and the Soviet State (1939–1950)*. Edmonton: Canadian Institute of Ukrainian Studies, 1996.

Bohachevsky, Danylo. *V im'ia pravdy: peredruk stattey z Shliakhu*. Philadelphia: Apostleship, 1965.

———. *Na vozi i pid vozom: Spomymy halyts'koho advokata*. Toronto: Dobra Knyzhka, 1976.

———. *Vladyka Konstantyn Bohachevsky: Pershy Mytropolyt Ukraiins'koii Katolyt'skoii Tserkvy v ZSA*. Philadelphia: America, 1980.

Bohachevsky-Chomiak, Martha. "The Ukrainian University in Galicia: A Pervasive Issue." *Harvard Ukrainian Studies* 5, no. 4 (December 1981): 497–545.

———. *Feminists Despite Themselves: Women in Ukrainian Community Life, 1884–1939*. Edmonton: Canadian Institute of Ukrainian Studies, 1988.

———. "Shadow Boxing: Ukrainian Greek Catholic Hierarchs and the Ukrainian Community, 1900–1930." *Journal of Ukrainian Studies* 37 (2012): 130–53.

———. "Conflict between Church and State in the Absence of Both." *Harvard Ukrainian Studies* 32–33 (2011–2014): 127–42.

———. "Mytropolyt Sheptyts'ky i rozvytok Ukraiins'koii Hreko-Katolyts'koii Tserkvy v SShA." *Kovcheh* 7 (2015): 87–102.

Budurowycz, Bohdan. "The Greek Catholic Church in Galicia, 1914–1944." *Harvard Ukrainian Studies* 26, nos. 1–4 (2002–3): 291–353.

Bukowski, Dorothy Ann, and Maria Rozmarynowycz, eds. *Basilian Sisters in America, Jesus, Lover of Humanity Province: The First Hundred Years*. Jenkintown, Penn.: n.p., n.d.

Chopek, Anna. "Recollections of Anna Chopek Regarding the Trials and Tribulations of the Ukrainian Catholic Church in Boston and its Parishioners." In *Christ the King Church: History of the Ukrainian Catholic Community in Boston 1907–2007*, 75–103. Boston: Christ the King Ukrainian Catholic Church, 2007.

Danko, Osyp. "Natsional'na polityka Madiarshchyny sered Rusyniv Zakarpattia v Spoluchenykh Shtatakh Ameryky." *Ukraiins'ky Istoryk: Zhurnal Istorii Ukraiinoznavstva* (New York), nos. 1–4 (1999): 191–208.

Diadiuk, Myroslava, ed. *Lysty Viacheslava Lypyns'koho do Osypa Nazaruka (1921–1930)*. Lviv: Lviv'ska Naukova Biblioteka im. V. Stefanyka, 2004.

Dolnyts'ky, Oleh, ed. *Litopys rodu Dolnyts'kykh: Dokumenty, Materialy, Spohady: Henealohichne doslidzhennia*. Lviv: Ukrainian Catholic University, 2004.

Dragan, Antin. *Luka Myshuha: Korotka biohrafia*. Jersey City, N.J.: Svoboda, 1973.

Dushnyk, Walter, and Nicholas I. Chirovsky, eds. *The Ukrainian Heritage in America*. New York: Ukrainian Congress Committee of America, 1991.

Fogarty, Gerald P. "The American Hierarchy and Oriental Rite Catholics, 1890–1907." *Records of the American Catholic Historical Society* 85, nos. 1–2 (March–June 1974): 17–28.

———. *The Vatican and the American Hierarchy from 1870 to 1965*. Collegeville, Minn.: Liturgical Press, 1982.

Galadza, Peter. *The Theology and Liturgical Work of Andrei Sheptyts'kyi (1865–1944)*. Rome: Pontifico Instituto Orientale, 2004.

Gotia, Ivan. *V oboroni prav nashoii Hreko-katol. tserkvy*. Lviv: n.p., 1929.

Gudziak, Borys. *Crisis and Reform: The Kyivan Metropolitanate, the Patriarchate of Constantinople, and the Genesis of the Union of Brest.* Cambridge: Harvard University Press, 2001.

Hentosh, Liliana. *Vatykan i vyklyky modernosti: skhidnoievropeis'ka polityka Papy Benedykta XV ta ukraiins'ko-pol'sky konflikt u Halychyni (1914–1923).* Lviv: Klassyka, 2006.

——. *Mytropolyt Sheptyts'ky, 1923–1939: Vyprobuvannia Idealiv.* Lviv: Klassyka, 2015.

Himka, John-Paul. *Socialism in Galicia: The Emergence of Polish Social Democracy and Ukrainian Radicalism (1860–1890).* Cambridge, Mass.: Harvard University Press, 1983.

——. *The Greek Catholic Church and the Ukrainian Society in Austrian Galicia.* Cambridge, Mass.: Harvard Ukrainian Studies, 1986.

——. "The Issue of Celibacy at the Lviv Provincial Synod of 1891: Unpublished Documents from Lviv and Przemysl (Peremyshl) Archives." In *Mappa Mundi: Zbirnyk naukovykh prats' na poshanu Yaroslava Dashkevycha z nahody yoho 70-richchia,* edited by Ihor Hyrych et al., 648–70. Lviv: Kots Publishing, 1996.

——. *Religion and Nationality in Western Ukraine: The Greek Catholic Church and the Ruthenian National Movement in Galicia, 1867–1900.* Montreal: McGill-Queens Press, 1999.

Hrytsak, Yaroslav. *Prorok u svoiiy zemli.* Kyiv: Krytyka, 2006.

Isajiw, Wsevolod, ed. *Ukrainians in American and Canadian Society.* Cambridge, Mass.: Harvard Ukrainian Research Institute, 1976.

Isajiw, Wsevolod, Yury Boshyk, and Roman Senkus, eds. *The Refugee Experience: Ukrainian Displaced Persons after World War II.* Edmonton: Canadian Institute of Ukrainian Studies, 1992.

Kaszczak, Ivan. *The Education of Ukrainian Catholic Clergy (1882–1946).* Lviv: Svichado Press, 2007.

——. *Metropolitan Andrei Sheptytsky and the Establishment of the Ukrainian Catholic Church in the United States.* Toronto: Basilian Press, 2013.

——. *Bishop Soter Stephen Ortynsky and the Genesis of the Eastern Catholic Churches in America.* Philadelphia: CreateSpace Independent Publishing Platform, 2016.

Kharyna, Myroslav, ed. *Ukraiins'ka Katolyts'ka Mytropolia v Zluchenykh Derzhavakh Ameryky, 1 Lystopada, 1958.* Philadelphia: Archbishop's Chancery, 1959.

Kolodny, Anatolii, ed. *Relihiia i Tserkva v Istoriii Ukraiins'koii Diaspory.* Vol. 9 of *Istoriia Relihii v Ukraiini.* Kyiv: Institute of Philosophy, Academy of Science Ukraine, 2012.

Korolevsky, Cyril. *Metropolitan Andrew (1865–1944).* Translated and Revised by Serge Keleher. Lviv: Stauropegion, 1993. Originally published as *Cyrille Korolevskij, Metropolite Andre Szeptyckyj, 1865–1944,* Pratsi Ukraiins'koho Bohoslovs'koho Naukovoho Tovarystva 16–17 (Rome: Ukrainian Theological Society, 1964).

Kravchuk, Andrii. *Christian Social Ethics in Ukraine: Legacy of Andrei Sheptytsky.* Edmonton: Canadian Institute of Ukrainian Studies Press, 1997.

Kuropas, Myron. *The Ukrainian Americans: Roots and Aspirations 1884–1954.* Toronto: University of Toronto Press, 1991.

————. *Ukrainian-American Citadel: The First One Hundred Years of the Ukrainian National Association*. Boulder, Colo.: East European Monographs, 1996.

Lebedovych, Ivan. *Polevi dukhovnyky Ukraiins'koii halyts'koii armii*. Winnipeg: self-published, 1963.

Lencyk, Vasyl. *Beresteis'ka Uniia (1596–1996)*. Lviv: Logos, 1996.

————. *Tireless Worker: Biography of Bishop John Stock*. Lviv: Svichado, 2006.

Liber, George O. *Total Wars and the Making of Modern Ukraine, 1914–1954*. Toronto: University of Toronto Press, 2016.

Likvidatsiia Ukraiins'koii Hreko-Katolyts'koii Tserkvy. Vol. 1. Kyiv: Shevchenko Ukrainian National University, 2006.

Losten, Basil H. *Archbishop Ambrose Senyshyn and His Vision of the Ukrainian Catholic Church in America*. Toronto: Basilian Press, 2016.

Lotots'ky, Volodymyr, ed. *Iuvileyny Al'manakh Ukraiins'koii Hreko-Katolyts'koii Tserkvy u Zluchenykh Derzhavakh z nahody 50-littiia iiii istnuvannia, 1884–1934*. Philadelphia: America, 1934.

Lukych, V. *Ivan Franko: Kilka spohadiv i kilka zdohadiv ioho suchasnyka i spivrobitnyka*. Philadelphia: Orphanage Publishing, 1927.

Luzhnytsky, Hryhor. *Ukraiins'ka Tserkva mizh Skhodom i Zakhodom*. Philadelphia: Providence Association of Ukrainian Catholics, 1954.

Lypynsky, Viacheslav. *Religiia i tserkva v istoriii Ukraiiny*. Philadelphia: Narodna biblioteka Ameryky No. 17, 1925.

————. *Collected Works, Letters, Papers and Miscellanea*. Vol. 7, *The Letters of Osyp Nazaruk*. Edited by Ivan L. Rudnytsky. Philadelphia: W.K. Lypynsky East European Research Institute, 1976.

Magocsi, Paul Robert. *Our People: Carpatho-Rusyns and Their Descendants in North America*. Toronto: Multicultural History Society of Ontario, 1984.

————, ed. *Morality and Reality: The Life and Times of Andrei Sheptyts'kyi*. Edmonton: Canadian Institute of Ukrainian Studies, 1989.

McVay, Athanasius D. *God's Martyr, History's Witness: Blessed Nykyta Budka, the First Ukrainian Catholic Bishop in Canada*. Edmonton: Ukrainian Catholic Eparchy of Edmonton and Metropolitan Andrey Sheptytsky Institute of Eastern Christian Studies, 2014.

Melnychuk, Petro. *Vladyka Hryhorij Khomyshyn*. Philadelphia: n.p., 1979.

Morozowich, Mark M. "The Liturgy and the Ukrainian Catholic Church in the United States: Change through the Decades." *U.S. Catholic Historian* 82, no. 1 (Winter 2014): 49–70.

Motiuk, David. *Eastern Christians in the New World: An Historical and Canonical Study of the Ukrainian Catholic Church in Canada*. Ottawa: Saint Paul University, Metropolitan Andrey Sheptytsky Institute of Eastern Christian Studies and Faculty of Canon Law, 2005.

Myshuha, Luka, ed. *Propamiatna Knyha: Vydana z nahody soroklitnioho Iuvyleiu Ukraiins'koho Narodnoho Soiuzu (Jubilee Book of the Ukrainian National Association in Commemoration of the Fortieth Anniversary of Its Existence)*. Jersey City, N.J.: Svoboda Press, 1936.

Nazaruk, Osyp. *Holos Ievropeis'koho Vladyky Preosviashchennoho Dioniziia: i inshi holosy pro nashi tserkovni spravy v Amerytsi.* Philadelphia: n.p., 1926.

———. *Nash Epyskopat v Amerytsi i Borot'ba Proty Nyoho* [Our Bishopric in America and the Attacks against It]. Philadelphia: n.p., 1926.

———. *Svitohliad Ivana Franka: Chy mozhe khrystiians'kiy narid pryniaty i shyryty kult ioho?* Philadelphia: n.p., 1926.

———. *Hreko-Katolyts'ka Tserkva I Ukraiins'ka Liberal'na Intelligentsia.* Lviv: Pravda, 1929.

Oleksiv, Petro, ed. *Nasha Shkola, Nasha Peremoha.* Philadelphia: n.p., 1940.

O'Malley, John W. *What Happened at Vatican II.* Cambridge, Mass.: Harvard University Press, 2008.

Paska, Walter. "The Ukrainian Catholic Church in the USA." In *The Ukrainian Heritage in America*, ed. Walter Dushnyk and Nicholas I. Chirovsky, 75–83. New York: Ukrainian Congress Committee of America, 1991.

Pavliuk, Oleskander. *Borot'ba Ukraiiny za nezalezhnist' i polityka SShA.* Kyiv: Akademia Press, 1996.

Pavlyshyn, Oleh. *Ievhen Petrushevych* . Lviv: Instytut istorychnykh doslidzhen', 2013.

Plokhy, Serhii and Frank Sysyn. *Religion and Nation in Modern Ukraine.* Edmonton: CIUS, 2003.

Pop, Ivan, ed. *Entsyklopediia Podkarpatskoj Rusy.* Uzhorod: Izdadelstvo V. Padiaka, 2001.

Pop, Ivan, and Paul Robert Magocsi, eds. *Encyclopedia of Ruthenian History and Culture.* Toronto: University of Toronto Press, 2005.

Pospishil, Victor J. *Final Tally: A Report on the Unremarkable Life of a Catholic Priest in the Twentieth Century.* Matawan, N.J.: self-published, 2001.

Prach, Bohdan. *Dukhovenstvo peremys'koii eparchiii ta apostol'skoii Administratsii Lemkivshchyny.* Vols. 1 and 2. Lviv: Ukrainian Catholic University, 2015.

Pravda pro Uniiu: Dokumenty I Materialy. 2nd expanded edition. Lviv: Kameniar, 1968.

Procko, Bohdan P. *Ukrainian Catholics in America: A History.* Lanham, Md.: University Press of America, 1982.

———. "Role of the Catholic Church in the Adjustment of Ukrainian Immigrants." In *The Ukrainian Heritage in America*, ed. Walter Dushnyk and Nicholas I. Chirovsky, 95–102. New York: Ukrainian Congress Committee of America, 1991.

Prokopik, Emellia, OSBM. *Keepers of the Flame: 90-Year Province History.* Fox Chase Manor, Pa.: Contemporary Graphics, Inc., 2005.

Propamiatna knyha Amerykan'skykh Ukraiintsiv vydana u stolitniu richnytsiu smerty o. Markiiana Shashkevycha 1843–1943. Philadelphia: America Publishers, 1943.

Propamiatna Knyha iz sviatochnoho obkhodu Ukraiins'koho Katolyts'koho Kaledzha, 24 Lystopada, 1940, u Filadelfiii. Philadelphia: America, 1941.

Propamiatna Knyha z nahody zolotoho iuvileiu poselennia Ukraiins'koho narodu v Kanadi. Yorkton, Saskatchewan: Redeemer's Voice, 1941.

Prystay, Oleksa. *Z Truskavtsia u svit khmaroderiv.* 4 vols. Vols 1–3: Lviv: Dilo, 1933–36;

vol. 4: Lviv: Naukove Tovarystvo im. T. Shevchenka [Shevchenko Scientific Society], 1937.

Saato, Fred J. *American Eastern Catholics*. Mahwah, N.J.: Paulist Press, 2006.

Schoenig, Steven A., SJ. *Bonds of Wool: The Pallium and Papal Power in the Middle Ages*. Washington, D.C.: The Catholic University of America Press, 2016.

Segre, Emilio. *A Mind Always in Motion: The Autobiography of Emilio Segre*. Berkeley: University of California Press, 1993.

Sochotsky, Isidore. "The Ukrainian Catholic Church of the Byzantine-Slavonic Rite in the USA." In *Kharyna, Ukraiins'ka Katolyts'ka Mytropolia v Zluchenykh Derzhavakh Ameryky*, 1 Lystopada, 1958, 199–292. Philadelphia: Archbishop's Chancery, 1959.

Sorokowsky, Andrew. *The Greek-Catholic Parish Clergy in Galicia, 1900–1939*. Ph.D. dissertation. London: University of London, 1990.

———. "The Lay and Clerical Intelligentsia in Greek Catholic Galicia, 1900–1939: Competition, Conflict, Cooperation." *Harvard Ukrainian Studies*, nos. 1–4 (2002–3): 261–90.

———, ed. *Materiialy do istorii ukraiins'koho patriarkhal'noho rukhu (1963–2001)*. Lviv: Svichado, 2009.

Stefan, Augustin. *For Justice and Freedom*, book one. Toronto: Toronto Free Press, 1973.

Stercho, Petro. *Karpato-Ukraiins'ka Derzhava*. Toronto: Shevchenko Scientific Society, 1965.

Sulyk, Stefan. *Yak Stefan stav mytropolytom*. Lviv: n.p., 2001.

Tarnawsky, Fylymon. *Spohady: Rodynna Khronika Tarnavs'kykh*. Edited by Anatol Bazylewycz and Roman Danylewycz. Toronto: Dobra knyzhka, 1981.

Temporary Diocesan Statutes of the Byzantine Rite Apostolic Exarchate of Philadelphia, PA, USA. Vol. 1. Philadelphia: Bishop's Chancery Office, 1953.

Tsehels'ky, Lonhyn. *Vid legend do pravdy*. New York: Bulava Publishing Company, 1960.

Ulam, Stanislaw. *Adventures of a Mathematician*. Los Angeles: University of California Press, 1975.

Wendland, Anna Veronika. *Die Russophilen in Galizien: Ukrainische Konservative zwischen Osterreich und Russland, 1848–1915*. Vienna: Studien der Oesterreich-ungarischen Monarchie, 2001.

Yak Tvoryt'sia Ukraiins'ky Kul'turny Tsentr v Stamfordi. Philadelphia: n.p., 1937.

Zahaykevych, Bohdan, ed. *Peremyshl': Zakhidny bastion Ukraiiny*. New York: America, 1961.

Zaiitsev, Oleksander ed. *Natsionalizm i Relihiia: Hreko-Katolyts'ka Tserkva ta ukraiins'ky natsionalistychny rukh v Halychyni (1920–1930-ti roky)*. Lviv: Ukrainian Catholic University, 2011.

INDEX

Ortynsky, Ivan, 166
Ortynsky, Joseph, 161–62
Ortynsky, Soter, 5, 7–8, 10, 94–95, 104, 124,
   128–35, 137, 153, 159–64, 173, 176n29, 271,
   280, 350, 357
Orun, Zakhariy, 135n20, 483n12
Ostap, Antin, 380n80
Ostap, Ivan, 244–45, 245n12
OUN. See Organization of Ukrainian
   Nationalists
outreach, 276, 308, 331–34

Pacelli, Eugenio, 335, 384. See also Pius XII
pallium, 499–501. See also vestments
Panchuk, John, 407
Papadopulos, Isaiah, 10n5, 97, 108n38, 111
Papp, Antoni, 105n29
Paris Peace Conference, 101n19
Pashuk, Antin, 364n40
Pasternak, Yaroslav, 369
pastoral letters, of Bohachevsky, 170–71,
   194, 311–12, 330, 334, 338n60, 352–53,
   357n20, 413n54, 422–23
patriarchate, 16, 489, 512–13
patriotism, 34–35, 171–72, 186, 193–94, 199,
   204, 207, 222, 231–32, 236, 442. See also
   nationalism
Pavliak, Oleksander, 331n37, 364n40
Pelekhovych, Joseph, 269n53
Pelesh, Julian, 70
Perekopane, 74
Peremyshl, 50n1, 65–66, 69–71, 74n30, 105–7,
   116, 176, 294–95, 328n28, 415; cathedral,
   6, 69, 72
Peremyshl Civic Committee, 11–12
Perth Amboy, N.J., 216, 320
Peter's Pence, 386n5, 473–74
Petliura, Symon, 235–36
Petranka, 28
Petrivsky, Volodymyr, 104, 175, 261, 263, 280
Petrushevych, Evhen, 140n30, 149n39,
   319–20
Philadelphia, 134, 137n24, 139, 149, 153–54,
   185, 187, 315–16, 323–24, 328, 331n37,
   357n24, 364n40, 366, 379n77, 450, 452–60,
   480–81, 487–88
Piddubcheshen, Eva, 332, 397
Pidhoretsky, Mykola, 135n20, 156–57, 206
Pittsburgh, 305, 315–16, 447, 486, 493

Pius X, Pope, 91, 95, 128, 198, 453
Pius XI, Pope, 1, 9, 11–12, 78, 87–89, 93,
   105–6, 108, 134n19, 264–65, 290–91,
   316n6, 347, 384, 386, 485. See also Ratti,
   Achille
Pius XII, Pope, 335, 384n2, 397, 423, 442, 453,
   468, 487, 494. See also Pacelli, Eugenio
Plast (organization), 449
Pluhiv, 18, 26n9, 28
Pobuk, 51
Pobutsky, Stephen, 315, 404
Podney, Bohdanna, 362n35
pogrom, 354
Poland, 5–7, 12–13, 67–69, 80–85, 96, 102,
   105–6, 142, 144n31, 148, 176, 185, 190,
   246–47, 340n63, 354, 384–85
Poles, in United States, 174–75; Catholics,
   11–12
Polishchak, Adam, 242n8
Polish Commonwealth, 19
Polish-Ukrainian War, 66–69, 96
Polish-Vatican Concordat, 85, 88, 185,
   190, 256
Polonization, 55, 58, 75–76, 158n8, 167, 188,
   190
Poloway, Michael, 439n38
Poniatyshyn, Petro, 14, 97, 101, 103, 106, 110,
   136–42, 138n26, 138n28, 140n30, 145–46,
   150–52, 159, 175, 179n34, 188n42, 201,
   218n27, 245, 320, 325–26
Pospishil, Victor, 469–70, 473, 475, 502,
   505–6
Potocki, Andrzei, 174
poverty, 29n14, 31, 34n28, 44, 73–75, 161, 170,
   185, 196, 301, 312, 349, 351, 373
Prashko, Ivan, 493
Priashiv, 99n13, 100, 104, 116, 325
priests. See clergy
Procko, Bohdan, 390, 409n46, 480, 484,
   506n57
Prokopik, Emellia (Julia), 332, 362n35, 384n1,
   441
property. See finances; real estate
Protestantism, 97, 132, 200, 395n21, 418
Protsko, Pavlo, 166, 239–40, 252, 344n74,
   362n35, 363, 369–70, 391, 393–94, 404
Providence Association, 131–32, 149, 187–88,
   205–6, 211, 216, 230–31, 256–57, 377, 401,
   484

Shashkevych, Markian, 175–76, 222, 330–31, 335n51, 336, 369, 398
Shchur, Lev, 423
Shenandoah, Penn., 8, 323
Sheptytsky, Andrey, 5–7, 10, 10n5, 28, 36–37, 39n38, 45n51, 50n1; and bishopric in U.S., 96–102; in Bohachevsky's education, 41–43; Bonzano and, 95n7; Cathedral of the Immaculate Conception and, 153–54; church unity and, 52–57; deportation of, 51; in ecumenical movement, 54, 54n4; exile of, 64n16; and expansion of Ukrainian Catholic Church, 88–89; Franko and, 225–29; incarceration of, 96n8; lack of support from, 201; liturgical texts and, 57; Lviv Theological Academy and, 347n2; Njaradi and, 98–101; and Paris Peace Conference, 101n19; Poland and, 68; Prystay and, 126n5; and public role of Ukrainian Catholic Church, 139; report to, on Ukrainian Catholic Church in North America, 132–33; return of, 64–65, 80–82; seminary and, 340–41; in South America, 96–97; in United States, 134–36; Zhuk and, 92, 263, 319
Shevchenko, Taras, 222, 284, 369
Shevchenko Scientific Society, 34, 124n3, 421, 442–43, 491
Shtaat (state), 196n1
Shukhovsky, John, 261
Shwed, Mary, 332n41
Sichynsky, Myroslav, 218n27, 262n36
Simenovych, Myroslav, 400
Simenovych, Nykolai, 337n56
Sincero, Luigi, 261, 266, 280, 282, 327
Sisters of the Sacred Heart, 397, 440, 441n44
Sisters Servants of Mary, 397
Skoropadsky, Danylo, 336–37, 377
Skoropadsky, Hetman Pavlo, 146, 184n40
Skrotsky, Yaroslav, 428n23
Slavonic language, 40, 175, 282, 284, 305–6, 434n31, 462, 484
Slipyj, Joseph, 16, 268n49, 308, 328n27, 340, 358n27, 377n70, 410, 412n50, 494, 512–14
Sloatsburg, N.Y., 373, 397
Sluzhebnyk (prayer book), 296
Smal-Stocki, Roman, 442–43, 448, 472
sobor (council), 295n36, 410–12, 464, 471, 502, 511

Sochotsky, Isidore, 264, 499
socialism, 22–23, 26n9. See also communism
Societies of the Sacred Heart, 497
Society of St. Joseph, 71
Society of St. Paul, 135
Society of Sts. Joseph and Nychodem, 74, 75n31
Sodalities of the Blessed Virgin, 497
Sokhotsky, Isidore, 157
Sokil, Maria, 399n28
Soviet Union, 6–7, 16, 67, 144, 174, 316–17, 354–55, 385–86, 395, 403–6, 410–15, 456, 489, 512
Spellman, Francis, 406
Spolitakevych, Volodymyr, 149, 271n58
Stamford, Conn., 333–34, 367–68, 396, 450–51, 471–72
Stanislaviv, 24
statues, 58, 61, 182, 301–2, 306, 462, 464
St. Basil Academy, 322, 362
St. Basil Preparatory School, 372–74
St. Basil's College, 333–34, 368–73, 377, 396, 471–72
Stebelsky, Vasyl, 428n23
Stetsiuk, Vasyl, 218n27, 262n36, 280
steyt (state), 196n1
St. John the Baptist School (Newark), 397
St. Josaphat Kuntsevych, 75, 75n21
St. Josaphat Seminary (Rome), 406n39
St. Josaphat Seminary (Washington), 380–82, 396–98, 446–49
St. Joseph's seminary (Baltimore), 366
Stock, John, 16, 380n80, 409, 513
Stratford, N.Y., 448
Stritch, Samuel, 454n10
Strotsky, Andriy, 260
Strutynsky, Mykola, 218n27, 260n33
Stryj, 22n4, 24–25, 31
suffrage, universal, 33n23
Sulyk, Stefan, 416, 447n1, 460, 467n25
summer camp, 332n41, 426, 448–49
Surovtseva, Nadia, 144, 174
Sventsitsky, Ilarion, 41, 64
Svoboda (newspaper), 139, 148n38, 192, 202–5, 207, 242–43, 246–51, 253–54, 258, 259, 260n33, 261n34, 264, 270, 273, 389n9, 399n28, 510
Swystun, Teofil, 318n8
Sydoriak, Stephanie Chopyk, 269n51

Ukrainian Bishop, American Church: Constantine Bohachevsky and the Ukrainian Catholic Church was designed in Quadraat and Quadraat Sans by Kachergis Book Design of Pittsboro, North Carolina. It was printed on 60-pound Natures Book Natural and bound by Thomson-Shore of Dexter, Michigan.